MW01092313

Novels Into Film
Adaptations & Interpretations

LIBRARY OF
CONGRESS
SURPLUS
DUPLICATE

Novels Into Film
Adaptations & Interpretations
Volume Two

Editor
D. Alan Dean, Ph.D.

SALEM PRESS
A Division of EBSCO Information Services, Inc.
Ipswich, Massachusetts

GREY HOUSE PUBLISHING

Copyright © 2021 by SALEM PRESS, Inc., A Division of EBSCO Information Services, Inc., and Grey House Publishing, Inc.

All rights in this book are reserved. No part of this work may be used or reproduced in any manner whatsoever or transmitted in any form or by any means, elecronic or mechanical, including photocopy, recording, or any information storage and retrieval system, without written permission from the copyright owner. For permissions request, contact permissions@ebscohost.com.

The paper used in these volumes conforms to the American National Standard for Permanence of Paper for Publications and Documents in Libraries and Archives, ANSI/NISO Z39.48-1992 (R2009).

Publisher's Cataloging-In-Publication Data
(Prepared by The Donohue Group, Inc.)

Names: Dean, D. Alan, editor.
Title: Novels into film : adaptations & interpretations. Volume two / editor, D. Alan Dean, Ph.D.
Description: Ipswich, Massachusetts : Salem Press, a division of EBSCO Information Services, Inc. ;
    [Amenia, New York] : Grey House Publishing, [2021] | Includes bibliographical references and indexes.
Identifiers: ISBN 9781637000366
Subjects: LCSH: Fiction—Film adaptations—History and criticism. | Film adaptations—History and
    criticism. | Motion pictures and literature.
Classification: LCC PN1997.85 .N68 2021 | DDC 791.43/6—dc23

Table of Contents

Introduction

In ninety two years of Academy Awards ceremonies (the first was in 1929), the award for Best Picture has gone a total of sixty times to movies that were adapted from either novels or plays. However, while adaptations have certainly been well-received by Oscar committees, the actual percentage of adaptations produced each year varies, ranging from only 10 percent in some years to as high as fifty percent in other years (take, for example, the banner year of 1955).[1] Why, exactly, have so many adaptations done so well at the Academy Awards?

One reason for the popularity and success of adaptations is straightforward: good novels typically feature strong stories and compelling, well-developed characters. In some cases, they also bring with them built-in audiences for the film. A good case in point is Peter Jackson's three-part *The Lord of the Rings*, adapted from the three-part novel by J.R.R. Tolkien, whose books are famous for their seminal influence on the fantasy genre and for their massive and enthusiastic fan-base around the globe.

But influential books are not always the basis for film adaptations. The source for an adaptation can be almost anything: a novel, novella, short story, play, biography, poem, comic book, non-fiction book or essay, scripture—even another film. For the sake of copyright law, an adaptation is considered a *derivative* work, meaning simply that it is a work based upon one or more works that already exist.[2] Derivative, in this usage is not a derogatory critical judgment; it simply describes the legal relationship of one work to another.

There are times, however, when a film's derivative status does come with derogatory critical judgment. For example, novel readers routinely criticize the adaptations of their favorite novels, claiming, as is often the case, that "the book was better." Questions about fidelity often drive this line of criticism: was the film true to the book or author, was the adaptation faithful? An adaptation might be viewed—or taught in the classroom—as less a text in its own right than as one that provides an interpretation of the novel. These ways of viewing adhere more or less to what we can call a "derivative" model of the adaptation process: the novel is the original and the film is somehow secondary, dependent, or a kind of copy.

This style of criticism—so-called fidelity criticism—dominated discussions of adaptation for many years, even among scholars, and it is still probably the most obvious and common critical language for casual film viewers. But there are distinct limitations to this approach. To what, exactly, is a filmmaker supposed to be faithful? One answer might be to the novel's plot and its characters. But of course it isn't possible to faithfully recreate on film each episode from the plot of a long novel. Novels typically have much more plot than films. The paradigmatic case study for an attempted faithful adaptation in this sense—one that translates every moment in the plot to the screen—is Erich von Stroheim's *Greed* (1924). Von Stroheim's film was an adaptation of the 1899 Frank Norris novel *McTeague*. The story of the film's making is legendary. In the interest of accomplishing a truly faithful adaptation of a novel, something that no director had done

---

1 An analysis of major motion pictures released since the 1980s shows that the number of adaptations of all kinds in Hollywood films has increased consistently—and fairly dramatically—over the last several decades. Most of the increase in adapted stories can be attributed to the growth in popularity of film franchises and films adapted from either real life stories or from comic books. However, adaptions from novels, novellas, and short stories remain strong.

2 "A 'derivative work' is a work based upon one or more preexisting works, such as a translation, musical arrangement, dramatization, fictionalization, motion picture version, sound recording, art reproduction, abridgment, condensation, or any other form in which a work may be recast, transformed, or adapted. A work consisting of editorial revisions, annotations, elaborations, or other modifications which, as a whole, represent an original work of authorship, is a 'derivative work.'" (United States Copyright Act, 17 U.S.C. §101.)

before, von Stroheim made creative decisions that are common today but were eccentric in 1924, like shooting on location—including in California's Death Valley—for the sake of authenticity. His final edit, which featured 42 reels, was more than nine hours long. The studio executives were horrified. The film was promptly taken out of von Stroheim's hands and re-edited. The edited version had a running time of two and a half hours. Some who saw the original nine-hour version of the movie called it the greatest film ever made, and its specter has haunted film history ever since.

The example of von Stroheim's film exposes the important differences between film and literature. In addition to being different media, they also operate under a different set of constraints and possibilities and, as a result, also afford different kinds of aesthetic experiences. A novel might have many sub-plots and many characters and take thirty or forty hours to read. Novels might put language at the fore. Think, for example, of the styles of writers like Virginia Woolf or of Henry James. In the condensation of a novel to a movie, changes are inevitable. Plots must be simplified, characters re-drawn, and the effects of language either ignored or hinted at through techniques unique to the visual medium of cinema.

Important works of film scholarship have focused on the distinctions between film and literature. Christian Metz, writing about the different capacities for narration in the two media of film and literature, has said, "Film tells us continuous stories; it 'says' things that could be conveyed also in the language of words; yet it says them differently. There is a reason for the possibility as well as for the necessity of adaptations."[3] One might add that the act of reading, rather than viewing, brings with it certain imaginative and affective pleasures and even an experience of time that differs from the pleasures and experiences of film, which has its own enjoyments and its own immersive temporal dimension.

In *Novels Into Film: A Critical Study* (1957), a path-breaking and seminal work on film adaptation, George Bluestone also reflects on the differences between the two genres. In his opening chapter, Bluestone characterizes the difference between the two media as "two ways of seeing." According to Bluestone's succinct formulation, the difference is "between the percept of the visual image and the concept of the mental image."[4] A filmmaker creates visual images, or percepts, that the viewer sees on the screen. A writer uses language to invoke mental images in the reader's mind. From this difference, others follow: the visual nature of the medium of film means that motion and the depiction of human actions are its real strengths. Alternatively, novels can convey more about the complexities of inner motivation and can also render time more substantially and with greater complexity.

Bluestone notes that in a successful adaptation, the essential features taken from a novel usually have little to do with language. In literature, language and thematic concerns are inseparable, and together they comprise much of the substance of the work. An adaptation cannot be very concerned with the language of a novel; instead, adaptations take certain "characters and incidents which somehow have detached themselves from language, and like the heroes of folk legends, have assumed a mythical life of their own." One has only to think of the difference between the novels of Henry James and the nearly 20 resulting film adaptations. What is essential in James is less what happens than the extraordinarily fine-grained observations and the sophisticated, layered complexity of his language. The adaptations cannot convey this level of linguistic complexity. Although the film versions are often quite fine period dramas and can succeed on their own cinematic terms, they can never really resemble James's novels.

---

3 Christian Metz, *Film Language: A Semiotics of the Cinema*, trans. Michael Taylor (Oxford University Press: New York, 1974), 44.

4 George Bluestone, *Novels into Film* (Johns Hopkins University Press: Baltimore, 2003), 1.

What ultimately serves to connect literature and feature film and what makes successful adaptation possible—perhaps, in the words of Christian Metz, even sometimes "necessary"—is that they are both narrative arts that employ parallel or even identical narrative strategies, analyzable in terms of plot, characterization, theme, mood, style, and so forth. Although employing different media, they marshal the resources that are unique to each medium in order to tell similar kinds of stories. These similarities and this deep parallelism between movies and novels are no accident. They are the result of the historical development of the art of narrative film out of the techniques and strategies of nineteenth-century fiction.

Early makers and distributors of movies wanted their product to be respectable, and so they turned to literature. The move had as much to do with money as with manners and social mores: middle-class film viewers were a lucrative market. Film scholar James Naremore writes that the film industry "recognized from the beginning that it could gain a sort of legitimacy among middle-class viewers by reproducing facsimiles of more respectable art or by adapting literature to another medium."[5] And Brian McFarlane suggests that "as soon as the cinema began to see itself as a narrative entertainment, the idea of ransacking the novel—that already established repository of narrative fiction—for source material got underway, and the process has continued more or less unabated for ninety years."[6]

In their turn to nineteenth-century novels, early filmmakers discovered not only kinds of stories and types of characters that they could make films about, but they also found a trove of techniques and strategies for narration. The pioneering American director D.W. Griffith, widely credited with consolidating if not inventing many of the major techniques of narrative film editing, once remarked that he learned the principles of editing by using the same story-telling techniques that he found in the novels of Charles Dickens. The Griffith-Dickens connection was the subject of a famous essay by Sergei Eistenstein, "Dickens, Griffith, and the Film Today."[7] Eisenstein found in the novels of Dickens the origins or models for such cinematic techniques as the close-up, parallel editing, the "cut-back," and even composition within the camera frame. Eisenstein tells the story of Griffith's decision while editing *Enoch Arden* (*After Many Years*, 1908) to cut away from the action to show another character located elsewhere and then to cut back to the first scene. Those around him asked, "How can you tell a story jumping about like that?" And Griffith supposedly responded, "Well, doesn't Dickens write that way?"

Film scholars now commonly emphasize that it was not only novels that provided the wealth of narrative techniques that enabled the feature film as we know it to come into being. Theater, both high and low, as well as painting and other arts impacted the story-telling strategies of film (as well as novels). The arts have always been in an intertextual or dialogic relation to one another. However, the novel and cinema are often considered to have a particularly close kinship. Christian Metz has even argued that in the twentieth century, film and film-viewing came to take over many of the social functions of novels and novel-reading.[8] These social functions vary but they are considerable. They include the circulation of ideas, stories, and characters in popular culture; the signaling of class or education among the middle classes; the provision of widely disseminated texts for criticism or commentary in magazines and newspapers, and so on. Finally, it

---

5   James Naremore. "Introduction: Film and the Reign of Adaptation." *Film Adaptation*. Ed. James Naremore. New Brunswick, NJ: Rutgers UP, 2000. 1-16

6   Brian McFarlane. *Novel to Film: An Introduction to the Theory of Adaptation*. Oxford: Clarendon, 1996.

7   Sergei Eisenstein. "Dickens, Griffith, and the Film Today." *Film Form: Essays in Film Theory*. Ed. Jay Leyda. New York: Harcourt Brace Jovanovich, 1977. 195-255.

8   Christian Metz. *The Imaginary Signifier: Psychoanalysis and the Cinema*. Trans. Celia Britton, Annwyl Williams, Ben Brewster, and Alfred Guzzetti. Bloomington: Indian University Press, 1977. 110.

remains uncontroversial to emphasize that cinema as we know it was formed through the adaptation of narrative techniques long practiced by writers to the visual medium of film.

Circling back to the unusually high number of esteemed Hollywood pictures that have been adaptations from novels, novellas, and short stories noted at the start of this Introduction, two main reasons exist. Firstly, existing literary works provide Hollywood scriptwriters with ready-made stories that have already proven to be interesting, durable, or compelling in other media; note the number of adaptations among award-winning films. Secondly, the profound historical relationship between novels and film no doubt plays an important role. Narrative film and literature have a strong genetic relationship to one another, and there are similarities buried deep in their DNA, just as there are similarities in the social functions that they play.

The essays in this volume provide readers and film viewers with concise analyses of 100 film adaptations. The films included range from classics of the silent era to recent blockbusters. Each essay focuses primarily on the film but also briefly addresses both the written work and the adaptation strategy. The essays are intended primarily for students of literature, and the use of language specific to film studies has been kept to a minimum and explained when it is used. The essays briefly contextualize both the novel and the film, offer an analysis of the film, and provide basic, important information about the film's reception and significance. It is hoped that the essays will be useful to students, teachers, and general readers who are interested in film and in the film adaptations of works of literature. A balance was struck between good films that are adaptations of canonical works of literature and canonical films that are adaptations of sometimes lesser-known but fine novels. Many more films could have been included.

—D. Alan Dean

Publisher's Note

We are pleased to add this second volume of *Novels into Film: Adaptations & Interpretations* to Salem Press' growing list of works that explore literature with expert critical analysis and original commentary. This work offers a unique look at how a story makes its way from the printed page to the screen.

The 128 novels covered in this work represent a wide range of years, genres, and stories. While most of the films in this work have been adapted from full-length novels, some come from novellas, short stories, or plays. You will find classics, such as *Age of Innocence* and *Alice in Wonderland*, as well as contemporary blockbusters, such as *Crazy Rich Asians* and *The Wolf of Wall Street*.

Essays are arranged alphabetically mostly by film title, with a few by book title if that is more widely recognized. Each essay offers valuable top matter about both the book (author and date of publication) and the film (year released, director, screenwriter and actors). The body of the essay is divided into detailed sections—Context, Film Analysis, and Significance—and all signed essays end with Further Reading and Bibliography lists. Each detailed essay is made all the more robust with images, including movie posters, stills from the film, and photographs of actors and directors at work.

In addition to the essays themselves, the back matter of *Novels Into Film* is comprised of six significant indexes:
  * Index of Print Works by Title, that includes the author of the work
  * Index of Print Works by Author, that includes the title of the work
  * Index of Print Works by Date of First Publication, chronological by work's published date with title of work
  * Index of Films by Screenwriter, that includes the name of the film
  * Index of Films by Director, that includes the name of the film
  * Index of Films by Release Date, chronological by film's release date with title of film

This Publisher's Note is preceded by an Introduction that includes a detailed look at the approaches that are used when studying those films that come from books, and differences between books and movies, some not so obvious.

This new work will appeal to both book and film lovers alike, as well as offer serious value to film study curricula. This volume, together with *Novels into Film* volume 1, published in 2018, offer unparalleled coverage of 228 of the most significant films adapted from the printed word.

About a Boy

The Novel
Author: Nick Hornby (b. 1957)
First published: 1998

The Film
Year released: 2002
Directors: Chris Weitz (b. 1969), Paul Weitz (b. 1965)
Screenplay by: Peter Hedges, Chris Weitz, Paul Weitz
Starring: Hugh Grant, Nicholas Hoult, Toni Collette, Rachel Weisz

Context
A funny, heartwarming story about unlikely friendships, *About a Boy* (1998) is Nick Hornby's second novel. Like his debut novel, *High Fidelity* (1995), it focuses on a hip but shallow thirty-something Londoner. The protagonist of *About a Boy*, the aptly named Will Freeman, lives a life devoid of obligations or attachments. Over the course of the novel, he is drawn into a friendship with an awkward twelve-year-old boy named Marcus, and ultimately learns how to connect with people. The book's title refers as much to Will as it does to Marcus, and by the novel's end both characters have grown.

Chris and Paul Weitz, the sibling team that directed *American Pie* (1999) also directed a film version of *About a Boy* in 2002. *High Fidelity* (2000), starring John Cusack, had already shown that Hornby's novels could work well on the big screen. While that production had relocated the story to Chicago, *About a Boy* would retain its London setting. This was important to Hugh Grant, who read the manuscript and attached himself to the production early on. The Weitz brothers showed that they could pivot to a more nuanced, bittersweet story and that they had the directorial chops for both comedy and romance. Grant, a Hollywood A-lister in the wake of *Four Weddings and a Funeral* (1994) and *Notting Hill* (1999), was matched by an impressive cast that included Toni Collette, Rachel Weisz, and newcomer Nicholas Hoult. Hoult's performance is flawless, and the film succeeds in large part due to his gifted performance as the odd, guileless Marcus. Collaborating with Peter Hedges on the script, the Weitz brothers made major changes to the last third of the novel, creating a conclusion that is in some ways more organically connected to the rest of the story and that possesses a distinctly cinematic quality.

Film Analysis
Hornby's novel alternates between the perspectives of Will and Marcus, establishing each of them as individual characters before bringing them together. The film takes the same approach and uses voice-overs to bring whole sections of Hornby's text from the novel into the film. The

Hugh Grant (Will). Photo by Tine Hemeryck Wikimedia Commons.

book begins with Marcus's point-of-view, but the film begins with Will's. Hugh Grant, after all, is the movie's star, and there is a subtle but pervasive reframing of the narrative to focus on him. In the opening scene, Will makes his way through his apartment, performing various tasks and talking about the importance of dividing one's time into manageable blocks. His apartment is a sleek bachelor pad, and his daily routine includes such indices of character as throwing away the name and phone number of a woman he has recently met. The audience does not see Grant's face until the final shot of the scene, and even then, it is viewed in the warped reflection of a toaster. The camera is doing to the audience what Will has done to so many people in his own life: guarding him against being truly seen or known.

The perspective then shifts to Marcus, a twelve-year-old boy played by Nicholas Hoult. Marcus and his bohemian mother, Fiona (Toni Collette), are newly arrived in London, and he is facing difficulties both at home and at school. His mother has been crying incessantly, and Marcus is not old enough to help. At his rough-and-tumble school, Marcus is bullied and ostracized. His bowl haircut, homemade sweaters, and tendency to sing Joni Mitchell songs in class all serve to make him an easy target.

Meanwhile, Will finds himself dating a single mother. He discovers that compared to an ex-husband, he comes across as a good guy. When he eventually becomes tired of the constraints of working around a toddler's schedule, he decides to break it off with his new girlfriend. Before he can do so, however, she breaks up with him. In a brilliantly realized comic scene, Will registers surprise and a barely suppressed delight that he has been released from the relationship while still retaining his good-guy status. Determined to meet more single mothers, Will seeks out a support group called SPAT, Single Parents Alone Together. Inventing a two-year-old son named Ned, he attends one of their meetings where he holds hands, shares stories, and mouths affirmations. His mission is a success and he meets a pretty single mother named Suzie (Victoria Smurfit).

It is through Suzie that Will meets Marcus. Knowing that her friend Fiona has been depressed, Suzie decides to take Marcus to a SPAT picnic so that Fiona can have a day to herself. Will offers to drive, leading to one of the film's many set pieces: Will purchasing a car seat for his imaginary son Ned and then "distressing" it in the parking lot by grinding potato chips into it. At the picnic, Will

shows little interest in Marcus, although he does come to the boy's defense after he accidentally kills a duck by throwing a piece of his mother's inedible homemade bread at it. Will also admits, during the day in the park, to the source of his financial independence: his father wrote a Christmas hit called "Santa's Super Sleigh," and Will lives off the royalties. When the group returns to Marcus's apartment that afternoon, they find that Fiona has overdosed on pills in an attempted suicide. Here, as in so many parts of the book and movie, Will's narrative helps to strike the right tone and keep the story grounded in the realm of comedy. Will acknowledges, for example, that the afternoon is a tragedy but admits that he enjoyed driving fast in the ambulance's wake. Bidding goodbye to Fiona and Marcus late that night, Will assumes that he will never see them again.

Marcus, however, has other ideas. In a clever set of scenes that build on the film's opening sequence, Marcus begins following Will through his vapid daily routine. He finally shows up at Will's door, accusing him of not actually having a son and making a series of demands. He tells Will to take his mother and him out to lunch—thinking that Will might make a good boyfriend or husband for his depressed mother—and he starts hanging around Will's apartment after school. A clever montage of the two of them watching television on the couch shows how their relationship develops over the course of days or weeks, until they seem to actually be enjoying each other's company. Grant and Hoult have terrific chemistry, and despite his youth, Hoult never seems self-conscious or overly rehearsed in front of the camera. Much of their comedic dynamic comes from the clash of Will's studied cool with Marcus's obliviousness to social norms. Clever cuts and pacing heighten the effect of this clash of personalities and worlds. For example, Will decides that he can help Marcus fit in at school by buying him an expensive pair of sneakers. In the next scene, Marcus comes home, barefoot and drenched from rain, because the sneakers have been stolen. This leads to a terrific, cringeworthy scene in which Fiona confronts Will in a trendy restaurant, asking why he is entertaining a twelve-year-old boy in his apartment. Screenwriters Peter Hedges and the Weitz brothers amplify the original scene from the book by transposing it to a public setting, underscoring the idea that Will's worlds are colliding.

Will had been revealed to be a fraud, leading to a very funny reunion with Suzie at Fiona and Marcus's Christmas party. Now it is Marcus's turn to defend Will, arguing that he should be allowed to stay at the party despite having pretended to have a son. A reference to the dead duck from the picnic reduces them all to laughter, and they emerge from the Christmas party as something like friends. In the story's next twist, Will falls for another single mother, Rachel (Rachel Weisz). Not having yet learned his lesson, Will implies that he, too, has a child, and must then enlist Marcus to play the role of his son.

The screenwriters take great liberties with the last third of the story, ultimately producing an ending that is as satisfactory as that of the book. In Hornby's novel, Marcus is befriended by a goth girl at school named Ellie. She accompanies him to Cambridge to visit Marcus's injured father. On the train, they learn that Kurt Cobain, the front man of the band Nirvana, has killed himself. Getting off the train in the next town, they find a record store displaying a Nirvana poster; incensed that the owners are making money from her hero's death, Ellie smashes the front window and the shop owner calls the police. All of the characters gather at the police station to get the children released. The trip marks a change for Marcus, as he decides to be more independent both from his parents and from Ellie. By novel's end, Will and Marcus have changed places. Because Will is smitten with Rachel, he is as guileless and confused as Marcus once was, while Marcus has become as cool and jaded as Will once was. Neither one is a boy anymore: Will is a sensitive man in a caring relationship, and Marcus is a sullen teenager. The book closes with Marcus telling his mother that he hates Joni Mitchell, while Will looks on with approval.

The film didn't include the train trip to Cambridge, but instead invents a new climax to the story: Marcus's decision to sing Roberta Flack's "Killing Me Softly" at his school's battle of the bands. Marcus is convinced that this is the way to rescue his mother from her depression. The script cleverly prepares for this scene, picking up on the novel's references to Fiona and Marcus singing together, showing a guitar in Will's apartment, and having Fiona tell Marcus how happy his singing makes her. Will, who has become estranged from both Rachel and Marcus, comes to the boy's rescue. Joining Marcus onstage with an electric guitar, Will salvages what would have been a dismal performance and a form of social suicide.

In the film's final scene, all of the principal characters gather at Will's apartment for Christmas, a surrogate family for a man who once thought he was an island.

Significance

About a Boy was a popular and critical success. Roger Ebert said that while the plot could "supply the materials for a film of complacent stupidity," *About a Boy* "is much more than that; it's one of the year's most entertaining films." A. O. Scott, writing for *The New York Times*, said "You succumb to the movie's warmth and bonhomie because the alternative is to remain in the isolating, self-protective cynicism from which Will has been lucky to escape." *About a Boy* is a film that seemed to catch its critics by surprise, winning them over despite its occasional rom-com chops and clichés. Nominated for an Academy Award for Best Adapted Screenplay, the film was a second successful adaptation of a Nick Hornby novel. It bolstered Hugh Grant's career as a leading man, expanding his range by moving him away from the floppy-haired, inoffensive protagonists of *Four Weddings and a Funeral* (1994) and *Notting Hill* (1999). While not necessarily the "Santa's Super Sleigh" of romantic comedies, *About a Boy* retains a strong fan base and has become something of a seasonal favorite.

—*Matthew Bolton*

Further Reading

"About Nick." *Nick Hornby*, 2020, www.nickhornbyofficial.com/about/. Accessed 13 July 2020.
Rennison, Nick. *Contemporary British Novelists*. Routledge, 2005.

Bibliography

Ebert, Roger. "About a Boy." *RogerEbert.com*, 17 May 2002, www.rogerebert.com/reviews/about-a-boy-2002. Accessed 13 Apr. 2020.
Hornby, Nick. *About a Boy*. Riverhead Books, 1998.
Scott, A. O. "Peter Pan Meets Another Lost Boy." *The New York Times*, 17 May 2002, www.nytimes.com/2002/05/17/movies/film-review-peter-pan-meets-another-lost-boy.html. Accessed 13 Apr. 2020.

The Age of Innocence

The Novel

Author: Edith Wharton (1862-1937)
First published: 1920

The Film

Year released: 1993
Director: Martin Scorsese (b. 1942)
Screenplay by: Jay Cocks, Martin Scorsese
Starring: Daniel Day-Lewis, Michelle Pfeiffer, Winona Ryder, Miriam Margolyes

Context

Edith Wharton was an incredibly prolific author who wrote more than forty books in forty years, from novels to nonfiction works on interior design and travel. She is best remembered, however, for her fiction, including such acclaimed works as *The House of Mirth* (1905) and *Ethan Frome* (1911), both mainstays of English literature classes.

Also ranked among her great works is *The Age of Innocence*, which won the Pulitzer Prize for Fiction in 1921, making Wharton the first woman to receive that honor. The book took a nuanced, sophisticated look at the New York City of the 1870s, the setting of Wharton's own coming of age. This restrictive upper-class world, with social rules that were never spoken and yet never openly flouted, often prevented intelligent and independent women like Wharton from expecting more from life than having a proper marriage and family. Wharton, however, would break free of that world, both by establishing herself as an acclaimed author and by divorcing her mentally unstable husband, Teddy Wharton, in 1913. Yet by the time of her middle age, she would look back on the world of her youth with a degree of sympathy. This was in large part because the horrors of World War I (1914-18), which she directly experienced while overseeing humanitarian organizations in France, largely ended such rigid restrictions.

Such an upper-class world seemed an unlikely subject to tackle for Martin Scorsese, the great Italian American film director who had risen to fame with gritty crime dramas like *Mean Streets* (1973), *Taxi Driver* (1976), and *Goodfellas* (1990). Yet, by the same token, a tightly controlled world with its own values and codes was not unfamiliar terrain to him. In the 1980s, Jay Cocks, a music critic who would go on to help draft the screenplay for *The Age of Innocence*, encouraged Scorsese to read Wharton's novel. Although Scorsese fell in love with the story and Wharton's writing, it would take him several years to find the time to make a film adaptation, because of his own work on other pictures and also because he had trouble finding a studio to produce it. Ultimately, the adaptation

Daniel Day Lewis played Newland Archer. Photo by Siebbi via Wikimedia Commons.

landed with Warner Brothers. Major stars Daniel Day-Lewis, Michelle Pfeiffer, and Winona Ryder were brought on for the lead roles.

Film Analysis

In drafting their screenplay, Cocks and Scorsese went to considerable effort to maintain the central storyline of the novel and included much of the dialogue. They also included many of Wharton's own deft descriptions and characterizations, primarily through a voice-over narration by Hollywood veteran Joanne Woodward. Both novel and film focus on the story of Newland Archer (Daniel Day-Lewis), the man torn between a safe marriage to May Welland (Winona Ryder) and the allures of her cousin, Countess Ellen Olenska (Michelle Pfeiffer), who has returned from Europe having left her very troubled marriage.

The film opens at the opera, where Archer, a respected lawyer in 1870s New York, is reintroduced to the countess. Ellen is in New York after having lived in Europe for some years, married to a Polish count who turned out to be a womanizer and gambler. She has left her husband, causing something of a scandal in New York high society. Privately, Newland questions why this should cause such a scandal, since Ellen is a woman of intelligence and self-respect and has done nothing wrong other than leave a terrible marriage. Later that evening, Newland announces his engagement to May at the home of the Beauforts, a well-connected family. Shortly thereafter, May shows off her engagement ring to her grandmother, Mrs. Manson Mingott (Miriam Margolyes), who urges them to marry as soon as possible, although society expects a long engagement. A good match between great families in old New York, to Mrs. Mingott's thinking, is of paramount importance. The only concern the families face, however, is the presence of Ellen among them, without her husband, and associating with men like Julius Beaufort (Stuart Wilson).

Although May frets about Ellen, Newland finds himself sympathetic to her plight and growing more attracted to her by the moment, especially when compared with May, who doesn't appear to express a thought outside of what is socially expected. After all of high society declines an invitation extended by Mrs. Mingott for a dinner in Ellen's honor, Newland appeals to the powerful van der Luydens family, who host a dinner in Ellen's honor at their home.

The dinner does not go as planned. Ellen shows up late, then speaks to Newland about what are considered inap-

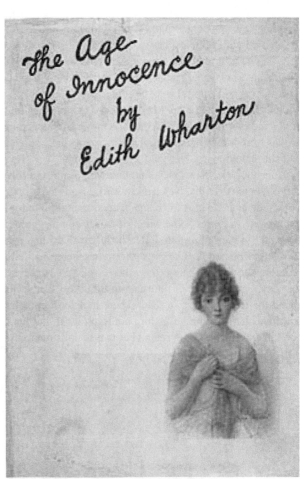

The Age of Innocence, *U.S. first edition dust-jacket. 1920. Image via Wikimedia Commons. [Public domain.]*

propriate subjects, such as his love for May. Later, Ellen invites Newland to her home, where she asks him how to adjust to the rules of New York society. Afterward, he sends her yellow roses. When Ellen tells her family that she intends to divorce her husband, the family begins to fear the scandal this would bring, particularly as Newland and May's wedding approaches. Newland is asked to intercede, and he goes to visit Ellen with the idea of persuading her not to seek divorce, since her reputation could be ruined, and that of the family could be harmed as well. She agrees, but he leaves feeling that he is falling deeply in love with her. Realizing this, Newland leaves New York to visit May and her family, who are on vacation, asking her that they speed up their engagement. She is initially suspicious, and believes the only reason for him to rush the engagement is because he is in love with another woman. Newland denies this, yet still finds himself feeling unsatisfied with May and her worldview.

When he returns to New York, Newland discovers that Ellen's husband wants her back. Newland tells her not to go back to him, and admits his love for her. She loves him too, but tells him that betraying May would go against his principles and everything he holds dear. As they talk, a telegram arrives from May, announcing that her parents have agreed that she should marry Newland within a month.

After their marriage, Newland and May settle into the sort of society life that Newland inwardly finds appalling. Sometime later, he sees Ellen again, after struggling to forget her. He first sees her at Mrs. Mingott's country home, from afar in the setting sun. Later, he learns that Ellen has traveled to Boston, and he goes to visit her there. She tells him that she was planning to see her husband's secretary that day, with the idea of returning to him. He asks her to spend the day with him instead, where he later admits he still loves her. She promises him not to return to her husband in exchange for him seeing her in a social situation.

Michelle Pfieffer played The Countess. Photo by joyparris via Wikimedia Commons.

When Ellen's grandmother, Mrs. Mingott, suffers a stroke, Ellen returns from Washington, DC, to be with her. Newland picks her up from the station, and they embrace and kiss passionately in the carriage. Ellen does not want him to abandon his marriage and does not want to be his mistress either. Yet the pair agrees to consummate their relationship just once before parting again. He sends her a key to an apartment, which she later returns to him unopened. She also tells her family that she has decided to return to Europe. He tries to find out why at a farewell party for her, but is prevented from doing so. He begins to suspect that all of society knew of his feelings for Ellen.

Later, Newland attempts to tell his wife of his feelings for Ellen, but May interrupts him to tell him that she is pregnant and had only just found out about it—but had told Ellen two weeks earlier when she only suspected it.

The years pass, and Newland proves to be a good husband and father of three. After May dies of pneumonia, he genuinely mourns her. When Newland is fifty-seven years old, some twenty-five years after he had last seen Ellen, his son Ted (Robert Sean Leonard) invites him to visit Paris, where he surprises his father with the knowledge that his fiancée is friends with Ellen. Ted then claims that when May was dying, she told Ted that they could always trust their father because, when she asked, he gave up the thing most important to him in life: Ellen. This news startles Newland, because it shows that May had known and understood. Ted then tells his father that Ellen is waiting for them now at her apartment, but when they get to the square, Newland says he will not go up, and he sends Ted on alone. Newland waits in the square, watching the apartment windows, thinking of Ellen. When a window closes, he is struck by the sunlight and the memory of seeing her years ago in the sun at Mrs. Mingott's. Then he leaves the square.

Significance

The novel version of *The Age of Innocence* remains a classic of American literature, taught in classrooms and read by generations since its first publication in 1920. In 2014, it made *The Guardian*'s list of the one hundred best English-language novels, coming in at number forty-five. It is considered to be among Wharton's best works, both because it casts a meticulously critical eye on the world she describes, while at the same time having considerable compassion for the characters that inhabit it.

Scorsese's 1993 film version has also weathered the test of time. Although the film performed poorly at the box office, *The Age of Innocence* received largely positive reviews from film critics. Roger Ebert considered it a successful blend of the source material and the work of a visionary director, declaring, "through some miracle it is all Wharton, and all Scorsese." Similarly, in *The New York Times*, Vincent Canby noted: "Scorsese has made a gorgeously uncharacteristic Scorsese film.... a big, intelligent movie that functions as if it were a window on a world he had just discovered, and about which he can't wait to spread the news."

The Age of Innocence earned Academy Award nominations for best adapted screenplay, best art direction, best original score, and best supporting actress (Ryder), and it won the award for best costume design. Ryder won the Golden Globe Award for Best Supporting Actress in a Motion Picture—Drama. Pfeiffer was nominated for a Golden Globe for Best Actress in a Motion Picture—Drama, but did not win. Today, *The Age of Innocence* is regarded as one of Scorsese's finest pictures.

—*Christopher Mari*

Further Reading

"Edith Wharton: A Biography." *The Mount: Edith Wharton's Home*, www.edithwharton.org/discover/edith-wharton/. Accessed 12 Feb. 2019.

Geldin, Brian. "Legendary Director Martin Scorsese Discusses 'The Age of Innocence.'" *Christian Science Monitor*, 25 June 2012, www.csmonitor.com/The-Culture/Culture-Cafe/2012/0625/Legendary-director-Martin-Scorsese-discusses-The-Age-of-Innocence. Accessed 15 Feb. 2019.

Bibliography

"The Age of Innocence." *AFI Catalog*, catalog.afi.com/Catalog/MovieDetails/59449. Accessed 12 Feb. 2019.

Canby, Vincent. "Review/Film: The Age of Innocence; Grand Passions and Good Manners." Review of *The Age of Innocence*, directed by Martin Scorsese. *The New York Times*, 17 Sept. 1993, www.nytimes.com/1993/09/17/movies/review-film-the-age-of-innocence-grand-passions-and-good-manners.html. Accessed 15 Feb. 2019.

Ebert, Roger. Review of *The Age of Innocence*, directed by Martin Scorsese. *RogerEbert.com*, 17 Sept. 1993, www.rogerebert.com/reviews/the-age-of-innocence-1993. Accessed 12 Feb. 2019.

Gilchrist, Andrew. "My Favourite Film: *The Age of Innocence*." Review of *The Age of Innocence*, directed by Martin Scorsese. *The Guardian*, 23 Dec. 2011, www.theguardian.com/film/filmblog/2011/dec/23/favourite-film-age-of-innocence. Accessed 12 Feb. 2019.

McCrum, Robert. "The 100 Best Novels: No 45—*The Age of Innocence* by Edith Wharton (1920)." *The Guardian*, 28 July 2014, www.theguardian.com/books/2014/jul/28/100-best-novels-age-of-innocence-edith-wharton-robert-mccrum. Accessed 15 Feb. 2019.

Rickey, Carrie. "Haunting, Powerful, Passionate: Martin Scorsese's *The Age of Innocence*." *Library of America*, 10 Feb. 2016, www.loa.org/news-and-views/1119-haunting-powerful-passionate-martin-scorseses-_the-age-of-innocence. Accessed 12 Feb. 2019.

Alexander and the Terrible, Horrible, No Good, Very Bad Day

The Novel
Author: Judith Viorst (b. 1931)
First published: 1972

The Film
Year released: 2014
Director: Miguel Arteta (b. 1965)
Screenplay by: Rob Lieber
Starring: Steve Carell, Jennifer Garner, Ed Oxenbould, Dylan Minnette, Kerris Dorsey

Context

When Judith Viorst published her children's book *Alexander and the Terrible, Horrible, No Good, Very Bad Day* in 1972, accompanied by striking illustrations from Ray Cruz, it quickly became a favorite among young readers. The picture book, which follows its preteen protagonist over the course of a day in which everything goes wrong, struck a chord because of its humor and relatability as well as its themes of fatality and acceptance. Capitalizing on the success of the title, which was named an ALA (American Library Association) Notable Children's Book of 1972, Viorst published three sequels over the next few decades, releasing *Alexander, Who Used to Be Rich Last Sunday* in 1977, *Alexander, Who Is Not (Do You Hear Me? I Mean It!) Going to Move* in 1995, and *Alexander, Who's Trying His Best to Be the Best Boy Ever* in 2014, all of which were warmly received by fans of the original title.

Author Judith Viorst reads at the 2014 National Book Fair. Photo by Slowking4, GFDL 1.2 Wikimedia Commons.

Although *Alexander* proved immediately popular, it was not until 1990 that Viorst's signature character was given life off the written page. In that year, HBO aired a thirty-minute animated television version of the original book that turned its young hero's ordeal into a musical. Following the book reasonably closely, the special nonetheless faced the problem of filling more time than it would take to read the book. While the television version of Alexander faces almost all of the same difficulties as his literary counterpart, he is made to suffer even more, enduring almost a dozen further indignities. To balance this increased load of misery, the makers of the animated special allow a few good things to happen to him as well. In addition, there are three musical numbers interspersed throughout the program.

Although the 1990 special brought the book to the small screen, and a Kennedy Center musical followed in 1998 with Judith Viorst collaborating with composer Shelly Markham, it was not until 2014 that *Alexander* was finally adapted into a full-length motion picture. First conceived in 2011, the film that would eventually be released three years later was initially developed by 20th Century Fox with Lisa Cholodenko set to direct. Steve Carell, who plays Alexander's father, joined in 2012 and things seemed to be moving along. By the end of that year, however, Fox had dropped the project, citing budget concerns. Luckily, Disney swooped in and picked it up, assigning Miguel Arteta as director and filling out the cast with a combination of established performers like Jennifer Garner and young up-and-comers like Ed Oxenbould (who would play Alexander) and Disney Channel star Bella Thorne. The film was completed over a few months in 2013 and was released in October 2014.

Film Analysis

At the beginning of Miguel Arteta's film adaptation of *Alexander and the Terrible, Horrible, No Good, Very Bad Day*, the 11-year-old protagonist informs the viewer in voice-over, "My parents say there's no such thing as a bad day. It all depends on how you look at it." This philosophy, which is held by his eternally optimistic father Ben, is not one that Alexander shares—at least not at the beginning of the film. Following the introduction of a framing device that starts the film *in media res*, the narrative flashes back and details a particularly difficult day in the life of its hero. This first, relatively brief section of the film is the part that most closely corresponds to Judith Viorst's 1972 picture book. Both narratives find the hapless preteen suffering a seemingly never-ending series of indignities, although the nature of these unfortunate events differs considerably from source to screen. In the book, Alexander's woes include getting no dessert with his lunch, having a cavity, and getting pushed into a mud puddle. In the film, Alexander accidentally sets fire to the notebook of the girl upon whom he has a crush, and he suffers the humiliation of having an embarrassing Photoshopped image of him make the rounds at school. The only thing the two Alexanders have in common is the threat of social demotion—in the book, Alexander's best friend tells him he has a new best friend, a boy named Philip Parker; while his cinematic counterpart's best friend tells him he will be attending Philip Parker's birthday party instead of Alexander's because the two parties are scheduled for the same time.

All of these misfortunes lead Alexander to question his parents' optimistic wisdom, which is both similar and different from that of the mom in the book. Viorst's story is told in the first person and mostly consists of Alexander's continuous narration that informs the reader of all the bad things that happen to him while repeatedly noting his plans to move to Australia to get away from his misfortunes. At the end of the book, though, Alexander's mom is given the final word. "It has been a terrible, horrible, no good, very bad day," Alexander narrates. "My mom says some days are like that. Even in Australia." In one sense, this attitude seems consistent with that of cinematic Alexander's parents. Both acknowledge the impossibility of controlling what happens to a person and encourage an acceptance of one's fate. But the attitude of the parents in the film suggests that by taking a positive attitude a person can at least control their perception of reality. The book's

mom offers very little positive advice and with her clipped utterance implies a more fatalistic attitude: one must simply accept what is bad and not try to run from it.

Alexander, after his bad day, concludes that his parents only maintain their positive attitudes because they do not know what it is like to share his misery. At midnight, when it technically becomes a new day (and his birthday at that), he lights a candle on a homemade ice cream sundae and places a curse on his family, wishing them all a bad day so they will be able to better relate to his plight. It is here that the film begins to veer dramatically away from the book, creating a whole new narrative independent from anything that Viorst had written and which comprises the bulk of the film's story. When adapting a story that is just over 700 words into a feature-length film, this expansion becomes a necessary.

The bulk of the film then follows the misfortunes suffered by the family in direct consequence of Alexander's curse. These misfortunes are extensive and afflict every member of the family. In the book, in addition to his parents, Alexander lives with two brothers of roughly the same age, Anthony and Nick. In the film, he lives with his parents, an older brother, also named Anthony, an older sister, Emily, and a baby brother, Trevor. It is not long before everything begins going wrong for this quintet. Alexander's mom has a major mix-up at work that could cost her a promotion; his out-of-work dad's job interview is seemingly sabotaged when he has to bring Trevor along and Trevor smudges a crayon all over his face; Anthony accidentally destroys school property and fails his driver's test; and Emily gets a cold just when she's about to star in a school play. No matter what the family tries to do, nothing seems to go right until suddenly things begin to turn around. Alexander confesses what he has done and, while no one in his skeptical family believes in the power of his curse, their fates soon take a turn for the better after Alexander's confession.

When an illness forces Philip Parker to cancel his birthday party, everyone heads to Alexander's instead. His parents, it turns out, have arranged for a great party, complete with a petting zoo of Australian animals. (The book's reliance on Australia as an imagined escape for Alexander manifests itself in the film as an obsessive interest in the country on Alexander's part.) Even the girl he has a crush on shows up. His mom gets the promotion, his dad gets the job, and the film ends happily. In the world of the film, it turns out that the bad day was simply an aberration. All this leads Alexander to finally conclude, "I just think you've gotta have the bad days so you can appreciate the good days." This would seem to bring his philosophy in line with his parents' and suggest that a positive attitude is the best approach to adversity and that things will generally work themselves out. This may strike the viewer as a little simplistic; it is certainly contrary to the message of Viorst's book. While the reader can certainly imagine that not every day will be as bad for Alexander as the one detailed in the book, there is no turn for the better in Viorst's narrative. We are left only with a few stoical words that speak to the inability to avoid one's fate. Things may improve or they may not—all a person can do is to passively accept what comes.

Significance

Alexander and the Terrible, Horrible, No Good, Very Bad Day opened in 2014 to modest reviews but a robust box office. It earned nearly $67 million domestically and over $100 million worldwide against a budget of just $28 million. No doubt sales were driven more by the longstanding appeal of the book than by what any individual critic had to say about it. Those who went to see it were treated to an appealingly good-natured film that had no shortage of comical moments. It is unclear how much cultural impact the movie had beyond simply being a diverting, momentarily popular film, but as such, it more than lived up to expectations.

The same year that the film was released, Judith Viorst published the fourth, and to date, last chapter in the Alexander series, *Alexander Who's Trying His Best to Be the Best Boy Ever*. In that book, which includes illustrations by Isidre Monés "in the style of" original illustrator Ray Cruz, Alexander eats a whole box of jelly donuts before bed only to wake up sick. Wary of the negative consequences of his behavior, he vows to be good but finds it more difficult than he thought. With an appealingly relatable plot, this latest *Alexander* book proved pleasing to fans, and in conjunction with the film, proved that Viorst's

most famous character continues to have massive appeal across the generations.

—Melynda Fuller

Further Reading

Chai, Barbara. "Writer Judith Viorst Finds Joy and Wisdom in Aging." *The Wall Street Journal*, 4 May 2019, www.wsj.com/articles/writer-judith-viorst-finds-joy-and-wisdom-in-aging-11556962200. Accessed 18 Mar. 2020.

Saval, Malina. "Steve Carell, Jennifer Garner and *Alexander* Stars Celebrate 'Love Letter to Family' at L.A. Premiere." *Variety*, 7 Oct. 2014, variety.com/2014/scene/vpage/jennifer-garner-steve-carell-alexander-and-the-terrible-horrible-no-good-very-bad-day-1201324109/. Accessed 18 Mar. 2020.

Sextro, Charlie. "Miguel Arteta on Learning How to Run a Movie Set." *The Creative Independent*, 15 Sept. 2017, thecreativeindependent.com/people/miguel-arteta-on-learning-how-to-run-a-movie-set/. Accessed 18 Mar. 2020.

Bibliography

Alexander and the Terrible, Horrible, No Good, Very Bad Day (2014). *Box Office Mojo*, www.boxofficemojo.com/title/tt1698641/?ref_=bo_se_r_1. Accessed 14 Mar. 2020.

Hoffman, Jordan. "*Alexander and the Terrible, Horrible, No Good, Very Bad Day*: Short on Drama but Lots of Fun—First Look Review." *The Guardian*, 2 Oct. 2014, www.theguardian.com/film/2014/oct/02/alexander-and-the-terrible-horrible-no-good. Accessed 14 Mar. 2020.

Mendelson, Scott. "Review: *Alexander and the Terrible, Horrible, No Good, Very Bad Day* Is a Funny, Progressive, Empathetic, Pretty Good Film." *Forbes.com*, 2 Oct. 2014, www.forbes.com/sites/scottmendelson/2014/10/02/review-alexander-and-the-terrible-horrible-no-good-very-bad-day-is-a-funny-progressive-empathetic-pretty-good-film/#31479bfc7ea1. Accessed 13 Mar. 2020.

O'Malley, Sheila. "*Alexander and the Terrible, Horrible, No Good, Very Bad Day*." *RogerEbert.com*, 10 Oct. 2014, www.rogerebert.com/reviews/alexander-and-the-terrible-horrible-no-good-very-bad-day-2014. Accessed 13 Mar. 2020.

Scott, A. O. "Be Careful What You Wish For." *The New York Times*, 9 Oct. 2014. www.nytimes.com/2014/10/10/movies/no-good-very-bad-day-with-steve-carell.html. Accessed 14 Mar. 2020.

Alice in Wonderland

The Novel
Author: Lewis Carroll (1832-98)
First published: 1865

The Film
Year released: 1951
Directors: Clyde Geronimi (1901-89), Wilfred Jackson (1906-88), Hamilton Luske (1903-68)
Screenplay by: Winston Hibler, Ted Sears, Bill Peet, Erdman Penner, Joe Rinaldi, Milt Banta, William Cottrell, Dick Kelsey, Joe Grant, Dick Huemer, Del Connell, Tom Oreb, John Walbridge
Starring: Kathryn Beaumont, Ed Wynn, Richard Haydn, Sterling Holloway

Context

Lewis Carroll was the pseudonym of Charles Lutwidge Dodgson, a nineteenth-century mathematician, photographer, and writer. He wrote *Alice in Wonderland* in 1865 and *Through the Looking-Glass* in 1871, books that have been called the "first significant works of fantasy for children." Carroll initially wanted to illustrate the books himself, before settling on John Tenniel to create the images that most readers associate with the work, including details such as Alice's blue dress. In the years following the author's death, numerous film and artistic versions of the books have been produced, with over fifty illustrators producing versions of the tale's characters and approximately twenty film variations. The first three films were silent versions directed by Cecil Hepworth and Percy Stow (1903), Edwin S. Porter (1910), and W. W. Young (1915). In 1933, Gary Cooper and Cary Grant starred in a Paramount version directed by Norman McLeod, Hugh Harman, and Rudolf Ising.

The 1951 Disney film version of *Alice in Wonderland* was a culmination of what some sources call Walt Disney's "longtime attraction to the novel." In 1933, he had discussed an option with Mary Pickford to portray Alice in a full-length film, but the work had to be delayed because Paramount had released its live-action version of the film that same year. The 1951 film came after a series of short films Disney had made between 1923 and 1927; these clips included a live actress who appeared in a cartoon world with animated backgrounds and animals. The first of these shorts was titled *Alice's Wonderland*, with the series titled the *Alice Comedies*. After Paramount preempted Disney's live-action film, he claimed rights to the book in 1938, committing to producing a film that some sources suggest he was not completely in favor of making.

Audience interest in the film was piqued in 1950, when Disney produced a television special, *One Hour in Wonderland*. As might be expected of an animated Disney film, the 1951 Alice adds a sense of whimsy that went beyond Tenniel's earlier illustrations and other film versions. For instance, one critic notes, "In place of the illustrator's [Tenniel's] austere Rabbit (and indeed Carroll's flustered and fussily bullying one) is a dumpy, goofy, bouncy, cutesy, ninny." This lighter version of the characterization might be a reflection of the popularity of Disney's short "Silly Symphonies" as well as *Fantasia* (1940) and competitor cartoons from companies such as Metro-Goldwyn-Mayer (MGM) and Warner Bros.

Alice in Wonderland was the thirteenth animated (or mostly animated) film for Walt Disney, but it was distributed by RKO (Radio-Keith-Orpheum) Radio Pictures. It followed

A Mad Tea-Party, illustration by John Tenniel, 1865. Image via Wikimedia Commons. [Public domain.]

Alice in Wonderland *(1951). Image via Walt Disney/Wikimedia Commons. [Public domain.]*

Cinderella (1950). Directors Clyde Geronimi, Wilfred Jackson, and Hamilton Luske had all worked on the previous year's *Cinderella*. Geronimi also worked on *Sleeping Beauty* (1959) and *Peter Pan* (1953), while Jackson's other Disney credits include *Snow White and the Seven Dwarfs* (1937) and *Peter Pan* (1953). Luske had worked on *Pinnocchio* (1940) as well as *Mary Poppins* (1964).

Film Analysis

The 1951 animated *Alice in Wonderland* is not on the level of Disney's best films, but it remains one of the most popular film versions of *Alice*. Disney himself was not particularly positive about the film. In 1956, he said, "We didn't feel a thing. But we were forcing ourselves to do it." A few years afterward, he noted, "The picture was filled with weird characters." He even claimed, "I got trapped into making *Alice in Wonderland* against my better judgment and it was a terrible disappointment. Frankly, I always liked the Tenniel illustrations in *Alice* but I never exactly died laughing over the story. It's terribly tough to transfer whimsy to the screen."

Conflicts between Disney and his illustrators during the production of the film may have caused further problems with the film itself. For instance, Frank Thomas reported to one interviewer that Disney did not seem to know what he wanted out of the film, so he contradicted what the illustrators were trying to do, and the results were less than satisfactory to either. This unrest is reflected in some ways in the storyline itself as well as in the characterization in the film.

The story of the film is based on a combination of Carroll's *Alice in Wonderland* as well as *Through the Look-*

ing-Glass. The film's creators chose bits of the second novella to incorporate into the main story from the first. As a result, the plot remains rather flat, including conflicts but never really building to one climax in the way that Carroll's first book did. In Carroll's book, Alice falls into the rabbit hole and spends most of her journey chasing after two things: the ever-present white rabbit, who works for a duchess, and admittance into a lovely garden that she sees through the little door she finds in the original hallway. While looking for the rabbit, Alice encounters a variety of situations and characters. Like in the film, she samples a drink and a cake that change her size, she has a crying fit that floods the hallway, and she encounters a dodo bird who participates in a Caucus race. The scene with the dodo is quite a bit different from the book, though, and here the dodo takes charge, trading places of importance with the dormouse, who is only a minor character in the film.

Though the scenes in the film serve as a way to entertain the audience, each scene throughout the novel has a specific purpose for Alice's story, serving as a test of her logical or linguistic ability or as a test of her identity. As a result, she learns something from her encounters, and each encounter leads her to the final croquet and court scenes, where she finally achieves her goals of finding the garden as well as understanding who she is. In the film, however, the screenwriters subtly change the trajectory of the story, leading Alice on a chase that does not seem to have much purpose. Although the film includes iconic characters such as the Cheshire Cat, the hookah-smoking caterpillar, the Mad Hatter, and the March Hare, the Duchess is left out, replaced with brief musical interludes with characters or scenes from the second book, such as Tweedledee and Tweedledum, who tell the story of the Walrus and the Carpenter. Carroll's novel ends on a positive note, with Alice's sister waking her up but then drifting into a daydream of her own based on Alice's adventures, thus affirming the benefits of imagination. The film, however, ends with Alice being scolded for falling asleep during a lesson, the older female character shooing her back home for tea.

The characterization is another critical element of the film. In Carroll's version, Alice is engaging, often arguing with herself and continuously seeking knowledge of who she really is. The encounters with the Cheshire Cat, the caterpillar, the Mad Hatter, and March Hare, as well as with the Queen of Hearts all lead to Alice understanding herself better. The film leaves this aspect of Alice's char-

Lewis Carroll in 1857. Photo via Wikimedia Commons. [Public domain.]

acter out for the most part, including only a few minor connections to the issue of identity, such as when the caterpillar asks her who she is. Both pieces do include Alice's humorously irritable attitude, but the film adds a sense of boredom with the trial scene while the book shows Alice as more exasperated by the hijinks. A second character of note is the Mad Hatter. The tea party scene provides a sense of comic relief to both the book and the film, with Disney's version emphasizing the humor while Carroll's version adds a logical element with more word play around the issue of time. In both instances, though, the Mad Hatter's zany and over-the-top actions provide a physical comedy that attracts audiences of all ages.

Finally, by fragmenting the original story and characters, Disney's film does include several features that are a reflection of successful stories of the time. For example, its musical style mirrors Disney's earlier works and the humorous tone further connects this film to Disney shorts as well as to competitor cartoons. The film's side stories, like the Walrus and the Carpenter or the interlude with the singing flowers, act as mini cartoons within the whole.

Significance

Alice in Wonderland's release in the summer of 1951 was hopeful; however, it lost money, with a $3 million creation budget but only grossing $2.4 million. In comparison, the cost was two-thirds more than *Cinderella*, Disney's previous release, which met with much greater success. Despite this disappointment, Disney's use of television to promote the film was notable for several reasons. In one respect, it predicted the success of the later Disney programming on ABC and in another respect, it allowed Disney to remind viewers of earlier films, thus producing positive memories of those previous experiences. The television program that introduced the film also introduced audiences to Kathryn Beaumont, the actress who voiced Alice. This allowed Disney to use the actress to promote the film in later venues as well. Another positive outcome of this promotion was that it showed the audience of children the possibilities of a joy-filled interaction with a fantasy world.

The film has been reintroduced to audiences several times in the years since it was first shown in theaters. Two television broadcasts, three years after its original release and then a decade after that, allowed Walt Disney to interact with the film as he presented information about Carroll's original novel as well as his own company's picture book version. It was aired on television again in 1987. All three television airings cut pieces out of the film to limit its showing to an hour.

Alice in Wonderland was critically recognized. Directors Geronimi, Jackson, and Luske were nominated for the Golden Lion at the Venice Film Festival in 1951. Oliver Wallace was nominated for an Oscar for Best Music-Scoring of a Musical Picture, at the Academy Awards in 1952.

—Theresa L. Stowell, PhD

Further Reading

Douglas-Fairhurst, Robert. *The Story of Alice: Lewis Carroll and the Secret History of Wonderland.* Harvard UP, 2015.

Holt, Nathalia. *The Queens of Animation: The Untold Story of the Women Who Transformed the World of Disney and Made Cinematic History.* Little, Brown and Company, 2019.

Ross, Deborah. "Escape from Wonderland: Disney and the Female Imagination." *Marvels & Tales: Journal of Fairy-Tale Studies,* vol. 18, no. 1, 2004, pp. 53-66. *EBSCOhost,* search.ebscohost.com/login.aspx?direct=true&db=edsglr&AN=edsgcl.122027830&site=eds-live. Accessed 31 Mar. 2020.

Bibliography

Alice in Wonderland (1951). *IMDb,* www.imdb.com/title/tt0043274/?ref_=fn_al_tt_2. Accessed 31 Mar. 2020.

Barrier, Michael. *The Animated Man: A Life of Walt Disney.* University of California Press, 2007.

Bonner, Frances and Jason Jacobs. "The First Encounter: Observations on the Chronology of Encounter with Some Adaptations of Lewis Carroll's Alice Books." *Convergence: The International Journal of Research into New Media Technologies,* vol. 17, no. 1, 2011, pp. 37-48.

Brooker, Will. "Chapter 6: Adapting Alice." *Alice's Adventures: Lewis Carroll in Popular Culture,* Bloomsbury, 2004, pp. 199-28.

Galda, Lee, et al. *Literature and the Child.* Wadsworth Publishing, 2017.

Sinker, Mark. "Alice Through the Lens." *Sight & Sound,* vol. 20, no. 4, Apr. 2010, pp. 35-38. *EBSCOhost,* search.ebscohost.com/login.aspx?direct=true&db=mzh&AN=2010440760&site=eds-live. Accessed 31 Mar. 2020.

All the Bright Places

The Novel
Author: Jennifer Niven (b. 1968)
First published: 2015

The Film
Year released: 2020
Director: Brett Haley (b. 1983)
Screenplay by: Jennifer Niven and Liz Hannah
Starring: Elle Fanning, Justice Smith, Alexandra Shipp, Kelli O'Hara, Lamar Johnson

Context

American author Jennifer Niven published the novel *All the Bright Places* in 2015. Niven had previously written in several different genres for adult readers, including nonfiction, a memoir, and a series of historical novels. *All the Bright Places* represented a notable shift for Niven as the book was aimed at young adults. In interviews, Niven noted that the book was loosely inspired by her own experiences as a teenager who dated someone with bipolar disorder. The novel quickly earned critical acclaim for its realistic portrayal of mental health issues, including teen suicide. It went on to become a *New York Times* best seller.

The success of *All the Bright Places* was part of a boom in young-adult fiction. The genre had grown in popularity through the late twentieth century, and became a major cultural force in the early 2000s with the immense success of series such as Harry Potter (1997-2007), Twilight (2005-08), and The Hunger Games (2008-10)—all of which were adapted into blockbuster film series as well, setting off a parallel trend in the film industry. While those series demonstrated the mainstream appeal of supernatural fantasy and dystopian stories, by the 2010s there was also a wave of Judy Blume-style realism in young-adult fiction. *All the Bright Places* is comparable to popular books such as John Green's *The Fault in Our Stars* (2012) and Angie Thomas's *The Hate U Give* (2017) in exploring serious issues teens might face in the real world. Both those titles were also turned into successful movies, as young-adult titles continued to be popular in Hollywood.

The film adaptation of *All the Bright Places* (2020) was directed by Brett Haley, mostly known writing and directing small independent films. He broke through to mainstream audiences with *The Hero* (2017) and *Hearts Beat Loud* (2018), two realistic comedy-dramas that earned largely positive reviews. *All the Bright Places* continued Haley's transition into mainstream cinema. It became part of a burgeoning trend of low- to mid-budget films based on best-selling young-adult novels and distributed by the popular streaming service Netflix, along with works such as *To All the Boys I've Loved Before* (2018) and *Dumplin'* (2018). The adaptation of *All the Bright Places* drew particular comparisons to the Netflix series *13 Reasons Why* (2017), based on Jay Asher's 2007 novel of the same name, which similarly focuses on teen suicide. Overall, these works represented an increase in demand for stories about teenagers going through real-world challenges and navigating the complex contemporary social landscape.

Film Analysis

While Haley's film adaptation of *All the Bright Things* differs at times from the novel, as a whole it remains true to its source material's central story and message. Both center on the lives of teenagers Violet Markey (Elle Fanning) and Theodore Finch (Justice Smith), who are drawn together as they each face mental health challenges. The film retains the book's small-town Indiana setting, which reinforces the fact that the characters are ordinary people. The narrative focuses on emotional tension and character building rather than action or a complex plot.

Most of the differences between book and film were in fact implemented by Niven herself, who cowrote the screenplay with novelist Liz Hannah, to ensure that her novel translated more effectively to the screen. Most notably, she removed many of the details of Finch's mental health struggles, leaving audiences with just the broad strokes. As a result, the film shows Finch grappling with some form of depression but never elaborates on a specific diagnosis. This is quite different from the book, which clarifies that the "awake" and "asleep" states that Finch vacillates between are a result of bipolar disorder. Furthermore, Finch does not talk about suicide in the film like he does in the book or make an unsuccessful attempt to end his own life. The decision to omit these pieces of dialogue and the significant plot point ultimately provide the film with a greater sense of suspense. It makes Finch's true identity and motivations ambiguous, which in turn creates propulsive dramatic tension that keeps the film moving steadily toward its climax.

All the Bright Places is primarily a love story between two characters struggling with serious issues. In this way, it is comparable to other dark romance films like Terrence Malick's *Badlands* (1973) and Jane Campion's *Bright Star* (2009)—both of which Haley cited as direct inspirations. While *All the Bright Places* does not have quite the same ominous sense of doom as those two works, it does lack the airiness of a typical teen romance. To establish a tone that fits between these two genres, Haley infuses the film with a gentle kind of realism. He accomplishes this by rejecting the heightened look, atmosphere, and pace of many romance films. Additionally, he lets the camera linger on silent moments between characters rather than engaging in quick cuts of snappy dialogue. As a result, much of what Violet and Finch are feeling about themselves and each other is communicated through their faces and body language. The end result is a film that is neither gritty nor saccharine, but one that feels authentic.

Haley uses numerous cinematic tools to infuse the film with a sense of intimacy and heightened emotion. Specifically, he uses primarily over-the-shoulder (OTS) shots when filming the dialogue between the characters. A technique in which the camera focuses on the speaker's face while including a piece of the listener's body in the frame, OTS shots are often used to establish spatial depth within a scene. They can also communicate character relationships through the space between two characters and their eyelines in relation to one another. In *All the Bright Places*, Haley often uses OTS shots when the characters are revealing their complicated emotions to one another. These visual cues help to show the characters' desires to connect with one another as well as the raw honesty of the things they are saying.

While the book alternates between Finch and Violet's first-person narratives throughout its chapters, the film is more subtle in the way that it strikes a balance between their two perspectives. Haley opts to "show, not tell" with the characters' thoughts and feelings by relying primarily on the camera rather than the tools of dialogue or voice-over. The scenes that demonstrate what Finch is truly feeling are shot predominantly when he is alone in his room. This is because when Finch is in public, he adopts the persona of someone who does not care what others think about him. When he is alone, he is his most authentic self. It is in Finch's room that audiences learn about the efforts that he must take to not succumb to depression. This includes decorating his ceiling and walls with color-coded sticky notes about the positive things that happened to him that day.

In contrast, Haley showcases Violet's internal experience through her interactions with other people. In the beginning of the film, when she is still reeling from her sister's death in a car crash, Violet comes across as forlorn and withdrawn from the world. Once she reluctantly agrees to work on a geography project with Finch, however, she begins to change. A key example of how Haley presents Violet's breakthrough from depression comes in the trip she takes with Finch to a nearby roller coaster. This sequence demonstrates how scared she is to be in a car by having the camera focus on her body language, with an insert close-up shot of her hands drumming nervously on her knees. After she rides on the roller coaster, Violet's face becomes more relaxed and cheerful. Her transformation culminates in the following scene when she rides home with Finch. At one point, he pulls the car over to the side of the road to kiss her for the first time. When she kisses him back, the sun comes out and the frame is flooded with bright light. The following scenes depict the two falling in love through a montage of joyful activities that show Violet smiling, running, and dancing. This stark contrast to where she was earlier in the film effectively brings out her character development even without words.

One of the biggest themes of the film is how life continues to be beautiful even in the midst of death—one just needs to know where to look to see it. Haley helps communicate this message through the film's color palette and set design. In addition to the film's overall yellow aesthetic tone, Violet and Finch are often depicted wearing red and brown in the early scenes of the film. These autumnal colors can be interpreted as suggestive of death and mourning. As Violet and Finch travel around Indiana, however, they are surrounded by glimpses of green trees. Haley places the green on the periphery of the frames to communicate the characters' burgeoning feelings of love and hope. As their time together continues and they fall deeper in love, Haley replaces the industrial and suburban architecture from the first act of the film with more romantic imagery. In turn, their environment no longer feels confining but like a magical place where anything is possible.

Significance

All the Bright Places premiered on Netflix on February 28, 2020. The film received mixed reviews. Several critics worried that the film's take on the issue of suicide was overly romanticized, shallow, or otherwise problematic. Writing for *The Guardian*, for example, Benjamin Lee complained that the film "lingers briefly in the deep end but remains disappointingly shallow." Other reviewers felt *All the Bright Places* in fact presented an admirably nuanced look at struggles with grief and depression. For example, writing for *Variety*, Courtney Howard called the movie a "standout" in the crowded young-adult genre thanks to its "extremely sensitive touch" and "humanistic undertones."

Notably, Netflix included messages in the film's credits directing audience members who may have struggled with mental health issues to resources for help. The decision to do so came after other works exploring such subject matter—particularly *13 Reasons Why*—had generated considerable controversy. Haley and others involved with *All the Bright Places* spoke about intentionally trying to raise awareness of mental health challenges while also attempting to craft a film that did not feel overly didactic or exploitative.

Aside from considerations of the subject matter, most critics praised the technical aspects of the film. Many remarked that Haley's direction helped the narrative pack an emotional punch without being overwrought or manipulative. The cinematography and the use of music also earned plaudits. Finally, reviewers commended the central performances of Fanning and Smith. While both had successful careers previous to *All the Bright Places*, the film showcased their potential as leads capable of bringing complex material to life.

—*Emily E. Turner*

Further Reading

Fanning, Elle, and Justice Smith. "'All the Bright Places' Stars Elle Fanning and Justice Smith on How the Film Portrays Mental Illness." Interview by P. Claire Dodson. *Teen Vogue*, 28 Feb. 2020, www.teenvogue.com/story/all-the-bright-places-elle-fanning-justice-smith-how-film-portrays-mental-illness. Accessed 10 Mar. 2021.

Gullickson, Brad. "Brett Haley on the Knee-Jerking Filmmaking Required for 'All the Bright Places.'" *Film School Rejects*, 19 Mar. 2020, filmschoolrejects.com/brett-haley-interview/. Accessed 10 Mar. 2021.

Bibliography

Frederick, Candice. "Love amid Trauma." Review of *All the Bright Places*, directed by Brett Haley. *The New York Times*, 28 Feb. 2020, www.nytimes.com/2020/02/28/movies/all-the-bright-places-review.html. Accessed 10 Mar. 2021.

Howard, Courtney. Review of *All the Bright Places*, directed by Brett Haley. *Variety*, 28 Feb. 2020, variety.com/2020/film/reviews/all-the-bright-places-review-1203518263/. Accessed 10 Mar. 2021.

Lee, Benjamin. "All the Bright Places Review—Teen Charm Can't Lift Maudlin Netflix Drama." Review of *All the Bright Places*, directed by Brett Haley. *The Guardian*, 28 Feb. 2020, www.theguardian.com/film/2020/feb/28/all-the-bright-places-review-netflix. Accessed 10 Mar. 2021.

Miller, Julie. "How Netflix's 'All the Bright Places' Tackled Teen Suicide in the Wake of '13 Reasons Why.'" *Vanity Fair*, 28 Feb. 2020, www.vanityfair.com/hollywood/2020/02/all-the-bright-places-movie. Accessed 10 Mar. 2021.

Niven, Jennifer. "Life is Too Short to Be Closed Off to Possibility." Interview. *The Guardian*, 26 Jan. 2015, www.theguardian.com/childrens-books-site/2015/jan/26/jennifer-niven-interview-all-the-bright-places. Accessed 10 Mar. 2021.

And Then There Were None

The Novel
Author: Agatha Christie (1890-1976)
First published: 1939

The Film
Year released: 1945
Director: René Clair (1898-1981)
Screenplay by: Dudley Nichols
Starring: C. Aubrey Smith, Judith Anderson, Walter Huston, Louis Hayward, June Duprez

Context

By the eve of World War II, British writer Agatha Christie, the "Queen of Crime," was world-famous. She introduced Belgian detective Hercule Poirot in her first novel *The Mysterious Affair at Styles* (1920), and he quickly became a mystery fan favorite. In 1926, the author herself was the subject of a real-life mystery. Christie vanished during an acrimonious breakup with her first husband and a nationwide search ensued. She reappeared eleven days later, apparently suffering from amnesia. The following year, with her mental health restored, she introduced amateur sleuth Jane Marple to the reading world. Christie continued to be beloved for ingenious plotting, inventive methods of murder, the skill with which she moved believable characters around colorful crime scenes, and the tension she created in the process of making mayhem.

Christie's most-recognized, most-purchased, and most-adapted novel is known by various titles. It debuted in England as *Ten Little Niggers* (1939) in both newspaper serial and book form. However, the racial epithet used in the title was widely recognized as offensive, especially in the United States, where the novel was published under a title borrowed from the last line of a nineteenth-century minstrel song that figures prominently throughout the plot—*And Then There Were None* (1940). Yet into the late 1990s, the original title did remain in use in various translations. The novel was also published as *Ten Little Indians* in paperback editions released between 1964 and 1986, before that title was also deemed politically incorrect.

Under any name, the novel was a success—even without the presence of Poirot or Marple. It featured one of the author's most diabolic plots. A group of strangers is lured one by one to a luxurious rendezvous. The characters are "types" from a range of social classes—a doctor, an el-

derly spinster, a retired judge, a military veteran. As the story unfolds, they gain dimension. Their hidden strengths and weaknesses are displayed publicly through words and deeds, and are revealed privately in memories, thoughts, hopes, and fears.

They arrive on a private island off the coast of Devon in southwest England, where a long-gone millionaire built a fabulous home. After they dine, a recording is played. An unidentifiable voice accuses each of the ten people present

The author, Agatha Christie. Photo by F l a n k e r via Wikimedia Commons.

A scene from And Then There Were None *(1945). Left to right: Louis Hayward, C. Aubrey Smith, Barry Fitzgerald, Richard Haydn, Mischa Auer, and Walter Huston. Photo via 20th Century Fox/Wikimedia Commons. [Public domain.]*

of a specific crime resulting in death. As they soon learn, there will be retribution for their actions, whether they feel guilty or not. The island is really a trap from which there is no escape. One by one, guests begin to die. Survivors ultimately realize that one of them must be the murderer. As bodies pile up, doubt, paranoia, and suspicion mount.

Film Analysis

A perfect example of the author's innovations, *And Then There Were None* provides a baffling mystery that allows readers to play along in the deadly guessing game. The novel combines multiple mystery tropes: revenge, locked-room puzzle, false protagonist, serial offender. At the end, ten corpses inhabit an otherwise deserted island. The complex story required two separate devices at the end to inform readers how the murders were committed and to identify the killer. First came an epilogue: a Scotland Yard inspector describes to a superior the results of the extensive investigations. This scene confirms the probable order of the killings and exposes the plots behind the crimes but leaves key questions unanswered. For example, who is the mysterious mastermind, U. N. Owen? Forensic evidence eliminates the last few victims as the killer. The best police theory is that an additional person must have been present—on a barren island with no hiding places and no means of escaping across rough seas to the mainland. These problems are only resolved via a final revelation. Christie's murderer writes a confession, puts it in a bottle, and tosses it into the ocean. The bottle is fortuitously retrieved by a fishing trawler and is turned over to the authorities who, along with readers, at last know motive, means, and culprit.

While the novel offered possibilities for dramatization, the killer's twelve-page bottled confession presented production difficulties. Christie, a talented playwright—her murder mystery play, *The Mousetrap*, has run continuously since 1952—revised the story for the stage. She changed some character names (like "General Macarthur," because there was already a prominent American officer with a similar surname—Douglas MacArthur). She eliminated the epilogue and incorporated elements from the confession, which added suspense and increased the pace. Most significantly, she added romance. This lightened the bleakness, imparting a more upbeat, wartime morale-boosting mood. As a play, it was produced first as *Ten Little Indians* (1940), then under its revised title in 1943. The second version, with certain adjustments, served as the basis for the 1945 film adaptation.

Exiled French filmmaker René Clair—famed for *Le Million* and *A Nous la Liberté* (both 1931)—was chosen to direct. Academy Award-winning (*The Informer*, 1935) screenwriter Dudley Nichols, who also wrote such screen hits as *Bringing Up Baby* (1938), *Stagecoach* (1939), *The Long Voyage Home* (1940), and *Mr. Lucky* (1943), handled the screenplay. His script powerfully complemented Christie's superior plotting and characterization skills.

One immediate refinement in the adaptation was the story's starting point. The novel takes pages to introduce and sketch each of the eight characters invited to the island and assemble them for the boat ride to their destination. The film eliminates the need to explain by showing. It starts with a motorboat full of people moving across the water. No dialogue is exchanged for four minutes as the camera travels across the passengers' faces. It is a brilliant use of silence. The interlude allows viewers to anticipate the roles of well-known character actors such as C. Aubrey Smith ("General Mandrake"), Barry Fitzgerald ("Justice Quincannon"), and Walter Huston ("Dr. Armstrong"). The sequence gives visual clues to personalities as they react wordlessly to stimuli. The stern-looking spinster Emily Brent (Judith Anderson) turns away in disgust from pipe smoke. One man looks queasy or drunk. The pretty young woman Vera Claythorne (June Duprez) attracts attention by letting her scarf blow across the faces of the men riding next to her.

They land on Indian Island (based on Burgh Island), the name of which agrees with the nursery rhyme Ten Little Indians used to tabulate victims and their method of demise. In the film it is documented through piano sheet mu-sic, rather than framed poems hanging in every room, as in the novel. One guest, Russian Prince Nikita Starloff (Mischa Auer), a cosmopolitan substitute for the novel's one-dimensional Marston, plays and sings the simple tune with verve. A dining room centerpiece reinforces the theme: ten little Indian figurines that are broken by the killer to mark each elimination.

The plot unfolds much as Christie wrote it with the novel's internalized text converted to dialogue or removed. Cinematographer Lucien N. Andriot's (1892-1979) subtle touches enhance viewing pleasure. In one sequence demonstrating heightened suspicion, ex-policeman Blore (Roland Young) spies on adventurer Philip Lombard (Louis Hayward) through a keyhole. The camera pulls back to reveal Dr. Armstrong watching Blore through another keyhole while he himself is being observed by yet another character. Many sequences are staged around a pool table, which allows ivory balls and sturdy cues to be useful dramatic props. In a scene not included in the novel, survivors vote for whom they think is Mr. Owen, their mysterious host, a serial killer. Unexpectedly, servant Thomas Rogers (Richard Haydn) receives the most votes. (Haydn, with one squeaking shoe and an exceedingly nasal delivery, provides several moments of comic relief.) Incensed at being thought of as a lunatic murderer, Rogers gulps down all the drinks he just served to prove they are not poisoned. He then staggers off through a downpour to the woodshed, his bedroom for the night, soon to become a fresh crime scene.

A streamlined script, excellent acting and crisp camera work make *And Then There Were None* a satisfying suspense film. Despite gory methods of dispatch described in the novel—axe murder, bludgeoning, skull-crushing—the violence mostly occurs off-screen. A limp hand here, a still foot there, are tasteful representations of death. The adaptation is self-contained, with no appendices necessary. A brief flashback near the end illustrates certain deceptions and misdirections, using passages taken from U. N. Owen's confession in the novel, and narrated in the killer's voice.

This entertaining film even created its own little riddle. In several scenes, a striped cat is seen strolling out of the kitchen, sunning on a windowsill, peering from a woodpile, playing with a ball of yarn, sitting on a lap. None of the ten guests brought the cat to what was an empty house on a long-unoccupied island more than a mile from the mainland across open water. Mystery lovers might question how the cat arrived on the island. Animal lovers would probably want to know what became of it after everyone died.

Significance

Critical reception of the first *And Then There Were None* film adaptation was uniformly positive. Reviewers praised the outstanding cast, tight screenplay, and evocative photography. Some singled out the music by composer-pianist Mario Castelnuovo-Tedesco, who had completed scores for suspense films like *Above Suspicion* (1943) and *The Mark of the Whistler* (1944). Commercially, it was not among the top-grossing films, but recouped 20th Century Fox's $1 million investment. With competition from other major releases like *Spellbound*, *The Lost Weekend*, and *Mildred Pierce*, the film did not receive any Academy Award nominations. However, it garnered the grand prize for best picture, the Golden Leopard, at the initial Locarno International Film Festival in Switzerland, and René Clair was tapped as best director.

While Christie's stories, plays and novels were adapted for film as early as 1928, a virtual avalanche of entertainment based on her work began after World War II. More than thirty film adaptations—some produced in places like France, Russia, and India—were released. Several of these (in 1965, 1974, and 1989) were remakes of *And Then There Were None*. There were, in addition to regular series (1980s- 1990s, 2000s-2010s) featuring Miss Marple and Hercule Poirot, also more than thirty full-blown television productions between 1947 and 2020. These included adaptations of *And Then There Were None* in 1949, 1959, and 2015. Christie's characters and novels have also been featured on radio, in graphic novels, video games, and Japanese animation. Christie's own stage version of *And Then There Were None* (1943) is also frequently produced.

—Jack Ewing

Further Reading

Aldridge, Mark. *Agatha Christie on Screen*. Palgrave Macmillan, 2016.

Green, Julius. *Curtain Up: Agatha Christie: A Life in the Theatre*. Harper, 2015.

Bibliography

Bunson, Matthew. *The Complete Christie: An Agatha Christie Encyclopedia*. Pocket Books, 2000.

Chhibber, Mini Anthikad. "*And Then There Were None* at 80: A Tribute." *The Hindu*, 5 Nov. 2019, www.thehindu.com/entertainment/movies/agatha-christies-and-then-there-were-none-tunrs-80/article29888710.ece. Accessed 20 Feb. 2020.

Christie, Agatha. *And Then There Were None*. William Morrow, 2011.

Flood, Alison. "*And Then There Were None* Declared World's Favourite Agatha Christie Novel." *The Guardian*, 1 Sept. 2015, www.theguardian.com/books/2015/sep/01/and-then-there-were-none-declared-worlds-favourite-agatha-christie-novel. Accessed 20 Feb. 2020.

Manus, Peter. "What Makes Agatha Christie's *And Then There Were None* Everyone's Favorite Murder Spree?" *Criminal Element*, 20 Jan. 2017, www.criminalelement.com/what-makes-agatha-christies-and-then-there-were-none-everyones-favorite-murder-spree/. Accessed 20 Feb. 2020.

Stein, Sadie. "Mystery." *Paris Review*, 5 Feb. 2016, www.theparisreview.org/blog/2016/02/05/mystery/. Accessed 20 Feb. 2020.

Turner, Camilla. "Mystery of Agatha Christie's Disappearance Is Solved' as Author Suggests She Considered Suicide over Husband's Affair." *The Telegraph*, 8 May 2017, www.telegraph.co.uk/news/2017/05/08/mystery-agatha-christies-disappearance-solved-author-suggests/. Accessed 20 Feb. 2020.

The Angel

The Novel
Author: Uri Bar-Joseph (b. 1949)
First published: 2010, in Hebrew (English trans., 2016)

The Film
Year released: 2018
Director: Ariel Vromen (b. 1973)
Screenplay by: David Arata, Uri Bar-Joseph
Starring: Marwan Kenzari, Toby Kebbell, Hannah Ware, Waleed Zuaiter, Tsahi Halevi, Sasson Gabai, and Maisa Abd Elhad

Context

The Angel is a 2018 Israeli American spy thriller based upon Uri Bar-Joseph's 2010 nonfiction work *The Angel: The Egyptian Spy Who Saved Israel*, which was updated and translated from Hebrew into English in 2016. The book is based on the real-life story of Ashraf Marwan, a prominent Egyptian official who spied for the Israeli government during the lead-up to the Yom Kippur War of 1973. That war against Israel had been launched by an alliance of Arab states, led by Egypt and Syria, in an effort to take back lands in the Sinai Peninsula and the Golan Heights that Israel had occupied since the Six-Day War of 1967. The loss of those lands was particularly vexing to the man who would spearhead the retaliatory war, Anwar Sadat, president of Egypt. Although the Israelis were initially taken by surprise—despite warnings from Marwan—they ultimately held off the invasion. After a ceasefire was negotiated by the United Nations following heavy losses on both sides, Egypt and Israel sought to normalize relations. With the help of US president Jimmy Carter, the 1978 Camp David Accords were signed between the two Middle Eastern powers, leading to the return of the Sinai to Egypt and the first-ever peaceful recognition of Israel by an Arab country.

Bar-Joseph's book on Israel's greatest spy grew out of his fascination with Marwan, who was the son-in-law of Egyptian president Gamal Abdel Nasser and later became a close adviser under Nasser's successor, Sadat, who ultimately secured peace with Israel before he was assassinated in 1981. Marwan died a very rich man under mysterious circumstances when he fell to his death from a balcony in London in 2007. Since Marwan had been revealed as a spy prior to his death, the intelligence community has debated whether he was a double agent who really worked for Egypt, or if he was simply a spy for Israel. Also debated are the full extent of his motives, which Bar-Joseph outlines in great detail in his book.

Bar-Joseph's interest in Marwan also came from experience; the author served for fifteen years as an intelligence analyst for the Israel Defense Forces (IDF) Intelligence/Research Division. He published several works about Israeli military and intelligence capabilities, as well as the history of the Arab-Israeli conflict. He also taught political science at the University of Haifa.

Israeli Ariel Vromen directed the film adaptation of Bar-Joseph's book, which had a $12 million budget and was an original movie developed by the streaming service Netflix. Vromen's other films include *Rx* (2005), *Danika* (2006), *The Iceman* (2012), and *Criminal* (2016). The screenplay based on Bar-Joseph's book was written by David Arata, a noted screenwriter who had earned an Oscar nomination for *Children of Men* (2006).

Film Analysis

Vromen's film adaptation of *The Angel* largely follows the facts presented in Bar-Joseph's account of Ashraf Marwan's life, though the timeline sometimes differs as the film employs flashbacks to tell its story. The film begins in Rome in 1973, at a dramatic moment: Marwan (Marwan Kenzari) is smuggling missile launchers to Arab terrorists. The terrorists are seeking to shoot down a passenger jet in retaliation for Israel accidentally shooting down a Libyan jet that had inadvertently crossed into its territory. Marwan tells the terrorists that he cannot stay with them since he is an Egyptian diplomat. At the moment the terrorists are getting ready to shoot down the plane, the film flashes back to London in 1970.

At this time, Marwan and his wife, Mona (Maisa Abd Elhadi), are living in London with their young son, while Marwan pursues an advanced degree. Mona is the daughter of President Nasser of Egypt (Waleed Zuaiter), who does not respect his son-in-law. Nasser urges his daughter to divorce him, in part because of Marwan's love of gambling. In conversation over dinner, Marwan suggests to his father-in-law to make peace with the Israelis, after Egypt's loss in the Six-Day War of 1967, with the help of the United States. Nasser's Egypt, however, is allied with the Soviet Union, a country Marwan believes is on its last legs. Nasser repudiates Marwan both at dinner and later to his daughter.

Embarrassed by his father-in-law's treatment of him, Marwan gets additionally frustrated when he discovers that Nasser is using undercover agents to spy on him. When Mona accuses him of having an affair with an English woman named Diana Ellis (Hannah Ware), Marwan tells her truthfully that he is not. These frustrations lead Marwan to call the Israeli embassy from a phone booth in London, to offer his services as a spy. When the embassy refuses to connect him with the Israeli intelligence service, the Mossad, he hangs up.

Later in 1970, Marwan is summoned from his university classes by Egyptian agents, who tell him Nasser has died of a heart attack. Nassar will be replaced in office by Vice President Sadat (Sasson Gabai). Back in Egypt, Marwan helps to secure a place for himself in Sadat's government by uncovering corruption. Now a highly valued advisor to Sadat, Marwan attempts to balance his burgeoning political career with his homelife. All seems well until Mossad agents approach Marwan by playing him a recording of his botched attempt to contact them previously. Under the threat of Mossad agents revealing him to Sadat, Marwan agrees to become a spy for them and meets his handler, Alex (Toby Kebbell). Marwan—now codenamed "The Angel"—begins to present Israeli officials with high-level intelligence, with which the Israelis are incredibly impressed. For his services, they pay him large sums of cash at each meeting. At two different times during his spying, Marwan gives the Israelis information suggesting that Sadat is preparing to launch a major military attack on Israel. Each time the Israelis call up reservists, who wait for months for surprise attacks that never come, at the cost of millions of dollars. Sadat postpones each invasion,

leading the Israelis to conclude that Marwan is purposely giving them faulty information.

The film then returns to 1973, the period just before the Arab terrorists attempt to shoot down an Israeli plane. The Libyan dictator Muammar Gaddafi (Tsahi Halevi) wants to take revenge on Israel for its accidental downing of the Libyan passenger jet, but Sadat refuses to join in. Marwan then presents a plan to Sadat: to give Gaddafi weapons to conduct the attack—but to have the weapons fail to work. In the film, Marwan is seen removing the firing pins from the missile launchers. As he continues to provide information to the Mossad, Marwan eventually regains their trust, but they remain hesitant to believe that Egypt and allied Arab powers will invade Israel on Yom Kippur, the holiest day of the Jewish religious year. Because the Israelis refuse to believe him, they do not mount as vigorous a defense as they might have otherwise.

On October 6, 1973, Egypt, Syria, and their allies invade. Three days into the fighting, Israeli leaders begin to fear that the Jewish state may be toppled, but Israeli forces rally against the invading armies and prevail after almost a month of intense fighting. After the Yom Kippur War ends in a brokered ceasefire, with a massive loss of life on both sides, Egypt and Israel ultimately negotiate a peace treaty in 1978, ending hostilities between the two powers and returning the Sinai to Egypt. The film ends with a coda that takes place in 1983, when Marwan and his former handler Alex meet in a park and exchange a copy of Aesop's Fables. Before the end credits, a statement notes that Marwan died in 2007 by falling from a balcony in London.

Though the main points of Marwan's career as a spy are highlighted in both the book and the film, the film's portrayal differs on several details. According to the film, the brokered peace deal was part of Marwan's plan all along: to goad the Israelis into a false sense of security so that they would come to the negotiating table. The film portrays Marwan as believing that a diplomatic solution is the only way to ensure peace and that only a humbled Israel would negotiate, thus suggesting that Marwan was a double agent—which in reality remains unclear.

The film also employs typical cinematic shortcuts to tell Marwan's life story. What was actually said in private meetings between Marwan and various Egyptian and Israeli officials remains largely unknown and unknowable, apart from official summary reports that have been disclosed. Also unknown is whether or not Marwan, who died a billionaire through various investments and connections, was really a double agent. He was honored as a national hero in both Israel and Egypt. Neither side has been willing to admit that he may have duped them. Additionally, the movie fabricates certain moments to increase dramatic tension. For example, Marwan did funnel arms to terrorists, but he did not remove the firing mechanisms, and the arms were brought to Rome not in his suitcase but in his wife's luggage. He did not, as the movie suggests, fake an affair with a British woman to throw Egyptian officials off his tracks, and Bar-Joseph's book gives no indication that Marwan ever had any extramarital affairs. He and his wife did not separate because of any perceived infidelity; in fact, they remained married until his death in 2007. Also not noted in the film is the fact that Marwan claimed to be writing a memoir shortly before his death—a manuscript that has never been found.

Significance

Whether the film version or the book endures as the more significant remains to be seen. Bar-Joseph's account of Marwan's life does not take liberties with the facts, as the film dramatization does. The book was highly lauded for its comprehensive research and attention to detail when it was published in the United States, but critics were not entirely lockstep in their praise for his efforts. For instance, Dan Raviv, writing for the magazine *Moment*, noted that the book was "an uneven read, unfortunately, with repetitions that more-stringent editing could have eliminated."

The film version of *The Angel*, however, received widespread acclaim when it was released on Netflix in 2018, with many critics lauding its actors, production values, and plotline. The film was also notable for its extensive use of Arabic dialogue—unusual for films released in the United States and a first for Netflix—and its cast of diverse and largely unknown actors. In the *Jerusalem Post*, Hannah Brown, praising the Dutch actor Marwan Kenzari, declared that he "gives an outstanding performance in the lead role, successfully embodying the contra-

dictions that drive many spies." Likewise, in the *Hollywood Reporter*, Frank Scheck applauded Kenzari's "consistently powerful" performance. Scheck found some faults in the film, however, citing "unanswered questions" and that, at times, the "emphasis of the screenplay...feels off." Overall, though, he called the film a "fascinating tale, delivered with just enough suspense to make it engrossing without feeling over the top," reflecting the general consensus.

—*Christopher Mari*

Further Reading

Bregman, Ahron. *The Spy Who Fell to Earth: My Relationship with the Secret Agent Who Rocked the Middle East*. CreateSpace Independent Publishing Platform, 2016.

Blum, Howard. *The Eve of Destruction: The Untold Story of the Yom Kippur War*. HarperCollins, 2003.

Blum, Howard. "Who Killed Ashraf Marwan?" *The New York Times*, 13 July 2007, www.nytimes.com/2007/07/13/opinion/13iht-edblum.1.6645021.html. Accessed 4 Apr. 2021.

Bibliography

Brown, Hannah. "'The Angel' Cometh to Netflix." *The Jerusalem Post*, 15 Sept. 2018, www.jpost.com/Israel-News/Culture/The-Angel-cometh-to-Netflix-567275. Accessed 4 Apr. 2021.

Gajanan, Mahita. "The True Story Behind the Movie *The Angel*." *Time*, 14 Sept. 2018, time.com/5386423/true-story-the-angel/. Accessed 4 Mar. 2021.

Keslassy, Elsa. "Netflix Boards Ariel Vromen's Spy Thriller 'The Angel.'" *Variety*, 25 July 2017, variety.com/2017/film/news/netflix-boards-ariel-vromen-spy-thriller-the-angel-1202504253/#!. Accessed 4 Mar. 2021.

Raviv, Dan. Review of *The Angel: The Egyptian Spy Who Saved Israel*, by Uri Bar-Joseph. *Moment*, July-Aug. 2016, momentmag.com/book-review-angel-uri-bar-joseph/. Accessed 4 Mar. 2021.

Scheck, Frank. Review of *The Angel*, directed by Ariel Vromen. *Hollywood Reporter*, 14 Sept. 2018, www.hollywoodreporter.com/review/angel-1143043. Accessed 16 Mar. 2021.

Animal Farm

The Novel
Author: George Orwell (1903-50)
First published: 1945

The Film
Year released: 1954
Directors: Joy Batchelor (1914-91), John Halas (1912-95)
Screenplay by: Lothar Wolff, Borden Mace, Philip Stapp, Joy Batchelor, John Halas
Starring: Gordon Heath, Maurice Denham

Context

George Orwell's parable *Animal Farm* was published in 1945, four years before the British author's most famous work, *Nineteen Eighty-four* (1949). Both novels explore the psychological mechanisms of totalitarianism. Orwell, who died in 1950, spent most of his life and career as an essayist and political advocate. Among other subjects, he wrote about poverty and classism (*Down and Out in Paris and London* in 1933; *The Road to Wigan Pier* in 1937), and fighting fascism in the Spanish Civil War (*Homage to Catalonia* in 1938). In a 1946 essay called "Why I Write," he wrote, "Every line of serious work that I have written since 1936 has been written, directly or indirectly, *against* totalitarianism and *for* democratic Socialism as I understand it."

Animal Farm is no different in this regard. Specifically, the book is a satire of the Russian Revolution, but it is also disdainful of capitalism and includes parodies of Western political figures as well as Soviet ones. In the fraught early years of the Cold War—a term that Orwell himself coined—a number of readers wondered if the book was meant to be a critique of revolution in general. Orwell addressed this idea in a 1946 letter that was later published in *George Orwell: Life in Letters* (2013). "I meant the moral to be that revolutions only effect a radical improvement when the masses are alert and know how to chuck out their leaders as soon as the latter have done their job," he wrote. "The turning-point of the story was supposed to be when the pigs kept the milk and apples for themselves.... If the other animals had had the sense to put their foot down then, it would have been all right." There is no such thing, he warned, as a "benevolent dictatorship."

Animal Farm was an instant hit with readers, though some critics were skeptical. George Soules of the *New Re-*public described it as "dull" and "clumsy." (In 2013, the magazine reprinted that review along with a retraction of its judgment.) Soules complained that the events of the story confuse the reader by being both too close and, in other cases, too far, from the actual events of the Russian

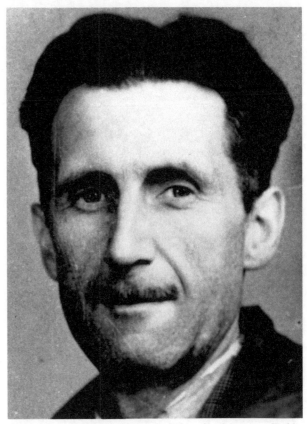

Author George Orwell. Photo via Wikimedia Commons. [Public domain.]

Revolution. To later readers, these discrepancies might be considered a blessing. They allow *Animal Farm* to stand independently as work of art, providing not a dry history but a resonant warning to future generations of people who hope to inhabit a more just world.

Film Analysis

Probably the most significant fact about the animated British film that one needs to know is that it was made at the behest of the US Central Intelligence Agency (CIA). Although ostensibly produced by the husband-and-wife production company Halas and Batchelor, the agency secretly financed the film and oversaw important editorial changes. It was part of a large-scale, secretive propaganda campaign whose activities, on the cultural front, included the secret sponsorship and direction of art exhibitions, movies, magazines and other publications, and much more.

Animal Farm, *first edition dust-jacket. Photo via Wikimedia Commons. [Public domain.]*

To understand the CIA's peculiar interest in *Animal Farm*, it is important to understand a few of the book's real-world corollaries, recognizable to most audiences of the era. The prophetic Old Major, an aged pig who incites the animals to revolt before dying, is understood to represent political philosopher Karl Marx. More importantly, Napoleon—guarded by his pack of dogs, i.e., the Soviet secret police—is the brutal Soviet dictator Joseph Stalin. It was important to the CIA that totalitarianism (or more specifically, Stalinism) and communism appear indistinguishable. (Why else would an avowedly capitalist country support a story that, at its outset, makes a compelling argument against capitalism?) In the era of the Red Scare, capitalism and Communism were positioned as polar forces of good and evil. This reductive conceit was odious to Orwell, who (in the same 1946 letter cited above) bemoaned unimaginative people in the world who "have grown pessimistic and assume that there is no alternative except dictatorship or *laissez-faire* capitalism."

Orwell died of complications from tuberculosis in 1950. Howard Hunt, a CIA agent who later became famous as a member of the team that broke into the Watergate Hotel in 1972, purchased the rights to *Animal Farm* from Orwell's widow, Sonia Brownwell, on behalf of the Orwellian-sounding Psychological Warfare Workshop. Hunt hired producer Louis de Rochemont, who in turn hired Joy Batchelor and John Halas. Batchelor and Halas had no idea that the project was being funded by the CIA, though they had launched their careers in Britain making government-funded propaganda films during World War II. They began work on *Animal Farm* in 1951. Batchelor and Halas worked with a small team of screenwriters, including Lothar Wolff, Borden Mace, and Philip Stapp.

The film is narrated by American actor Gordon Heath; all of the characters in the film are voiced by English actor Maurice Denham. As in the book, the story concerns farm animals who rise up against their drunken, incompetent farmer. Led by two pigs, Snowball and Napoleon, they rename Manor Farm as Animal Farm, and create a set of governing rules. The primary tenet of their new government: all animals are equal. Things start out well enough, until, lacking any meaningful ideas to challenge his political opponent, the tyrannical Napoleon ousts visionary leader Snowball. Napoleon, aided by a ferocious pack of dogs and a loyal constituency of pigs, consolidates his power. He spreads misinformation through the cunning pig Squealer, brutally silences protest, and does business with the human world to enrich himself—all while blaming the farm's increasing woes on the long-absent Snowball. Along the way, he tweaks the farm's original set of rules. His crowning achievement: "All animals are equal, but some are more equal than others." In the end, the animals of the farm cannot tell the difference between their former human rulers and the pigs.

At least, that was the ending as Orwell conceived it. Batchelor and Halas and their team simplified the story—cutting prominent characters and suggesting a unity of character among the non-pig animals—but they also changed the ending. This change was important to the larger propaganda goals of the film, though the production crew, years later, disagreed about who ultimately made the decision. (Batchelor was initially against the change; Halas supported it because it provided a more uplifting conclusion.) Regardless, in the film, the animals rally other animals from neighboring farms to overthrow the pigs and start again. The propaganda aim, important to the CIA, was to show the defeat, or possible defeat, of a communist regime by means of a popular uprising (with the help of a foreign power). The CIA also had a hand in the BBC film adaptation of Orwell's *Nineteen Eighty-four*, which was also released in 1954. Against the late author's explicit instructions, the ending of that story was significantly changed as well. The protagonist Winston Smith submits to the regime in the book; in the film, he dies in defiance of it.

Animal Farm was Britain's first animated feature-length film. It was strongly influenced by the pioneering animated films of Walt Disney. Recent Disney films of the era included *Cinderella* in 1950, *Alice in Wonderland* in 1951, and *Peter Pan* in 1953 *Animal Farm*'s animation lacks the technical precision of those films, and unlike Disney films, *Animal Farm* was intended for adults, not children. Still, Batchelor and Halas incorporated distinctly Disney-inspired elements in *Animal Farm*. For instance, they include a character of a baby chick, who is unnamed and largely unimportant to the story, but like the best animal sidekicks from Disney—such as the mice in *Cinderella* or the tiny mouse at the Mad Hatter's tea party in *Alice in Wonderland*—provides moments of levity through physical comedy. Moments of levity are welcome in *Animal Farm*. The story is quite dark, though moments of extreme violence are suggested rather than explicitly shown. Sometimes this choice emphasizes the horror, as when the workhorse

Boxer, braying and trying to break free from his cart, is shipped off to the glue factory. The moral is clear: a totalitarian regime can and will turn on anyone, even its most loyal supporters.

Significance

The film premiered in New York in 1954, and was later distributed around the world by the United States Information Agency (USIA). It performed well with audiences, and it was praised by most contemporary critics. Bosley Crowther of *The New York Times* wrote, "The shock of straight and raw political satire is made more grotesque in the medium of cartoon. The incongruities of recognizable horrors of some political realities of our times are emphasized and made more startling by the apparent innocence of their surrounding frame." He warned that the film was not for children.

Delmore Schwartz of the *New Republic* was more critical, finding the technical construction of the film wanting. He argued that, while the film remained (for the most part) true to Orwell's text, it lacked the spirit of the book, which he felt came originally from "being the product of sophistication, innocence, hope and suffering combined." Schwartz struggled to understand what a person unfamiliar with historical events would make of the film, noting the resemblance of the pigs to not just Soviet leaders but also British politicians and suggesting that people might misinterpret the story. This raises again the important question of how to approach the film given its "Orwellian" origins as a piece of propaganda from the CIA, itself guilty of large-scale, anti-democratic actions on behalf of a nation widely considered imperialist (actions not excluding the secret production and dissemination of propaganda.) One response to this criticism is to suggest that it ignores those nuances that makes *Animal Farm* more than a simple piece of propaganda—even with the altered ending of the film version. The film, it can be argued, does not merely describe twentieth-century historical events, or only argue for the overthrow of particular twentieth-century communist regimes who were enemies of the United States. In demonstrating the various methods by which tyrants have gained, and continue to gain, power, the film can be seen to be as relevant in the twenty-first century—and beyond—as it was when it was made.

—Molly Hagan

Further Reading

Soules, George. "In 1946, The New Republic Panned George Orwell's 'Animal Farm.'" Review of *Animal Farm*, by George Orwell. *The New Republic*, 26 Sept. 2013, newrepublic.com/article/114852/1946-review-george-orwells-animal-farm. Accessed 19 Nov. 2018.

Zuckerman, Laurence. "How the C.I.A. Played Dirty Tricks with Culture." *The New York Times*, 18 Mar. 2000, www.nytimes.com/2000/03/18/books/how-the-cia-played-dirty-tricks-with-culture.html. Accessed 20 Nov. 2018.

Bibliography

Chilton, Martin. "How the CIA Brought Animal Farm to the Screen." *The Telegraph*, 21 Jan. 2016, www.telegraph.co.uk/books/authors/how-cia-brought-animal-farm-to-the-screen/. Accessed 21 Nov. 2018.

Cohen, Karl. "The Cartoon That Came in from the Cold." *The Guardian*, 6 Mar. 2003, www.theguardian.com/culture/2003/mar/07/artsfeatures.georgeorwell. Accessed 20 Nov. 2018.

Crowther, Bosley. "The Screen in Review; Orwell's 'Animal Farm' Emerges as Cartoon." Review of *Animal Farm*, directed by Joy Batchelor and John Halas. *The New York Times*, 30 Dec. 1954, www.nytimes.com/1954/12/30/archives/the-screen-in-review-orwells-animal-farm-emerges-as-cartoon.html. Accessed 19 Nov. 2018.

Orwell, George. "Why I Write." *The Orwell Foundation*, 1946, www.orwellfoundation.com/the-orwell-foundation/orwell/essays-and-other-works/why-i-write/. Accessed 11 Dec. 2018.

Schwartz, Delmore. "TNR Film Classics: 'Animal Farm' (January 17, 1955)." Review of *Animal Farm*, directed by Joy Batchelor and John Halas. *The New Republic*, 17 Jan. 1955, newrepublic.com/article/102820/tnr-film-classics-animal-farm-january-17-1955. Accessed 19 Nov. 2018.

Annihilation

The Novel
Author: Jeff VanderMeer (b. 1968)
First published: 2014

The Film
Year released: 2018
Director: Alex Garland (b. 1970)
Screenplay by: Alex Garland
Starring: Natalie Portman, Oscar Isaac, Jennifer Jason Leigh, Gina Rodriguez, Tessa Thompson, Tuva Novotny

Context

A science-fiction novelist whose work often focuses on the relationship between human beings and the environment, Jeff VanderMeer earned the nickname the "weird Thoreau" from a writer for the *New Yorker* in 2015. While much of his early fiction is composed of award-winning short fantasy and horror stories, his reputation for psychedelic nature writing was solidified with his Southern Reach trilogy. His style is experimental, dark, and often challenging to read, and the Southern Reach trilogy falls firmly in the science-fiction genre. *Annihilation* (2014), the first book in the trilogy and the winner of the 2014 Nebula Award for Best Novel, follows four female scientists as they venture out to a mysterious place known only as Area X. Its sequel, *Authority* (2014), explores the politics of the organization that sent these scientists on their mission while the final installment, *Acceptance* (2014), concludes the stories of the characters introduced in the first two novels. VanderMeer released all three of the novels, largely to critical acclaim, in the same year in an attempt to appeal to the popular "binge" style of consuming contemporary popular culture commonly associated with the streaming platform Netflix.

The decision to adapt *Annihilation* into a feature film occurred in March 2013, a year before the book's release. The film rights were acquired by Paramount Pictures and Scott Rudin Productions. British filmmaker Alex Garland was brought on the following year as a director. Acclaimed as a writer with the publication of his novel *The Beach* in 1996, Garland made his directorial debut in 2014 with *Ex Machina*, a film about the godlike delusions of humans with regards to their machines. *Ex Machina* established Garland as one of the industry's most visionary science-fiction filmmakers, and its script, which he also

penned, earned an Academy Award nomination. In addition to directing, Garland decided to write the *Annihilation* screenplay.

Annihilation was released in the winter of 2018. It exemplified a cinematic trend of science-fiction films produced with sizeable budgets despite belonging to a niche

Author Jeff VanderMeer. Photo by SouthernNights via Wikimedia Commons.

genre. The film is perhaps most comparable to the film *Arrival* (2016), which tells the story of a scientist attempting to communicate to aliens who have come to Earth. Other big-budget science-fiction films released around the same period as *Annihilation* include *Interstellar* (2014), *The Martian* (2015), and *Blade Runner 2049* (2017).

Film Analysis

In interviews, director Alex Garland said that he read Jeff VanderMeer's novel only once before adapting it into a screenplay. Because Garland wanted to focus on the atmosphere of the book and did not feel that the work's very internal, abstract narration lent itself to a strict adaptation for the screen, the film takes many liberties with the original narrative. It should be said that most of the main plot points are the same; in both iterations, a group of female scientists are sent to explore a mysterious stretch of land near the coast after the members of previous expeditions were affected by the area in a variety of ways and failed to provide any real insight into the area. The characters in both the novel and the film are subjected to strange phenomena once they arrive in the area—in addition to their sense of reality and time being altered, they also encounter bizarre biological mutations among the plants and predators living there. Furthermore, the main protagonist's decision to go into the quarantined area is motivated by the fact that her husband was on one of the earlier failed missions. After returning from the area alive, he ultimately dies from cancer in the novel but falls into a coma in the film.

There are also a lot of differences between both versions of the *Annihilation* story. For example, Southern Reach, the organization that sends the scientists out into Area X, plays a fairly prominent role in the novel. In the film, Southern Reach is named but exists somewhat in the periphery of the experience of protagonist Lena (Natalie Portman). Additionally, while VanderMeer keeps many details regarding the characters and their motivations vague, Garland fleshes them out more clearly. There are four female scientists in the novel, and the first-person narrator refers to them only by their professional roles. Contrarily, Garland has five women on the expedition and gives them all names in order to keep the cinematic narrative more natural. The protagonist, known as "the biologist" in the book, is called "Lena" in the film. Furthermore, while the psychologist uses hypnosis on the members of the expedition in the novel, this element is left entirely out of the film.

Most of the changes that Garland made were to enhance the viewer's experience. Certain elements of VanderMeer's narrative, including its vaguer approach, that work on the page would not have translated well to the screen. For example, there is no clear physical boundary separating the rest of the world from Area X in the novel. In the film, however, there exists a thin, colorful barrier that looks like a soap bubble that leads to the area; this is called "the Shimmer." This vivid barrier provides moviegoing audiences with a distinct visual clue that the characters are leaving the normal world and entering an alien one. Without it, their journey into the area might be less interesting to watch and follow. Additionally, by making the choice to turn the journal that the scientists find from a previous expedition in the novel into a video in the film, Garland amplifies the drama. Rather than read about the horrifying things that Lena's husband, Kane (Oscar Isaac), endured and participated in, viewers watch and interact with them, making them significantly more terrifying.

The one way that the film stays especially true to the book is in tone. Garland conveys and builds upon the quiet eeriness of VanderMeer's book by concretely illustrating the mysterious area's appearance and contents. The set design is deceptively simple. There is a kind of beautiful, peaceful disorientation to the film's environment. The characters tramp through the overgrown landscape toward their final destination of a lighthouse, and they are almost always in wide open spaces—whether it is outdoors or in abandoned government buildings. The natural world around them looks unnatural—the colors of plants and animals are so artificial looking that it is almost jarring. The only creatures the women come across are mutated animals, including oversized alligators with rows of sharks' teeth and a terrifying "bear" with a distorted face and a growl that emanates the screams of the people it has eaten.

The cinematography of *Annihilation* is lush. Everything in the natural world has a soft, luminescent glow to it. The color palette runs on the spectrum of mossy green to silver grey. Garland has long, sequential scenes during which the characters trek through the woods. These are mostly long shots in which the women's relatively small frames are contrasted with the expansive wildness of their environment. Through this imagery, Garland conveys how much danger they are in as nature clearly has the upper hand over the humans. The film's action and horror scenes occur in short, unexpected bursts. The characters will be outside in the daylight when one of them is snatched up. In another scene, Anya (Gina Rodriguez) begins unraveling after one of their colleagues gets eaten by a mysterious creature. She ties the remaining women up and starts threatening them with a gun. Repeatedly, Garland interrupts a false sense of peace and safety with bizarre violence, creating an unsettling viewing experience. Overall, the film does not have a lot of action and its dialogue is spare. However, it remains highly engaging thanks to the mysteriousness of the characters' environment and circumstances.

Thematically, the film *Annihilation* explores the idea that, somehow, biological life has developed a new way to reproduce itself, and to produce novel living beings, through rapidly occurring mutations in the DNA of living things. The Shimmer is the place where life, seemingly of its own evolutionary whim, has learned to "refract" in weird and new ways, much the way that light can be refracted into myriad colors—or, more ominously, the way that cancer cells reproduce quickly and pathologically. The film also explores the human psychological tendency towards self-destruction, or the death drive. At one point, Lena has a conversation with her colleague, psychologist Dr. Ventress (Jennifer Jason Leigh), about why anyone would want to volunteer to explore the area, which is clearly a "suicide mission." All of the women on the expedition were chosen because they want to destroy themselves in some capacity. Dr. Ventress is dying from terminal cancer while Cass (Tuva Novotny) is mourning the loss of her young daughter. Meanwhile, Lena seems to be punishing herself for cheating on Kane; it was because of her infidelity that Kane accepted the Southern Reach mission in the first place. The Shimmer area, symbolic of biological life's mindless reproductive vitalism, is also symbolic of death, as it causes the cells of the humans that enter it to break down and mutate into something else.

The scene most demonstrative of this central theme is the ending, which also varies significantly from the book. Lena finally arrives at the lighthouse, which is surrounded by crystalline structures and bizarre tree roots. Inside, she finds human bones and a video camera with footage of her husband engaging in self-immolation. She descends into a hole in the floor to find Dr. Ventress being overtaken by a strange, colorful energy. The energy surrounds her too, eventually taking the form of a green-silver humanoid. The humanoid is Lena's exact shape and size, and mimics her every move, trying to overtake her. Eventually, it adopts Lena's face. She destroys it with a grenade, escaping back outside—however, it is not clear whether she is the original Lena or not.

Significance

Annihilation was released in theaters in North America on February 23, 2018. Produced on a budget of $40 million, it was considered a box-office flop because it earned only $32.7 million in domestic gross, according to the website Box Office Mojo. The film's poor reception among audiences has been attributed to insufficient promotion by its production company, which also controversially gave the international distribution rights to Netflix. Therefore, the film did not premiere in many theaters abroad but became part of the streaming platform's massive content collection, where many viewers did not get the full cinematic experience.

Although the film did not do well at the box office, it became a considerable critical success. Most of the film's reviews remarked on Garland's deft screenwriting and superb direction. Natalie Portman's nuanced performance as the film's strong, albeit nihilistic, protagonist was another common point of praise. Overall, most critics found the film to be an intelligent, compelling work of science fiction that celebrates the genre but is never predictable. While some fans of the novel were turned off by the many changes made for the film, others considered the film to be a different but elevated take on the concepts introduced by the book.

Ultimately, *Annihilation* is an impressive work of cinematic art. Instead of risking the integrity of the film by trying to appeal to mainstream audiences, as Garland was reportedly encouraged to do following a screen test, the director allowed *Annihilation* to be intellectual and challenging. In this way, the film succeeds in achieving the underlying goal of any work of science fiction: to get audiences to think in new, unexpected ways about themselves and the future of humanity.

—*Emily E. Turner*

Further Reading

Garland, Alex. "'Annihilation' Director Alex Garland Wants You to Interpret the Film's Ending on Your Own." Interview by Jennifer Vineyard. *Thrillist*, 31 May 2018, www.thrillist.com/entertainment/nation/annihilation-director-alex-garland-interview. Accessed 9 Feb. 2019.

Sims, David. "The Mind-Bending Final Confrontation of *Annihilation*." *The Atlantic*, 25 Dec. 2018, www.theatlantic.com/entertainment/archive/2018/12/dissecting-final-scene-annihilation-natalie-portman-alex-garland/578989. Accessed 9 Feb. 2019.

Bibliography

"Annihilation." *Box Office Mojo*, www.boxofficemojo.com/movies/?page=main&id=annihilation.htm. Accessed 9 Feb. 2019.

Garland, Alex. "Alex Garland Leaves Nothing Behind." Interview by Sean Fennessey. *The Ringer*, 23 Feb. 2018, www.theringer.com/movies/2018/2/23/17036466/alex-garland-annihilation-interview-ex-machina. Accessed 9 Feb. 2019.

Lee, Benjamin. "Annihilation Review—Natalie Portman Thriller Leaves a Haunting Impression." Review of *Annihilation*, directed by Alex Garland. *The Guardian*, 21 Feb. 2018, www.theguardian.com/film/2018/feb/22/annihilation-review-natalie-portman-thriller-leaves-a-haunting-impression. Accessed 9 Feb. 2019.

Nordine, Michael. "'Annihilation': How the Movie Differs from the Book It's Based On (and Why It's Better)." *IndieWire*, 23 Feb. 2018, www.indiewire.com/2018/02/annihilation-movie-vs-book-adaptation-spoilers-1201929719/. Accessed 9 Feb. 2019.

Pendle, George. "Alex Garland Mutated Annihilation into a Psychedelic Sci-Fi Horror." *Esquire*, 21 Feb. 2018, www.esquire.com/entertainment/movies/a15895685/annihilation-alex-garland-interview. Accessed 9 Feb. 2019.

Rothman, Joshua. "The Weird Thoreau." *The New Yorker*, 14 Jan. 2015, www.newyorker.com/culture/cultural-comment/weird-thoreau-jeff-vandermeer-southern-reach. Accessed 9 Feb. 2019.

A Bear Called Paddington / Paddington

The Novel
Author: Michael Bond (1926-2017)
First published: 1958

The Film
Year released: 2014
Director: Paul King (b. 1978)
Screenplay by: Paul King
Starring: Hugh Bonneville, Sally Hawkins, Nicole Kidman, Ben Whishaw

Context

One day in 1956, Michael Bond noticed a teddy bear sitting on a shelf at a London store, right near the Paddington train station, and he decided to pick it up as a last-minute Christmas gift for his wife. It fulfilled its role as a present, but its lasting influence proved to be far greater. Bond was an aspiring writer who had published his first short story during his time in the British army at the end of World War II, and he was mostly content to work as a television cameraman while penning the occasional play or story. With the teddy bear serving as inspiration, he decided to write a series of vignettes for children about just such a toy. In his imagination, the bear was a sentient, talking creature who had come to London as a stowaway from "darkest Peru."

In 1958, having written eight interconnected stories, Bond put them together in a book, publishing them as *A Bear Called Paddington*, with illustrations by Peggy Fortnum, and detailing the bear's adventures, beginning with his discovery and adoption by the Brown family. The book was an immediate success and the following year, Bond wrote a sequel, *More About Paddington*, in the same format. For the next three years, a volume was published each year. Bond kept adding more to the Paddington opus and he ended up producing more than a dozen collections, completing two final volumes, the collection *Paddington's Finest Hour* and the standalone picture book, *Paddington at St. Paul's*, just before his death in 2017.

Paddington first came to the screen, albeit the small one, in 1976. In that year, he appeared on a British television series called simply *Paddington*. This popular children's program was shot using stop-motion animation and featured a three-dimensional Paddington interacting with two-dimensional hand-drawn characters. Although the original run was short-lived, it was followed by two Christmas specials in December 1976 and a new series, *The Adventures of Paddington*, in 1979. In 2007, the first full-length film production of Paddington was announced, although no further developments were undertaken until 2013. At that time, the production proceeded quickly and the film, which combined live-action and animation, was eventually released as *Paddington* in 2014 to box-office success and critical acclaim. A sequel followed in 2017 with a third film reportedly in the works.

Film Analysis

Far more than the book *A Bear Called Paddington* on which it is based, Paul King's 2014 film is about the nature of families. Late in the film, the Brown family's housekeeper, Mrs. Bird, chides the head of the household, Mr. Brown, for his behavior toward the talking bear that had so far been merely a provisional member of the family. As Mrs. Bird admonishes him, Mr. Brown and his family need Paddington just as much as their charge needs them. In this moment, Mr. Brown realizes that Paddington is truly a member of his family and that family is a question of mutual need, love, and protection.

But it is a long journey for the film version of Mr. Brown. In the book, Paddington is brought into the family quickly and unequivocally. Mr. Brown expresses some vague misgivings when they discover the stowaway bear at Paddington Station, but he is quickly overruled by his wife. Their daughter Judy, who they are at the station to pick up, immediately takes to the bear, as does her brother Jonathan, and Paddington is given his own room with the understanding that he will stay indefinitely. Thus, Paddington does not have to earn his place in the family; it is understood that once the Browns made the decision to take him in, he would be well cared for. When Paddington worries about the cost of his food, Mrs. Brown quickly dismisses his worries. "We wouldn't dream of charging you anything," she tells him. "We shall expect you to be one of the family."

It is quite different in the film, where Paddington immediately splits the family in two. While Mrs. Brown and Jonathan take an instant liking to the bear and want to bring him home, Mr. Brown and Judy feel very differently. As played by Hugh Bonneville, the film version of Mr. Brown is presented as an uptight man who is (and it turns out, rightfully) concerned with Paddington wreaking havoc on his perfectly appointed home. For Judy, it is more a question of social embarrassment. As a result of these split viewpoints, a compromise is struck. Paddington can stay for one night, but he has to sleep in the attic.

The action of the film then becomes a dual narrative of Paddington earning his way into the family and Mr. Brown realizing that he needs Paddington to be part of his family. While Judy is quickly won over after Paddington inadvertently stops a serial pickpocket, Mr. Brown is a more difficult convert. He remains suspicious of Paddington until late in the film. Nonetheless, in the film's warm conception of human nature, people are capable of changing for the good. After revealing that before the birth of his first child, Mr. Brown was an adventurous type, and thus signaling to the audience that his uptightness is born out of a concern for his family, he is allowed to regain some of his old personality, ultimately putting his life on the line to save Paddington.

In the film, Paddington indeed needs saving, for just as he finally masters the art of living in the human world, and thus proving himself an appropriate family member for the Browns, he is targeted by the villainous taxidermist Millicent Clyde, who is determined to capture Paddington, stuff him, and display him at the natural history museum.

The Paddington Bear movie awakened childhood nostalgia for the character: here, a London shop window is filled with stuffed Paddingtons, Christmas 2014. Photo by Rick Ligthelm via Wikimedia Commons.

As the film progresses, this plot takes over the action and turns the film in a direction quite different from the book, moving into the territory of a thriller. Paul King stages several nail-biting set-pieces that work very well on the screen but, even if original author Michael Bond had been so inclined, would have been far harder to pull off on the page. In one particularly tense scene, Paddington has to climb up a chimney using two hand-held vacuums to suction himself to the wall while flames rise below him. When the vacuums start to lose their charge and die down, the tension ratchets up considerably.

If the film's plot seems a little bit rote, particularly the alteration in Mr. Brown's character, it is presented in a manner that is both warm and thrilling. Even the villainous Millicent, although not redeemed, is at least granted a somewhat sympathetic reason for hatching her plot: she has strong memories of her father, the explorer who first discovered Paddington in his native Peru, being mocked by his colleagues for refusing to bring back stuffed specimens, and she wants to redeem his honor. In this way, Millicent stands as a kind of perverse mirror to the Brown family. The Brown's familial loyalty is in every way endorsed by the film, while Millicent's own devotion to her father's memory is not, but it at least presents her motives in a way that is understandable. In the end, though, the viewer is expected to take glee in the fate that befalls Millicent, as she is sentenced to do community service at a petting zoo.

Altogether, though, Paddington makes the case for inclusiveness and generosity, and in that it is not too different from the book. The book's Paddington gets in just as many misadventures as his film counterpart, but he is always supported by the Brown family. If the film Paddington has to earn that support, it only makes Mr. Brown ultimately championing Paddington all the more satisfying. Whether familial ties and responsibility are taken as something that is understood or something that all parties must constantly work to achieve and maintain, the world of Paddington ultimately affirms these values. If anything, the film offers a more mature and thoughtful vision of family life than the book, but both understand fully the pleasures and satisfactions of belonging.

Significance

Although Paddington was expected to do well at the box office, it became a surprise critical favorite as well. Earning an overwhelming 97 percent fresh rating from Rotten Tomatoes, Paddington was singled out for special excellence by a number of critics. Dan Kois at Slate Magazine called the film "a wonder: warm, gentle, well-acted, visually stylish and inventive" while at The New York Times, Jeannette Catsoulis felt that it "delivered a knockout blend of fluid animation and live action," even if she considered the adaptation to be a bit too "safe." The film, though, also lived up to expectations at the box office. Opening on November 28, 2014, in the United Kingdom, it was the most popular film in the country for two weeks. It was just as successful upon its release in the United States when it opened on January 16, 2015, earning over $76 million. Worldwide, the film ended up grossing more than $282 million.

Buoyed by the success of the film, Paddington became a wide-ranging franchise. The next entry in the series, Paddington 2 was released in 2017 to even greater acclaim than its predecessor. Justin Chang of the Los Angeles Times wrote that the film is "an exquisite reminder of the wondrous things that can happen when a storyteller of boundless imagination avails himself of some rigorous discipline." In his capsule review of the film for Slant Magazine's best films of the year feature, Keith Watson wrote that it was "wilder, weirder, funnier, more heartfelt and eye-popping, and, above all, more fully realized" than the original. Following the release of the sequel, producers announced two additional projects, a third film in the series, and an animated television show. The latter, known as The Adventures of Paddington, began airing in December 2019. Paddington 3 was delayed because of the Coronavirus pandemic in 2020 and 2021.

—Melynda Fuller

Further Reading

Horwell, Veronica. "Michael Bond Obituary." The Guardian, 28 June 2017, www.theguardian.com/books/2017/jun/28/michael-bond-obituary. Accessed 9 Apr. 2020.

Pauli, Michelle. "Michael Bond: 'Paddington Stands up for Things, He's Not Afraid of Going to the Top and Giving Them a Hard Stare.'" The Guardian, 28 Nov. 2014, www.theguardian.com/books/2014/nov/28/michael-bond-author-paddington-bear-interview-books-television-film. Accessed 9 Apr. 2020.

Shoard, Catherine. "How Paddington Took Paul King from Mighty Boosh to Almighty Blockbuster." The Guardian, 23 Mar. 2015, www.theguardian.com/film/2015/mar/23/paddington-mighty-boosh-paul-king-garth-marenghi. Accessed 10 Apr. 2020.

Bibliography

Catsoulis, Jeannette. "Adventures of a Peruvian Immigrant (the Furry Variety)." *The New York Times*, 15 Jan. 2015, www.nytimes.com/2015/01/16/movies/paddington-an-adaptation-of-michael-bonds-books.html?partner=rss&emc=rss. Accessed 10 Apr. 2020.

Kois, Dan. "A Very Rare Sort of Movie." *Slate Magazine*, 16 Jan. 2015, slate.com/culture/2015/01/paddington-movie-reviewed-adaptation-of-childrens-book-is-surprisingly-good.html. Accessed 10 Apr. 2020.

Paddington. Box Office Mojo, www.boxofficemojo.com/release/rl1466533377/. Accessed 10 Apr. 2020.

Paddington. Rotten Tomatoes, www.rottentomatoes.com/m/paddington_2014. Accessed 10 Apr. 2020.

Paddington 2. Rotten Tomatoes, www.rottentomatoes.com/m/paddington_2/reviews. Accessed 10 Apr. 2020.

Preston, John. "Michael Bond Interview: 'The Modern World Is Depressing. Paddington Is My Escape.'" *The Telegraph*, 28 June 2017, www.telegraph.co.uk/books/authors/michael-bond-interview-modern-world-depressing-paddington-escape/. Accessed 10 Apr. 2020.

Staff. "The 25 Best Films of 2018." *Slant Magazine*, 14 Dec. 2018, www.slantmagazine.com/film/the-25-best-films-of-2018/. Accessed 10 Apr. 2020.

Beautiful Boy

The Novel
Author: David Sheff (b. 1955)
First published: 2008

The Film
Year released: 2018
Director: Felix van Groeningen (b. 1977)
Screenplay by: Luke Davies, Felix van Groeningen
Starring: Steve Carell, Timothée Chalamet, Maura Tierney, Amy Ryan

Context

Journalist David Sheff's memoir of his experience with his son's addiction to methamphetamines, *Beautiful Boy* (2008), made *The New York Times* bestseller list and was recognized by many critics as one of the best works of nonfiction to be published that year. Sheff's book, sensitive and vulnerable, avoided stereotypes and was open and honest about his son's experience and his own. In addition to assessing his personal role in Nic's addiction, he wrote about the emotional challenges that he endured as a parent whose every effort to save his child continuously failed. The book was developed from an essay that Scheff had published in *The New York Times Magazine* in 2005 called "My Addicted Son." The essay received an enormous response from thousands of people who were also struggling with addiction or had family members who were. The book's publication marked a transition in Sheff's career—previously, he had been known for interviewing cultural icons like John Lennon, Keith Haring, Steve Jobs, Betty Friedan, and Carl Sagan. After *Beautiful Boy*'s publication, he became one of the most authoritative voices on the increasingly serious issue of addiction in America. Nic became a prominent voice on the subject, publishing another memoir, *Tweak: Growing Up on Methamphetamines* in 2008.

The film rights to both *Beautiful Boy* and *Tweak* were optioned by actor Brad Pitt's production company, Plan B Entertainment, in 2008. Although filmmaker Cameron Crowe was originally tapped to write and direct the adaptation of these books, he eventually dropped out. In 2015, it was announced that Belgian director Felix van Groeningen would be leading the project instead. He partnered with Australian screenwriter Luke Davies to write the script for *Beautiful Boy*. After van Groeningen's film *The Broken Circle Breakdown* (2012) earned an Academy Award nomination, American producers had been pursuing him to direct an English language film. *The Broken Circle Breakdown* followed the story of a couple who falls in love through bluegrass music and later must endure the death of their young daughter. In interviews, van Groeningen stated that he chose *Beautiful Boy* to be his Hollywood debut because he was drawn to the father-son

Timothée Chalamet's performance received positive reviews from critics and he received numerous award nominations. Photo by Elena Ringo via Wikimedia Commons.

relationship at the heart of the story, having lost his own father in his twenties. Additionally, van Groeningen liked the idea of exploring the perspectives of two different characters on opposite sides of a traumatic event.

Film Analysis

The *Beautiful Boy* film differs from the book in myriad ways. The first major difference between the two iterations of the story is that the book is written exclusively from author David Sheff's perspective. As a result, it is more expansive and all-encompassing in the timeline that it covers. Specifically, it begins with Nic's birth and follows him throughout his childhood, preteen years, and adolescence, until his mid-twenties. Sheff also digs deeper into the details of events that had a profound impact on his son's young life like his divorce from Nic's mother and their subsequent custody battle. He also makes sure to thoroughly capture what a bright, talented, and friendly individual Nic was growing up while also highlighting his underlying rebellious tendencies. His purpose in providing such an in-depth portrait of Nic is to ensure that readers have the full context of who he was before he started using drugs. It makes Nic's addiction feel like a tragedy incongruent to his character and in turn allows readers to understand Sheff's shock and disbelief. Furthermore, it illustrates how addiction can affect anyone—even children raised by loving, attentive parents from upper middle-class backgrounds.

The film does not hew especially close to Sheff's original narrative. In part, this is because van Groeningen and Davies' script combines both Sheff and Nic's memoirs. Sheff's book is ultimately about the experience of a parent who must watch helplessly from the sidelines as drugs push his son further and further away from him. As such, there are long stretches of the book where he and the readers do not know where Nic is or what he is doing. If the film were to stay true to this, Nic would rarely appear on-screen once he started using drugs. However, by weaving in scenes from Nic's memoir *Tweak*, these large gaps in time are filled. The end result is a film that demonstrates what it is like for a father to lose his son to addiction as well as what it is like for a young man to become addicted to methamphetamines.

One of the boldest choices that van Groeningen makes as both a screenwriter and a director is to allow *Beautiful Boy* to unfold in a nonlinear fashion. Rather than follow Nic's (Timothée Chalamet) descent into addiction chronologi-

cally, the film weaves back and forth in time. As such, scenes that are intended to be set in the present are often followed by flashbacks to different moments in Nic's childhood. Sometimes these flashbacks act as a stark contrast to who Nic is in the throes of his addiction. For example, a scene of him struggling with drugs is followed by one where he is a sweet ten-year-old, holding his baby brother in his arms, completely awestruck. Other times, the flashbacks are intended to provide insight into Nic's relationship with his father, David (Steve Carell). At one point, for example, there is a flashback to Nic as a high school senior planning to go off to college. He offers his dad a joint. After some resistance, David ends up smoking with him. Throughout the flashback, Nic tells David about how hard he worked in high school and how he deserves the opportunity to unwind with marijuana. Here, van Groeningen wants audiences to see the thinking that may have led Nic to drugs and make them wonder if David was complicit.

By telling the story in a nonlinear fashion, van Groeningen infuses the film with a dreamlike quality. This atmosphere is exacerbated by the fact that each scene is presented as an independent vignette. The creative decision to tell the characters' stories through short, loosely connected moments demonstrates how van Groeningen was in many ways more focused on conveying the characters' emotions than moving the plot forward. To ensure that the surreal circumstances that Sheff and Nic are experiencing are successfully translated on-screen, van Groeningen uses soft, warm lighting with lots of shadows and blacks, which generates a surreal feeling. This is intended to communicate the protagonists' perspective and experience. On drugs, Nic is no longer anchored in reality. Meanwhile, David feels as though he is stuck in a waking nightmare that simply will not end.

The set design of *Beautiful Boy* is used to communicate how the characters' relationships to one another change over time. This is primarily evident in the Sheffs' house. Located in Northern California just outside of San Francisco, the Sheff house is large with a dark, earthy, wooden interior. It has large windows with views of the peaceful woods. It is a beautiful refuge, protected by its natural surroundings. As Nic's addiction worsens, however, the house no longer feels safe. In the scenes where David waits up all night wondering where his son is, the house's windows start to look like terrifying holes out into the darkness. The feeling that their family house is a sanctuary is completely destroyed at the beginning of the climax of the film when Nic breaks in by smashing a window so that he can steal belongings for drug money. Another important set in the film is that of the diner, where David and Nic like to meet. The diner has a fun and playful atmosphere—it is where David used to take Nic when he was a young boy. His request to have Nic meet him there while at the worst stage of his addiction seems to be an effort to remind him of who he used to be. Yet it is at this same diner where Nic insists that the drug addict version of himself is who he "really is." As the two men meet several times at the diner throughout the course of the film, it becomes a kind of symbolic battleground for Nic's soul.

Significance

Beautiful Boy debuted at the Toronto International Film Festival on September 7, 2018. It was subsequently released in American theaters on October 12, 2018. The film was met with mostly positive reviews from critics, who were quick to commend Chalamet and Carell's performances. In his review for the *Financial Times*, Nigel Andrews wrote, "Carrell is heroically good as the father vexed by his powerless compassion and Chalamet equal to him in his wrestling, restless awareness of his own path to destruction." Despite such praise for the acting, however, the film was deemed inadequate in its exploration of addiction by some. For example, A. O. Scott wrote for the *The New York Times* that, "*Beautiful Boy* is not a bad movie. It was made with earnest care and honorable intentions and concludes with a recitation of one of Charles Bukowski's best poems. But as much as it may want to illuminate the realities of addiction, it mystifies David and Nic's experiences, leaving too many questions—how and what as well as why—swirling in the air."

Public reception to *Beautiful Boy* proved to be middling. Filmed on a $25 million budget, it only grossed $16 million in the theaters. Arguably the biggest impact of the film was solidifying Chalamet's career as a notable actor. Chalamet had already earned acclaim for his role in the coming-of-age film *Call Me by Your Name* (2017), and *Beautiful Boy* further demonstrated his dramatic range as well as his willingness to take on difficult roles. For his performance in *Beautiful Boy*, Chalamet earned Golden Globe, British Academy Film Awards, and Screen Actors Guild Awards nominations for best supporting actor.

—*Emily E. Turner*

Further Reading

Jordan, Richard. "*Beautiful Boy Director:* 'There Are No Easy Answers When It Comes to Addiction.'" *Den of Geek*,16 Jan. 2019, www.denofgeek.com/movies/beautiful-boy-director-there-are-no-easy-answers-when-it-comes-to-addiction. Accessed 23 Apr. 2020.

Scott, A. O. "Review: In *Beautiful Boy*, a Writer Confronts His Son's Meth Addiction." *The New York Times*, 11 Oct. 2018, www.nytimes.com/2018/10/11/movies/beautiful-boy-review-steve-carell.html. Accessed 23 Apr. 2020.

Sheff, David. "My Addicted Son." *The New York Times Magazine*, 6 Feb. 2005, www.nytimes.com/2005/02/06/magazine/my-addicted-son.html. Accessed 23 Apr. 2020.

Bibliography

Andrews, Nigel. "*Beautiful Boy*—Steve Carell and Timothée Chalamet Are Heroically Good." *Financial Times*, 16 Jan. 2019, www.ft.com/content/e55e368a-199c-11e9-b93e-f4351a53f1c3. Accessed 23 Apr. 2020.

Combemale, Leslie. "Writer/Director Felix van Groeningen on Music, Catharsis, and Crafting *Beautiful Boy*." *Motion Picture Association*, 22 Oct. 2018, www.motionpictures.org/2018/10/writer-director-felix-von-groeningen-on-music-catharsis-and-crafting-beautiful-boy/. Accessed 23 Apr. 2020.

Gilbey, Ryan. "Steve Carrell and Timothée Chalamet on Drugs, Disillusionment and Playing Father and Son." *The Guardian*, 13 Dec. 2018, www.theguardian.com/film/2018/dec/13/steve-carell-and-timothee-chalamet-on-drugs-disillusionment-and-playing-father-and-son. Accessed 23 Apr. 2020.

Gross, Terry. "Father and Son behind *Beautiful Boy* Share Their Story of Addiction and Recovery." *NPR*, 19 Oct. 2018, www.npr.org/2018/10/19/658781285/father-and-son-behind-beautiful-boy-share-their-story-of-addiction-and-recovery. Accessed 23 Apr. 2020.

Before I Fall

The Novel
Author: Lauren Oliver (b. 1982)
First published: 2010

The Film
Year released: 2017
Director: Ry Russo-Young (b. 1981)
Screenplay by: Maria Maggenti
Starring: Zoey Deutch, Halston Sage, Logan Miller

Context

Before I Fall is a young-adult novel by Lauren Oliver published in 2010 about a teenager who relives the last day of her life over and over again. The book was well received, described by a reviewer for *Kirkus* as "unexpectedly rich." In a starred review for *Publishers Weekly*, another reviewer deemed it "raw, emotional, and, at times, beautiful." *Before I Fall* was Oliver's first novel. She has since published a number of books, including a dystopian young-adult trilogy called Delirium. The books take place in a society where love is considered a disease. Her 2015 young-adult novel *Vanishing Girls* is a thriller about a girl on the hunt for her missing sister. Her adult novel, a family drama titled *Rooms* (2014), is narrated by two ghosts. Thematically, *Before I Fall* fits neatly into Oliver's larger oeuvre, combining realism and elements of fantasy to tell a suspenseful story. The production company Fox 2000 optioned the rights to *Before I Fall* and hired screenwriter Maria Maggenti to adapt it the same year the book was published. Maggenti is also the screenwriter of the teen adventure comedy *Monte Carlo* (2011), starring Selena Gomez. In 2011, Maggenti's script appeared on the annual Hollywood Black List of best unproduced screenplays.

The film was directed by Ry Russo-Young, known for her 2012 film *Nobody Walks*, starring John Krasinski. (She wrote the film with *Girls* creator Lena Dunham.) Star Zoey Deutch, then best known for the comedy *Vampire Academy* (2014), was cast in 2015. Deutch went on to star in Richard Linklater's *Everybody Wants Some!!* (2016) and the indie film *Flower* (2017). *Before I Fall* is one of a handful of dramas in the 2010s based on young-adult novels that features a dying teenage girl. Among them are *The Fault in Our Stars* (2014), *Me and Earl and the Dying Girl* (2015), and *If I Stay* (2014). In these films, dying offers a new way of looking at life. *Before I Fall* is no different in this regard. Russo-Young's film, like Oliver's novel, explores Sam's relationships with her family and friends through the lens of her death.

Film Analysis

Though the novel and film follow the same story, there are a few key differences between the two. Both begin with a prologue (in the film, this happens in voice-over) in which the protagonist, a teen girl named Samantha Kingston, ponders the last moments of her life. Crucially, in both the book and the film, the audience understands before the story begins that Sam will die. In the film, though, exactly how she dies remains a mystery until it happens. The audience follows Sam (Zoey Deutch) through her entire day at her school, which is holding a Valentine's Day celebration called Cupid's Day. The day was supposed to be a momentous one. Sam plans to lose her virginity to her jock boyfriend, Rob (YouTube star Kian Lawley). A member of the popular clique at school, she receives an armful of Cupid's Day roses from admirers and joins her friends in jeering a lonely, awkward girl named Juliet (Elena Kampouris) in the cafeteria. That night, Sam and her friends attend a party where the girls tussle with Juliet. On the way home, with Sam's friend Lindsay (Halston Sage) at the wheel, the car hits something on the road, flips, and crashes.

A few seconds after the crash, Sam wakes up in her bed on the morning of Cupid's Day. In the film as in the book, Sam tries to convince herself that the crash was merely a bad dream, but as the day proceeds, ending, again, with the fatal car crash, Sam realizes that something very strange is happening. When she wakes up on Cupid's Day again,

Sam begins to change her behavior in an attempt to prevent her own death. Though she succeeds in convincing her friends to stay in—thus preventing the car crash—the night ends with the discovery that Juliet has committed suicide. Sam wakes up on Cupid's Day again, suggesting that the two girls are linked in a significant and mysterious way, and that Sam must figure out why. In the book, Sam relives her last day seven times. Some readers have suggested that each of these seven days is linked to a stage of grief—among them denial, anger, bargaining, and acceptance. On each day, Sam learns more about the people around her and uses that information in subsequent days to forge new bonds and repair broken relationships—all while trying to figure out why she is trapped in this strange purgatory. In the film, it is unclear how many times Sam relives her last day. Montages suggest that it happens far more than seven times. Other key differences involve male characters. In the film, Sam, on what could be described as her "anger" day, has sex with Rob. In the film, she boldly flirts with an attractive teacher, but in the book, she actually kisses him (and regrets it). One interesting cosmetic change: in the book, many of the characters smoke.

Nearly every review of *Before I Fall* compares it to the classic 1993 comedy *Groundhog Day*. The time loop trope has been used in other stories—including the horror film *Happy Death Day* (2017), the action film *Edge of Tomorrow* (2014), and the novel *Life After Life* (2013), in which the main character is forced to repeat her entire life each time she dies—but the Bill Murray film remains the most enduring example. In it, a television weatherman named Phil Connors (Murray) is covering the annual Groundhog Day event in the small town of Punxsutawney, Pennsylvania. Phil is forced to relive the day over and over again, for reasons he must discover over the course of the film. *Before I Fall* and *Groundhog Day* share a number of common moments and structural devices. For instance, both Sam and Phil wake to the sounds of a familiar song—"I Got You Babe," by Sonny and Cher, for Phil, and "Dangerous (featuring Joywave)," by Big Data, for Sam (it was the evocative "No More Drama," by Mary J. Blige, in the book). They are also both, at the outset, unlikable characters. Phil is rude, arrogant, and self-important; Sam is a bully, or more accurately, complicit in the school's mechanisms of cruelty. She also distances herself from her parents and younger sister. Both characters have lessons to learn about other people and themselves, and both develop a romantic relationship with an unlikely partner. Both also experience a period of frustration (in a famous montage, Phil tries to kill himself in various ways to end the loop) and a period of exhilaration after realizing the extent of their consequence-free existence. Ultimately, both find a way to accept their circumstances and use their acquired knowledge to live the day to benefit the people around them.

Unlike *Groundhog Day*, *Before I Fall* does not have a romance at its center. (Sam falls in love with a fellow student named Kent, played by Logan Miller, but their relationship does not constitute the heart of the film.) As Anthony Kaufman pointed out in his review for *Screen Daily*, the film explores love and compassion in a more general sense. Sam's most important relationships are with her friends and family. Kaufman also noted the film's superior photography. Set in the Pacific Northwest, the story unfolds against the backdrop of fairytale-like forests and ominous winding, foggy roads. The film's central party scene takes place at Kent's house, an enormous cabin-like mansion that appears to be located deep in the woods. These images evoke the fantastical elements of the story and emphasize the story's suspense. Shots of car headlights moving through the night and Juliet, in flapping, layered sweaters, running through the fog are eerie and strange.

Significance

Before I Fall premiered at the Sundance Film Festival in January 2017. It received moderately positive to mixed reviews. Emily Yoshida of *Vulture* offered one of the latter. She wrote that the film "can't decide how deep it wants to go." Sam and her friends are not one-dimensional but they fall short of true complexity. Subtle moments are followed by clunky dialogue and a heavy-handed emphasis on theme. (The film returns again and again to a shot of a print-out on Kent's wall that says, "Become who you are.") "But the film mostly retains its humanity, largely thanks to Deutch's performance and Russo-Young's insistence on keeping her at the forefront of almost every shot," Yoshida wrote. "Deutch takes Sam through adolescent naiveté, angst, and wonder—and getting through it completely alone." A. O. Scott, writing for *The New York Times*, was more critical, complaining that the film has no realistic characters, calling them archetype "avatars." His tepid praise was that the story is "tactful rather than maudlin, tasteful rather than lurid, soothing rather than creepy." He added that *Before I Fall* lacks the more "intriguing" qualities of Russo-Young's previous film, *Nobody Walks*. Peter Debruge of *Variety* offered a more positive take. Though he raised some important questions about the nature of the story—"Is Sam trying to save her own life, or is she trying to make a positive change that will leave the world better once she's gone?"—he described the film as "an impressively stylish adaptation" with "a look, feel, and voice that's distinct from the vast swatch of YA movies." By comparison to many other young-adult films, though, the indie film fared modestly at the box office, bringing in just over $12 million.

—Molly Hagan

Further Reading

Berman, Eliza. "Director Ry Russo-Young on Dignifying the Female Teenage Experience." *Time*, 13 Mar. 2017, time.com/4695790/ry-russo-young-before-i-fall-interview/. Accessed 10 Jan. 2019.

Erbland, Kate. "'Before I Fall': Why Indie Auteur Ry Russo-Young Embraced the YA Genre." *IndieWire*, 26 Jan. 2017, www.indiewire.com/2017/01/before-i-fall-ry-russo-young-sundance-1201773430/. Accessed 10 Jan. 2019.

Bibliography

Debruge, Peter. Review of *Before I Fall*, directed by Ry Russo-Young. *Variety*, 21 Jan. 2017, variety.com/2017/film/reviews/before-i-fall-review-sundance-1201966093/. Accessed 10 Jan. 2019.

Kaufman, Anthony. "'Before I Fall:' Sundance Review." Review of *Before I Fall*, directed by Ry Russo-Young. *Screen Daily*, 21 Jan. 2017, www.screendaily.com/reviews/before-i-fall-sundance-review/5114011.article. Accessed 10 Jan. 2019.

Review of *Before I Fall*, by Lauren Oliver. *Kirkus*, 15 Feb. 2010, www.kirkusreviews.com/book-reviews/lauren-oliver/before-i-fall/. Accessed 9 Jan. 2019.

Review of *Before I Fall*, by Lauren Oliver. *Publishers Weekly*, 25 Jan. 2010, www.publishersweekly.com/978-0-06-172680-4. Accessed 9 Jan. 2019.

Scott, A. O. "Review: 'Before I Fall,' a Melodramatic 'Groundhog Day.'" Review of *Before I Fall*, directed by Ry Russo-Young. *The New York Times*, 1 Mar. 2017, www.nytimes.com/2017/03/01/movies/before-i-fall-review-zoey-deutch.html. Accessed 9 Jan. 2019.

Yoshida, Emily. "In *Before I Fall*, the Instagram Generation Gets Its *Groundhog Day*." Review of *Before I Fall*, directed by Ry Russo-Young. *Vulture*, 28 Feb. 2017, www.vulture.com/2017/02/before-i-fall-movie-review-teen-weepie-is-no-groundhog-day.html. Accessed 9 Jan. 2019.

Beloved

The Novel
Author: Toni Morrison (1931-2019)
First published: 1987

The Film
Year released: 1998
Director: Jonathan Demme (1944-2017)
Screenplay by: Akosua Busia, Richard LaGravenese, Adam Brooks
Starring: Oprah Winfrey, Danny Glover, Thandie Newton, Kimberly Elise, Beah Richards, LisaGay Hamilton, Albert Hall

Context

Beloved, both as a novel and as a film, exemplifies several important developments in the history of American fiction and moviemaking. One of those developments was the rise of women as major creators and cultural figures. Even before she wrote *Beloved*, but especially after the novel was published, Toni Morrison enjoyed growing prominence as an important American novelist. In fact, it was largely because of *Beloved* that in 1993 she won the prestigious Nobel Prize in Literature. No other American would win that prize again until 2016, when it was awarded to songwriter Bob Dylan. In contrast, ten Americans had won the prize between 1930 and 1987, and only one of them—Pearl Buck in 1938—was a woman.

By the same token, the person who spearheaded, produced, and starred in the film version of *Beloved* was Oprah Winfrey, who by the late 1990s had firmly established herself as one of the most prominent and prosperous media figures in the United States. Winfrey's early commitment to turning the novel into a film was an important vote of confidence from a figure widely admired by a huge American audience. In fact, the rise of both Morrison and Winfrey to such significant cultural positions exemplified the rise of women in general to increasing positions of influence in practically all spheres of American life. And these were women whose achievements were rooted in their intelligence and creativity, not (as in the case of such earlier female icons as Marilyn Monroe) their physical beauty. Morrison and Winfrey were valued, above all else, for their skill in language and for their interest in exploring important issues.

But of course, another reason that both *Beloved* the novel and *Beloved* the film were significant was that Mor-

rison and Winfrey were *Black* women. Powerful women were rare enough in the 1980s; powerful African American women were even rarer. Morrison and Winfrey helped shatter barriers not just for others of their gender but for others of their race. They helped exemplify the talents that

Oprah Winfrey starred as Sethe. Photo by INTX: The Internet & Television Expo via Wikimedia Commons.

existed in two large but previously under-represented "minority groups" (although women, of course, make up the numerical majorities in most countries). *Beloved* centers mainly on the experiences of Black *women* rather than on the experiences of men, either Black or White. Morrison, in the novel, and then also Winfrey in the film, especially explored the lives of persons who were doubly disempowered, both because of their race and because of their gender. But both the novel and the film showed the kind of power, endurance, and resilience that not only Black people in general but by Black women in particular could display under incredibly harsh circumstances.

Finally, one more way in which both the novel and the film versions of *Beloved* are significant is in both works' willingness to present, in unvarnished fashion, the horrific legacy of American slavery. Many novels and films, in the decades before the 1970s and 1980s, offered sanitized versions of that legacy. *Beloved*, both on-screen and on the page, helped to break new ground, presenting slavery and

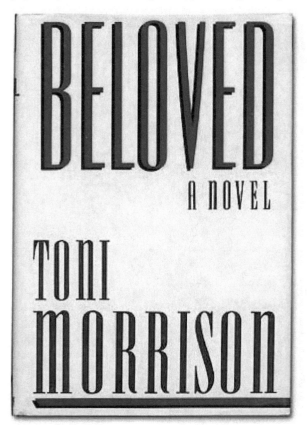

Beloved, by Toni Morrison. First edition dust-jacket, Alfred A. Knopf, 1987. Photo via Wikimedia Commons. [Public domain.]

its results in sickening and repulsive detail. Both the book and the film showed the damaging effects of slavery long after slavery had been technically abolished.

Film Analysis

Beloved the film was not as well received, at least by critics, as *Beloved* the novel. Reviewers' reactions were mixed, with some commentators greatly admiring the film and others harshly condemning it. Significantly, it was nominated for only one Academy Award (for Best Costume Design) but failed to win even that honor. Any hopes that Jonathan Demme may have had to be selected as 1998's best director were dashed, and the same was true of any hopes his cast may have had to be recognized for their skill as actors. Participants in the film did receive various important awards from the National Association for the Advancement of Colored People (NAACP), but it failed to garner the kind of recognition that matters most in Hollywood.

One almost universal complaint about the film—lodged both by people who admired it and by those who did not—involved its great length. At almost three hours long, it was often called far too leisurely for its own good. Various reviewers suggested that it could have been a much more effective film if it had simply been shorter and thus less tedious. Some reviewers accused the filmmakers of sticking too faithfully to the plot of Morrison's lengthy novel, and even many admirers of the film expressed relief that it was not even longer than it was. Critics of the film also faulted it for following too closely the complicated, convoluted structure of the novel. They argued that while the complex book could be read at a leisurely pace, the complex film was difficult to digest and make sense of in the time available, especially if viewers had not already read the novel. Some reviewers wished that the film had dispensed with some elements of the novel, especially its heavy emphasis on the supernatural, but often they acknowledged that if Demme had decided to simplify the novel's plot he would have been accused of failing to do proper justice to the book. A few reviewers even wondered whether this innovative, idiosyncratic novel could ever be made into a successful, or at least widely popular, film. They suggested that viewers lacking prior knowledge of the novel would likely find the film especially mystifying.

Finally, another feature of the film that attracted very strong criticism was the performance of Thandie Newton in the title role. Reviewers who disliked her acting found it hysterical, histrionic, excessive, and even unintentionally laughable. They considered her performance hard to accept or take seriously, especially because of her exaggerated facial expressions and the odd sounds and gestures that often accompanied them. A few reviewers found the film too preachy, too obvious, and too closely indebted to horror movies, but the most common complaint was its sheer length.

On the other hand, critics who admired the film often had high praise for the actors and acting. Oprah Winfrey, playing the key role of Sethe, was often commended for submerging herself in the part and resisting the impulse to make the film all about her. Kimberly Elise, playing Sethe's daughter Denver, won widespread praise. In fact, many critics considered her performance the best in the film. Danny Glover, playing Paul D., the major male role, was also frequently commended. But perhaps the most surprising aspect of the various positive reactions the film received was the praise directed at Thandie Newton for her performance as Beloved. People who hated the film often hated this performance in particular, but people who admired it often admired what Newton had done with an exceptionally difficult and challenging role. They called her performance innovative, exciting, and inventive, unlike almost anything ever seen in a film before.

Likewise, while some negative critics of the film disliked its heavy emphasis on horror and the supernatural, some positive commentators admired precisely those aspects of the film. It was often praised for sticking close to the plot of the book and for trying to be a faithful adaptation, even though negative critics often attacked it for exactly those same reasons. Janet Maslin, writing for *The New York Times*, admired the way that "Demme affectingly mixes faded color with glorious bursts of light, jarring angles with startling flashbacks, the vitality of nature with the harshness of man" to convey the complicated plot and texture of the book, thereby achieving a film that she found quite compelling in its own right.

Often, then, critics paid attention to the very same features of the film but came to diametrically opposed conclusions about them. Some commentators admired the film for sticking close to the plot, themes, and characters of the book, while others attacked what they saw as the film's excessive fidelity to the novel. For example, some reviewers appreciated Demme's decision to include elements of horror and the supernatural, while other writers saw this decision as seriously flawed. In particular, they often found the special effects used in these sequences unconvincing and even comical.

Significance

If reactions on sites such as *Rotten Tomatoes* are any indication, "regular people" seem to admire the film more than many early critics did. It was not the box office "smash" its makers surely hoped it would be, but neither was it by any means a critical or financial failure.

Demme was a greatly respected director, Oprah Winfrey was and is one of the most popular Americans of her generation, and right up until her death in 2019, Morrison continued to win acclaim as one of the most important literary figures in America and around the world. The book and the film tell the story of a significant period in American history—a period when women in general and Black women in particular were finally winning major recognition for their contributions to culture. For all these reasons, the film version of *Beloved* is likely to remain a noteworthy cultural achievement and the novel will continue to be widely taught in high schools and colleges. Teachers will almost surely continue to use the film to help cast extra light on the book. The mere fact that both the book and film deal thoughtfully with such important issues as race, gender, class, and slavery will contribute to their endurance. As the United States becomes increasingly multicultural, the voices of people such as Morrison and Winfrey are likely to receive even more respect and attention.

—*Robert C. Evans, PhD*

Further Reading

Alleva, Richard. "Mistranslated." *Commonweal*, vol. 125, no. 20, 1998, p. 18. EBSCOhost, search.ebscohost.com/login.aspx?direct=true&db=lkh&AN=1329910&site=ehost-live. Accessed 20 Apr. 2020.

Wardi, Anissa Janine. "Freak Shows, Spectacles, and Carnivals: Reading Jonathan Demme's *Beloved*." *African American Review*, vol. 39, no. 4, Winter 2005, pp. 513-526. EBSCOhost, search.ebscohost.com/login.aspx?direct=true&db=lkh&AN=20597824&site=ehost-live. Accessed 20 Apr. 2020.

Bibliography

Ebert, Roger. Review of *Beloved*, directed by Jonathan Demme. *RogerEbert.com*, 16 Oct. 1998, www.rogerebert.com/reviews/beloved-1998. Accessed 13 July 2020.

Hudson-Weems, Clenora. "*Beloved*: From Novel to Movie." *Western Journal of Black Studies*, vol. 23, no. 3, 1999, p. 203. EBSCOhost, search.ebscohost.com/login.aspx?direct=true&db =lkh&AN=2807463&site=ehost-live. Accessed 20 Apr. 2020.

Maslin, Janet. "*Beloved*: No Peace from a Brutal Legacy." *The New York Times*, 16 Oct. 1998, archive.nytimes.com/ www.nytimes.com/library/film/101698beloved-film-review.html. Accessed 20 Apr. 2020.

The Big Sleep

The Novel
Author: Raymond Chandler (1888-1959)
First published: 1939

The Film
Year released: 1946
Director: Howard Hawks (1896-1977)
Screenplay by: William Faulkner, Leigh Brackett, Jules Furthman
Starring: Humphrey Bogart, Lauren Bacall, Martha Vickers, John Ridgely, Dorothy Malone

Context

Raymond Chandler was a primary developer of the hard-boiled detective story, marked by naturalism and a lack of sentimentality. Though Carroll John Daly and Dashiell Hammett are credited with pioneering the subgenre in the 1920s, Chandler helped bring the concept to iconic status. His character Philip Marlowe exhibited an ideal balance of physical presence, mental acuity, moral principles, and human flaws that made him a template for the no-nonsense private detective. Marlowe's exploits were chronicled in Chandler's well-wrought, simile-saturated, jaundiced, lyrical prose across seven novels and a short story collection, beginning with *The Big Sleep* (1939).

The strength of these works (and their commercial success) inspired a multitude of hard-boiled emulators, many of whom imparted their own spin on the genre. Some practitioners (such as Ross Macdonald, Bill Pronzini, and Robert B. Parker) created detectives who could have been Marlowe's direct descendants. Others took a more lighthearted (John D. MacDonald) or more violent (Mickey Spillane) approach. And still others changed the gender (Sue Grafton, Sara Paretsky), the sexual orientation (Joseph Hansen), or the race (Walter Mosley) of the protagonist.

Chandler's work first appeared on-screen in 1942 with *Time to Kill*, an adaptation of his novel *The High Window* (1942). However, Marlowe was replaced with the similar private-eye character Mike Shayne, portrayed by Lloyd Nolan. That same year, an adaptation of Chandler's *Farewell, My Lovely* (1940), titled *The Falcon Takes Over*, appeared but starred George Sanders as gentleman detective the Falcon. The first film featuring Marlowe as the lead character was *Murder, My Sweet* (1944), a well-received faithful adaptation of *Farewell, My Lovely* starring Dick Powell. This was released several months after another significant Chandler project: with director Billy Wilder, he wrote the screenplay for the outstanding film noir *Double Indemnity* (1944), adapted from the 1943 James M. Cain novel of the same name.

The year 1946 was especially fruitful for Chandler. His first original screenplay, *The Blue Dahlia*, was released as a critically acclaimed film noir (the author was nominated for an Academy Award, as he had been for *Double Indem-*

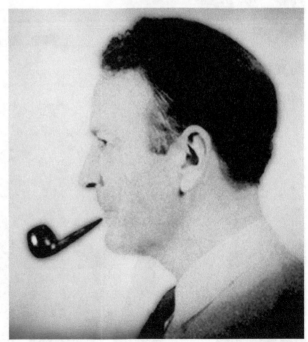

Author Raymond Chandler. Photo via Wikimedia Commons. [Public domain.]

nity, but did not win an Oscar either time). Then, *The Big Sleep* premiered in the United States to become the first film based on a Chandler novel to retain the work's original name. The project was directed at Warner Brothers by the versatile Howard Hawks, whose credits included *The Dawn Patrol* (1930), *Scarface* (1932), *Bringing Up Baby* (1938) and *Sergeant York* (1941). The adaptation had been in the works since late 1944, but the film's release was delayed by a number of unforeseen difficulties.

Film Analysis

That Chandler's *The Big Sleep*—a novel crafted by combining parts of earlier stories—would need to be extensively edited for the big screen was a foregone conclusion. The novel contained explicit references to many contro-

versial subjects, including drug abuse, pornography, sexual promiscuity, homosexuality, and government and law enforcement corruption. Such material would need to be toned down or eliminated completely to avoid the wrath of film censors. Chandler was a popular commodity in Hollywood in the 1940s, but was unavailable to adapt his own material due to a contract at a different studio. In his absence, two impressive substitutes were hired to handle the task of translating the novel to film. Novelist William Faulkner had worked with director Hawks adapting Ernest Hemingway's novel for the film *To Have and Have Not* (1944), which featured star Humphrey Bogart and the debut of Lauren Bacall. Hawks paired Faulkner with writer Leigh Brackett, based on strength of her hard-boiled novel *No Good from a Corpse* (1944).

Humphrey Bogart and Lauren Bacall in The Big Sleep *(1946). Photo via the National Motion Picture Council/Wikimedia Commons. [Public domain.]*

Faulkner divided Chandler's novel in half, and the two screenwriters worked alone on alternate chapters, seldom comparing notes. Once they were done, screenwriter-script doctor Jules Furthman was brought in to merge Faulkner's and Brackett's contributions into a cohesive shooting script. The end result was a screenplay that tracked closely with the novel's dark tone and complex plot. Many of Chandler's exchanges of dialogue were lifted verbatim.

In both novel and film, the story begins in classic fashion. Private investigator Philip Marlowe (Bogart) is summoned by a wheelchair-bound widower, General Sternwood (Charles Waldron). The aged millionaire is being blackmailed because of the antics of his wild young children. Libidinous younger daughter Carmen (Martha Vickers) is involved in gambling, drugs, and pornography with erotic book dealer Arthur Geiger (Theodore von Eltz, uncredited). Cool, snobby elder daughter Vivian Rutledge (Lauren Bacall) is in debt to casino owner Eddie Mars (John Ridgely), who seems to have something more incriminating on her. Marlowe begins work by trailing Geiger from his bookstore to his bungalow. While on stakeout, he hears shots inside the home and a car speeds away. Marlowe breaks into the home, finds Geiger shot to death and Carmen drugged into a giggling stupor. A hidden camera, used to take compromising pictures, is missing its film.

As Marlowe works to recover photos of Carmen, he undertakes a related, unpaid job: learning the whereabouts of General Sternwood's friend and surrogate son, Sean Regan, who suddenly disappeared. In the course of the convoluted investigation, Marlowe unravels a series of interrelated crimes. Several people die violently. The Sternwoods' chauffeur Owen Taylor (Dan Wallace, uncredited) drowns. A shady character involved in the blackmail scheme, Joe Brody (Louis Jean Heydt), is shot to death. Peripheral character Harry Jones (Elisha Cook Jr.), connected to Geiger's bookstore clerk Agnes Lozelle (Sonia Darrin, uncredited), is poisoned. Regan may be dead, too, but how and why and where nobody knows.

The film's plot is often said to be confusing and complicated. This was partly an artistic choice, a way of drawing the audience into the suspense and excitement. Over time, the complicated plot has become an offbeat hallmark of the film, generally considered part of its—somewhat dizzying—charm. But it was also the result of a series of production quirks that eventually led to two substantially different versions of the film, with an early version shown in 1945 to servicemen abroad, before it was reworked into the final version of 1946. The 1945 version, shown to military personnel, received generally favorable reactions, with particular kudos to the high-contrast black-and-white photography shot by cinematographer Sidney Hickox. It also included a sequence about halfway through in which Marlowe discusses events with the authorities, offering explanations of who did what to whom. However, as World War II wound down, studios wanted to rush war-oriented films into production before the subject became obsolete, so the general release of *The Big Sleep* was postponed.

In the meantime, *To Have and Have Not* proved highly popular, especially because of the strong chemistry between Bogart and Bacall. Bacall also made another film, *Confidential Agent* (1945), but her performance was widely maligned. Hawks—whose wife had discovered Bacall—Warner Brothers studio heads, and Bacall's agent, who all had considerable investments in the young star, agreed that rewrites to *The Big Sleep* should expand Bacall's role (her character, Vivian, has few scenes in the novel) to capitalize on her dynamic with Bogart and boost her suddenly tarnished acting reputation. Screenwriter Philip Epstein, who had contributed to the screenplay of *Casablanca* (1942), was called in to do the work.

Epstein cut about twenty minutes of footage from the 1945 version of the film, including the explanatory scene in the middle. He then added in rewritten, condensed, or completely new scenes that were reshot. Most changes featured Bogart and Bacall together—with more flattering lighting, better camera angles and wittier dialogue—to take advantage of the chemistry that had progressed into a real-life romance. One of most significant additions to the script was a sequence extraneous to the plot, in which Bogart and Bacall talk about horse racing in sexually suggestive terms. (Chandler himself later suggested that Vickers's screen time was reduced to prevent her own highly sensual performance distracting from Bacall.) The ending of the film was also extensively reworked to adhere to a Production Code requirement to show that crime does not pay. Retakes were accomplished in early 1946, and the film, expertly edited by Christian Nyby and featuring a memorable score by Max Steiner, was released in August of that year.

The resulting wide-release version of *The Big Sleep* notably, eccentrically, trades plot coherence for dramatic energy. Several plot threads are left wholly unexplained, and Hawks himself frequently commented that even he did not understand the story. But, he said, the plot was incidental to the film's entertainment power. And indeed, the film is captivating, with Bogart and Bacall living up to the success of their previous pairing and the rest of the performances perfectly serving Hawks's skilled direction.

Significance

The Big Sleep was very commercially successful, tripling its $1.6 million budget in domestic and foreign box office sales. Most critics of the time praised the film, even despite frequent confusion about the plot. Today it is considered a masterpiece of film noir that holds up well despite its age. Bogart's portrayal of Marlowe is considered definitive and continually influential, and his chemistry with Bacall remains legendary. The film has been included on critics' lists of the greatest films of all time. It was not until the late 1990s that the original 1945 version was discovered, restored, and released. It too was acclaimed, though most viewers of both adaptations have concluded that the faster-paced later version is more entertaining.

Many of those associated with the film flourished in the wake of its success. Chandler continued to publish Marlowe novels, winning an Edgar Award for *The Long Goodbye* (1953), itself made into a critically acclaimed film in 1973. Despite personal struggles late in life, his literary reputation has only increased posthumously. Hawks expanded upon his already stellar career as a versatile director, adding features like *Red River* (1948), *I Was a Male War Bride* (1949), and *Gentlemen Prefer Blondes* (1953) to his filmography. Brackett worked on a number of later Hawks features—including *Rio Bravo* (1959), *El Dorado* (1966), and *Rio Lobo* (1970)—and wrote the screenplay for the film of *The Long Goodbye*. She also contributed an early draft of the screenplay for the Star Wars film *The Empire Strikes Back* (1980). Faulkner, meanwhile, won the Nobel Prize for literature in 1949 and garnered two Pulitzer Prizes (1955 and 1963) on the way to becoming one of the most celebrated American writers of the twentieth century.

Arguably the biggest beneficiary of *The Big Sleep*'s success, however, was Bacall. Whereas her counterpart Bogart was already an established star, Bacall's burgeoning career—almost derailed by *Confidential Agent*—was put back on track thanks in large part to the new material added to the film. Her sensuous sparring with Bogart, intentionally recalling her alluring performance in *To Have and Have Not*, cemented her status as one of the leading stars of her time. As husband and wife, Bacall and Bogart went on to appear together in two additional noir-flavored films, *Dark Passage* (1947) and *Key Largo* (1948). Another detective film from Bacall's long career was *Harper* (1966), adapted from Ross Macdonald's novel *The Moving Target* (1949) featuring the Marlowe-like private eye Lew Archer.

—*Jack Ewing*

Further Reading

Bacall, Lauren. *Now*. Knopf, 1994.

McCarthy, Todd. *Howard Hawks: The Grey Fox of Hollywood*. Grove Press, 2000.

Bibliography

"The Big Sleep (1946)." *Turner Classic Movies*, 2018, www.tcm.com/tcmdb/title/45/The-Big-Sleep/. Accessed 11 Dec. 2018.

Carr, Jeremy. "A Masterpiece of Moments: 'The Big Sleep' Turns 70." *Movie Mezzanine*, 31 Aug. 2016, moviemezzanine.com/the-big-sleep-at-70/. Accessed 26 Nov. 2018.

Chandler, Raymond. *The Annotated Big Sleep*. Annotated and edited by Owen Hill, Pamela Jackson, and Anthony Dean Rizzuto. Vintage Crime/Black Lizard, 2018.

Dirks, Tim. "The Big Sleep (1946)." *AMC Filmsite*, 2018, www.filmsite.org/bigs.html. Accessed 11 Dec. 2018.

Grimes, William. "Mystery of 'The Big Sleep' Solved. *The New York Times*, 9 Jan. 1997, www.nytimes.com/1997/01/09/movies/mystery-of-the-big-sleep-solved.html. Accessed 26 Nov. 2018.

McCrum, Robert. "The 100 Best Novels: No. 62—*The Big Sleep* by Raymond Chandler (1939). *The Guardian*, 24 Nov. 2014, www.theguardian.com/books/2014/nov/24/100-best-novels-the-big-sleep-raymond-chandler. Accessed 26 Nov. 2018.

Phillips, Gene D. *Creatures of Darkness: Raymond Chandler, Detective Fiction, and Film Noir*. UP of Kentucky, 2000.

The Blind Side

The Novel
Author: Michael Lewis (b. 1960)
First published: 2006

The Film
Year released: 2009
Director: John Lee Hancock (b. 1956)
Screenplay by: John Lee Hancock
Starring: Sandra Bullock, Tim McGraw, Quinton Aaron, Kathy Bates

Context

Over the course of a career that has spanned more than three decades, author Michael Lewis has astutely spotted and chronicled zeitgeist-defining trends in American culture. His books include *Liar's Poker: Rising Through the Wreckage on Wall Street* (1989), a look at 1980s Wall Street culture that was partially based on Lewis's own experiences working as a bond trader; *Moneyball: The Art of Winning an Unfair Game* (2003), about the Oakland Athletics baseball team and its general manager, Bill Beane; and *The Big Short* (2010), which chronicles the crash of the housing market which precipitated the 2008 global financial crisis.

The first of Lewis's books to be adapted for the screen was *The Blind Side: Evolution of a Game*, published in 2006. The book focuses on the evolution of football strategy since the early 1980s. Through the remarkable life story of former National Football League (NFL) player Michael Oher, it also investigates the lucrative rise of the left tackle position. Lewis became inspired to write the book in the fall of 2003, following a meeting with his childhood friend, former University of Mississippi basketball star Sean Tuohy, about an unrelated writing project. It was then when Lewis first heard about Michael Oher, who at the time was living at Tuohy's house as an unofficial member of his family. One of thirteen children born to a crack-addicted mother, Oher grew up in a tough area of Memphis, Tennessee, and bounced between foster care and the streets before being taken in by the Tuohy family during his junior year of high school. By his senior year, Oher, under the guidance of Tuohy, his indomitable wife Leigh Anne, and others, had risen to become one of the top left tackle prospects in the country. Intrigued, Lewis began digging further into Oher's background, which coalesced with research into the rapidly evolving NFL game.

The Blind Side became a bestseller and earned widespread critical praise for its deft analysis of the NFL and poignant portrait of the human condition. John Lee Hancock, a well-known screenwriter who had made his directorial debut with the well-received baseball drama *The Rookie* (2002), adapted the book for the screen in 2007. Hancock's script lagged in development for over a year before it was picked up by Alcon Entertainment, and the film went into production in the spring of 2009. Starring Sandra Bullock as Leigh Anne Tuohy, *The Blind Side*, which Hancock also directed, premiered in New York City on November 17, 2009, and also had other premieres in Nashville and New Orleans.

Film Analysis

Like Lewis's book, *The Blind Side* opens with a sequence that deconstructs an infamous 1985 NFL play, one in which New York Giants star linebacker Lawrence Taylor violently sacked the Washington Redskins quarterback Joe Theismann from the blind side and broke his leg in two places. The play effectively ended Theismann's career and helped reinforce the importance of the left tackle position, which protects the blind side for right-handed quarterbacks. The sequence is narrated by a spunky southern woman, later revealed to be Leigh Anne Tuohy (Sandra Bullock), which signals to viewers who the film will center around. However, unlike the book, which includes lengthy digressions into football history, the film uses this sequence as a context-setting prologue to its central story about an impoverished inner-city African American teenager who is adopted by a white, well-to-do Memphis family.

That teenager is Michael Oher (Quinton Aaron), who is introduced in the following scene. He is being questioned by a National Collegiate Athletic Association (NCAA) investigator for an unknown reason and then the film segues to a flashback from two years earlier. Bouncing from home to home due to an absent, drug-addicted mother, Oher ends up being taken in by a mechanic and inner-city youth mentor named Tony Hamilton, who, despite his nearly nonexistent academic record, helps him win acceptance to the Wingate Christian School, an exclusive, predominantly white private school in Memphis. Oher's size and athleticism intrigues the school's head football coach, Burt Cotton (Ray McKinnon), who recruits him to play football. It is not long after enrolling at the school that Oher discovers that his father, largely absent from his life, has died in an accident. Still living on the streets, Oher soon comes to the attention of Sean (Tim McGraw) and Leigh Anne Tuohy, whose children also attend Wingate. While walking alone at night, Oher is spotted by Leigh Anne and Sean, who invite him to sleep at their home. This ultimately sets in motion a series of events that results in Oher becoming an official member of the Tuohy family.

Hancock condenses and alters information from Lewis's book to heighten drama. *The Blind Side* is shot in a slick but straightforward and unobtrusive style and features a lighthearted soundtrack, both of which serve to reinforce the film's heartwarming and inspirational nature and appeal to a wide audience. Characters like Tony Hamilton (who is based on a man named Tony Henderson) only appear briefly in the film, despite playing a larger role in Oher's life. Also, plot details surrounding Oher and his entry into Wingate (based on Briarcrest Christian School) are slightly more complicated, as he was required to participate in a home school program for several months before gaining admission. Such uses of dramatic license are on one level meant to make the film more streamlined—and by extension, more entertaining—but on another level, aimed to highlight the central relationship that forms its emotional core: that of Oher and the Tuohys.

While the transition period from the time Oher first met the Tuohys to the time he started living with them was much longer, Hancock effectively portrays the transformative role they played in his life. Leigh Anne and Sean stepped in and became surrogate mother and father figures, respectively, and their children, Collins and S. J., be-

Sandra Bullock won numerous awards for her role in The Blind Side, *including the Screen Actors Guild Award for Best Actress. Photo by djtomdog via Wikimedia Commons.*

come surrogate siblings. Together, they put him on a path toward academic success and football greatness. The self-confident and dauntless Leigh Anne, in particular, emerges as Oher's chief protector and champion, feeding him, taking him clothes shopping, and helping him obtain a driver's license, among other things. She is even portrayed showing Oher how to play football, both in practice and in games, and directing coach Cotton, who is based on former Briarcrest coach Hugh Freeze, how to use him properly. These details, however, did not happen in real life as Oher had played football prior to attending Briarcrest. In Lewis's book, Freeze is depicted as a football savant, but the Cotton character is stereotypically clueless and headstrong. This nonetheless adds another layer of dramatic conflict, and in viewers' minds, further builds up Leigh Anne's influence.

More negative aspects of Oher's early life are largely glossed over, though there are several scenes in which

Oher returns to the rough-and-tumble neighborhood he grew up in. He is shown uncomfortably interacting with former football players-turned-drug dealers, illustrating the palpable and pervasive lure of gang life. At one point, Leigh Anne pays a visit to Oher's mother Denise (Adriane Lenox) to ask for her permission to obtain legal guardianship. Rather than presenting her in an unflattering light, however, Hancock takes a sentimental approach, portraying her sympathetically. The only major roadblock to Oher's future as a professional football player, after the Tuohys become his legal guardians, is his academic performance, and thus the collective efforts of the Tuohys, his teachers, and his full-time private tutor Miss Sue (Kathy Bates) to help him meet necessary academic requirements. This facet of Oher's story is also effectively dramatized as he was also required to take correspondence courses to bring his grades up.

One of the more memorable sequences in the film shows Oher being courted by some of the most renowned college football coaches in America. Adding a dash of realism to the picture, Hancock opted to have such coaches—Nick Saban, Phillip Fulmer, Lou Holtz, Tommy Tuberville, and Ed Orgeron—play themselves in scenes that are not much different from what transpired in real life. Upon raising his grades, Oher chooses to play under Ed Orgeron at the University of Mississippi, also known as "Ole Miss." This decision is revealed to be the source of Oher's troubles depicted at the beginning of the film, as the Tuohys, besides being well-known alumni, are unabashed boosters for the school. Oher is consequently interviewed by an NCAA investigator to determine whether he was inappropriately influenced by the Tuohys to attend Ole Miss. A climactic confrontation between Oher and Leigh Anne ensues, propelling the film to its uplifting resolution. Ultimately, Oher and the Tuohys' conflict with the NCAA is settled without incident and Oher is accepted to Ole Miss. The film ends with a photo montage of the real-life Oher and Tuohys, which culminates with Oher being drafted into the NFL by the Baltimore Ravens in the first round of the 2009 draft. This serves as an appropriate addendum to Lewis's book, which concludes just as Oher starts his college career at Ole Miss.

Significance

Following its premieres, *The Blind Side* opened in theaters throughout the United States on November 20, 2009. The film was met with mixed reviews. While acknowledging its inspirational nature, many critics commented negatively on its sentimental tone, sugarcoated depictions of reality, and deliberate departures from Lewis's book to heighten drama. Bullock's dynamic, no-nonsense lead performance, however, was widely praised; newcomer Quinton Aaron and country music star Tim McGraw also earned positive notices for their portrayals. For her work on the film, Bullock garnered numerous awards and nominations, most notably winning an Academy Award, Golden Globe, and Screen Actors Guild Award for best actress in a leading role.

Thanks to a savvy marketing campaign, *The Blind Side* was a smash commercial hit, grossing more than $34 million its opening weekend—$5 million more than its modest $29 million production budget. It went on to earn more than $255 million at the domestic box office and $309 million globally, which at the time made it the highest-grossing sports drama of all time. Despite a mixed critical response, the film became a surprising Oscar contender, and it was one of ten films nominated for best picture at the 82nd Academy Awards. It helped revive Bullock's career and also served as a Hollywood launchpad for Lewis, paving the way for the film adaptations of two of his other books, *Moneyball* and *The Big Short*, in 2011 and 2015, respectively.

Sadly, Michael Oher was not a fan of the film. While commending Aaron for his acting, Oher took particular exception to the film's portrayal of his intellectual ability. Oher had an IQ of 80 as a boy; this was dramatically amended later in life, once his learning disability was identified and addressed. To tell this story and to set the record straight, Oher published an autobiography, *I Beat the Odds: From Homelessness, to The Blind Side, and Beyond* (2011). The book made *The New York Times* Best Seller list. Still, *The Blind Side*, released during Oher's rookie season, made the left tackle one of the most popular players in the NFL, in which he played for three teams over eight seasons; in 2013, he won a Super Bowl ring as a member of the Baltimore Ravens. Although the film would later be accused of reinforcing negative racial stereotypes, *The Blind Side* is regarded as one of the most inspirational sports films of all time.

—*Chris Cullen*

Further Reading

Abramowitz, Rachel. "The Making of *Blind Side* a Real-Life Drama." *Los Angeles Times*, 17 Jan. 2010, www.latimes.com/archives/la-xpm-2010-jan-17-la-et-blindside17-2010jan17-story.html. Accessed 15 Apr. 2020.

Higgins, Brendan. "The Real Story behind *The Blind Side*." *Collider*, 20 Aug. 2019, collider.com/galleries/the-blind-side-true-story-differences/. Accessed 15 Apr. 2020.

Will, George F. "The Next Big Thing." *The New York Times*, 12 Nov. 2006, www.nytimes.com/2006/11/12/books/review/Will.t.html. Accessed 15 Apr. 2020.

Bibliography

Cieply, Michael, and Paula Schwartz. "*Blind Side* Finds a Path to the Oscars by Running Up the Middle." *The New York Times*, 5 Feb. 2010, www.nytimes.com/2010/02/06/movies/awardsseason/06blind.html?auth=loginemail&login=email. Accessed 15 Apr. 2020.

Holmes, Linda. "Beyond *The Blind Side*, Michael Oher Rewrites His Own Story." *NPR*, 8 Feb. 2011, www.npr.org/2011/02/08/133590180/beyond-the-blind-side-michael-oher-rewrites-his-own-story. Accessed 15 Apr. 2020.

Levin, Josh. "Illegal Use of Sandra Bullock." *Slate*, 20 Nov. 2009, slate.com/culture/2009/11/the-blind-side-reviewed.html. Accessed 15 Apr. 2020.

Lewis, Michael. *The Blind Side: Evolution of a Game*. Kindle ed., W.W. Norton & Company, 2007.

Leydon, Joe. "*The Blind Side*." *Variety*, 15 Nov. 2009, variety.com/2009/film/reviews/the-blind-side-1200477424/. Accessed 15 Apr. 2020.

Rechtshaffen, Michael. "*The Blind Side*: Film Review." *The Hollywood Reporter*, 15 Nov. 2009, www.hollywoodreporter.com/review/blind-side-review-movie-2009-93755. Accessed 15 Apr. 2020.

Scott, A. O. "Steamrolling over Life's Obstacles with Family as Cheerleaders." *The New York Times*, 19 Nov. 2009, www.nytimes.com/2009/11/20/movies/20blindside.html. Accessed 15 Apr. 2020.

"The Blindside: Evolution of a Game." *Publishers Weekly*, 28 Aug. 2006, www.publishersweekly.com/978-0-393-06123-9. Accessed 15 Apr. 2020.

The Book of Negroes

The Novel
Author: Lawrence Hill (b. 1957)
First published: 2007

The Film
Year released: 2015
Director: Clement Virgo (b. 1966)
Screenplay by: Lawrence Hill, Clement Virgo
Starring: Aunjanue Ellis, Kyle M. Hamilton, Lyriq Bent, Cuba Gooding Jr., Louis Gossett Jr., Ben Chaplin, Allan Hawco, Greg Bryk, Jane Alexander

Context

The Book of Negroes (2007) is an award-winning novel written by Canadian author Lawrence Hill, who began his writing career as a newspaper reporter for *The Globe and Mail* and *The Winnipeg Free Press*. The son of civil rights activists, Hill was interested in the issue of race from an early age. He published several nonfiction books on the subject, including *Trials and Triumphs: The Story of African-Canadians* (1993) as well as *Women of Vision: The Story of the Canadian Negro Women's Association, 1951-1976* (1996). Like his historical works on African Americans and African Canadians, much of Hill's other writing explores the theme of identity. This is evident in his 2001 memoir *Black Berry, Sweet Juice: On Being Black and White in Canada* (2001); his novel *Any Known Blood* (1998), which follows five generations of an African Canadian American family; and *The Book of Negroes*.

The Book of Negroes (titled *Someone Knows My Name* in its American edition) is a book about the life of an enslaved African woman named Aminata Diallo who is sent to live in Canada by the British after the American Revolutionary War. Upon its publication, Hill's novel earned significant critical acclaim as well as the 2007 Rogers Writers' Trust Fiction Prize and the 2008 Commonwealth Writers' Prize. The book's title pays homage to the actual historical document that contained the names of three thousand African American slaves who were granted land and freedom in Nova Scotia after crossing over to the British side during the American Revolution.

In 2009, the rights to *The Book of Negroes* were optioned by filmmakers Clement Virgo and Damon D'Oliveira. The following year, television networks CBC and BET came onboard and the project was changed from a film to a six-part miniseries. The scripts were cowritten by Hill and Virgo, who also served as director. Born in Jamaica but raised in Toronto, Virgo was educated at the Canadian Film Centre. Previous to *The Book of Negroes*, he was best known for his directorial work on film and television projects that explored African Canadian and African American lives like *The Planet of Junior Brown* (1997), *Soul Food* (2000), *The Wire* (2002), and *Poor Boy's Game* (2007). American actress Aunjanue Ellis was cast in the lead role of Aminata with Jamaican Canadian actor Lyriq Bent playing her husband Chekura. Filming of the international co-production began in 2014. *The Book of Negroes* was shot in South Africa and Canada. It is comparable to other African American historical series like *Roots* (1977) and *Underground* (2016).

Film Analysis

The Book of Negroes miniseries stays true to its source material. This can be partially attributed to the fact that Hill cowrote the scripts with Virgo to ensure that they felt like a faithful retelling of his novel. Most of the differences between the two iterations of Aminata Diallo's story are minor and involve superfluous characters and plot points. Ultimately, Hill and Virgo condensed Aminata's journey so that it comprised only its most dramatically essential elements. This meant omitting anything that either did not directly propel the narrative forward or did not visually translate to the screen.

Like the novel, the miniseries begins with an aged Aminata (Ellis) telling her life story to a group of British legislators in London before quickly transitioning into a flashback scene to her younger years. This setup creates a feeling of suspense as viewers are left to wonder how Aminata ended up in London and why she is speaking to these men. As the flashback scene demonstrates, Aminata's journey began in West Africa, where she was born and raised. There, her father was a Muslim jeweler while her mother worked as a midwife "catching" babies. Although Aminata enjoyed helping her mother catch babies, as a young girl she wanted to one day be a "djeli" or the village storyteller who learns and shares the stories of everyone in the community. This idea that recording someone's existence validates their humanity proves to be a reoccurring theme throughout the miniseries.

Virgo's onscreen depiction of Africa is intended to reflect the fact that it is Aminata's home. Consequently, the director amplifies the natural beauty that surrounds her village—the landscape, sea, and sky are all bright and joyful in appearance. This is a stark contrast to the way that he later portrays America, Canada, and England, which feel more claustrophobic, dirty, and manmade in comparison. Aminata's introduction into these foreign Western lands begins tragically one day when she and her family are attacked while walking through the forest. Marauders working for white slavers end up killing her parents and kidnapping her. As she is marched toward the ocean with other captured Africans, a boy about her age named Chekura treats her with kindness. Although he does not wear chains and assists the slavers, the reality is that he has no choice in the matter. Later he is enslaved as well.

While the filmmakers never mitigate the suffering and terror that Aminata and other enslaved African's experience, they also try to balance such events with empowering stories and imagery. Scene after scene, they demonstrate the bravery and perseverance of enslaved African people to show that they are not victims but survivors. This is first evident on the slave ship where Aminata and the other captives stage a coup and almost successfully overthrow their European captors. Once in America, Aminata is sold to Robinson Appleby, an indigo plantation owner who tries repeatedly to break her sense of hope. After learning that she has romantically reconnected with Chekura, Appleby rapes her. Instead of having the audience watch this, however, Virgo has the camera outside of the closed door where it is happening. It is a powerful scene without being exploitative. Later, when Aminata is pregnant with Chekura's child, Appleby drags her out where the other enslaved workers can see her and shaves her head. It is a disturbing scene intended to demonstrate

his power and ability to violate her. However, this does not stop Aminata who continues fighting for her freedom as well as the freedom of other enslaved people in the years that follow. In this way, she embodies the spirit of African American people.

Many of the characters have a nuanced, complex relationship with slavery. While there are some characters who are wholly good or evil, others are not as easy to define. For example, Chekura must live with the fact that he helped enslave Aminata as well as dozens of other Africans. The character of Mr. Lindo, a Jewish man who later purchases Aminata, provides Aminata with a significantly better life than Appleby. Despite the fact that he gives her more liberties and celebrates her intellect, at the end of the day he still considers her his property and consequently is not a good man. Perhaps one of the most complex characters in *The Book of Negroes* is that of Samuel Fraunces (Gooding Jr.), a tavern owner who helps Aminata escape Lindo and gives her a job. Although he is a free African American man who wants to liberate others, he sides with the Americans during the Revolutionary War even though they will allow slavery to continue once free from England.

Unlike many other dramas about American history, *The Book of Negroes* does not portray the American Revolution in a positive light. Instead, it showcases the many hypocrisies of the American people who claimed to live in a land where every man was created equal and yet practiced slavery. The miniseries focuses on the British experience during the American Revolution, revealing a little-known chapter of history in which they offered freedom and land in Nova Scotia to any slaves who helped them fight the Americans. Aminata earns this privilege by recording the names and occupations of three thousand African Americans who would be sent to Canada in a document called "The Book of Negroes." After things prove to be too difficult in Nova Scotia, she, Chekura, and other freed slaves are sent to settle Sierra Leone by the British government. Once back in Africa, Aminata returns to her village where she realizes that she must do more to help enslaved people. It is then that she decides to head to London to share her story in an effort to end the slave trade. Her contributions prove to be successful.

In many ways, *The Book of Negroes* is a love story. The relationship between Aminata and Chekura prevents the miniseries from becoming nothing more than a dry historical drama. After forming an unshakeable bond at the age of eleven, the two are repeatedly separated and reunited in the years that follow. Years after being sold to different plantations, Chekura eventually finds Aminata at Appleby's. In an especially powerful scene, Virgo has Chekura bring Aminata a scarf, which he wraps around her head upon her request. In addition to it being a deep red color that symbolizes his love for her, the scarf is representative of their homeland. By continuously weaving tender scenes of love and joy between Aminata and Chekura throughout the miniseries, Hill and Virgo depict African American history in a way that feels celebratory and hopeful.

Significance

The *Book of Negroes* premiered in Canada on CBC on January 7, 2015. It debuted on February 16, 2015, in the United States on BET. Reception of *The Book of Negroes* was favorable. 1.9 million Canadians watched the first episode of the series, which made it the highest-rated original scripted drama on CBC since 1990. In the United States, critics were mostly positive in their reviews. Writing for *The Hollywood Reporter*, Whitney Matheson concluded that it was "One of BET's most notable offerings to date." While the actors' performances and the production design were ubiquitous points of praise among critics, certain aspects of the storytelling fared harsher criticism. For example, Hank Stuever argued in his *Washington Post* review that the series' writing was occasionally problematic. He said, "Although the script (by Hill and series director Clement Virgo) opens with a poetic, almost liquid quality to its story and words, *The Book of Negroes* quickly suffers in the second night, when it starts racing along the timeline with clumsy dialogue that exists mainly to push along the plot." Brian Lowry makes a similar comment in his *Variety* review, claiming that the narrative suffers from a pacing and meandering problem. Despite these grievances, *The Book of Negroes* would go on to win a number of awards and accolades, including Best TV Movie/Miniseries from the Directors Guild of Canada and Best Dramatic Miniseries or TV Movie from the 2016 Canadian Screen Awards.

—*Emily E. Turner*

Further Reading

Foster, Kimberly. "*Book of Negroes* Star Discusses Why We Cannot Stop Telling the Stories of the Enslaved." *For Harriet*, 17 Feb. 2015, www.forharriet.com/2015/02/book-of-negroes-star-on-why-we-must.html. Accessed 20 May 2020.

Mochama, Vicky. "'The Stakes Are Higher, but Those Are the Stories I Want to Tell': An Interview with Clement Virgo." *Hazlitt*, 31 May 2016, hazlitt.net/feature/stakes-are-higher-those-are-stories-i-want-tell-interview-clement-virgo. Accessed 20 May 2020.

Bibliography

Bethune, Brian. "Blood and Belonging in *The Book of Negroes*." *Maclean's*, 4 Jan. 2015, www.macleans.ca/culture/television/blood-and-belonging-in-the-book-of-negroes. Accessed 20 May 2020.

Lowry, Brian. "TV Review: BET's *The Book of Negroes*." *Variety*, 12 Feb. 2015, variety.com/2015/tv/reviews/tv-review-bets-the-book-of-negroes-1201424143. Accessed 20 May 2020.

Matheson, Whitney. "*The Book of Negroes*: TV Review." *The Hollywood Reporter*, 16 Feb. 2015, www.hollywoodreporter.com/review/book-negroes-tv-review-773708. Accessed 20 May 2020.

Sagawa, Jessie. "Projecting History Honestly: An Interview with Lawrence Hill." *Studies in Canadian Literature*, vol. 33, no. 1, 2008, journals.lib.unb.ca/index.php/SCL/article/view/11222. Accessed 20 May 2020.

Stuever, Hank. "BET's *The Book of Negroes* Rushes Past Its Best Moments." *The Washington Post*, 15 Feb. 2015, www.washingtonpost.com/entertainment/tv/bets-book-of-negroes-a-slavery-story-that-rushes-past-its-best-moments/2015/02/15/75bc0d54-b53a-11e4-aa05-1ce812b3fdd2_story.html. Accessed 20 May 2020.

Boy Erased

The Novel
Author: Garrard Conley (b. ca. 1985)
First published: 2016

The Film
Year released: 2018
Director: Joel Edgerton (b. 1974)
Screenplay by: Joel Edgerton
Starring: Lucas Hedges, Nicole Kidman, Russell Crowe, Troye Sivan, Joel Edgerton

Context

In 1993 *The Wall Street Journal* became one of the first national publications to bring attention to the effects of conversion therapy on the LGBTQ community when it published Michael Ybarra's article on the subject. In his article, Ybarra documented the experience of his friend Jack McIntyre, who wrote about the struggles he experienced over his four years at the Love in Action (LIA) conversion therapy facility before his suicide in 1977. Since then, the medical and mental health community has declared the practice of conversion therapy not only unethical, but also ineffective and dangerous. In 2009 the American Psychological Association found that most people who go through the therapy not only do not experience any change in their sexual orientation, but become more likely to suffer from depression, substance abuse, self-destructive behavior, and suicide. Between 2013 and 2018, the year the film was released, fourteen US states had banned conversion therapy. By that year, according to a report by the University of California School of Law, an estimated 698,000 adults had received conversion therapy in the United States. Of these, 350,000 were minors when they received treatment. By 2021, the number of US states banning conversion therapy had grown to twenty.

McIntyre's account of his experience was the first in what become a conversion therapy memoir subgenre. As advocacy groups such as Born Perfect carry the fight forward to ban conversion therapy centers, these memoirs continue to raise public awareness about the detrimental effects conversion centers have on the individuals exposed to them. In 2016, several such memoirs were released, including *One of These Things First*, by Steven Gaines; *Saving Alex*, by Alex Cooper; and *Boy Erased* by Garrard Conley.

Conley's memoir focuses on his experience in a conversion therapy facility during a week in June 2004, when he was nineteen. Taking an intimate look at the relationship between faith and identity in the LGBTQ community, Conley captures a snapshot of himself as he reconciles the belief that he was created in the image of God with his true self, which, according to his Baptist upbringing, puts him at odds with God. After being outed, Conley's parents give him an ultimatum: lose his place with his family—and, they say, with God—along with financial support for college, or agree to go to LIA, located in Memphis, Tennessee, which they hope will cure him of what they believe is both sexual deviance and sin. Conley's memoir and the film version of his story both resonate at a time when members of the LGBTQ community still suffer from varying degrees of social disapproval, especially difficult for young people, and the facts about conversion therapy are becoming more widely known.

Film Analysis

Boy Erased is a 2018 film based on Conley's memoir of the same name. Like the memoir, the film is about a nineteen-year-old college student coming to terms with his faith, identity, and the freedom that comes with leaving home. Opening with actual footage of Garrard Conley as a child with his family, the film then shifts to a scene of protagonist Jared Eamons (Lucas Hedges) from behind as he dresses for his first day at Love in Action. The movie weaves in and out of Jared's week at LIA as well as his memories at home and college prior to being evaluated for the conversion therapy program. It offers a quicker pace, with cinematic structuring that is similar to the literary structuring of the memoir. The scenes build with memories strategically placed in between therapy sessions, as well as the inclusion of nonlinear private emotional moments, giving the film an arc in an otherwise evenly toned story.

The book and the film each tackle intimacy in rather nuanced ways. In the film, just before leaving for college, Jared's high-school girlfriend Chloe (Madelyn Cline) expects that they will become intimate. Jared's parents do not directly encourage their intimacy, but coyly approve. When Jared declines Chloe's advances, he finds comfort in playing video games in his room. These scenes are casually framed and crafted depicting the ease with which this should occur, whereas in the book Conley renders these scenes with such tension, which lends itself more to the inner turmoil he experienced.

Once at college, Jared befriends a dormmate named Henry (Joe Alwyn) and acknowledges that he broke up with his girlfriend. In the movie, as he and Henry get closer, the scenes are cut rather staccato-like, and even the half-on, medium shot framing of their bodies lends itself to the tension between them. They become running partners and Henry invites Jared to his Pentecostal church one day where there is an awkward introduction with one of the other congregants, a young man who is very reserved and appears shaken by Henry's presence, as conveyed by his back and his shadow-covered profile.

Henry eventually rapes Jared in a visceral scene that also conveys how Jared buries the trauma, in that the sequence of the scenes are jumbled like puzzle pieces. After the rape, Jared goes to great lengths to avoid Henry on campus. His trauma intensifies when Henry calls his house and outs him to his mother, Nancy Eamons (Nicole Kidman). When confronted, Jared refrains from telling his parents that he was raped. The blocking of the distance between the characters builds creatively up to when, in his attempt to prove his desires to his parents, he takes his game console and dumps it in the bathtub, running water over it while declaring that he is done playing games.

Jared's appointment with Dr. Muldoon (Cherry Jones), ostensibly to have his testosterone level tested to see if it is a contributing factor to his sexual orientation, is a pivotal scene in the film, and one that offers a moment of reprieve not overtly recognizable in the book. In the privacy of her office, Dr. Muldoon offers Jared much more than medical advice when she tells him that she disagrees with his parents' stance on his sexuality. With just the two of them in a well-lit office, she lets him know that she can test his testosterone levels, but that is not going to indicate anything

of substance. She indicates that she is a Baptist too, but believes he can live his life in his own way—even if that means leaving all that he knows in this small town in search of a community that will accept him just as he is.

Back at home, Jared's father Marshall Eamons (Russell Crowe), a car dealership owner and pastor, invites his church peers over to the house and they recommend the church-based conversion therapy facility Love in Action, where the promise of being cured of homosexuality is heralded. In this scene, the distance between Jared and his parents is back, but the lighting on his mother indicates that she may not be in agreement with the men at the table. On the drive to the facility, the tension between Jared and Nancy is only cut briefly when she asks Jared to stop putting his hand out of the window into the wind. She says that she's heard of a kid who lost his hand in a freak accident while doing the same thing; Jared does not believe the anecdote is true. The scene does not appear in the book, but was inserted by director-screenwriter Joel Edgerton to remind the audience of the close mother-child dynamic between the two characters: parents are protectors and worriers, while children often feel the need to go with the flow and to ride the wind.

At the LIA facility, the film is effective at bringing to life the descriptions in the book. Jared turns in his cell phone and journal and receives his LIA handbook, which is laced with incorrect spelling, typos, and other grammatical errors. He's advised to destroy any evidence of "False Images," and is welcomed into the group of others who have been labeled sexual deviants and are looking to be cured of their so-called sins.

Jared attends these sessions, including a gender-conditioning exercise in which participants are told how to posture themselves as men and women. The other patients around him exhibit repressed behavior patterns that are cause for concern. Withholding eye contact, provoked anger outbursts, and suicidal ideation are common at LIA under the guidance of counselors whose qualifications are unknown. Participants are forced to express feelings they do not have and also forced to share personal and intimate thoughts with each other. One of the most traumatizing scenes is when the group stages a funeral for Cameron (Britton Sear), after he is unable to summon any anger toward his father in a mock role-playing conversation. Cameron's family attends his funeral while he sits in the audience. As he watches what will become of his life if he fails LIA, the effects of the drastic measures of the program begin to build. When a boy goes home concussed, his parents arrive at the facility and reprimand the head counselor Victor Sykes (Edgerton) for his negligence. The confrontation begins to unravel the authority Victor tries to wield over the participants.

Unsure if the therapy is working or not, Jared begins to have a nervous breakdown. While out on a run in Memphis, he passes a bus stop where the advertisement displays a male model that Jared finds attractive. He curses and destroys the advertisement, then tilts his head toward the sky to curse God.

When it is Jared's turn to have the mock conversation, Victor tries to provoke him to be angry with his father, but Jared cannot summon any rage. He instead becomes angry with Victor and storms out of the session. He struggles against the others to gather his things and then calls his mother to pick him up. She does not hesitate and when she arrives, Victor demands that Jared stay and work through the feelings that are rising. Finally, Cameron steps in and makes Victor allow Jared to leave the facility.

In a liberating moment with his mother at a restaurant, Jared is able to let his guard down as she assures him that he does not have to go back to the facility. She says that she will talk to his father and also acknowledges that she should have spoken up for him at their kitchen table when his father's church peers prayed over him. This turning point carries all the emotional weight that has built up throughout the film and diffuses it with the subtle realization that Jared's parents have a lot of work to do in order to accept their son for who he is.

The movie jumps to Jared as a twenty-something writer in New York City, living with those who accept him for who he is, in a community just as Dr. Muldoon had described. When his mother texts him an article about a kid who lost his hand from hanging it out the window and shares that she has read Jared's latest work, they say that they are looking forward to seeing each other for Thanksgiving. There are still unresolved issues between Jared and his father, however. Back at home, at the car dealership, Jared confronts his father about the gulf between them and stands up for himself, even if it that means jeopardizing the future of their relationship. Marshall shares what his dreams had been for his son, of leaving him the dealership, and when he leaves his son with the pen he uses to write his sermons, the scene portrays a deep sense of acceptance and the possibility that they can right their relationship.

As much as *Boy Erased* portrays the dangers and ineffectiveness of conversion therapy, it also explores something more subtle, the experience of guilt over one's identity. The film delves into both spiritual and secular understandings of life, and the film makes effective use of close-up shots, suggesting that there is much going on beneath underneath the surface of these characters as they struggle to live their lives, feeling guilty for not being who they are asked to be. Their faces are tense, and their eyes are averted, but when the turning point in the film occurs and Jared and his mother leave the facility once and for all, the camera gives us wider angles to suggest that the characters are now more free to live their lives with a sense of openness.

Significance
The film received critical acclaim and twenty-nine award nominations, including a Golden Globe for Best Performance by an Actor in a Motion Picture-Drama (Lucas Hedges). It also won best studio film at the San Diego International Film Festival. The book also earned warm reviews from readers, who have attested to the honest portrayal of this devastating reality of conversion therapy for so many in the LGBTQ community, whether they had previous knowledge of the issue or whether this book opened their eyes. Some reviewers suggested that the book lacked context about conversion therapy because it was just a musing of the author's one-week experience at LIA and otherwise an underdeveloped story about his life before and after. However, both book and film are generally praised for showing the detrimental effect that conversion therapy has on the self and the identities of adolescents in the LGBTQ community.

—Dominique Taylor

Further Reading
Emezi, Akwaeke. "Who Is Like God." *Granta*, 2017, granta.com/who-is-like-god/. Accessed 2 Dec. 2018
"Facts You May Not Know about Conversion Therapy: A Note from the Boy Erased Team." *Garrard Conley*, 26 Oct. 2018, garrardconley.com/news/2018/10/26/facts-you-may-not-know-about-conversion-therapy-a-note-from-the-boy-erased-team. Accessed 10 Jan. 2019.
Turban, Jack. "Gay Conversion Therapy Associated with Suicide Risk." *Psychology Today*, 14 Nov. 2018, www.psychologytoday.com/intl/blog/political-minds/201811/gay-conversion-therapy-associated-suicide-risk. Accessed 2 Dec. 2018.

Bibliography

Hicklin, Aaron. "I Was 19, Gay and Ready to Be 'Cured' by Conversion Therapy." *The Guardian*, 10 June 2018, www.theguardian.com/lifeandstyle/2018/jun/10/i-was-19-gay-and-ready-to-be-cured-by-conversion-therapy. Accessed 2 Dec. 2018

McLaughlin, Don James. "The Gay Conversion Therapy Memoir." *Public Books*, 14 Nov 2018, www.publicbooks.org/the-gay-conversion-therapy-memoir/. Accessed 7 Jan. 2019

Stack, Liam. "Mike Pence and 'Conversion Therapy': A History." *The New York Times*, 30 Nov 2016, www.nytimes.com/2016/11/30/us/politics/mike-pence-and-conversion-therapy-a-history.html. Accessed 7 Jan. 2019

The Boy Who Harnessed the Wind

The Novel
Authors: William Kamkwamba (b. 1987) and Bryan Mealer
First published: 2009

The Film
Year released: 2019
Director: Chiwetel Ejiofor (b. 1977)
Screenplay by: Chiwetel Ejiofor
Starring: Maxwell Simba, Chiwetel Ejiofor, Aissa Maiga, Lily Banda

Context

The Boy Who Harnessed the Wind (2009) is a memoir written by William Kamkwamba, who was born and raised in a small village in Malawi that lacked running water or electricity. The book follows his journey from the time he was a poor student forced to drop out of school to his decision to build an electricity-generating windmill to save his family's farm. *The Boy Who Harnessed the Wind* was published after Kamkwamba had given a talk at the 2007 TED (Technology, Entertainment and Design) conference in Tanzania and subsequently became a famous international figure.

The early 2000s and 2010s saw an increase in the availability of books by African writers among Western readers. The trend was especially evident in the popularity of authors like Chimamanda Ngozi Adichie, who is best known for her novels *Half of a Yellow Sun* (2006) and *Americanah* (2013). Several autobiographies were popular as well, such as Kenyan writer Binyavanga Wainaina's *One Day I Will Write About This Place* (2011) and Liberian writer Ellen Johnson Sirleaf's *This Child Will Be Great* (2009). Although *The Boy Who Harnessed the Wind* is autobiographical, it differs from these titles in being lighter in tone and written for young readers.

In 2019, *The Boy Who Harnessed the Wind* was adapted into a film by British actor Chiwetel Ejiofor. At the time, Ejiofor was best known for his performances in *Kinky Boots* (2005) and *12 Years a Slave* (2013) and had never directed before. In many ways, his debut film is difficult to categorize. *The Boy Who Harnessed the Wind* aims to depict African life in an authentic, respectful way. In addition to being shot on location in Malawi with many local actors, the film's dialogue includes both English and Chichewa, a Bantu language that is one of Malawi's official languages. The film is part of a small genre of films that depict African stories and are intended for international audiences.

Film Analysis

The book was written for children ages 10 and up. As a result, Kamkwamba is lighthearted when discussing the challenges his family faced before he built the windmill that ultimately saved them. In particular, Kamkwamba describes famine, cholera, poverty, and the death of his beloved dog in a delicate, matter-of-fact way that children can easily comprehend. He ensures that such events are not too overwhelming by balancing them with positive anecdotes, avoiding upsetting details, and maintaining an overall optimistic perspective. The combination of these elements ultimately upholds his message that any challenge can be overcome if someone is curious and determined.

By contrast, Ejiofor's adaptation of Kamkwamba's story is much more somber. The director, who also wrote the screenplay, aimed the film at adult audiences. Although the film still focuses on Kamkwamba, whose character goes by his first name William (Maxwell Simba), it also aims to capture some of the socio-political events that defined Malawi in the early 2000s. This includes a tumultuous election and a nationwide food shortage. These events heighten the drama surrounding William's journey and make it more compelling. For example, at one point in the film William's mother Agnes (Aissa Maiga) and sister Annie (Lily Banda) are robbed by a group of starving men while he and his father are away. Agnes and Annie are so desperate to protect their food stores that they try to stand up to the men and ultimately jeopardize their physical

William Kamkwamba and co-author Bryan Mealer at a book signing for Kamkwamba's autobiographical story, The Boy Who Harnessed the Wind. Photo via Wikimedia Commons. [Public domain.]

safety. This heightens the stakes for William, making his development of a scientific solution to the famine that much more essential.

The film develops significantly the character of William's father, Trywell (Ejiofor), making him an integral part of the story. In the book, Trywell is a loving father but otherwise marginal to the narrative. In the film, Kamkwamba's relationship to his father is a key source of dramatic tension. Trywell struggles to provide for his family as the droughts and floods decimate his crops; he is a proud man who has always done things his own way—even when it created more challenges for him. When William tells Trywell that he wants to build a windmill to pump water from the well so that they can grow crops year-round, he is resistant. In one of the film's most cli-

mactic scenes, William gets a group of his friends to confront his father and demand his bicycle so he can use the parts for the windmill. Still, Trywell refuses to give in. It is not until his wife Agnes reveals how much she has lost because of his stubbornness that Trywell concedes and the windmill is built.

Like the book, the film is an ingenuous celebration of technology, "modernization" in the developing world, conflict with tradition depicted as superstition, and youthful pluck. Like an African Bill Gates tinkering in his garage, William is shown tinkering with old radios and car batteries, and his plans are doubted by his tradition-bound father. In one of the film's earliest scenes, William and his family are attending his uncle's funeral. The priest enunciates the old world view in a heavy-handed way, saying that God decides people's fates and that they have no control over whether they live or die. By the end of the film, William has disproven this logic, and his determined focus on education, science, and technology wins the day.

William encounters many obstacles throughout film. His father's farm is failing, his family is starving, and there is not enough money for him to finish school. However, he is optimistic, resourceful, and exceedingly resilient—three qualities that make him a highly compelling protagonist. After he is told that he can no longer attend school, for example, he continues sneaking into science class. He even blackmails his teacher, who is dating his sister Annie in secret, into letting him use the library. It is in the library that William finds the science books he needs to build the windmill. In the book, William has six sisters and never needs to threaten his teacher in order to get to the library.

In addition to the African village society, William's other antagonist in the film is nature. Ejiofor communicates this to audiences by including many wide shots to ensure that the natural world always appears powerful and inescapable. Furthermore, the film's golden color palette creates a warm, dry aesthetic that amplifies the feeling of the drought that has decimated Trywell's maize farm. William's triumph over the elements by using science ultimately disproves his community's belief that they are at the complete mercy of bigger forces. Ejiofor depicts their acceptance of William's worldview as a kind of enlightenment. When he climbs the tower as the windmill's blades are being hoisted upward, it is a scene reminiscent of a cross being hoisted atop a church steeple. Similarly, when the windmill succeeds in pumping water from the well by running on scrap wires and bicycle parts, it feels like a miracle. This imagery pays tribute to the first chapter of Kamkwamba's book, which comments on how spirituality and science were once seen as being at odds with one another. Now, science and its miracles will replace superstitions and bring legitimate "salvation" to the villagers.

Significance

The Boy Who Harnessed the Wind premiered at the Sundance Film Festival on January 25, 2019, to an enthusiastic audience. On March 1, 2019, it debuted worldwide on the Netflix streaming platform. *The Boy Who Har-* nessed the Wind was overwhelmingly popular among critics as it earned an aggregate score of 87 percent on *Rotten Tomatoes*. Most critics were quick to commend the film's script as well as its direction. In his review for *The Atlantic*, David Sims writes, "It builds realism and context into both sides of the story and manages to be a winning adaptation as a result." Another common point of praise for *The Boy Who Harnessed the Wind* was for its balanced tone and worldview. Robert Abele writes in his *Los Angeles Times* review that the film, "feeds our hunger for inspiring tales in these desperate times with a beautifully engineered narrative latticework of hardship, hope, and know-how." Although *The Boy Who Harnessed the Wind* did not earn any awards, it did inspire numerous think pieces and reviews from the mainstream media.

—*Emily E. Turner*

Further Reading

Shapiro, Ari. "Chiwetel Ejiofor's Directing Debut Takes Him to Malawi to Capture 'the Wind.'" *NPR*, 28 Feb. 2019, www.npr.org/2019/02/28/699060631/chiwetel-ejiofors-directing-debut-takes-him-to-malawi-to-capture-the-wind. Accessed 4 Mar. 2020.

Tenreyro, Tatiana. "What's William Kamkwamba Doing in 2019? *The Boy Who Harnessed the Wind* Inventor is Making a Difference Globally." *Bustle*, 28 Feb. 2019, www.bustle.com/p/whats-william-kamkwamba-doing-in-2019-the-boy-who-harnessed-the-wind-inventor-is-making-a-difference-globally-16103209. Accessed 4 Mar. 2020.

Bibliography

Abele, Robert. "Review: Chiwetel Ejiofor's Directing Debut *The Boy Who Harnessed the Wind* Inspires." *Los Angeles Times*, 28 Feb. 2019, www.latimes.com/entertainment/movies/la-et-mn-mini-boy-who-harnessed-wind-review-20190228-story.html. Accessed 4 Mar. 2020.

Catsoulis, Jeannette. "*The Boy Who Harnessed the Wind* Review: Saving a Village, Using Books and Brains." *The New York Times*, 28 Feb. 2019, www.nytimes.com/2019/02/28/movies/the-boy-who-harnessed-the-wind-review.html. Accessed 4 Mar. 2020.

Sims, David. "Netflix's *The Boy Who Harnessed the Wind* Is a Winner." *The Atlantic*, 27 Feb. 2019, www.theatlantic.com/entertainment/archive/2019/02/the-boy-who-harnessed-the-wind-netflix-review-william-kamkwamba-chiwetel-ejiofor/583720/. Accessed 4 Mar. 2020.

Zetter, Kim. "Teen's DIY Energy Hacking Gives African Village New Hope." *Wired*, 2 Oct. 2009, www.wired.com/2009/10/kamwamba-windmill/. Accessed 4 Mar. 2020.

The Breadwinner

The Novel
Author: Deborah Ellis (b. 1960)
First published: 2001

The Film
Year released: 2017
Director: Nora Twomey (b. 1971)
Screenplay by: Anita Doron, Deborah Ellis
Starring: Saara Chaudry, Soma Chhaya, Ali Badshah, Noorin Gulamgaus, Kane Mahon, Laara Sadiq, Kanza Feris, Shaista Latif, Kawa Ada, Ali Kazmi, Reza Sholeh

Context

Deborah Ellis, a Canadian author, activist, and philanthropist, gained international acclaim for her debut novel, *Looking for X*, published in 1999, and winner of the Canadian Governor General's Literary Award for 2000 in Children's Literature. Her second novel, *The Breadwinner*, was published in 2001, close on the heels of the nonfiction *Women of the Afghan War*, published in 2000. *The Breadwinner*, a novel for middle readers (eight- to twelve-year-olds), is based on stories Ellis heard while interviewing refugees in Pakistan, including the story of a girl who dressed as a boy.

In *The Breadwinner*, eleven-year-old Parvana must disguise herself as a boy in order to support her family. Her father, a teacher with a foreign education, is arrested and imprisoned, and her older brother was killed years earlier by a landmine. Parvana, her mother, her older sister Nooria, and younger brother are trapped in the house because women in Afghanistan are not allowed out in public unescorted by a man. Parvana's disguise provides her with a measure of independence and allows her to provide for her family. As Parvana tries to find a way to free her father, she tells a story that she and her father had begun to tell each other, a tale of a brave young man who confronts an elephant king who has stolen the seeds from his village. The story of the elephant king is told in the film in cut-out animation style and parallels the challenges that Parvana faces.

The resourcefulness of the female protagonist balances a truly harrowing tale set in a brutally repressive time, with war looming. The characters seem doomed and are constantly facing ever more daunting obstacles. As *The New York Times* review concluded, "they are depicted frankly, but in a way that encourages young viewers to form an affinity with the characters rather than cringe in terror."

In keeping with the author's personal activism, all royalties from the sale of the book are donated to Canadian Women for Women in Afghanistan, a fund for the education of Afghan girls in refugee camps in Pakistan. *The Breadwinner* is part of a body of work that brought attention to the challenges facing girls in Afghanistan, the most famous of which is *I Am Malala: The Girl Who Stood Up for Education and Was Shot by the Taliban* by Malala Yousafzai, published in 2013. Malala, who at sixteen was the youngest person nominated for the Nobel Peace Prize, identified *The Breadwinner* as one of her favorites, and suggested that all girls should read the book because it "reminds us how courageous and strong women are around the world."

Film Analysis

The film differs from the book in several key plot points, which were streamlined to fit the time and narrative order best suited to film. Some changes are simple—in the book Parvana has two younger siblings, while in the film she has only one. Perhaps the character that is the most changed between the book and the film is Parvana's mother, who spends most of the film version recovering from being beaten at the prison where she tries to get information about her husband or begging Parvana not to go outside. In the book, Parvana's mother writes a magazine called *Afghanistan National Magazine*, with the help of Mrs. Weera, a former teacher who lives with the family, and they manage to smuggle magazine copy into and out of Pakistan for printing. She is also responsible, along with Mrs. Weera, for the idea of Parvana passing as a boy. A deeply troubling scene in the book where Parvana and her friend Shauzia, who is also passing as a boy, go to see what they believe to be a sporting event, but instead witness mutilations performed as punishment by the Taliban. In the book, Noori and her mother and siblings leave for Noori's wedding of their own volition, leaving Parvana at home with Mrs. Weera. In the film they are dragged off by a relative of the young man Noori has promised to marry. In the book, Parvana's father comes back to the apartment on his own, while in the film he is rescued from prison by a Taliban member whose letters Parvana had translated in the market. At the end of the book, Parvana and Shauzia plan to meet in Paris at the Eiffel Tower in twenty years. At the end of the film, they will meet on a beach.

The New York Times review of the film adaptation of *The Breadwinner* commented on its most glaring flaw. "An animated film set in Afghanistan, made largely by westerners and based on a western source, might raise some red flags." However, the issue of cultural appropriation was balanced by a concerted effort to focus the film on Afghan voices and stories. First, Ellis, who cowrote the screenplay with Anita Doron, had spent significant time with refugees from Afghanistan and used these relationships to inform her book.

When Irish director Nora Twomey was brought into the project, she reached out to Angelina Jolie, even though the project was fully financed. Twomey, who had never directed a film alone before, looked to Jolie to share her perspective on Afghanistan, where Jolie has built schools for girls and served as a United Nations Goodwill Ambassador. The story required a high level of sophistication and sensitivity as it tackles harrowing subject matter in an animated film that must be accessible to older children. Jolie, who has significant experience with refugees, but also a deep knowledge of the culture and history of Afghanistan, was involved in many different aspects of this film, from the color of the sky over Kabul to the casting of the voice actors. Jolie said, "we want people to respect what these young children go through and understand this magical culture with a rich, deep history." She wanted the viewer to think of more than just suffering and oppression, and see the rich history, the human relationships, and the real cost of years of war and brutality.

The decision to turn the story into an animated feature was a bold one. Writing for *Variety*, Peter Debruge points out that this is not the first time animation had been used to

represent extremely difficult topics. "At Studio Ghibli, both Isao Takahata and Hayao Miyazaki used the medium to address difficult memories of wartime Japan—in *Grave of the Fireflies* and *The Wind Rises*," and says the Ireland-based "Cartoon Saloon follows their lead." Twomey worked on two other Oscar-nominated animated films from the studio, *The Secret of Kells* (2009) and *Song of the Sea* (2014) and brought its solid-line graphic style to her solo debut in *The Breadwinner*, a style that is hand-drawn using a program called TVPaint. The story of the elephant king is drawn to look like stop-motion paper cut animation, highlighting the folkloric elements of the story, an element that is visually pleasing but also can distract the viewer from the plot, picking up during moments of dramatic tension that may have been best left alone.

The *Variety* review also recalls the iconic 1985 *National Geographic* cover, a close-up of the face of an Afghan girl, her green eyes staring defiantly into the camera. Throughout the film adaptation of *The Breadwinner*, Parvana stares directly at the audience, her green eyes wide and determined, a nod to this portrait, and to the spirit of Afghan women and girls through decades of conflict. It invites the viewer to look directly at this society, torn apart by brutality to its most vulnerable members, and dares them not to look away.

Significance

Reviews of the film, which was nominated for an Academy Award for best animated feature, were generally positive. Some, like Peter Debruge in *Variety*, felt that changes to the plot from book to film hurt the overall direction of the story, as it remains unclear what Parvana is planning to do once she gains access to her father in prison. The *RogerEbert.com* review by Peter Sobczynski agrees that the storyline is clunky and doesn't flow smoothly. "Although we are always behind the brave and resourceful Parvana, there never seems to be a clear idea of what she is hoping to ultimately accomplish." In the *Washington Post*, Vanessa H. Larson calls the film "narratively uneven."

The story of the elephant king, while praised by most reviewers for its visual quality, was found by others to detract and distract. The *Washington Post* review found it "hard to follow, and key clues to its deeper meaning take too long to become clear." The *Variety* review found the story to be "meandering," and that it tended to "interrupt the overall flow."

Glenn Kenny of *The New York Times* had high praise for the characterization and the cast, something shared by most of his peers. "The director, Nora Twomey, has a nuanced way with characterization and action, and the voice cast, led by Saara Chaudry...is terrific." Also garnering praise from many reviewers was the score, composed by Jeff and Mychael Danna, which *Variety* praised for "capturing that essential sense of optimism that makes Parvana such a remarkable heroine."

Overall, the strength of the film is its unflinching look at hope and courage amid suffering and brutality. Parvana looks to storytelling to provide an escape during times of darkness and fear, which seems to be most of the time in Kabul. She comforts her brother and her friend and summons reserves of courage through the story of the young man taking on the elephant king and winning. The stories Parvana invents and those she remembers from her father provide the one beautiful thing amid such dark times—hope that things can change.

—*Bethany Dorau, MA*

Further Reading

Ellis, Deborah. *The Breadwinner: A Graphic Novel*. Groundwood Books, 2018.

Ellis, Deborah. *Parvana's Journey*. Groundwood Books, 2002.

Bibliography

"The Breadwinner." *Publishers Weekly*, 1 Mar. 2001, publishersweekly.com/978-0-88899-419-6. Accessed 29 June 2020.

Debruge, Peter. "Film Review: *The Breadwinner*." *Variety*, 3 Nov. 2017, variety.com/2017/film/reviews/the-breadwinner-review-1202606241/. Accessed 29 June 2020.

Kenny, Glenn. "Review: In *The Breadwinner*, a Girl Bravely Provides for Her Family." *The New York Times*, 16 Nov. 2017, www.nytimes.com/2017/11/16/movies/the-breadwinner-review.html. Accessed 29 June 2020.

Larson, Vanessa H. "*The Breadwinner*, about a Kabul Girl, Features Gorgeous Animation but a So-So Story." *The Washington Post*, 20 Nov. 2017, www.washingtonpost.com/goingoutguide/movies/the-breadwinner-about-a-kabul-girl-features-gorgeous-animation-but-a-so-so-story/2017/11/20/948626fc-ca4a-11e7-8321-481fd63f174d_story.html. Accessed 29 June 2020.

"Malala Yousafzai: By the Book." *The New York Times*, 19 Aug. 2014, www.nytimes.com/2014/08/24/books/review/malala-yousafzai-by-the-book.html. Accessed 29 June 2020.

Sobczynski, Peter. "*The Breadwinner*." *RogerEbert.com*, 17 Nov. 2017, www.rogerebert.com/reviews/the-breadwinner-2017. Accessed 29 June 2020.

Thompson, Anne. "The Mind of Angelina Jolie: How *The Breadwinner* Leaned on Her Work More Than Her Name." *IndieWire*, 15 Feb. 2018, www.indiewire.com/2018/02/the-breadwinner-angelina-jolie-nora-twomey-best-animated-feature-oscar-afghanistan-1201928392/. Accessed 29 June 2020.

Brighton Rock

The Novel
Author: Graham Greene (1904-91)
First published: 1938

The Film
Year released: 1947
Director: John Boulting (1913-85)
Screenplay by: Graham Greene, Terence Rattigan
Starring: Richard Attenborough, Hermione Baddeley, William Hartnell, Carol Marsh

Context

Graham Greene was among the most prolific and significant British authors of the twentieth century. Often drawing on his wide travels for inspiration, his works explore a number of subjects including relationships, politics, and espionage. Greene divided his own work into two categories: what he called "entertainments," which modern readers would regard as thrillers, and his more literary works. As intuitive as that division might seem, many of his most notable novels span both categories. These include *The Power and the Glory* (1940), *The Heart of the Matter* (1948), *The Third Man* (1949), *The End of the Affair* (1951), *The Quiet American* (1955), *Our Man in Havana* (1958), *The Comedians* (1966), *Travels with My Aunt* (1969), *The Human Factor* (1978), *Monsignor Quixote* (1982), and *The Captain and the Enemy* (1988). He also wrote journalistic pieces, short stories, and plays.

A convert to Roman Catholicism, Greene factored religion into a number of his novels, including *Brighton Rock*, first published in 1938. He described it as an entertainment because it explores the criminal underworld in the British resort town of Brighton before World War II, but the novel also has significant religious themes, and it deals with its material with the subtlety and intelligence we normally associate with "literary" works. It touches on the Catholic faith of Pinkie Brown, the teenage sociopath who is the main character of the novel; Rose, a waitress he forces himself to marry to maintain his alibi on a murder charge; and Ida, the humanist seeking to bring Pinkie to justice. The complexity of characterization throughout the book distinguishes it from typical lowbrow thrillers.

The film adaptation of *Brighton Rock*, first released in 1947, was directed by John Boulting, whose twin brother, Roy Boulting, served as producer of the movie. The twins often wrote, directed, and produced their films together at British Lion Films and through their own production company, Charter Film Productions. Some of John Boulting's most notable works as director include *Journey Together* (1945), *The Magic Box* (1951), *Private's Progress* (1956),

Novelist Graham Greene. Photo via National Potrait Gallery/ Wikimedia Commons. [Public domain.]

Lucky Jim (1957), *I'm All Right Jack* (1959), *Heavens Above!* (1963), and *Rotten to the Core* (1965). Among them, *Brighton Rock* is widely considered his masterpiece.

Greene himself was directly involved with the adaptation of *Brighton Rock*. The screen rights to the book had been owned by a group that included playwright Terence Rattigan, who insisted on writing the script for the film. However, the Boultings felt Rattigan was not a good fit for the project, so they had Greene heavily rework the script. Thus, the book author himself was responsible for many of the film's similarities and differences to his original work.

Film Analysis

The film version of *Brighton Rock* in general hews very closely to its source material. In fact, entire scenes seem to be lifted directly from the novel's text, although compressed and reimagined for the visual medium of film. The black-and-white tones set the mood of the noir piece, and the filming in Brighton provides a level of authenticity to the work. In fact, the crime and violence are so realistically portrayed for the time that the filmmakers agreed to include a preface indicating that the city of Brighton was no longer anything like the film's seedy 1930s setting.

The film begins much as the novel does, with the murder of William Kite, a gang leader who was the mentor to Pinkie Brown (Richard Attenborough). Pinkie discovers that the reporter Fred Hale (Alan Wheatley), who exposed Brighton's criminal rackets and whom the gangsters therefore consider responsible for their leader's death, will be in town that day. Hale is doing a promotional stunt for the paper, posing as a character named Kolley Kibber and leaving cards around Brighton; whoever discovers a card and calls Kibber out wins a prize. As the new gang leader, Pinkie has the other members—Dallow (William Hartnell), Spicer (Wylie Watson), and Cubitt (Nigel Stock)—stalk Hale through the streets of Brighton. As Hale attempts to evade them, he meets Ida Arnold (Hermione Baddeley), an entertainer who takes a liking to him and agrees to stay with him throughout the day. When Ida goes to the ladies' room, Hale buys tickets to a ride they want to go on and discovers Pinkie is waiting for him. In the ride's tunnel, Pinkie throws him into the water below.

The police rule Hale's death a heart attack. But Ida becomes suspicious and begins her own investigation. At the same time, Pinkie has sought to create an alibi for himself by having Spicer continue to distribute Hale's cards around town. When he learns Spicer put a card under a tablecloth in a restaurant, Pinkie worries that the waitress there might be able to identify Spicer as not being Kolley Kibber. When Pinkie goes to retrieve the card, he is discovered taking it by Rose (Carol Marsh), a sweet and innocent girl who, like Pinkie, is Roman Catholic. The pair discuss issues of faith, with Pinkie declaring that he firmly believes in hell and damnation. He also suggests that she not speak to anyone about who left the card. To further pull her into his clutches, he asks her out on a date.

Shortly thereafter, Pinkie meets with Colleoni (Charles Goldner), the leader of a rival, more powerful gang, who tells Pinkie to clear out of town. Leaving the meeting, Pinkie is taken in by the police and told not to cause any trouble during the races, which begin the next day. The police warning gives Pinkie an idea—to get rid of Spicer by having Colleoni's men kill him at the races, which he believes will help his alibi. But when he goes with Spicer to the races, they are both slashed with razors by Colleoni's men. Pinkie returns home believing Spicer has been killed. When Spicer turns up alive, Pinkie kills him by shoving him off a landing with a rickety bannister, to make it look like an accident.

During their time together, the innocent Rose falls in love with the malevolent Pinkie, believing that he loves her too. Soon Pinkie realizes that the only way to keep Rose from talking to the police is by marrying her, even though they are both only seventeen and the idea of sexual love is repellant to him. The theme of sexuality, closely linked to religious guilt, contributes heavily to the brooding atmosphere of the film. The two ultimately marry with the aid of a corrupt lawyer, and Rose asks Pinkie to record his voice for her on a record. Alone in the recording booth, Pinkie says that he does not love her but in fact hates her and calls her names. Rose, who cannot listen to the record as she has no player, treasures it in the belief that it contains his profession of love.

Meanwhile, Ida has grown ever more convinced that Pinkie was not only involved with Hale's death but Spicer's as well. Posing as her mother, Ida visits Rose while Pinkie is out and tries to convince her that Pinkie is irredeemable, without mercy, compassion, or pity. Rose refuses to hear this and sends Ida away, but Pinkie sees Ida leaving. When he asks Rose if her mother had been to see her, Rose says yes. Pinkie becomes suspicious of Rose and decides he must kill her too. So he tells her they must enter a suicide pact, as the police are closing in on him. At first

Rose refuses—suicide being a mortal sin in Roman Catholic teaching—but Pinkie persuades her to agree, ostensibly so they can both be together in the afterlife.

In reality, Pinkie has no plans to kill himself, but only wants Rose to shoot herself first. Dallow protests this plan, however. He wants to protect Rose and believes they are in the clear because Ida is leaving Brighton without evidence against them and Colleoni is offering them money to leave town. Yet Pinkie persists and takes Rose down to the pier to carry out the pact. Knowing Rose is in danger, Dallow enlists the aid of Ida and the police to help save Rose. Seeing the police coming, Rose tosses the gun into the water. As Pinkie attempts to escape from the police, he falls into the surf below and is killed.

The most significant difference between the book and the film is the conclusion. In the novel, Rose goes to confession with a local priest, convinced that Pinkie loved her. The priest tells her that if there was any love in his heart, Pinkie might be saved from damnation, and that they should pray for him. She then goes home to listen to the recording of Pinkie's voice for the first time, only to discover that he was in fact the unrepentant monster everyone told her he was. This extremely bleak ending would have likely been rejected by British censors at the time, so the filmmakers altered it to be more ambiguous. The final scene of the movie shows Rose discussing Pinkie with a nun, who offers a similar message to the priest of the novel about the mercy of God. When Rose plays the record, which has been damaged, the needle gets stuck and it repeats only the part where he says, "I love you." Therefore, Rose is never shown to hear Pinkie's true hatred of her, though viewers are left to determine for themselves whether she might ultimately discover that part.

Significance

When *Brighton Rock* first appeared in theaters, some critics condemned the film's violence, particularly the razor-slashing scenes. The film was even banned in New South Wales, Australia. Despite this concern, the movie proved popular among British audiences. It was somewhat less successful in the United States, where it was released under the title *Young Scarface*.

Both the novel and the film versions of *Brighton Rock* have weathered the years well, with critics and audiences holding them in high regard. Greene's novel is often ranked among his best works and is counted as one of his "Catholic novels," which debate complex questions of faith and doctrine. The 1947 adaptation is ranked among the best of British film noir and is also considered one of director John Boulting's most memorable efforts. In a 1999 survey by the British Film Institute, *Brighton Rock* was cited as one of the best British films of all time, at number fifteen overall. Much praise has been directed at the acting performances, especially Richard Attenborough's iconic lead role (which he had first developed in a stage production of the work). In an article on the film for *BFI Screenonline*, Tony Whitehead noted: "Attenborough's astonishing performance as perversely puritanical teenage gang leader Pinkie has an edgy intensity.... *Brighton Rock* was not the only new and distinctive British crime movie to appear in the immediate post-war years, but the fine contributions of its participants, both behind and in front of the cameras, have made it the most memorable."

Brighton Rock's enduring legacy is indicated by the novel having been adapted again in 2010, by writer and director Rowan Joffe. The update kept the basic plot but moved the action from prewar Brighton to Brighton of 1964, when the resort town was besieged with fighting between Mods and Rockers. However, it received mixed reviews as many critics compared it unfavorably to the earlier film.

—*Christopher Mari*

Further Reading

Falk, Quentin. *Travels in Greeneland: The Cinema of Graham Greene*. Revised and updated 4th ed. UP of North Georgia, 2014.

Greene, Graham. "Selection; The Uneasy Catholicism of Graham Greene." Interview by Marie-Francoise Allain. *The New York Times*, 3 Apr. 1983, www.nytimes.com/1983/04/03/books/selection-the-uneasy-catholicism-of-graham-greene.html. Accessed 5 Mar. 2019.

Newton, Michael. "The Boulting Brothers: Holy Fools." *The Guardian*, 26 July 2013, www.theguardian.com/film/2013/jul/26/boulting-brothers-holy-fools. Accessed 5 Mar. 2019.

Bibliography

Arnold, Jeremy. "Brighton Rock (1947)." *Turner Classic Movies*, 2019, www.tcm.com/tcmdb/title/69716/Brighton-Rock/articles.html. Accessed 5 Mar. 2019.

Arnott, Jake. "Mad, Bad and Dangerous to Know." *The Guardian*, 19 July 2002, www.theguardian.com/books/2002/jul/20/featuresreviews.guardianreview14. Accessed 5 Mar. 2019.

"Brighton Rock (1948)." *IMDb*, 2019, www.imdb.com/title/tt0039220. Accessed 5 Mar. 2019.

Rizov, Vadim. "Brighton Rock at Film Forum." Review of *Brighton Rock*, directed by John Boulting. *The Village Voice*, 17 June 2009, www.villagevoice.com/2009/06/17/brighton-rock-at-film-forum. Accessed 5 Mar. 2019.

Thomson, David. "David Thomson on Films: Skip This Remake of 'Brighton Rock' and Catch the Grim, 1947 Original." *The New Republic*, 30 Apr. 2011, newrepublic.com/article/94308/brighton-rock-remake-sam-riley. Accessed 5 Mar. 2019.

Whitehead, Tony. "Brighton Rock (1947)." *BFI Screenonline*, 2014, www.screenonline.org.uk/film/id/458657/index.html. Accessed 5 Mar. 2019.

Brooklyn

The Novel
Author: Colm Tóibín (b. 1955)
First published: 2009

The Film
Year released: 2015
Director: John Crowley (b. 1969)
Screenplay by: Nick Hornby
Starring: Saoirse Ronan, Domhnall Gleeson, Julie Walters, Emory Cohen

Context
Irish writer Colm Tóibín began his career as a journalist, which included working for publications such as the monthly news magazine *Magill* in the early 1980s. In the 1990s, he began writing novels at a prolific pace, starting with *The South* (1990), *The Heather Blazing* (1992), *The Story of the Night* (1996), and *The Blackwater Lightship* (1999). His work quickly became known for the way it examines the themes of Irish identity, loss, and homosexuality. His fifth novel, *The Master* (2004), which explores the life of American author Henry James, established Tóibín as a formidable talent for historical fiction. In 2009, Tóibín published *Brooklyn*, a novel about the journey of a young woman named Eilis Lacey who leaves Ireland in the 1950s to start a new life on her own in New York City. Set, in part, in Tóibín's hometown of Enniscorthy, County Wexford, *Brooklyn* quickly became critically acclaimed and was long-listed for the Man Booker Prize before winning the 2009 Costa Novel Award.

Once the film rights for *Brooklyn* were optioned, Nick Hornby, a British novelist famous for such best sellers as *Fever Pitch* (1992), *High Fidelity* (1995), and *About a Boy* (1998), was tapped to adapt Tóibín's novel into a screenplay. Up to that point, his experience as a screenwriter had largely been in adapting nonfiction, having penned the scripts for the acclaimed films *An Education* (2009) and *Wild* (2014), both based on memoirs; he was nominated for an Academy Award for his screenplay for *An Education*. After initial difficulty attracting a director to take on the seemingly simple script, Irish director John Crowley was eventually brought on board to direct. Previously, Crowley was known for his independent features *Intermission* (2003) and *Boy A* (2007) as well as his work in the London theater scene.

As Rooney Mara, initially approached to star in the film, had dropped out by that point, Academy Award-nominated actor Saoirse Ronan was cast in the lead role of Eilis. The relatively unknown American actor Emory Cohen was hired to play her American love interest, Tony Fiorello. Shooting began in Ireland in April 2014, and the production then moved to Montreal, which acted as a stand-in for much of the scenes taking place in New York City. As the film was produced for only an estimated $11 million, there was a lot of pressure on the cast and crew. In an interview for *The Moveable Feast* in November 2015, director Crowley stated, "It was a crazy schedule, trying to get this done on this budget. Nothing was ever shot as one would wish in sequence that would help psychology. It put a lot of pressure on Saoirse."

Brooklyn proved to be a unique film in several ways. While period pieces are often fodder for Academy Awards, most depict significant historical events or famous personalities. Contrarily, *Brooklyn* is a relatively uneventful film about a fictional young woman who must choose between living in New York City and Ireland. Her dilemma is quiet, even ordinary, compared to flashier Irish American immigrant stories such as Martin Scorsese's *Gangs of New York* (2002) or Jim Sheridan's *In America* (2002). In this way, *Brooklyn* does not represent a cinematic trend but rather more of an anomaly.

Film Analysis
Screenwriter Nick Hornby stays true to Tóibín's novel throughout *Brooklyn*, deviating from the original plot in only a few instances and therefore retaining the quiet, incremental, but emotionally powerful and complex effect of the novel. One such change is evident in the film's end-

ing. Where the book concludes in Ireland, Hornby actually depicts Eilis's (Saoirse Ronan) return to America. This allows the audience to clearly see how much she has grown from the beginning of her story. For example, on the boat ride West, Eilis acts as a sage by giving another young Irish girl advice for starting a life in New York. This scene directly harkens back to an earlier one in which a fellow traveler had given the inexperienced Eilis advice during her initial voyage from Ireland. In the film's final scene, Eilis waits for Tony (Emory Cohen) outside of his work. She waits for him across the street, looking confident and beautiful. They embrace in a loving way and it is clear that she is happy that she chose to return to Brooklyn. Another difference in the film is Hornby's decision to omit a dream sequence in which Eilis's homesickness manifests into a fantasy in which she flies over the cliffs of Ireland. While deeply powerful in the novel, this scene would have felt out of place and possibly, Crowley felt, cliché in the decidedly naturalistic film.

Director John Crowley divides the film into three distinct parts. He accomplishes this through different camera shots, color palettes, and Eilis's general appearance on screen. In the beginning, for example, when Eilis is still living in Ireland, the camera stays in tight close-ups; there are no wide shots used. This filming strategy suggests that Eilis lives in an insular, somewhat claustrophobic community. Her world is small; she works in a shop for the horrible Miss Kelly (Brid Brennan) and has very little of a social life. The town of Enniscorthy, which is literally brought to life as the scenes were shot in the real-life Irish town, is beautiful, but does not offer anything especially exciting for a woman her age.

Things begin to change on screen once Eilis begins her journey to America. The film's first wide shot occurs when she is on the boat, when the whole world opens up for her. Once in America, Crowley begins to introduce more bright, playful colors. This happens slowly, in congruence with Eilis's growth as a character. At first, she is homesick and wants to return to Ireland. Then, Father Flood (Jim Broadbent) offers to pay for her to take college courses and she meets a handsome young Italian man named Tony. Suddenly, Eilis's fashion becomes more glamorous. She dresses in yellows, pinks, blues, and reds. The film's palette grows brighter and more playful along with her. Here, Crowley opts for more natural light whenever possible. Simultaneously, the camera frames are looser—more adventurous.

When Eilis returns to Ireland, after the sudden death of her sister, Rose (Fiona Glascott), she is in a place of uncertainty and denial. Before she leaves America, Tony asks her to marry him because he is worried she will never return, and she accepts. Back in Enniscorthy, she keeps her marriage a secret from her family and friends. Everything seems to be better than before—not only is handsome suitor Jim Farrell (Domhnall Gleeson) interested in her, but she is offered a well-paying job. Eilis keeps pushing her return date to America back, unsure of what she really wants. Crowley depicts her state of denial and uncertainty by using the camera to create a soft, dreamy aesthetic. At first, everything has a glossy, appealing shine to it. However, when Eilis learns that Miss Kelly knows about her marriage to Tony and that she plans to tell the whole town, she realizes how small and petty her hometown can be. She tells her mother the truth and returns to America.

The film version of *Brooklyn*, in its devotion to its source material and focus on characters, effectively conveys its themes of home, family, and the circuitous journey of finding one's self. It depicts the twentieth-century immigrant experience with detail, care, and a distinctly Irish perspective. Eilis's experience is one shared by the tens of millions of people who came from Europe and other continents to the United States throughout the 1800s and 1900s. When the film begins, Eilis is timid but feels as though she deserves a better life. This enables her to take the terrifying risk to leave her mother and sister behind and move to New York City, where she does not know anyone. She quickly becomes overwhelmed with homesickness and regrets her decision, spending every night crying herself to sleep. It is not until Eilis starts pushing herself to try new things that her world expands and she becomes happier. When she returns to Ireland, everything seems better than before. At first, she mistakenly believes that is because Enniscorthy has changed. The reality is that her town is just as restrictive—she is the one who has changed and, though it is painful, she must reckon with the fact that America is now her home and Tony her family.

Significance

Brooklyn premiered at the Sundance Film Festival in January 2015, launching a bidding war among several distribution companies. Eventually, its rights were won by Fox Searchlight Pictures for $9 million. The film would be released to select theaters on November 4, 2015, before going on to a wide release on November 25, 2015. A box-office success, the film went on to earn just over $62 million worldwide. It was also well received by critics. Peter Bradshaw wrote for *The Guardian*, "Brooklyn is a robust drama with big flavours.... Hornby's screen translation and John Crowley's sure-footed direction have, I think, let the discreet intelligence in Tóibín's prose migrate to the lead actor, to be embodied by Ronan, who gives such a tremendous performance."

Brooklyn was nominated for the Academy Award for Best Picture. Its writer, Hornby, received a nomination for Best Writing (Adapted Screenplay), and its star, Ronan, earned a nomination for Best Actress in a Leading Role. Although the film didn't win any Academy Awards, it bolstered Ronan's reputation as a formidable talent in Hollywood. Playing the role of Eilis earned Ronan additional nominations for the Screen Actors Guild Awards, the Golden Globe Awards, and the British Academy of Film and Television Arts Awards and gave her the opportunity to take on more leading roles, such as in *Lady Bird* (2017) and *Mary Queen of Scots* (2018). While appreciated by American audiences, the film seemed to resonate especially well with viewers in Ireland and the United Kingdom. Several Irish writers produced think-pieces about how well *Brooklyn* captured their experiences as immigrants to America, Canada, or Australia. The BBC would later rank *Brooklyn* as forty-eighth in the top one hundred films of the twenty-first century.

Brooklyn is a significant film in that it has a small narrative scope. Where Hornby and Crowley could have packed the film with action and conflict, instead they chose to extract drama from Eilis's internal struggle—the feeling that she is torn between two different places and identities. In this way, *Brooklyn* is timelessly relatable. The film is also significant in that it is from a female perspective, which is more unusual for an immigrant narrative. In a February 2016 interview for *The Guardian*, the film's producers Amanda Posey and Finola Dwyer stated that they feel most of history's untold stories are female and they intend to correct this. Remarking on their motivation for making *Brooklyn*, Dwyer said, "There's never been an immigration story from a female's perspective,

where she hasn't been diseased, or had to prostitute herself, or been very vulnerable in some way."

—*Emily E. Turner*

Further Reading

Kermode, Mark. "'Brooklyn' Review—This Fairytale of New York Casts a Spell." Review of *Brooklyn*, directed by John Crowley. *The Guardian*, 8 Nov. 2015, www.theguardian.com/film/2015/nov/08/brooklyn-observer-film-review-saoirse-ronan. Accessed 4 Mar. 2019.

Tóibín, Colm. "Colm Tóibín on Filming His Novel Brooklyn: 'Everyone in My Home Town Wanted to Be an Extra.'" *The Guardian*, 10 Oct. 2015, www.theguardian.com/books/2015/oct/10/colm-toibin-film-brooklyn-novel. Accessed 4 Mar. 2019.

Bibliography

Bradshaw, Peter. "'Brooklyn' Review—Saoirse Ronan Shines in Heartfelt and Absorbing Adaptation." Review of *Brooklyn*, directed by John Crowley. *The Guardian*, 5 Nov. 2015, www.theguardian.com/film/2015/nov/05/brooklyn-review-saoirse-ronan-shines-in-nick-hornby-colm-toibin-drama. Accessed 4 Mar. 2019.

Crowley, John. "Interview: John Crowley on Finding the Face of 'Brooklyn.'" Interview by Stephen Saito. *The Moveable Feast*, 8 Nov. 2015, moveablefest.com/john-crowley-brooklyn/. Accessed 4 Mar. 2019.

Crowley, John. "Interview: John Crowley Talks 'Brooklyn,' The Heartsickness of Leaving Home & Dramatizing a Movie That Shouldn't Work." Interview by Rodrigo Perez. *IndieWire*, 16 Nov. 2015, www.indiewire.com/2015/11/interview-john-crowley-talks-brooklyn-the-heartsickness-of-leaving-home-dramatizing-a-movie-that-shouldnt-work-104719. Accessed 4 Mar. 2019.

Crowley, John. "Recreating '50s NYC in Montreal: Director John Crowley on 'Brooklyn' at TIFF 2015." Interview by Trevor Hogg. *Filmmaker*, 17 Sept. 2015, filmmakermagazine.com/95670-recreating-50s-nyc-in-montreal-director-john-crowley-on-brooklyn-at-tiff-2015. Accessed 4 Mar. 2019.

Ellis-Petersen, Hannah. "'Brooklyn' Producers: 'A Lot of the Untold Stories Are Female.'" *The Guardian*, 27 Feb. 2016, www.theguardian.com/film/2016/feb/27/brooklyn-producers-a-lot-of-the-untold-stories-are-female. Accessed 4 Mar. 2019.

Tóibín, Colm. "Colm Tóibín Loves the New Movie Version of His 'Brooklyn.'" Interview by Carole Burns. *The Washington Post*, 2 Nov. 2015, www.washingtonpost.com/entertainment/books/colm-toibin-loves-the-new-movie-version-of-his-brooklyn/2015/11/02/14db7ce6-8103-11e5-8ba6-cec48b74b2a7_story.html. Accessed 4 Mar. 2019.

The Call of the Wild

The Novel
Author: Jack London (1876-1916)
First published: 1903

The Film
Year released: 2020
Director: Chris Sanders (b. 1962)
Screenplay by: Michael Green
Starring: Harrison Ford, Omar Sy, Cara Gee, Dan Stevens, Karen Gillan, Bradley Whitford

Context

The Call of the Wild was written by American author and social activist Jack London. It appeared in four installments in the *Saturday Evening Post* in the summer of 1903 before being published as a book. *The Call of the Wild* was inspired by a year that London spent in the Yukon during the Klondike Gold Rush in the late 1890s, where he was exposed to the harshness of the wilderness. *The Call of the Wild* follows a dog named Buck as he is transformed from a domesticated beast back into a wild one. The novel explores the inherent tensions that exist between civilization and nature. London would continue exploring this theme in the follow-up novel *White Fang* (1906), in which a wild wolf-dog becomes a domesticated pet. His dystopian novel *The Iron Heel* (1907) is a science fiction work about the rise of a tyranny in the United States.

In October 2017, 20th Century Studios announced plans to turn London's book into a film. The script was written by Michael Green, known for adapting Neil Gaiman's *American Gods* (2001) into a television series. Chris Sanders was tapped to direct the film. Sanders's version of *The Call of the Wild* was not the first to grace the big screen—the classic American story had been adapted into a film several times before, beginning with a silent feature film released in 1923. Later versions include a 1935 film starring Clark Gable and a 1972 British adaptation starring Charlton Heston. Sanders's version targets a younger audience than these early adaptations, and it makes heavy use of computer-generated imagery (CGI). The decision to use CGI instead of real dogs was met with a mixed reception. Some animal activists commended the decision, others felt that it undermined the film's realism.

Film Analysis

The film's plot differs from the book's in several ways. When the book begins, for example, readers learn that Buck had been owned by a judge in Northern California before he was kidnapped and sold to traders in the Klondike region of Canada, where there was a demand for sled dogs. The film, however, provides its audience with glimpses of Buck's time with the judge (Bradley Whitford). It demonstrates that Buck had a comfortable life in California—one where he could act how he wanted without any real consequences. As a result, he is somewhat undisciplined when he first arrives to Canada, which makes his transition into the demanding work of a sled dog that much more difficult. Ultimately, the filmmaker's decision to showcase Buck's backstory as a dog that lived in leisure is an effort to make his narrative arc more compelling. By the end of the film, he has completely transformed in personality and returned to the wild.

Although the film maintains most of London's original story, there are some amendments and omissions. In the book, Buck is sold off to a Canadian mail service dogsled team run by two men named Perrault and François. In the film, the character of François is a First Nations woman named Françoise (Cara Gee) and she and Perrault (Omar Sy) prove to be much kinder to the dogs than the original characters. Specifically, they never use violence against the dogs or pit them against each other. The decision to change these characters speaks to the film's overall mitigation of violence and death. Buck's world is bloody, competitive, and vicious in the book. The film, intended for children, limits such upsetting scenes. For example, Buck's rivalry with another sled dog named Spitz still exists in the film but the showdown between the two does not end in Spitz's death. Similarly, the film alters the fate of Buck's fellow sled dogs at the hands of a later master named Hal so that they escape rather than starve and drown. These changes combined with some small, humorous sequences ensure that the film's tone stays mostly lighthearted—a stark contrast to the dark, gritty feeling of the book.

Where Buck encounters many bad men throughout London's novel, Hal is the primary antagonist in the film. The filmmakers ensure that Hal stands out as a different kind of human within Buck's world through his clothing. In the town where Perrault and Françoise leave Buck and his sled mates, the people wear blue, brown, and gray utilitarian clothing designed for the snow and cold weather. In stark contrast, Hal wears a bright red suit and ornate accessories that demonstrate his wealth. This fact is exacerbated by the

Harrison Ford, star of the 2020 Call of the Wild movie. Photo by Gage Skidmore via Wikimedia Commons.

luxury belongings he expects his sled dogs to pull for him, which include a Victrola record player as well as a case of champagne. Hal proves to be a selfish character—he is determined to go and find gold in a remote part of the country when the snow is melting, making it difficult for the dogs to pull him. He does not care about their well-being, pushing them to the brink of starvation and exhaustion.

The filmmakers utilize Hal's character to embody everything that London believed was wrong with modern twentieth=century society. Hal is symbolic of capitalist greed and its lack of humanity. Meanwhile, the character of John Thornton (Harrison Ford) is presented as his foil. The film amplifies Thornton's role so that it is more prominent than it is in the book. Thornton narrates the film in voice-over, providing the audience with insights into Buck's journey and inner transformation. Thornton is loyal, kindhearted, and selfless. After saving Buck from Hal, he decides to take Buck on an adventure into the Yukon to look for a place that his deceased son once talked about. They find an abandoned cabin near the river, which they quickly realize is filled with gold. In the end, Thornton does not take more gold than is necessary to pay for groceries for the rest of his life, ultimately rejecting the excessive greed that Hal represents. This is slightly different than the book, in which Thornton had two companions with whom who he and Buck traveled out to the wilderness specifically to find gold.

The character of Buck is increasingly drawn to his ancestral instincts the longer he spends time in the wilderness. The filmmakers use the image of a black wolf with green eyes that match the aurora borealis of the night sky to represent this growing feeling. The image is something that only Buck can see, and it appears whenever he is feeling more drawn to his inner nature than to his human masters. Initially Buck tries to ignore this feeling because it scares him, and he stays loyal to Thornton. However, the more time he spends in nature, the more he is overcome. Buck finally returns to the wild. The last image of the film shows him years later, an older, slower dog but with his head held high as he hunts with the rest of his pack.

There are very few interior shots throughout the film—most of it takes place outdoors in the Canadian wilderness. When a scene is set inside, the space often appears small, claustrophobic, and flimsy. Interestingly, *The Call of the Wild* was predominantly shot on a soundstage and not on location, and most of the imagery of the Canadian wilderness is in fact CGI.

Significance

The Call of the Wild was released in theaters nationwide on February 21, 2020. Produced on a budget of $125 million, the film performed poorly and did not break even at the box office. There were several factors that contributed to the film's financial failure. For one, it received mediocre critical reviews. While a handful of critics labeled it as an entertaining children's movie, others argued that it was a poor adaptation of London's novel and ultimately too saccharine and sentimental in tone. For example, Charlotte O'Sullivan wrote for the *London Evening Standard* that the script was, "flagrantly sappy and frequently ridiculous." Meanwhile, many other critics disliked *The Call of the Wild* because of its use of CGI, especially when it came to Buck's appearance. Finally, the film failed to attract a wide audience because its heartfelt story and characters, including Buck, don't align well with the tastes of contemporary young audiences for CGI and animated features.

—Emily E. Turner

Further Reading

Brandt, Kenneth. "The Short, Frantic, Rags-to-Riches Life of Jack London." *Smithsonian Magazine,*22 Nov. 2016, www.smithsonianmag.com/smithsonian-institution/short-heroic -rags-riches-life-jack-london-180961200/. Accessed 15 Mar. 2020.

Roeper, Richard. "Chicago Kid Harrison Ford Felt the Call of the *Call of the Wild.*" *Chicago Sun Times*, 18 Feb. 2020, chicago.suntimes.com/2020/2/18/21138752/harrison-ford-interv iew-cgi-dog-call-wild-jack-london. Accessed 15 Mar. 2020.

Bibliography

Gleiberman, Owen. "Why Did *The Call of the Wild* Cost $125 Million? It's a Mid-Budget Film That Caught Budget-itis (Column)." *Variety*, 23 Feb. 2020, variety.com/2020/film/ news/why-did-the-call-of-the-wild-cost-125-million-its-a-mid-budget-film-that-caught-budget-itis-1203511978/. Accessed 15 Mar. 2020.

Jacobs, Julia. "*Call of the Wild* Casts a Digital Star. Is He a Good Dog?" *The New York Times*, 23 Feb. 2020, www.nytimes.com/ 2020/02/23/movies/call-of-the-wild-dog.html. Accessed 15 Mar. 2020.

O'Sullivan, Charlotte. "*The Call of the Wild* Review: Harrison Ford and His Dead-Eyed CGI Dog Take a Walk on the Mild Side." *London Indoors*, 18 Feb. 2020, www.standard.co.uk/ go/london/film/the-call-of-the-wild-film-review-a4365161.html. Accessed 15 Mar. 2020.

Rubin, Rebecca. "Harrison Ford's *Call of the Wild* to Lose $50 Million at Box Office." *Variety*, 1 Mar. 2020, variety.com/ 2020/film/box-office/harrison-ford-call-of-the-wild-to-lose-50-million-1203520284/. Accessed 15 Mar. 2020.

Captain Underpants: The First Epic Movie

The Novel
Author: Dav Pilkey (b. 1966)
First published: 1997-2015

The Film
Year released: 2017
Director: David Soren (b. 1973)
Screenplay by: Nicholas Stoller
Starring: Kevin Hart, Thomas Middleditch, Ed Helms, Nick Kroll, Jordan Peele

Context

The DreamWorks feature film *Captain Underpants: The First Epic Movie*, was released in the United States in 2017, adapted from the Captain Underpants series of children's novels, a long-running series by American writer and illustrator Dav Pilkey. Consisting of twelve books, the series began in 1997 with the publication of *The Adventures of Captain Underpants* and concluded with 2015's *Captain Underpants and the Sensational Saga of Sir Stinks-A-Lot*. The series proved particularly popular among children and became best sellers both in the United States and abroad, spawning a variety of tie-in publications as well as spin-offs focused on the superheroes Dog Man and Super Diaper Baby. In light of their popularity among young readers, the books in the Captain Underpants series were often the target of challenges from parents and other concerned individuals, largely due to their emphasis on the inherently humorous nature of bodily functions, and they became some of the most frequently banned and challenged books in US schools.

DreamWorks Animation acquired the rights to the series in 2011, with the goal of adapting the series for the screen. The Captain Underpants film adaptation was initially set to be directed by Rob Letterman, who left the film and was replaced by David Soren in 2015. Soren had long worked for DreamWorks Animation in roles such as storyboard artist and head of story and made his feature-length directorial debut with the company's 2013 animated film *Turbo*, which he also cowrote. The screenplay for the Captain Underpants adaptation was credited primarily to screenwriter Nicholas Stoller, who was known for his work on children's films such as *The Muppets* (2011) and *Storks* (2016), and featured contributions from Soren. Titled *Captain Underpants: The First Epic Movie* and featuring the voices of actors Kevin Hart, Thomas Middleditch, Ed Helms, Nick Kroll, and Jordan Peele, among others, the film premiered in the United States in May 2017.

Film Analysis

In adapting the Captain Underpants series for the screen, the filmmakers faced several key challenges, including the need to select which book or books of the series to adapt. As a series consisting of twelve books published over the course of nearly two decades, the Captain Underpants series provided ample content from which to draw; however, with its numerous adventures and villains for the titular superhero to face, the series also provided more content than could reasonably be contained in a single film. At the same time, adapting only a single book would limit the scope of the narrative and the characters able to be included. In light of that, the filmmakers struck a balance between adhering strictly to the source material and deriving inspiration from the series as a whole. The early events of the film strongly reflect the events of the first book in the series, *The Adventures of Captain Underpants*, which details both the creation of the character of Captain Underpants, the protagonist of a comic created by fourth-graders George Beard and Harold Hutchins, and the transformation of school principal Mr. Krupp into the superhero himself. The film begins as George (Kevin Hart) and Harold (Thomas Middleditch) complete a homemade comic detailing the origin of their superhero, the pages of which come to life on the screen. The Captain Underpants comic created in the world of the film goes beyond the comic depicted in the first book of the series, showing the destruction of the superhero's home planet, Underpantyworld, the flight of the infant Captain Underpants through space, and his eventual arrival on Earth, where he is raised by a pair of dolphins. In addition to providing further context for the character as George and Harold have imagined him, the events of that portion of the comic draw heavily from the origin story of the DC Comics hero Superman, thus firmly rooting Captain Underpants in the established superhero tradition and demonstrating how George and Harold's creative points of view have been shaped by the imaginative works that came before.

Captain Underpants: The First Epic Movie follows the events of the first book in the series relatively closely for a time, chronicling the fictional Captain Underpants's entry into the real lives of his creators. Early in the film, George and Harold face the threat of being placed in separate classes after their cruel and fun-hating principal, Mr. Krupp (Ed Helms), discovers that they were responsible for sabotaging a project showcased by their classmate Melvin (Jordan Peele) at the school's Invention Convention. Although Mr. Krupp has long suspected the boys of having been responsible for numerous pranks carried out at the school, the incident at the Invention Convention provides sufficient evidence for him to take action. While the Mr. Krupp of *The Adventures of Captain Underpants* gathers evidence of the boys' wrongdoing in school on his own, through the use of hidden cameras installed specifically for that purpose, the film incarnation of the character does so with the assistance of Melvin, who disapproves of their behavior. The character of Melvin is not present in *The Adventures of Captain Underpants* and is not introduced until the second book in the series, *Captain Underpants and the Attack of the Talking Toilets* (1999). While his inclusion in the film represents a diversion from the series and to an extent renders Mr. Krupp's vendetta against George and Harold somewhat less personal, Melvin ultimately serves as a useful counterpart to his troublemaking classmates and plays a key role in the development of the film's conflict.

To prevent Mr. Krupp from separating them, George and Harold hypnotize their principal and tell him to become Captain Underpants, and he takes on the identity and personality of the good-natured superhero. However, the school faces a new threat in the form of newly hired teacher Professor Pee-Pee Diarrheastein Poopypants, Esq. (Nick Kroll), who seeks to eliminate laughter from the world with the aid of the humorless Melvin. Known in the books as Professor Pippy P. Poopypants, the character was

Self-published in 1989, "The Really Cool Adventures of Captain Underpants" was a limited edition run sold in Kent, Ohio. Dav Pilkey donated 50% of the profits to Goodwill and the United Way. Photo by Ohiobusinessboy, CC BY-SA 4.0, via Wikimedia Commons.

introduced in *Captain Underpants and the Perilous Plot of Professor Poopypants* (2000), the fourth installment in the series. The character's perspective in the film is in many ways the supervillainous equivalent to Krupp's own, and Professor Poopypants's threat to eliminate the human capacity for laughter is effectively a global-scale version of Krupp's threat to separate George and Harold. Captain Underpants's defeat of Professor Poopypants thus represents a powerful victory in the name of fun and friendship and, to an extent, Krupp's victory over the mean-spirited part of himself, which in turn paves the way for Krupp's eventual change of heart.

In addition to determining which elements of the source material to include in the film, the filmmakers sought to create a work that captured the distinctive visual elements of the original series while transforming them into a visual narrative suitable for the screen. The books in the main Captain Underpants series mix a prose narrative with illustrations depicting the events taking place as well as in-universe media elements, perhaps most notably the comic books written and drawn by the characters. Although the illustrations in the book are the work of author and illustrator Pilkey, they vary stylistically based on whether they reflect the real world of the books or the imagined world of George and Harold's comics. *Captain Underpants: The First Epic Movie* aptly demonstrates and arguable intensifies that distinction, as the boys, their environment, and the people they encounter are typically animated in a style that reflects their design in the original books while bearing some of the roundness and polish characteristic of much three-dimensional computer-generated animation. The comic-book sequences, in contrast, closely resemble the childish drawings seen in the comics in the original books, with the added addition of motion made possible through the medium of film. The film likewise incorporates several other visual styles, including a sequence in which the boys and other characters are depicted as live-action sock puppets. A climactic battle sequence near the film's conclusion begins in the computer-generated animation style used in most of the film but switches to a flipbook style after George and Harold pause the action to tell the viewer that the coming sequence is too violent, intense, and expensive to be depicted through any other medium but flip book or "flip-o-rama." As director David Soren noted in interviews following the film's release, the sequence is a deliberate reference to the original books, which prominently feature such flip-o-rama sequences. Overall, in addition to reflecting the style of the original books, the film's mixed-media aesthetic emphasizes the imagination of the protagonists, which is key to the film as a whole.

Significance

Following its US premiere in May 2017, *Captain Underpants: The First Epic Movie* opened in theaters throughout the United States in June of that year. The film performed well at the box office, grossing nearly 74 million dollars domestically, according to the website Box Office Mojo. *Captain Underpants* continued to open in cinemas around the world over the summer and fall of 2017 and ultimately grossed more than another 51.5 million dollars interna-

tionally, proving particularly financially successful in the United Kingdom, Australia, and Spain.

The critical response to the film was generally positive, with many readers commenting that the film's characteristic humor—generally considered to be consistent in nature with the humor in Pilkey's original books—translated well to the screen and entertained both children and adults while ultimately remaining innocent and good hearted. Reviewers also commented on the film's innovative shifts in animation styles, which distinguished *Captain Underpants* from many other animated films aimed at children and families. Although Pilkey had previously expressed reservations about having his work adapted for the screen, he was likewise pleased with the resulting film and in interviews noted that he had collaborated with Soren at various stages during the project. Following the film's release in theaters, *Captain Underpants* won the Behind the Voice Actors Awards for best male lead vocals in a feature film (Ed Helms) and best male supporting vocals in a feature film (Jordan Peele), as well as the International Film Music Critics Award for best original animated film score (Theodore Shapiro), and received nominations for a number of awards, including the Annie Award for best animated feature.

Although the subtitle of the film, "The First Epic Movie," suggested the possibility of one or more sequels, no sequel films were announced within the year following the film's release. However, in late 2017, DreamWorks Animation announced that a spin-off television series would be released through the streaming content provider Netflix, becoming one of many Netflix series based on existing DreamWorks properties. Titled *The Epic Tales of Captain Underpants*, the series premiered on Netflix in July 2018 and featured a different stable of writers and directors as well as a new voice cast that included Nat Faxon as Captain Underpants and Mr. Krupp, Jay Gragnani as Harold, and Ramone Hamilton as George.

—*Joy Crelin*

Further Reading

Pilkey, Dav. *The Adventures of Captain Underpants*. Scholastic, 1997.
Soren, David. "'Captain Underpants' Director David Soren on Importance of Experimenting with Narrative Style in Animation." Interview by Matt Grobar. *Deadline*, 5 Dec. 2017, deadline.com/2017/12/captain-underpants-david-soren-oscars-interview-news-1202218402/. Accessed 30 Nov. 2018.

Soren, David. "David Soren Interview: *Captain Underpants* Six Months On." Interview by Simon Brew. *Den of Geek*, 15 Feb. 2018, www.denofgeek.com/uk/movies/captain-underpants-the-first-epic-movie/55231/david-soren-interview-captain-underpants-six-months-on. Accessed 30 Nov. 2018.

Bibliography

Andersen, Soren. "'Captain Underpants' Review: Kids Flick Outfunnies the Books." *The Seattle Times*, 1 June 2017, www.seattletimes.com/entertainment/movies/captain-underpants-review-kids-flick-outfunnies-the-books/. Accessed 30 Nov. 2018.

Burnett, Matia. "Movie Alert: 'Captain Underpants.'" *Publishers Weekly*, 11 May 2017, www.publishersweekly.com/pw/by-topic/childrens/childrens-book-news/article/73566-movie-alert-captain-underpants.html. Accessed 30 Nov. 2018.

"Captain Underpants." *Box Office Mojo*, www.boxofficemojo.com/movies/?id=captainunderpants.htm. Accessed 30 Nov. 2018.

Giardina, Carolyn. "'Captain Underpants' and the New Push to Make Cheaper Animated Movies." *Hollywood Reporter*, 2 June 2017, www.hollywoodreporter.com/news/captain-underpants-new-push-make-cheaper-animated-movies-1008170. Accessed 30 Nov. 2018.

Gleiberman, Owen. "Film Review: 'Captain Underpants: The First Epic Movie.'" *Variety*, 1 June 2017, variety.com/2017/film/reviews/captain-underpants-the-first-epic-movie-review-1202449135/. Accessed 30 Nov. 2018.

Otterson, Joe. "Netflix, Dreamworks Partner for Six Animated Shows in 2018, Including 'Trolls,' 'Boss Baby' Series." *Variety*, 12 Dec. 2017, variety.com/2017/tv/news/trollhunters-season-3-trolls-boss-baby-netflix-1202637829/. Accessed 30 Nov. 2018.

Rottenberg, Josh. "Why 'Captain Underpants' Author Dav Pilkey Played Hard to Get with Hollywood." *Los Angeles Times*, 1 June 2017, www.latimes.com/entertainment/movies/la-et-mn-captain-underpants-dav-pilkey-20170601-story.html. Accessed 30 Nov. 2018.

VanDerWerff, Todd. "Captain Underpants Is Better Than Any Movie Named Captain Underpants Has a Right to Be." *Vox*, 2 June 2017, www.vox.com/culture/2017/6/2/15726584/captain-underpants-movie-review. Accessed 30 Nov. 2018.

Casino

The Novel
Author: Nicholas Pileggi (b. 1933)
First published: 1995

The Film
Year released: 1995
Director: Martin Scorsese (b. 1942)
Screenplay by: Nicholas Pileggi, Martin Scorsese
Starring: Robert De Niro, Sharon Stone, Joe Pesci

Context

Although director Martin Scorsese has worked in a variety genres, many of his most characteristic contributions—beginning with his early films *Mean Streets* (1973) and *Taxi Driver* (1976)—feature gritty New York City locales, portrayals of lively violence and machismo, Italian-American culture, Catholic themes, and the Mafia. He grew up in the Little Italy neighborhood of New York City in the 1950s and was influenced heavily its environment and the social structures around him. Films reflecting Scorsese's long-standing interests in the relationships and socioeconomic factors underlying crime include *Mean Streets*, a fictional narrative inspired in part by events he observed during his youth, and 1990's *Goodfellas*, based on the life and career of real-world Mafia associate Henry Hill. For the latter work, Scorsese collaborated with writer Nicholas Pileggi, an established crime journalist who originally chronicled Hill's coming-of-age in the Mafia in the book *Wiseguy*(1985). Scorsese and Pileggi went on to be nominated for the Academy Award for best adapted screenplay for their work on the film.

Following their successful collaboration on *Goodfellas*, Pileggi introduced Scorsese to the story of Frank "Lefty" Rosenthal, who began his career in gambling and bookmaking operations run by the Chicago Outfit and who was later sent to Las Vegas to run several Mafia-connected casinos throughout the 1970s. Intrigued by the story and seeking to make a film to fulfill the terms of his contract with Universal Pictures, Scorsese opted to collaborate with Pileggi to adapt Rosenthal's story for the screen. Although Pileggi had already been working on the manuscript for the nonfiction book *Casino: Love and Honor in Las Vegas*, which chronicles the events in question and incorporates extensive first-person recollections from Rosenthal himself

as well as other individuals involved, the two ultimately agreed that Pileggi would, rather uncharacteristically, work on cowriting the script at the same time; the film and book were ultimately released within weeks of one another. Titled *Casino*, Scorsese and Pileggi's film draws heavily from Pileggi's factual research for his book but takes a degree of artistic license with the material, including changing the names of its characters. Released in US theaters in late 1995, *Casino* stars Robert De Niro as Sam "Ace" Rothstein, a character based on Rosenthal; Sharon Stone as Ginger McKenna, based on Rosenthal's wife, Geri McGee; and Joe Pesci as Nicky Santoro, based on Rosenthal's childhood friend and Mafia associate Anthony Spilotro.

Film Analysis

In adapting the story of Frank "Lefty" Rosenthal for the screen, Scorsese and Pileggi faced a different set of challenges than they had when adapting Pileggi's book *Wiseguy* into *Goodfellas*. At the time that they began that earlier project, the manuscript for *Wiseguy* had already been finalized for publication, and the two were tasked with adapting the narrative presented in the book into one fit for the screen. With *Casino*, however, the book and the film were in progress contemporaneously; while Pileggi had already researched and written a chronological narrative, the structure of his work was not yet set, and the book would not be made available for purchase until around the time that the film was in theaters. As such, the book and the film closely reflect each other in numerous ways, and the simultaneous nature of their development renders it difficult to determine which elements of the film's structure originated within Pileggi's manuscript and which originated within the film itself and subsequently shaped the structure of the published book. The film's opening sequences, for example, closely reflect the book's introduction, which begins with the 1982 car bombing that failed to kill Rosenthal and goes on to provide a brief overview of Rosenthal's criminal history and the operations of casinos and their count rooms. The film likewise begins with the car bombing, showing Sam "Ace" Rothstein (Robert De Niro) start a car that is quickly engulfed in flames. In addition to mirroring the start of the book and providing a visually compelling opening scene, the sequence aptly creates a sense of inevitability that is pervasive throughout the film. Ace's downfall is coming, and the audience can ask only how and when.

Moving on from that opening scene, the film goes on to provide a similar overview of the Las Vegas casino environment of the early 1970s, focusing in particular on the flow of money in and out of the casino's count room, where a portion of the casino's earnings are skimmed off to be delivered to Mafia leaders outside of Nevada. *Casino: Love and Honor in Las Vegas* provides ample trivia pertaining to the count room, noting, for example, that $1 million in quarters weighs twenty-one tons. The corresponding scene in the film, however, makes the true extent of the wealth passing through Rothstein's casino visible, showing countless loose coins being dumped out of buckets, traveling down conveyer belts, and eventually emerging in paper-wrapped rolls. Much like the bright colors and glittering lights of the casino floor itself, through which Ace travels in the course of his duties, the constant flow of shiny coins in the counting room makes the allure of the casino visually evident and supports the film's assertion that the period depicted on screen was, in large part, the golden age of mob-controlled Las Vegas—an age that, as the film's apparently cataclysmic opening suggests, is on the verge of its own dramatic combustion. However, as the film's conclusion indicates, the ultimate collapse of Ace's Las Vegas came not through the sudden violence exemplified by the car bombing but through the demolition of the old casinos and the rise of family-friendly corporate resorts financed through an entirely different form of financial trickery. The actions of the film's characters, though of great significance on a micro level, mean nothing in the face of the passage of time and broad cultural shifts.

Among the most characteristic features of *Casino* is its use of voice-over, a feature previously used to great effect in films such as *Goodfellas*. As with that earlier film,

Director Martin Scorcese. Photo by the Peabody Awards via Wikimedia Commons.

which was based on a book containing extensive first-person quotations from its subjects, *Casino* draws heavily from factual material even though many of the details of the story, such as the names of the individuals and locations involved, were changed for the film. Just as he had previously done for *Wiseguy*, Pileggi made extensive use of interviews and first-person narratives in *Casino: Love and Honor in Las Vegas*, focusing particularly on Rosenthal, the sole living member of the trio of figures on whom the film would later focus. In a 1995 interview with Steve Daly for *Entertainment Weekly*, Pileggi commented that his goal in doing so was to tell the story "in the voices of these real people" and that he, as the author, sought to "disappear and become an invisible, omniscient narrator."

In adapting his research and manuscript for the screen, however, Pileggi and Scorsese had to move beyond the

Actress Sharon Stone received acclaim for her role. Photo by Georges Biard, CC BY-SA 3.0, via Wikimedia Commons.

role of invisible narrator due to their decision to feature dual voice-overs, one from Ace and one from Nicky Santoro (Joe Pesci). While Rosenthal was still alive at the time and was able to be interviewed by Pileggi, Anthony Spilotro, on whom Nicky was based, was murdered in 1986 and was therefore largely unable to speak for himself in the book, other than through the recollections of others and transcriptions of telephone conversations intercepted by the authorities. Portions of Nicky's voice-over, then, reflect Pileggi's statements rather than Spilotro's. At the beginning of the film, for instance, Nicky comments through voice-over that his and Ace's tenure in Las Vegas represented "the last time that street guys like us were ever given anything that f—— valuable again," while a similar statement from Pileggi—minus the profanity characteristic of Nicky's voice-overs and dialogue—concludes *Casino: Love and Honor in Las Vegas*. The screenwriters likewise exhibited further artistic license by attributing

statements truly made by other individuals to the film's central characters: Spilotro associate Frank Cullotta's description of Las Vegas as "paradise on earth" is given to Ace in the film, for instance, while his subsequent statement that the gangsters had "f—— it all up" was given to Nicky. While such additions and altered attributions, along with the changes made to names and various other details, render *Casino* not wholly factually accurate, they enabled the filmmakers to entertainingly explore the mindsets and motivations of two very different characters over the course of the film, thus shedding light on the inner workings of a Las Vegas that no longer exists.

Significance

Following its premiere, *Casino* opened in theaters throughout the United States in November 1995 and went on to open worldwide over the course of 1996. The film performed relatively well at the box office, accumulating a domestic lifetime gross of more than $42 million, according to the website Box Office Mojo. The film grossed an additional $73 million internationally. Reviews of *Casino* were generally positive, with many critics commenting approvingly on Scorsese's depiction of 1970s Las Vegas and the intriguing, factually inspired narrative. Stone's portrayal of Ginger also drew extensive praise, with many critics identifying the role as her most challenging and complex to date. She was ultimately nominated for the Academy Award for Best Actress in a Leading Role for her work on the film and won the Golden Globe Award in that category. Additionally, Scorsese was recognized for his work on *Casino*, including with a nomination for the Golden Globe for Best Director—Motion Picture.

While much of *Casino*'s contemporary reception was positive, some critics did object to the film's nearly three-hour length as well as to its multiple scenes featuring graphic violence. In addition, the film's perceived similarities to *Goodfellas*—which included their shared genre; the presence of De Niro and Pesci in both films and the similarities between Pesci's characters in both; and their origins in the collaboration between Scorsese and Pileggi—prompted both contemporary and later reviewers and commentators to compare the two films, often to *Casino*'s detriment. In his review for *Rolling Stone*, critic Peter Travers commented on that phenomenon, noting that "expectations could kill *Casino* faster than any potshots from critics" while asserting that the film "is not the equal of *Mean Streets* or *Goodfellas*." Despite such comparisons, the critical view of *Casino* improved over the decades following the film's release, and *Casino* has come to be regarded as one of Scorsese's key films. It was to be the last collaboration between Scorsese and actor Robert DeNiro until 2019s *The Irishman*.

—*Joy Crelin*

Further Reading

Schickel, Richard. *Conversations with Scorsese*. Knopf, 2011.
Snider, Eric D. "12 High-Stakes Facts about *Casino*." *Mental Floss*, 8 Sept. 2015, mentalfloss.com/article/68258/12-high-stakes-facts-about-casino. Accessed 31 Dec. 2018.

Bibliography

"*Casino*." *Box Office Mojo*, www.boxofficemojo.com/movies/?id=casino.htm. Accessed 31 Dec. 2018.
Daly, Steve. "An Interview with Nicholas Pileggi." *Entertainment Weekly*, 6 Oct. 1995, ew.com/article/1995/10/06/interview-nicholas-pileggi/. Accessed 31 Dec. 2018.
Ebert, Roger. Review of *Casino*, directed by Martin Scorsese. *RogerEbert.com*, 22 Nov. 1995, www.rogerebert.com/reviews/casino-1995. Accessed 31 Dec. 2018.
Maslin, Janet. "Film Review; A Money-Mad Mirage from Scorsese." Review of *Casino*, directed by Martin Scorsese. *The New York Times*, 22 Nov. 1995, www.nytimes.com/1995/11/22/movies/film-review-a-money-mad-mirage-from-scorsese.html. Accessed 31 Dec. 2018.
McCarthy, Todd. Review of *Casino*, directed by Martin Scorsese. *Variety*, 16 Nov. 1995, variety.com/1995/film/reviews/casino-1200443792/. Accessed 31 Dec. 2018.
Travers, Peter. Review of *Casino*, directed by Martin Scorsese. *Rolling Stone*, 22 Nov. 1995, www.rollingstone.com/movies/movie-reviews/casino-112912/. Accessed 31 Dec. 2018.

Cat on a Hot Tin Roof

The Play
Author: Tennessee Williams (1911-83)
Premiered: 1955

The Film
Year released: 1958
Director: Richard Brooks (1912-92)
Screenplay by: Richard Brooks, James Poe
Starring: Elizabeth Taylor, Paul Newman, Burl Ives

Context

Tennessee Williams's classic drama *Cat on a Hot Tin Roof*, about a washed-up football star in denial about his own sexuality, opened on Broadway on March 24, 1955. *The New York Times* critic Brooks Atkinson deemed it the playwright's "finest drama." Other critics of the time were similarly effusive. The play ran for nearly 700 performances, and was awarded the Pulitzer Prize for Drama in 1955. Set in the 1950s on a plantation home in the Mississippi delta, the play begins with a family gathering to celebrate the sixty-fifth birthday of patriarch, Big Daddy. Big Daddy's alcoholic son, a former football star named Brick, has just broken his ankle drunkenly trying to clear hurdles on the high school track. Brick's wife, Maggie, stews in her own desires, as Brick refuses to sleep with her since the death of his best friend, Skipper. Their marital drama dovetails with a larger family drama, as Big Daddy, who has yet to make out his will, does not know what most members of the family already do: that he is dying of cancer. As Brick's brother and sister-in-law vie to prove their love for Big Daddy in hopes of inheriting his vast estate, each character is forced to part with the lies they tell themselves to avoid confronting unpleasant realities.

Williams, regarded as one of the greatest dramatists of the twentieth century, was at the height of his career when he wrote *Cat on a Hot Tin Roof.* In 1951, his play *A Streetcar Named Desire* (1947), which also won a Pulitzer Prize, was adapted into an Academy Award-winning film starring Marlon Brando and Vivien Leigh. Still, the famously tempestuous writer was anguished by the success of the play for reasons that would further manifest themselves in the film adaptation. Working with famous director Elia Kazan, Williams rewrote the play's third act for its Broadway debut. In that version, Brick moves toward self-reflection and crucially, displays some tenderness toward his wife, Maggie. In Williams's original version, Brick remains impenetrable. The audience understands that an important buried truth—his true feelings for Skipper—has been revealed, but that revelation has no bearing on Brick's "moral paralysis," as Williams puts it in the script. His final exchange with Maggie is ambivalent. Today, one can read both versions of act three—and a note from Williams explaining their difference—in the pub-

Tennessee Williams. Photo by Orlando Fernandez/World Telegram, via Wikimedia Commons. [Public domain.]

lished script. Williams makes clear that he felt pressured to change the ending to make the play, which for him was always a tragedy, into a drama with a more palatable resolution. The film version, written and directed by Academy Award-winner Richard Brooks, incorporates elements of the Broadway script and moves even further from Williams's original intent.

Film Analysis

The considerable differences between stage and film versions of *Cat on a Hot Tin Roof* are usually attributed to the Hays Code. Named for Will Hays, the first chairman of the Motion Picture Producers and Distributers of America, the code was a strict set of censorship guidelines. The code prohibited, among other things, nudity, "lustful kissing," "suggestive dances," and "ridicule of religion." Brick's homosexuality, unfortunately, fell under the code's ban on "discussions of sexual perversion." The play's entire dramatic core—Brick's alcoholism and chilly ambivalence, stemming from his struggle to repress his romantic feelings for his dead friend—was considered too controversial for movie-going audiences. Thus it was necessary, in adapting the play, to tell an entirely different story. Following scene for scene, the dialogue in the two versions is nearly the same until the climax, a scene between Brick and Big Daddy. In the play, Big Daddy, a self-described tolerant man, coaxes Brick to be honest with himself about Skipper. Brick cruelly rebukes him by telling him what the audience already knows: Big Daddy is lying to himself, too, about the fact that he is dying of cancer. In the film, the scene follows a very different path. The details are a bit convoluted, but in its essence, Skipper becomes a kind of false idol. Brick worships his friend, who is, in Maggie's eyes, a lesser football talent. In the play, the story goes, Skipper tries to prove he is straight by seducing Maggie. In the film, Maggie seduces Skipper to prove that Skipper is a disloyal friend, completely changing Skipper's role in the conflict between Brick and Maggie.

The filmmakers use the momentum of this new story to reach a totally different conclusion as well. Using elements of Williams's discarded Broadway draft, they build on the reappearance of Big Daddy to create an original scene in which Brick and Big Daddy share an emotional exchange about Big Daddy's father, a boxcar-hopping tramp. This resolution between them further propels Brick to embrace Maggie in an alliance against his brother, Gooper, and sister-in-law, Mae, who represent stifling so-

Poster for Cat on a Hot Tin Roof. *Photo via Wikimedia Commons. [Public domain.]*

cial mores and greed. What was perhaps most odious to Williams—who reportedly hated the film—is the ending, in which Brick calls Maggie upstairs and kisses her. He takes charge to "make the lie true"—a line from the play about Maggie having told the family she was pregnant with Brick's child. In the play, he shirks her advances. The play is pointedly about homophobia and sexism; the film merely gestures toward these themes, and more so the latter than the former. It is also about truth and "mendacity," or untruthfulness, a word Brick repeats over and over. Both the play and the film are about the comforting lies people tell themselves and each other, though ironically, the film perpetuates its own comforting lies about the story—that Big Daddy learns how to tell his family that he loves them, and that Brick and Maggie were meant to be together after all. By expunging Brick's homosexuality, it succumbs to the same harmful mores that Williams bemoans in the play. In a stage direction after Brick spits out the word, "Fairies," a gay slur, Williams writes in the stage directions, "In his utterance of this word, we gauge the wide and profound reach of the conventional mores he got from the world that crowned him with early laurel."

Angelica Jade Bastién wrote for the *Village Voice* that *Cat on a Hot Tin Roof* is "not a good adaptation" but is a "great film" in its own right. This is in large part thanks to its talented, star-studded cast. It stars a twenty-six-year-old Elizabeth Taylor as Maggie and Paul Newman as Brick. Burl Ives, who plays Big Daddy, was the only member of the Broadway cast to reprise his role in the film. (The role of Maggie was originated by Barbara Bel Geddes; the role of Brick was originated by Ben Gazzara.) It was written and directed by Richard Brooks, who would go on to win an Academy Award for his adaptation of the Sinclair Lewis novel *Elmer Gantry*. While the play takes place within the confines of Brick and Maggie's bedroom, the film uses the entirety of the Pollitt plantation. A sudden rainstorm, a car stuck in the mud and the smashing of old artifacts in the basement add to the drama inherent in the script. The film also features several black actors playing (largely nameless) servants and field workers. Their presence underscores the irony of Big Daddy's boasts about how he rose from nothing with help from no one, another comforting lie.

Significance

Despite Williams's displeasure with the film, it was a huge hit with audiences. Critics praised aspects of the film, though several noted its divergence from the source material. *The New York Times* critic Bosley Crowther described it as "a ferocious and fascinating show." (Elements of his review also touch on Williams's reputation as a vulgar sensationalist; he describes the characters as "trashy.") He goes on to write that the alterations of the original material in the film "do not represent supreme achievements of ingenuity or logic in dramatic art" and describes the resolution between Brick and Big Daddy as "glib." He concluded that although the conflicts between the characters no longer made sense, the actors did their best to make up for it with performances full of "violent emotion," singling out Newman for particular praise. A critic for *Variety* was more positive, describing the film as "intense" and "important." "By no means is this a watered-down version, though 'immature dependence' has

replaced any hint of homosexuality. Motivations remain psychologically sound." Today, critics are compelled to wrestle more directly with the film's omissions in their assessments of it. Peter Bradshaw, for *The Guardian*, wrote that the film's conspicuous side-stepping and clunky attempts to sanitize Williams's script seem almost stylized, like something out of a Modernist play. In its day, and for those who did not know the story of the play, the film provided a welcome return to Williams's sensual Southern world. It also provided for one of Taylor's most memorable performances as the prowling and complex "Maggie the Cat." *Cat on a Hot Tin Roof* was nominated for six Oscars, including best picture as well as best actor and best actress for Newman and Taylor. Though Williams likely disagreed, it was also nominated for best script adaptation.

—*Molly Hagan*

Further Reading
Atkinson, Brooks. "Theatre: Tennessee Williams' 'Cat.'" Review of *Cat on a Hot Tin Roof*, by Tennessee Williams, directed by Elia Kazan. *The New York Times*, 25 Mar. 1955, movies2.nytimes.com/books/00/12/31/specials/williams-cat.html. Accessed 13 Nov. 2018.
Lahr, John. *Tennessee Williams: Mad Pilgrimage of the Flesh.* W.W. Norton & Company, 2014.

Bibliography
Bastién, Angelica Jade. "The Contradictory Power of 'Cat on a Hot Tin Roof.'" *The Village Voice*, 16 Nov. 2016, www.villagevoice.com/2016/11/16/the-contradictory-power-of-cat-on-a-hot-tin-roof/. Accessed 14 Nov. 2018.
Bradshaw, Peter. "The Cat on a Hot Tin Roof Film May Be Censored—But in Some Ways It's Superior." *The Guardian*, 17 Oct. 2012, www.theguardian.com/stage/2012/oct/17/cat-hot-tin-roof-film-censored. Accessed 14 Nov. 2018.
Review of *Cat on a Hot Tin Roof*, directed by Richard Brooks. *Variety*, 31 Dec. 1957, variety.com/1957/film/reviews/cat-on-a-hot-tin-roof-2-1200419154/. Accessed 14 Nov. 2018.
Crowther, Bosley. "The Fur Flies in 'Cat on a Hot Tin Roof.'" Review of *Cat on a Hot Tin Roof*, directed by Richard Brooks. *The New York Times*, 19 Sept. 1958, www.nytimes.com/1958/09/19/archives/the-fur-flies-in-cat-on-a-hot-tin-roof-talent-galore-found-in-music.html. Accessed 13 Nov. 2018.
Mondello, Bob. "Remembering Hollywood's Hays Code, 40 Years On." *NPR*, 8 Aug. 2008, www.npr.org/templates/story/story.php?storyId=93301189. Accessed 14 Nov. 2018.
Quart, Leonard. Review of *Cat on a Hot Tin Roof*, directed by Richard Brooks. *Cineaste*, 2016, www.cineaste.com/winter2016/cat-on-a-hot-tin-roof/. Accessed 13 Nov. 2018.
Zinoman, Jason. "Theater: Excerpt; Cat on a Hot Tin Roof." *The New York Times*, 2 Nov. 2003, www.nytimes.com/2003/11/02/theater/theater-excerpt-cat-on-a-hot-tin-roof.html. Accessed 12 Nov. 2018.

A Clockwork Orange

The Novel
Author: Anthony Burgess (John Anthony Burgess Wilson, 1917-1993)
First published: 1962

The Film
Year released: 1971
Director: Stanley Kubrick (1928-99)
Screenplay by: Stanley Kubrick
Starring: Malcolm McDowell, Warren Clarke, Patrick Magee, Michael Bates, Anthony Sharp

Context

A Clockwork Orange is a dystopian satirical novel written by English author Anthony Burgess and published in 1962. In the novel, set in a near-future England, a youth subculture of extreme violence is ravaging society. The film adaptation, directed by Stanley Kubrick, was released in 1971. As Burgess himself explains in "The Clockwork Condition," a short essay written in the early 1970s, his intent was to write a novel critical of efforts to cure juvenile delinquency. What gave the story impetus was the use of aversion therapy, as espoused by psychologist-philosopher B.F. Skinner, "to liquidate the criminal impulse." Burgess noted, "It is better to be bad of one's own free will than to be good through scientific brainwashing."

In the novel, events unfold over a three-year period in an unidentified city that combines attributes of Manchester in England (where Burgess was born), Leningrad in the Soviet Union (now St. Petersburg, Russia), and New York City. The story focuses on first-person narrator Alex DeLarge, a teenager who leads one of many small gangs that run wild at night when police are scarce. Alex and his thuggish "droogs" (friends) dress fashionably in "Nadsat" (teen) style. They speak a patois combining Slavic and Romani words, and Cockney rhyming slang that, along with their clothes, distinguishes them from the rest of society. They drink drug-laced milk to get pumped up for ultraviolence: committing muggings, vandalism, holdups, car theft, home invasions, rape, and worse.

Caught and convicted for murder after his friends betray him, Alex is sentenced to a long prison term. In prison, he learns of the Ludovico Technique, a new treatment that is supposed to eliminate criminal behavior, leading to quick release. Accepted as the first test subject—which also makes him a political pawn—Alex is injected with experimental drugs. He is then forced to watch films of beatings, rapes, and wartime atrocities. The scientific tactics make him feel sick whenever he observes violence or thinks violent thoughts. However, the films have classical music soundtracks. As a result, Alex also becomes ill when he hears the classical music—especially Ludwig van Beethoven's *Ninth Symphony*—he has grown to love.

Released back into society as cured, Alex finds no refuge. His parents reject him. Former friends are now policemen who beat him. Old crimes return to haunt him. Victims take revenge, driving Alex to attempt suicide by jumping from a window. Severely injured, he becomes a rallying point for forces that accuse the government of inhumane treatment. The government compensates Alex for mental and physical injuries, offering him a high-paying job. While he recuperates, scientists operate on his brain. His violent impulses return, and Alex can enjoy his favorite music again.

Film Analysis

Director-producer Stanley Kubrick is credited as screenwriter of the 1971 film. In reality, much of the dialogue and large excerpts of Alex's narrative voice-over monologue are taken directly from the Burgess novel. Kubrick certainly deserves credit for what he left out of the adaptation—the film is fast-paced and seems shorter than its 137 minutes. There are, for example, many more crimes committed in the novel, which serve a thematic purpose. They did not, however, all need to be seen onscreen to illustrate the vicious nature of Alex and his friends. The film was already controversial, and showing Alex kicking a man to death in prison, or sexually assaulting ten-year-old girls would have been difficult to portray on film at the time while still maintaining the ethos of a "black comedy."

Malcolm McDowell as Alex DeLarge in Stanley Kubrick's 1971 film A Clockwork Orange. Photo via Wikimedia Commons. [Public domain.]

The director is also responsible for the startling contrasts between the bright, modernistic look and simultaneously dark, dystopian feel of the finished film. Kubrick was assisted in this effort by cinematographer John Alcott. A talented crew of production and costume designers, art directors, prop masters, painters, and sculptors provided interesting sets, with a focus on an ultramodern aesthetic.. There are also erotic paintings and sculptures, and kitsch, such as a chorus line of naked dancing Jesuses. The sound features electronic renditions of classical music and original compositions by Wendy Carlos (born Walter Carlos, 1939). Malcolm McDowell was an excellent choice to play protagonist Alex DeLarge. The actor (though obviously older than the 15-year-old antihero in the novel) had his first leading role as a similarly rebellious youth in *If....* (1968). Seasoned character actors filled memorable key roles in a large, colorful cast.

Kubrick's unique vision is immediately apparent in the film's opening scene, which establishes the exotic nature of the story to be told. Like the novel, the film begins inside the Korova (cow) Milkbar. Alex is the focus because the story will be told exclusively from his earnest, but unreliable perspective. He stares confidently and malevo-

lently between false eyelashes. The camera moves back to reveal his friends/accomplices: Georgie (James Marcus), Pete (Michael Tarn), and Dim (Warren Clarke). They are similarly dressed in white bodysuits with studded belts and crotch protectors. Each of them wears a hat and heavy boots. (In the novel, the bodysuits are black, and the groin guards, worn beneath the cloth, have personalized embossed designs.) They are drinking milk-plus, an amphetamine-laced concoction that will spur them to participate in ultraviolence. As the camera retreats, impressive props come into view. The tables of the milk bar are shaped like life-sized naked women. Milk dispensers are nude crouching women on pedestal-style vending machines. Other small groups of young men in different costumes—rival gangs—can be seen also getting stoked for the evening, foreshadowing events to follow.

The action soon begins. The boys assault an old drunk. They interrupt an attempted rape and fight a rival gang. They steal a car and go for a joyride at top speed, running other vehicles off the road. They talk their way into a rural home, where they beat the owner, writer Frank Alexander (Patrick Magee), and gang-rape his young wife (Adrienne Corri). The last sequence is particularly graphic. It is just one of many such scenes featuring female (and occasionally male) nudity. Highlights include a three-way sexual encounter, performed to the "William Tell Overture"—a memorable, humorous scene that momentarily lightens the grim mood. The home invasion is an important element, however, because it will figure again later in the story. In the novel, Alex sees the title of the manuscript Frank is working on—"A Clockwork Orange"—and reads a nonsensical passage aloud before tearing up the pages. In the film, the self-reference is omitted. Instead, Alex fatefully belts out "Singin' in the Rain," punctuating the song's phrases with kicks and blows from his walking stick on his victims' bodies.

There are many small and relatively unimportant cosmetic differences between the novel and the film, which otherwise track quite closely. The stark, overcrowded prison cell where Alex is housed for two years in the novel, for instance, becomes a homey room in the film where he can keep a bust of Beethoven and hang pictures of naked women. Alex's former friend Georgie—killed in the novel during a burglary—shows up later in the film as a policeman, partner to his other ex-comrade, Dim; in the novel, the partner is former gang rival Billyboy (Richard Connaught). The Nadsat language, which is used liberally throughout the novel, has been toned down in the film. The foreign words, even for those unfamiliar with Russian, are readily understandable when heard in context. Although the location of the story is purposely not mentioned in the novel in order to give the story universality, the film is obviously set in London. Many familiar landmarks are seen. Newspaper mastheads and headlines that are used as transitional devices are all from British publications. (Kubrick pays sly tribute to the novel's author by having article ledes name the protagonist "Alex Burgess.")

The most significant change between the novel and the film was the elimination of the final chapter, Chapter 21, which completes the symmetrical structure as Anthony Burgess had originally conceived. The British (but not the American) version contained the last chapter, which shows Alex, now 18, with a new gang. The thrill of ultraviolence is fading for him, and he envisions getting married and becoming a father. Kubrick eschewed the hopeful ending and opted instead for a darker vision. Alex is cured of society's hypocrisy. He has been returned to his original state. He retains all of the qualities that the government minister (Anthony Sharp) considered when choosing him for treatment: he is just as "aggressive, enterprising, outgoing, young, bold, and vicious" as he was at the beginning.

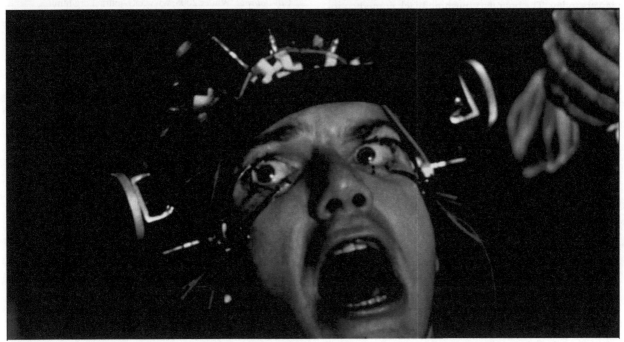

The Ludovico test. Photo via Wikimedia Commons. [Public domain.]

Significance

By any standard of measurement, the film *A Clockwork Orange* was a commercial and critical success despite its initial X rating. (Banned in several countries for the sex, violence, and language, it was later re-released after editing to tone down particularly intense scenes, with the more widely acceptable R rating.) Box office revenues paid back the $2.2 million budget more than tenfold.

Although reviews were mixed, the film was nominated for four Academy Awards (best picture, director, adapted screenplay, editing), but lost most of those honors to *The French Connection*, which won five of eight nominations. *A Clockwork Orange* was likewise shut out at the British Academy Film Awards, despite seven nominations, and at the Golden Globe Awards (three nominations). The film did, however, score a Hugo Award (best dramatic presentation), two New York Film Critics Circle Awards (best film and director), honors at the Venice Film Festival, and the Silver Ribbon award given by the Italian National Syndicate of Film Journalists.

The film (like the novel) explores themes like the perils of psychiatry, the problem of juvenile delinquency, gangs and violence, and nihilism in modern society. These were highly topical in the period in which both the novel and the film were made, and they still resonate with readers and viewers today. The boundary-pushing black comedy, violence, and stylization in the film make Kubrick with *A Clockwork Orange* a forerunner to later filmmakers such as Quentin Tarantino. The film is frequently included on lists of the 100 greatest films. In 2020, it was selected for preservation in the United States National Film Registry by the Library of Congress for being "culturally, historically, or aesthetically significant."

Not everyone was pleased with the film, however. Anthony Burgess, for one, always had mixed feelings about it. In 1986, he wrote, "The book I am best known for, or only known for, is a novel I am prepared to repudiate: written a quarter of a century ago, a *jeu d'esprit* knocked off for money in three weeks, it became known as the raw material for a film which seemed to glorify sex and violence. The film made it easy for readers of the book to misunderstand what it was about, and the misunderstanding will pursue me until I die. I should not have written the book because of this danger of misinterpretation."

—*Jack Ewing*

Further Reading

Burgess, Anthony. *Little Wilson and Big God: Being the First Part of the Autobiography*. Weidenfeld & Nicolson, 1986.

Heller, Agnes. *Wind and Whirlwind: Utopian and Dystopian Themes in Literature and Philosophy*. Brill/Rodopi, 2019.

Bibliography

Burgess, Anthony. "The Clockwork Condition." *The New Yorker*, 28 May 2012, www.newyorker.com/magazine/2012/06/04/the-clockwork-condition. Accessed 26 Feb. 2020.

Burgess, Anthony. *The Novel Now: A Guide to Contemporary Fiction*. W.W. Norton & Company, 1967.

Burgess, Anthony, and Andrew Biswell, editors. *A Clockwork Orange: The Restored Text*. W.W. Norton & Company, 2012.

Dalrymple, Theodore. "A Prophetic and Violent Masterpiece." *City Journal*, Winter 2006, www.city-journal.org/html/prophetic-and-violent-masterpiece-12926.html. Accessed 26 Feb. 2020.

Flood, Alison. "'The Clockwork Condition': Lost Sequel to *A Clockwork Orange* Discovered." *The Guardian*, 25 Apr. 2019. www.theguardian.com/books/2019/apr/25/the-clockwork-condition-lost-sequel-to-a-clockwork-orange-discovered. Accessed 26 Feb. 2020.

McCrum, Robert. "The 100 Best Novels: No 82—*A Clockwork Orange* by Anthony Burgess (1962)." *The Guardian*, 13 Apr. 2015. www.theguardian.com/books/2015/apr/13/100-best-novels-clockwork-orange-anthony-burgess. Accessed 26 Feb. 2020.

Crazy Rich Asians

The Novel
Author: Kevin Kwan (b. ca. 1974)
First published: 2013

The Film
Year released: 2018
Director: Jon M. Chu (b. 1979)
Screenplay by: Peter Chiarelli, Adele Lim
Starring: Constance Wu, Henry Golding, Michelle Yeoh

Context

Crazy Rich Asians is an adaptation of the novel of the same name published in 2013 by writer and visual-design professional Kevin Kwan. Born in Singapore, Kwan drew on his observations of Singaporean society and its wealthy and connected residents when writing the novel. *Crazy Rich Asians* proved popular among readers upon its publication, and Kwan followed the book with the sequels *China Rich Girlfriend*, published in 2015, and *Rich People Problems*, published in 2017. In addition to its widespread readership, *Crazy Rich Asians* attracted the attention of a variety of film studios. The production company Color Force ultimately won the rights to the film and began to work on developing the film prior to finding a distribution partner. Following a bidding war, the team behind the film opted to turn down a multimillion-dollar upfront offer from the video-streaming service Netflix in favor of a less lucrative offer from Warner Bros. Pictures that would enable the film to be distributed as widely as possible.

The film adaptation of Kwan's novel was directed by Jon M. Chu, then known for his work on several dance-focused projects, musical biopics, and the 2016 thriller *Now You See Me 2*. The screenplay for the work was written by Peter Chiarelli and Adele Lim, each of whom was tasked with developing different portions of the film's narrative and characterization. Released in the United States in August 2018, *Crazy Rich Asians* featured a large ensemble cast that included Constance Wu, Henry Golding, Michelle Yeoh, Awkwafina, Ken Jeong, Gemma Chan, and many other actors.

The film mingles romance, comedy, and drama, touching on topics like fraught family relationships, social pressures and expectations, and socioeconomic class. Its central story concerns the romance between Chinese American economics professor Rachel Chu and her Singaporean boyfriend, Nick Young. Their relationship faces a series of hurdles when they travel to Singapore, where Rachel meets Nick's ultrawealthy family for the first time. The ensuing conflicts are both universal and highly specific to the wealthy characters of the film.

Film Analysis

In adapting *Crazy Rich Asians* for the screen, screenwriters Chiarelli and Lim worked to transform a novel featuring an extensive cast of characters and multiple interwoven story lines into a single, cohesive narrative appropriate for the screen. The complexity of the novel is immediately signaled by the presence of a family tree explaining the relationships between the Young, Shang, and T'sien families, who collectively make up the extended family of major character Nick Young. Rather than mere bonus material, the family tree plays a key role in helping the reader keep track of Nick's large family and gain a fuller understanding of the family and the socioeconomic dynamics at play. This is particularly essential due to the structure of the novel, which is divided into chapters focusing on a range of different characters. While some chapters focus on Rachel and Nick, others center on Eleanor Young, Nick's cousin Astrid, Rachel's friend Peik Lin and her family, and other characters, a strategy that enables Kwan both to tell the core stories of the novel's protagonists but also to comment satirically on the lives of Singapore's wealthy elite. When watching a film, however, audiences cannot refer back to a family tree, and frequent shifts between focal characters could render the overall narrative disjointed and confusing. In light of such factors, the screenwriters condensed Kwan's work significantly when adapting the novel for the screen. The film version of *Crazy Rich Asians* focuses more tightly on the romance between Rachel (Constance Wu) and Nick (Henry Golding) and the challenges they must overcome before reaching the film's triumphant conclusion, although some subplots from the novel are also touched on during the film—or even explored at length, as in the case of the subplot concerning the troubled relationship between Astrid (Gemma Chan) and her husband, Michael (Pierre Png).

In addition to the relationship between Rachel and Nick, the film particularly highlights the character of Eleanor (Michelle Yeoh), Nick's mother, and the role her disapproval of that relationship plays in the work's central conflict. The opening scene of the film emphasizes Eleanor's importance while illustrating the screenwriters' approach to paring down the number of characters and story

Awkwafina wins audiences over in her hilarious supporting role. Photo by Casi Moss via Wikimedia Commons.

lines featured in the novel. The opening scene—set in 1995 in the film, 1986 in the book—begins as Eleanor, Eleanor's sister-in-law Felicity (Janice Koh), and the young Nick (Nevan Koit) and Astrid (Amanda Evans) enter an exclusive London hotel. Although they have a reservation, the hotel staff turns them away, believing that they do not belong there. After calling her husband, however, Eleanor returns to the hotel with her family and the hotel owner appears, revealing that she is henceforth the new owner of the establishment. A similar scene is featured in the novel's prologue, yet there are a number of key differences, including the presence of two additional characters, Eleanor's sister-in-law Alexandra and nephew Edison. Perhaps most important, however, is that the novel's prologue ends with Felicity's husband as the new owner of the hotel, not Eleanor. By reducing the number of characters in the scene and giving the climactic purchase of the hotel to Eleanor rather than Felicity, the screenwriters simplified the scene while also placing greater emphasis on Eleanor as a character, highlighting the wealth of the Young family, and demonstrating the lengths to which Eleanor is willing to go to ensure that her family is respected.

The film's enhanced focus on Rachel, Nick, and Eleanor further plays a substantial role in *Crazy Rich Asians'* conclusion. Unlike the novel, which is the first in a series and features a relatively open-ended conclusion, the film adaptation features a more traditional story arc that culminates in a conclusive ending befitting the genre to which the film belongs. After Rachel and Nick travel to Singapore to attend Nick's best friend's wedding, Rachel meets with disapproval from some of Nick's relatives, particularly Eleanor, who identify her as an outsider because she was raised in the United States, was born in mainland China rather than overseas, and does not come from a wealthy family. Over the course of the film, Eleanor tells Rachel that she is an unsuitable partner for Nick and reveals that Eleanor herself was once not considered to be a good choice for her own husband, which is why her engagement ring is a distinctive emerald ring rather than the family heirloom engagement ring. Rather than bonding with Rachel over their shared difficulties in winning over their prospective spouses' families, however, Eleanor states that she was able to make sacrifices for the sake of her marriage and ultimately prevail, but Rachel will never be enough for Nick. Although the core of this conflict is present in the novel, and the novel does hint at Eleanor having sacrificed to reach her present position, the plot point concerning the engagement ring is unique to the film, and the ring itself serves as a powerful visual reminder of the conservatism and traditionalism of portions of Nick's family.

In events that adhere closely to those in the novel, Eleanor concludes her campaign against Rachel by hiring a private investigator to seek out information about Rachel's father, whom Rachel believes to be dead. Eleanor reveals that Rachel's mother had been married but, after becoming pregnant through an affair, took the baby and fled to the United States. Although Rachel's mother, Kerry Chu (Tan Kheng Hua), later explains that her husband was abusive and that Rachel's biological father helped her escape from that abuse, Eleanor and her mother-in-law, Ah Ma (Lisa Lu), care only about the scandal that Nick marrying a woman with such a background would create. Nick, however, proposes to Rachel anyway and offers to leave his family behind. Not long afterward, Rachel meets with Eleanor in a scene that functions as the final showdown between the two characters. However, Rachel does not go on the offensive against Eleanor: rather, she reveals that she rejected Nick's proposal because she did not want him to have to turn his back on his family. As Rachel later boards a plane to leave Singapore, Nick finds her and proposes once again, this time with his mother's emerald ring. Both the meeting between Rachel and Eleanor and the final proposal are original to the film adaptation of Crazy Rich Asians and provide a fitting end to the conflict that developed over the film. Having come to accept Rachel because of her actions, Eleanor signals that acceptance through her emerald ring, thus removing the major factor limiting Rachel and Nick's relationship. Concluding with a lavish party in honor of Rachel and Nick's engagement, Crazy Rich Asians ultimately features a satisfying conclusion to its central narrative arc.

Significance

Crazy Rich Asians premiered on August 7, 2018, and opened in theaters throughout the United States on August 15. The film proved to be a significant financial success, nearly equaling its $30 million production budget with its opening-weekend box-office revenue. In total, Crazy Rich Asians went on to gross more than $174 million domestically and amass an additional $64 million internationally, with particularly strong performances in Australia, the United Kingdom, Indonesia, New Zealand, and Taiwan.

Upon its release, Crazy Rich Asians received largely positive reviews from critics, many of whom highlighted the film as a strong addition to the romantic comedy genre and called attention to the generational, class, and cultural clashes that fuel the narrative's conflicts. Critics also particularly appreciated the film's contribution to the representation of actors of Asian descent in American film, noting that it was one of few American commercial films to be set in the present day and feature a predominantly Asian and Asian American cast. In addition to the film's romantic leads, reviewers praised Yeoh for her complex portrayal of Eleanor and highlighted the comedic contributions of rapper-actor Awkwafina in her role as Rachel's friend Goh Peik Lin. While some reviewers, including New York Times critic A. O. Scott, found the film felt rushed despite the consolidation that had taken place during the adaptation process, the overall reception of the film was generally favorable, and Crazy Rich Asians went on to be nominated for the Golden Globe Award for Best Motion Picture-Musical or Comedy. Wu was likewise nominated for the award for Best Performance by an Actress in a Motion Picture-Musical or Comedy for her portrayal of Rachel. In light of the success of the film, the creative team behind Crazy Rich Asians announced plans to reunite for a sequel based on Kwan's novel China Rich Girlfriend.

—Joy Crelin

Further Reading
Ho, Karen K. "Crazy Rich Asians Is Going to Change Hollywood. It's about Time." Time, 15 Aug. 2018, time.com/longform/crazy-rich-asians. Accessed 31 Dec. 2018.
Kwan, Kevin. Crazy Rich Asians. Anchor, 2014.
Lee, Chris. "The Long Crazy Road to Crazy Rich Asians." Vulture, 9 Aug. 2018, www.vulture.com/2018/08/the-long-crazy-road-to-crazy-rich-asians.html. Accessed 31 Dec. 2018.

Bibliography
Chiu, Allyson. "An All-Asian Cast and No Martial Arts: Why the Crazy Rich Asians Movie Matters." The Washington Post, 26 Apr. 2018, www.washingtonpost.com/news/morning-mix/wp/2018/04/26/an-all-asian-cast-and-no-martial-arts-why-the-crazy-rich-asians-movie-matters. Accessed 31 Dec. 2018.
"Crazy Rich Asians." Box Office Mojo, www.boxofficemojo.com/movies/?id=crazyrichasians.htm. Accessed 31 Dec. 2018.
Lenker, Maureen Lee. "Crazy Rich Asians: All the Differences between the Book and the Movie." Entertainment Weekly, 19 Aug. 2018, ew.com/movies/2018/08/19/crazy-rich-asians-book-movie-differences. Accessed 31 Dec. 2018.

McHenry, Jackson. "*Crazy Rich Asians*: The Biggest Changes from the Book to the Movie." *Vulture*, 17 Aug. 2018, www.vulture.com/2018/08/crazy-rich-asians-the-biggest-changes-from-book-to-movie.html. Accessed 31 Dec. 2018.

Scott, A. O. "Review: *Crazy Rich Asians* Is a Party with a First-Rate Guest List. "Review of *Crazy Rich Asians*, directed by Jon M. Chu. *The New York Times*, 14 Aug. 2018, www.nytimes.com/2018/08/14/movies/crazy-rich-asians-review.html. Accessed 31 Dec. 2018.

Sun, Rebecca, and Rebecca Ford. "*Crazy Rich Asians* Sequel Moves Forward with Director Jon M. Chu." *Hollywood Reporter*, 22 Aug. 2018, www.hollywoodreporter.com/news/crazy-rich-asians-sequel-plans-revealed-jon-m-chu-returning-1135890. Accessed 31 Dec. 2018.

Zhang, Jenny G. "How the *Crazy Rich Asians* Movie Departs from the Book." *Slate*, 17 Aug. 2018, slate.com/culture/2018/08/crazy-rich-asians-movie-vs-book-differences-between-the-film-adaptation-and-the-novel.html. Accessed 31 Dec. 2018.

The Crucible

The Play

Author: Arthur Miller (1915-2005)

First published: 1953

The Film

Year released: 1996

Director: Nicholas Hytner (b. 1956)

Screenplay by: Arthur Miller

Starring: Daniel Day-Lewis, Winona Ryder, Paul Scofield, Joan Allen, Bruce Davison

Context

In 1953, the United States was in the early stages of the Cold War and things were tense both at home and abroad. As the Korean War (a proxy war with the Soviet Union) winded down, paranoia gripped the home front, stirred by politicians and the media who insisted Communists were infiltrating every aspect of American life. Starting in 1950, Joseph McCarthy, a senator from Wisconsin, began listing the names of government officials that he believed to be communist spies. Over the next four years, McCarthy's efforts expanded, with hundreds of people falling under suspicion of having communist ties. Many were forced to testify before Congress and many others lost their jobs despite lack of real evidence against them. Hollywood, too, came under suspicion, with the House Un-American Activities Committee (HUAC) convening and forcing many actors, writers, and directors to out each other as Communists. This campaign on the part of McCarthy and his allies was alarming to many Americans, and the phenomenon known as McCarthyism was often labeled a "witch hunt" for its mostly baseless persecution of individuals.

Among those who were disturbed by McCarthy's campaign was the playwright Arthur Miller. Thanks to hit productions such as *All My Sons* (1947) and *Death of a Salesman* (1949), he was already among the country's best-known writers and intellectuals. Allegorizing the hysteria that accompanied McCarthyism and literalizing the witch hunt metaphor, Miller reached back into the nation's history for a parallel and found it in the Salem witch trials of 1692 and 1693, in which twenty people were killed for suspected witchcraft in the heart of Puritan New England. Miller took the real-life events and characters and lightly fictionalized them, creating a drama that, in the written text interpolated into the play proper, made clear the parallels between 1693 and his own time.

Miller's play debuted at the Martin Beck Theater in 1953; the reception was mixed but the work went on to win a Tony Award for best play. A new production of *The Crucible* began a year later and became a huge hit. From there, the play went on to be considered a contemporary classic, often performed and taught in schools. Early ef-

Arthur Miller. Photo via Wikimedia Commons. [Public domain.]

forts at adapting the work included a mostly forgotten 1957 French film with a screenplay by Jean-Paul Sartre and the 1961 opera by Robert Ward which became an enduring classic.

Given the play's success, it is somewhat surprising that it only came to Hollywood in 1996. Chosen to direct was noted British theater director Nicholas Hytner, who had adapted another play for his first film, *The Madness of King George* (1994). The producers' biggest coup, however, was landing Miller himself to write the screenplay.

Film Analysis

The film version of *The Crucible* opens with a scene that is not acted out in the play, only described. As the credits roll, the camera tracks through the mist of a dark night, finally alighting on a group of teenage girls engaged in what looks like the devil's work. The girls, accompanied by an older woman—later revealed to be Tituba (Charlayne Woodard), a Barbadian slave—are dancing around a boiling cauldron, calling out spells to make boys like them and generally engaging in some mostly innocent fun. Then, things start to get a little bit out of hand. One of the girls strips naked. Another calls for the death of her lover's wife. Then, a gray-haired man shows up and one of the girls, who is later revealed to be his daughter, drops into a faint.

This gathering proves to be the precipitating event that throws all of Salem, Massachusetts, into a turmoil, setting the stage for all the accusations of witchcraft and subsequent executions to follow. In the play, though, there is some question as to what exactly happened. On one hand, there is the eyewitness account of the Reverend Samuel Parris (played in the film by Bruce Davison), the man who interrupted the proceedings. On the other hand, there is the changing testimony of the girls themselves. Ringleader Abigail Williams (Winona Ryder)—the one who wants her former lover John Proctor's (Daniel Day-Lewis) wife, Elizabeth Proctor (Joan Allen), dead—first insists that the girls did nothing but dance, and then entirely switches her story, claiming she was possessed.

The filmmakers' decision to show rather than just report the forest ritual scene is important, as it subtly changes the knowledge and therefore the experience of the viewer. Crucially, this removes much of the ambiguity and uncertainty of the following scenes. Rather than have to piece together what actually happened in the woods, the viewer is placed in the more passive position of simply watching the various testimonies unfold. After all, he or she already knows that the truth is somewhere between witchcraft and innocent dancing. This arguably robs the film of some of the power of the play, as the plot and the ultimate message both hinge on how the threat of witchcraft is one that preys on the imagination. In Miller's original work, the viewer or reader experiences a share of the anxiety occurring in Salem in 1692, as they, like the majority of the town residents, are not privy to the actual nature of the events in the woods. As critic Roger Ebert put it in his review of the film, "the play is not about literal misbehavior but about imagined transgressions," but this cannot be developed as fully in the adaptation after showing the original incident. Instead, the film increases the emphasis on the erotic undertones of the witch trials and the tension of repressed sexuality.

In most other particulars, the film follows the play fairly closely. There are a few new scenes, most of which turn greater focus onto the lead character of John Proctor, making it a true starring role for the dynamic Day-Lewis. The chain reaction of accusations plays out as Abigail calls Tituba a witch, the slave confesses in order to avoid hanging, and the girls use their newfound credibility to name other women—including Elizabeth Proctor—as witches. The Reverend Hale (Rob Campbell) and Judge Danforth (Paul Scofield) are brought in to sort out the situation, but it continues to spiral out of control. John Proctor attempts to stop the hysteria by insisting that the girls are faking their accusations, even confessing his affair with Abigail. However, the fear-driven frenzy overwhelms the truth and John himself is accused of witchcraft and arrested. Eventually Abigail goes too far in her claims and the townspeople stop blindly believing the girls. John, however, remains in jail awaiting execution with several others, rebuffing Abigail's suggestion that they flee together. Though he agrees to a written confession that would spare his life, the demand that his name be publicly displayed to urge others to falsely confess proves too much. He recants the confession and is hanged alongside other accused witches.

Themes such as the coercive power of fear, the complexity of power and gender dynamics, and the value of truth above even personal safety are all carried over from play to film. However, in addition to the differences caused by slight narrative changes, the adaptation carries differences from the play based on the contexts in which each work was created. When Miller's *The Crucible* originally appeared, critics and the general public alike widely read it as a very clear condemnation of McCarthyism, the HUAC, and the pressure to name names in order to save oneself. Notably, Miller had a major falling out with his longtime friend, the theater and film director Elia Kazan, after Kazan named colleagues with communist ties to the HUAC in 1952 in order to avoid being blacklisted himself. Miller's portrayal of the dangers of giving into a witch hunt and his hero John Proctor's refusal to confess resonated strongly in the political climate of the time. By contrast, the film version of *The Crucible* appeared at a much more stable time in United States history. By 1996 the paranoia of the Cold War was receding into the past, as was Hollywood's own shame over its blacklisting of the 1950s. However, the early 1990s saw a wave of media attention to crimes allegedly committed by satanic cults, providing a new subtext to the film as noted by reviewers such as Ebert.

Satanism aside, the film version of *The Crucible* is typically considered more a generalized statement about human nature than a political allegory like the play. Director Nicholas Hytner ramps up the drama with an assortment of cinematic techniques, including the frequent use of wide-angle lenses and the grouping of the accusing girls in sinister arrangements, and the audience understands that there is plenty at stake. Who, watching this movie, would not recognize the temptation to turn on their fellow citizens if it meant either personal gain or a form of vengeance? The idea of jealous vengeance is most specifically channeled through Abigail, but she is portrayed with nuance as a truly human figure rather than a purely evil villain. Her actions are extreme, but are realistically driven by love (or at least lust)—and a modern interpretation of her sexual relationship with her much older employer as a young, essentially powerless woman presents further opportunity for sympathy.

Ultimately, it is the humanization of the characters caught up in the heavy drama around them that gives the film its power, not its reliance on any kind of subtext. As critic Owen Gleiberman concluded in his rave review of the film for *Entertainment Weekly*: "The way *The Crucible* speaks to us today has less to do with any specific instance of collective indictment than it does with the relentless group-think mentality of modern America, where people, crushed under by a bureaucratic/consumerist/media culture, rely more and more on forces outside themselves to determine what to like, what to say, what to believe."

Significance

The Crucible is a play that since its debut in 1953 has held an outsized place in the American literary imagination. This is in part because the message at its core is a flexible allegory. While its scathing response to McCarthyism continues to memorialize a dark chapter of US history, even as the threat of communist witch hunts has disappeared the play can be applied to other instances of paranoia and scapegoating—situations that are never very far from erupting whether in the United States or elsewhere. Miller's shrewd understanding of human nature ensures that *The Crucible* has never lost its power or appeal, and it continues to be read and produced regularly around the world.

In contrast, the film version was met with decidedly mixed reviews from critics and was not a major box-office success. Some reviewers hailed it as a wholly successful work, praising everything from the acting and directing to the sets and costumes. Others, however compared it unfavorably to the original play. It did earn a pair of Academy Award nominations, for Miller's screenplay and for Joan Allen's supporting performance. And even despite the mixed reception, the film remains the best-known (and a relatively faithful) adaptation of one of the most iconic plays of all time. As such, it is often used in schools as an aid in teaching the text.

—*Andrew Schenker*

Further Reading
Miller, Arthur. "Arthur Miller, The Art of Theater No. 2." Interview by Olga Carlisle and Rose Styron. *The Paris Review*, 1996, www.theparisreview.org/interviews/4369/arthur-miller-the-art-of-theater-no-2-arthur-miller. Accessed 10 Dec. 2018.
Stapinski, Helene. "Arthur Miller's Brooklyn." *The New York Times*, 22 Jan. 2016, www.nytimes.com/2016/01/24/nyregion/arthur-millers-brooklyn.html. Accessed 10 Dec. 2018.

Bibliography
Bloom, Harold, ed. *Arthur Miller's The Crucible*. Chelsea House, 2004.
Ebert, Roger. Review of *The Crucible*, directed by Nicholas Hytner. *RogerEbert.com*, 20 Dec. 1996, www.rogerebert.com/reviews/the-crucible-1996. Accessed 10 Dec. 2018.

Gleiberman, Owen. Review of *The Crucible*, directed by Nicholas Hytner. *Entertainment Weekly*, 29 Nov. 1996, ew.com/article/1996/11/29/movie-review-crucible/. Accessed 10 Dec. 2018.

Lanzendorfer, Joy. "10 Powerful Facts about *The Crucible*." *Mental Floss*, 31 Aug. 2015, mentalfloss.com/article/67433/10-witchy-facts-about-crucible. Accessed 10 Dec. 2018.

Maslin, Janet. "The Bewitching Power of Lies." Review of *The Crucible*, directed by Nicholas Hytner. *The New York Times*, 27 Nov. 1996, movies2.nytimes.com/books/00/11/12/specials/miller-cruciblefilm.html. Accessed 10 Dec. 2018.

The Curious Case of Benjamin Button

The Novel
Author: F. Scott Fitzgerald (1896-1940)
First published: 1922

The Film
Year released: 2008
Director: David Fincher (b. 1962)
Screenplay by: Eric Roth
Starring: Brad Pitt, Cate Blanchett, Julia Ormond, Tilda Swinton, Taraji P. Henson, Elias Koteas

Context

F. Scott Fitzgerald wrote some of the greatest American novels of the twentieth century, including *The Great Gatsby* (1925), *The Beautiful and Damned* (1922), and *This Side of Paradise* (1920). Fitzgerald was also a prolific short story writer, who during the 1920s kept himself afloat financially by publishing dozens of tales in popular magazines. "The Curious Case of Benjamin Button" is one such story, a strange and comical piece first published in *Collier's Magazine* in the spring of 1922. It follows the life of its title character, Benjamin Button, who is born as an old man and ages in reverse, growing younger each year. Much of the conflict and comedy in this story come from the disparities between the protagonist's chronological age and the "age" of his unusual body. Benjamin lives a thoroughly conventional life—but does so in reverse. The story ends with him as a mewling baby, forgetful of everything, even "the warm sweet aroma of milk."

In 2008, director David Fincher and screenwriter Eric Roth released a film version of *The Curious Case of Benjamin Button*. It was an interesting departure for Fincher, who had directed violent thrillers like *Se7en* (1995), *Fight Club* (1999), and *Zodiac* (2007). Roth was an experienced screenwriter who was best known for writing *Forrest Gump* (1994). However, adapting the work of a classic author would be new territory for him as well. Roth and Fincher deviated dramatically from the original story, changing its plot and setting, adding new characters, threading a love interest throughout, and, perhaps most significantly, changing its satirical tone. With Fincher directing, and Brad Pitt and Cate Blanchett playing the leads, *Benjamin Button* was designed to be a tentpole film, a literary adaptation whose A-list cast and high production values would appeal to a wide range of viewers.

Film Analysis

Short story and film alike follow the protagonist, Benjamin Button, from birth through death. In Fitzgerald's story, Benjamin's birth scene is played for laughs: emerging from the womb as a little old man, Benjamin immediately demands to be given a rocking chair. Fincher and Roth, how-

F. Scott Fitzgerald, author. Photo via Wikimedia Commons. [Public domain.]

ever, approached Benjamin's birth differently. First, they created a frame story for the film as a whole, which now begins in a New Orleans hospital in the wake of Hurricane Katrina. A dying old woman, played by Cate Blanchett, recalls her life and tells the story of Benjamin. The film then flashes back to the end of World War I. A clockmaker whose son died in the trenches has been commissioned to create a grand clock in New Orleans. When he unveils it, the clock is revealed to be running backward; its maker wishes to turn back time and bring back the generation that was lost in the war. That night, Benjamin is born. The implication seems to be that Benjamin's condition is somehow the product of the reversed clock or the clockmaker's grief. There is an element of magical realism to this material that is quite different from Fitzgerald's humor. In contrast to Fitzgerald's story, the film's Benjamin is born as a sickly, wrinkled baby. He does not speak cantankerously or demand the trappings of old age the way Fitzgerald's character does. An infant trapped in a body that is unnaturally aged, he can only suffer. All of this produces a dramatic shift in tone, away from the comedic and satirical, to the tragic, melodramatic, and sentimental. Although the arc of Benjamin's life is similar across the two versions, it is a life that is seen through a very different sensibility and told for very different purposes.

In Fitzgerald's short story, Benjamin eventually decides, as he gets younger, to marry a woman named Hildegarde. She is a two-dimensional character who serves a convenient foil. For a decade and a half, Benjamin enjoys respectability as a married pillar of the community and the proprietor of a family dry goods business. But he finds, as the age difference between him and his wife keeps widening, that his affections have shifted. Fitzgerald writes: "And here we come to an unpleasant subject which it will be well to pass over as quickly as possible. There was only one thing that worried Benjamin Button; his wife had ceased to attract him." For her part, Hildegarde views Benjamin's condition as an affront to propriety and convention: "There's a right way of doing things and a wrong way. If you've made up your mind to be different from everybody else, I don't suppose I can stop you, but I really don't think it's very considerate." Benjamin goes on to fight in the Spanish American War and to play football for Harvard. Marriage is just another phase of life that Benjamin leaves behind him, and the satirical nature of Fitzgerald's story leaves little room for broken hearts or regrets.

Brad Pitt, star of Benjamin Button (2008). Photo by Georges Biard via Wikimedia Commons.

Fincher and Roth dramatically alter the nature of Benjamin's romantic life. Hildegarde is replaced by Daisy, played by Cate Blanchett, a character who meets Benjamin not once, but at several points in their lives. The character shares a name with Daisy Buchanan, whom Jay Gatsby pined for in *The Great Gatsby*, and possesses some of the qualities and interests of Fitzgerald's wife Zelda. Daisy and Benjamin first meet when she is a child and he an old man, and they reencounter each other several times before finding a point in their respective aging processes when they can be happy together. "We're meeting in the middle," Daisy tells Benjamin during their period as contemporaries and lovers. As time goes on, however, they will be pulled apart. Both Blanchett and Pitt are powerful actors who turn in fine performances throughout the film, and who have real chemistry during the scenes they share at the center of the film. However, the scenes in which their age difference is pronounced—and particularly, when they meet as an old man and a young girl—can be a little unsettling. Though they have a child together, Benjamin must leave home to spare his family from watching him devolve into an ever-younger version of himself. The satirical tone of the original story is nowhere to be found, and the film instead creates an anguished sense of loss as its two protagonists surrender each other to forces outside of their control. In the final phase of their relationship, an elderly Daisy will care for a childlike Benjamin, who is struggling with Alzheimer's. The frame story helps to make Daisy's role more prominent—a considerable challenge given the drama and interest inherent in Benjamin's condition.

In Fincher's film, Benjamin wanders the world twice, once as a young man in an old body and, later, as an old man in a young one. As its protagonist explores the American century, the film takes on a sweeping, cinematic quality. With its southern setting and its structure of following one unusual man through several tumultuous decades of American history, the script bears no small resemblance to Roth's *Forrest Gump*. Coupled with scenes set in atmospheric New Orleans and with Fincher's love for period details, the film is grander and more romantic than it would have been had it stayed rooted in the story's setting of Baltimore. There is a crowd-pleasing, big-screen quality to Benjamin's travel sequences and to Fincher's evocative and beautiful images of bygone eras. Some critics, however, saw this as so much window dressing. One of the questions that viewers will have to answer for themselves is whether Fitzgerald's lean, satirical story can really support the weight of Roth's historical scene setting and his narrative of star-crossed lovers.

The Curious Case of Benjamin Button represented a breakthrough in computer-generated imagery (CGI). Fincher, working with special effects studio Digital Domain, grafted Pitt's digitally aged image onto a series of actors who played his part. In fact, Pitt himself doesn't appear until nearly an hour into the film; the wizened Benjamin of the first part of the film is a digital archetype. Simply put, this film could not have been made five or ten years earlier, as it is grounded in 2008's cutting-edge technology. This is not to say that every audience member or critic thought these effects were worthwhile. In a biting review of the film, Roger Ebert said, "It expends Oscar-worthy talents on an off-putting gimmick." This is a sentiment that several other reviewers echoed, seeing *Benjamin But-*

ton as a film that was impressively constructed but ultimately hollow.

Significance

With *The Curious Case of Benjamin Button*, Paramount Pictures aimed to produce a film that would be both a blockbuster and an award winner. In the final analysis, the film had only moderate success in each arena. With a $150 million budget and another $135 million plowed into marketing and distribution, *Benjamin Button* was an expensive proposition that demanded high market returns. Because it approached the $335.8 million mark in domestic and international sales, it proved narrowly profitable, but it was by no means the runaway hit that the studio had hoped for.

By the same token, the film received mixed reviews from critics. There seems to have been a polarizing quality to its earnestness and sentimentality, causing reviewers to either love or hate the film. A. O. Scott wrote glowingly of *Benjamin Button*, terming it a "triumph of technique" that "sighs with longing and simmers with intrigue while investigating the philosophical conundrums and emotional paradoxes of its protagonist's condition." Peter Bradshaw, on the other hand, called it an "incredible shaggy-puppy of a movie, a cobweb-construction patched together with CGI, prosthetics, gibberish and warm tears."

Benjamin Button had a strong showing in the lead-up to the Academy Awards, garnering thirteen nominations, including Best Picture, Best Actor, Best Director, and Best Adapted Screenplay. It only won, however, in three humbler categories: Production Design, Visual Effects, and Makeup. In the long run, these may be the qualities that *The Curious Case of Benjamin Button* is best remembered for. It represents a remarkable step forward in CGI technology and draws on the talents of some of Hollywood's top actors and filmmakers. Yet none of this seemed to coalesce into a wholly satisfying film that would please either audiences or critics. In the end, *Benjamin Button* may not age well.

—*Matthew Bolton*

Further Reading

Gawande, Atul. *Being Mortal*. Metropolitan Books, 2014.

Meyers, Jeffrey. *Scott Fitzgerald: A Biography*. HarperCollins, 1994.

Raftery, Brian. *Best. Movie. Year. Ever.: How 1999 Blew Up the Big Screen*. Simon & Schuster, 2019.

Bibliography

Bradshaw, Peter. "*The Curious Case of Benjamin Button*." *The Guardian*, 5 Feb. 2009, www.theguardian.com/film/2009/feb/ 06/ benjamin-button-brad-pitt-cate-blanchett. Accessed 13 Apr. 2020.

Ebert, Roger. "And Down He Forgot as Up He Grew." *Roger Ebert.com*, 23 Dec. 2008, www.rogerebert.com/reviews/the-curious-case-of-benjamin-button-2008. Accessed 13 Apr. 2020.

Eller, Claudia. "The Curious Case of Film Economics." *Los Angeles Times*, 23 Jan. 2009, www.latimes.com/archives/ la-xpm-2009-jan-23-fi-button23-story.html. Accessed 13 Apr. 2020.

Fitzgerald, F. Scott. "The Curious Case of Benjamin Button." *The Short Stories of F. Scott Fitzgerald*, edited by Matthew J. Bruccoli, Charles Scribner's Sons, 1998.

Scott, A. O. "It's the Age of a Child Who Grows from a Man." *The New York Times*, 24 Dec. 2008, movies.nytimes.com/2008/12/ 25/movies/25butt.html. Accessed 13 Apr. 2020.

Death of a Salesman

The Play
Author: Arthur Miller (1915-2005)
First published: 1949

The Film
Year released: 1985
Director: Volker Schlöndorff (b. 1939)
Screenplay by: Arthur Miller
Starring: Dustin Hoffman, Kate Reid, John Malkovich, Stephen Lang

Context

Arthur Miller's 1949 play *Death of a Salesman* is considered one of the most important dramas of the twentieth century, not only because of its excellence as a work of art but also because it showed—or at least sought to show—that important tragedies could be written about the lives of "ordinary" people. Greek and Renaissance tragedy, of course, is usually associated with the lives of kings, queens, or other kinds of aristocrats. Miller, whose politics were definitely left-wing and even for a time Communist, sought to show that the "common man" could be the subject of tragic drama. *Death of a Salesman*, moreover, can also be read as a work that indicts larger social forces, especially competitive capitalism, for helping to cause individual tragedies. The "salesman" of the title, Willy Loman, has spent his whole adult life trying to achieve commercial success. His entire self-worth is bound up with his sense of his success as a salesman. As he ages and begins to lose customers, he begins to consider himself a failure, both financially and socially and also as a husband and father. By the end of the play he has committed suicide, partly out of desperation, partly out of guilt, and partly out of love: he hopes that the insurance money his family will receive will help them (especially his son Biff) survive and even succeed.

The 1985 televised film of the play, which was based on a 1984 New York stage production, won wide critical acclaim. It was seen as an unusually successful adaptation of a major drama for television, partly because it was filmed rather than merely videotaped. Critics hailed the broadcast as an example of what television could do at its best. Starring such notable actors as Dustin Hoffman and John Malkovich, this adaptation is still regarded as one of the best filmed versions of any Miller play. The broadcast version was largely faithful to Miller's original script. In fact, Miller, rather than an adaptor, is given credit as the writer of the screenplay. The fact that the play was broadcast on CBS—at that time one of the three major commercial networks—shows several things: first, how much this drama had come to be considered an American classic; second, how well the 1984 stage production had been received; and, finally, how much the television networks during this period wanted to enhance their own stature by being associated with prestigious productions.

Some critics have suggested that the play was relevant not only to the America of the late 1940s but also to the United States of the 1970s and 1980s. Much of the 1970s had been an era of great economic uncertainty. The economy had been suffering from the strange, seemingly unsolvable problem of "stagflation," with prices rapidly rising even as the overall economy seemed stagnant. This economic malaise had helped doom Jimmy Carter's efforts to be reelected President in 1980. Instead, Ronald Reagan swept into office with promises to kill inflation and restore economic growth. After a very painful recession in 1982—partly designed by the Federal Reserve to crush inflation—the economy began booming and continued to boom throughout the 1980s. Reagan was easily reelected in a 49-state landslide in 1984. Miller's play, then, could be seen as especially relevant when it was broadcast in 1985. On the one hand, it probably spoke to many who had endured the same fear of financial failure that Willy Loman feels. On the other hand, the television production could be seen as a warning against the dangers of the materialism that is often associated with the late 1980s. Most Americans, however, were more than happy to escape from the gloom of the 1970s—and materialism seemed an attractive alternative to stagflation.

Film Analysis

The 1985 televised film starred Dustin Hoffman as Willy Loman; Kate Reid as Willy's wife, Linda; John Malkovich as their adult son, Biff; and Stephen Lang as their other adult son, Happy. Some critics complained that the director, Volker Schlöndorff, had failed to turn the play entirely into a full-blown motion picture with consistently "real" settings and outdoor locations. Instead, he had chosen to highlight the work's origins as a play intended for the stage, especially when presenting flashbacks to the family's earlier life and particularly when presenting flashbacks set outside, such as in the family's backyard. Even when focusing on relatively realistic indoor settings, Schlöndorff often deliberately undermined the illusion by letting obviously artificial outdoor settings be seen through windows. These unrealistic settings and locations were *stage* settings and *stage* locations.

Schlöndorff's staging struck some critics as *too* "stagey" and unrealistic. They would have preferred a production similar to the 1951 film starring Fredric March, which opens with Willy driving a car over an obviously real and massive bridge. It features mostly realistic settings of the kind found in the majority of movies, both of that era and of most eras before and since. Many other critics, however, defended Schlöndorff's approach, which must also surely have been approved by Miller. The production's admirers claimed that Schlöndorff had managed to retain all of the virtues of a stage production without simply offering a videotaped recording of one. He had managed to combine realism and symbolism, especially when depicting settings outside the strict confines of the Loman home. Some reviewers saw Schlöndorff's overall approach and achievement as path-breaking, combining the best traits of high-quality filmmaking with the immediacy of a stage production. The film *looks* like a film. When compared with videotaped programs from the 1980s, it still seems fresh and sharp, with strong colors and fine resolutions.

The fact that Schlöndorff could pause and shoot scenes in any order he chose and then string them all together at a later time definitely worked to his artistic advantage. He did not simply have to rely on pointing a few fixed cameras at a stage and recording what happened there. He could arrange shots from many different angles, with much cross-cutting and many close-ups. He could film his characters both in their younger years and again as they aged and then easily shift between time periods in ways that would have been much more difficult to do if recording a stage production in real time. In the film, the Loman family members look young and vigorous; and sometimes they look older and more worn down. When Willy is young, his hair looks blond and relatively full; when he is older, near the end of his life, his hair is thin and gray. Filming the play as a film rather than merely videotaping an actual stage production allowed Schlöndorff to achieve a kind of realism.

The film inevitably differs from the play in various respects. For example, the play opens with a long discussion between Willy and Linda, which is then followed by a similarly long discussion between Biff and Happy. In the film, the two discussions are combined and intercut: the perspective shifts back and forth, sometimes focusing on the parents and sometimes on their sons. This, once again, illustrates how the film allowed for a more complex, more nuanced effect than would have been possible onstage. Such rapid intercutting between one pair of characters and another pair would not have worked as well if performed live: one pair would be seen and awkwardly silent while the other pair was talking. On film, the intercutting and the switching back-and-forth, seems perfectly natural.

For the most part, the film is remarkably faithful to the text and structure of the play—a fact that is especially obvious if one compares and contrasts the 1985 and 1951 films. The conclusion of the latter seems extremely overblown and melodramatic. It spends much time depicting Willy's final drive (a drive that is merely implied in the play). It shows Willy talking to his brother Ben, a figment of his imagination, inside his car as he drives down a main city street passing one brightly lit city block after another with glaring lights and blaring music. In contrast, the 1985 film, like the original play, leaves the final drive to the audience's imagination—a much more effective and understated choice. Whereas Willy's final moments in the 1951 film seem exaggerated and sensational, in the play, as in the 1985 film, those moments are effectively implied rather than blatantly depicted.

Significance

The 1985 film was widely praised when it was originally broadcast and has, perhaps, been even more widely praised in the years since then. It is generally seen as a landmark production and is often used when teaching the play. The film did not do as well in the contemporary television ratings as its producers had hoped, but CBS's decision to air the work and thereby garner prestige paid off. Schlöndorff's *Death of a Salesman* remains famous and important long after the popular fare it competed against has been forgotten. Critics at the time generally praised Hoffman's performance, and so have most critics since then. Some reviewers, however, both then and later, considered him ill-suited to the role. Some thought he was too young for the part; some thought his performance was too intense too early, diminishing some of the impact of the play's forceful later scenes. Others argued that Hoffman, who had not appeared on stage very much for two decades, seemed rusty. For the most part, though, critics then and since greatly admired Hoffman's performance, and indeed the entire cast was strongly praised, especially Kate Reid as Linda.

Some critics actually considered the film superior to the 1984 New York theater revival on which the film was based. They thought the roles were more evenly balanced in the film and that the use of close-ups allowed each actor/character his or her own moment to shine. The television production was sometimes praised as a masterpiece. It was often called one of the best examples imaginable of what television, as a medium, could do when presenting "serious" or "substantial" literature. Miller himself had urged Hoffman to take the role, and the fact that the playwright allowed the stage production to be transferred to the small screen suggests that he must have been pleased with the results Hoffman and his fellow actors had

achieved. Interestingly, few contemporary or later reviewers commented on the play's political implications. Instead, most commentators discussed the film in aesthetic terms, focusing on the acting, the sets, and especially the decision to use high-quality film rather than low-budget videotape. The film, now widely available online and on DVD, does look crisp and fresh with none of the worn-out, washed-out colors of most videotaped programs from the early 1980s.

—*Robert C. Evans, Phd*

Further Reading

Hart, Jonathan. "The Promised End: The Conclusion of Hoffman's *Death of a Salesman*." *Literature Film Quarterly*, vol. 19, no. 1, 1991, p. 60. EBSCOhost, search.ebscohost.com/login.aspx?direct=true&db=lkh&AN=9609033892&site=ehost-live. Accessed 7 Apr. 2020.

Murphy, Brenda, editor. *Critical Insights: Death of a Salesman.* Salem Press, 2010.

Sickels, Amy. "Critical Contexts: Arthur Miller's *Death of a Salesman*: History of Criticism." *Critical Insights: Death of a Salesman*, edited by Brenda Murphy, Jan. 2010, pp. 76-91. EBSCOhost, search.ebscohost.com/login.aspx?direct=true&db=lkh&AN=48218066&site=ehost-live. Accessed 7 Apr. 2020.

Bibliography

Abbotson, Susan C. W. *Critical Companion to Arthur Miller: A Literary Reference to His Life and Work.* Facts on File, 2007.

Ferres, John H. *Arthur Miller: A Reference Guide.* G. K. Hall & Co., 1979.

Koorey, Stefani. *Arthur Miller's Life and Literature: An Annotated and Comprehensive Guide.* Scarecrow Press, 2000.

Doctor Zhivago

The Novel
Author: Boris Pasternak (1890-1960)
First published: 1957

The Film
Year released: 1965
Director: David Lean (1908-91)
Screenplay by: Robert Bolt
Starring: Geraldine Chaplin, Julie Christie, Tom Courtenay, Omar Sharif, Rod Steiger

Context

Both the novel and the film versions of Doctor Zhivago were significant at the time of their release partly for providing inside views of the birth and development of the Soviet Union, the communist regime that replaced Czarist Russia following World War I. The revolution of 1917, followed by several years of civil war before the Communists finally gained complete control, resulted in a sprawling dictatorship that dominated much of Europe and northern Asia. The Soviet Communists sought world revolution, supposedly to free workers everywhere from capitalist domination. By the early 1940s, however, the Soviet Union, ruled by the tyrant Joseph Stalin, was fighting for its very existence. It had been surprise-attacked by Nazi Germany, ruled by the fascist tyrant Adolf Hitler, Stalin's one-time foe, then ally, then foe again. From 1941 to 1945 the United States and other capitalist Allied nations joined Stalin to defeat Hitler in World War II. After that war's end, however, a Cold War soon arose between the western democracies (especially the United States) and the Soviet Union, eventually aligned with Communist China.

During the immediate postwar period, Russian author Boris Pasternak began intensive work on the novel *Doctor Zhivago*. Like many Russian intellectuals, he had first sympathized with the communist revolution and supported the czar's fall. But soon, he and many others began suffering under Stalin's bloody dictatorship. By the time *Doctor Zhivago* was smuggled out of the Soviet Union and first published, in Italian, in 1957, the Cold War had the real potential to devolve into an nuclear holocaust. In fact, it almost did so, in 1962, during the Cuban missile crisis.

For all these reasons, Americans and others in the west were eager to read books (and see films) about the rise and evolution of Soviet communism and about the lives of people trapped behind the Iron Curtain. Western publication of Pasternak's novel—which was banned inside the Soviet Union—was thus considered a provocation by the Soviets. When Pasternak won the 1958 Nobel Prize in Lit-

Author Boris Pasternak. Photo via Wikimedia Commons. [Public domain.]

Omar Sharif and Julie Christie from the 1965 film Doctor Zhivago. Photo via Wikimedia Commons. [Public domain.]

erature, he was told he could never return to his homeland if he left to accept the prize. He therefore declined it. In 1960, he died. Not until the late 1980s, when the Soviet Union was on its last legs, could the novel finally be published in Russia and Pasternak's son finally retrieve his father's Nobel Prize.

Both on the page and on the screen, therefore, *Doctor Zhivago* was interesting partly because it seemed politically timely. Both works showed the nature and value of mere existence for people who had had to endure the loss of political, social, moral, intellectual, and personal freedom. By the time the book and film were released, the world had suffered through two massive wars and seemed faced with the prospect of nuclear annihilation. Individual bravery and integrity, the consolations of personal love and loving family ties, and the sheer strength of human nature when faced with severe physical and psychological threats are all key themes of *Doctor Zhivago*, both as fiction and as cinema.

Film Analysis

Director David Lean and screenwriter Robert Bolt faced a daunting task in trying to squeeze the complicated plot of Pasternak's massive novel into a film—even with the three-hour running time of the final cut. While the title character, played by Omar Sharif, remains central, the filmmakers inevitably jettisoned various plot developments and major characters (such as Zhivago's close boy-

hood friend). They also radically revised the book's structure, particularly by treating the main plot as a flashback reported from the perspective of Zhivago's Communist half-brother, General Yevgraf Zhivago (Alec Guinness). He tells one of Zhivago's grown daughters (Rita Tushingham) about the parents she never knew: her dashing, romantic, poetic father and her beautiful, captivating, heroic mother (Lara, played by Julie Christie).

Their tale is both tragic and inspiring. Yevgraf begins by describing the death of Zhivago's mother when Zhivago was still a young boy; the absence and death of Zhivago's father; the privileged life Zhivago enjoyed while living with wealthy friends of his mother; and his love for and eventual marriage with Tonya (Geraldine Chaplin), their attractive daughter. Yevgraf also recounts the tragic life of the beautiful Lara, whose widowed mother, a dress-maker, is romantically involved with a wealthy, well-connected cynic named Victor Komarovsky (Rod Steiger). Komarovsky soon seduces the teenaged Lara. When Lara's mother learns of this affair, she tries to commit suicide but is saved by a prominent physician who, coincidentally, is Zhivago's mentor. Zhivago meets Lara for the first time while accompanying the physician on this emergency call. He sees her again later, at a high-society Christmas party, where she arrives with a gun and tries to kill Komarovsky, who has recently raped her, but only succeeds in wounding him. Having destroyed her old life, she marries a young, idealistic revolutionary named Pasha (Tom Courtenay), who has long loved her.

Lean depicts ruling-class extravagance and brutal czarist oppression, but he shows disaster truly descending on Russia during World War I. Practically all the major characters suffer not only during that war but also during the ensuing revolution, the resulting civil war, and the final establishment of Communism. Pasha volunteers and is soon apparently killed (although he later reemerges as a brutal revolutionary nicknamed "Strelnikov"). In the meantime, Zhivago, serving as a frontline physician, accidentally encounters Lara again. Although searching for Pasha, she soon begins assisting Zhivago as a nurse. Love develops, but their true affair only begins later, after both have moved east, away from Moscow. Zhivago, torn between his love for his devoted wife and little son and his secret passion for Lara, eventually loses touch with the now-pregnant Tonya when he is kidnapped by partisans needing a doctor's services.

When he finally escapes and begins looking for his wife and children, he learns that they have been exiled. But he does meet Lara again, and they enjoy a brief, precarious bliss. Eventually the hard-edged Komarovsky shows up and tries to persuade them to flee further east with him, to safety. Although Zhivago refuses, the pregnant Lara goes, intent on protecting the child she is carrying—the child who is later tracked down, as an adult, by Yevgraf. Zhivago himself has one more chance encounter with Lara when he is older, worn down, and extremely weak. He sees her walking in a Moscow street, but unfortunately, she does not see him. When he tries to chase her, a heart attack kills him. Lara does, however, briefly attend his funeral, as he has become a famous poet who has written a whole series of popular poems about her.

The film above all is a love story. Although the character of Zhivago is sometimes condemned as a self-centered philanderer who cheated on a loving, loyal, intelligent, and beautiful wife, the complexity of the romantic relationships is realistic and compelling. Zhivago has also been criticized as passive, but he does display physical strength, bravery, and endurance, especially when he trudges for months across grim frozen landscapes driven only by a passion to return to his long-lost wife and child. Furthermore, virtually all the major characters are sympathetic, rounded human beings whose motives and behaviors seemed both comprehensible and morally complicated. Even the obvious villains—Komarovsky and Strelnikov—cannot be dismissed as mere brutes. Steiger as Komarovsky, in particular, is a fascinating rogue: suave and cruel, abusive and eloquent.

The film's physical settings are as vividly memorable as the characters. The diverse landscapes and changing seasons become characters in themselves: the early beauty of snow-covered Moscow; the blood-covered streets of the capital after imperial troops cut down peaceful protestors; the depressing makeshift hospital, packed with wounded soldiers; the endless, unforgettable train ride in a stinking cattle car, into which Zhivago and his family are packed with scores of other suffering people; the stunning speed of the short, clean, bright-red train that races by, carrying the fearsome Strelnikov. Perhaps above all is the haunting beauty of the snow- and ice-saturated dilapidated mansion where Lara and Zhivago enjoy a few weeks of fragile, loving peace together before Komarovsky reappears.

Lean effectively employed similarities and contrasts of all sorts. The movie both opens and closes with scenes of Yevgraf talking with Zhivago's daughter. Early in the film, Zhivago sits next to Lara on a streetcar, not suspecting her later significance in his life, and near the end he sees her again from yet another streetcar, just before he collapses, dead, while trying to pursue her. Sharif changes from a fresh-faced, bright-eyed young man to a wrinkled, worn-down, worn-out old man whose heart is broken both symbolically and in fact. Similarly, Pasha changes from a young, determined idealist into the dreaded, hard-hearted killer Strelnikov. The film shows history's often tragic impact on individuals, but it also shows the courage and resilience some people muster to cope with tragedies they cannot escape.

Love is a major theme of the film, but the love presented is not sappy. It is instead hard-won and difficult to preserve, and the film manages to present characters who seem ethically complex: Zhivago both loves his wife and cheats on her; he both loves Lara and knows that his love in some ways is wrong. Lara deceives her mother with her mother's boyfriend but still manages to seem, especially by the end of the film, like a young woman who learns from her mistakes. Even Komarovsky has his good points, especially near the end, when it is he who prevents Lara and the baby she is carrying from being slaughtered, whatever his darker motives.

But the film, importantly, resists any easy, happy ending. Tanya, the now-grown daughter of Lara and Zhivago, may have some hope of happiness in her future, but she probably will never experience the kind of opulence and prospects her father enjoyed when he was her age. If the movie ends with a shot of a rainbow, that shot is simply one last reminder, by Lean, that nature can be beautiful even when humans make a mess of their own and others' lives.

Significance

Lean's film at first received chilly responses from prominent reviewers. Many attacked him and Bolt for treating a major historical period as mere backdrop to a love story. They thought the movie simplified the book's plot, structure, character, and themes and showed more interest in panoramas of stunning landscapes than in insightful treatment of larger issues or complex characters. The film was often condemned as sentimental. But the public soon disagreed. Helped by a twenty-minute cut from the first version of the film, an expensive publicity campaign, and a brief, recurring musical motif that became an earworm, *Doctor Zhivago* became, and has remained, one of the highest-grossing films of all time.

In the twenty-first century *Doctor Zhivago* is considered a classic and remains popular with viewers. Critical opinion has improved not only in the West but also in Russia, and the film has been both shown and taught since the fall of the Soviet Union. In some ways, the movie has fared better than the book: few literary critics now regard Pasternak's novel as nearly as important as it first seemed, and it is probably more often the film that leads people to the book rather than vice versa. Although at first regarded by some critics as too romantic and insufficiently historical, Lean's movie now seems anything but naïve in its depiction of the ways historical change can crush the lives of individual persons and of whole societies.

—Robert C. Evans, PhD

Further Reading

Melnerney, John M. "Lean's *Zhivago*: A Reappraisal." *Literature Film Quarterly*, vol. 15, no. 1, Mar. 1987, p. 43. *Literary Reference Center*, search.ebscohost.com/login.aspx?direct=true&db=lfh&AN=6904729&site=ehost-live. Accessed 26 Dec. 2018.

Morson, Gary Saul. "Crimes against Culture." *New Criterion*, vol. 35, no. 9, May 2017, pp. 13-18. *Literary Reference Center*, search.ebscohost.com/login.aspx?direct=true&db=lfh&AN=122884602&site=ehost-live. Accessed 26 Dec. 2018.

Tarr, Kathleen. "The Trappist Monk and Pasternak's Tree." *Sewanee Review*, vol. 121, no. 3, Summer 2013, pp. 449-59. *Literary Reference Center*, search.ebscohost.com/login.aspx?direct=true&db=lfh&AN=89882463&site=ehost-live. Accessed 26 Dec. 2018.

Tomei, Christine D. "*Doctor Zhivago*." *Masterplots II: Juvenile & Young Adult Literature Series*, Supplement, Mar. 1997, pp. 1-2. *Literary Reference Center*, search.ebscohost.com/login.aspx?direct=true&db=lfh&AN=103331JYS10919720000021&site=ehost-live. Accessed 26 Dec. 2018.

Bibliography

Anderegg, Michael A. *David Lean*. Twayne, 1984.

Brownlow, Kevin. *David Lean: A Biography*. St. Martin's, 1996.

"Dr. Zhivago (1965)." *Internet Movie Database*, www.imdb.com/title/tt0059113/externalreviews?ref_=tt_ov_rt. Accessed 26 Dec. 2018.

Phillips, Gene D. *Beyond the Epic: The Life and Films of David Lean*. UP of Kentucky, 2006.

Santas, Constantine. *The Epic Films of David Lean*. Scarecrow, 2012.

Williams, Melanie. *David Lean.* Manchester UP, 2014.

Don't Look Now

The Novel
Author: Daphne du Maurier (1907-89)
First published: 1971

The Film
Year released: 1973
Director: Nicolas Roeg (1928-2018)
Screenplay by: Allan Scott, Chris Bryant
Starring: Julie Christie, Donald Sutherland, Hilary Mason, Clelia Matania

Context
Best-selling novelist Daphne du Maurier is mostly known for her historical romances set in or near her beloved Cornwall, England. Although she had a devoted following and financial success, literary critics often voiced various complaints about her novels, taking issue with their formulaic plots, stock characterizations, and a failure to deal with contemporary issues. Later critics, however, have been more generous, appreciating her creative incorporation of gothic elements. *My Cousin Rachel* (1951), for example, opens with a child observing a dead body, swinging, after a public hanging. The dark and ominous tone of the beginning resonates throughout the rest of the novel. Du Maurier also explores the darker aspects of love and human nature in *Jamaica Inn* (1936) and *Rebecca* (1938); her short story "The Birds" was famously adapted into a film of the same name by Alfred Hitchcock in 1963.

As the example of "The Birds" illustrates, du Maurier's short stories often focus on a mysterious paranormal phenomenanon, in contradistinction to the novels, which tend to focus on gothic-infused love relationships. In "Don't Look Now," first published in the collection of the same name in 1971, the parents of a recently deceased child meet a psychic who has communicated with their daughter. Equally eerie is "The Breakthrough" (1971), in which a scientist works on a secret project to separate and trap the soul, or the body's energy, after death. In these stories and others, du Maurier builds mystery and suspense using paranormal elements, such as psychics, unexplained phenomena, and life-afer-death exploration.

Her body of work remains widely read and has proven to be attractive material for translation to the big screen on several occasions. The film adaptations *Jamaica Inn* (1939; 1983 for television), *Rebecca* (1940), *My Cousin Rachel* (1952, 2017), *The Birds*, and *Don't Look Now* (1973), all of which focus on gothic or paranormal aspects, have been largely successful and well received.

Film Analysis
Overall, the film adaptation of Daphne du Maurier's short story "Don't Look Now" adheres to the original short story's plot, characters, and tone, while adding several scenes to help to flesh out the short story. Director Nicolas Roeg, working on only his third project in that role following mixed commercial and critical success with the films *Performance* (1970) and *Walkabout* (1971) but having spent several years as a cinematographer, took a story around fifty pages long and developed it into a two-hour film. To accomplish this, he created a backstory for the Baxter family on the day of their daughter's death and altered some elements to establish symbolic significances for water, glass, and the color red.

Du Maurier's story centers on the loss of a child and the impact of that loss on the child's parents, John and Laura. Du Maurier sets her story entirely in Venice, Italy, weeks after their daughter's death. Readers only understand the aftermath of their loss and how the parents have continued to struggle. Roeg, however, sets the film in England first, at the family's home on the day of the death of their daughter, Christine (Sharon Williams). This added scene is lengthy and significant in that it introduces the symbolism and foreshadows an important plot element. In this scene, Christine and her brother, Johnny (Nicholas Salter), are playing outside, unsupervised. Christine is wearing a red raincoat and playing with a ball near a pond. Johnny is riding his bicycle and punctures his tire when he runs over and breaks a pane of glass. Their parents are in the house working, with Laura (Julie Christie) reading and John (Donald Sutherland) preparing slides for his architectural restoration of a church in Venice. John spills a glass of water on the slide, and the slide bleeds red. Shortly after the spill, John gets a premonition and runs outside, where he finds Christine under water in the pond. She has drowned, and John cannot resuscitate her.

The scene establishes John's psychic abilities early on, much earlier than in du Maurier's story. John does not yet realize he has psychic abilities and will resist that notion for the duration of the film. One of the key conflicts of the film, and of the original story, is John's skepticism about the psychic they encounter and Laura's firm belief in her. By including John's premonition of Christine's death in this added scene, the conflict is established earlier and developed more fully over the course of the film. Roeg also adds several other scenes, such as Laura talking with the psychic in the restaurant bathroom, a lovemaking scene between John and Laura, and John's near-fatal fall from a scaffold while directing the church restoration. These scenes develop, visually and emotionally, the story's paranormal themes and heightened suspense as well as the reconciliation after loss that John and Laura experience.

Additionally, the opening scene sets the stage for the symbolism of broken glass, water, and the color red throughout the work. Although these elements are largely absent in the short story, as symbols they are an important part of the film, and Roeg develops them fully. Du Maurier uses body stature to connect Christine with the person later identified as a killer who has been terrorizing Venice, while in the film, Roeg enhances that connection by also having both characters wear red coats. This highlights the emotional and psychological aspects of death and loss. Roeg also employs the color red to signify blood, such as in the moving stain created when the slide becomes wet; Christine's red-striped ball, which Laura brings to Venice in her suitcase; and the blood pooling under John's head when he is stabbed.

To a somewhat lesser degree, Roeg emphasizes water and broken glass as symbols. First, he changes the way Christine dies. In the short story, she dies of meningitis, but in the film, she dies by drowning (which also adds another level to the parents' grief, as the death was caused by a potentially preventable accident rather than illness). Wa-

ter imagery is then repeated in all the numerous shots of John and Laura walking along the Venetian canals and the floating vaporettos. John also sees a body pulled up from the depths of the canal and later finds a naked doll, reminiscent of a dead baby, near the canal's edge, all reinforcing Christine's death and how it haunts him. There are also several depictions of broken glass, such as when Laura faints and falls after her encounter with the psychic in the restaurant bathroom, leading to a close-up of spilled water and broken glass on the floor. In their totality, these repeated images of red, water, and broken glass signify the near constant presence of Christine and her parents' feelings of loss.

Another distinct aspect of the film is Roeg's use of montage editing, defined as a series of short clips organized sequentially to condense information and time. Roeg uses this technique to great effect in several situations, including the opening, where images of the red stain, growing and moving in the spilled water, is sequenced between shots of John trying and failing to revive Christine after she drowned. Here, the water and red symbolism, seen in both shots, strengthens the emotional impact and horror of Christine's death. Roeg also employs montage editing in Laura and John's sex scene, where they reconnect for the first time since Christine's death. Brief, explicit clips of the sexual encounter are intercut with equally brief clips of the couple separately getting dressed afterwards, creating the effect of blending the past, present, and future to suggest that all moments in time are interconnected. Another example comes during the scene near the end of the film in which John experiences flashbacks from throughout his life. The rapid succession of shots suggests the fleeting nature of time and reinforces a sense of John's psychic sensitivity.

In *Don't Look Now*, Roeg enhances and develops on du Maurier's story. The result is a suspenseful and poignant film that makes strong use of added scenes, an emphasis on symbolism, and the montage style of film editing.

Significance

Since its release in 1973, critics have come to appreciate *Don't Look Back* for its innovative editing and cinematography, as well as its psychological approach to horror. The following year, the film was nominated for several BAFTA (British Academy of Film and Television Arts) Awards, including best film, best direction, best actress for Christie, best actor for Sutherland, and best film editing, and won the award for best cinematography. In addition to its innovative qualities, the adaptation also stirred controversy due to Roeg's inclusion of the explicit sex scene between protagonists John and Laura. In the United States, Roeg cut nine frames from the film to avoid the X rating, while in the United Kingdom, no cuts were required. Although the film did receive an X rating in the United Kingdom, the controversy fueled ticket sales.

Perhaps the most criticized aspect of the film has been its ending. Michael Dempsey, reviewing the film for *Film Quarterly*, and Sam Jordison, writing for *The Guardian*, thought the final reveal of the serial killer was gimmicky rather than shocking. Almost thirty years later, however, in a 2002 review, critic Roger Ebert reassessed the film's ending, suggesting that the killer can be viewed as symbolic rather than literal. Many critics have since noted the film as a classic, with especial appreciation for Roeg's innovative montage editing, use of symbolism, and the portrayal of the psychological aspects of dread and loss associated with the death of a child.

—*Marybeth Rua-Larsen*

Further Reading

Tooze, Jessica. "Daphne Du Maurier's Cornwall." *Britain*, Mar. 2014, pp. 54-60.

Von der Lippe, George B. "Death in Venice in Literature and Film: Six 20th-Century Versions." *Mosaic: An Interdisciplinary Critical Journal*, vol. 32, no. 1, 1999, pp. 35-54.

Wisker, Gina. "Don't Look Now! The Compulsions and Revelations of Daphne du Maurier's Horror Writing." *Journal of Gender Studies*, vol. 8, no. 1, 1999, pp. 19-33.

Bibliography

Dempsey, Michael. Review of *Don't Look Now*, directed by Nicolas Roeg. *Film Quarterly*, vol. 27, no. 3, 1974, pp. 39-43.

Ebert, Roger. Review of *Don't Look Now*, directed by Nicolas Roeg. *RogerEbert.com*, 13 Oct. 2002, www.rogerebert.com/reviews/great-movie-dont-look-now-1974. Accessed 22 Dec. 2018.

Jordison, Sam. "*Don't Look Now*: Reading the Film." Review of *Don't Look Now*, directed by Nicolas Roeg. *The Guardian*, 27 Oct. 2011, www.theguardian.com/books/2011/oct/27/dont-look-now-film-du-maurier. Accessed 22 Dec. 2018.

Ohlin, Alix. "Life Was Sometimes Lovely and Sometimes Rather Sad: Du Maurier Reconsidered." *Los Angeles Review of Books*, 21 June 2012, lareviewofbooks.org/article/life-was-sometimes-lovely-and-sometimes-rather-sad-du-maurier-reconsidered/#!. Accessed 9 Dec. 2018.

Dr. Strangelove or: How I Learned to Stop Worrying and Love the Bomb

The Novel
Author: Peter George (1924-66), writing as Peter Bryant
First published: Two Hours to Doom, 1958, in the United Kingdom

The Film
Year released: 1964
Director: Stanley Kubrick (1928-99)
Screenplay by: Stanley Kubrick, Peter George, Terry Southern
Starring: Peter Sellers, George C. Scott, Sterling Hayden, Slim Pickens, James Earl Jones

Context

The Cold War (1945-89) began just after World War II. The term "cold war" was popularized by writer George Orwell in a 1945 essay, "You and the Atom Bomb," in which Orwell correctly predicted that geopolitical and ideological hostility would prevail between superpowers, or those nations best able to afford to build and stockpile nuclear weapons. Two such superpowers emerged postwar: the United States and the Soviet Union. The Cold War heated up and cooled down several times before petering out in the early 1990s with the dissolution of the Soviet Union. Flashpoints included the Soviet occupation of European nations like Hungary and Czechoslovakia in the late 1940s; the first Russian atomic bomb detonation in 1949, and the Korean War between 1950 and 1953. The superpowers came perilously close to waging nuclear war in October 1962, during the Cuban Missile Crisis.

Between the late 1940s and early 1960s, Cold War tensions yielded an outpouring of literature. Writers became preoccupied with various aspects of the superpower standoff and the prospect of mutually assured destruction. Espionage, political machinations, sinister conspiracies, nuclear holocaust, and postapocalyptic scenarios all became subjects of interest. Orwell's *1984* (1949) and Jack Finney's *Invasion of the Body Snatchers* (1954), for example, metaphorically explored the possibilities of Soviet dominance. Works like Graham Greene's *The Quiet American* (1955) focused on behind-the-scenes manipulations. Spies were especially popular, as in Ian Fleming's *From Russia with Love* (1957), John le Carré(c)'s *Call for the Dead* (1961), and Len Deighton's *Ipcress File* (1962). The aftereffects of atomic warfare were brilliantly de-

picted in novels like Nevil Shute's *On the Beach* (1957) and Pat Frank's *Alas Babylon* (1959).

In 1958, Peter Bryan George, a Royal Air Force Bomber Command flight officer who wrote as Peter Bryant, published *Two Hours to Doom*, a realistic novel that showed how a nuclear war might plausibly start. Pub-

Stanley Kubrick. Photo via Columbia Pictures/Wikimedia Commons. [Public domain.]

lished that same year in the United States as *Red Alert*, George's novel centers around a simple but frightening idea. A deranged US Air Force general, for his own twisted reasons, launches an entire wing of nuclear bombers against the Soviet Union. Both governments frantically attempt to recall or eliminate the bombers to prevent triggering a secret doomsday device that will kill all life on Earth.

Film Analysis

In 1964, director Stanley Kubrick, who for years was interested in nuclear strategy, bought the rights to *Red Alert*. George's novel served as the basis of a project that would become *Dr. Strangelove or: How I Learned to Stop Worrying and Love the Bomb* (1964). Initially, Kubrick planned to make a serious film, reflecting both the sus-

penseful plot and the crisp, well-informed tone of *Red Alert*. The film's first working title, influenced by the book's British title, was *Edge of Doom*. However, as Kubrick and George worked on the screenplay, the director envisioned the story as a black comedy. A later title—*The Delicate Balance of Terror*—indicated the change in direction.

At the recommendation of actor Peter Sellers, who had appeared in Kubrick's *Lolita* (1962) and was impressed by Terry Southern and Mason Hoffenberg's satirical novel *Candy* (1958), Kubrick invited Southern to contribute his unique brand of humor to the script. George's novelization of the almost-completed screenplay (both 1963) included a prologue and epilogue that made it seem as if the script was part of an alien report on the causes of the Earth's demise. The novelization, screenplay, and film all

Peter Sellers in the title role. Photo via Columbia Pictures/Wikimedia Commons. [Public domain.]

share the same title: *Dr. Strangelove or: How I Learned to Stop Worrying and Love the Bomb*. The plotline of the source material was essentially retained, with certain embellishments. Like the novel, the film setting focused upon three locations: a US Air Force base, a Strategic Air Command B-52 bomber, and a meeting place where the US President and upper-echelon military and political leaders plan strategy.

In turning the story into dark satire, the first things to change were character names. Their new handles instantly alert viewers that proceedings should not be taken at face value. The demented Air Force brigadier general Quinten in George's novel became General Jack D. Ripper (Sterling Hayden), a man obsessed with the purity of "precious bodily fluids" in the film. The general's executive officer, an American named Major Paul Howard, was turned into a British exchange officer, Group Captain Lionel Mandrake (Peter Sellers), a subtle reference perhaps to the hallucinogenic qualities of the narcotic mandrake root. The pilot of the featured B-52 bomber (*Alabama Angel*, renamed *Leper Colony*), Clint Brown, transformed into Major "King" Kong (Slim Pickens). The president of the United States, unnamed in the novel, is suggestively called President Merkin Muffley (Peter Sellers). Likewise, the unseen Soviet Union leader, simply called "the Marshal" in *Red Alert*, now has a name: Premier Dimitri Kissoff. The officer directing the attack on the air base (once "Sonora," later "Burpelson"), originally named Lieutenant Colonel Andrew Mackenzie, performs in *Dr. Strangelove* as Colonel "Bat" Guano (Keenan Wynn). The Air Force chief of staff with the confidence-boosting name General Steele morphed into unhinged General Buck Turgidson (George C. Scott)—a bizarre practice run for the actor's next role as a high-ranking military officer, his Academy Award-winning performance as the titular lead in *Patton* (1970).

The film's title character does not appear in the novel. Dr. Strangelove (Peter Sellers) was the third of four roles Sellers was scheduled to play. Though he mastered a Texas accent, he bailed on the part of "King" Kong after breaking a leg. Sellers had often played multiple characters in film shorts and television programs from the early 1950s. He continued the practice throughout his career in such features as *The Mouse That Roared* (1959) and *The Prisoner of Zenda* (1979), among others. Strangelove—his unusual name is explained on-screen as a rough translation of his German surname Merkwürdigliebe—does not show up until late in the film and is present in only a

few scenes. Yet the character is indelibly associated with the film, thanks to Sellers's manic, largely improvised and laugh-inducing performance. A former Nazi scientist, now a presidential adviser confined to a wheelchair, Strangelove is physically characterized by his ruthlessly right-leaning hairdo, tinted glasses, clenched voice, peculiar accent, and a black- gloved hand seemingly with a mind of its own. He sometimes forgets where he is and addresses the president as "Mein Führer." Strangelove expresses practical, if licentious, ideas about preserving the human species after the apocalypse.

Kubrick devoted much time and thought to *Dr. Strangelove*'s film sets. The interior mock-up of the B-52 was afterward declared by experts to be astonishingly accurate. This was in keeping with the underlying truth of the outlandish concept propelling the plot. Nuclear command-and-control was an actual US policy authorizing military commanders to launch nuclear attacks that were almost impossible to recall once they passed a fail-safe point. A more original visual was the film's War Room, a fictional location that substituted for the novel's Pentagon conference room. Said to be deep beneath the White House, the strikingly designed War Room graphically displays US bombers as they penetrate Russian territory, aimed at lighted targets representing military bases and missile complexes. The set provides an opportunity to use one of the film's most memorable lines. As General Turgidson wrestles the Russian ambassador, Alexi de Sadeski (Peter Bull), for control of a tiny spy camera, the president declares: "You can't fight in here! This is the War Room!"

The film's stark, dynamically lit black-and-white look is faithful to the novel's underlying theme of the absurdity of war. The exciting, accelerating pace of the novel, with chapters set just moments apart to show how much can happen in so little time, is reproduced with quick cuts between the three settings. Martial music (a taut instrumental version of "When Johnny Comes Marching Home") builds as the B-52 bomber, crippled by Russian defensive weapons, limps toward its target. A viewer might be forgiven for secretly rooting on the crewmen (including James Earl Jones, in his film debut), even if their mission's success means the end of the world. The image of Kong straddling the bomb and riding it like a bronco to the ground (a sequence not found in the novel) will linger long in the memory, as will the sight of Strangelove, who regains the use of his legs just before multiple nuclear bombs of the doomsday device explode to Vera Lynn's 1939 song "We'll Meet Again (Don't Know Where, Don't Know When)." A slapstick pie-fight sequence originally intended to close the film was mercifully edited out of the finished product. In the novel, the Doomsday device does not go off and the world is saved.

Significance

Dr. Strangelove was scheduled to open on November 22, 1963. However, the assassination of US President John F. Kennedy that day pushed the film's release date to January 29, 1964. A further complication was the existence of a competing film with an almost identical plot also being produced at Columbia Pictures: Sidney Lumet's *Fail-Safe* (1964), from the 1962 novel of the same name by Eugene Burdick and Harvey Wheeler. The two films were so similar, in fact, that Stanley Kubrick and Peter George sued for copyright infringement and settled out of court. *Fail-Safe*, though critically praised when it was released more than eight months after *Dr. Strangelove*, failed at the box office.

Kubrick's film returned more than $9.4 million in US box office revenues on a $1.8 million budget. Reviews were mostly positive. The novel and film can perhaps even be jointly credited with helping to improve security measures surrounding nuclear weapons, as crucial members of the Department of Defense were already aware of *Red Alert*.

Dr. Strangelove received four Academy Award nominations, including for best picture, best director, best adapted screenplay, and best actor (Sellers). Although the film did not go on to win any Oscars, it won several prestigious awards including three British Academy of Film and Television Arts (BAFTA) awards, a Writers Guild of America best comedy award, a Hugo Award, and a New York Film Critics best director award.

Appreciation of *Dr. Strangelove* has grown in the decades since its initial release. The film was ranked thirty-ninth on the American Film Institute's (AFI) 2007 100 Years...100 Movies—Tenth Anniversary Edition list, and number three on the AFI's 100 Funniest Movies of All Time list. Many critics feel that the film is one of Kubrick's best, in a canon that includes such outstanding and well-known visual entertainments as *The Killing* (1956), *Paths of Glory* (1957), *Spartacus* (1960), *Lolita* (1962), *2001: A Space Odyssey* (1968), *A Clockwork Orange* (1971), *The Shining* (1980) and *Full Metal Jacket* (1987).

—*Jack Ewing*

Further Reading

Craig, Campbell, and Fredrik Logevall. *America's Cold War: The Politics of Insecurity*. Belknap Press, 2012.

Ruchti, Ulrich, Sybil Taylor, and Alexander Walker. *Stanley Kubrick, Director:* A Visual Analysis. W.W. Norton & Company, 2000.

Bibliography

Bonanos, Christopher. "How Weegee Gave Dr. Strangelove His Voice." *Slate*, 5 June 2018, slate.com/culture/2018/06/the-photographer-weegee-captured-the-pie-fight-scene-on-the-set-of-dr-strangelove.html. Accessed 16 Dec. 2018.

Denby, David. "The Half-Century Anniversary of 'Dr. Strangelove.'" *The New Yorker*, 13 May 2014, www.newyorker.com/culture/culture-desk/the-half-century-anniversary-of-dr-strangelove. Accessed 16 Dec. 2018.

Gady, Franz-Stefan. "'Dr. Strangelove' and the Insane Reality of Nuclear Command-and-Control." *The Diplomat*, 5 Jan. 2018, thediplomat.com/2018/01/dr-strangelove-and-the-insane-reality-of-nuclear-command-and-control/. Accessed 16 Dec. 2018.

George, Peter. *Dr. Strangelove or: How I Learned to Stop Worrying and Love the Bomb*. Expanded edition. Candy Jar Books, 2015.

Hayles, David. "Is This the Best Film Set Ever Designed? On 'Dr. Strangelove's' War Room." *New Statesman*, 5 Nov. 2014, www.newstatesman.com/culture/2014/11/best-film-set-ever-designed-dr-strangelove-s-war-room. Accessed 16 Dec. 2018.

Schlosser, Eric. "Almost Everything in 'Dr. Strangelove' Was True." *The New Yorker*, 17 Jan. 2014, www.newyorker.com/news/news-desk/almost-everything-in-dr-strangelove-was-true. Accessed 16 Dec. 2018.

Drive

The Novel
Author: James Sallis (b. 1944)
First published: 2005

The Film
Year released: 2011
Director: Nicolas Winding Refn (b. 1970)
Screenplay by: Hossein Amini
Starring: Ryan Gosling, Carey Mulligan, Bryan Cranston, Oscar Isaac, Christina Hendricks, Ron Perlman

Context

Drive is a short novel written by American crime writer James Sallis. Dark, gritty, and existential, it follows the journey of an unnamed man who spends his days as a stunt driver and his nights driving for the criminals of Los Angeles. The first book in the two-part series, it reflects Sallis's myriad literary influences. Sallis began his career as a short story science fiction writer in the 1960s. He would go on to write the well-received *Lew Griffin* series about an alcoholic amateur detective as well as the *John Turner* series about an ex-con who becomes a deputy sheriff. Like these previous series, *Drive* focuses on a complex antihero whose good intentions are often muddied by his morally questionable behavior. In many ways, the book is reminiscent of the early twentieth century pulp and noir movements in its celebration of lurid crimes, overt violence, double crossing, and revenge. Although stylistically more experimental, tonally *Drive* can be compared to the works of crime writers like Dennis Lehane, Elmore Leonard, and Richard Price.

Drive received positive reviews upon its publication in 2005. Shortly after, its film rights were optioned by producers Marc Platt and Adam Siegel. When actor Ryan Gosling signed on to play the lead, he was given the power to choose a director and subsequently tapped Danish filmmaker Nicolas Winding Refn. At that time, Refn was best known for making dark, violent films like *Pusher* (1996), *Valhalla Rising* (2009), and *Bronson* (2008). Although *Drive* was Refn's first American film, it proved to be a thematic continuation of his previous work by focusing on violence, crime, and masculinity. *Drive* was highly anomalistic for its time. Where most action films of the early 2010s focused on outlandish stunts, *Drive* focused primarily on its protagonist's experience. In this way, it is a neo-noir reminiscent of a previous cinematic era and is most comparable to films like *Point Blank* (1967), *The Driver* (1978), *Thief* (1981), and *To Live and Die in L.A.* (1985). Furthermore, the car chases in *Drive* differed from those in the early 2000s. Instead of emulating the style made popular by *The Fast and the Furious* (2001) film series, its car chase sequences are more comparable to those in Philip D'Antoni's *Bullitt* (1968), *The French Connection* (1971), and *The Seven-Ups* (1973).

Film Analysis

There are many similarities between the novel *Drive* and its film adaptation. Both versions are dark, gritty crime stories that follow the journey of an unnamed protagonist known simply as "Driver" as he faces down a gang of criminals to protect the woman he loves. The film stays true to most of Sallis's original plot. When it begins, Driver (Gosling) is a stuntman by day and a getaway driver by night. Although this means he regularly works with criminals, he does not get involved in their actual crimes—he just drives for them. His life remains simple and lonely until one day he befriends his next-door neighbor, Irene (Carey Mulligan) and her four-year-old son Benicio (Kaden Leos). Everything changes, however, when Irene's husband Standard (Oscar Isaac) is released from prison and must rob a pawn store to pay off the debt he owes the men who protected him while he served time. Determined to keep Irene and Benicio safe, Driver offers his getaway services to Standard who ends up getting killed. Driver is then forced to track down the men behind Standard's murder, and in turn puts his own life in danger.

While the film reprises the main plot points of Sallis's novel, it also differs in some significant ways. Screenwriter

Hossein Amini condensed, simplified, and reorganized the source material. Where the novel jumps back and forth in time, the film has a linear narrative. Additionally, Amini omits and combines some of the original characters. The film's Shannon (Bryan Cranston), for example, is an amalgam of characters from the novel, including a stunt driver named Shannon, Driver's screenwriter friend Manny, and a crooked physician called Doc. In the novel, these three men function as pseudo father figures to Driver. In the film, Shannon fulfills a similar role by giving Driver jobs and generally looking out for his well-being. Another difference between the two iterations of the story is the character of Irene. Originally, she is written as a tough Mexican American woman named Irina who has no interest in reviving her relationship with Standard when he gets out of jail. The film's Irene is Caucasian, cherubic, and seemingly willing to pick up with Standard where they left off before he was arrested. These changes to the Irene character add another layer of drama to the film as she comes across as more naive and vulnerable. In turn, Driver's decision to protect her feels more compelling.

Arguably the biggest difference between the film and the novel is how Driver is depicted. In the book, Driver comes across as guarded and reticent to the outside world, but can also be quite affable to the few people he calls friends. Meanwhile, the film's version of this character barely speaks at all and appears to have no one in his life. There is no real insight into his backstory, and it is unclear both why he is so quiet and where his violent tendencies, which he tries to suppress, come from. This paring down or minimalism helps the film seem more like an existential parable or fable than the short novel. Within the first act of the film, the director Refn reveals that the one thing that motivates Driver is his desire to protect the innocent. Irene and especially Benicio are presented as the embodiment of innocence. So, when their lives are threatened by hitmen, something snaps inside of Driver and he becomes violently protective. In some ways, it appears that Driver's determination to save Benicio is an attempt to save his own inner child.

Drive may pay tribute to Sallis's novel, but at the end of the day the film is distinctly Refn's vision. Highly stylized, it borrows heavily from the 1980s in both its aesthetic as well as its soundtrack. Another unique quality of the film is the gratuitous way that Refn depicts violence. In the scene after the pawn shop robbery goes awry, for example, Driver and Blanche (Christina Hendricks) wait in a motel for further instructions. Two armed men break into their room, shooting Blanche in the head. Refn chooses to show this image in slow motion rather than cut away, illustrating the bodily effects of the bullet in detail. Similarly, in a later scene, Driver begins fighting with a hitman and brutally kicks his head in. The violence here is comparable to that of director David Cronenberg, who is known for his depiction of body horror. While violence is not uncommon in neo-noir films, what makes *Drive* different is the way that it depicts it in such disturbingly heightened, detailed, and almost cartoonish ways.

Most of the characters in *Drive* are trying to get to a new, better place in their lives. The ubiquitous presence of cars speaks to this theme. In most scenes, the characters are shown either in cars, next to them, or are speaking about them. What makes the film unique in this regard is the fact that most of these cars are not fancy or exciting, but average everyday vehicles. For example, the first scene begins with Driver getting into a Chevy Impala. Even though it is a common sedan, Driver uses it to escape the police. To ensure that the film's chase sequences are exciting, Refn shoots them primarily from the interior of the car from low angles. This provides audiences with Driver's perspective and essentially makes them feel as though they are along for the ride.

Significance

Drive proved to be a commercial success. Filmed on a modest budget of $15 million, it earned $76.9 million at the box office worldwide. In addition to being popular with audiences, *Drive* also resonated with most critics, earning a positive 92 percent aggregate rating on the *Rotten Tomatoes* website. Furthermore, it was dubbed the best film of the year by *Rolling Stone* magazine. Common among most of the critics' favorable reviews was commendation for Refn and his highly stylized, neo-noir aesthetic. Writing for *Time Out*, Tom Huddleston states, "*Drive* never drags: this is an entirely welcome riff on old material, a pulse-pounding electronically enhanced cover version of a beloved standard. Sure, it's shallow, but it's also slickly compelling, beautifully crafted and so damn shiny." Another central point of praise among critics was for the actors' performances. Many remarked that a large part of the film's appeal was how Gosling and Mulligan played stereotypical roles in fresh, unconventional ways. A. O. Scott commented on this in his review for *The New York Times* where he wrote, "The softness of Mr. Gosling's face and his curiously high-pitched, nasal voice make him an unusually sweet-seeming avenger, even when he is stomping bad guys into a bloody pulp. And Ms. Mulligan's whispery diction and kewpie-doll features have a similarly disarming effect."

The few critics who disliked *Drive* noted its excessive violence and familiar plot. These individuals argued that the film relied too much on style and failed to deliver real substance. Despite their detraction, however, *Drive* made a quiet but noticeable cultural impact. In the months that followed, pieces of the film's 1980s male fashion enjoyed a brief revival. Additionally, *Drive* influenced several films in the years that followed. This was first evident in *Nightcrawler* (2014), a dark film that also followed a male antihero who trolled the city's streets at night alone in his car. *Nightcrawler* differs from *Drive* in that it is not as stylized. Still, its depiction of Los Angeles as well as the young, disturbed anti-hero at its helm is highly reminiscent of Refn's film. Another film that was clearly shaped by *Drive* was Edgar Wright's film *Baby Driver*. Like *Drive*, *Baby Driver* follows a loner who works as a getaway driver for criminals. In addition to many shared plot points, the films both portray cars and driving in a comparable way. Where they differ greatly, however, is in tone. *Drive* has a nihilistic worldview, where *Baby Driver* is more optimistic and comedic.

—Emily E. Turner

Further Reading

Barone, Matt. "Interview: *Drive* Director Nicolas Winding Refn Talks Ryan Gosling's Clout and Artistic Violence." *Complex Magazine*, 14 Sept. 2011, www.complex.com/pop-culture/2011/09/interview-drive-director-nicolas-winding-refn. Accessed 4 Mar. 2020.

Gilchrist, Todd. "Nicolas Winding Refn Says *Drive* Was about the Purity of Love with His Wife; Says Driver Was a Werewolf." *IndieWire*, 1 Feb. 2012, www.indiewire.com/2012/02/nicolas-winding-refn-says-drive-was-about-the-purity-of-love-with-his-wife-says-driver-was-a-werewolf-253963/. Accessed 4 Mar. 2020.

Bibliography

Heath Jr, Glenn. "Interview: Nicolas Winding Refn Talks *Drive*, Ryan Gosling, and More." *Slant Magazine*, 12 Sept. 2011, www.slantmagazine.com/film/interview-nicolas-winding-refn/. Accessed 4 Mar. 2020.

Huddleston, Tom. "*Drive*." *Time Out*, 20 Sept. 2011, www.timeout.com/london/film/drive. Accessed 5 Mar. 2020.

McGillicuddy, Louisa. "An Interview with Nicolas Winding Refn, the Director of *Drive*." *Vice*, 23 Sept. 2011, www.vice.com/en_uk/article/ex77we/nicolas-winding-refn-movie-drive-ryan-gosling-cars. Accessed 4 Mar. 2020.

Scott, A. O. "Fasten Your Seat Belts, the Chevy Is Taking Off." *The New York Times*, 15 Sept. 2011, www.nytimes.com/2011/09/16/movies/drive-with-ryan-gosling-review.html. Accessed 4 Mar. 2020.

Outlaw, Kofi. "*Drive* Ending Explained." *Screen Rant*, 16 Sept. 2011, screenrant.com/drive-movie-ending/. Accessed 4 Mar. 2020.

Dumplin'

The Novel
Author: Julie Murphy (b. 1985)
First published: 2015

The Film
Year released: 2018
Director: Anne Fletcher (b. 1966)
Screenplay by: Kristin Hahn
Starring: Danielle Macdonald, Jennifer Aniston, Hilliary Begley, Luke Benward, Odeya Rush

Context

Dumplin' (2015) is a young adult novel written by American author Julie Murphy. A *New York Times* bestseller, it tells the story of an overweight Texas teenager named Willowdean Dickson who decides to enter a beauty pageant and subsequently learns to navigate the rocky terrain of adolescent love, friendship, body image, and self-acceptance. *Dumplin'* is Murphy's second book after her debut *Side Effects May Vary* (2014), which followed the journey of a sixteen-year-old diagnosed with leukemia. Like *Side Effects May Vary*, *Dumplin'* also centers around a young, headstrong female protagonist who feels that she is at odds with the world around her. In *Dumplin'*, however, the author explores issues of identity and difference in the experience of a socially marginalized person.

The years leading up to the publication of *Dumplin'* saw an explosion of young adult fiction. From 1997 to 2009 alone, the number of YA novels published each year increased from 3,000 to 30,000. Much of this growth was an effort to capitalize on the success of the Harry Potter franchise, which demonstrated that there was a significant demand for young adult fiction. Since about 2010, an increasing number of books about the experience of characters who are different in their race, gender, or sexual orientation were published. While *Dumplin'* is part of this trend, it remains something of an anomaly because of its focus on the issue of body image, although other young adult books to feature overweight protagonists include *Eleanor & Park* (2012), *To Be Honest* (2018), and *Leah on the Offbeat* (2018).

Dumplin' was adapted into a film by screenwriter Kristin Hahn and director Anne Fletcher in 2018. A seasoned filmmaker, Fletcher is best known for her work on comedies like *27 Dresses* (2008), *The Proposal* (2009), and *The Guilt Trip* (2012). *Dumplin'* differs from other, contemporaneous films and television shows about overweight heroines, such as *Brittany Runs a Marathon* (2019) and *Insatiable* (2018), in that the story prioritizes acceptance over weight loss.

Film Analysis

When the novel *Dumplin'* begins, Willowdean "Will" Dickson is a high school junior whose life is in a state of transition. A few months earlier, her beloved Aunt Lucy died. She is growing apart from Ellen, her best friend since childhood, and she has started seeing her work crush, Bo, in secret. While this would be a lot for any teenaged girl to endure, it is especially difficult for Will, who is constantly told by the world around her that her body is problematic because she is overweight. Although Will loves herself and does not feel the need to change, she is bullied at school and her former beauty pageant mother clearly wishes she looked different. Combined with the fact that everything in her life seems to be changing, Will begins to question her own self-acceptance. When she discovers that her Aunt Lucy had wanted to enter the local beauty pageant but never did, she drums up enough gumption to do it.

The film version of *Dumplin'* stays true to the broad strokes of the book's plot. In it, Will (Macdonald) spends most of her time either hanging out with her best friend Ellen (Rush) or working as a waitress at the local fast-food joint. She is still grieving the loss of her Aunt Lucy (Begley), trying to process her complex feelings for Bo (Benward), and defying her mother by participating in the beauty pageant that she runs. However, there are many details, characters, and storylines that the film omits. For example, the film does not show the extent of Will and Bo's relationship and how they met secretly for months before she calls it off. Similarly, the film does not introduce the character of Mitch who Will feels obligated to date because he is "big like her." Will and Ellen drift apart for different reasons in the film. In the book, Ellen begins having sex with her boyfriend and spending time with thinner, more popular girls causing Will to feel as though she is being left behind. In the film, the two girls grow apart after they both join the pageant and they have different ideas of how to protest it.

The film is narrower in its scope, focusing primarily on Will's journey as a contestant in the Miss Bluebonnet pageant. Although her entry into the pageant is intended to both honor her aunt and defy her mother Rosie (Aniston), Will ends up inspiring a group of misfits to follow her lead. Despite her initial instincts, she quickly realizes that she can affect more change if she does well in the pageant than if she does not try. She and her friends end up getting to know a group of drag queens who help them improve their costumes, performances, and overall confidence. The drag queens play a much larger role in the film than in the book. Director Anne Fletcher leverages their presence to infuse the film with energy and excitement.

The character of Aunt Lucy is arguably one of the most important of the book. It was Aunt Lucy who not only taught Will to love herself but also introduced her to Ellen and Dolly Parton. However, Aunt Lucy also represents the dangers of being overweight: she died of a heart attack in her 30s. In the film, sequences using voice-over and flashbacks show Will when she was a child spending time with Aunt Lucy. These are scattered sparingly throughout the film and have a dreamier look. They are typically accompanied by voice-over in which Will speaks about how Aunt Lucy made her feel.

The film is about the importance of self-acceptance. One way the film communicates this, borrowing the trope from the book, is through its music. Will and Ellen are Dolly Parton fans, thanks to the influence of Aunt Lucy. In the book, which is narrated from a first-person perspective, Will examines her life through the lens provided by Dolly Parton lyrics, expressions, and anecdotes. The film uses Parton's music to establish a strong, upbeat sensibility. According to Dumplin' screenwriter Kristin Hahn, the reason the filmmakers felt Parton's music was so essential to the film was because it captured the central message, saying, "A lot of what she's (Parton) written about through the decades has been about loving who you are, the way you are, and accepting others for who they are."

Significance

Dumplin' was released on December 7, 2018, on Netflix. Although the film received predominantly positive reviews, it was criticized for being too lightweight or superficial. In The New York Times review, Manohla Dargis wrote, "The filmmakers never give this character a real, searching, complex inner life. They give her problems to solve, hurdles to clear. They turn emotional complexity into affirmations, a potentially transformational character into a you-go-girl cliché."

As a lighthearted comedy, however, with a positive message, the film was praised by Sophie Gilbert in The Atlantic: "Dumplin' isn't a story that uses a skinny, conventionally pretty protagonist to pick apart a realm that rewards women exactly like her. It's more imaginative than that, open to the idea that beauty itself is more expansive and subjective."

—Emily E. Turner

Further Reading
Arreola, Cristina. "The Dumplin' Book Ending Is a Reminder to Surround Yourself with the People Who See Your Beauty." Bustle, 7 Dec. 2018, www.bustle.com/p/the-dumplin-book-ending-is-a-reminder-to-surround-yourself-with-the-people-who-see-your-beauty-13256121. Accessed 4 Mar. 2020.
Shorr-Parks, Sadie. "Dumplin' and the Fat Female Protagonist." LA Review of Books, 3 Feb. 2019, lareviewofbooks.org/article/dumplin-fat-female-protagonist/. Accessed 4 Mar. 2020.

Bibliography
Dargis, Manohla. "Dumplin' Shares an Ordinary Girl's Truth." The New York Times, 5 Dec. 2018, www.nytimes.com/2018/12/05/movies/dumplin-review.html. Accessed 9 Mar. 2020.
Gilbert, Sophie. "What Dumplin' and Queen America Say about Female Beauty." The Atlantic, 13 Dec. 2018, www.theatlantic.com/entertainment/archive/2018/12/what-dumplin-and-queen-america-say-about-female-beauty/577951/. Accessed 4 Mar. 2019.
Keaney, Quinn. "Why Making Dumplin' Was a 'Dream Come True' for Screenwriter Kristin Hahn and Jennifer Aniston." Pop Sugar, 16 Dec. 2018, www.popsugar.com/entertainment/Dumplin-Interview-Screenwriter-Kristin-Hahn-45569920. Accessed 4 Mar. 2019.
Marine, Brooke. "Dumplin' Star Danielle Macdonald Explains the Terror of Beauty Pageants, and Singing with Jennifer Aniston and Dolly Parton." W Magazine, 9 Dec. 2018, www.wmagazine.com/story/dumplin-netflix-danielle-macdonald-interview/. Accessed 4 Mar. 2020.
Radish, Christina. "Dumplin' Director on Casting the Netflix Dramedy and Getting Dolly Parton Onboard." Collider, 3 Dec. 2018, collider.com/dumplin-interview-anne-fletcher/. Accessed 4 Mar. 2020.

East of Eden

The Novel
Author: John Steinbeck (1902-1968)
First published: 1952

The Film
Year released: 1955
Director: Elia Kazan (1909-2003)
Screenplay by: Paul Osborn
Starring: Julie Harris, James Dean, Raymond Massey, Richard Davalos, Burl Ives, Jo Van Fleet

Context

John Steinbeck was one of the most popular and influential authors of the twentieth century. Over the course of a writing career that spanned four decades, Steinbeck authored approximately thirty books. He worked in a variety of literary forms, genres, and styles, but is best known for his realist novels that dealt with the economic and social effects of the Great Depression. The most famous of these novels, *The Grapes of Wrath*(1939), which follows the perilous journey of a downtrodden Oklahoma farming family as they are forced to migrate west to California during the Dust Bowl, is considered by many to be Steinbeck's greatest achievement and an indispensable part of the American literary canon.

Not long after completing *The Grapes of Wrath*, Steinbeck began thinking about what would become his most personal and ambitious novel, the 1952 epic *East of Eden*. Steinbeck did not actually start writing *East of Eden* until early 1941, but in the decade-plus run-up to its realization, the author came to describe the novel as "the first book," which represented a culmination of all his previous work and all his literary talents. Like much of Steinbeck's most beloved fiction, the lengthy novel is set in his native Salinas Valley, an expansive agricultural region in northern California. That Edenic setting serves as the symbolic backdrop for a saga about three generations of two families—the Trasks and the Hamiltons—whose intertwined stories crystallize into a modern retelling of the book of Genesis. Covering the period from the American Civil War to the end of World War I, the novel centers around Adam Trask, his estranged former wife, Cathy, and their twin sons, Caleb and Aron, who reenact the fall of Adam and Eve and the deadly rivalry of Cain and Abel. *Eden* became an instant bestseller, and despite receiving a mixed critical reception, it would come to be regarded not only as one of Steinbeck's major works but the true *magnum opus* of his storied career.

Among the first people to read *East of Eden* was the critically acclaimed theater director and filmmaker Elia Kazan, who had previously collaborated with Steinbeck on *Viva Zapata!* (1952), an Oscar-nominated biopic in which actor Marlon Brando starred as the Mexican revolu-

John Steinbeck, *author of* East of Eden. *Photo via Wikimedia Commons. [Public domain.]*

tionary Emiliano Zapata. Kazan, who formed a close friendship with Steinbeck after *Zapata*, obtained financial backing from Warner Brothers to purchase the rights to *Eden* while the novel was still in its advance galley stages. He turned to another friend, the noted playwright Paul Osborn, to draft the film's script.

When *Eden* went into production in 1954, Kazan was coming off the heels of *On the Waterfront* (1954), an eight-time Academy Award-winning crime drama that had helped transform him into a big-time Hollywood director. Kazan initially considered casting *Waterfront*'s star Marlon Brando in the leading role of Cal, but he ultimately decided against it because at thirty, the actor was too old for the role. Instead, Kazan, at the suggestion of Osborn, opted to cast a virtually unknown stage and television actor by the name of James Dean. Rounding out the film's cast was Julie Harris, Raymond Massey, Richard Davalos, Burl Ives, and Jo Van Fleet. The first Kazan production to be shot in color and in widescreen Cinema-Scope, *East of Eden* premiered at the Astor Theatre in New York City on March 9, 1955.

Film Analysis

Befitting the epic nature of Steinbeck's novel, the 1955 film adaptation of *East of Eden* is preceded by a rousing three-minute overture, which is set against panoramic images of an idyllic coastal town on a headland.

Though introduced in the credits as a production of "John Steinbeck's *East of Eden*," Kazan's film adaptation only covers the last quarter of the novel and in the process very much becomes his own original work. This is evident from the opening scenes, in which Kazan's focal point is firmly established: through soft and almost dreamlike morning imagery, Cal Trask (James Dean), a seemingly emotionally anguished teenage boy, is shown surreptitiously following the movements of a well-dressed woman (Jo Van Fleet) who, after making a sizable deposit at the local bank, makes her way to an upscale brothel. The woman is Cal's mother Cathy Ames, who, under the alias Kate, serves as the successful madam of a brothel. This brings Cal to the painful realization that his mother is not only alive—after growing up thinking otherwise—but is also depraved.

In the book, Steinbeck chronicles Cathy's backstory and portrays her as a monster. Among other things, she falsifies her own rape, incinerates her parents, sleeps with her brother-in-law Charles on her wedding night, and then

James Dean in East of Eden. Photo via Wikimedia Commons. [Public domain.]

shoots and deserts her husband Adam after giving birth to their twin boys. All these details, save for references to her shooting of Adam, are left out of Kazan's film, but viewers are able to make inferences about Cathy's dark and violent past both through Jo Van Fleet's cold-hearted, albeit more humanized, portrayal and through subsequent dialogue exchanges. (A major criticism of Steinbeck's book revolves around the idea that Cathy is too inexplicably evil to be credible as a character, so by eliminating much of this backstory, Kazan and Osborn are able to make her more accessible to viewers.)

At the heart of Kazan's film is the conflict between Cal and his pious, Bible-thumping father Adam (Raymond Massey), which is established soon after Cal returns home to Salinas from Monterey. Cal is reprimanded by Adam for not returning home the previous night, and in retaliation, Cal destroys blocks of ice Adam has just purchased for an idealistic lettuce preservation venture. During this sequence, Adam is cold and stern toward Cal. Aron (Richard Davalos), who is clearly the favored son, enthusiastically supports his father's venture. Cal, on the other hand, unsuccessfully tries to convince his father to invest in beans, which, with the United States' entry into World War I, will undoubtedly reap greater financial rewards. Through clever intercutting, Kazan illustrates the desperate pain and torment Cal feels in trying to win Adam's love and approval.

Later that night, at Adam's direction, Cal and Aron participate in a Bible-reading session at the family dinner table. Adam forgives Cal for his actions, but as a form of re-pentance, he instructs Cal to read from a specific Bible passage. Surly and largely uncooperative, Cal provokes Adam by delivering a halfhearted reading, prompting Aron to excuse himself from the table. It is then when Cal confronts Adam about the lies he has told them about their mother. According to Adam, Cathy moved east after her twin boys were born and he assumed she died there. During this exchange, Adam, after acknowledging that he lied to save his sons from pain, mentions his former wife's lack of kindness and conscience and dodges a question from Cal about the scar on his shoulder, which instead of being a wound suffered "in the Indian campaigns" was caused by Cathy shooting him. Adam nonetheless pleads with Cal to keep the truth from Aron. These domestic scenes—and others throughout the film—are shot at slightly askew angles, which, besides further highlighting the palpable tension between Cal and Adam, produce a disorienting effect on viewers, conveying the sense that the Trask home is not only unstable but is on the verge of collapse.

By this point, readers of Steinbeck's novel will have noticed one major omission—the Trask family's Chinese American cook and housekeeper Lee. One of the most important characters in the book, Lee runs the household for Adam after he is shot by Cathy, which leaves him in a decade-long state of shock. Lee helps raise Cal and Aron and even plays a role in naming them when Adam proves unable to do so. Highly intelligent, well-read, and compassionate, Lee is the philosophical backbone of Steinbeck's novel, serving as the conduit for many of its themes, and acts as a voice of reason in the Trask household, providing stability in the midst of conflict. By eliminating Lee from their highly condensed adaptation, Kazan and screenwriter Osborn are able to home in on Cal's troubled relationship with his father without interference, allowing them to heighten tension between the two characters more effectively. In place of Lee, two characters in Kazan's film stand in as quasi-surrogate father figures for Cal: Will Hamilton (Albert Dekker), a close family friend and businessman, and Sam (Burl Ives), the town sheriff. Over the course of the film, both characters offer Cal advice and guidance and fill him in on details about his mother.

Nevertheless, *East of Eden* remains largely faithful to the last quarter of Steinbeck's novel. Cal eventually confronts his mother and attempts to reach an understanding of her actions. Eventually, a love triangle emerges between Cal, Aron, and his girlfriend Abra (Julie Harris). In a climactic scene, Cal presents Adam with the profits from his bean business, but upon discovering their source, Adam disdainfully rejects the gift. Distraught, Cal retreats to the yard, where he is consoled by Abra, but the two are interrupted by Aron, who orders Abra to stay away from Cal. In vengeful anger, Cal takes Aron to their mother's brothel, which drives the disillusioned Aron into a maniacal drunken frenzy. Aron rashly enlists in the army and dies in the war, causing Adam to suffer a paralyzing stroke. The film ends with Cal, through Abra's mediation, coming to his father's bedside, seemingly initiating a path toward reconciliation and acceptance.

Though Kazan and Osborn compress events from Steinbeck's novel, and in some cases, invent new ones to meet their narrative goals, they ultimately maintain its true essence and preserve its themes. The most significant of these themes revolves around the Hebrew word *timshel*, which appears in the biblical story of Cain and Abel. Meaning "thou mayest," *timshel* represents free will and the ability to choose between good and evil. While the word is never explicitly mentioned in Kazan's film—unlike in the novel where it is dealt with at length—it is largely understood by viewers that Cal must come to terms with this dilemma before moving forward with his life. By the film's conclusion, Cal has not only begun the reconciliation process with his father but, it can be safely inferred, has also accepted the idea that evil can be overcome, therefore completing his emotional and spiritual transformation. This somewhat sentimental ending proves to be a much more appealing alternative to the novel's, where Adam utters the word *timshel* to a guilt-ridden Cal before drifting off to sleep.

Significance

Following its world premiere in New York, *East of Eden* opened in theaters throughout the United States on April 10, 1955. The film received widespread acclaim from critics, many of whom praised Ted McCord's lush color cinematography, Leonard Rosenman's moody score, and the performances of Dean, Davalos, Harris, and Van Fleet. All, of course, worked under the direction of Kazan, a quintessential actor's director who was equally recognized for his deft use of the then novel widescreen CinemaScope format to frame both vast California landscapes and intimate family scenes. The film earned four Academy Award nominations, including Best Director for Kazan, Best Writing, Screenplay for Osborn, and acting nods for

Dean and Van Fleet (both in their first feature film roles). Van Fleet took home the sole award for the film, winning the Oscar for Best Actress in a Supporting Role.

More than anything else, *East of Eden* is notable for marking the mesmerizing film debut of James Dean, who despite only making three films over a sixteen-month period, would go on to become one of the most iconic and legendary actors in film history. A proponent of the immersive method style of acting, Dean thrust himself into the role of Cal with a rebellious verve and emotional vulnerability that immediately struck a chord with the 1950s teenage generation. He instantly became an archetype for the misunderstood teenager filled with angst, which helped play a considerable role in making *Eden* a commercial hit and cult phenomenon. The film was the only one released during Dean's lifetime as well as the only one the actor personally saw in its entirety. (Dean died in a car accident on September 30, 1955, when he was just twenty-four years old.)

Not all reviewers embraced Dean's acting in *East of Eden*. Most famously, *The New York Times'* Bosley Crowther compared the actor unfavorably to Marlon Brando and likened his performance to "a mass of histrionic gingerbread." Still, to other critics and countless filmgoers over the subsequent decades, Dean in *Eden* came to represent "the determining and turning-point performance of the 1950s," as David Thomson declared in a review of the film for his compendium *Have You Seen...?* (2010). Kazan, who considered *Eden* the most personal film he ever made, later regarded his casting of Dean as one of the savviest decisions of his legendary career. Thanks in part to the Dean legend, *East of Eden* became a classic and widely influential film and in 2016 was se-lected for preservation by the Library of Congress's National Film Registry.

—*Chris Cullen*

Further Reading
Benson, Jackson J. *John Steinbeck, Writer: A Biography*. Penguin Books, 1990.
Dalton, David. *James Dean: The Mutant King*. Chicago Review Press, 2001.
Schickel, Richard. *Elia Kazan: A Biography*. Harper Perennial, 2006.

Bibliography
Crowther, Bosley. "The Screen: *East of Eden* Has Debut; Astor Shows Film of Steinbeck Novel." *The New York Times*, 10 Mar. 1955, www.nytimes.com/1955/03/10/archives/the-screen-east-of-eden-has-debut-astor-shows-film-of-steinbeck.html. Accessed 19 Mar. 2020.
Langberg, Eric. "*East of Eden* Review." *Medium.com*, 25 Sept. 2015, medium.com/everythings-interesting/east-of-eden-review-43605f33f671. Accessed 19 Mar. 2020.
O'Malley, Sheila. "Unforgettable Lonely Boy James Dean Carries *East of Eden* on His Narrow Shoulders." *Library of America*, 19 Apr. 2017, www.loa.org/news-and-views/1274-unforgettable-lonely-boy-james-dean-carries-_east-of-eden_-on-his-narrow-shoulders. Accessed 19 Mar. 2020.
Reid, Monica. "Film Review: John Steinbeck's *East of Eden* Directed by Elia Kazan." *Far Out Magazine*, 29 Nov. 2016, faroutmagazine.co.uk/film-review-john-steinbecks-east-of-eden-directed-by-elia-kazan/. Accessed 19 Mar. 2020.
Steinbeck, John. *East of Eden*. 1952. Penguin Classics, 1992.
———. *Journal of a Novel: The East of Eden Letters*. 1969. Penguin Books, 1990.
Thomson, David. "*East of Eden*." *Have You Seen...?* Knopf, 2010, p. 250.
Wyatt, David. Introduction. *East of Eden*, by John Steinbeck, 1952. Penguin Classics, 1992, pp. vii-xxviii.

Election

The Novel
Author: Tom Perrotta (b. 1961)
First published: 1998

The Film
Year released: 1999
Director: Alexander Payne (b. 1961)
Screenplay by: Alexander Payne and Jim Taylor
Starring: Reese Witherspoon, Matthew Broderick, Chris Klein, Jessica Campbell

Context
Election is a 1999 film based on Tom Perrotta's 1998 novel of the same name. Inspired by the 1992 presidential election and first written in 1993, *Election* was Perrotta's second novel. The publisher was not initially clear about the book's intended audience. Centered on the story of an ambitious teenage girl, was it for young people or for adults? (The ambiguity lingered: although the novel was ultimately published as adult fiction, the film was produced by the youth-oriented MTV.) Several years after Perrotta completed the manuscript, Hollywood producers expressed interest in another of his works, the then-unfinished novel *The Wishbones* (1997), which focuses on a guitarist and his New Jersey wedding band. Instead, Perrotta gave them *Election*. The producers, very enthused about the material, handed it off to director and screenwriter Alexander Payne. Thus, *Election* was born as both a published novel and a film at essentially the same time.

As a novel and a film, *Election* was an early work in the careers of both Perrotta and Payne, respectively. Both are considered satirists with a soft edge. Perrotta would later become known for the darkly comic 2004 novel *Little Children*, which explores parenthood and suburban malaise. He also went on to enjoy a successful screenwriting and production career adapting his own work—he cowrote the 2006 screenplay for the film version of *Little Children* and helped adapt his 2011 novel *The Leftovers* into a critically acclaimed series for HBO that ran between 2014 and 2017. However, he played no part in the adaptation of *Election*. Payne wrote the script with longtime collaborator Jim Taylor.

Before *Election*, Payne, a native Nebraskan who graduated in 1990 with a master's degree from the University of California, Los Angeles's film school, had made just one film as a professional director. The critically acclaimed *Citizen Ruth* (1996), starring Academy Award-winning actor Laura Dern, is a satire about abortion in which an opportunistic woman ends up at the center of a heated national debate. Payne's effective handling of his subject and the moral ambivalence of his characters are echoed in *Election*, the film that is widely credited with making his reputation. His subsequent films, such as *About Schmidt* (2002), *Sideways* (2004), and the Academy Award-nominated *Nebraska* (2013), often explore down-on-their-luck, middle-class characters who seek redemption in unusual and extraordinary ways.

Film Analysis
Perrotta has conceded that Payne's film version of *Election* has largely overshadowed his book in the popular imagination and noted that he is a fan of the film. Despite some differences from the source material, the movie follows the plot of its literary inspiration fairly closely. Jim McAllister (Matthew Broderick), affectionately known to students as Mr. M., teaches at a high school. He claims to be happy with his job, but in retrospective voice-over narration—a technique used by different characters to represent the narrative form of the book, structured by multiple points of view—he suggests that something is amiss at the school, and it has to do with a student named Tracy Flick (Reese Witherspoon). Tracy is running for student body president. An ambitious perfectionist, she is both painfully intelligent and irritatingly self-assured. She often wears her perfectly coiffed blonde hair in a bob, and her headband always matches her tasteful sweaters and neatly pleated skirts. There is a determined edge, communicated effectively by Witherspoon, to Tracy evident in the tightness of her set jaw and the rigid-

ity of her arm when she raises her hand in class. Even her politeness feels combative.

However, there is more to Tracy than meets the eye. In the film's first few minutes, Mr. M. lets the audience in on a secret: Tracy had an affair with his adult, married friend, Dave Novotny (Mark Harelik), another teacher at the school. (Mr. M. describes Dave as "one of those guys who taught because they never wanted to leave high school in the first place.") When Tracy's mother discovers the affair, Dave is fired, his wife divorces him, and he moves back in with his parents. Mr. M. is critical of his friend's choices, but the fallout from the affair breeds in him lust-driven contempt for Tracy. He sets out to destroy her to punish her for the affair, but also to quell his own desire.

The central conflict of the film, as with the novel, revolves around Mr. M.'s unhinged quest to rob Tracy of her most fervent want: to win the election for student body president. To this end, he convinces a sweet but dense athlete named Paul Metzler (Chris Klein) to run against her as a spoiler candidate. Paul is hesitant to run at first, arguing that Tracy, who is running unopposed, would make a great president. His apprehension is a part of the film's larger theme: Who is allowed to project power? Who is supposed to project weakness? While Paul is happy to cede power to Tracy, Mr. M. is not. Paul's candidacy has its own unintended consequence of inspiring his lovelorn little sister, Tammy (Jessica Campbell), to run as well, advocating for the overthrow of the student government altogether. The election pits undeserving privilege against unpopular competence against nihilist anarchy, but *Election* is most directly a satire about power and weakness as it applies to gender, and how those ideas undergird the American political system and everyday life.

Both Tracy and Mr. M. are unreliable narrators, and the complexities of their lives and their relationship to each other are communicated visually. The dissonance between how the characters describe events and what the audience actually sees creates moments of irony that are sometimes quite dark. Take, for instance, how Tracy characterizes her relationship with Dave, saying that Dave was not actually taking advantage of her. Payne's visuals suggest, however, that this was indeed the case. Tracy describes her early relationship with Dave, her teacher, as "professional," implying that they were of equal status. It was not until they were left alone at a pizza parlor, following a meeting of the high school yearbook staff of which Dave was the supervisor, that Tracy says they began to talk as adults rather than as a

student and teacher. Few would describe the following scene that way, though. Dave begins by telling Tracy that she appears to be a "loner" without close friends. He implies that, given her superior intellect, it must be hard for her to be close to someone, and, inevitably, suggests that he could fill that role. As *New York Times* critic A. O. Scott pointed out in an essay reassessing the power dynamics of *Election*, Dave's overtures are a "textbook case of predatory grooming." Subsequent scenes reinforce this point of view. Tracy is visibly uncomfortable before her first sexual experience with Dave. It would be unfair to characterize Tracy solely as a victim in the film, but Payne's nuance bears note. Her relationship with Dave is consensual insofar as Tracy is an active participant in it, but the opinion, held by Dave and Mr. M., that Tracy held more power in the relationship is presented as absurd.

The irony of Mr. M.'s narration is even more overt, as he repeatedly—and in increasingly absurd ways—denies attraction and contempt for Tracy. Within the first few

Reese Witherspoon, star of Election *(1999). Photo by dtstuff9 via Wikimedia Commons.*

minutes of the film, he poses a question to his class probing the difference between what is ethical (the rules set by society) and what is moral (one's internal sense of right and wrong). Mr. M. presents himself as a moral guide while engaging in conduct that is immoral, from cheating on his wife to trying to fix the school election. This theme, regarding morals and ethics, is one of the significant differences between the book and Payne's film. While the film questions the morality of Dave and Tracy's relationship, the book merely uses it as a catalyst for the plot. The book is much more concerned with the then-recent events Perrotta was preoccupied with when he wrote it. Specifically set in 1992, it begins with a very different question, one regarding the overlap between private virtue and public responsibility. It was a pressing quandary that year as voters wondered if Bill Clinton could be a good president if he had committed adultery as had been alleged, or if Clarence Thomas could effectively serve as a US Supreme Court justice when he had been accused of harassing his colleague Anita Hill.

There are several other noted differences between the film and its source material. For example, the Tracy of the book is more overtly sexual and wears sexy clothes, and the film's ending has a more cynical tone that was considered more of a suitable fit for the rest of the feature. A more minor difference is indicative of Payne's style: the book is set in suburban New Jersey, but the film takes place in Omaha, Nebraska, Payne's hometown. Payne shot the film at a real Nebraska high school that was in session during filming.

Significance

Election performed rather poorly at the box office, even as it won critical praise. It has since become a cult classic, however, one of Payne's most popular films and one of Witherspoon's most beloved roles. The film's evolving cultural significance is largely due to the character of Tracy Flick. Tracy, basically conceived as a comic figure and drawing on what is almost a stereotype—an annoying, straight-A female student, the kind who runs for class president—was reclaimed by some writers as a sort of feminist hero. She was the recognizable archetype, as Elisabeth Donnelly wrote for *Vanity Fair*, of "a woman who is just too much—too accomplished, too hardworking, too ambitious."

In a 2019 essay for *The Guardian*, critic Charles Bramesco argued against this embrace of Tracy, empha-

sizing that she is ruthless, cynical, and "surprisingly entitled for someone resentful of the upper class." *New York Times* critic Scott, in an essay that referenced Bramesco's piece, was more inclined to the elevation of the character: "She cares. She participates. She works hard. She refuses to see herself as a victim," he wrote. "She's everything America celebrates in theory and, as often as not, despises in practice." Tracy remains compelling for some because although she isn't a hero, at least she isn't a victim, and this has made *Election* a provocative litmus test for some writers, a gauge of how people view society and each other.

—*Molly Hagan*

Further Reading

Perrotta, Tom. "Tom Perrotta on the Origins of *Election*, Tracy Flick's Legacy, and Adapting His Own Work." Interview by Tyler Aquilina. *Entertainment Weekly*, 7 May 2019, ew.com/movies/2019/05/07/election-20th-anniversary-tom-perrotta-interview/. Accessed 25 Mar. 2021.

Talbot, Margaret. "Home Movies: Alexander Payne, High Plains Auteur." *The New Yorker*, 21 Oct. 2013, www.newyorker.com/magazine/2013/10/28/home-movies-4. Accessed 25 Mar. 2021.

Bibliography

Bramesco, Charles. "Election at 20: Assessing the High School Satire's Brutal Politics." *The Guardian*, 23 Apr. 2019, www.theguardian.com/film/2019/apr/23/election-20th-anniversary-tracy-flick-reese-witherspoon. Accessed 29 Mar. 2021.

Donnelly, Elisabeth. "Why Tracy Flick Is Still Inescapable." *Vanity Fair*, 2 May 2019, www.vanityfair.com/hollywood/2019/05/election-movie-anniversary-tracy-flick-reese-witherspoon. Accessed 26 Mar. 2021.

Howe, Desson. "'Election' Wins by a Landslide." Review of *Election*, directed by Alexander Payne. *The Washington Post*, 7 May 1999, www.washingtonpost.com/wp-srv/style/longterm/movies/videos/electionhowe.htm. Accessed 25 May 2021.

Perrotta, Tom. "Novelist Tom Perrotta Looks Back on His Most Famous Creation: Election's Tracy Flick." Interview by Emily VanDerWerff. *Vox*, 28 Sept. 2017, www.vox.com/2017/9/27/16369542/tracy-flick-election. Accessed 25 Mar. 2021.

Pirnia, Garin. "13 Facts about *Election*." *Mental Floss*, 22 Aug. 2016, www.mentalfloss.com/article/84190/13-focused-facts-about-election. Accessed 29 Mar. 2021.

Review of *Election*, by Tom Perrotta. *Publishers Weekly*, 30 Oct. 2000, www.publishersweekly.com/978-0-399-14366-3. Accessed 25 Mar. 2021.

Scott, A. O. "What America Gets Wrong about Tracy Flick." *The New York Times*, 1 Aug. 2019, www.nytimes.com/2019/08/01/movies/tracy-flick-reese-witherspoon.html. Accessed 25 Mar. 2021.

Every Day

The Novel
Author: David Levithan (b. 1972)
First published: 2012

The Film
Year released: 2018
Director: Michael Sucsy (b. 1973)
Screenplay by: Jesse Andrews
Starring: Angourie Rice, Justice Smith, Owen Teague

Context

David Levithan's acclaimed, bestselling 2012 young-adult novel *Every Day* effectively combines a meet-cute teen romance, an intriguing science-fiction puzzle, and a meditation on the nature of gender, identity, and sexuality. High schooler Rhiannon falls in love with an incorporeal being who inhabits the body of a different high-school age student each day. Rhiannon and this being, named "A," tackle the challenges of developing a relationship under such existentially difficult circumstances, and ultimately must decide whether they can imagine a future together. The book earned considerable positive attention both for Levithan's strong writing style and for raising a series of important questions about the nature of love and about the fluidity of orientation and attraction. Reviewing the novel for the *Los Angeles Times*, Susan Carpenter wrote, "It's the rare book that challenges gender presumptions in a way that's as entertaining as it is unexpected and, perhaps most important, that's relatable to teens who may not think they need sensitivity training when it comes to sexual orientation and the nature of true love."

A prolific novelist, Levithan began his career with the novel *Boy Meets Boy* (2003), which, like several of his later novels, features lesbian, gay, bisexual, transgender, and queer (LGBTQ) themes. He also collaborated with fellow novelists, most notably with Rachel Cohn on *Nick and Norah's Infinite Playlist* (2006), which was adapted for the screen in 2008. As an editorial director at Scholastic and the founding editor of the PUSH imprint, Levithan edited several anthologies, including *The Full Spectrum: A New Generation of Writing about Gay, Lesbian, Transgender, Questioning, and Other Identities* (2006). *Every Day* grew out of a set of questions Levithan asked himself about identity. He wanted to explore what it would be like to develop as a person without any of the typical ways people categorize themselves and others, and also what a relationship would be like with a person whose identity was continually changing. Levithan went on to publish *Another Day* (2015), a retelling of the events of *Every Day* from Rhiannon's perspective, and the sequel *Some Day* (2018).

The 2018 film adaptation of *Every Day* was scripted by Jesse Andrews. It was directed by Michael Sucsy, whose previous films included the 2012 romance *The Vow*. Distributed by Orion Pictures, the film was made for approximately $4.9 million. Levithan was unofficially consulted in the production process and was made aware of the more substantial changes to the source material.

Film Analysis

Every Day begins with a young man waking up and inspecting his hands. This, viewers later discover, is "A," a being who inhabits the body of a different teenager each day. The visual trope of A's morning routine is one which will run through the film: looking at the hands of the new body, looking about the room of the teenager whose body it is, and then setting a series of phone alarms to warn when midnight is approaching and the current host must be relinquished. Normally, A tries not to deviate much from the host's personality and normal daily activities.

On this particular day, A is living the life of Justin (Justice Smith), a popular high school basketball player. At school, A encounters Rhiannon (Angourie Rice), Justin's girlfriend, and decides to break character by treating her better than Justin typically does. The two of them sneak out to play hooky and to have a platonically ideal day off together. Rhiannon is charmed by the change in her boyfriend, who has suddenly become attentive and thoughtful. She confides in him the struggle she is having trying to connect with her father, who has had a nervous breakdown and rarely leaves the house.

Back at school the next day, Rhiannon finds that Justin has reverted to his sullen and puerile ways. For his part, Justin can barely remember what they did the day before. A, meanwhile, has fallen in love with Rhiannon. Through a series of new hosts, A confesses to her the truth of the identity-swapping existence. Though understandably skeptical, Rhiannon begins to entertain the idea that this might be something other than an elaborate practical joke. This part of the film is anchored by a series of compelling performances by its young actors. These include not only Rice and Smith, but the various actors who play hosts for A—characters that can be male, female, nonbinary, and diverse in all manner of other characteristics such as ethnicity and sexual orientation.

In a scene that plays out in a diner, A, in the body of James (Jacob Batalon), tells Rhiannon about life as a transient spirit, including the challenges and rewards that come with having no identity of one's own. The diner booth setting has a long history in cinema, and *Every Day* makes great use of the device. Rhiannon sits down a skeptic, but gradually begins, with the viewer, to see things from A's point of view. Smith's performance is likewise an important one. He is convincing both as the A-inhabited Justin and as the caddish everyday Justin, and his performance therefore helps the viewer to believe that we have seen two different people in one body. Lukas Jade Zumann is similarly convincing as Nathan, a dorky partygoer who dances with Rhiannon as A and who later believes that he has been possessed by a demon.

The fact that A also inhabits the bodies of girls and of people who do not identify with either of the binary genders is key to the film's message. When Rhiannon asks at one point whether A identifies as a boy or a girl, A answers, "Yes." One of the predominant themes is the fluidity of gender and of sexual attraction, and therefore the limitations inherent in thinking of other people in overly gendered or deterministic ways. As Christy Lemire puts it in her review of the film for RogerEbert.com, *Every Day* carries a "worthwhile, fundamental message about the importance of getting to know people for who they truly are inside, regardless of the expectations you might have about them based on their appearance, race, gender, or sexual orientation."

One of the strengths of *Every Day* is that it establishes a convincing science-fiction or fantasy premise without the use of any special effects. We learn the lineaments of A's existence—such as retaining a core personality while also having access to a host's memories—through dialogue and through solid acting. A operates by a self-enforced series of rules, including trying to leave the host's life mostly undisturbed (but also being willing to chase the host's dreams a little more fervently than they might on their own). This is put to the test when A wakes up in Rhiannon's body. This is a moment where the romantic comedy and science-fiction elements of the story fully gel, as the premise has been solidly set up and the viewer can enjoy watching how things play out. A seeks out Rhiannon's father and has the kind of meaningful conversation that Rhiannon herself longs for but struggles to start. The next day, Rhiannon thanks A for not breaking up with Justin on her behalf—something she promptly does herself. In a different subplot, A inhabits the body of a girl who is clearly suicidal. Rhiannon convinces A to learn how to stay in her body longer than one day in order to get her the help she needs.

The film approaches its dramatic climax when A inhabits the body of Alexander (Owen Teague) and Rhiannon helps convince him to remain in the host indefinitely so they can be together. However, A ultimately decides it is wrong to co-opt another's life forever and determines that the real Alexander would in fact be a great match for Rhiannon. Alexander has the things that A has always wanted—a loving family and a real home—and would be able to give Rhiannon a life that A cannot. A flashforward montage expresses A's concerns about the instability and uncertainty of trying to stay with Rhiannon for good. The film seems committed to validating a realistic range of expressions of gender and sexuality, so it is perhaps a little surprising that it ultimately validates the dream of a highly conventional heterosexual marriage arrangement. Nevertheless, the two young people are right to see that their future together would be a difficult one, and the ending brings strong character development as well as emotional impact.

Every Day is undeniably derivative. Sometimes A seems very close to Scott Bakula's character in the television series *Quantum Leap* (1989-93), a body-hopping do-gooder who changes the lives of his hosts for the better. Various other films also make use of some kind of body-swapping premise, and some are clearly echoed here. There is a dynamic akin to the several versions of *Freaky Friday* in many scenes, particularly the ones where A inhabits Rhiannon's body. Several reviewers noted particular similarities to screenwriter Charlie Kaufman's *Being John Malkovich* (1999), albeit with more family-friendly material. Meanwhile, A's wake-up routine owes much to the alarm clock trope in *Groundhog Day* (1993) and similar works, while A and Rhiannon's star-crossed relationship is reminiscent of countless romantic dramas. Yet, even with all these influences, *Every Day* blends its source materials well and notably addresses issues important to a generation of young-adult viewers.

Significance

Every Day performed reasonably well at the box office, bringing in about $6.1 million during its four-week theatrical run. It received qualified but fairly positive reviews both from audiences and from critics. While reviewers often found fault with aspects of the film's plot and direction, they were generally impressed by its actors' performances and by its empathic and accepting message.

For example, Owen Gleiberman, writing for *Variety*, described the film as "highly derivative" in some ways but ultimately "a surprisingly original entry in the genre of fanciful mismatched love story." Like many critics, he found Suscy's direction to be tepid, yet commended an overall sense of "playfulness" in the film and singled out for praise the performances of several of its young cast members. *The New York Times* Glenn Kenny likewise saw Every Day as derivative but winning, calling it a "heartwarmingly benign" young-adult take on the metaphysical style of screenwriter Charlie Kaufman. In general, critics thought enough of *Every Day* to parse out what does and does not work about the film. Reviewing it for *The Wrap*, William Bibbiani wrote that "*Every Day* is a fascinating movie with flaws inherent to its concept, and it's easy to forgive it that."

—*Matthew Bolton*

Further Reading
Levithan, David. "About Me." *David Levithan*, 2019, www.davidlevithan.com/about/. Accessed 7 Jan. 2019.

Levithan, David. "David Levithan on the Future of YA: 'The Path of Queer YA Is the Path of Inclusion.'" Interview by M. J. Franklin. *Mashable*, 26 Feb. 2018, mashable.com/2018/02/26/mashreads-podcast-david-levithan/#kB_YqBMA6kqI. Accessed 7 Jan. 2019.

Bibliography
Bibbiani, William. "*Every Day* Film Review: Girl Meets Disembodied Soul in Thought-Provoking Teen Romance." Review of *Every Day*, directed by Michael Sucsy. *The Wrap*, 22 Feb. 2018, www.thewrap.com/every-day-film-review-david-levithan/. Accessed 7 Jan. 2019.

Carpenter, Susan. "Not Just for Kids: *Every Day* has Heart and Soul." Review of *Every Day*, by David Levithan. *Los Angeles Times*, 1 Sept. 2012, articles.latimes.com/2012/sep/01/entertainment/la-et-book-20120901. Accessed 7 Jan. 2019.

Gleiberman, Owen. Review of *Every Day*, directed by Michael Sucsy. *Variety*, 22 Feb. 2018, variety.com/2018/film/reviews/every-day-review-1202706500/. Accessed 7 Jan. 2019.

Kenny, Glenn. "Review: In *Every Day*, Each 24 Hours Brings Another Boyfriend." Review of *Every Day*, directed by Michael Sucsy. *The New York Times*, 22 Feb. 2018, www.nytimes.com/2018/02/22/movies/every-day-review.html. Accessed 7 Jan. 2019.

Lemire, Christy. Review of *Every Day*, directed by Michael Sucsy. *RogerEbert.com*, 23 Feb. 2018, www.rogerebert.com/reviews/every-day-2018. Accessed 7 Jan. 2019.

Levithan, David. "Interview: David Levithan Discusses *Every Day* and Its Journey from Page to Screen." Interview by Jason Palmer. *Entertainment Focus*, 20 Apr. 2018, www.entertainment-focus.com/film-section/film-interviews/interview-david-levithan-discusses-every-day-its-journey-from-page-to-screen/. Accessed 7 Jan. 2019.

Ferdinand

The Novel
Author: Munro Leaf (1905-76)
Illustrator: Robert Lawson (1892-1957)
First published: 1936

The Film
Year released: 2017
Director: Carlos Saldanha (b. 1965)
Screenplay by: Robert L. Baird, Tim Federle, Brad Copeland
Starring: John Cena, Kate McKinnon, Anthony Anderson, Bobby Cannavale, David Tennant, Peyton Manning

Context

The Story of Ferdinand, written by Munro Leaf and illustrated by Robert Lawson, came to be regarded as a classic of children's literature in the years following its publication in 1936. The book's publishers initially had little expectation of it being a major hit, printing just 5,200 copies. After selling a respectable 14,000 copies in its first year, it then sold 68,000 copies in 1937. By 1938, it had shunted Margaret Mitchell's blockbuster *Gone with the Wind* (1936) from atop the bestseller lists. Around the same time Ferdinand merchandising began to appear, everything from toys to women's accessories—even a Cartier brooch. Ferdinand received his own balloon in the annual Macy's Thanksgiving Day Parade in New York City. In 1939, Walt Disney earned an Academy Award for his adaptation of *The Story of Ferdinand* into a cartoon short.

Part of the story's phenomenal success was due to the simplicity of Leaf's tale and the charm of Lawson's illustrations, as noted by Michael Patrick Hearn for the *Washington Post*: "Each figure is individualized, each spread a new surprise as Lawson expanded the understated humor of Leaf's tale through the beautiful and hilarious pictures." Hearn continued to explain its popularity among young audiences, specifically admiring the book's overall message. "Every child knows what it is like to be forced to do something that he or she just does not want to do," Hearn wrote. "Another writer would have clumsily transformed timid Ferdinand into a hero of the bullring. But Leaf knew that true courage is being true to one's self, no matter what anyone else might say. And it is within himself that Ferdinand finds true happiness."

The book's success was also likely due to the fact that it was published right at the outbreak of the Spanish Civil

War (1936-39), which made many readers wonder if the pacifism Ferdinand projected was suggestive of political motivations on the part of the book's author and illustrator. Prominent figures like Thomas Mann, H. G. Wells, Mahatma Gandhi, and Franklin and Eleanor Roosevelt admired the children's book. Dictators Adolf Hitler of Germany and Francisco Franco of Spain had it burned and banned it from being published. Some critics saw communist or fascist leanings in Ferdinand's behavior. Leaf and Lawson, however, possessed no ulterior motive when creating the book. In October 1935, before the start of the Spanish Civil War, Leaf was looking to put together a new children's book that would highlight the work of his friend Lawson. He decided on writing a book about a bull in Spain, a place he had never been. In less than an hour, he had written the whole story and Lawson, inspired, quickly worked on the illustrations. *The Story of Ferdinand* has been published consistently since its origination and is included on the Time 100 Best Children's Books of All Time list.

Demonstrating *The Story of Ferdinand*'s popularity, the book inspired a computer graphic full-length film directed by Carlos Saldanha more than eighty years after the book's release.

Film Analysis

In order to adapt *The Story of Ferdinand* into a full-length film, Saldanha had to greatly expand on the picture book's story. The story presented by Leaf and Lawson is a fairly simple one: Ferdinand does not want to play with the other little bulls, who want nothing more than to butt heads and grow up to fight in the bullrings. He would rather sit under a cork tree and smell flowers, which his mother, a cow, lets him do because she knows it makes him happy. After accidentally getting stung by a bee, Ferdinand begins snorting, butting, and stomping in front of five men who have come from Madrid to choose the next bull to fight in the ring. Mistaking Ferdinand's reaction to the bee for fierceness, the men bring him to the bullring, where the matador and his picadores and banderilleros do their best to get Ferdinand to fight. Instead, he just sits in the ring smelling the flowers in the ladies' hair. Since he will not fight no matter what anyone does, Ferdinand is sent back home, where he happily returns to his favorite spot under the cork tree.

To expand the tale, *Ferdinand*'s screenwriters, Robert L. Baird, Tim Federle, and Brad Copeland, added numerous characters and plot elements. They also brought the story ahead in time, moving it away from Spain in the 1930s and into the modern era. A young Ferdinand (Colin H. Murphy) still begins his life as a gentle calf who refuses to fight, but now he is watched over by his father (Jeremy Sisto) instead of his mother. Ferdinand's father encourages him to be aggressive while getting ready for his own fight in the bullring, which he believes he has a chance of winning. The calves who enjoy butting heads in the book are given names and personalities in the film. As calves, Bones (Nile Diaz), Guapo (Jet Jurgensmeyer), and Valiente (Jack Gore) make fun of Ferdinand, believing him to be weak and scared. When Ferdinand's father is chosen for the bullring but does not return, Ferdinand escapes to a farm. There he becomes a beloved pet to the farmer's daughter, Nina (Julia Saldanha), even as he grows to his full, massive size.

After an adult Ferdinand (John Cena) has grown to his full size, the farmer and Nina must leave him out of their trip to the village for a flower show. Ferdinand decides to follow on his own. When he gets stung by a bee, however, he accidentally destroys the village, causing the townspeople to see him as a rampaging menace. The authorities capture him and send him back to the place where he was born. Now full grown, Bones (Anthony Anderson), Guapo (Peyton Manning), and Valiente (Bobby Cannavale) continue to make fun of Ferdinand for his unwillingness to fight, although they are astounded by his size. They have also been joined by two more bulls, Angus (David Tennant) and Maquina (Tim Nordquist). But Ferdinand becomes friends with a goat named Lupe (Kate McKinnon) and three hedgehogs.

Ferdinand slowly befriends the other bulls. When a legendary matador is unimpressed with the group, however, Guapo is sent to the local slaughterhouse. During an escape attempt, Ferdinand sees his father's horns mounted to a wall. He tries to convince the other bulls that they need to escape. All the bulls agree except Valiente, who tries to get Ferdinand to fight him but succeeds only in breaking off one of his horns. Valiente is sent to the slaughterhouse and the matador, who saw the fight, chooses Ferdinand for the bullring. In a final attempt at freedom, Ferdinand, with the help of Lupe and the hedgehogs, manages to free both Guapo and Valiente from the slaughterhouse and escape with the rest of the bulls in a truck.

A madcap car chase ensues, ending in a train station in Madrid, where Ferdinand is captured helping the others to escape. Lupe follows Ferdinand, who is sent to the bullring in Madrid. Nina and her father hear of Ferdinand's fight and travel to Madrid to help him. Here, like in the book, the bullfighters do their best to force Ferdinand to fight but he resists to smell a flower thrown into the ring. The crowd throws more flowers and calls out to the bullfighters to let him live. The matador ends the bullfight and Ferdinand is reunited with Nina and her father. He, Lupe, and the other bulls go to live on Nina's farm together. The last shot of the film is of the entire gang watching the sun set over the farm.

Although readers have interpreted *The Story of Ferdinand*'s main point in a variety of ways over the years, most critics agree that pacifism and the willingness to stay true to oneself are the most common conclusions most people draw. Saldanha also sought to highlight these aspects to his audience.

Significance

Ferdinand debuted in American theaters on December 15, 2017, the same weekend that *Star Wars: The Last Jedi* (2017) was first released in theaters. Because the animated film premiered the same weekend as the ninth installment of the blockbuster Star Wars film series, it opened in second place, garnering a little more than $13 million in its first weekend. It went on to gross more than $84 million domestically in its theatrical run and another $211 million internationally, bringing its worldwide total to more than $296 million, but was not considered to be a blockbuster success.

The movie earned a nomination for Best Animated Feature Film at the 90th Academy Awards, losing out to Pixar's *Coco* (2017). It also was nominated for Golden

Globe Awards for Best Motion Picture: Animated and Best Original Song (for "Home").

Ferdinand met its greatest success with critics and filmgoers, who gave the film mostly positive reviews. For *Variety* (7 Dec. 2017), Peter Debruge called it "sincere, likable, surprisingly funny, and overall true to its source material" and went on to declare, "'Ferdinand' may have a serious message—'It looks like weird is the new normal,' argues a movie whose hero is a selfless, non-violent fella with the courage to do his own thing—but it never forgets that it's a cartoon. As such, it's free to indulge in the sort of silliness the medium so wonderfully supports." Ben Kenigsberg, for *The New York Times* (14 Dec. 2017), was more reserved in his assessment: "'*Ferdinand*,'...speaks to its own time in a different way, dutifully adhering to the template for contemporary children's films while avoiding much personality or distinction.... And the movie is bright and peppy enough to hold young viewers' attention, though a faithful 1938 Walt Disney short showed more inventiveness in eight minutes." Despite some complaints, most critics agreed that *Ferdinand* held an important message on contesting typical norms in order to be true to oneself.

—*Christopher Mari*

Further Reading

Franklin, Ben A. "Munro Leaf, Author, Dead at 71; Creator of Ferdinand the Bull." *The New York Times*, 22 Dec. 1976, www.nytimes.com/1976/12/22/archives/munro-leaf-author-dead-at-71-creator-of-ferdinand-the-bull.html. Accessed 9 Jan. 2019.

Saldanha, Carlos. "Carlos Saldanha on Expanding the World of 'Ferdinand.'" Interview by Matt Grobar. *Deadline*, 8 Dec. 2017, deadline.com/2017/12/ferdinand-carlos-saldanha-blue-sky-studios-animation-interview-1202221411/. Accessed 9 Jan. 2019.

Bibliography

Debruge, Peter. Review of *Ferdinand*, directed by Carlos Saldanha. *Variety*, 7 Dec. 2017, variety.com/2017/film/reviews/ferdinand-review-blue-sky-bull-1202632821/. Accessed 9 Jan. 2019.

Handy, Bruce. "How 'The Story of Ferdinand' Became Fodder for the Culture Wars of Its Era." *The New Yorker*, 15 Dec. 2017, www.newyorker.com/books/page-turner/how-the-story-of-ferdinand-became-fodder-for-the-culture-wars-of-its-era. Accessed 9 Nov. 2019.

Hearn, Michael Patrick. "Ferdinand the Bull's 50th Anniversary." *The Washington Post*, 9 Nov. 1986, www.washingtonpost.com/archive/entertainment/books/1986/11/09/ferdinand-the-bulls-50th-anniversary/3325d6dc-cc68-4be7-9569-408439896098/. Accessed 9 Jan. 2019.

Kenigsberg, Ben. "Review: 'Ferdinand' Delivers a Timeless Be-Yourself Message." Review of *Ferdinand*, directed by Carlos Saldanha. *The New York Times*, 14 Dec. 2017, www.nytimes.com/2017/12/14/movies/ferdinand-review.html. Accessed 9 Jan. 2019.

MacPherson, Karen. "Hitler Banned It; Gandhi Loved It: 'The Story of Ferdinand,' the Book and, Now, Film." *The Washington Post*, 12 Dec. 2017, www.washingtonpost.com/entertainment/books/hitler-banned-it-gandhi-loved-it-the-story-of-ferdinand-the-book-and-now-film/2017/12/11/43a03e8c-de7f-11e7-bbd0-9dfb2e37492a_story.html. Accessed 9 Jan. 2019.

Fight Club

The Novel
Author: Chuck Palahniuk (b. 1962)
First published: 1996

The Film
Year released: 1999
Director: David Fincher (b. 1962)
Screenplay by: Jim Uhls
Starring: Ed Norton, Brad Pitt, Helena Bonham Carter, Meat Loaf

Context

Chuck Palahniuk's debut novel, *Fight Club*, was published in 1996. It received positive reviews from *Publishers Weekly* and *Kirkus*. "This brilliant bit of nihilism succeeds where so many self-described transgressive novels do not: It's dangerous because it's so compelling," a reviewer for the latter wrote. Still, several years passed before the novel gained in popularity. The idea for *Fight Club*—about an insomniac who forms an unlikely friendship, and a secret club in which members pummel each other to exhaustion, with an anarchic prankster—grew out of a short story Palahniuk wrote for a writing workshop with author Tom Spanbauer. Spanbauer teaches a concept called "dangerous writing," which encourages writers to access the most frightening parts of themselves in their work. Palahniuk, Spanbauer's most successful adherent, wrote *Fight Club* as a rejoinder to publishers who found his first, rejected novel too disturbing. Buoyed by the release of the film, the novel has inspired a cult following; Palahniuk's die-hard fans refer to themselves collectively as "the Cult." Palahniuk has since written about twenty other books, including *Choke* (2001), a novel about a sex addict who pays for his abusive mother's hospital expenses by pretending to choke on food at expensive restaurants. The Good Samaritans who save him inevitably offer to give him money. *Choke* was made into a film in 2008, starring Sam Rockwell.

Producers Ross Grayson Bell and Josh Donen bought the rights to *Fight Club* soon after it was published, though Palahniuk's agent warned him not to get his hopes up about it getting made. Screenwriter Jim Uhls and director David Fincher, who had already made the blockbuster crime drama *Seven*, starring Brad Pitt and Morgan Freeman in 1995, acquired the book around the same time.

Given the green light to develop the project, Uhls wrote a first draft of the screenplay before Fincher made *The Game* (1997), starring Michael Douglas. In 1997, Fincher hired Pitt (sharply increasing the film's budget) and Edward Norton to play the lead roles, and shooting began in 1998.

Director David Fincher. Photo by Raffi Asdourian via Wikimedia Commons.

The principal cast of Fight Club: (L-R) Edward Norton, Brad Pitt, Helena Boham Carter. Photos by by David Shankbone, Foreign and Commonwealth Office and Siebbi via Wikimedia Commons.

With a star-studded cast and visceral, violent appeal, *Fight Club* was as shocking as the novel on which it was based. Ads for the film ran during World Wrestling Federation (WWF) matches, and the official poster featured Pitt holding a pink bar of soap—a baffling teaser to those unfamiliar with the story. It was pitched to Fox executives as a 1990s version of the subversive coming-of-age satire *The Graduate* (1967). However, executives were taken by surprise upon being shown the film's final edit. *Fight Club* inspired deeply divided responses from critics and audiences.

Film Analysis

The film follows the same trajectory of the book. It adheres to Palahniuk's clever structure in which the story opens at the end, with Tyler Durden (Brad Pitt) shoving a gun inside the mouth of the unnamed narrator (Edward Norton). (This literary technique itself was borrowed from film conventions.) Other aspects of the film are quite different from the source material. The basic plot of *Fight Club* follows the tribulations of an unnamed thirty-something first-person narrator. He works a boring, white-collar job for a car company, assessing whether faulty parts need to be recalled. He lives comfortably in a meticulously furnished high-rise apartment, but he has a problem. He cannot sleep. Inspired by an exasperated remark from his doctor, he begins attending support groups for people with terminal illnesses. He meets Robert "Big Bob" Paulson (Meat Loaf) at a support group for men with testicular cancer. He also meets Marla Singer (Helena Bonham Carter), an emotionally unhinged chain-smoker and support-group "tourist" like the narrator. Most important among the story's other characters, though, is Tyler, a raffish prankster who lives in a dilapidated old house on a vacant street. In the book, the narrator meets Tyler on a nude beach; in the film, the two men meet on an airplane. After the narrator's apartment explodes, he moves in with Tyler. Hungry to emote and, perhaps, gain a sense of community, the men found an underground boxing club called "fight club."

At its inception, fight club consists of one-on-one bareknuckle brawls, but Tyler has a larger purpose. The single gathering becomes many gatherings and eventually evolves into a prank-oriented terrorist endeavor called Project Mayhem. The narrator becomes increasingly uncomfortable with Tyler's methods and aims, only to discover at the story's climax that he *is* Tyler. Tyler is not a flesh-and-blood human being but rather the narrator's more self-assured alter ego. The story returns to the scene in which Tyler is threatening to kill the narrator. In the film, the narrator shoots himself, surviving, but effectively "killing" Tyler, or rather, successfully silencing that part of himself that Tyler once embodied. In the book, things happen a bit differently. The narrator shoots himself and wakes up in a mental institution, convinced he has died and gone to heaven. All the orderlies are members of Project Mayhem who call him Mr. Durden, and say, in the book's last line: "We look forward to getting you back."

The idea for *Fight Club* came in part from the Cacophony Society, a real group of which Palahniuk is a member. The Cacophony Society was based on the West Coast in the 1980s and 1990s. Creators of chaos, they aimed to shake people out of complacency by orchestrating large-scale spectacles and pranks, or as Palahniuk called them, "liminoid events." The Cacophony Society was part of a tradition dating at least to the 1960s; the paradigmatic instance of a prank society was Ken Kesey's band of "Merry Pranksters," whose exploits were documented in a famous book by Tom Wolfe. The Situationists also employed humor and disruption to make political statements about life in a capitalist society. The fight club in the book is a liminoid event, Palahniuk told Kathryn Borel for *Believer* magazine, consisting of "small social experiments where people could try out a different way of being," he said. In the film, the fight club comes to fulfill Tyler's militantly anticorporate, anticonsumerist vision. Among the many riddles he offers the narrator: "The things you own end up owning you," and "It's only after we've lost everything that we're free to do anything." Reflecting a more nihilist sensibility than the Cacaphony Society and its 1960s forebears, however, Tyler's vision of self-improvement is realized through self-destruction.

In the film, Fincher sets up a visual dichotomy between the narrator's sleek but drab corporate environs—the office, interchangeable hotels and airplanes, his apartment furnished with mass-produced furniture—and the bloody, sweaty, muddy, chaotic world of Tyler. Fincher, with cinematographer Jeff Cronenworth, unites the two worlds with a very specific style and "lurid" colors, as he said in an interview with Gavin Smith for *Film Comment* magazine. He went on to cite an unusual source of inspiration. "We didn't want to be afraid of color, we wanted to control the color palette. You go into 7-Eleven in the middle of the night and there's all that green-fluorescent. And like what green light does to cellophane packages, we wanted

to make people sort of shiny." Fincher also found a way, again visually, to mimic Palahniuk's choppy, purposefully jumbled narrative. He told *Film Comment* that he wanted the first half of the film, and the establishment of the plot, to move at "the speed of thought." The beginning of the film, for instance, leaps from the gun-in-the-mouth scene back in time to the introduction of Bob and then back even further, as the narrator says in voice-over (a controversial choice that Fincher advocated for), to the introduction of the narrator himself.

Significance

The dissatisfaction of the film executives presaged the film's reception by critics. Few liked *Fight Club*, and some found the film either merely repellent or dishonest or both. Reflecting the first judgment, Roger Ebert described it as "macho porn," writing that it contained "some of the most brutal, unremitting, nonstop violence ever filmed." Reflecting the second judgment, at the heart of Ebert's critique was his frustration that the film celebrated viscerally what it criticized intellectually; the film was having it both ways. "Although sophisticates will be able to rationalize the movie as an argument against the behavior it shows, my guess is that audiences will like the behavior but not the argument," he wrote. It received a rare positive review from Janet Maslin for *The New York Times*. "'Fight Club' sounds offensive from afar," she wrote. "If watched sufficiently mindlessly, it might be mistaken for a dangerous endorsement of totalitarian tactics and super-violent nihilism in an all-out assault on society...." But, she explained, "It means to explore the lure of violence in an even more dangerously regimented, dehumanized culture. That's a hard thing to illustrate this powerfully without, so to speak, stepping on a few toes."

Fight Club was booed when it premiered at the Venice Film Festival. It enjoyed a strong audience during its first week in theaters, but it was ultimately deemed a box-office flop, earning only half the amount of money that it cost to make the film. The film soon found a cult audience through DVD sales, and it went on to be recognized as a cult classic. In 2015, Palahniuk began publishing a series of graphic novels called *Fight Club 2*, in which Tyler Durden strikes again. Visceral reactions to the film and its philosophy continue to make it a cultural touchstone.

—*Molly Hagan*

Further Reading

Maslin, Janet. "Film Review; Such a Very Long Way from Duvets to Danger." Review of *Fight Club*, directed by David Fincher. *The New York Times*, 15 Oct. 1999, www.nytimes.com/1999/10/15/movies/film-review-such-a-very-long-way-from-duvets-to-danger.html. Accessed 1 Mar. 2019.

Smith, Gavin. "Inside Out: David Fincher." *Film Comment*, vol. 35, Sept.-Oct. 1999, pp. 58-68.

Bibliography

Ebert, Roger. Review of *Fight Club*, directed by David Fincher. *RogerEbert.com*, 15 Oct. 1999, www.rogerebert.com/reviews/fight-club-1999. Accessed 1 Mar. 2019.

Lambie, Ryan. "The Difficult History of David Fincher's Fight Club." *Den of Geek*, 15 Oct. 2018, www.denofgeek.com/us/movies/fight-club/239904/the-difficult-history-of-david-finchers-fight-club. Accessed 1 Mar. 2019.

Naughton, John. "Fight Club: An Oral History." *Men's Health*, 2 Feb. 2016, www.menshealth.com/uk/building-muscle/a755460/fight-club-an-oral-history. Accessed 1 Mar. 2019.

Palahniuk, Chuck. "A Conversation with Chuck Palahniuk." Interview by Kathryn Borel. *The Believer*, 1 May 2014, believermag.com/a-conversation-with-chuck-palahniuk. Accessed 1 Mar. 2019.

Review of *Fight Club*, by Chuck Palahniuk. *Kirkus*, 1 June 1996, www.kirkusreviews.com/book-reviews/chuck-palahniuk/fight-club. Accessed 1 Mar. 2019.

First Man

The Novel
Author: James R. Hansen (b. 1952)
First published: 2005

The Film
Year released: 2018
Director: Damien Chazelle (b. 1985)
Screenplay by: Josh Singer
Starring: Ryan Gosling, Claire Foy, Jason Clarke, Kyle Chandler, Corey Stoll

Context

Twelve men walked on the moon over the course of the National Aeronautics and Space Administration's (NASA) Apollo landings from 1969 to 1972. None, however, earned the global celebrity and lasting fame as astronauts Neil Alden Armstrong and Edwin "Buzz" Aldrin, the first two humans ever to set foot on the moon when they landed on July 20, 1969. Thanks to this coveted "first man" status, Armstrong became arguably the most famous astronaut in the world, but upon retiring from NASA in 1971, he eschewed the limelight, leading a mostly private life in his home state of Ohio as a teacher, researcher, and businessman. Very little was known to the public about the famously reserved and unassuming Armstrong, other than mythical and speculative anecdotes, until 2005, when former NASA scientist James R. Hansen published his widely acclaimed book *First Man: The Life of Neil A. Armstrong*, the first authorized biography to detail the cultural icon's life.

Efforts to bring Armstrong's life to the silver screen began as early as 2003, when famed actor-director Clint Eastwood acquired the film rights to Hansen's book prior to its publication. Eastwood had previously produced, directed, and starred in the well-received science-fiction western *Space Cowboys* (2000), and seemed like an apt choice to direct the film adaptation of *First Man*. However, a meeting that Hansen brokered between Eastwood and Armstrong did not prove fruitful, resulting in Eastwood eventually giving the rights to Universal Studios. The project languished in development until 2014, when wunderkind director Damien Chazelle, who had then just completed his second feature, the smash-hit music-themed drama *Whiplash* (2014), developed an interest in it. Chazelle crafted a new seventy-two-page treatment based on Hansen's book. He then set aside the project to film *La Land* (2016), for which he won an Academy Award for best director. During this time, Chazelle and his fellow producers brought in screenwriter Josh Singer to fashion a script from Chazelle's *First Man* treatment.

The resulting film, also titled *First Man*, went into preproduction in 2017, with Chazelle directing and Singer serving as the sole screenwriter. Drawing on only parts of Hansen's meticulously researched book, which offers an all-encompassing look at Armstrong's life and career, the film focuses exclusively on the momentous eight-year period leading up to Armstrong's historic mission to the moon. During this time, NASA, answering a challenge issued by US president John F. Kennedy, launched its landmark Gemini and Apollo programs and overtook the Soviet Union in the space race. The film, on which Hansen served as a coproducer, saw Chazelle team up again with Gosling. Gosling signed on to portray Armstrong, who died at the age of eighty-two in 2012. Gosling starred alongside English actor Claire Foy, who was cast as Armstrong's first wife, Janet. They headed an ensemble cast that included actors Jason Clarke, Kyle Chandler, Corey Stoll, and Ciarán Hinds. Distributed by Universal and cofinanced by Steven Spielberg's DreamWorks Pictures, *First Man* premiered at Italy's Venice International Film Festival on August 29, 2018.

Film Analysis

Unlike Hansen's book, which is structured as a conventional chronological biography, beginning with an extensive account of Armstrong's early life and upbringing, Chazelle's film opens with a bravura sequence that works as a composite of the years Armstrong spent as a NASA research test pilot at Edwards Air Force Base in southern

California. The year is 1961 and Armstrong (Ryan Gosling) is shown flying an X-15 rocket-powered plane that inadvertently bounces off the Earth's atmosphere. Using a combination of claustrophobic, convulsing cinematography, bone-rattling sound design, and breathtaking visual effects, Chazelle and his collaborators expertly hook the viewer by creating a visceral, first-person experience of hypersonic flight.

Upon landing safely in the Mojave Desert, Armstrong returns to Edwards, where he is soon informed that he will be grounded for this latest mishap. The film then transitions to a shot of his two-year-old daughter, Karen, receiving treatment for a brain tumor. The analytically minded Armstrong, whose love for flying was only outweighed by his passion for aeronautical engineering, is subsequently shown poring over a personal log of her symptoms and possible treatment methods. Karen soon dies, however, devastating him and his wife Janet (Claire Foy). In his book, Hansen notes that Karen's death "shattered Neil to the core," and illustrates how this traumatic event could have been partly responsible for several flying "mishaps," including the one portrayed in the opening sequence of Chazelle's film. Though Armstrong claimed otherwise, Chazelle and screenwriter Josh Singer use the grief caused by Karen's illness and death, which is only given a brief four-page chapter in the book, to form the emotional center of the film. That emotional emphasis is strengthened by composer Justin Hurwitz's sublimely poignant theremin-laden musical score, which features variations on a motif that can be interpreted as an extended lullaby to Armstrong's daughter.

Both the book and the film speculate that Karen's death was likely an impetus behind Armstrong joining NASA and becoming an astronaut. Adhering closely to events and incidents chronicled in the book, the rest of *First Man* follows Armstrong as he becomes part of NASA's second group of astronauts, known as the "New Nine." These men played instrumental roles in the launching of the highly successful Gemini and Apollo programs, which culminated with Apollo 11's first manned landing on the moon in July 1969. After officially being selected as an astronaut in September 1962, Armstrong moves to Houston, Texas, with Janet and their young son, Rick; the couple have a second son, Mark, in 1963. In Texas, Armstrong becomes close friends with fellow incoming astronauts Ed White (Jason Clarke), who lives across the street, and Elliot See (Patrick Fugit).

In depicting Armstrong's transition from research test pilot to astronaut, Chazelle uses artistic license to effectively dramatize certain events and to offer a more well-rounded, three-dimensional portrait of the man. In the film, for example, Armstrong is shown receiving the news of his selection as an astronaut from NASA chief Deke Slayton (Kyle Chandler) while sitting at the dinner table with Janet at their home in Juniper Hills, California—making the event emotionally and visually striking. However, according to Hansen's book, Armstrong actually received the news while working at his office at Edwards. Following his selection, Armstrong, along with his New Nine cohorts, had to undergo two years of intensive basic training that included a rigorous academic curriculum and strenuous physical tests. Though this training is only given cursory mention in the book, the film dedicates several scenes to it, offering Chazelle an opportunity to subtly reveal aspects of Armstrong's character, such as his deadpan wit, laconic demeanor, and determined temperament.

Though *First Man* does feature scenes showing the strong camaraderie that Armstrong forms with his New Nine peers, particularly See and White, the film is mostly an intimate character study of an intensely private man who struggles to balance the demands of work and family. Armstrong's unfailing commitment to his job takes a major toll on his marriage to Janet, whom he struggles to open up to on an emotional level, especially as it pertains to Karen. As Armstrong endures more personal loss after becoming an astronaut, the couple's interactions become fraught with tension. This is conveyed visually through uncomfortable silences, terse exchanges, and heated blow-ups. Throughout the film, there are a number of shots of Armstrong alone at his desk at home from outside of doorways, an effective framing device to illustrate his introspective, solitary nature. Recurring images of the moon nonetheless repeatedly remind viewers of Armstrong's overall goal.

To achieve that goal, Armstrong must overcome more obstacles and adversity. Further highlighting the theme of loss and grief, Chazelle and Singer home in on two tragic events that would also have a major impact on Armstrong's life: the deaths of See and White. Armstrong is shown receiving the news of the former just two weeks before he almost dies himself while carrying out his fateful Gemini 8 mission, on March 16, 1966, in which he and copilot Dave Scott successfully conducted the first docking of two spacecraft in orbit. That mission and White's death—less than a year later in the 1967 Apollo 1 capsule fire that also killed two other astronauts—are harrowingly reenacted in the docudrama mold. Armstrong's second near-death experience a little more than a year later while testing the Lunar Landing Research Vehicle (LLRV) is also depicted, albeit in a slightly different way than in the book. In the film, after being forced to eject from the LLRV's rocket-powered seat just seconds before crashing, Armstrong, bloodied and partially covered in soot, briefly returns home to wash up, quickly gulping down an iced tea before returning to work to write up an accident report. The book only includes the story of an incredulous colleague, astronaut Al Bean, who witnessed Armstrong calmly working on the report an hour after the accident occurred.

All of these events effectively build up to the film's final climactic sequence of Armstrong's Apollo 11 mission to the moon, which is also reenacted in vivid detail. Chazelle eschews predictable biopic tropes by not wasting screen time on the weighty and oft-debated decision behind Armstrong being the first out of the lunar module, which is discussed at length in Hansen's book. Instead, he focuses on his brief, tense interactions with Apollo 11 crewmates Buzz Aldrin (Corey Stoll), who up until this sequence is portrayed as highly assertive, and Mike Collins (Lukas Haas), the mission's command module pilot, prior to his historic moonwalk. After delivering his famous "one small step" speech, which is carefully recreated, Armstrong drops Karen's baby bracelet inside the moon's Little West crater, an action that is speculated on in the book. Upon completing their mission, Armstrong, Aldrin, and Collins return home and are placed in a mandatory three-week quarantine. There, President Kennedy's famous 1962 "moon speech" is shown on a television, demonstrating that Armstrong and his copilots have fulfilled his challenge. The film then concludes with Armstrong and Janet tenderly pressing their palms together on opposite sides of a glass partition in the quarantine facility.

Significance

Following its world premiere, *First Man* screened at the United States' Telluride Film Festival and at Canada's Toronto International Film Festival, among others. It was released in theaters throughout the United States and the United Kingdom on October 12, 2018. Over the following months, *First Man* opened in numerous other countries around the world. After taking in $16 million in box office receipts during its opening weekend, the film grossed a total of $44.9 million in the United States. The film fared better abroad, amassing $60.5 million in total from other markets, helping it to recoup its $59 million production budget.

Despite earning $104 million worldwide, *First Man* was considered a commercial disappointment. Still, the film received mostly rave reviews from critics, many of whom praised its direction, script, cinematography, sound design, and score, as well as Gosling and Foy's performances. Widely considered to be a significant technical achievement of sight and sound, the film made numerous critics' top-ten lists for 2018, including that of *Variety*'s Owen Gleiberman, who commented that it "redefines what space travel is, the way it lives inside our imaginations, by capturing what the stakes really were." The film received many accolades, most notably Academy Award nominations for best sound editing, best sound mixing, best production design, and best visual effects, winning in the latter category.

Notwithstanding its critical success, *First Man* unexpectedly became the subject of controversy due to its decision not to portray the planting of the American flag during the Apollo 11 moon landing sequence. Deemed by some to be un-American, the omission sparked heated reactions from a range of conservative politicians and pundits, US president Donald Trump, and even Buzz Aldrin, who weighed in on the flap by posting several cryptic Twitter messages alongside images of the flag planting. In response to the furor, Chazelle, who opted to show the flag in the background of the moon landing sequence, refuted claims that it was a politicized artistic decision, instead explaining that it represented the film's overall aim of focusing on aspects of Armstrong and the Apollo 11 moon mission that were previously unknown to the American public. Chazelle was supported by Hansen and Armstrong's sons, and most critics, in fact, considered the film, which featured numerous American flag images, to be highly patriotic.

Released one year before Apollo's 11's fiftieth anniversary, *First Man* is ultimately a celebration of not just a remarkable American achievement but one for all humankind. The film sheds meaningful light on a reluctant and deeply complex figure, and contrary to its Hollywood predecessors, such as Philip Kaufman's *The Right Stuff* (1983) and Ron Howard's *Apollo 13* (1995), it reinvents the space docudrama as an immersive and intimate character study.

—Chris Cullen

Further Reading

Hansen, James R. *First Man: The Life of Neil A. Armstrong*. Simon & Schuster, 2005.

Kluger, Jeffrey. "Space is Terrifying. Ryan Gosling and Damien Chazelle Prove It in Their New Movie." Review of *First Man*, directed by Damien Chazelle. *Time*, 11 Oct. 2018, time.com/5421573/first-man-damien-chazelle/. Accessed 18 Feb. 2019.

Tapley, Kristopher. "How Neil Armstrong Biopic 'First Man' Achieved Lift Off." *Variety*, 3 Sept. 2018, variety.com/2018/film/in-contention/how-neil-armstrong-biopic-first-man-achieved-lift-off-1202925131/. Accessed 18 Feb. 2019.

Bibliography

Edelstein, David. "First Man Is Laborious—and Stupendous." Review of *First Man*, directed by Damien Chazelle. *Vulture*, 12 Oct. 2018, www.vulture.com/2018/10/first-man-review-a-laborious-stupendous-space-movie.html. Accessed 18 Feb. 2019.

"First Man." *Box Office Mojo*, www.boxofficemojo.com/movies/?id=firstman.htm. Accessed 18 Feb. 2019.

Gleiberman, Owen. Review of *First Man*, directed by Damien Chazelle. *Variety*, 29 Aug. 2018, variety.com/2018/film/reviews/first-man-review-ryan-gosling-damien-chazelle-1202920157/. Accessed 18 Feb. 2019.

Rose, Steve. "'If Anyone Can Maga, It Is Nasa': How First Man's Flag 'Snub' Made Space Political Again." *The Guardian*, 6 Sept. 2018, www.theguardian.com/film/2018/sep/06/if-anyone-can-maga-it-is-nasa-how-first-man-put-a-rocket-up-the-politics-of-space. Accessed 18 Feb. 2019.

Scott, A. O. "Review: 'First Man' Takes a Giant Leap for Man, a Smaller Step for Movies." Review of *First Man*, directed by Damien Chazelle. *The New York Times*, 10 Oct. 2018, www.nytimes.com/2018/10/10/movies/first-man-review-ryan-gosling-damien-chazelle.html. Accessed 18 Feb. 2019.

Seitz, Matt Zoller. Review of *First Man*, directed by Damien Chazelle. *RogerEbert.com*, 12 Oct. 2018, www.rogerebert.com/reviews/first-man-2018. Accessed 18 Feb. 2019.

Travers, Peter. "'First Man' Review: Neil Armstrong Biopic Brings a Hero Back to Earth." Review of *First Man*, directed by Damien Chazelle. *Rolling Stone*, 10 Oct. 2018, www.rollingstone.com/movies/movie-reviews/first-man-movie-review-734973/. Accessed 18 Feb. 2019.

Freak the Mighty / The Mighty

The Novel
Author: Rodman Philbrick (b. 1951)
First published: 1993

The Film
Year released: 1998
Director: Peter Chelsom (b. 1956)
Screenplay by: Charles Leavitt
Starring: Kieran Culkin, Elden Henson, Sharon Stone

Context

Freak the Mighty is a young adult novel about an unlikely friendship between two teenaged boys, Max and Kevin, who both have challenges that make them outsiders in their community. Max has a learning disability, which has resulted in him repeating seventh grade multiple times. He is large for his age and is unfairly judged by many for his imprisoned father's crimes. Kevin, nicknamed Freak, suffers from Morquio Syndrome, making him extremely small and fragile, and unable to walk without crutches and braces. Despite his physical disabilities, Kevin is incredibly smart. Both boys are bullied for their differences and soon join forces, each one using his strengths to bolster the other's weaknesses. As a team they are known as "Freak the Mighty" with Max acting as Kevin's legs by letting him ride on his shoulders, and Kevin acting as the "brains" of the duo.

Although the plot is fictional, the main characters of Max and Freak were inspired by real-life childhood acquaintances of the author, Rodman Philbrick. Growing up, there was a small boy in his neighborhood who was very smart and would ride on the shoulders of another taller boy. The author recalls that the real person who inspired the character of Kevin "had an advanced vocabulary at a young age. So, I wanted him to express himself in a way that might be above a reader's vocabulary level," thus inspiring the dictionary that appears in the back of the book to help readers who may not be familiar with some of the words Kevin uses. Philbrick wanted readers to understand Kevin without having to look up terms in a separate dictionary. "This way, all the reader has to do is flip to the end of the book. Of course, once I started writing word definitions in Kevin's voice, I got carried away and wanted it to be interesting and funny, just like Kevin,"

Philbrick explains. In the film, Kevin's mom alludes to this quirk, stating "I gave birth to a 7 1/2-pound dictionary."

The book was well-received by readers and critics alike and was the recipient of various awards, including the American Library Association's Best Books for Young Adults. After the success of the first novel, Philbrick wrote a sequel to *Freak the Mighty*, which was published in 1998 entitled *Max the Mighty*.

Film Analysis

As with the novel, the film adaptation of *Freak the Mighty* follows the unlikely friendship and ensuing adventures of Max (Elden Henson) and Kevin (Kieran Culkin). Renamed simply *The Mighty*, the film follows the general plot of the book with some differences. While Philbrick, the book's author, submitted a screenplay for the film early on, the studio ultimately decided to go with Charles Leavitt's version. Despite this, Philbrick said he was satisfied with how the film turned out, acknowledging that sometimes it is necessary to make changes for cinematic purposes.

The film takes place in Cincinnati, Ohio, a change from the far less urban, industrial setting of Portsmouth, New Hampshire, where the book is set. This change of setting adds a certain edginess to the atmosphere of the film with the city becoming almost a character in and of itself. Kevin and his mom, Gwen (Sharon Stone), have recently moved next door to Max's grandparents, with whom he has lived since his mother's death at the hands of his father, who is now in prison. Our first glimpse of Kevin is in his backyard flying his ornithopter, a toy aircraft that has flapping wings like a bird. Max is intrigued by his new neighbor with leg braces and a larger-than-life attitude despite his small stature and twisted body.

Both the book and the film are told from the perspective of Max, who up until this time has led a lonely existence being tormented by a group of bullies led by Blade (Joe Perrino). When Blade and his cohorts throw a basketball at Kevin in gym class, knocking him over, Max is blamed for the incident. Later, when he is waiting for a tutor to arrive, he is surprised to see Kevin, who arrives to help him with reading. The two sort out the misunderstanding from gym class and Kevin introduces Max to King Arthur and the Knights of the Round Table. Kevin says, "The knights were like the first human version of robots. They wore this metal armor to protect them and make them invincible." It is clear in a way that Kevin uses fantasy as a coping mechanism, the braces on his legs, like the armor of the knights. This becomes a reoccurring theme in the film, the knights appearing whenever the two friends go on adventures and perform good deeds, sabotaging the misdeeds of Blade and his gang of troublemakers. At one point, we see Kevin on Max's shoulders as they walk across a bridge giving the visual impression that Kevin is a knight riding atop his horse.

It is on one of these occasions, when riding on Max's shoulders, that Kevin leads him to a building he describes as a laboratory where he claims he is part of a secret experiment and "likely within the next year, I will enter that lab. I am going to be the first biogenetically improved human." Max does not realize at the time that the building they are looking at is actually an industrial laundromat and that Kevin likely will not survive another year with his medical condition. Kevin's story about a body transplant is merely his way of coping with the unthinkable.

Like Kevin, Max has his own coping strategies for the darkness and trauma surrounding the death of his mother and his hatred and fear of his father, her murderer. There is a scene in the film where Max lies under his bed and imagines looking up into the clouds saying, "There's a place I go in my head sometimes. It's cool and dim in there and you float like a cloud. No, you are a cloud. You don't have to think about anything. You're nothing, you're nobody." This is Max's safe space, where the world and its cruelty cannot touch him. While a similar scene appears in the book, it is somehow more powerful seeing it on-screen, Max's large body squeezed beneath his bed, effectively trying to disappear from a world that has wronged him in so many ways.

Later, when Max's father, "Killer Kane" (James Gandolfini), is let out of prison, he kidnaps Max from his room on Christmas Eve. He brings him to the apartment of his accomplices Loretta Lee (Gillian Anderson) and Iggy (Meat Loaf), unaware that Max had been to the apartment earlier with Freak to return Loretta's wallet. When Killer Kane finds Loretta trying to help Max escape, he violently attacks her, triggering traumatic memories of Max's own mother's brutal murder. Meanwhile, Kevin has connected the dots and realizes where Max has been taken, and he takes matters into his own hands and absconds with his mother's van on his way to save Max. When the van breaks down en route, he creates a makeshift sled, zooming through the park determined to be the hero.

After some tense moments in which Max's father realizes that Freak knows where he is holding Max, Kevin and Max are able to escape and Kane is taken into custody by the police. The kidnapping scene is far less dramatic in the book, where Kevin rescues Max by calling the police and telling them to look for Iggy, rather than taking matters into his own hands and asking someone else to call the police. Max is finally able to confront the demons related to his mother's murder and healing can begin. Once Max and Kevin are reunited with Gwen, Gram (Gena Rowlands), and Grim (Harry Dean Stanton), the group celebrates Christmas together, happy to turn over a new leaf with Killer Kane back in prison. However, their happiness is short-lived when Kevin passes away in his sleep. Max is devastated and the scene in which he runs through the laundromat thinking he will find Kevin is poignant and heartbreaking.

Both Henson and Culkin give strong performances as Max and Kevin. They have good chemistry and despite some unrealistic action sequences in the film, the friendship conveyed by the actors is real and touching. Even though the two are almost opposites, both in terms of physicality and intellect, Max and Kevin are truly "two peas in a pod" and have similar demons. They each bring something unique to the friendship that makes the other person somehow more complete. By the time Kevin dies, Max is finally beginning to see himself in a more positive light because of Kevin's friendship. Though the ending is sad due to Kevin's passing, there is also a sense of optimism as Max is able to overcome his challenges and recognize his own self-worth.

Significance

Although *The Mighty* was not a big budget film and only grossed $2.6 million at the box office, it received many positive reviews from critics. It was also nominated for two Golden Globe awards and has achieved a cult following of adoring fans over the years. Roger Ebert gave the film three stars stating in reference to the Arthurian theme of the film, "No child is completely a captive of a sad childhood if he can read and has books; they are the window to what can be, and that is the underlying message of *The Mighty*." Janet Maslin of *The New York Times* praises director Peter Chelsom, "his sense of visual enchantment easily accommodates the boys' preoccupation with all things Arthurian and the story's way of letting dreams of knighthood loom large and literal from time to time. From the directorial standpoint, this was no easy task."

The Mighty is a film about friendship first and foremost and how the effects of that relationship can allow for amazing individual growth. Max and Kevin are so much more than they appear on the surface; and only when they join forces, do they realize how powerful they really are.

The lasting impression the friendship leaves on Max, despite the untimely death of his partner in crime, finally allows him to fully come into his own.

—Aimee Chevrette Bear

Further Reading

Philbrick, Rodman. *Freak the Mighty*. Blue Sky Press, 1993.
———. "Rodman Philbrick Interview Transcript." *Scholastic*, www.scholastic.com/teachers/articles/teaching- content/rodman-philbrick-interview-transcript/. Accessed 10 May 2020.

Bibliography

Ebert, Roger. "*The Mighty*." *RogerEbert.com*, 16 Oct. 1998, www.rogerebert.com/reviews/the-mighty-1998. Accessed 10 May 2020.
Errigo, Angie. "*The Mighty* Review," *Empire*, 1 Jan. 2000, www.empireonline.com/movies/reviews/mighty-review/. Accessed 10 May 2020.
Maslin, Janet. "Film Review; Talents to Make Buddies: Walking and Wisecracking," *The New York Times*, 9 Oct. 1998, www.nytimes.com/1998/10/09/movies/film-review-talents-to-make-buddies-walking-and-wisecracking.html. Accessed 10 May 2020.

Fugitive Pieces

The Novel
Author: Anne Michaels (b. 1958)
First published: 1996

The Film
Year released: 2007
Director: Jeremy Podeswa (b. 1962)
Screenplay by: Jeremy Podeswa
Starring: Stephen Dillane, Rade Serbedzija, Rosamund Pike, Ayelet Zurer

Context

Fugitive Pieces (1996) is a novel written by the Canadian author Anne Michaels, who first earned critical acclaim as a poet with her award-winning collections *The Weight of Oranges* (1986) and *Miner's Pond* (1991). A native of Ontario, she attended the Vaughn Road Academy as well as the University of Toronto. Michaels has said that she transitioned from poetry to prose because she wanted to explore certain themes more thoroughly. It took her nearly a decade to write *Fugitive Pieces*, which was met with overwhelmingly positive reviews from readers and critics alike. In addition to earning the Orange Prize for Fiction and *The Guardian* Fiction Prize, it remained on the Canadian bestseller list for two years and was translated into twenty languages. Exploring the relationship between history and memory, *Fugitive Pieces* follows the story of Jakob, a Holocaust survivor, as well as his neighbor Ben, who is the son of Holocaust survivors. Michaels's second novel, *The Winter Vault* (2009), was published thirteen years later. Both books are thematically about loss, history, displacement, and human connection. As a writer, Michaels is comparable to other Canadian poet-novelists such as Margaret Atwood, Jane Urquhart, and Michael Ondaatje.

The film adaptation of *Fugitive Pieces* was led by Canadian filmmaker Jeremy Podeswa. Prior to *Fugitive Pieces*, Podeswa was best known as a television director for prestigious dramas like *Queer as Folk* and *Six Feet Under*. Podeswa's desire to write the screenplay and direct *Fugitive Pieces* was in part due to his personal connection to the material. Of Polish Jewish descent like the character of Jakob, Podeswa is also the son of a Holocaust survivor. The development of *Fugitive Pieces* took place over the course of seven years. Podeswa chose to shoot it in Can- ada and Greece, casting mostly unknown actors, including Stephen Dillane, Rade Serbedzija, Rosamund Pike, and Ayelet Zurer. Podeswa has since been involved in directing *Game of Thrones* and *Boardwalk Empire*, among others.

Film Analysis

The film *Fugitive Pieces* differs from the book in several important ways. Arguably the most noticeable is the way in which Podeswa organizes the narrative. Michaels's book is divided into two parts, the first of which follows the experience of Jakob Beer from the time he was a little boy in Poland during World War II to adulthood in Canada and Greece. The second part of the book is told from the perspective of Ben, who grew up across the hallway from Jakob in Toronto. While Ben is still an important character in this iteration of the story, his role is much smaller in the film than in the book. To ensure the film feels like it is told exclusively from Jakob's point of view, Podeswa uses excerpts from Jakob's writing in the form of voice-over to narrate certain scenes. Additionally, the director does not include many scenes in which Jakob is not present.

Like the book, the film *Fugitive Pieces* is about Jakob (Dillane) grappling and eventually reconciling with his grief, fear, and survivor's guilt. Podeswa begins the film by intercutting scenes of the events responsible for such complex feelings: Jakob as a young boy (Robbie Kay) watching from behind a crack in the wall while his family prepares for the imminent arrival of Nazi soldiers and him running through the woods soon after. Podeswa does not linger on the disturbing imagery of Jakob's father being shot or his sister being taken away by the soldiers, but rather shows it in brief fragments with the walls encroaching on the frame so that it feels as though it is truly from the perspective of a child in hiding.

The event that begins Jakob's story of being a survivor is when he is discovered in the woods by Athos Roussos (Serbedzija), a Greek archeologist who is working in Poland during the Nazi invasion. Athos brings Jakob back to Greece and keeps him safe until the end of the war. To mark this transition in Jakob's life, Podeswa uses different colors and light. For example, the scenes in Poland appear dark and cold as though they have been shot through a blue-gray filter, while the sunshine and whitewashed houses of Greece feel optimistic and hopeful. In many ways, Podeswa depicts the physical landscape of Greece as a reflection of Athos's character. Throughout Jakob's life, Athos proves to be a light in the darkness. Ultimately, he is the one who takes Jakob to Canada to start over and later teaches him to turn his negative feelings into something valuable by writing.

Podeswa jumps back and forth in time throughout the film, from Jakob's childhood with Athos to his adult years as a published writer and husband. The story slowly moves forward in a linear fashion, however, demonstrating Jakob's evolution over time. The introduction of the character of Ben provides a kind of reflection of Jakob's experience. Where Jakob is haunted by his past, Ben is haunted by his parents' past. In the book, Ben finds comfort in reading Jakob's poems. In the film, Ben serves more as a tool that allows Jakob to better understand himself. In one scene, for example, Jakob witnesses Ben's father screaming at him for not finishing an apple, declaring that there was no point in him surviving the Nazis if his son could not understand the value of things. Here, Jakob witnesses how harmful it can be when people hold onto the tragedies of their pasts.

The film ending differs radically from the novel. At the end of Michaels' book, Jakob dies. In the movie, however, Jakob returns to Toronto and meets Ben and his girlfriend for dinner. They introduce him to Michaela, a woman he will eventually marry. Jakob is willing to share his past with Michaela and be honest about his pain. For the first time, he is also willing to allow himself to let go of these feelings. The two travel to Greece together and it is there in Athos's homeland that he allows himself to feel happiness again. Michaela becomes pregnant and, for the first time since he was a little boy, Jakob is able to look to the future.

Significance

Fugitive Pieces debuted on the opening night of the Toronto International Film Festival on September 6, 2007. It went on to a limited release in the United States on May 2, 2008, at just thirty-eight theaters. Filmed on a budget of $12 million CAD, it grossed a total of $843,945 worldwide and consequently can be considered a financial failure.

Fugitive Pieces received mostly positive reviews from critics, earning a favorable aggregate score of 68 percent on *Rotten Tomatoes*. Most praised the way that the film explored difficult historical events in a delicate way. In his review for *IndieWire*, Leo Goldsmith wrote that it was, "Nostalgic, deeply felt, and refreshingly astute, *Fugitive Pieces* is something of a rare bird these days—a big-budget, transnational, historical drama that actually justifies its scope and subject matter with more than visual opulence." Not all critics agreed, however. Some felt as though Podeswa's decision to jump back and forth in time was clunky and disorienting. Others argued that the film's biggest problem was its failure to capture the brilliance of its source material. Philip French wrote in *The Guardian* that, "Michaels's novel is a complex, literary work about memory, history, and survival guilt. Much of its appeal resides in a precise, poetic diction, a subtle allusiveness and the seamless interweaving of past and present. Podeswa's confusing, commonplace film lumbers along with a painful sincerity." Although it did not perform well at the box office, *Fugitive Pieces* did win a handful of rewards, including Best Film at the 2008 Sydney Film Festival and the Audience Award at the Sarasota Film Festival.

—Emily E. Turner

Further Reading

Botez, Catalina. "Liquefactions: River Floods and Tides of Memory in Anne Michaels' *Fugitive Pieces*." *Social Alternatives*, vol. 33, no. 2, 2014, pp. 23-30. *EBSCOhost*, search.ebscohost.com/login.aspx?direct=true&db=f6h&AN=98 001671&site=ehost-live. Accessed 31 May 2020.

Goldsmith, Leo. "The Archaeologist's Dilemma: Jeremy Podeswa's *Fugitive Pieces*." *IndieWire*, 28 Apr. 2008, www.indiewire.com/2008/04/review-the-archaeologists-dilemma-jeremy-podeswas-fugitive-pieces-72507/. Accessed 20 May 2020.

Kakutani, Michiko. "Surviving the Past through the Power of Words." *The New York Times*, 7 Mar. 1997, www.nytimes.com/1997/03/07/books/surviving-the-past-through-the-power-of-words.html. Accessed 20 May 2020.

Bibliography

Crown, Sarah. "Anne Michaels, Fugitive Author." *The Guardian*, 1 May 2009, www.theguardian.com/books/2009/may/02/interview-anne-michaels. Accessed 20 May 2020.

Di Piero, W. S. "Fossil Remains." *The New York Times*, 20 Apr. 1997, archive.nytimes.com/www.nytimes.com/books/97/04/20/reviews/970420.20dipiert.html. Accessed 20 May 2020.

French, Philip. "*Fugitive Pieces*." The Guardian, 30 May 2009, www.theguardian.com/film/2009/may/31/fugitive-pieces-film-review. Accessed 20 May 2020.

Vaughan, R. M. "'A Feeling of Awe' for Toronto-Born, Emmy-Nominated Director Jeremy Podeswa." *The Globe and Mail*, 16 Sept. 2018, www.theglobeandmail.com/arts/television/article-a-feeling-of-awe-for-toronto-born-emmy-nominated-director-jeremy/. Accessed 20 May 2020.

The Goldfinch

The Novel
Author: Donna Tartt (b. 1963)
First published: 2013

The Film
Year released: 2019
Director: John Crowley (b. 1969)
Screenplay by: Peter Straughan
Starring: Ansel Elgort, Oakes Fegley, Finn Wolfhard, Luke Wilson, Nicole Kidman, Jeffrey Wright, Sarah Paulson, Aneurin Barnard

Context

Publishing a novel every ten or eleven years, Donna Tartt has become one of America's most important novelists and has inspired something of a cult following. Tartt grew up in Mississippi and studied Creative Writing at The University of Mississippi and Bennington College. At Bennington, she rubbed shoulders with other members of the 1980s literary brat pack, including Bret Easton Ellis (to whom she would dedicate her first novel), Jill Eisenstadt, and Jonathan Lethem. Tartt waited longer than many of her contemporaries to publish her first novel, 1992's *The Secret History*. A brilliant fusion of thriller and literary fiction, *The Secret History* was a critically lauded bestseller. It would be another decade before Tartt released her next book, *The Little Friend* (2002). In this novel, Tartt returned to her native Mississippi, writing a Southern-Gothic inflected slow-burn of a mystery about the death of a child and the effect the loss has on his family.

The release of Tartt's third novel was a much-anticipated literary event. *The Goldfinch* (2013) was a runaway bestseller and was the winner of the Pulitzer Prize for fiction. While critics like Michiko Kakutani of *The New York Times* and author Stephen King praised it, others—including James Wood in *The New Yorker* and novelist Francine Prose—dismissed it as implausible and juvenile.

The book is centered around Theo Decker, a young man whose world is shattered when his mother is killed in a bombing at the Metropolitan Museum of Art. Theo survives the blast, and takes with him Carel Fabritius's painting, "The Goldfinch," as he escapes the museum. Over this sprawling, Dickensian story, Theo passes through various stages of life and deals with both the loss of his old world and with the weight of being responsible for a great work of art.

In 2019, director John Crowley's film version of *The Goldfinch*, based on Peter Straughan's screenplay, was released. Crowley had garnered strong reviews with a previous literary adaptation, *Brooklyn* (2015). In the film version of *The Goldfinch*, Ansel Elgort and Oakes Fegley play the older and younger versions of Theo, respectively. The cast is rounded out by better-known actors, including Finn Wolfhard (star of *Stranger Things*), Luke Wilson, Jeffrey Wright, and Nicole Kidman. Released at the Toronto Film Festival, the film seemed designed to replicate on the silver screen the success of the novel: it was meant to be a literary crowd-pleaser that would earn both accolades and box-office returns.

Film Analysis

Crowley's film version of *The Goldfinch* stays true to the novel's plot, carefully recreating scenes like the bombing in the museum and settings like the antique workshop that becomes a second home for Theo, and the windswept desert around Las Vegas. Yet Cowley and screenwriter Peter Straughan choose to fracture the chronology of this plot. Rather than telling the story linearly, as Tartt does, the film transitions back and forth between scenes of Theo as a boy and as a young man. This structure creates some interesting parallels, juxtaposing the two parts of Theo's life as mirrors of each other. At its best, this structure demonstrates the lingering trauma of Theo's loss of his mother. But Tartt's plot relies so much on happy accidents and absurd twists that it may suffer when reconstructed in this more formal way, which stresses parallelism and correspondence, but also highlights the plot's inherent implausibility.

One of the challenges in adapting *The Goldfinch* lies in capturing, in one way or another, Theo's first-person narration. Theo's voice is the engine of Tartt's novel; it is what carries the reader across the disparate parts of Theo's fractured life and of the novel's sprawling plot. While the film uses occasional first-person voice-overs to incorporate some aspects of Theo's narration, it struggles to replicate the novel's sense of intimacy. The visual medium of film ultimately distances the viewer from Theo, and in particular from the older version played by Ansel Elgort. Without the ability to narrate his own story, Theo becomes a mystery. His practiced urbanity and unflappability wall off the viewer just as effectively as they do his contemporaries.

The Goldfinch may ultimately be more successful at portraying places and objects than it is at revealing characters' inner lives. Cinematographer Roger Deakins, who has been nominated for fourteen Academy Awards, brilliantly realizes one location after another. Theo's life is an odyssey, a long struggle to find his home again. After the bombing in the museum, he is taken in by the Barbours, the wealthy family of a classmate. Mrs. Barbour (Kidman) has filled her Park Avenue apartment with antiques and paintings, and it is, for a brief period of time, a refuge for Theo. He also begins frequenting the antiques workshop of Hobie (Wright), a father figure whose partner was killed in the blast. Deakins's ability to capture on film the heft and texture of antique furniture is critical to the success of these scenes; he lends the viewer the practiced eye of Mrs. Barbour, Hobie, or, eventually, Theo himself. Filming on location in New York City is likewise critical to the success of the film. Crowley and Deakins evoke a timeless, well-heeled Manhattan that will always be Theo's true home. When Theo's "no good" father (Luke Wilson) spirits him away to Las Vegas, the foreclosed tract houses and windswept scrublands of this setting stand in sharp contrast to the permanence of Manhattan. The film juxtaposes these two settings, making them the spiritual poles of Theo's life.

The film assembles a solid cast to support Fegley and Elgort. Wilson and Sarah Paulson, as Theo's father and his girlfriend, each bring a brash crudeness to their roles that is a striking contrast to the sophistication of the Barbours and the gentleness of Hobie. On a similar note, Finn Wolfhard infuses some much-needed energy into the story as Boris, the wild friend whom Theo meets in Las Vegas. Wolfhard and Fegley capture the odd-couple dynamic and the deep affection between the two boys. Aneurin Barnard struggles gamely as a grown-up Boris, but never quite matches his youthful counterpart's energy. Perhaps the strongest performances belong to Wright and Kidman, as Hobie and Mrs. Barbour, Theo's surrogate father and mother. The color-blind casting of Wright (who is African American) as Hobie, who is described as being white in the novel, helps to diversify the cast and to deepen a character whose infinite patience can, even in the novel's treatment of him, seem like a form of wish fulfilment.

The scenes between Theo and Hobie are perhaps the most powerful ones in the film. In particular, the exchange in which Theo confesses that he has been selling chimeras—faux antiques cobbled together out of cast-off original parts and cleverly disguised new ones—is particularly devastating. Wright's performance is tremendously compelling, and he brings the kind-hearted antiquarian to life. Likewise, Kidman is riveting as Mrs. Barbour, both in the earlier and later stages of the story. Ultimately, however, she is a minor character in this story, and Kidman's impressive turn in this role serves a disappointingly limited purpose. While she is thoroughly convincing as a luminous, genteel society type, one almost wonders whether it would have been better to cast her as the woman who truly haunts this story: Theo's mother.

These casting issues go hand-in-hand with a central shortcoming of the film. Its fidelity to the novel's plot causes it to rush through a great many scenes, events, and characters at a harried pace that is quite different from the overbearing passage of the novel itself. Some characters, such as Pippa, a young girl orphaned in the same blast that killed Theo's mother, are therefore given short shrift. The film's latter half feels increasingly rushed, and Theo and Boris's third-act attempt to regain the lost Goldfinch painting shifts too suddenly into a crime caper. Taking greater liberties with the novel's plot and characters might have freed Crowley and his team to tell a story that was more cinematic and that better lent itself to the scope of a feature film. At its worst, the film can feel like one of the chimeras that Theo sells from Hobie's store: a beautiful but fraudulent imitation of the real thing.

Significance

After premiering at the Toronto Film Festival, *The Goldfinch* was released by Warner Bros. in the United States and internationally in September 2019. The film was meant to capitalize on the runaway success of Tartt's novel. A literary thriller that draws big audiences could garner a trifecta of rewards: good reviews in prominent outlets, nominations at the Academy Awards and other events, and a strong box office return. Casting prestigious actors like Nicole Kidman might help to bring in a wider audience and to signal that this is a serious film. Crowley's previous adaptation, *Brooklyn*, had been nominated for Best Picture, Best Actress, and Best Adapted Screenplay, and with him leading the film, it seemed to promise that it would be in consideration for similar honors.

In the end, *The Goldfinch* failed to deliver in any of these areas. It received withering reviews, becoming something of a critical punching bag. The film was ridiculed by fans of the book and by people who had never read it; by professional critics and casual internet commenters; and by both highbrow magazines and popular websites. Richard Brody, writing for *The New Yorker*, summed up in the title of his review the problem that so many viewers identified in the film: its "wan faithfulness." Brody argued, "Any novel can be the basis for a good movie, if the filmmakers only dare to betray the book." With *The Goldfinch*, the filmmakers' dutiful reverence to their source has led them to produce a film that is lifeless and inert. As Peter Bradshaw puts it in his review for *The Guardian*, "The film always looks good under the eye of cinematographer Roger Deakins, and screenwriter Peter Straughan renders some elegant and amusing dialogue, but this Goldfinch stays earthbound." The film was not nominated for any major awards.

Financially, *The Goldfinch* lost a great deal of money for Warner Bros. Produced for $45 million, the film took in a little under $10 million worldwide, according to the website *Box Office Mojo*. A $35 million loss sends a pow-erful message to a studio, and one has to wonder what lessons producers will take from the critical and commercial failure of *The Goldfinch*. In a perfect world, they might learn that tasking a director with dutifully recreating a hit novel is not a surefire way to produce a successful film.

—*Matthew Bolton*

Further Reading

Alpers, Svetlana. *The Art of Describing: Dutch Art in the Seventeenth Century*. John Murray General Publishing Division, 1983.
Ellis, Bret Easton. *Less Than Zero*. Simon & Schuster, Inc., 1985.

Bibliography

Bradshaw, Peter. "*The Goldfinch* Review—Donna Tartt's Art-Theft Epic Has Its Wings Clipped." *The Guardian*, 26 Sept. 2019, www.theguardian.com/film/2019/sep/26/the-goldfinch-review. Accessed 28 Apr. 2020.
Brody, Richard. "Review: The Wan Faithfulness That Made *The Goldfinch* Movie a Flop." *The New Yorker*, 18 Sept. 2019, www.newyorker.com/culture/the-front-row/review-the-wan-faithfulness-that-made-the-goldfinch-movie-a-flop. Accessed 28 Apr. 2020.
Diamond, Jason. "Sex, Drugs, and Bestsellers: The Legend of the Literary Brat Pack." *Harper's Bazaar*, 2 Nov. 2016, www.harpersbazaar.com/culture/art-books-music/a18422/literary-brat-pack-donna-tartt-jay-mcinerney/. Accessed 28 Apr. 2020.
"*The Goldfinch* (2019)." *Box Office Mojo*, www.boxofficemojo.com/title/tt3864056/. Accessed 22 Apr. 2020.
Peretz, Evgenia. "It's Tartt—But Is It Art?" *Vanity Fair*, 11 June 2014, www.vanityfair.com/culture/2014/07/goldfinch-donna-tartt-literary-criticism. Accessed 22 Apr. 2020.
Scott, A. O. "*The Goldfinch* Review: Strictly for the Birds." *The New York Times*, 11 Sept. 2019, www.nytimes.com/2019/09/11/movies/the-goldfinch-review.html. Accessed 22 Apr. 2020.
Tartt, Donna. *The Goldfinch*. Little, Brown and Company, 2013.

Gone Girl

The Novel
Author: Gillian Flynn (b. 1971)
First published: 2012

The Film
Year released: 2014
Director: David Fincher (b. 1962)
Screenplay by: Gillian Flynn
Starring: Rosamund Pike, Ben Affleck, Neil Patrick Harris

Context

Known for their suspenseful narratives and explorations of societal fears and preoccupations, thrillers have remained popular into the first decades of the twenty-first century. Recent filmmakers in the genre have drawn upon shifts in technology, the media, and the global economy to create films that often amplified the concerns of their audiences, taking common anxieties to new and sometimes shocking extremes. Among the most popular and critically acclaimed thriller films of the era was the 2014 film *Gone Girl*, a work that, like many of its predecessors, reflects preoccupations of the times in which it was made. Exploring topics such as marriage, the sensationalism of the news media, and the lingering effects of the global recession that began late in the first decade of the twenty-first century, the film embeds these relatable concerns in a tortuous plot that won the film widespread critical acclaim.

The film *Gone Girl* was adapted from the novel of the same name, published in 2012 by Gillian Flynn. A former journalist and critic for *Entertainment Weekly*, Flynn had previously published the mystery novels *Sharp Objects* (2006) and *Dark Places* (2009) but found particular success with *Gone Girl*, which became a bestseller and received numerous positive reviews. When selling the film rights to the novel, Flynn stipulated that she be personally involved in the process of adapting the novel for the screen, and she went on to write the initial draft of the screenplay. Her work proved promising, and Flynn remained with the project as the sole credited screenwriter and worked closely with the film's director, David Fincher. A critically acclaimed director who began his career in music videos, Fincher had established himself as a key figure in mystery and thriller cinema during the late twentieth and early twenty-first centuries with films such as *Se7en* (1995), *Fight Club* (1999), *Zodiac* (2007), and *The Girl with the Dragon Tattoo* (2011). He had likewise directed *The Curious Case of Benjamin Button* (2008) and *The Social Network* (2010), which earned him two nominations for the Academy Award for Best Directing and a British Academy of Film and Television Arts (BAFTA) Award for the latter. Flynn and Fincher together refined the film's screenplay, developing a narrative that captured the core of the original novel in a form appropriate for the screen. Starring Rosamund Pike, Ben Affleck, and Neil Patrick Harris, *Gone Girl* premiered at the New York Film Festival in September 2014.

Film Analysis

Adapted for the screen by the author of the original novel, *Gone Girl* adheres closely to the plot of Flynn's book, de-

Gone Girl *stars Ben Affleck and Rosamund Pike. Photo by aphrodite-in-nyc from new york city, CC BY 2.0, via Wikimedia Commons.*

picting many of the crucial events that set up and ultimately resolve the novel's central mystery. The film begins when one of the film's two protagonists, Nick Dunne (Ben Affleck), arrives at his Missouri home to discover his wife, Amy Elliott (Rosamund Pike), gone and the home in partial disarray. Evidence at the home suggests that Amy was murdered, and Nick becomes the prime suspect due to his infidelity, extensive consumer debt, and reportedly hostile relationship with Amy. However, the film goes on to reveal that Amy has attempted to frame Nick for her murder as revenge for both his infidelity and the lack of effort he has put into their marriage, and she is hiding out and watching the ensuing media circus from a distance. Amy is forced to alter her plan after her money is stolen, and she takes refuge with ex-boyfriend Desi Collings (Neil Patrick Harris), who proves to be controlling. After deciding to return to Nick, she kills Desi and, upon returning home, successfully convinces the media and law enforcement that Desi had abducted her and held her captive. Nick is aware that Amy tried to frame him for murder, but he decides to remain in a relationship with her anyway when she confesses to having had herself artificially inseminated with his child. The film concludes with the couple tied together indefinitely in an uneasy truce, each fully aware of the other's worst qualities. Although the film omits or reduces the roles of several characters from the novel, including those of Amy's parents and Nick's father, and simplifies the novel's plot and the protagonists' backstories, the film adaptation of *Gone Girl* ultimately captures the overall story arc of the novel as well as much of the source material's commentary on relationships, gender roles, and the media and the public's approaches to criminal investigations.

In addition to cutting down the length and scope of her original narrative, Flynn sought to translate the unique narrative characteristics of the novel into a form suitable for the screen. As a work that could be classified as part of the thriller, mystery, and crime genres, *Gone Girl* is perhaps at its most intriguing when the plot takes twists and turns that surprise both its characters and the audience. In Flynn's original novel, such surprises are in part made possible through shifts in point of view that take place throughout the book. In the first of the book's three parts, chapters alternate between Nick's present-day, first-person point of view and extracts from Amy's diary, which span the period between January 2005, when the couple first meet, and June 2012, shortly before her disappear-

ance. When adapting the novel, Flynn sought to retain the shifts in point of view yet avoid having the film simply "be two people talking to the camera," as she later told Joe Berkowitz in a 2014 interview for *Fast Company*. While many films adapted from books or stories written in the first-person point of view rely heavily on voice-over narration, Flynn chose to limit the use of that device in the scenes focusing on Nick. While brief voice-overs by Nick begin and end the film, his inner thoughts are largely inaccessible to the reader, which renders the questions concerning Nick's role in his wife's disappearance—and presumed murder—all the more essential. The scenes illustrating Amy's diary entries, on the other hand, do feature voice-over narration that introduces the audience to the various extracts from Amy and Nick's past relationship as they are presented on screen. Following the reveal that

Author Gillian Flynn. Photo by aphrodite-in-nyc via Wikimedia Commons.

Amy is still alive, the film continues to shift between its focal characters, continuing to show the events taking place around Nick in addition to depicting Amy's present and recent past. This in keeping with the structure of the novel, which alternates between similar chapters over the course of the final two segments of the narrative.

Alongside maintaining the narrative structure of the novel and presenting a compelling onscreen narrative, the shifting points of view in *Gone Girl* facilitate Flynn's use of unreliable narrators, a key characteristic of both the novel and the film. Early on, the film suggests that all the events presented in the narrative thus far are events that really happened in the lives of the protagonists: the flashbacks presented via Amy's diary entries are as truthful and valid as the events Nick is experiencing in the present. For a viewer who believes that the film is presenting the truth, Nick—who is seen onscreen but whose mindset and thoughts are largely unknown—may seem particularly untrustworthy, especially after his infidelity is revealed. The mystery, then, may seem to be whether Nick did truly kill his wife and, if so, how and why. Upon reaching the turning point of the film, however, Flynn subverts such expectations by revealing that Amy is not only alive but also the mastermind behind the whole investigation, having planned an elaborate revenge scheme that has fooled both many of the characters within the film and, possibly, a portion of the film's audience. The diary is revealed to have been fabricated, written after Amy began to plan her scheme with the express goal of inventing a history of domestic abuse as well as motives for the supposed murder. Just as Amy has lied about Nick by constructing a misleading alternative narrative, the film has lied about its own truthfulness, presenting Amy's diary entries as factual within the context of the narrative when many of them are not. The viewer's willingness to believe that false narrative is in some ways indicative of the same preconceptions that lead law enforcement and the media in the film to assume Nick's guilt, and *Gone Girl* ultimately makes use of such preconceptions to create a complex, suspenseful, and thought-provoking narrative.

Significance

Following its debut at the New York Film Festival, *Gone Girl* opened in theaters throughout the United States in October 2014. The film performed well at the box office, grossing more than $167 million domestically, according to the website Box Office Mojo. *Gone Girl* also screened in numerous countries worldwide and grossed more than $200 million internationally, performing particularly well in the United Kingdom, Australia, France, and South Korea. Reviews of the film were largely positive and focused on the actors' strong performances, Fincher's characteristic style, and the work's overall plot and key twist. Although some critics commented that the work could be seen as misogynistic and antifeminist, particularly in the latter portion of the narrative, reviewers took particular note of the film's depiction of the media circus surrounding the characters, which Flynn noted in interviews was inspired in part by her observations of media involvement in real-world murder and missing-person cases.

Gone Girl also earned a variety of award nominations, many of them in recognition of Pike's performance as Amy. She was nominated for the Academy Award for Best Actress in a Leading Role and was similarly recognized at the Golden Globe, BAFTA, and Screen Actors Guild Awards. Fincher likewise received widespread acclaim for his work as director and was nominated for the Golden Globe in that category. In addition to the film's actors and director, Flynn herself received extensive recognition for the strength of her screenwriting debut, earning Golden Globe and BAFTA nominations for her screenplay. Building upon the success of *Gone Girl*, she went on to adapt her earlier novel *Sharp Objects* into the 2018 HBO television miniseries of the same name, cowrite the screenplay for the 2018 crime film *Widows*, and write for and executive-produce the Amazon Studios television series *Utopia*.

—*Joy Crelin*

Further Reading

Berkowitz, Joe. "How Gillian Flynn Adapted Her Biggest Novel, 'Gone Girl,' into Her First Screenplay." *Fast Company*, 3 Oct. 2014, www.fastcompany.com/3036579/how-gillian-flynn-adapted-her-biggest-novel-gone-girl-into-her-first-screenplay. Accessed 31 Dec. 2018.

Fincher, David. "Interview: David Fincher." Interview by Amy Taubin. *Film Comment*, Film Society of Lincoln Center, 26 Sept. 2014, www.filmcomment.com/blog/interview-david-fincher. Accessed 31 Dec. 2018.

Flynn, Gillian. *Gone Girl*. Crown, 2012.

Bibliography

Brockes, Emma. "The *Gone Girl* Phenomenon: Gillian Flynn Speaks Out." *The Guardian*, 3 Oct. 2014, www.theguardian.com/books/2014/oct/03/gone-girl-phenomenon-gillian-flynn. Accessed 31 Dec. 2018.

Dargis, Manohla. "No Job, No Money and Now, No Wife." Review of *Gone Girl*, directed by David Fincher. *The New York Times*, 25 Sept. 2014, www.nytimes.com/2014/09/26/movies/ben-affleck-in-david-finchers-gone-girl.html. Accessed 31 Dec. 2018.

Dockterman, Eliana. "The 13 Biggest Differences between the *Gone Girl* Movie and the Book." *Time*, 4 Oct. 2014, time.com/3466109/gone-girl-movie-book. Accessed 31 Dec. 2018.

Flynn, Gillian. "'Gone Girl' Author Gillian Flynn on Adapting It for Film." Interview by Carla Meyer. *Sacramento Bee*, 29 Sept. 2014, www.sacbee.com/entertainment/movies-news-reviews/article2615304.html. Accessed 31 Dec. 2018.

"Gone Girl." *Box Office Mojo*, www.boxofficemojo.com/movies/?id=gonegirl.htm. Accessed 31 Dec. 2018.

McIntyre, Gina. "Thrills, Chills for Gillian Flynn in Adapting 'Gone Girl.'" *Los Angeles Times*, 5 Sept. 2014, www.latimes.com/entertainment/la-et-mn-ca-sneaks-gone-girl-20140907-story.html. Accessed 31 Dec. 2018.

Rothman, Joshua. "What 'Gone Girl' Is Really About." *The New Yorker*, 8 Oct. 2014, www.newyorker.com/books/joshua-rothman/gone-girl-really. Accessed 31 Dec. 2018.

Travers, Peter. Review of *Gone Girl*, directed by David Fincher. *Rolling Stone*, 23 Sept. 2014, www.rollingstone.com/movies/movie-reviews/gone-girl-101407. Accessed 31 Dec. 2018.

Goodfellas

The Novel
Author: Nicholas Pileggi (b. 1933)
First published: 1985

The Film
Year released: 1990
Director: Martin Scorsese (b. 1942)
Screenplay by: Martin Scorsese, Nicholas Pileggi
Starring: Ray Liotta, Lorraine Bracco, Robert De Niro, Joe Pesci

Context

The nonfiction book *Wiseguy* (1985) was written by Nicholas Pileggi, a journalist who worked on the organized crime beat in New York City. Pileggi had grown up in an Italian American neighborhood in New York and consequently had a deep familiarity with the far-reaching Italian American criminal organization known as the Mafia. *Wiseguy*, his best-known book, came about after he was approached by the lawyer of a former "wiseguy," or gangster: Henry Hill. After a life of crime, Hill had been arrested and faced years in prison. He was cut a deal, however, in exchange for informing on his associates—a violation of one of the Mafia's central codes. When Hill reached out to Pileggi about writing his life's story, he had been in witness protection for several years.

The publication of *Wiseguy* arrived at a time in American culture when gangster stories were in vogue. Most influential was Mario Puzo's novel *The Godfather* (1969), which sold nine million copies in the span of two years. It was adapted into the equally popular and critically acclaimed film *The Godfather* (1972), directed by Francis Ford Coppola, which generated two sequels and won several Academy Awards. Quickly regarded as one of the greatest films of all time, it shaped public perception of organized crime and spawned numerous imitators over the decades.

Both were best sellers about organized crime, but *Wiseguy* was quite different from *The Godfather*, a work of fiction famous for its over-the-top style and romanticized qualities. Pileggi's book, by contrast, is a work of true crime that tells the everyday stories of street-level crooks. It is gritty and realistic, mostly made up of verbatim interviews with Henry Hill, his wife Karen, and other people who knew him. The book is also engaging because of the real-life notoriety of events Hill was involved with—including the over $5 million Lufthansa heist in 1978, one of the biggest robberies in history.

The success of *Wiseguy* quickly led to it being optioned for a film. Italian American filmmaker Martin Scorsese was

Robert DeNiro. Photo by Petr Novák via Wikimedia Commons.

impressed by the book, and contacted Pileggi. Soon, the two were collaborating on a screenplay. Scorsese's decision to adapt *Wiseguy* came at an interesting point in his career. The director had built his reputation on films about seedy street life, including *Who's That Knocking at My Door* (1967) and the crime drama *Mean Streets* (1973), but had declared his intent to avoid projects about the Mafia. By the late 1980s, however, he had endured the commercial and critical failure of *The King of Comedy* (1982) and attempted to reboot his career by returning to a bare bones production style with *After Hours* (1985). He returned to box office success with *The Color of Money* (1986), giving him more freedom to pursue his passion projects.

Scorsese soon involved his frequent collaborator, the actor Robert De Niro, on the *Wiseguy* adaptation, casting him as Hill's fellow gangster Jimmy "the Gent" because he was too old to play Hill himself. The two had worked most famously together on *Mean Streets* and *Raging Bull* (1980). Joe Pesci, whom Scorsese had also worked with in *Raging Bull* and who was mainly a character actor known for his gangster roles, took the part of Tommy, who like Jimmy was based on a real-life figure but was given a different last name. The director ended up fighting the studio to cast the relative newcomer Ray Liotta in the lead role, and eventually won. Because several other works released in the late 1980s had similar titles to *Wiseguy*, the film project changed its title to *Goodfellas*, another word for gangsters.

Film Analysis

Both *Wiseguy* and *Goodfellas* became touchstones in American popular culture and are now considered classics. Yet there are a number of significant differences between the two, with the book presenting a more comprehensive biography of Hill and the film providing a more artistic, stylized look at a life in crime. In writing the screenplay, Scorsese and Pileggi omitted certain details about the gangster-turned-informant's life. For example, the film never addresses the time Hill (Ray Liotta) spent in the army as a paratrooper or the fact that he and his wife Karen (Lorraine Bracco) originally eloped. Additionally, there are a number of events and characters that are changed for the screen. Tommy DeVito (Joe Pesci) in the film, for example, is a composite of the book's Tommy DeSimone, Lenny Vario, and Paulie Vario, Jr.

Similarly, Hill's time in prison is condensed into a single sentence where in fact he was incarcerated several times throughout the 1960s and 1970s. The choice to effectively pare down and merge such details makes for a smoother, more traditional film narrative structure. The book is overflowing with highly amusing tangential anecdotes that do not necessarily move the story forward. Ultimately, Scorsese and Pileggi carefully selected and rearranged the best details and lines of dialogue to craft a cohesive, engaging story suitable for the medium of film.

Wiseguy is a book that explores violence and organized crime from a journalistic perspective. *Goodfellas* takes a more literary approach to the subject, presenting Hill's story as an engaging morality tale about the effects of greed and materialistic consumption on the human soul. This is evident in Hill's devolution throughout *Goodfellas*: he begins as a clever kid eager to join the seemingly glamorous gangster life and eventually becomes a drug-addled middle-aged man, with friends who want him dead and a family in danger.

Other characters endure similar fates. Karen, for example, is complicit in Hill's crimes and can be seen as losing a piece of her humanity in the process. Scorsese uses the wedding scene to showcase her indoctrination into this world of immorality. Karen is shown as a new bride being handed envelopes of money by dozens of Henry's mob associates. She is a Jewish girl from a good neighborhood who recognizes that something is not quite "right" about these people, yet being in their company excites her. In a later scene, which is intended to take place years later when Karen knows exactly what Henry does for a living, she asks him for money. He hands her a stack of bills and she responds by performing a sexual act on him. Her actions demonstrate that not only does she know about her husband's crimes, but she actively encourages them to continue. The scene also emphasizes the interconnected themes of materialism and eroticism that the film explores in the context of organized crime.

Scorsese uses stylized or self-consciously cinematic techniques throughout *Goodfellas*, reflecting the director's well-known love for the medium of film, its techniques, and its history. This creates interest and excitement. An example of these techniques is the film's flamboyant use of voice-over. After an introductory action scene, the film begins with Hill's voice describing his life and associates using lines that are often taken verbatim from *Wiseguy*. This is significant because in the year the film was released, 1990, the use of voice-over was considered old-fashioned. Scorsese pushes the envelope further by also including voice-over narration from Karen. In some ways, Karen is a stand-in for the audience; she is an outsider entering Henry's world for the first time. Her thoughts and remarks reflect viewers' naiveté and disbelief.

Some film historians have pointed out that *Goodfellas* mainstreamed cinematic techniques associated with the sixties-era French New Wave. Spearheaded by Jean-Luc Godard and Francois Truffaut, the French New Wave employed novel and exciting camera movements, editing styles, and screenwriting techniques to play with audience expectations. Scorsese's use of freeze frames and jump cuts is clearly an homage to the New Wave style and, in particular, to Godard's emblematic crime movie, *Breathless*. Again, in the scene where Hill's criminal associates are introducing themselves, the director has the actors break the fourth wall by speaking directly to the camera. The technique goes back to the days of silent cinema, but its use as a creative, fun, stylized gesture is associated with Godard.

A famous example of the influence of the New Wave style on Scorsese is in *Goodfellas'* Copacabana scene. During it, Hill takes Karen to the nightclub for the evening, but rather than wait in line with everyone else, the two are ushered in through the back door. They travel through the basement hallways and kitchen where chefs are busy at work until they arrive in the packed main room and waiters quickly set up a table for them. Scorsese follows their journey the entire time, using a single Steadicam tracking shot that is uninterrupted for over three minutes. The long tracking shot is a cinematic technical flourish that had been employed by classic American directors like Hitchcock and was beloved by Godard, whose film *The Weekend* (1967), contains a famous sequence in which the camera moves alongside a traffic jam in a single seven-minute take. The use of the technique in Goodfellas is effective in that it provides audiences with the feeling of the couple's experience—the energy and excitement of their privilege. This further highlights the money, power, and connections at Hill's disposal because of his gangster status.

Significance

Goodfellas was a critical and commercial success, earning $46.8 million domestically at the box office. It was quickly labeled one of the best films of the year by critics across the country. In his original review, noted critic

Roger Ebert wrote, "Most films, even great ones, evaporate like mist once you've returned to the real world; they leave memories behind, but their reality fades fairly quickly. Not this film, which shows America's finest filmmaker at the peak of his form. No finer film has ever been made about organized crime—not even *The Godfather*." *Goodfellas* went on to earn six Academy Award nominations, including for best picture and best director, with Joe Pesci winning for best supporting actor. The film continues to be lauded as one of the best films of all time, and certainly one of the best gangster movies.

The impact of *Goodfellas* on the filmmaking world was enormous. Many film historians argue that Scorsese generated a new prototype for the gangster movie, one marked by excessive violence and highly profane dialogue. This influence quickly became evident throughout the 1990s, with examples including director Quentin Tarantino's bloody, dialogue-driven films *Reservoir Dogs* (1992) and *Pulp Fiction* (1994) and Scorsese's own *Casino* (1995), starring De Niro. In addition to the way it portrayed gangsters, *Goodfellas'* highly stylized, rule-breaking filmmaking techniques gave rise to an era of more experimental cinema. Directors such as Stephen Soderbergh, David Fincher, and Paul Thomas Anderson began aiming to push boundaries in new ways.

Goodfellas was a pervasive influence on the television series *The Sopranos* (1999-2007). That award-winning show similarly focuses on the world of street criminals and explores themes of violence, humanity, and material consumerism, and its creators noted that it would not exist without *Goodfellas*. The character of Henry Hill in many ways became the archetype for later television antiheroes, the immoral but likeable protagonists whom audiences simultaneously cheer for and root against. The antihero has defined the Golden Age of television with characters including Tony Soprano, Don Draper of *Mad Men*, and Walter White of *Breaking Bad*.

—*Emily E. Turner*

Further Reading

Merry, Stephanie. "'Goodfellas' Is 25. Here's a List of All the Movies That Have Ripped It Off." *The Washington Post*, 29 Apr. 2015, www.washingtonpost.com/news/arts-and-entertainment/wp/2015/04/29/goodfellas-is-25-heres-an-incomplete-list-of-all-the-movies-that-have-ripped-it-off. Accessed 15 Jan. 2019.

Vlastelica, Ryan. "*Goodfellas* Turned *Wiseguy*'s Simple Prose into Cinematic Gold." *AV Club*, 18 Sept. 2015, aux.avclub.com/ goodfellas-turned-wiseguy-s-simple-prose-into-cinematic-1798284739. Accessed 15 Jan. 2019.

Bibliography

Behar, Henri. "Classic Feature: Scorsese Talks *Goodfellas*." *Empire*, Nov. 1990, www.empireonline.com/movies/features/ goodfellas-classic-feature/. Accessed 15. Jan. 2019.

Dirks, Tim. "GoodFellas (1990)." *AMC Filmsite*, 2019, www.filmsite.org/goodf.html. Accessed 4 Feb. 2019.

Ebert, Roger. Review of *Goodfellas*, directed by Martin Scorsese. *RogerEbert.com*, 2 Sept. 1990, www.rogerebert.com/reviews/ goodfellas-1990. Accessed 4 Feb. 2019.

Hemphill, Jim. "Of Tarantino and TV: The Legacy of *Goodfellas*." *Filmmaker Magazine*, 22 Apr. 2015, filmmakermagazine.com/ 93889-of-tarantino-and-tv-on-goodfellas-legacy. Accessed 15 Jan. 2019.

Linfield, Susan. "*Goodfellas* Looks at the Banality of Mob Life." Review of *Goodfellas*, directed by Martin Scorsese. *The New York Times*, 16 Sept. 1990, www.nytimes.com/1990/09/16/ movies/film-goodfellas-looks-at-the-banality-of-mob-life.html. Accessed 15 Jan. 2019.

The Good Liar

The Novel
Author: Nicholas Searle
First published: 2015

The Film
Year released: 2019
Director: Bill Condon (b. 1955)
Screenplay by: Jeffrey Hatcher
Starring: Helen Mirren, Ian McKellen, Russell Tovey

Context

The best-selling British spy thriller *The Good Liar* was published in 2015. It follows an aging con man named Roy Courtnay. Intent on pulling off one last con, Courtnay aims to defraud Betty, a wealthy widow he has met on an internet dating site—but neither character, as the book progresses, is what they seem. *The Good Liar* was the literary debut of the pseudonymous Nicholas Searle, a long-time British intelligence agent. Searle has subsequently published two other novels, both thrillers, including *A Traitor in the Family* (2017) and *A Fatal Game* (2019). Upon publishing *The Good Liar*, Searle won comparisons to John le Carré and Patricia Highsmith, titans of the espionage and crime genres, although Lucy Scholes of the London *Independent* wrote that the book itself was more difficult to quantify. She called it a "character study meets mystery meets historical fiction," concluding that it was "a wily tale of a much larger, more traumatic and multifaceted deception than initially anticipated."

The Good Liar was adapted for film by American writer Jeffrey Hatcher. As a playwright, Hatcher is best known for his period comedy, *Compleat Female Stage Beauty* (1999); as a screenwriter, he wrote the 2005 film, *Casanova*, starring the late Heath Ledger, and *The Duchess* (2008), starring Keira Knightly, about the Duchess of Devonshire. *The Good Liar* was directed by Bill Condon, who won an Academy Award for Best Adapted Screenplay for *Gods and Monsters*, starring Ian McKellen, in 1999. Condon's output has been surprisingly diverse. He has directed horror films, like *Candyman: Farewell to the Flesh* (1995), as well as the film adaptation of the musical *Dreamgirls* (2006), starring Beyoncé. He also directed the two final *Twilight* films, in 2011 and 2012, and the live-action version of Disney's *Beauty and the Beast* (2017). His

most celebrated films include *Gods and Monsters*, about Hollywood film director James Whale, and *Kinsey* (2004), about the pioneering researcher of human sexuality, Alfred Kinsey.

Film Analysis

To discuss the various elements of *The Good Liar*, a twisting crime mystery and thriller, it is necessary to spoil the

Screenwriter Jeffrey Hatcher. Photo by August Schwerdfeger via Wikimedia Commons.

plot. In the film, as in the book, Roy (Ian McKellen) is an aging con man. His mark is Betty (Helen Mirren), a wealthy widow. In the film, the viewer follows a subplot in which Roy and his criminal partner, Vincent (Jim Carter), run a scam—foreshadowing the scam Roy plans to run on Betty—on two wealthy businessmen. Roy and Betty's companionable relationship progresses quickly. Roy moves into Betty's house, and eventually convinces her to combine their finances in a joint account. Roy's efforts are occasionally thwarted by Betty's grandson, Stephen (Russell Tovey), a graduate student studying history with a special focus on Nazi Germany. Late in the film, Stephen reveals Roy's secret: that he was born in Germany and stole the identity of one of his dead English colleagues, Roy Courtnay, after World War II. Roy's true origin plays an important part in the climactic moment of the film, when Betty reveals that her relationship with Roy has been an elaborate scheme on her part, all orchestrated as revenge for the fact that Roy raped her when they were teenagers living in Germany. Betty, who is also of German origin, reveals that Roy was once her English teacher. He also turned her father in to the Nazi secret police, upending her entire family.

One of the biggest differences between the book and film versions of *The Good Liar* is how much the audience knows about Roy as the plot progresses. The book contains more flashbacks to Roy's earlier life as a criminal, offering more evidence of his callousness and cruelty. In the film, though, the viewer immediately understands that Roy is a liar, the depth of his depravity emerges more slowly, culminating in Betty's revelation in the last twenty minutes of the film. When *The Good Liar* was published, Searle was compared to legendary crime writer, Patricia Highsmith. Roy's story invokes one of Highsmith's most famous characters, Tom Ripley, of *The Talented Mr. Ripley* (1955). In that story, the protagonist, Tom, kills his friend Dickie, assuming both his identity and his trust fund. Highsmith presents Tom as calm, cool, and rational—a disposition totally at odds with his increasingly heinous crimes. Roy, the protagonist of *The Good Liar*, forces a similar reckoning. At first, the audience might be inclined to sympathize with him, a dashing con man in his twilight days, far more charming than the creepy, social climber, Tom. But Roy's crimes escalate—at one point, he pushes a man in front of a train before joining Betty for tea—culminating in Betty's revelation of his cruelty as a young man, forcing the audience to assess his character in total.

Helen Mirren. Photo by Harald Krichel via Wikimedia Commons.

Betty's backstory, and in fact, her entire character, are also re-imagined in the film. The details of the assault are different, as is Betty's experience of the war. In the book, Betty is sent to a concentration camp. Her parents are executed, and her sisters disappear. After the war, she is taken in by a wealthy couple in England. In the film, Betty tells Roy that her father was executed, and her mother committed suicide. She and her sisters stayed in Germany during the war, and her three sisters were killed by a bomb. After Russia's invasion of Germany at the end of the war, she suggests that she prostituted herself to Russian soldiers to survive. Her journey to England and to Oxford is unclear.

The book weaves together stories of past and present; only at the end does Betty reveal that Roy is Hans Taub, telling the story of the stolen identity placed earlier in the film version. In the book, Betty cons Roy out of his life's savings, but returns his money to him by check. Her grandson takes it upon himself to tear up the check, leaving Roy destitute. Later, Roy dies alone in a hospital. In the film, the ending is far more dramatic. Betty, in the hands of Academy Award-winner Mirren, is shrewder—the obvious architect of both the plan itself and the inevitable final confrontation. Director Condon and cinematographer, Tobias A. Schliessler invoke a familiar trope, orchestrating a scene in which Roy returns to the house he once shared with Betty. The house is dark and totally empty. The flick of a light switch reveals Betty sitting in an armchair, waiting for him. In the book, Betty is uneasy about revealing her ploy; in the film, she immediately begins pressing buttons on her keypad, depleting Roy's savings for every lie he tells. In the book, their confrontation ends with an uncomfortable lunch. She even lets him squat in the empty house. Not so in the film. After her revelatory monologue, Roy dives for the keypad. After a mad scramble, Betty gives it to him, revealing a total of 100,000 pounds—the exact amount he owes one of the businessmen he had earlier conned. That businessman then appears, alongside a crony who Roy had ordered beaten earlier in the film. Betty leaves the house as the sound of Roy's screams fade behind her.

As this climactic scene, and its radical divergence from the book, demonstrate, the film doubles down on *The Good Liar* as a rape revenge narrative. This may explain why Condon and Hatcher chose to make the rape itself more graphic than it is in the book, and further, why they suggest that the rape led to the degradation of Betty's body after the war. Betty's violation is placed front and center among her many grievances against Roy and gives her plot to con him an air of righteousness. Right or wrong, the purpose of a rape revenge tale is eye-for-an-eye justice; in the film, Betty even orchestrates the violation of Roy—in the form of a brutal beating—at the hands of his former associates. In a rape revenge narrative, revenge equals justice and justice equals peace. In the final scene of the film, Betty, appearing for the first time as her true self, hosts a party for friends and family at her sprawling estate. She is untroubled by remorse, though the ambiguous screams—delight or terror?—of her grandchildren playing in the pond give her pause. In the film's last line, she warns them that the water is "deeper than it looks," suggesting that her mind is more concerned with protecting young women from harm than with the fate of her former abuser.

Significance

The Good Liar performed moderately well at the box office when it opened in November 2019. It fared less well with critics, who awarded it with mixed to negative reviews. Ben Kenigsberg, who reviewed it for *The New York Times*, complained that it "tips its hand" in the first scene, a montage that toggles between Betty and Roy as they set up their online dating profiles, revealing that both of them are lying. (He says he is a non-smoker while smoking a cigar; she says she is a non-drinker while nursing a bottle of wine.) When they meet for the first time, both confess that they have used a fake name. Kenigsberg was frustrated with director Condon for the "layers of misdirection." The question of why Betty, a confident, former Oxford professor, would believe the folksy, slow-talking Roy in the first place is never adequately explained. He lamented that Condon was not the famous mystery filmmaker Alfred Hitchcock, or Brian De Palma—the director of *Scarface* (1983) and *Carrie* (1976), among others—"a filmmaker with a visual style seductive enough to offer distraction from the grinding plot mechanics, which are especially clunky here." Hau Chu of *The Washington Post* was more magnanimous, calling *The Good Liar* a "taut acting showcase," though he conceded that Hatcher's script was "less than satisfying."

In an interview for the *Los Angeles Times*, Condon, Mirren, and McKellen noted that the film was made during the rise of the #MeToo movement, in which women all over the world came forward to detail their experiences of sexual assault and harassment at the hands of men. Condon said that movement made the film, particularly Betty's decision to confront her abuser fifty years after the fact, unintentionally timely.

—*Molly Hagan*

Further Reading
Kenigsberg, Ben. "*The Good Liar* Review: For Helen Mirren and Ian McKellen, the Truth Hurts." *The New York Times*, 14 Nov. 2019, www.nytimes.com/2019/11/14/movies/the-good-liar-review.html?searchResultPosition=1. Accessed 7 Mar. 2020.

Scholes, Lucy. "*The Good Liar* by Nicholas Searle, Book Review: Engaging and Poised." *The Independent*, 14 Jan. 2016, www.independent.co.uk/arts-entertainment/books/reviews/the-good-liar-by-nicholas-searle-book-review-engaging-and-poised-a6813011.html. Accessed 4 Mar. 2020.

Bibliography

Appler, Michael. "*The Good Liar* Director Bill Condon Praises 'Legends' Helen Mirren and Ian McKellen." *Variety*, 7 Nov. 2019, variety.com/2019/scene/news/good-liar-helen-mirren-ian-mckellen-bill-condon-1203397094/. Accessed 7 Mar. 2020.

Chu, Hau. "Helen Mirren and Ian McKellen Have a Blast in *The Good Liar*, a Silly, Cat-and-Mouse Game." *The Washington Post*, 13 Nov. 2019, www.washingtonpost.com/goingoutguide/movies/helen-mirren-and-ian-mckellen-have-a-blast-in-the-good-liar-a-silly-cat-and-mouse-game/2019/11/13/ec2a90a8-0307-11ea-8501-2a7123a38c58_story.html?arc404=true. Accessed 7 Mar. 2020.

Zemler, Emily. "*Good Liar* Ending Explained: How the Stars Flip the Script on Gender Roles." *Los Angeles Times*, 18 Nov. 2019, www.latimes.com/entertainment-arts/movies/story/2019-11-18/good-liar-ending-explained-twist. Accessed 7 Mar. 2020.

The Great Gilly Hopkins

The Novel
Author: Katherine Paterson (b. 1932)
First published: 1978

The Film
Year released: 2015
Director: Stephen Herek (b. 1958)
Screenplay by: David Paterson
Starring: Sophie Nélisse, Kathy Bates, Glenn Close, Octavia Spencer

Context

The Great Gilly Hopkins is a beloved 1978 young adult novel by Katherine Paterson, author of *Bridge to Terabithia* (1977) and *Jacob Have I Loved* (1980). The novel centers on an eleven-year-old girl named Galadriel "Gilly" Hopkins who—after being abandoned by her mother—has grown up in a series of foster homes. At the start of the novel, she is placed with the big-hearted Maime Trotter and a younger foster child, William Ernest (W. E.). In a hunt for her birth mother, Gilly lies, steals, and ultimately sets in motion a series of events that lead to her being taken away from Trotter. She realizes too late that Trotter's was the right home for her, and that she has forever removed herself from the closest thing she has had to a real family.

Like so many of Paterson's stories, *The Great Gilly Hopkins* is realistic and bittersweet, presenting childhood and adolescence not in idealized terms, but as a time that can be full of difficulty and loss. *The Great Gilly Hopkins* was awarded the 1979 National Book Award and was named a Newbery Honor Book the same year. In the 1980s, however, the novel was frequently included in school lists of banned books because of its use of offensive language.

In 2007, Paterson's son David Paterson adapted *Bridge to Terabithia* for the big screen. Paterson loved the result and enthusiastically supported his decision to write and produce the film adaptation of *The Great Gilly Hopkins*. The film was produced for about five million dollars in 2015. It was directed by Stephen Herek, whose other works include family comedies like *Bill & Ted's Excellent Adventure* (1989), *The Mighty Ducks* (1992), and *101 Dalmatians* (1996). Paterson was as enthusiastic about the film version of *The Great Gilly Hopkins* as she had been

about her son's previous adaptation, saying in an interview with Luann Toth for *School Library Journal* (12 Oct. 2016), "I've seen the movie at least nine times. And I love it every time. I think I'm the only one among my writer friends who truly loves to see adaptations of their work into film."

Film Analysis

The film adaptation of *The Great Gilly Hopkins* hews closely to the storyline of the novel. As in the book, the film begins with a social worker bringing his young charge, twelve-year-old Gilly (Sophie Nélisse), to live with a new foster family. The social worker in the novel, Ms. Ellis, becomes Mr. Ellis (Billy Magnussen) in the film. Gilly's new foster mother, Maime Trotter (Kathy Bates), has a limited education and limited financial resources, but a huge heart and an outsized personality. She has been raising foster children for twenty years and welcomes Gilly to her home.

Gilly is determined not to connect emotionally to her new family or teachers, because she believes that her mother, Courtney (Julia Stiles), will one day rescue her from the foster system. A fantasy sequence early in the film shows a glamorous Courtney arriving at the house to whisk Gilly away. To keep her autonomy, Gilly is mean and sarcastic to young W. E. (Zachary Hernandez) and Trotter. At school, she rebuffs Agnes (Clare Foley), who tries to be Gilly's friend, and starts a fight with a group of boys.

One of the greatest differences between the novel and the film is in how they approach race, something that Paterson was careful to address sensitively in her book. At the start of the book, Gilly is asked by Trotter to guide their neighbor,

Author Katherine Paterson. Photo by Politics and Prose Bookstore via Wikimedia Commons.

the blind Mr. Randolph (Bill Cobbs), over to the house for dinner. Reflecting attitudes that were more prevalent in the era in which the book was written, Gilly is surprised that he is African American, saying, "I never touched one of those people in my life." The film doesn't include this. The film does retain a scene in which Gilly gives her African American teacher, Ms. Harris (Octavia Spencer), an intentionally racist card. But without the broader context provided by the book, it is hard to understand why Gilly did this. While Ms. Harris's scene confronting Gilly about the card is still a powerful moment, it loses some of the importance that it has in the book. Writing for the *Los Angeles Times* (6 Oct. 2016), Gary Goldstein noted that the film has "a miscalculated racial element that may offend or confuse." The screenwriter and director may have gotten the balance wrong, cutting either too much or too little of Gilly's initial racism for her encounters with Mr. Randolph and Ms. Harris to make sense.

There are other ways in which the film is thrown off by adaptive miscalculations, hewing too closely to its source

in some ways and deviating from it in others. The overall time setting of the story can be seen as problematic. The book was written in 1978, but the film is set in the present. This makes it difficult for some aspects of the novel, such as the lack of technology, to appear natural in the film. Modern technology should have made Gilly's search for her mother easier; however, that would have removed important aspects of the plot. Therefore, the film's removal of most modern technology makes the appearance of a laptop and video chatting near the end of the film seem out of place. Jesse Jassenger, in a review for the *A. V. Club* (5 Oct. 2016), suggested, "a film can be utterly faithful to its source and still not feel quite right." By neither setting the film firmly in the 1970s nor updating aspects of its setting and plot to ground it in the present day, the producers somewhat weaken *The Great Gilly Hopkins* in an unconvincing amalgam of the two.

When Gilly does learn of her mother's address in San Francisco, she concocts a plan to reunite with her. Gilly first sends her mother a letter exaggerating the conditions in which she has been living and tells Courtney that she hopes to come live with her. She then sets about getting herself to the West Coast. Gilly begins to put on an act at home, helping both Trotter and W. E. to gain their trust. With an unwitting W. E.'s help, she steals money from both Mr. Randolph and Trotter in order to buy a bus ticket to California. (In the bus station, author Katherine Paterson makes a cameo appearance as a salesperson who urges Gilly to pick out a book for the long ride.) When the ticket agent sees that Gilly is too young to travel on her own, he calls the police and Gilly is brought back to Trotter's house.

Mr. Ellis wants to remove Gilly from Trotter's care after her attempt to run away, but Trotter delivers a passionate speech in which she refuses to give up on Gilly. Overhearing this, Gilly is finally won over, and the transformation that she had once feigned becomes real. She lowers her guard and commits fully to her new family; she teaches W. E. how to stand up for himself, apologizes to and befriends some of her classmates, and cares for W. E., Trotter, and Mr. Randolph when they get sick with the flu. But Gilly has already set in motion a series of events that she cannot undo. On Thanksgiving Day, she is visited by a woman who identifies herself as Gilly's grandmother, Nonnie (Glenn Close). Having heard from Gilly's mother about the neglectful foster situation that Gilly claimed to be living in, her grandmother, who had not previously known of Gilly's existence, is determined to take her away from Trotter's home.

Despite Gilly's protests, she must part with Trotter and the family she has come to love. Nonnie takes her to her impressive house in the Maryland countryside and enrolls her in an upscale school. Gilly pines, however, for the warmth of Trotter's humble household and for her old classmates and teacher. The silver lining to all of this seems to come with the arrival of Courtney, who has agreed to spend Christmas with her estranged mother and daughter. Courtney turns out to be both calculating and volatile, however, and Gilly realizes within moments of her landing that she has come not to see Gilly, but to collect the money that Nonnie promised her in exchange for this visit.

In the book, Gilly reaches Trotter over the phone, and has a heartbreaking conversation in which her foster mother tells her that "all that stuff about happy endings is lies." Trotter tells Gilly that she loves her, but that Gilly will have to make her home with her grandmother. The film reworks this scene by having Gilly run away to Trotter's house, which allows them to speak in person. It illustrates Gilly's sadness at losing Trotter and W. E., and shows her moving forward with Nonnie. But the film also adds a final scene in which Gilly and her grandmother have a joyous Easter dinner with Trotter, W. E., and Mr. Randolph. While the scene leaves the film ending on a happy note, it seems to undercut the central message of the book and Trotter's stoic parting words.

Significance

The Great Gilly Hopkins premiered at the SCHLINGEL International Film Festival in October 2015, and Lionsgate then released the film widely in the United States in October 2016. The film was commercially successfully, but received mixed reviews from critics. The cast was widely praise, with Bates singled out for having turned in a particularly strong performance.

The script and overall tone of the film were less well-regarded. Many critics cited an unresolved tension between the film's tween-pleasing hijinks and its more sentimental side. In a review for the *Hollywood Reporter* (7 Oct. 2016), Frank Shenk wrote that "the alternately farcical and melodramatic tones never fully cohere, and the title character is so abrasive that it's hard to muster much sympathy for her." Peter Debruge for *Variety* (7 Oct. 2016) praised Nélisse, Bates, and other cast members, but was somewhat disappointed with Herek's directing, concluding that there is "an overall clumsiness to *The Great Gilly Hopkins*" despite "terrific performances from the entire cast."

Some critics wished that the film had focused more steadily on character development. Writing for *The New York Times*, Neil Genzlinger says that "Gilly's transformation isn't entirely convincing, partly because not enough time is spent exploring the roots of her initial hostility." Genzlinger nevertheless concludes that "the story is beautifully ambivalent." Despite its unevenness in tone, the film marshals a universally praised cast that created some moments of real emotional impact.

—*Matthew Bolton*

Further Reading

Paterson, Katherine. "Going to the Movies with Katherine Paterson: 'The Great Gilly Hopkins.'" Interview by Luann Toth. *School Library Journal*, 12 Oct. 2016, www.slj.com/?detailStory=going-to-the-movies-with-katherine-patersonthe-great-gilly-hopkins. Accessed 14 Jan. 2019.
———. *The Great Gilly Hopkins*. Harper Collins, 1978.

Bibliography

Debruge, Peter. "Film Review: The Great Gilly Hopkins." Review of *The Great Gilly Hopkins*, directed by Stephen Herek. *Variety*, 7 Oct. 2016, variety.com/2016/film/reviews/the-great-gilly-hopkins-review-1201881956/. Accessed 14 Jan. 2019.

Genzlinger, Neil. "Review: The Great Gilly Hopkins, A Child's Story Elevated by Grown-Ups." Review of *The Great Gilly Hopkins*, directed by Stephen Herek. *The New York Times*, 6 Oct. 2016, www.nytimes.com/2016/10/07/movies/the-great-gilly-hopkins-review.html. Accessed 14 Jan. 2019.

Goldstein, Gary. "*The Great Gilly Hopkins* is Stuck in Retrograde (but Kathy Bates Impersonates a Chicken)." Review of *The Great Gilly Hopkins*, directed by Stephen Herek. *The Los Angeles Times*, 6 Oct. 2016, www.latimes.com/entertainment/movies/la-et-mn-mini-gilly-hopkins-review-20161001-snap-story.html. Accessed 14 Jan. 2019.

Hassenger, Jesse. "*The Great Gilly Hopkins* Is Faithful to the Letter but Not Always the Spirit." Review of *The Great Gilly Hopkins*, directed by Stephen Herek. *The A. V. Club*, 5 Oct. 2016, film.avclub.com/the-great-gilly-hopkins-is-faithful-to-the-letter-but-n-1798188972. Accessed 14 Jan. 2019.

Shenk, Frank. "*The Great Gilly Hopkins*: Film Review." Review of *The Great Gilly Hopkins*, directed by Stephen Herek. *The Hollywood Reporter*, 7 Oct. 2016, www.hollywoodreporter.com/review/great-gilly-hopkins-review-936253. Accessed 14 Jan. 2018.

The Guernsey Literary and Potato Peel Pie Society

The Novel
Author: Mary Ann Shaffer (1934-2008), Annie Barrows (b. 1962)
First published: 2008

The Film
Year released: 2018
Director: Mike Newell (b. 1942)
Screenplay by: Kevin Hood, Don Roos, Tom Bezucha
Starring: Lily James, Michiel Huisman, Glen Powell, Jessica Brown Findlay, Katherine Parkinson

Context

The Guernsey Literary and Potato Peel Pie Society (2008) was written by American novelist Mary Ann Shaffer, who stated that the idea for the book came to her in a sudden burst of inspiration. In the 1980s, she had traveled to England with the intention of writing a biography about Kathleen Scott, the wife of Antarctic explorer Robert Falcon Scott. When she discovered that Kathleen Scott's diaries were illegible, she gave up on the project and decided on a whim to spend some time on Guernsey in the Channel Islands. There, she learned about the unique history of the island, which was the only part of the United Kingdom to be occupied by the Germans during World War II, and she felt inspired to write about it.

It wasn't until twenty years later, in 2006, that Shaffer's manuscript about how a ragtag book club on Guernsey defied the Nazis was accepted for publication. The publishers requested that Shaffer rewrite a significant portion of the novel, but her deteriorating health prevented her from doing so. She requested that Annie Barrows, her niece and an experienced children's book author, help with editing and rewrites. Both women were credited as coauthors in the manuscript's final iteration, entitled *The Guernsey Literary and Potato Peel Pie Society*. Shaffer, who had spent her life as a librarian and bookstore worker, passed away in February 2008, just a few months before the novel's publication. It became a bestseller.

The film adaptation of *The Guernsey Literary and Potato Peel Pie Society* was a British-French venture that began in 2010, but it took several years for the project to get underway. Originally Kenneth Branagh was on board to direct, with actor Kate Winslet attached as the lead character, Juliet Ashton. Both dropped out in 2013 and the film's production did not gain momentum again until 2016,

when British director Mike Newell was brought on. Newell had cut his teeth as a producer and director of television in the 1960s. He began directing feature films in 1977 with *The Man in the Iron Mask* before going on to direct classics such as *Four Weddings and a Funeral* (1994) and *Donnie Brasco* (1997). In interviews, Newell said that he did not expect to make many more films after *Guernsey*.

Guernsey was demonstrative of a resurgence in the popularity of historical romantic dramas.. While extremely common during the 1980s and 1990s, the genre began to dwindle in the 2000s. In part, this was because studios had started to focus so heavily on action films such as superhero blockbusters and dystopian science fiction. As a result, projects with medium-sized budgets were less likely to get financed. By the late 2010s, however, audience and critical attention to dramas and romances rose once more, especially with the influence of the online streaming service Netflix. Increasingly influential as a producer and distributor of original content, Netflix took up distribution of *Guernsey* in the United States and some other markets.

Film Analysis

The Guernsey Literary and Potato Peel Pie Society is a historical romantic drama that aims to depict the devastating impact of World War II on British citizens. Set in 1946, the film uses flashback sequences to bring some of these wartime horrors to life. Presented as the characters' memories, these flashbacks include imagery of violence against prisoners of war, children being separated from their parents, and bombed-out buildings in central London. They are employed sparingly and for dramatic purpose. Much of the protagonist Juliet's (Lily James) journey is centered around learning what happened to Elizabeth McKenna (Jessica Brown Findlay), the founder of the book club known as the Guernsey Literary and Potato Peel Pie Society, at the hands of the Nazis. It is Juliet's quest for the truth about Elizabeth that provides the film's narrative with suspense and forward momentum.

Despite its serious historical themes, *Guernsey* has a light and playful tone, and much of the film's energy focuses on a romance between Juliet and Dawsey Adams (Michiel Huisman). The two initially meet through a correspondence that begins when he writes her to say that he found a book inscribed with her name in Guernsey, where he lives. Several letters later, Dawsey describes how the development of their impromptu book club allowed him and some other citizens to resist the Nazis. Juliet, a journalist, subsequently decides to travel there so that she can write their story. Although she is engaged to a wealthy American when she arrives to Guernsey, Juliet quickly develops feelings for Dawsey, which he reciprocates.

Director Mike Newell crafted a sumptuous visual experience for viewers, evident in the cast's costumes as well as the set design. Juliet's London is brimming with an elegant 1940s aesthetic. Although there is evidence that the country is still recovering from the Blitz, Newell does not focus on that, but instead on the more beautiful parts of the characters' world. This is also evident in the way that he chooses to shoot the island of Guernsey. In the film's opening scene, the book club members walk back after their first unofficial meeting. It is dark outside and all that can be seen are their silhouettes against the night sky, which is full of stars. The imagery is so striking and beautiful that it almost looks as though it is animated. In later scenes, Newell shoots the Guernsey landscape with wide, open angles in an effort to showcase the beauty and unique qualities of the place. This infuses the film with a feeling of whimsy, which the director seems to want audiences to get lost in.

Guernsey is unabashedly a light-hearted, clever, and fun "women's film." When the film begins, Juliet is a successful writer known for her comical wartime novels, but she is struggling to decide what to write next. Although things are going well for her career and love life, she is still mourning the loss of her parents, who were killed during the Blitz when a bomb took out their family home. Juliet's decision to travel to Guernsey to learn more about the book club is what drives the plot. The other character responsible for creating narrative momentum is another

woman, Elizabeth. It was she who defied the Nazis by starting the book club. Additionally, she was brave enough to try to help a prisoner of war. Both Juliet and Elizabeth are strong, independent women willing to stand up against their antagonists to do what is right. In a strong showing of the film's pop-feminism, it ends with Juliet taking the lead and asking Dawsey to marry her.

Thematically, *Guernsey* is about the love of books and about the power and joys of reading fiction. In this, the film has stayed true to Shaffer's original intention. The Guernsey characters were able to temporarily escape the terror and oppression of Nazi occupation through their book club, and Juliet finds her books provide readers with lighthearted relief during the war. There are a few differences between the two iterations of the story, however. For one, the film portrays the character of Amelia

Co-author Annie Barrows. Photo by Larry D. Moore via Wikimedia Commons.

(Penelope Wilton) as an antagonist, whereas in the book she is more welcoming to Juliet. Arguably the biggest difference is that the novel uses an epistolary format, telling the story through a series of letters between the characters. It is an interesting stylistic choice that provides readers with a clear sense of each character's unique perspective and feelings.

Significance

The Guernsey Literary and Potato Peel Pie Society premiered in London on April 20, 2018. During its theatrical run in twenty-one countries, mainly in Europe, the film earned $23 million at the box office. It was later released in the United States directly to Netflix. In many ways, *Guernsey* was indicative of the changing state of the film industry at the time of its release. In previous decades, films would generally only get funding if they were destined for a widespread, theatrical release. By 2018, that was no longer true thanks to outlets such as Netflix.

Furthermore, films made specifically for streaming platform distribution were beginning to earn serious critical attention and film industry accolades. This was especially evident with the Netflix original *Roma* (2018) by director Alfonso Cuarón. Despite being screened in only a few theaters nationwide, *Roma* went on to be nominated for ten Academy Awards, winning three. Although it did not enjoy as many accolades as *Roma*, *Guernsey* received mostly positive ratings from critics. In his review for the *Los Angeles Times*, Kenneth Turan called the film "an old-school, old-fashioned entertainment, a romantic drama bursting with scenic vistas and earnest charm that contains just enough mystery to keep us involved." Newell's direction and James's performance received particular praise from reviewers, while most negative comments were directed at the plot, which some found to be too cloying or quaint. In one notable critical take, Peter Bradshaw wrote for *The Guardian* that the film was "a glutinous 40s-period exercise in British rom-dram solemnity, as if *Downton Abbey* were subject to a very polite Nazi occupation."

—*Emily E. Turner*

Further Reading

Benson, Heidi. "Literary Labor of Love Gave Way to Guernsey." *SF Gate*, 27 Aug. 2008, www.sfgate.com/entertainment/article/Literary-labor-of-love-gave-way-to-Guernsey-3271560.php. Accessed 8 Mar. 2019.

Venning, Nicola. "Director Mike Newell: I Have One More Film in Me." *Readers Digest*, 9 Apr. 2018, www.readersdigest.co.uk/culture/celebrities/director-mike-newell-i-have-one-more-film-in-me. Accessed 8 Mar. 2019.

Bibliography

Bradshaw, Peter. "The Guernsey Literary and Potato Peel Pie Society—An Outbreak of World War Twee." Review of *The Guernsey Literary and Potato Peel Pie Society*, directed by Mike Newell. *The Guardian*, 20 Apr. 2018, www.theguardian.com/film/2018/apr/20/the-guernsey-literary-and-potato-peel-pie-society-review-lily-james. Accessed 8 Mar. 2019.

Lodge, Guy. Review of *The Guernsey Literary and Potato Peel Pie Society*, directed by Mike Newell. *Variety*, 18 Apr. 2018, variety.com/2018/film/reviews/the-guernsey-literary-and-potato-peel-pie-society-review-1202753994. Accessed 8 Mar. 2019.

Martinelli, Marissa. "Netflix's New Movie Is Perfect Comfort Food for Fans of Downton Abbey or the Brontes." Review of *The Guernsey Literary and Potato Peel Pie Society*, directed by Mike Newell. *Slate*, 20 Aug. 2018, slate.com/culture/2018/08/the-guernsey-literary-and-potato-peel-pie-society-movie-review-netflixs-adaptation-is-perfect-comfort-food.html. Accessed 8 Mar. 2019.

Turan, Kenneth. "Review: Netflix's 'The Guernsey Literary and Potato Peel Pie Society' Is a Pleasant Throwback Romance with a Sparkling Lily James." Review of *The Guernsey Literary and Potato Peel Pie Society*, directed by Mike Newell. *The Los Angeles Times*, www.latimes.com/entertainment/movies/la-et-mn-guernsey-literary-and-potato-peel-pie-society-review-20180809-story.html. Accessed 8 Mar. 2019.

The Hate U Give

The Novel
Author: Angie Thomas (b. 1988)
First published: 2017

The Film
Year released: 2018
Director: George Tillman Jr. (b. 1969)
Screenplay by: Audrey Wells
Starring: Amandla Stenberg, Regina Hall, Russell Hornsby

Context

Police shootings of unarmed African Americans became a critical issue in American public life thanks to the efforts of the Black Lives Matter movement and hashtag, formed in the aftermath of the shooting of African American teenager Trayvon Martin in 2012. It was in the wake of another such incident, the killing of Oscar Grant III by a Bay Area Rapid Transit police officer in Oakland, California, that Angie Thomas wrote her award-winning young adult novel *The Hate U Give*. The book is narrated by sixteen-year-old Starr, an African American girl who carefully navigates the starkly different worlds of her predominantly African American neighborhood of Garden Heights and the affluent, predominantly white, private school she attends. Thomas drew on her own experiences in creating the character of Starr. As she said in an interview on NPR, "I lived in a mostly poor, black neighborhood...and I went to a mostly white, upper-class private school just ten minutes away from my home. But in ten minutes it was like going into an entirely different world. So I overcompensated by doing what they call code switching." Starr is an adept code switcher, slipping into the identity that she refers to as "Starr Version 2" during her own commute from home to school. When Starr is the only witness to the killing of her childhood friend during a police traffic stop, her worlds collide and she must find the courage to speak for herself and for her community.

The book was released to critical acclaim, with Anna Diamond for the *Atlantic* calling it "an incisive and engrossing perspective of the life of a black teenage girl." It was also a bestseller, staying on *The New York Times* Best Seller list for more than eighty-five weeks. When director George Tillman Jr. read the book, he connected with Starr's authentic voice. Tillman's film is faithful to the novel, and Amandla Stenberg's performance and voice-over narrative as Starr help to preserve that authentic voice. Thomas was involved in various aspects of the production—appearing in a cameo role during the film's protest scene—and was enthusiastic about the adaption of her novel.

The Hate U Give was released in 2018, and joined a burgeoning field of films created by African American writers and directors. During the 2010s, increasing importance was placed on the need for diversity and representation in Hollywood. A growing number of feature films centering on African American protagonists, including such films as *Hidden Figures* (2016), *Get Out* (2017), and *Black Panther* (2018), were critically lauded and drew wide, diverse audiences.

Film Analysis

Thomas's novel begins as Starr (Amandla Stenberg) and her childhood friend Khalil (Algee Smith) are pulled over while driving home from a party. During the course of this traffic stop a police officer shoots Khalil, killing him in front of Starr. Tillman's film, by contrast, takes its time in reaching this scene, choosing instead to establish the critical themes that it will address and to establish Starr's voice and character. The film begins with Mav (Russell Hornsby), Starr's father, telling his children how to act and speak when he or they are inevitably pulled over by the police. Starr and her brother are portrayed by younger actors in this opening scene, which adds to its poignancy and impact. It also effectively foreshadows the fatal traffic stop that will be the inciting incident of the film. Tillman then explores Starr's life at sixteen years old, with a series of scenes following her through a typical morning of commuting from Garden Heights to her school, the upscale Williamson Prep.

Starr's voice-over narration helps to establish her voice and to retain much of the language of the novel. The film also introduces the other members of Starr's family, including her older half-brother Seven (Lamar Johnson), as well as prominent characters in the neighborhood and at school. As a visual medium, film allows Tillman to conjure up the fictional Garden Heights—depicted through shots of struggling black- owned businesses and faded houses and housing projects —and contrast it with the well-manicured suburban arcadia in which Williamson Prep sits. This reordering of events and establishing of context helps to draw the audience into the film and to invest them in its protagonist. By the time the film arrives at the tragic killing of Khalil, the audience already knows Starr and the two worlds that she inhabits.

Chronology is only one of several liberties that the film takes with the novel. At more than 450 pages in length, Thomas's book has more subplots and characters than could be fully explored in a feature film. As such, the screenplay scales back the roles of some characters, including neighborhood barber Mr. Lewis (Tony Vaughn) and Starr's friend Maya (Megan Lawless). Starr's boyfriend, Chris (K. J. Apa), likewise plays a smaller role in the film than in the book. In an unusual and telling turn of events, the actor who originally played Chris, Kian Lawley, was removed from the film after a video surfaced of him using a racial slur and making racially charged comments. All of his scenes were reshot with actor K. J. Apa assuming the role of Chris.

One major character and subplot disappeared almost entirely in the film adaptation. The character DeVante, who in the book steals money from local gang leader King (Anthony Mackie), is limited to little more than a cameo. In the book, this storyline plays a critical role in the story's climax. As such, the climax of the film unfolds along somewhat different lines. Yet despite scaling back the role of several characters, the film does choose to represent Starr's family in the complex manner in which it was presented in the book. Starr's half-brother Seven, for example, is the child of Mav and of King's girlfriend Iesha (Karan Kendrick). This creates tension between and within the two families, and calls on Seven too choose between the very different kinds of lives that Mav and King represent. Whereas King is profiting from a life of crime and violence, Mav is struggling to make a living and to support his community by running a local store. Starr's uncle Carlos (Common) is a police officer, which adds to the complex relationship between the police and the black community in the film.

Perhaps the most significant departure from the book comes during the traffic stop. In the book, Khalil does nothing to suggest that he has a weapon or is a threat. In the film, however, he reaches into his car to take out a hairbrush, which the police officer mistakenly believes is a gun. It is a softening of the incident, a choice that makes the officer's actions fall into a grayer zone than they do in the book. A later scene in which Starr threatens her former friend Hailey (Sabrina Carpenter) with a hairbrush is likewise an addition to the film.

The film's dramatic climax centers on Starr's choice to speak at a demonstration again police violence, and on the chaos that follows when the police department turns on the crowd. The film's various plotlines converge and resolve themselves in a satisfying and dramatic way, and Starr, her family, and her neighborhood emerge better able to face whatever challenges still lie ahead of them.

Director George Tillman, Jr. Photo by Montclair Film Festival via Wikimedia Commons.

Significance

The Hate U Give was released to limited theaters on October 5, 2018, and nationwide on October 19, 2018. It earned $7.5 million on its opening weekend. With a production budget of $23 million, the film quickly proved itself to be profitable.

The film was very well received by critics, with *Time* calling it "marvelous and provocative." Some critics saw the film as a step forward for young-adult fiction and their film adaptations; Scott Mendelson wrote in Forbes that "*The Hate U Give* strips the YA fantasy of its comforting fantasy sheen." Whereas a film like *The Hunger Games* raises social issues metaphorically and allegorically, *The Hate U Give* addresses them explicitly. *The Hate U Give* provides an important look at society in the twenty-first century, giving voice to the experiences of African American teenage girls, a group not usually represented as the protagonists in films. Mendelson continued, "The picture operates...as an indictment of a societal and institutional mindset, one obviously rooted in racism, where the same behavior...can lead to either a verbal warning or violent death depending on skin color. The movie indicts a system where benign actions can be considered just cause for getting shot by a police officer."

Other critics took issue with various aspects of the film; Aisha Harris, writing in *The New York Times*, praises the actors for "exploring their characters' depths," but argues that "a wonky script can only get them so far." These occasional objections seem not to have put a dent in the positive buzz and word of mouth around this film. The strong reviews and high box office return of this film indicate its crossover appeal and its ability to draw a wide and diverse audience.

—*Matthew Bolton*

Further Reading

Diamond, Anna. "*The Hate U Give* Enters the Ranks of Great YA Novels." Review of *The Hate U Give*, by Angie Thomas. *The Atlantic*, 28 Mar. 2017, www.theatlantic.com/entertainment/archive/2017/03/the-hate-u-give-angie-thomas-review/521079/. Accessed 15 Nov. 2018.

Thomas, Angie. *The Hate U Give*. Blazer + Bray, 2017.

Bibliography

Harris, Aisha. "Review: In 'The Hate You Give', A Police Shooting Forces a Teen to Find her Voice." Review of *The Hate U Give*, directed by George Tillman Jr. *The New York Times*, 3 Oct. 2018, www.nytimes.com/2018/10/03/movies/the-hate-u-give-review-amandla-stenberg.html. Accessed 15 Nov. 2018.

Ito, Robert. "Microaggressions at School? 'The Hate U Give' Team Has Been There." *The New York Times*, 17 Oct. 2018, www.nytimes.com/2018/10/17/movies/microaggressions-hate-u-give.html. Accessed 15 Nov. 2018.

Mendelson, Scott. "Review: 'The Hate U Give' Is an Oscar-Worthy Masterpiece." Review of *The Hate U Give*, directed by George Tillman Jr. *Forbes*, 1 Oct 2018, www.forbes.com/sites/scottmendelson/2018/10/01/review-the-hate-u-give-is-an-oscar-worthy-masterpiece/. Accessed 15 Nov. 2018.

Thomas, Angie, and George Tillman Jr. "'The Hate U Give' Creators Tell Their Story through a 16-Year-Old Black Girl." Interview by Mallory Yu and Ailsa Change. *All Things Considered*, NPR, 8 Oct. 2018, www.npr.org/2018/10/08/655635859/the-hate-u-give-author-and-director-discuss-representing-the-black-community. Accessed 15 Nov. 2018.

Young, Daniel. "*The Hate U Give* Aims to Create Empathy While Offering a Portrait of Why Black Lives Matter." *The Grapevine*, 7 July 2018, thegrapevine.theroot.com/the-hate-u-give-aims-to-create-empathy-while-offering-a-1827590605. Accessed 15 Nov. 2018.

Zacharek, Stephanie. "Review: *The Hate U Give* is a Galvanizing Drama About Young People—For Everybody." Review of *The Hate U Give*, directed by George Tillman Jr. *Time*, 5 Oct. 2018, time.com/5417038/the-hate-u-give-movie-review/. Accessed 15 Nov. 2018.

Hold the Dark

The Novel
Author: William Giraldi (b. 1974)
First published: 2014

The Film
Year released: 2018
Director: Jeremy Saulnier (b. 1976)
Screenplay by: Macon Blair
Starring: Jeffrey Wright, Alexander Skarsgård, James Badge Dale, Riley Keough, Tantoo Cardinal, Julian Black Antelope

Context

The 2018 film *Hold the Dark*, directed by Jeremy Saulnier and starring acclaimed actor Jeffrey Wright, is based on the 2014 novel of the same name by author William Giraldi. *Hold the Dark* was Giraldi's second novel and, along with his first, established Giraldi as one of a number of popular voices in the evolving genre of surreal fiction. Giraldi's debut novel, *Busy Monsters*, which was released in 2011 to critical acclaim, tells the story of a man chasing an estranged girlfriend, who in turn has gone in search of a giant squid. Giraldi's second novel, *Hold the Dark*, is a different kind of effort for the author, allowing him to explore the gritty mystery genre with an entry that is extreme, violent, and somewhat surreal. However, like his first novel, there is an underlying theme of wildness and the savage powers of nature.

The novel *Hold the Dark* was well received by critics. In *The New York Times*, reviewer John Wilwol called the book "fierce" and "extraordinary," and he praised the richness and depth of Giraldi's prose. Other reviewers also found much to admire in Giraldi's writing skill and ability to build suspense and mystery. Some suggested that the book at times felt a bit overwritten, or excessive in its repetitive imagery and symbolism, and a few noted that the book was likely to divide readers. One of the ways in which Giraldi enhances the mystery of his story is through animal symbolism. *Busy Monsters* has its characters in pursuit of a giant squid, echoing Herman Melville's Moby Dick; *Hold the Dark* uses the figure of the wolf as a symbol of human violence and to suggest the mystery of wildness. The wolves are the vehicle that launches the action of the story, as a biologist specializing in wolf behavior is brought in to investigate allegations of wolves stealing and/or eating children, but the literal wolves are only one of the many ways in which Giraldi evokes this totemic animal and its representations in human culture. There is, for instance, a wolf mask donned by several characters in various scenes, creating a physical manifestation of the "wolf within" these characters. Allusions to wolves or other lupine characteristics, such as howling, snarling, growling, and having one's hackles up, appear repeatedly in the dialogue and in the descriptions of the characters and their interactions. Some reviewers noted that the constant lupine language might be seen as overdone, but Giraldi's intention may have been precisely to call attention to the way that humans obsessively search for clues, meaning, and symbols, whether or not they are there to be seen. The mystery of the wolf thus encourages readers to search for meaning in a story that, at its core, is about nihilistic violence and cruelty.

Less than a year after *Hold the Dark* was released, industry publications reported that VisionChaos Productions was in the process of creating a theatrical version of the novel, with up-and-coming director Jeremy Saulnier at the helm. Saulnier won audience and critical recognition for his previous films, *Blue Ruin* (2013) and *Green Room* (2015), both of which were suspenseful, violent films dealing with crime and murder. *Green Room* was nominated for a number of critical awards in the drama and horror categories and was on several lists as one of the top suspense/horror films of the year. Actor and director Macon Blair, who starred in both of Saulnier's previous films, wrote the screenplay adaptation of Giraldi's novel. It was later announced that the film would be released directly through Netflix.

Jeffrey Wright. Photo by Gage Skidmore via Wikimedia Commons.

Film Analysis

The film, *Hold the Dark*, released in 2018, stars acclaimed actor Jeffrey Wright, who plays a nature writer and researcher named Russell Core asked to come to the isolated Alaskan village of Keelut to investigate a case of wolves allegedly stealing three small children from the village. The woman who calls for Core's assistance is Medora Slone (Riley Keough), whose six-year-old son, Bailey, is one of the children who has gone missing. The opening sections of the film are laden with long, meaningful spaces and slow dialogue punctuated by images of stark, beautiful Alaskan scenery. Everything is shot in darkness, with grey light punctuating inky frames. A ghostly voice-over from Slone sets up the story as audiences are told that her child has gone missing, that wolves have taken the child, and that she is hoping that Core can find the wolves and the child's body. She also mentions that her husband is at war but will soon be coming home, and there is a note of fear in the way she says this.

Core stays with Slone, whose behavior is peculiar, lonely, and detached. Slone, like many of the other charac-

ters he meets, is strange and seemingly haunted. Scattered remarks seem to indicate that the community itself is malignant, and the residents of the strange, grey village are lost or trapped. On the first night Core spends in Slone's house, he witnesses her scrubbing her body and chanting to herself, then sees her emerged, naked and wearing a wooden wolf mask. The action then shifts immediately to an entirely different kind of landscape—a dusty desert in which Slone's husband, Vernon (Alexander Skarsgård), is fighting in a war. We see Vernon Slone using a vehicle-mounted machine gun to gun down some people in a fleeing truck. Then, in a moment of rest, Vernon hears a fellow soldier raping a local woman. He walks in, fatally stabs the rapist, hands the weapon to the victim, and leaves; soon after, he is shot and the resulting injury sends him home, back to Alaska.

Core eventually sets out to track the wolves. Along the way he meets a woman, Illanaq (Tantoo Cardinal), who plays the role of the hermetic mystic, warning him that there is darkness and evil in their town. After tracking the wolves to a hot spring, Core finds the animals eating something that might be a child until it is revealed that the wolves are actually cannibalizing their own young. Core returns to the village having found no evidence of wolves stealing or eating children. When he returns to Medora Slone's house, and finds her missing, he discovers another hidden truth that reframes the entire story. There is some suggestion that Medora might be possessed, though Core seems skeptical. Villagers speak of wolves and demons, but Sheriff Donald Marium (James Badge Dale) is not convinced by rumors of evil forces and thinks that the events in the town are more realistically psychopathic and murderous.

At this point, *Hold the Dark* veers into film noir territory. Vernon and his friend Cheeon (Julian Black Antelope), whose child has also gone missing, begin their own strange, mystical effort to solve the mystery of what is killing the children. Cheeon, meanwhile, raises the issue of the government's neglect and the way that their village, and more specifically the state's indigenous inhabitants, have been ignored by the state and the nation. Vernon's problems are far deeper. It is revealed that young Vernon was treated with some sort of wolf-based medicine for a condition that sounds very much like psychopathic violent behavior. The specter of the deadly wolves, or a wolf demon, becomes a shadow of Vernon's own savagery.

The violence in the film grows more and more intense. There is a massive gun battle in the middle of the film that is presented in grisly detail in the midst of a bleak, dark snowscape. There are other moments of intense, personal violence and many moments in which characters, mainly Core and Marium, contemplate the aftermath of the film's murderous rage. Core is the true outsider of the book, a vehicle through which the audience can contemplate the nihilistic violence of the film, which comes without any reason and has very little depth. Like Core, the audience is lured into paying attention to the signs and symbols that pervade the film—the wolf masks, the scattered scenes of wolves walking through the snow and in the tree line, taxidermized animals, and whispers of ancient wolf demons. At its core, *Hold the Dark* is a film about the wildness within humanity and about the ways in which these impulses, this natural penchant for violence, is released.

The film follows the plot of the novel, but there are some notable differences. In the novel, for example, it is implied that Vernon and Medora might be siblings, even that they might be twins, adding another twisted level to their macabre, malignant relationship. Are they battling to escape from each other and the darkness of their relationship, or is there something else at play? The film does not suggest the relationship between these characters as explicitly, though there are hints at this twist. It is unusual that both Vernon and Medora have a Scandinavian appearance, and commentary from other residents highlights their sameness—as well as their otherness from the rest of the community. What is never fully answered is why the violence of the book takes place to begin with. Why did this child die? Why is Vernon so violent? What is wrong with Medora? It is suggested, in both the novel and the film, that Vernon and Medora are "wolf-like" in character and nature and thus that there is something primal about their violence. It is also suggested that the violence is a response to the darkness, both literal and metaphorical, that the characters inhabit. In the Alaskan wilderness in which the book is set, the sun sets in midafternoon, but this too might be a symbol for the darkness Vernon and Medora wish to escape, which is each other and their own twisted union.

Significance

The film version of *Hold the Dark* was not nearly as well received as the novel from which it was adapted. Writing in *The Atlantic*, David Sims said it is "disappointing" and "confusing," but also praised the way that the film draws audiences in and called the overall experience fascinating, if not satisfying. Writing for *RogerEbert.com*, Brian Tallerico said that while the film has the essential elements of a great mystery, it is "humorless" and "unforgiving." Other reviewers noted that the overall impression of the film's violent savagery is meaningless and empty, without enough of a plot to draw the elements together to a satisfying conclusion. Though there were many criticisms, reviewers, in general, found the film intriguing and stylish, even as it fell short of perfection in plot and characterization. Some reviewers felt that *Hold the Dark* is a letdown from Saulnier's previous films, lacking the depth and narrative propulsion that attracted critical acclaim for *Green Room* and *Blue Ruin*. Overall, the film version of *Hold the Dark* did not attract as much attention as the novel, and this may reflect the fact that some of the narrative questions made explicit in the novel are not drawn as cleanly in the film.

—Micah Issitt

Further Reading

Blanchard, Nathan. Review of *Hold the Dark*, by William Giraldi. *Washington Independent Review of Books*, 12 Nov. 2014, www.washingtonindependentreviewofbooks.com/index.php/bookreview/hold-the-dark. Accessed 10 Mar. 2021.

Giraldi, William. *Hold the Dark*. Norton, 2014.

Bibliography

Barker, Andrew. "Toronto Film Review: 'Hold the Dark.'" Review of *Hold the Dark*, directed by Jeremy Saulnier. *Variety*, 12 Sept. 2018, variety.com/2018/film/reviews/hold-the-dark-review-toronto-1202937717/. Accessed 10 Mar. 2021.

Fear, David. "'Hold the Dark' Review: Blood, Snow and Wolves Are Just the Tip of Thriller's Iceberg." Review of *Hold the Dark*, directed by Jeremy Saulnier. *Rolling Stone*, 27 Sept. 2018, www.rollingstone.com/movies/movie-reviews/hold-the-dark-movie-review-728103/. Accessed 10 Mar. 2021.

Sims, David. "*Hold the Dark* Is a Revenge Epic That's Not Quite What It Seems." Review of *Hold the Dark*, directed by Jeremy Saulnier. *The Atlantic*, 28 Sept. 2018, www.theatlantic.com/entertainment/archive/2018/09/hold-the-dark-review/571120/. Accessed 10 Mar. 2021.

Tallerico, Brian. Review of *Hold the Dark*, directed by Jeremy Saulnier. *RogerEbert.com*, 28 Sept. 2018, www.rogerebert.com/reviews/hold-the-dark-2018. Accessed 10 Mar. 2021.

Wilwol, John. "Hour of the Wolf." Review of *Hold the Dark*, by William Giraldi. *The New York Times*, 5 Sept. 2014, www.nytimes.com/2014/09/07/books/review/hold-the-dark-by-william-giraldi.html. Accessed 10 Mar. 2021.

The House with a Clock in Its Walls

The Novel
Author: John Bellairs (1938-91)
First published: 1973

The Film
Year released: 2018
Director: Eli Roth (b. 1972)
Screenplay by: Eric Kripke
Starring: Jack Black, Cate Blanchett, Owen Vaccaro, Kyle MacLachlan, Renée Elise Goldsberry

Context

The House with a Clock in Its Walls is a 1973 young-adult novel beloved for its winning characters and its Gothic atmosphere. Written by John Bellairs and illustrated by Edward Gorey, the book tells the story of Louis Barnavelt, an orphan who comes to live with his Uncle Jonathan in a rambling old house that is full of secrets. A warlock, Uncle Jonathan is searching for a doomsday clock that the house's previous owner—an evil warlock named Isaac Izard—has hidden someplace inside its walls. Jonathan is aided in his search by Mrs. Zimmerman, a powerful witch who lives next door. In a bid to impress a classmate, Louis visits the town graveyard and uses one of his uncle's books of magic to bring Izard's wife back from the dead, setting in motion a disastrous series of events and bringing the doomsday clock that much closer to tolling. Uncle Jonathan, Mrs. Zimmerman, and Louis must work together to defeat the witch and to find and destroy the clock before it spells doom for humanity.

The novel—originally intended for adult readers before being reworked at the suggestion of an editor—earned critical acclaim (including a *New York Times* Outstanding Book of the Year citation) and launched Bellairs's career as a popular author of young-adult fiction. He went on to write two sequels as well as numerous other supernatural-themed books, and further continuations of the Louis Barnavelt series were published posthumously with contributions from other authors. Bellairs's works remained popular into the twenty-first century, by which time supernatural young adult fiction had become increasingly desirable in Hollywood thanks to the success of series such as J. K. Rowling's Harry Potter books and their film versions. Efforts arose to adapt *The House with a Clock in Its Walls* for the big screen, and as early as 2011 screenwriter Erick Kripke, a longtime Bellairs fan, started work on a script treatment of the novel.

Eventually filmmaker Eli Roth signed on to direct the film adaptation based on Kripke's screenplay. Roth was seen by many as an uncomfortable fit for a children's movie, thanks to his reputation as a horror auteur known for directing violent R-rated features such as *Cabin Fever* (2002) and *Hostel* (2005). (He has also worked as an actor, most notably as the baseball-bat wielding Donnie "The Bear" Donowitz in Quentin Tarantino's 2009 war film *Inglourious Basterds*). Yet Roth was intrigued after learning that many people considered Bellairs's novel their introduction to the horror genre, and sought to craft a family-friendly film that might have a similar effect. He also drew inspiration from the project's production company, Amblin Entertainment, known for its critically acclaimed family films of the 1980s, including some with horror elements, such as *Gremlins* (1984) and *The Goonies* (1985).

Film Analysis

Like the book, the film version of *The House with a Clock in Its Walls* begins with young Louis (Owen Vaccaro) taking the bus to New Zebedee, Michigan. Recently orphaned, Louis is coming to live with his only remaining relative, Uncle Jonathan (Jack Black). Uncle Jonathan is eccentric, absentminded, and larger than life. Louis is soon introduced to his uncle's neighbor and friend Mrs. Zimmerman (Cate Blanchett), who is just as quirky as Jonathan. In their roles, Black demonstrates the trademark humor that has made him a mainstay in children's adventure-comedy films, while Blanchett brings a dry wit and restraint that provides a counterbalance to Black's zaniness. Perhaps inevitably, Vaccaro at times struggles to hold his own with these two actors.

The film has high production values, with a number of sets that are beguiling and immersive. The depiction of the town of New Zebedee, with its movie marquee and classic cars, is a standout. It effectively renders the mid-twentieth century setting, and thereby also evokes a sense of the classic horror and science-fiction films of that era. It is also a more integrated and diverse locale than one might have assumed from reading the novel, and the filmmakers deserve credit for casting actors of color in several key roles.

Uncle Jonathan's grand, spooky Victorian house is the film's other great set, and is where most of its action takes place. Some of its elements, like a stained-glass window that keeps depicting different images, are taken from the book. Others are embellishments, like the affectionate armchair in the front room or the griffin-shaped topiary that wanders around the backyard and refuses to use a litterbox. (The latter creature's leafy droppings are just one of several scatological elements added to the film to appeal to younger viewers.) Yet perhaps the most notable change from the source material is that while the book takes a gentle and wistful approach to magic, Roth's house bristles with computer-generated imagery (CGI)-enhanced magical elements. The film version of Uncle Jonathan's house seems influenced by the look of the Harry Potter blockbusters and their various imitators. Indeed, within short order Louis is being put through his paces as an apprentice wizard as the film grafts further Harry Potter-like sensibilities onto Bellairs's story.

The film is more tightly constructed than the book, streamlining Bellairs' ambling plot. Kripke's deft screenplay moves at a brisker pace and creates more connections among the various characters and story elements. In Bellairs's narrative, items and information appear when they become necessary; for example, Louis produces a Magic 8-Ball toward the end of the novel and uses it as part of a spell. In the film, Louis consults the ball as he arrives in New Zebedee in the opening scenes. He later tells his uncle that it is the last thing his parents gave him before their fatal car crash. Therefore, when Louis uses the Magic 8-Ball in a critical scene at the end of the film, it has a symbolic resonance that it does not possess in the book. Perhaps more significantly, Kripke's script has Louis resurrect Isaac Izard (Kyle MacLachlan) himself, rather than Izard's wife, Selena (Renée Elise Goldsberry), and the

Jack Black. Photo by Toglenn, GNU Free Documentation License via Wikimedia Commons.

evil warlock becomes an active character in the film in a way he is not in the book. The script likewise finds a clever way to bring Selena Izard into the story and connect her to previous events.

The film also gives each of the main characters backstories that inform their present actions and draw them into a closer web of associations and parallelisms. Louis, for example, is more affected by his parents' death in this film than he seems to be in the book, and is visited at night by what seems to be the ghost of his mother. Uncle Jonathan is given a history as Isaac Izard's former partner; he also discusses his estrangement from his father, who disapproved of his learning magic, and explains why he has been out of touch with Louis's mother. Both Isaac Izard and Mrs. Zimmerman are shown to be profoundly affected by World War II. Indeed, the film notes that Izard

Director Eli Roth. Photo by Sgt. Michael Connors, Public domain via Wikimedia Commons.

created his doomsday clock out of a desire to undo all of the damage that mankind has inflicted on the world by rolling time back to before the dawn of humanity. However, the film is not fully successful in integrating such weighty backstories, as references to grave subjects such as the Holocaust clash with what is otherwise a CGI-laden romp.

Like the production itself, the script has a slickness to it that gives the film a different feel from the book. Each character is given a neatly plotted journey, with moments of doubt followed by moments of insight and redemption. Uncle Jonathan learns that he is capable of taking care of a child, Mrs. Zimmerman faces her trauma and regains her magical mojo, and Louis saves the day and settles into his new life in New Zebedee. In contrast, Bellairs's original story is as creaky, odd, and rambling as Uncle Jonathan's

old house. Ultimately, Roth and Kripke have done a cinematic gut-renovation, adding many shiny new features to *The House with a Clock in its Walls* at the expense of some of the original's eccentric charm.

Significance

The House with a Clock in Its Walls film was commercially successful, earning over $131 million in domestic and foreign release against an approximately $42 million production budget. Its opening weekend domestic box office take of $26.9 million well outdid projections and easily became Roth's highest-grossing effort. Critically, however, it received decidedly mixed reviews. While acknowledging some effective aspects, many reviewers found the film to be derivative and unoriginal overall, especially in light of the strength of the source material. Writing in *Variety*, Peter Debruge termed it "yet another in a pipeline of vaguely Harry Potteresque wish-fulfilment fantasies," though he praised Roth's ability to tone down his signature horror style for younger viewers. Debruge also noted that children in the audience might one day look back on the film as favorably as many have come to view Amblin Entertainment's 1980s hits.

Other reviewers were more sharply critical. In a review for *NPR*, Scott Tobias echoed the charge that the production apes previous children's franchises, while suggesting that "Roth's instinct for horror maximalism is precisely the wrong approach to the material." Like several other critics, Tobias deplored what he saw as the use of cheap thrills and CGI distractions out of an apparent fear that children's attention spans are too short to handle less-frenetic fare. In his review for *Newsday*, Rafer Guzmán had similar objections, while arguing that Roth attempted to mimic the style of filmmaker Tim Burton but ultimately failed. "Despite its special effects and two proven stars, *The House with a Clock in Its Walls* never manages to create the magic we keep hoping will materialize," he wrote.

Despite such widespread criticisms, some critics had more positive reactions to the film. In *The New York Times*, Ben Kenigsberg called it a "nostalgic fun house movie" and suggested the influence of Tim Burton was a strength. He also detected inspiration from the works of noted director Steven Spielberg (the founder of Amblin Entertainment), and singled out the set design and Blanchett's performance for particular praise.

—*Matthew Bolton*

Further Reading

Hutman, Jon. "How *The House with a Clock in Its Walls* Was Actually Built." Interview by Susannah Edelbaum. *The Credits*, Motion Picture Association of America, 21 Sept. 2018, www.mpaa.org/2018/09/the-house-with-a-clock-in-its-walls-production-designer/. Accessed 17 Jan. 2019.

Roth, Eli, and Owen Vaccaro. "Eli Roth & Owen Vaccaro Interview: *The House with a Clock in Its Walls*." Interview by Joe Deckelmeier. *ScreenRant*, 17 Dec. 2018, screenrant.com/house-clock-walls-owen-vaccaro-eli-roth-interview/. Accessed 17 Jan. 2019.

Bibliography

Burnett, Matia. "Movie Alert: 'The House with a Clock in Its Walls." *Publishers Weekly*, 20 Sept. 2018, www.publishersweekly.com/pw/by-topic/childrens/childrens-industry-news/article/78085-movie-alert-the-house-with-a-clock-in-its-walls.html. Accessed 17 Jan. 2019.

Debruge, Peter. Review of *The House with a Clock in Its Walls*, directed by Eli Roth. *Variety*, 18 Sept. 2018, variety.com/2018/film/reviews/the-house-with-a-clock-in-its-walls-review-1202946627/. Accessed 17 Jan. 2019.

Guzmán, Rafer. "'The House with a Clock in Its Walls' Review: It's Not Magic Time." Review of *The House with a Clock in Its Walls*, directed by Eli Roth. *Newsday*, 19 Sept. 2018, www.newsday.com/entertainment/movies/house-with-a-clock-review-1.21127226. Accessed 17 Jan. 2019.

Kenigsberg, Ben. "Review: *The House with a Clock in its Walls* is Demented Fun (for Kids)." Review of *The House with a Clock in Its Walls*, directed by Eli Roth. *The New York Times*, 20 Sept. 2018, www.nytimes.com/2018/09/20/movies/the-house-with-a-clock-in-its-walls-cate-blanchett-jack-black.html?referrer=google_kp. Accessed 17 Jan. 2019.

Tobias, Scott. "'The House with a Clock in Its Walls' Is an Eyesore." Review of *The House with a Clock in Its Walls*, directed by Eli Roth. *NPR*, 20 Sept. 2018. www.npr.org/2018/09/20/647874840/the-house-with-a-clock-in-its-walls-is-an-eyesore. Accessed 17 Jan. 2019.

How to Train Your Dragon

The Novel
Author: Cressida Cowell (b. 1966)
First published: 2003

The Film
Year released: 2010
Directors: Chris Sanders (b. 1962) and Dean DeBlois (b. 1970)
Screenplay by: Will Davies, Dean DeBlois, and Chris Sanders
Starring: Jay Baruchel, Gerard Butler, America Ferrera, Craig Ferguson

Context

The film *How to Train Your Dragon* was loosely based on the 2003 book of the same name, by British writer Cressida Cowell. Building upon the characters and world that Cowell initially introduced in the 2000 picture book *Hiccup—the Seasick Viking*, the book *How to Train Your Dragon* and subsequent installments in the series were aimed at a somewhat older audience and would go on to be categorized primarily as middle-grade works. Published between 2003 and 2015, the series came to encompass twelve books, concluding with the book *How to Fight a Dragon's Fury*. All of the books focus on the adventures of young Viking Hiccup Horrendous Haddock III, his dragon companion Toothless, and the other residents of the island of Berk, who overcome a variety of challenges and defeat numerous enemies. Popular among readers in the United Kingdom, the United States, and elsewhere, the series also spawned several tie-in publications focusing on the world and characters presented in the series.

The 2010 film adaptation of *How to Train Your Dragon* was directed by Chris Sanders and Dean DeBlois, veterans of animation who had previously been associated primarily with Disney Animation projects. Sanders had previously contributed to the screenplays or stories for major Disney films such as *Beauty and the Beast* (1991), *Aladdin* (1992), and *Mulan* (1998), while DeBlois had worked on *Mulan* and *Atlantis: The Lost Empire* (2001). The pair made their feature-length directorial debut in 2002 with the release of the animated Disney film *Lilo & Stitch*, which they also cowrote. Both later left Disney for DreamWorks, where DeBlois focused primarily on the *How to Train Your Dragon* franchise while Sanders went on to work on projects such as 2013's *The Croods*. In addition to serving as codirectors, DeBlois and Sanders were credited as writers on *How to Train Your Dragon* alongside Will Davies, who had previously contributed to the 2006 DreamWorks Animation feature *Flushed Away*.

DreamWorks Animation became a major player in the US animation industry in the late 1990s, creating computer-animated films that led to comparisons with the company's rival, Pixar. The studio's first film, *Antz* (1998), was moderately successful. They became a household name with *Shrek* (2001) and the subsequent Shrek franchise. The films and related media in the *How to Train Your Dragon* franchise have been among the most critically and commercially successful animated adaptations released by the studio.

Film Analysis

In adapting *How to Train Your Dragon* for the screen, the filmmakers sought to balance concepts and characters drawn from Cowell's original series with the needs of the screen, creating a film that was recognizably based on her work yet featured an engaging narrative suited for a feature film. To do so, Sanders, DeBlois, and Davies made a variety of key changes when adapting the work. Perhaps the most important of these is a crucial shift in the relationship between humans and dragons that shapes the narrative as a whole.

In the original book, the Vikings of Berk are accustomed to capturing dragons and training them, and the process holds a great degree of cultural significance for the society; in fact, young men who are unable to train a dragon successfully are exiled from their village. The book begins as its young protagonist, Hiccup, and the other young men of his tribe are on a planned outing to capture their own dragons, which they will be tasked with training in accordance with their society's coming-of-age tradition. Much of the book's conflict centers on Hiccup's difficulty in completing his traditional duty successfully. As Hiccup's quest is to become a true member of his tribe, the challenges he faces fall largely within the bounds of his society's traditions rather than outside of them. He faces additional challenges in the form of unfriendly dragons that threaten his home, but those external threats do not come into significant conflict with his people's entire way of life.

The film adaptation of *How to Train Your Dragon* takes a different approach, as is initially signaled through the narration by Hiccup (Jay Baruchel) that opens the movie. In the world of the film, dragons are dangerous pests known for stealing livestock and threatening the Viking village. The relationship between the Vikings of Berk and the dragons is solely combative—an excursion with the goal of capturing dragons to be trained for useful purposes, as seen in the book, would be unheard of. Indeed, while young Vikings take part in training exercises in the film, the goal of the training is for the humans to learn how to kill dragons above all. Hiccup's eventual training of and friendship with the dragon Toothless, then, run counter to the norms of his society. This change raises the stakes of the narrative's conflict and enhances the impact of Hiccup's coming-of-age narrative. In addition to undergoing the transformative experiences of training a dragon and defeating a powerful enemy, he must overcome the long-held beliefs of his people and ultimately transform his society for the better.

Growing out of the crucial reshaping of the relationship between Vikings and dragons, the plot of the film version of *How to Train Your Dragon* diverges significantly from that of the book. The film opens with a dragon raid on the Viking village, during which Hiccup, the teenage son of chief Stoick the Vast (Gerard Butler), attempts to prove himself by fighting the dragons using a weapon he designed. He succeeds in shooting down a dragon, and finds where it crash-landed with the intention of killing it to prove his competence as a warrior. However, he ultimately shows the injured dragon mercy. In turn, the dragon—later known as Toothless—decides not to kill Hiccup when given the opportunity. The two begin a friendship, and Hiccup creates a prosthetic tail fin to replace the one Toothless lost when he was shot down.

Through his interactions with Toothless, Hiccup learns nonviolent means of interacting with dragons that conflict

Jay Baruchel. Photo by Gage Skidmore via Wikimedia Commons.

greatly with the skills he learns in his village, where his training is set to culminate in him killing a dragon in front of his father and peers. He eventually learns to ride Toothless, who shows Hiccup and his friend Astrid (America Ferrera) that the dragons have not been raiding the human village of their own free will but instead are forced to bring food to a giant, terrifying dragon known as the Red Death, who lives within a nearby volcano. Although Hiccup initially attempts to keep this information secret, fearing that his people will kill Toothless if they find out about him, the truth is eventually revealed. Hiccup is deemed a traitor for defending Toothless, and the Viking warriors set out to destroy all the dragons. Although the Viking fleet is unable to defeat the Red Death, Hiccup and his friends arrive to join the battle, having flown there on dragons. Working together, Hiccup and Toothless succeed where humans alone failed, ultimately killing the Red Death and removing the root cause of the conflict between humans and dragons.

As the ending of the *How to Train Your Dragon* demonstrates, Hiccup's actions within the film bring humans and dragons together, forming a productive interspecies relationship and bringing peace to the island of Berk. This establishes a new status quo that is more reminiscent of the state of Viking society presented at the start Cowell's original series, creating a fruitful jumping-off point for further adventures. In addition to changing his society, Hiccup has changed in a multitude of ways by the end of the film, including physically through the loss of part of his leg in the final battle, an injury that mirrors Toothless's injury at the start of the film. Perhaps most important, however, is the personal growth Hiccup experiences through his time teaching and learning from Toothless, which not only enabled him to end the threat to his people but also helped him lead the people of Berk into a new era of peace and possibility. While diverging significantly from the source material, *How to Train Your Dragon* ultimately presents a strong coming-of-age narrative, emphasizing the value of positive traits such as kindness, understanding, nonconformity, and teamwork.

Significance

How to Train Your Dragon was released in the United States and in many international markets, reaching audiences around the world in 3D and IMAX as well as standard versions. It performed very well at the box office, grossing more than $217 million domestically and $277 million in other countries against a budget of approximately $165 million, according to the website Box Office Mojo. In addition to proving popular among audiences, *How to Train Your Dragon* was generally well received by critics, and was nominated for Academy Awards for best animated feature film and best original score. It was likewise nominated for the Golden Globe and British Academy of Film and Television Arts (BAFTA) awards for best animated film and won several awards at the animation-focused Annie Awards. The film also won praise from Cressida Cowell, who approved of the changes made in adapting her work and noted in interviews that she viewed the film and the book as separate entities. Cowell particularly appreciated the filmmakers' decision to have Hiccup lose part of his leg, which she noted could render him a helpful role model for children with disabilities.

DreamWorks released two sequels to the film. The first, *How to Train Your Dragon 2*, was directed and written by DeBlois. The second sequel, *How to Train Your Dragon:*

The Hidden World, was released in 2019. In addition to feature-length films, the *How to Train Your Dragon* franchise came to include several short films, video games, and comic books based on the film series as well as a television series, *DreamWorks Dragons*, that premiered in 2012. Although primarily building on the world of the first film, these sequels and spin-offs continued to draw inspiration from Cowell's original series.

—*Joy Crelin*

Further Reading

Cowell, Cressida. "Cressida Cowell, Author of 'How to Train Your Dragon' Interview." Interview by Eric Sundermann. *Hollywood.com*, HYPERLINK "http://www.hollywood.com/movies/cressida-cowell-author-of-how-to-train-your-dragon-interview-57200749/" www.hollywood.com/movies/cressida-cowell-author-of-how-to-train-your-dragon-interview-57200749/. Accessed 30 Nov. 2018.

Cowell, Cressida. *How to Train Your Dragon*. Little, Brown, 2003.

Bibliography

D'Alessandro, Anthony. "'How to Train Your Dragon: The Hidden World' to Fly a Week Earlier in February." *Deadline*, 27 Sept. 2018. deadline.com/2018/09/how-to-train-your-dragon-3-everest-dreamworks-animation-1201864844/. Accessed 30 Nov. 2018.

Foutch, Haleigh. "Collider Gets a Behind-the-Scenes Look at *How to Train Your Dragon 2* with Director Dean DeBlois at DreamWorks Animation Studios." *Collider*, 11 June 2014, collider.com/how-to-train-your-dragon-2-interview-dean-deblois/. Accessed 30 Nov. 2018.

Honeycutt, Kirk. Review of *How to Train Your Dragon*, directed by Chris Sanders and Dean DeBlois. *The Hollywood Reporter*, 14 Oct. 2010, www.hollywoodreporter.com/review/how-train-your-dragon-film-29387. Accessed 30 Nov. 2018.

"How to Train Your Dragon." *Box Office Mojo*, www.boxofficemojo.com/movies/?id=howtotrainyourdragon.htm. Accessed 30 Nov. 2018.

Murray, Noel. "Source Material: The *How to Train Your Dragon* Books Are Very Different from the Movies." *Dissolve*, 12 June 2014, thedissolve.com/news/2462-source-material-the-how-to-train-your-dragon-books/. Accessed 30 Nov. 2018.

Scott, A. O. "No Slaying Required: A Viking Aids an Enemy and Wins a Friend." Review of *How to Train Your Dragon*, directed by Chris Sanders and Dean DeBlois. *The New York Times*, 25 Mar. 2010, www.nytimes.com/2010/03/26/movies/26howto.html. Accessed 30 Nov. 2018.

Wood, Helen. "Revisiting *How to Train Your Dragon*." *Den of Geek*, 14 May 2018, www.denofgeek.com/uk/movies/how-to-train-your-dragon/56978/revisiting-how-to-train-your-dragon. Accessed 30 Nov. 2018.

The Hunt for Red October

The Novel
Author: Tom Clancy (1947-2013)
First published: 1984

The Film
Year released: 1990
Director: John McTiernan (b. 1951)
Screenplay by: Larry Ferguson and Donald E. Stewart
Starring: Sean Connery, Alec Baldwin, James Earl Jones, Scott Glenn, Sam Neill

Context

In 1984, insurance broker Tom Clancy launched his writing career with *The Hunt for Red October* (1984), a novel about a rogue Soviet nuclear submarine. Although Clancy had no direct military experience (he was rejected from service because of poor eyesight), he was able to craft a compelling naval thriller thanks to his lifelong deep interest in military technology. He also loosely based his plot on a true incident of mutiny on a Soviet warship, giving the story an edge of realism in the midst of the Cold War. *The Hunt for Red October* was the first work of fiction ever published by Naval Institute Press, a long-standing maritime nonfiction specialist. This helped Clancy's debut novel quickly win approval among those with military ties, which in turn boosted its overall popularity. A notable public endorsement came from US president Ronald Reagan, and the book became a bestseller.

Indeed, *The Hunt for Red October* proved so successful that it is widely credited with making the political/military techno-thriller one of the leading subgenres in popular fiction. The category is known for including detailed technical information and professional jargon alongside often-complex action plots. There are whole alphabets of interagency acronyms for governmental entities, secret resources, and sophisticated armaments and other advanced technology. Heroes of military techno-thrillers exhibit keen intelligence, adaptability, and good instincts as they improvise their way through bureaucratic mazes to solve one problem after another. The subgenre is closely connected to traditional espionage fiction, such as John le Carré's books featuring the character George Smiley. Later techno-thriller heroes include Lee Child's Jack Reacher and Dan Brown's Robert Langdon, both featured in successful novel series and film adaptations. Yet Clancy's Jack Ryan character, first introduced in *The Hunt for Red October*, is among the most influential. Ryan is a bookish Central Intelligence Agency (CIA) analyst, all about facts and figures; who is drawn into a dangerous mission out of his sense of duty to his country.

Despite detailed passages about esoteric technological subjects, *The Hunt for Red October* illustrates Clancy's cinematic writing style. His prose includes quick cuts to far-flung locations and vivid contrast between claustrophobic spaces and wide-open seascapes. He effectively controls the pace through narrative and flashback, while steadily developing the rising conflict. Unsurprisingly, the book's film potential was quickly realized, and the option rights were sold in 1985.

However, because of the scope and complexity of the novel, five years passed before an adaptation was brought to screen. By that time, the Cold War had ended with the breakup of the Soviet Union, leading to some worries that the material was outdated. Nevertheless, Paramount Pictures and its production partners invested $30 million in the project. The US Navy also cooperated with the filmmakers, in part out of hope that the film would provide a public image boost much like the Paramount production *Top Gun* (1986) had.

The film was helmed by director John McTiernan, who was fresh off notable action hits with *Predator* (1987) and *Die Hard* (1988). Although the part of Jack Ryan was initially earmarked for Kevin Costner, he turned it down in favor of *Dances with Wolves* (1990), and the role went to rising star Alec Baldwin. The other lead role, that of Soviet submarine captain Marko Ramius, was supposed to be played by Austrian actor Klaus Maria Brandauer, but he dropped out after production had begun. Sean Connery, best known for portraying iconic spy James Bond, ultimately stepped in.

Film Analysis

The film adaptation of *The Hunt for Red October* was written by Larry Ferguson and Donald E. Stewart (with some uncredited contributions by John Milius). In general, it is faithful to the basic plot of the source material: the captain of the advanced Soviet nuclear submarine *Red October*, Marko Ramius (Connery), goes rogue, and CIA analyst Jack Ryan (Baldwin) must determine whether he intends to defect or poses a threat. However, as with many adaptations, the original story is greatly condensed: more than five hundred pages of text are compressed into a film with a running time of 135 minutes.

To accomplish this, dozens of scenes set at globe-spanning locations in the novel are absent. Many technical explanations are excised, minimized, simplified, or changed. For example, the innovative propulsion system responsible for the silence of the Soviet sub is reworked. The massive Soviet response to the rogue sub crisis (a fleet of nearly one hundred vessels in the novel) is mostly reduced to shots showing officers tracking ship movements on naval charts. The American military operation is similarly downsized, and a collaborative British effort is left out altogether.

The film also deletes many characters from the novel. The unnamed American president, for example, and his counterpart, an invented Soviet premier, are left out. Their elimination de-emphasizes the political maneuvering woven into the novel to complement military tactics. Negotiations are instead handled by less important underlings: National Security Advisor Jeffrey Pelt (Richard Jordan) and Soviet ambassador Andrei Lysenko (Joss Ackland). With politics relegated to the background, the film focuses on a suspenseful hide-and-seek, predator-versus-prey theme, in the tradition of earlier submarine action features like *Run Silent, Run Deep* (1958) and *Das Boot* (1981), but on a grander scale, with more modern accoutrements.

The film is noted for its realistic portrayal of military equipment, due both to Clancy's expertise and the involvement of the US Navy in the production. Because the story concerned potentially sensitive military information, the script was reviewed and—with certain suggested changes incorporated—approved by Navy authorities. Such cooperation had many benefits that added to the film's verisimilitude. Set designers and prop makers were

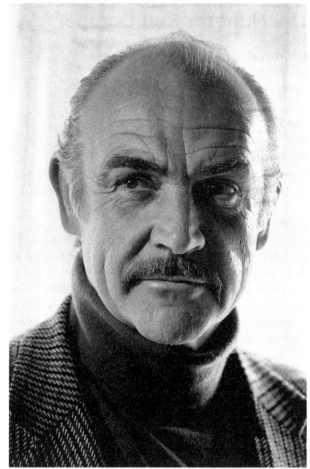

Sean Connery. Photo by Rob Bogaerts / Anefo, CC BY-SA 3.0 NL, via Wikimedia Commons.

allowed to board actual submarines, surface ships, aircraft, and other military resources for photographic purposes. Access to naval ports was granted; Port Valdez, Alaska, substituted for northern Russia, where the film opens, and Point Loma near San Diego, California, was a stand-in for East Coast shipyards, where some scenes occur. Actual sailors served as crew and extras. Since filming on real submarines presented problems, sets replicating portions of the interiors of both American and Russian subs were constructed upon platforms that allowed simulation of movement. For exterior shots, a large-scale model of the *Red October* was built atop barges. Underwater scenes featured remote-controlled models.

The film opens with superimposed type explaining that in late 1984 a Typhoon-class Soviet sub apparently sank, though the Soviet and American governments both disavowed the event. Plot points generally follow the novel, though their order is at times shuffled. Ramius, the captain of the Soviet Union's largest, most lethal, virtually undetectable ballistic missile submarine, is seen putting out to sea on the *Red October*'s maiden voyage. Ryan, who in the novel does not enter until the fourth chapter, is then introduced. He is shown arriving at CIA headquarters and meeting with Deputy Director James Greer (James Earl Jones). They examine secretly obtained photos of the sub and discuss its unique features. Also inserted early are scenes of the American attack sub USS *Dallas*, which is shadowing the *Red October*. Two characters who will figure prominently are introduced: *Dallas* commander Bart Mancuso (Scott Glenn) and sonar operator Jones (Courtney B. Vance), who develops a way to read the phantom *October*'s almost-silent signature.

Focus returns to the Soviet sub, where some dialogue is in Russian before switching to English. Other supporting characters comes into focus, each with their own agenda, including Soviet political officer Ivan Putin (Peter Firth) and Ramius's executive officer Vasily Borodin (Sam Neill). Connery's acting performance is key, as he depicts Ramius as a complex character with deep motivations. Eventually the captain's intentions become clear: to defect to America and deliver his vessel as a gift to seal the deal. He posts fake orders and tells the crew they are heading to Communist Cuba for rest and relaxation, a possibility that excites all except for the suspicious cook, Loginov (Tomas Arana), who is an undercover government spy.

Moscow, of course, will not allow its expensive prize to be lost easily. The Soviets dispatch a massive fleet to find and destroy the *October* without starting World War III. The effort is headed by a Ramius protégé, ambitious submarine commander Tupelov (Stellan Skarsgård), who vows to find and kill his mentor. They also invite the Americans to help, claiming that Ramius seeks to attack the United States. As US forces scramble to act, Ryan is the lone voice to suspect Ramius's true intentions—and he must not only convince others but also pull off a daring plan to avert catastrophe. The Cold War heats up in a hurry as the opposing submarines perform a sinister underwater ballet on the way to an explosive finale.

Much of the film relies on character-based drama in the tight confines of the submarines. Still, special effects-heavy shots of the vessels maneuvering underwater play a significant role in establishing atmosphere. Computer-generated imagery (CGI) was not yet dominant in Hollywood at the time of the production, but was used to add certain effects like bubbles that heightened the realism of these scenes. Sound effects also contribute strongly to the overall tense tone of the film. Perhaps most notable is the sound of the sonar "pings," which McTiernan carefully selected out of hundreds of options.

Significance

The film version of *The Hunt for Red October* was a commercial success. Half the budget was recouped during its opening week, on the way to a worldwide gross of more than $200 million. Reviews were generally positive. Noted critic Roger Ebert's take was representative, calling it "a skillful, efficient film that involves us in the clever and deceptive game being played." The film earned an Academy Award and a Motion Picture Editors Award for sound effects editing, as well as further Oscar nominations for Best Sound and Best Film Editing. Musical score composer Basil Poledouris (also known for *Conan the Barbarian*, 1982; *Red Dawn*, 1984; and *RoboCop*, 1987) won a Broadcast Music, Inc. (BMI) Award for his work. Among negative reactions to the film, Peter Travers, writing in *Rolling Stone*, spoke for numerous critics who found the film dramatic and proficient but ultimately empty, without real human drama. Travers also spoke for a sizable minority when he pointed out the cheesy propaganda aspects of the film (and the novel): "As right-wing, redbaiting, kick-ass techno-thrillers go, you can't do better than Clancy's *Hunt*," opined Travers. The film was "tub thumping for a strong defense capability," he wrote.

As a novel, *The Hunt for Red October* launched Clancy's writing career, and the success of the adaptation furthered his success as a major best-selling author. Jack Ryan would become his best-known character, featured in several further novels by Clancy himself as well as many other works across various media. On the big screen, Ryan has reappeared in various incarnations, most of which have been profitable if not always critically acclaimed. Harrison Ford took over the part in the well-received releases *Patriot Games* (1992) and *Clear and Present Danger* (1994), while Ben Affleck played Ryan for *The Sum of All Fears* (2002) and Chris Pine stepped in for *Jack Ryan: Shadow Recruit* (2014). The television series *Tom Clancy's Jack Ryan*, starring John Krasinski, debuted in 2018.

—Jack Ewing

Further Reading

Terdoslavich, William. *The Jack Ryan Agenda: Policy and Politics in the Novels of Tom Clancy; An Unauthorized Analysis.* Forge Books, 2005.

Young, Gregory D., and Nate Braden. *The Last Sentry: The True Story that Inspired* The Hunt for Red October. Naval Institute Press, 2005.

Bibliography

Axe, David. "'The Hunt for Red October' Is a Submarine Movie Masterpiece." Review of *The Hunt for Red October*, directed by John McTiernan. *The National Interest*, 14 Apr. 2020, nationalinterest.org/blog/buzz/%E2%80%98-hunt-red-october%E2%80%99-submarine-movie-masterpiece-144037. Accessed 18 Mar. 2021.

Berardinelli, James. Review of *The Hunt for Red October*, directed by John McTiernan. *ReelViews*, 5 Oct. 2018, www.reelviews.net/reelviews/hunt-for-red-october-the. Accessed 17 Feb. 2021.

Clancy, Tom. "PW Interviews Tom Clancy." Interview by John Mutter. *Publishers Weekly*, 8 Aug. 1986, www.publishers weekly.com/pw/by-topic/authors/interviews/article/59383-pw-interviews-tom-clancy.html. Accessed 18 Mar. 2021.

Ebert, Roger. Review of *The Hunt for Red October*, directed by John McTiernan. *RogerEbert.com*, 2 Mar. 1990, www.rogerebert.com/reviews/the-hunt-for-red-october-1990. Accessed 18 Mar. 2021.

Haglund, David. "How *The Hunt for Red October* Movie Revealed Classified Information about U.S. Submarines." *Slate*, 2 Oct. 2013, slate.com/culture/2013/10/the-hunt-for-red-october-movie-revealed-classified-information-about-u-s-submarines-because-tom-clancy-knew-his-stuff.html. Accessed 18 Mar. 2021.

"The Hunt for Red October." *Movie-Locations.com*, movie-locations.com/movies/h/Hunt-For-Red-October.php. Accessed 18 Mar. 2021.

"The Hunt for Red October." *Turner Classic Movies*, www.tcm.com/tcmdb/title/22092/the-hunt-for-red-october#overview. Accessed 18 Mar. 2021.

Snider, Eric D. "14 Deep Facts about *The Hunt for Red October*." *MentalFloss*, 12 June 2015, www.mentalfloss.com/article/64931/14-deep-facts-about-hunt-red-october. Accessed 18 Mar. 2021.

If Beale Street Could Talk

The Novel
Author: James Baldwin (1924-87)
First published: 1974

The Film
Year released: 2018
Director: Barry Jenkins (b. 1979)
Screenplay by: Barry Jenkins
Starring: KiKi Layne, Stephan James, Regina King, Colman Domingo, Michael Beach, Brian Tyree Henry, Emily Rios, Teyonah Parris

Context
If Beale Street Could Talk is a novel written by author and civil rights activist James Baldwin. Set in 1970s Harlem, it follows the love story of two young African Americans named Fonny and Tish. Although the world around them is racist, their love for one another protects them. Everything falls apart, however, when Fonny is arrested and is accused of rape and Tish's family must find a way to exonerate him. *If Beale Street Could Talk* was Baldwin's fifth novel and in some ways was an anomaly. In his previous novels *Another Country* (1962) and *Tell Me How Long the Train's Been Gone* (1968), Baldwin explored love and sexuality. However, most of the relationships in these novels were interracial or homosexual. *If Beale Street Could Talk* is different in that it focuses on a heterosexual African American couple. Furthermore, it is the only novel written by Baldwin that has a female narrator. As he did with all of his works, Baldwin used the narrative as an opportunity to shine a light on racist systems and their impact on African American people.

If Beale Street Could Talk was adapted into a feature film in 2018 by director Barry Jenkins. Best known for his Academy Award-winning film *Moonlight* (2016), Jenkins's work is comparable to Baldwin's in its determination to depict the aspects of the African American experience that rarely get mainstream media attention. Throughout the 1980s, 1990s, and early 2000s, most critically acclaimed films featuring African Americans revolved around slavery or Jim Crow narratives. This was evident in Academy Award-winning and -nominated films like *The Color Purple* (1985), *Amistad* (1997), and *12 Years a Slave* (2013). In addition to portraying African Americans through a myopic frame, many of these films had white directors. Jenkins belongs to a new wave of African American filmmakers like Jordan Peele, Ryan Coogler, and Ava DuVernay. Like Peele's *Get Out* (2017) and Coogler's *Black Panther* (2018), Jenkins's *If Beale Street Could Talk* explores the African American experience and anti-Black racism in new, more empowering ways.

Film Analysis
Beale Street is a street in New Orleans where James Baldwin's father was born. According to Baldwin, however, all African Americans live on Beale Street. To him, it was symbolic—a small, safe place where African Americans could gather, live, love, and exist freely amidst the oppressive white culture. Set in Harlem, Baldwin used the New Orleans street name in the title to pay tribute to its legacy and everything that it represented. Director Barry Jenkins stayed true to Baldwin's idea of Beale Street in his film, which can best be described as a celebration of African American love, family, and friendship. The story focuses on Fonny (Stephan James) and Tish (KiKi Layne), two young lovers whose blissful life together is derailed when Fonny is falsely accused of rape and is arrested. The film toggles back and forth between the "present day" storyline of Tish trying to prove Fonny's innocence and the past storyline of how they fell in love.

Jenkins uses different visual and narrative tools to showcase the prejudiced systems that prevent Tish and Fonny from being together. In several of the film's sequences, for example, Tish's voice-over is used to describe the anti-Black racism that she and Fonny have been surrounded by their entire lives. Jenkins complements her narration with black-and-white photographs of African

Americans in the 1970s experiencing everything that she is describing, such as extreme poverty and police brutality. These images bring gravity and truth to Tish's words. They are real photographs of people suffering and subsequently ensure that viewers cannot dismiss what she is saying as fiction simply because it is in a film. Another way that Jenkins ensures that racism feels omnipresent is through the characters' casual dialogue with one another. When Fonny meets up with his friend Daniel (Brian Tyree Henry), for example, the two share stories about the injustices they must endure as African American men. Fonny describes how difficult it has been for him and Tish to find an apartment because none of the landlords want African American tenants. Daniel reveals that he was arrested for stealing a car—a crime he did not commit.

The film ensures that there is never any doubt surrounding Fonny's innocence. At one point, Tish plainly describes the police's charges and then explains how it would have been impossible for Fonny to have committed the crime because he was with her and Daniel. However, this explanation is almost unnecessary. After getting to know Fonny throughout the first act of the film, viewers already know he is a good person incapable of harming someone else. It is important to note that Jenkins does not use Fonny's innocence as a way to mitigate the experience of his accuser, a Puerto Rican woman named Victoria Rogers (Emily Rios). The film makes it clear that although Rogers is mistaken about Fonny being her attacker, she was still assaulted. In one of the most climactic scenes, Tish's mother Sharon (Regina King) goes to Puerto Rico where Victoria has fled and begs her to try to understand that Fonny could not be her rapist. Victoria becomes overwhelmingly upset when forced to talk about the rape—her pain is palpable. Here, Jenkins shows that Fonny is not the only victim. Victoria also has been hurt by the system.

Although it addresses myriad issues, Jenkins's *If Beale Street Could Talk* is primarily a love story. The director communicates this fact through the film's color palette, imagery, and shot choices. Specifically, Jenkins opts for rich, saturated reds and yellows in much of the set design and costumes. These colors create a warm, celebratory atmosphere that is reflective of Fonny and Tish's feelings for one another. For example, in one scene the two are walking in the rain, sharing a bright red umbrella. The umbrella is symbolic of their love—just as the umbrella protects them from the rain, their love protects them from the harsh world around them. This idea of the power of Afri-

can American love is explored repeatedly throughout the film. Whenever Tish and Fonny are together, Jenkins ensures it feels like the rest of the world does not exist. He accomplishes this by utilizing close-up shots in most of the scenes where they are speaking to one another. In addition to shutting the rest of the world out, these close-ups provide audience members with the characters' perspectives. Tish is beautiful, kind, and familiar because that is how Fonny sees her. Similarly, Fonny is handsome, gentle, and loving. This makes the impact of the imagery of him imprisoned wearing a jumpsuit even more upsetting.

The film adaptation of *If Beale Street Could Talk* stays true to Baldwin's novel, making only a few small changes. Still, these changes make a significant impact on the film's tone. For example, in the novel, Fonny's father becomes so overwhelmed with despair over his son's imprisonment that he commits suicide. This happens at the same time that Tish gives birth, which makes her next phone call to Fonny one mixed with equal parts tragedy and joy. In some ways, the phone call feels representative of Baldwin's presentation of the African American experience—one that is marred with misfortune but still has hope for a better future. Jenkins ultimately omits Fonny's father's death from the film altogether and chooses a different, slightly more positive ending. Where the novel leaves Fonny's trial and fate ambiguous, the film concludes with him taking a plea bargain, forcing him to serve time in prison. Jenkins does not make it clear how long Fonny will be in prison although it is suggested in the last scene that it will be a long time. In it, Fonny is visited by Tish and their son who is now walking and talking. This indicates to the audience that many years have passed, and Fonny is still locked away. Despite this fact, Jenkins ensures that the scene feels hopeful by having the three characters talk about their future together and demonstrating that Fonny and Tish's love for one another has not wavered and will continue to endure until he is free.

Significance

If Beale Street Could Talk enjoyed moderate success at the box office. Filmed on a budget of $12 million, it opened on December 16, 2018, in select theaters before moving to an expanded release on December 25. The film ultimately grossed almost $20.6 million worldwide. Although it did not reach a wide breadth of audiences, it still earned nearly unanimous critical acclaim with 95 percent of reviews giving it a positive rating. A common point of praise among critics was for the film's ability to capture Baldwin's delicate balance of being both a love story as well as a protest against anti-Black racism. Additionally, many critics extolled Jenkins' ability to depict the African American experience with depth and nuance. In her review for *The Atlantic*, Hannah Giorgis writes, "Jenkins's *If Beale Street Could Talk* is a gorgeous, enveloping film—and one of its most poignant triumphs is how vividly it captures the depth and complication of intimacy among its Black characters."

If Beale Street Could Talk went on to be nominated for several Golden Globes, including Best Motion Picture-Drama, Best Screenplay, and Best Supporting Actress. It received similar recognition at the Academy Awards, being nominated for Best Adapted Screenplay, Best Original Score, and Best Supporting Actress, which it won for Regina King's performance. Although the film was not especially successful commercially or in the awards circuit, it was lauded as one of the most important films of the year by many critics.

—*Emily E. Turner*

Further Reading

Dorman, John L. "*If Beale Street Could Talk* Offers a Tour of a Lost New York." *The New York Times*, 3 Feb. 2019, www.nytimes.com/2019/02/03/travel/if-beale-street-could-talk-new-york-james-baldwin-barry-jenkins.html. Accessed 4 Mar. 2020.

Shaffer, Marshall. "Interview: Barry Jenkins on *If Beale Street Could Talk* and Generational Joy." *Slant Magazine*, 19 Dec. 2018, www.slantmagazine.com/film/interview-barry-jenkins-on-if-beale-street-could-talk-and-generational-joy/. Accessed 4 Mar. 2020.

Bibliography

Giorgis, Hannah. "*If Beale Street Could Talk* and the Urgency of Black Love." *The Atlantic*, 25 Dec. 2018, www.theatlantic.com/entertainment/archive/2018/12/if-beale-street-could-talk-channels-baldwins-vision-of-black-love/576751/. Accessed 7 Mar. 2020.

Overbey, Erin. "Barry Jenkins on *The Fire Next Time* and *If Beale Street Could Talk*." *The New Yorker*, 1 Dec. 2018, www.newyorker.com/books/double-take/barry-jenkins-on-the-fire-next-time-and-if-beale-street-could-talk. Accessed 4 Mar. 2020.

Saxena, Jaya. "An Interview with the Stars of *If Beale Street Could Talk*." *GQ Magazine*, 24 Dec. 2018, www.gq.com/story/an-interview-with-the-stars-of-if-beale-street-could-talk. Accessed 4 Mar. 2020.

Woubshet, Dagmawi. "How James Baldwin's Writings about Love Evolved." *The Atlantic*, 9 Jan. 2019, www.theatlantic.com/entertainment/archive/2019/01/james-baldwin-idea-of-love-fire-next-time-if-beale-street-could-talk/579829/. Accessed 4 Mar. 2020.

It

The Novel
Author: Stephen King (b. 1947)
First published: 1986

The Film
Year released: 2017
Director: Andy Muschietti (b. 1973)
Screenplay by: Chase Palmer, Cary Joji Fukunaga, Gary Dauberman
Starring: Bill Skarsgård, Jaeden Martell, Jeremy Ray Taylor, Sophia Lillis, Finn Wolfhard

Context

It is a 2017 horror film directed by Andy Muschietti, based on the 1986 Stephen King novel of the same name. King came up with the idea for *It* while living in Colorado in the late 1970s. Influenced by Norwegian fairy tales, King was interested in crafting a coming-of-age story framed within a modern horror setting. The idea would be to tell the story by interweaving the experiences of the main characters as children and as adults, flashing back and forth through time as a narrative device. While the book initially received mixed reviews from critics, it became hugely popular with readers. In 1987, King was awarded the British Fantasy Award and the book was featured as the bestselling hardcover novel in North America by *Publisher's Weekly*.

In 1990, ABC adapted the novel into a two-part miniseries, which, despite King's reservations, ended up being the most successful television program of the year, attracting some 30 million viewers over its two-night run. In fact, the 1990 adaptation was so popular that it spawned its own adaptation, a 1998 Indian television series, consisting of fifty-two episodes entitled *Woh*. Since the success of the 1990 miniseries, there had been much interest in Hollywood for a feature-length adaptation, however, it was not until 2009 that Warner Bros. Pictures announced its intention to produce the film.

Initially David Kajganich, fresh off the 2007 reboot of *The Invasion of the Body Snatchers*, was brought in to write the script for a single standalone film. However, in 2012 Kajganich's script was dropped and a new production team led by director Cary Joji Fukunaga, best known for his 2011 adaptation of *Jane Eyre*, was brought in. Working with cowriter, Chase Palmer, Fukunaga rewrote the script, splitting the story between two films. Ultimately however, Fukunaga dropped off the project in May

2015 after clashing with the studio over the vision and direction of the film. In July of that year it was announced by New Line Cinema, which had taken over principal production, that Andy Muschietti would lead the new film. Muschietti had previously only directed one feature film, the 2013 horror *Mama*, which the director had adapted from his own short film. To rewrite the script, New Line

Stephen King, author of It. *Photo by Pinguino Kolb via Wikimedia Commons.*

brought in Gary Dauberman, known for several horror television and film adaptations, including the 2014 film, *Annabelle*. By June 2016 much of the principal cast was selected, including Swedish actor Bill Skarsgård for the role of Pennywise the clown. Principal photography began in July 2016 in Port Hope, Ontario, and then moved to Oshawa and eventually to Toronto. Muschietti purposefully kept Skarsgård isolated from his young cast during production so as to preserve the tension and uncertainty between Pennywise and the kids he terrorizes.

Film Analysis

King's story follows the experiences of seven children who are terrorized by an evil entity, called "It," an ancient, obscure evil that appears every twenty-seven years in the town of Derry, Maine, to feed on its victims. It appears primarily in the form of Pennywise the Dancing Clown in order to attract its preferred prey—young children. Drawing on the fairy-tale archetype of trolls living under bridges, King placed Pennywise in the local sewer system. The children in the story form a club and fight It. King's story is the basis for the omnipresent popular culture trope of the "evil clown" in the sewer.

The principal theme of the film *It*, like the novel, is the loss of innocence and the tension between dangerous, primal forces and civilization (or adulthood). It's worth remembering that the Freudian "id" is literally the "it." The book examines the fears and anxieties of postwar America including scenes that take place in the 1950s and in the 1980s. The film updates the story so that the main characters are growing up in the 1980s, therefore changing the themes and motifs of the original novel. Gone are the references to Eisenhower's America, canned patriotism and tepid optimism masking the fears of global thermonuclear conflict. In the film, loss of innocence is tied to the loss of identity, wherein the principal characters battle, not fears of mummies and werewolves, but of childhood trauma and abuse. As the film is rated R, with special effects added, the violence and gore that the children experience becomes more visceral and in itself more traumatizing, adding to the overall despair felt by and for the characters.

Another major change to the source material has to do with the main characters themselves. The film's main protagonist is Bill Denbrough (Martell, credited as Jaeden Lieberher), whose brother Georgie (Jackson Robert Scott) is viciously and graphically murdered by the demonic clown Pennywise (Skarsgård) in the film's opening. In the novel, Bill was presented as a more flawed character, suffering from a severe stutter and social anxiety, only to emerge as the hero of the story. He did have a stutter in the film and it's mentioned throughout—but it finally disappears when he approaches the run down house to confront Pennywise. Bill's driving force in the film then becomes not about overcoming his own disabilities, but about wrestling with the guilt of Georgie's death, as in the film Bill fakes being ill so as not to have to play with him. Similar changes and deviations are rife throughout the film, shifting the core of the story thematically, and by doing so simplifying the narrative, making it more traditional and straightforward.

Through fighting Pennywise and the evil that he represents, the principal characters are able to face their fears and come into their own identities. With that said, the climax of the transition between childhood and adulthood is handled very differently in the film as opposed to the novel. In the book, the Losers, as the kids call themselves, have an orgy following the defeat of Pennywise, an awkward, sloppy release of the tension and horror the characters have felt throughout the story, as Beverly (Sophia Lillis) lets each one of the boys lose their virginity to her. The film takes a more conservative approach, framing the transition into adulthood through the development of the romance between Bill and Beverly whose relationship climaxes in a kiss. While some critics questioned King's choice of sexualizing his young characters, others saw it as the heart of the novel.

Ultimately, the film gives a somewhat neutered version of the source material, elevating gore and violence over the psychological and emotional complexities of the novel's narratives. Good and bad are presented in starker terms and the decisions made by the principal characters are ultimately in service to the sequel, rather than to their own development. The film also forgoes much of the magic and mysticism of the book, dialing back much of the lore and otherworldly story building so rife in King's novel. What remains is a more traditional horror narrative.

Significance

It was released on September 8, 2017 and promptly made a staggering $123 million in its opening weekend. Critics praised the film for its direction, cinematography, and especially its performances with most reviewers singling out Skarsgård's turn as the murderous Pennywise. Throughout its entire run, *It* earned a cumulative worldwide gross of nearly $702 million, destroying all previous records for a horror movie release, becoming the fifth-highest-grossing R-rated film and the highest-grossing horror film of all time. It also earned numerous honors, including the top prize at the German Bogey Awards and the Best On-Screen Team Award at the MTV Movie & Video Awards. While some critics floated the idea that *It* might stand as an Oscar contender, ultimately, the Academy of Motion Arts and Sciences snubbed the film entirely. Perhaps the greatest praise, however, came from Stephen King himself, who lauded the adaptation, saying, "I had hopes, but I was not prepared for how good it really was. It's something that's different, and at the same time, it's something that audiences are gonna relate to. They're gonna like the characters. To me, it's all about character. If you like the characters...if you care...the scares generally work."

As the film was a huge commercial and critical success, there was little doubt that the sequel would be made. Sure enough, within weeks of the film's premier, New Line Cinema announced that *It Chapter Two* would be released in September 2019. Ultimately, the sequel did not see the same critical and commercial success, but it certainly proved profitable, and all told the two films earned a combined box office of over $1 billion.

—*KP Dawes, MA*

Further Reading

King, Stephen. *On Writing*. Hodder Paperbacks, 2012.

Nathan, Ian. *Stephen King at the Movies: A Complete History of the Film and Television Adaptations from the Master of Horror*. Palazzo Editions, 2019.

Spignesi, Stephen. *Stephen King, American Master: A Creepy Corpus of Facts about Stephen King & His Work*. Permuted Press, 2018.

Bibliography

Bradley, Laura. "How the New *It* Became the Best Stephen King Adaptation in Decades." *Vanity Fair*, 8 Sept. 2017, www.vanityfair.com/hollywood/2017/09/it-movie-stephen-king-andy-muschietti-director-producer-interview. Accessed 26 Mar. 2020.

Hayman, Amanda. "Stephen King 'Was Not Prepared' for How Good the *It* Movie Is." *Business Insider*, 31 Aug. 2017, www.businessinsider.com/stephen-king-it-movie-reaction-praise-2017-8. Accessed 26 Mar. 2020.

Hendrix, Grady. "The Great Stephen King Reread: *It*." *Tor.com*, 25 Sept. 2013, www.tor.com/2013/09/25/the-great-stephen-king-reread-it/. Accessed 26 Mar. 2020.

"*It*." *IMDb*, www.imdb.com/title/tt1396484/. Accessed 26 Mar. 2020.

Setoodeh, Ramin. "Cary Fukunaga Offers New Details on Why *It* Remake Fell Apart." *Variety*, 2 Sept. 2015, variety.com/2015/film/news/cary-fukunaga-it-exit-1201584416/. Accessed 26 Mar. 2020.

Jackie Brown

The Novel
Author: Elmore Leonard (1925-2013)
First published: 1992

The Film
Year released: 1997
Director: Quentin Tarantino (b. 1963)
Screenplay by: Quentin Tarantino
Starring: Pam Grier, Samuel L. Jackson, Robert Forster, Bridget Fonda, Robert De Niro, Michael Keaton

Context

Beginning in the 1950s, Elmore Leonard published forty-five novels and sold millions of copies during a career that spanned six decades. He acquired legions of additional fans when many of his fictional works were adapted for film and television. Leonard's early writing, primarily in the Western genre, resulted in such big-screen releases as *3:10 to Yuma* (1957; 2007) and *Hombre* (1967). He also wrote the original screenplay for *Joe Kidd* (1972) and created the Desperado series of made-for-TV movies (1987-89). When audience tastes changed and interest in Westerns waned, Leonard successfully transitioned to contemporary crime stories. His later novels were adapted for such films as *52 Pick-Up* (1986), *Get Shorty* (1995), and *Out of Sight* (1998). His work has also served as the basis for several television series.

Much of Leonard's popularity as a source for visual adaptation derives from his cinematic writing style. He makes it easy to see and hear the action, and to feel shades of emotions his characters experience. The author typically uses third-person narrators who describe the questionable activities of fully rounded individuals involved in nefarious plans. This technique makes it difficult for readers to separate heroes from villains, or to guess in advance who will win or lose, who will live or die. The characters themselves add layers of uncertainty before the unpredictable outcome of the story, revealing positive and negative qualities through quirky actions and sharp dialogue. Leonard's protagonists are often witty, sometimes profound, frequently profane, and his characters are morally flexible and not averse to using subterfuge or violence to achieve goals.

Leonard likewise has an uncanny ability to place these interesting characters in recognizable settings and quickly set them into motion. Scenes, as viewed from multiple perspectives—like different camera angles with changing focal lengths—add dimension to the author's always readable prose. Conflicts appear to arise organically, due to friction among characters of differing abilities and mo-

Director Quentin Tarantino. Photo by Gage Skidmore, CC BY-SA 3.0, via Wikimedia Commons.

tivations. Unforeseen complications—bad weather, health concerns, accidents, unexpected setbacks, chance encounters—add drama and suspense. Leonard's stories also incorporate references to current social issues (such as economic, gender, or racial inequality) that, in conjunction with other literary qualities, lift the author's work beyond the limitations of genre.

Film Analysis

Leonard's 1992 caper novel *Rum Punch* features three characters previously seen in his 1978 novel *The Switch*—would-be mastermind Ordell Robbie, clumsy ex-con Louis Gara, and pothead surfer Melanie Ralston—who interact with aging flight attendant Jackie Burke in the process of carrying out risky schemes. Quentin Tarantino adapted *Rum Punch* for his third feature film, *Jackie Brown* (1997), following *Reservoir Dogs* (1992) and *Pulp Fiction* (1994), which he wrote and directed.

Rum Punch revolves around criminal enterprise. Ordell steals or purchases illegal firearms, transporting them from Florida to the Bahamas, where they are sold to Colombian drug-runners. He has cash in the Bahamas, but does not have ready access to it, because he is being watched by Alcohol, Tobacco and Firearms (ATF) agents and other law enforcement entities. He therefore uses Jackie, who flies with a low-rent shuttle airline, to transport bundles of cash (and occasional bags of cocaine for Melanie) into the United States. When Jackie is caught bringing back a shipment of drugs and money, she has a dilemma. If she does not cooperate with authorities, she will go to prison, and her future will be bleaker than her present. If she snitches on Ordell, she is likely to end up dead. The plot focuses on Jackie's efforts to extricate herself from a desperate, seemingly inescapable situation.

Jackie Brown follows the essential structure of Leonard's convoluted plot. The pacing of the film mirrors that of the novel—sometimes contemplative, sometimes frenetic. The film's tone, mixing the dark with the humorous, reflects the tone of the novel. Many scenes in the film are depicted as described in the novel, and much of the dialogue is taken directly from the book. *Jackie Brown*, however, is also a Tarantino film through-and-through, reflecting Tarantino's personal directorial style and sensibilities. The film pays homage to 1970s blaxploitation films, revels in bawdy and extreme language and violence, and unfolds with Tarantino's characteristic stylistic energy. Writing in the *Chicago Sun Times*, Roger Ebert described

the director's moves this way: "Tarantino leaves the hardest questions for last, hides his moves, conceals his strategies in plain view, and gives his characters dialogue that is alive, authentic and spontaneous."

Certain key differences, liberties taken in the adaptation, exemplify the director's proclivities and show his personal stamp. For example, the setting of *Rum Punch* was an East Coast metropolis (Miami, Florida, and environs) and its nearby foreign satellite (Freeport, Bahamas). *Jackie Brown* was moved to Southern California (Los Angeles, California, and suburbs), with Cabo San Lucas in Baja California as a stand-in for the place where black-market firearms are sold and ill-gotten revenues are banked. The different venue is not only more Tarantino-esque; it saved considerable time and budget in terms of on-location work.

The most significant change was in the casting of the film's title character. In *Rum Punch*, protagonist Jackie Burke is described as a forty-four-year-old white woman with blond hair and green eyes. For the film, Tarantino chose African American actor Pam Grier. In this way, with a stroke, Tarantino recast the story in a way that allowed him to draw heavily on the tropes of blaxploitation films, a controversial cinematic subgenre that appeared in the late 1960s and early 1970s. Blaxploitation pictures were made to appeal to urban African Americans, starring actors of color in plots that dealt with issues of importance to their community. Some critics decried blaxploitation films' portrayals of black men as problematic for glamorizing violence and criminal behavior, while proponents praised what they saw as challenging stereotypes with proud and strong depictions of individuals and the community. Grier had played lead roles in several such films, including *Coffy* (1973), *Foxy Brown* (1974), and *Sheba, Baby* (1975).

Tarantino's selection of Grier broadened and deepened the film. The racial element added another layer to the protagonist's problems; not only is she an aging woman with big trouble and dim prospects, but a black woman living in a white, male-dominated world. The complexity of her position reveals the essence of her character: she is a skilled manipulator, capable of employing a range of different approaches to defeat the forces arrayed against her. With macho killer Ordell (Samuel L. Jackson), his inept pal Louis (Robert De Niro), and stoned hanger-on Melanie (Bridget Fonda), Jackie can talk tough, feign fear, or confide in intimate fashion as appropriate. Dealing simultaneously with

ATF agent Ray Nicolette (Michael Keaton) and Los Angeles Police Department (LAPD) detective Mark Dargus (Michael Bowen) requires deft deceit: quick wits, bold lies, and sudden tears. Turning her world-weary, no-nonsense bail bondsman Max Cherry (Robert Forster) into a willing accomplice in a scheme to avoid incarceration, eliminate physical threat, and acquire a fortune in untraceable cash takes a whole new set of skills.

In adapting *Rum Punch* for the screen, Tarantino sacrificed a number of subplots and character development passages. A major thread—concerning a triple homicide that Ordell commits in league with Melanie, Louis, and a trio of crack-crazed "jackboys" while robbing a neo-Nazi's armory of military weapons—was completely eliminated. To compensate, the director expanded upon a concept outlined in the novel, of a gun demonstration video. For the film, Tarantino wrote and directed an actual video, with shapely, bikinied women firing automatic weapons and praising their advantages.

Another subplot, involving the relationship between Louis and Max, was likewise cut. In the novel, Louis works as muscle capturing bail jumpers after being placed in Max's office by a mob that took over the honest insurance agency that had backed the business for years. When Louis leaves, he steals guns from Max and uses them to hold up a liquor store. In the film, Louis is only known to Max as Ordell's companion.

Further details of Max's history were likewise deleted. In the novel, Max is married but separated from his wife, Renee, who runs a gallery in the mall where Ordell's money eventually changes hands. Renee is cultivating David, a young Cuban American felon, as an artist and her lover. In *Rum Punch*, Max enjoys several sexual interludes with Jackie and they declare their love for one another. In *Jackie Brown*, Max and Jackie are confined to amorous glances, long conversations with romantic undertones, and a brief hug and chaste kiss as they part, probably forever.

Dropping such side stories streamlined the plot of *Jackie Brown* (though the film still clocks in at 154 minutes), removing distractions from the central focus of the story: a character study of a strong woman who will do whatever is necessary to survive.

Significance
Jackie Brown, with an estimated budget of $12 million, grossed nearly $75 million at the box office. Reviews were generally positive. Praise was especially heaped on Grier's performance, although it was her costar Forster who was nominated for an Academy Award for best supporting actor. The film's place in the body of work produced by Tarantino remains an open question. Jay Carr, writing in the *Boston Globe*, lamented that the film lacked the confidence and bravura of Tarantino's earlier work in the same vein; critic Jason Bailey, writing in *Vice*, countered that the film "may be the only Quentin Tarantino movie that gets noticeably better with each viewing."

Tarantino's adaptation of *Rum Punch* completed an outstanding year for Elmore Leonard. Besides *Jackie Brown*, there were four other 1997 releases based on the author's work: the TV movies *Last Stand at Saber River*, *Pronto*, and *Gold Coast*, and the theatrical feature *Touch*. In the years since then, Leonard's novels and stories have been frequently mined for film and television. In the twenty-first century, Leonard-inspired features such as *The Big Bounce* (2004), *Be Cool* (2005), a *3:10 to Yuma* remake (2007), *Killshot* (2008), and *Freaky Deaky* (2012) have all appeared. Four television series were also based on Leonard plots or characters: *Maximum Bob* (1998), *Karen Sisco* (2003-4), *Justified* (2010-15), and *Get Shorty* (2017). The *Rum Punch* characters Ordell, Louis, and Melanie were resurrected for an adaptation of *The Switch*, the novel where they first appeared, titled *Life of Crime* (2013).

—*Jack Ewing*

Further Reading
Clarkson, Wensley. *Quentin Tarantino: The Man, the Myths, and His Movies*. John Blake, 2007.
Devlin, James E. *Elmore Leonard*. Twayne Publishers, 1999.
Sims, Yvonne D. *Women of Blaxploitation: How the Black Action Film Heroine Changed American Popular Culture*. McFarland, 2015.

Bibliography
Berlatsky, Noah. "The One Time Quentin Tarantino Got Blaxploitation Masculinity Right." *The Atlantic*, 19 Dec. 2012, www.theatlantic.com/sexes/archive/2012/12/the-one-time-quentin-tarantino-got-blaxploitation-masculinity-right/266469/. Accessed 6 Dec. 2018.
Collar, Cammila. "How Tarantino Made Race a Central Theme of 'Jackie Brown.'" *Outtake*, 10 June 2017, outtake.tribecashortlist.com/how-tarantino-made-race-a-central-theme-of-jackie-brown-848466ef430a. Accessed 6 Dec. 2018.
Hensher, Philip. "Elmore Leonard: The Great American Novelist." *The Guardian*, 27 Jan. 2012, www.theguardian.com/books/

2012/jan/27/elmore-leonard-great-american-novelist. Accessed 6 Dec. 2018.

Leonard, Elmore. *Rum Punch*. Dell Publishing, 1993.

Maslin, Janet. "Film Review: Smarter Than She Is? Hah!" Review of *Jackie Brown*, directed by Quentin Tarantino. *The New York Times*, 24 Dec. 1997, www.nytimes.com/1997/12/24/movies/film-review-smarter-than-she-is-hah.html. Accessed 6 Dec. 2018.

Michel, Lincoln. "'Jackie Brown,' the Best Quentin Tarantino Film, Is Streaming on Netflix. *GQ*, 21 Aug. 2017, www.gq.com/story/jackie-brown-the-best-quentin-tarantino-film-is-streaming-on-netflix. Accessed 6 Dec. 2018.

Williams, David E. "Beyond the Frame: 'Jackie Brown.'" *American Cinematographer*, 15 Oct. 2016, ascmag.com/articles/beyond-the-frame-jackie-brown-1997. Accessed 6 Dec. 2018.

The Joy Luck Club

The Novel
Author: Amy Tan (b. 1952)
First published: 1989

The Film
Year released: 1993
Director: Wayne Wang (b. 1949)
Screenplay by: Amy Tan, Ronald Bass
Starring: Tsai Chin, Kieu Chinh, Lisa Lu, France Nuyen, Rosalind Chao, Lauren Tom, Tamlyn Tomita, Ming-Na Wen

Context

The Joy Luck Club was a groundbreaking work, both as a novel and as a film. It was one of the first widely popular novels written not only by an Asian American writer but also by an Asian American *woman*. The fact that this highly successful work was also a *first* novel—rather than a work that came late in Amy Tan's career—was also impressive. The novel reflected various important trends not only in American culture but also in the culture of the world in general. For example, it was part of a broader movement toward multiculturalism in American society and culture. African American and Jewish writers had already, by the 1980s, achieved widespread recognition for their contributions to the nation's cultural heritage, but Asian American writers (with the obvious exception of Maxine Hong Kingston in the 1970s) had not yet attained that sort of national and international notoriety. Tan was one of the first—and remains one of the most prominent and influential—Asian American writers of fiction. By the 1980s, people of Asian backgrounds were becoming a larger and larger part of the population in the United States, and they were also becoming more and more important in contributing to all aspects of American culture. Tan's novel and the film adaptation were important events in the growing recognition of Asian Americans as major forces in the country's culture.

Tan wrote *The Joy Luck Club* implicitly from a feminist perspective. Most of the major characters in both the novel and the film are women. Moreover, both the book and the film are centrally concerned with the experiences of women *as* women, not only in their complex relationships with other females but also in their often-oppressive relationships with men. The 1970s and '80s, like the decades that have followed, saw an increasing interest in, and emphasis on, feminism in practically every area of American life. Tan's book and the film both reflected and contributed to that kind of focus on women's experiences, struggles, and alliances, and even on their tensions with one another.

The book was clearly concerned with the sort of generation gap that had been a concern in American culture since at least the 1960s. In Tan's novel, that gap largely involves mothers who grew up in China and their daughters, who were raised in the United States. Men played far less important roles, both in the novel and the film, and it seems safe to say that most of Tan's earliest readers were women. In any case, the film version of *The Joy Luck Club* was often perceived as a "woman's picture."

Finally, another trend reflected both by the novel and the film was the growth of China as a world power, espe-

Director Wayne Wang. Photo by Nancy Wong, CC BY-SA 3.0, via Wikimedia Commons.

cially in economic terms. For most of the twentieth century, China had been a severely impoverished country. Its economy and its cultural life had stagnated and even retreated under the hard-line Communist rule of Mao Zedong, who had seized power during a revolution in the late 1940s. Mao's attempts to impose his own peculiar ideas about economics and social structure had led to widespread poverty, in contrast with the freer economic system practiced on the island of Taiwan, which was ruled by his opponents, the "Nationalist" Chinese. Taiwan soon developed into one of the most prosperous countries in Asia, while Communist China stagnated, just as Communist North Korea fell further and further behind an increasingly vibrant and free South Korea. However, after Mao's death, the Chinese Communists slowly embraced more and more elements of western-style capitalism. By the late 1980s, there were hopes that China might someday evolve into a freer, more democratic society, as Taiwan and South Korea had done. Tan's novel, and the resulting film, reflected a growing American interest in China, Chinese life, and the contributions of Chinese immigrants to American culture.

Film Analysis

Tan's novel was innovative not only in its content and concerns but also in its structure. Rather than offering a conventional, chronological narrative focused on one relatively confined set of characters, the novel was a complex mosaic of interrelated chapters, each with a distinct focus. The novel was often seen as a collection of mutually reinforcing short stories rather than as a simple, straightforward narrative. In this respect, *The Joy Luck Club* resembles another important work of fiction from around the same period—Tim O'Brien's *The Things They Carried*. The complex structure of Tan's novel led some observers to conclude that it could never be made into a successful film—that it was *too* complicated in structure to be rendered on screen without radical reorganization and significant simplification.

But in fact, many critics praised the film for staying remarkably faithful to Tan's original design. The fact that Tan herself had a major hand in crafting the screenplay undoubtedly helped the film remain reasonably close to the book's original architecture. Praise of both the complexity and coherence of the film's structure was widespread and reflected similar praise of those same aspects of the book. The film's frequent use of flashbacks was often commended as an ingenious solution to the task of conveying the complexity of the book's interwoven narratives. The film was also praised for using distinct color schemes (associating different pairs of characters with different basic colors) as a way of helping viewers keep the characters and their stories straight. Readers of the novel often found it a bit difficult to keep the characters distinct; this was easier to do watching the film because the physical appearances of the various actors and the various settings were easier to keep track of when watching the film than had sometimes been the case when reading the book. The film features many close-ups—a technique that not only emphasizes its interest in the psychology of the characters, but also helps establish each woman in memorable ways.

Both the film and the book were praised for dealing with universal issues and themes even though almost all the characters were Asian women. The novel and the book were admired for exploring the complex relationships between mothers and daughters as well as, by implication, between parents and children of any gender. Both works dealt with parents' desires to see their children succeed in ways the parents valued, and both works also dealt with the frequent desire of children to chart their own paths, free—or at least not rigidly influenced—from parental control. These, of course, are archetypal issues and have been the subjects of literature and film since the beginnings of both kinds of artwork. By exploring such matters in an Asian American context, Tan the novelist and Wang the filmmaker helped, ironically, illuminate their universality. Daughters and mothers of all ethnic backgrounds found that they could relate to the characters in the novel and the film. In fact, many male readers and viewers could relate as well. Several reviewers of the film specifically stressed that it would appeal to viewers of all genders and ethnic backgrounds as well as people of various generations.

Just as Tan's novel was praised for prose that could be alternately lucid, lyrical, evocative, and symbolic, so the film was praised for similar reasons. Critics admired the historical range of both works, which dealt with characters, events, and settings both in China and the United States from at least the 1930s until the 1980s. Critics also frequently praised both works for presenting stories centered on distinct characters—stories that were definitely different yet also had much in common, so that each tale functioned as a variation on the basic theme of daughters' often tense but fundamentally loving relationships with their mothers. Both works were admired for dealing with serious (indeed, sometimes tragic) matters without being relentlessly gloomy. In fact, humor was a frequently admired feature in both works, especially when they dealt with the relationships between mothers and daughters in the modern United States rather than in the past in China. Both the novel and the film were praised for handling often tragic issues and events in ways that mostly managed to avoid melodrama and sentimentality, although some critics did find the film a bit too syrupy in this respect. The film, in particular, was often hailed as a deeply emotional film that managed to provoke tears (both of sadness and of joy) without being too manipulative, although some critics did fault it in the latter respect.

The film was an important adaptation of the novel precisely because its cast consisted almost entirely of Asian actors. In fact, few other films before or since were so heavily populated by Asian performers. It was one thing to read about Asian characters on the page and try to imagine them in one's own mind; it was another thing altogether to see so many very talented Asian actors on-screen, all together, bringing those characters to vivid life. The acting in the film was almost universally praised; reviewers frequently said that there was not a weak performance in the entire work. For this reason, the film was seen as, perhaps, even more a landmark cultural event than the novel had been. Directed by an Asian American, based on a hugely popular novel by an Asian American who also contributed decisively to the screenplay, and featuring a largely Asian American cast, the film was in many ways a truly unprecedented achievement—an achievement that has, unfortunately, not really been replicated in the decades since. And, just as Tan's book has sometimes been criticized for reinforcing various limiting stereotypes about Asians, so the film has suffered some of the same accusations. Both, however, are widely regarded as landmark works in the history of American fiction and film.

Significance

Some film reviewers accused The Joy Luck Club of being too sentimental, of ignoring or maligning male characters, and of focusing on daughters who were all uniformly attractive, successful, urban, sophisticated, and upper class. Negative reviewers also found the film manipulative, too repetitive, too long, and too confusing in structure and plot. They called the film overwrought, unsubtle, too reliant on unnecessary narration, and too dependent on the use of flashbacks. Positive reviews, however, heavily outnumbered negative assessments. Admirers of the film praised its clever, symmetrical structure, its skillful transitions, its well-developed characters, and its vivid cinematography, especially in the scenes set in China. Admirers also commended the ways the various subplots reinforced one another, contributing to the work's major themes, and they also extolled the impressive musical score and the use of symbolic colors and costuming. Numerous critics hailed the film for its strong emotional impact, often warning viewers to bring tissues with them to the theaters because the film, especially in its conclusion, was deliberately intended to provoke tears. The film was praised for being by turns funny and moving, lyrical and tragic, and for being able to appeal to viewers of all sorts, not just female Asian Americans.

The screenplay was nominated for several important awards, but neither the film itself nor its director nor its actors nor any of the other people (the cinematographer, the composer, the costume designers, or make-up artists, for instance) involved in making it were nominated for any Academy Awards. Assessments by professional reviewers on such aggregator sites as *Rotten Tomatoes* were overwhelmingly positive, and the film has also been highly rated by the general public. It remains one of the best possible representations not only of Tan's novel but also of Asian American life and the experiences of Chinese immigrants, both before and after their departures from China.

—*Robert C. Evans, PhD*

Further Reading

Eder, Doris L. "Critical Contexts: The Structure of *The Joy Luck Club*: Themes and Variations." *Critical Insights: The Joy Luck Club*. Salem Press, 2010, pp. 48-64. *EBSCOhost*, search.ebscohost.com/login.aspx?direct=true&db=lkh&AN=48267626&site=ehost-live. Accessed 22 Apr. 2020.

Ghymn, Esther Mikyung. "Critical Readings: Mothers and Daughters." *Critical Insights: The Joy Luck Club*. Salem Press, 2010, pp. 145-172. *EBSCOhost*, search.ebscohost.com/login.aspx?direct=true&db=lkh&AN=48267631&site=ehost-live. Accessed 22 Apr. 2020.

Koven, Mikel J. "Feminist Folkloristics and Women's Cinema: Towards a Methodology." *Literature Film Quarterly*, vol. 27, no. 4, Oct. 1999, pp. 292-300. *EBSCOhost*, search.ebscohost.com/login.aspx?direct=true&db=lkh&AN=2825255&site=ehost-live. Accessed 22 Apr. 2020.

Bibliography

Tibbetts, John C. "A Delicate Balance: An Interview with Wayne Wang about *The Joy Luck Club*." *Literature Film Quarterly*, vol. 22, no. 1, Jan. 1994, pp. 2. *EBSCOhost*, search.ebscohost.com/login.aspx?direct=true&db=lkh&AN=9503101638&site=ehost-live. Accessed 22 Apr. 2020.

Tseo, George K. Y. "Joy Luck: The Perils of Transcultural 'Translation.'" *Literature Film Quarterly* v. 24, no. 4, 1996, p. 338. *EBSCOhost*, search.ebscohost.com/login.aspx?direct=true&db=lkh&AN=9702271947&site=ehost-live. Accessed 22 Apr. 2020

Julius Caesar

The Play

Author: William Shakespeare (1564-1616)
First performed: 1599

The Film

Year released: 1953
Director: Joseph L. Mankiewicz (1909-1993)
Screenplay by: Joseph L. Mankiewicz
Starring: Marlon Brando, James Mason, John Gielgud, Louis Calhern

Context

One of William Shakespeare's most popular plays, *The Tragedy of Julius Caesar* is believed to have originally been performed in 1599. The earliest recorded mention of a performance of the play comes from the diary of the Swiss physician Thomas Platter the Younger, who notes having seen it in September of that year. The play, which was first published in the First Folio of 1623, a text that remains the definitive version of the work, was based largely on Shakespeare's reading of Plutarch's *Lives of the Noble Greeks and Romans*, in the then-popular English translation by Thomas North. *Julius Caesar* details the assassination of its title character by a group of conspirators and reflects the contemporary anxiety that many people in England felt about Queen Elizabeth's increasing age. At the time the play was written, Elizabeth was nearing seventy and had not named a successor, leading many to fear a tumultuous struggle following her death.

The play, which was believed to have been one of the first to be performed in the legendary Globe Theatre, has had a very long afterlife, remaining among Shakespeare's most performed works. Among the more notable twentieth and twenty-first century performances are Orson Welles's 1937 Mercury Theater production (which commented specifically on European fascism), Denzel Washington's turn as Brutus in a 2005 Broadway revival, and a 2017 Shakespeare in the Park production in which Caesar appeared in the guise of President Donald Trump.

The play has also proved to be a popular source for film and television adaptations, beginning as early as 1908, when the Vitagraph Company of America produced a silent film version. It was in the 1940s and 1950s, though, that the film industry turned to Shakespeare in a significant way, producing film versions of most of his major plays as high-toned prestige projects. Orson Welles alone filmed *Macbeth* in 1948 and *Othello* in 1951 (and would later anthologize the Falstaff plays into *Chimes at Midnight* in 1965), while Laurence Olivier made *Henry V* in 1944 and *Hamlet* in 1948. *Julius Caesar*, which was the subject of a low-budget film adaptation in 1950 starring a then-unknown Charlton Heston as Marc Antony, was finally given the full studio treatment in 1953 by Metro- Goldwyn-Mayer (MGM). With Joseph L. Mankiewicz both adapting the play and directing it, the film starred such heavyweights as Marlon Brando, James Mason, and John Gielgud. Nominated for five Academy Awards, including Best Picture, the film took home the Oscar for Best Art Direction-Set Direction, Black-and-White.

Film Analysis

One of the central questions posed by Shakespeare's play is how to read the character of Brutus. Although he is among the conspirators who murders Caesar, delivering the final blow, he provides something of a contrast with his fellow assassins, particularly the other most prominent of their lot, Cassius. Praised in death by Marc Antony at the play's end as "the noblest Roman of them all," Brutus appears to be motivated less by personal ambition and more by a fear of Caesar potentially becoming a tyrant once he agrees to take the crown and become ruler of Rome. Whereas Cassius's argument in the discussion leading up to the assassination weighs his own personal merits against Caesar's and finds himself not inferior to the newly crowned king, Brutus's arguments are less about self-interest and are made more out of concern for Caesar's subjects.

In Joseph L. Mankiewicz's film, Brutus is set apart even more, particularly in the central scene, the assassination itself, which occurs roughly halfway through the narrative. In the play, Brutus is differentiated from the other conspirators in that he is the last man to stab Caesar and is addressed by Caesar directly, who in surprise and accusation, asks the famous question of his former ally, "Et tu, Brutè?" ("And you, Brutus?") But Brutus is otherwise not clearly differentiated from his fellow assassins in the act of killing. The stage direction for the murder reads simply, "*They stab Caesar, Casca first, Brutus last.*"

In Mankiewicz's staging, Brutus is literally set apart. As the other conspirators stab Caesar, Brutus retreats to the far end of the courtyard, the camera angle emphasizing the physical distance between Brutus and the others. Building in a lengthy pause before Brutus turns his sword on Caesar, Mankiewicz fixes his camera on Brutus's tortured face as he hesitates to perform the murderous act. In that moment, all of Brutus's mixed feelings, torn as he is between a genuine love for Caesar and his sense that he must do what is right for Rome, is revealed in a way that is beyond anything indicated in Shakespeare's directions for the same scene. Shakespeare may have wanted us to think of Brutus as being more noble than the other conspirators, but in this scene, Mankiewicz underscores this point in a way that cannot be missed by the viewer.

James Mason, playing Brutus, convincingly portrays Brutus's tortured feelings, using both his body movements and especially his facial expressions to wordlessly convey his character's ambivalence. In any Shakespeare production, whether for the stage or the screen, the acting is the principal determinant of that production's success and Mankiewicz's film makes use of a strong cast of British and American actors of varying styles. In fact, although some traditionally minded studio executives had favored using only British actors, producer John Houseman decided at the outset that he would incorporate American actors into the production as well. While the majority of the cast, including Mason, John Gielgud as Cassius, Deborah Kerr as Portia, and Greer Garson as Calpurnia, were British, two of the more notable roles were given to American actors. While the relatively minor title role went to the veteran Brooklyn-born thespian Louis Calhern, the more significant role of Marc Antony was granted to Marlon Brando.

Brando was a controversial choice for the role; often considered the greatest film actor of all time, trained as a "method actor," and famous for the intensity and realism he brought to his roles, many wondered at the time, including the Hollywood gossip columnists of the day, whether he was capable of pulling off a Shakespearean role and Shakespearean technique. In fact, Brando's performance is different from the performances of his costars, registering a particular contrast with Gielgud's. The differences in technique between the two major actors, though, gives the film much of its charge, elevating it above its status as simply another filmed Shakespeare play.

Whereas Gielgud, with his classical training, brings a balance and orderliness and a certain formal stiffness to his performance as Cassius, Brando simmers with suppressed energy that frequently bursts forth. Brando, who studied acting with Stella Adler, was one of the first actors to bring the style known as "method acting" to Hollywood. The "method" encouraged a new form of expression and emotional honesty that was in contrast to the more detached performances of classical performers. From Brando's first major soliloquy, as, over Caesar's body, he angrily calls for vengeance, the difference is immediately made clear. With his fiery outburst, Brando communicates more directly with the viewer than any of the actors who had been on screen before.

A more measured but equally exciting moment comes for Brando during his major speech, as he addresses the Roman people after the death of Caesar. Unlike his earlier soliloquy, he builds up to anger, striking notes of thoughtfulness and irony along the way. Here, Brando shows that he is more than just a brute, given to passionate outbursts, but is rather a complete actor, capable of packing a range of emotions into a few minutes of screen time. When, about halfway through the film, Brando's Antony becomes a central figure in the narrative, he brings a new charge to the film that was not present earlier. Gielgud and Mason, the British actors who take on the biggest roles in the film apart from Brando, offer strongly measured and highly convincing performances in their own right. The contrast between the styles offers viewers a wealth of riches and creates a tension that mirrors that of the film's central story.

Significance

Julius Caesar proved to be both a critical and commercial success upon its release in 1953. *The New York Times*, for example, noted that it was "a production that pulls the full potential of point and passion from this classic of the stage," while *Time* magazine called it "the best Shakespeare that Hollywood has yet produced." It earned just over $3.9 million domestically and has continued to be popular on television and in repertory screenings, in no small part because of Marlon Brando's dramatic, Oscar-nominated performance. The film came right at the peak of Brando's early screen career, during which he brought his intense method-influenced performances to numerous films and changed the style and expectations of film acting. His nod for *Julius Caesar* was the third of four consecutive Oscar nominations he would earn for Best Actor in a Leading Role. He would win the next year for *On the Waterfront* and again in 1972 for *The Godfather*.

More importantly, *Julius Caesar* illustrated the continuing viability of Shakespeare as a prestigious film source. Coming in the golden age of Shakespearean films, Mankiewicz's production pointed the way to such later films as Franco Zeffirelli's 1968 version of *Romeo and Juliet* and, more recently, Kenneth Branagh's series of adaptations (*Henry V*, 1989; *Much Ado About Nothing*, 1993; *Hamlet*, 1996; *Love's Labour's Lost*, 2000; and *As You Like It*, 2006.) The Bard's work has also lent itself to looser adaptations such as the 1999 teen comedy *10 Things I Hate About You* (based on *The Taming of the Shrew*) and Baz Luhrmann's heavily stylized 1996 adaptation, *William Shakespeare's Romeo + Juliet*, proving that the possibilities of adaptation are far from limited to the reverent high-toned treatment typified by Mankiewicz's film.

—*Melynda Fuller*

Further Reading

Julius Caesar. Folger Shakespeare Library, 31 Jan. 2018, www.folger.edu/julius-caesar. Accessed 1 Apr. 2020.

Shakespeare's Life. Folger Shakespeare Library, 4 Nov. 2019, www.folger.edu/shakespeares-life. Accessed 1 Apr. 2020.

Soloski, Alexis. "Review: In *The Tragedy of Julius Caesar*, the Political Thrill Is Gone." *The New York Times*, 28 Mar. 2019, www.nytimes.com/2019/03/28/theater/the-tragedy-of-julius-caesar-review.html. Accessed 1 Apr. 2020.

Bibliography

"About the Play: *Julius Caesar*." *Utah Shakespeare Festival*, www.bard.org/study-guides/about-the-play. Accessed 1 Apr. 2020.

Crowther, Bosley. "*Julius Caesar* and Two Other Arrivals; Shakespeare Tragedy, Filmed by M-G-M with a Notable Cast, Unfolds at Booth." *The New York Times*, 5 June 1953, www.nytimes.com/1953/06/05/archives/julius-caesar-and-two-other-arrivals-shakespeare-tragedy-filmed-by.html. Accessed 1 Apr. 2020.

Julius Caesar. IMDb, www.imdb.com/title/tt0045943/. Accessed 1 Apr. 2020.

Julius Caesar (1953). *Rotten Tomatoes*, www.rottentomatoes.com/m/1011328_julius_caesar. Accessed 1 Apr. 2020.

Julius Caesar (1953). *Turner Classic Movies*, www.tcm.com/watchtcm/movies/79974/Julius-Caesar/. Accessed 1 Apr. 2020.

"Kenneth Branagh." *IMDb*, www.imdb.com/name/nm0000110/'ref_=fn_al_nm_1. Accessed 1 Apr. 2020.

Land, Graham. "10 Films and Television Series about *Julius Caesar*." *History Hit*, 9 Aug. 2018, www.historyhit.com/films-and-television-series-about-julius-caesar/. Accessed 1 Apr. 2020.

The Last of the Mohicans

The Novel
Author: James Fenimore Cooper (1789-1851)
First published: 1826

The Film
Year released: 1992
Director: Michael Mann (b. 1943)
Screenplay by: Michael Mann, Christopher Crowe
Starring: Daniel Day-Lewis, Madeleine Stowe, Jodhi May, Russell Means, Wes Studi, Eric Schweig, Steven Waddington

Context

Widely regarded as America's first major novelist, James Fenimore Cooper was credited with inventing frontier fiction, which helped lay the seeds for the western genre in literature, film, and television. A prolific author, Cooper wrote roughly fifty books over a career that spanned three decades, including thirty-two novels. While Cooper's writings traversed a wide range of subjects, from the sea to politics to history, he is best known for a series of five novels about the northeastern frontier collectively called the "Leatherstocking Tales." Published between 1823 and 1841, the novels center around the exploits of an indomitable frontiersman named Nathaniel "Natty" Bumppo, a child of white parents who is raised by Native Americans. The second and most famous installment of the series, *The Last of the Mohicans* (1826), is considered Cooper's masterpiece. Set in 1757 during the French and Indian War, the novel follows Bumppo, also known as Hawkeye, as he and his Mohican brethren, Chingachgook and Uncas, lead two daughters of a British army colonel to safety. One of the most popular English-language novels of the nineteenth century, *The Last of the Mohicans* would go on to inspire numerous film and television adaptations.

Most of those adaptations, however, have deviated greatly from Cooper's novel, which, despite its enormous popularity, has drawn criticism over the years for its length, verbose prose style, and racist depictions of Native Americans. Still, Cooper's American frontier myth has never ceased to captivate Hollywood filmmakers, who have utilized various plot elements from the novel for their own interpretations. Among them have included D.W. Griffith, who directed *Leather Stocking* in 1909; Maurice Tourneur and Clarence Brown, whose 1920 silent version

is regarded as the most faithful of all adaptations; and George B. Seitz, who handled the material twice, first as a silent serial film (*Leatherstocking*, 1924) and then as a feature-length film in 1936. It was Seitz's 1936 film, which stars Randolph Scott as Hawkeye and features a screenplay by Philip Dunne, that left a lasting impression on visionary filmmaker Michael Mann as a child and which ultimately prompted him to begin developing his own version in the late 1980s.

Admittedly not a fan of the Cooper novel, Mann, then known for writing and directing highly stylized crime dramas like *Thief* (1981) and *Manhunter* (1986), became particularly intrigued by Dunne's script, which was one of the first to romanticize Hawkeye as a symbol of the new American landscape. Teaming up with cowriter Christopher Crowe, Mann crafted a script that drew from Dunne's, as well as from the diary of the French admiral Louis-Antoine de Bougainville and from a history of the French and Indian War by the American historian Francis Parkman. For the lead role of Hawkeye, Mann cast the Academy Award-winning British method actor Daniel Day-Lewis, whose full-on immersion into the heroic frontiersman character during the film's shoot became the stuff of legend.

In making the film, Mann, a notorious perfectionist, led a quest for authenticity that was equally legendary. Among other things, he commissioned the recreation of Fort William Henry from 200-year-old schematics along with countless facsimiles of colonial-era costumes and props. The director rounded out the rest of the film's principal cast with actors Madeleine Stowe, Jodhi May, Russell Means, Eric Schweig, Steven Waddington, and Wes

Studi. Shot mostly in North Carolina's Blue Ridge Mountains, *The Last of the Mohicans* had its world premiere in Paris, France, on August 26, 1992.

Film Analysis

As is typical for a Michael Mann film, *The Last of the Mohicans* features a powerfully sublime opening sequence, one that not only stands out from its predecessors but also signals a radical departure from Cooper's novel. Over title cards establishing time and place, rolling drums build to a crescendo and then segue into a stirring orchestral arrangement of trumpets and strings as images of a majestic fog-covered mountain landscape appear. After slowly panning over the mountains, Mann then immediately immerses viewers into the action, following three men—protagonist Nathaniel Poe, or Hawkeye (Daniel Day-Lewis), and his Mohican kin, Chingachgook (Russell Means) and Uncas (Eric Schweig)—as they dash through a dense forest in search of an unknown quarry. Their search culminates in a slow-motion close-up on Hawkeye as he raises his rifle to fatally shoot an elk. Like opening up a dusty leather-bound book into a pristine, unspoiled past, Mann expertly melds action, sound, and style to transport viewers to 1757 America. In the process, he overcomes the plodding nature of Cooper's narrative, cutting out unnecessary exposition in favor of a visceral sensory experience that suits an epic historical adventure film.

Though not a single line of dialogue is uttered during the film's four-minute opening credit-hunt sequence, save for a ritual prayer Chingachgook chants to honor the dead elk, Mann makes it clear to viewers that Day-Lewis's sinewy Hawkeye, bare-chested with long flowing black hair, will serve as the focal point of the story. Here the director continues the narrative pattern popularized by Dunne with his script for Seitz's 1936 film adaptation. Unlike in that adaptation and others, Mann eventually introduces a love affair between Hawkeye and Cora Munro (Madeleine Stowe), the eldest daughter of British army colonel Edmund Munro (Maurice Roëves), commander of Fort William Henry. One of Mann's many revisions to the original Cooper novel, this relationship becomes a primary plot concern, making the film as much of a sweeping romance as it is an action-adventure epic.

In Cooper's novel, Hawkeye, Chingachgook, and Uncas first encounter Cora, her younger sister Alice, and two other British characters, army major Duncan Heyward and psalmodist David Gamut, as they have been

Director Michael Mann. Photo by Gage Skidmore via Wikimedia Commons.

led astray in the forest by a Huron chief, Magua. Out for revenge against his sworn enemy, Colonel Munro, who has exiled him and uprooted his family, Magua ambushes the protagonists with a group of fellow Huron warriors and takes Cora, Alice, Heyward, and Gamut captive. The rest of the novel follows Hawkeye, Chingachgook, and Uncas, as they pursue and try to rescue the captives. All the while, a series of plot twists ensues, among which include Magua professing his love for and unsuccessfully proposing marriage to Cora, and burgeoning romances between Uncas and Cora and Heyward and Alice. Throughout the narrative, Hawkeye, though still serving a central role, is not portrayed as a romantic hero but rather as an astute, and largely asexual, woodsman, guide, and protector.

Contrarily, Mann embraces Hawkeye's more alluring qualities to portray him not just as a self-reliant individualist but also as a ravishing leading man, thus making him more appealing to mass film audiences. He departs from Seitz's script, however, in introducing a love triangle with

Hawkeye, Cora, and Heyward (Steven Waddington), rather than one involving Hawkeye, Alice (Jodhi May), and Heyward. The biggest change Mann makes is to the dark-haired Cora character, who is of mixed-race background in Cooper's novel and is portrayed as such in other Hollywood adaptations. Here Cora is depicted as being all-white. Mann's Magua (Wes Studi), however, has no romantic interest in Cora or any other female character, as he is unwaveringly driven by his vengeful bloodlust. Meanwhile, like in most previous film versions, psalmodist David Gamut, who is largely used in Cooper's novel for comic relief, is completely eliminated from the plot.

In Mann's film, Hawkeye and Cora first meet when Magua, posing as a Mohawk guide for the British, leads Cora's traveling party into a Huron ambush. The Hurons massacre a troop of British soldiers, but Hawkeye, Chingachgook, and Uncas intervene before the war party kills Cora, Alice, and Heyward, the latter of whom has been charged with leading the Munros to their father at Fort William Henry. Magua escapes alone, but the trio agree to lead Cora, Alice, and Heyward to the fort. During their journey, Hawkeye and Cora grow attracted to each other, provoking jealousy in Heyward, who by this time has already unsuccessfully asked Cora to marry him. Alice and Uncas also develop feelings for one another, but this romantic subplot is deliberately left undeveloped to avoid convoluting the narrative.

A major and visually stunning set piece in the film is the siege of Fort William Henry by French forces, who, under the direction of General Louis-Joseph de Montcalm (Patrice Chéreau), overtake Colonel Munro's greatly outnumbered British army. Before this occurs, Hawkeye and his Mohican brethren safely guide Cora, Alice, and Heyward to the fort. While there Hawkeye and Cora pursue their mutual attraction: in a smoldering and wordless three-minute sequence, the two characters find each other amidst the mayhem and flee to a secluded area to passionately embrace. Here Mann again exploits the powers of the film medium, mixing sound, image, and action to solidify his narrative's overarching romance plot. That romance becomes comprised, however, when Hawkeye is found guilty of sedition and sentenced to hang after he helps a group of militiamen desert so they can protect their homesteads.

During the second half of the film, Mann teases out Hawkeye and Cora's tenuous, star-crossed union for full dramatic effect. After reaching favorable surrender terms with Montcalm, Munro leads his British troops out of the fort, but not long afterward, they are massacred by Magua and his band of Huron warriors. Hawkeye and Cora escape, along with Chingachgook, Uncas, Alice, and Heyward, and the group finds refuge behind a waterfall. Magua soon catches up with them, however, and again takes the women and Heyward captive. Hawkeye is then reunited with Cora a second and final time after he reaches the Huron settlement and pleads for the captives' lives. Heyward, serving as a French translator for the ruling Huron chief Ongewasgone (Dennis Banks), sacrifices his life for Cora's and is burned at the stake, while Alice is given to Magua as reparation for Munro's misdeeds.

The film culminates in another breathtaking, and mostly wordless, score-accompanied sequence that follows Hawkeye, Cora, Chingachgook, and Uncas, as they pursue Magua and his party into the high mountains to rescue Alice. During the pursuit, Uncas is killed by Magua, prompting Alice, hopeless and inconsolable, to jump off a cliff. Hawkeye and Chingachgook subsequently wipe out the remaining Hurons, and Chingachgook avenges Uncas's death by killing Magua. Chingachgook then offers a poignant prayer to his fallen son, one in which he declares himself to be "the last of the Mohicans." Mirroring its opening, the film concludes with Hawkeye, Cora, and Chingachgook looking out at the vast landscape before them as the score's main theme plays. This conclusion is much more agreeable to the one in Cooper's novel, which includes the funerals of Cora and Uncas, the former of whom is rashly killed by a Huron, and a final scene with Hawkeye, who shoots Magua with his rifle, comforting Chingachgook as a sage utters a lament about the decline of the Indians at the hands of the "palefaces." By preserving the film's central love story, Mann fulfills audience expectations with a more uplifting ending, one that suggests a sense of hope, rather than sorrow, for the new and rapidly changing frontier.

Significance

Following its world premiere, *The Last of the Mohicans* was released theatrically in the United States on September 25, 1992. The film received largely positive reviews, with many critics praising Day-Lewis's performance and Mann's direction as well as the film's breathtaking visuals (by Italian cinematographer Dante Spinotti), highly realistic action sequences, painstaking production design, intricate period costumes, and intensely rousing score. It was also a commercial hit, grossing more than $75 million and becoming the seventeenth highest-grossing film in the United States in 1992. The film's honors included an Academy Award for Best Sound and British Academy Film Awards (BAFTA) for Best Cinematography and Best Makeup Artist.

One of the most enduring legacies of *The Last of the Mohicans* is its musical soundtrack by Trevor Jones and Randy Edelman, which, despite being overlooked by the Academy Awards, garnered Golden Globe and BAFTA award nominations for best original score. In the decades since the film's release, their score has permeated the cultural consciousness, as it has been used in commercials, played as entrance music for professional athletes, showcased in military tattoos, and sampled in songs by other musical artists.

In no small part due to its score and other aesthetic qualities, *The Last of the Mohicans* has come to be regarded as a major work in Mann's oeuvre and as a classic of the historical action-adventure romance genre. Though the film remains Mann's only foray into historical period drama set before the twentieth century, it helped prove that the director was capable of deftly handling material outside of contemporary crime drama fare. The film, in fact, helped set in motion a period of high artistic achievement for Mann, who would follow it with two of the most critically acclaimed films of the 1990s: the sprawling Los Angeles crime saga *Heat* (1995) and the gripping docudrama *The Insider* (1999).

Some Cooper scholars have nonetheless expressed disappointment with Mann's adaptation and with Hollywood's treatment of *The Last of the Mohicans* in general. According to Jeffrey Walker, by largely focusing their narratives on the escapades of a romantic frontiersman in Hawkeye, Hollywood filmmakers have lost the novel's central commentary on the destruction of the Native American race. Notwithstanding such criticism, Mann's film is notable for being the first adaptation to feature Native American actors and the first to portray Native Americans in a mostly sympathetic light.

—*Chris Cullen*

Further Reading

Rayner, Jonathan. *The Cinema of Michael Mann: Vice and Vindication (Director's Cuts)*. Kindle ed., Wallflower Press, 2013.

Sragow, Michael. "Michael Mann's *The Last of the Mohicans*." *Library of America*, 27 Jan. 2016, www.loa.org/news-and-views/1115-michael-manns-_the-last-of-the-mohicans. Accessed 23 Mar. 2020.

Walker, Jeffrey. "Deconstructing an American Myth: Hollywood and *The Last of the Mohicans*." State University of New York College at Oneonta, 1999, pp. 77-84.

Bibliography

Chaberski, Chris. "25 Years Later, *The Last of the Mohicans* Score Makes It a Masterpiece." *ScreenCrush*, 25 Sep. 2017, screencrush.com/last-of-the-mohicans-25th-anniversary/. Accessed 23 Mar. 2020.

Cochrane, Glenn. "Interview with Michael Mann—*The Last of the Mohicans*." *STACK Magazine*, 1 Sept. 2019, stack.com.au/film-tv/film-tv-interview/interview-with-michael-mann-the-last-of-the-mohicans/. Accessed 23 Mar. 2020.

Cooper, James Fenimore. *The Last of the Mohicans*. 1826. Paper Mill Press, 2018.

Franklin, Kelly Scott. "Master of the Frontier." *National Review*, 13 Sept. 2018, www.nationalreview.com/magazine/2018/10/01/james-fenimore-cooper-americas-novelist/. Accessed 23 Mar. 2020.

Galbraith, Jane. "Facts of the *Mohicans*: A Historian Is Impressed by the Details in the Movie but Sees Inaccuracies in the Depiction of Frontier Life." *Los Angeles Times*, 10 Oct. 1992, www.latimes.com/archives/la-xpm-1992-10-10-ca-753-story.html. Accessed 23 Mar. 2020.

Kempley, Rita. "*The Last of the Mohicans*," *The Washington Post*, 25 Sept. 1992, www.washingtonpost.com/wp-srv/style/longterm/movies/videos/thelastofthemohicansrkempley_a0a32a.htm. Accessed 23 Mar. 2020.

"Michael Mann Looks Back on *The Last of the Mohicans* 20 Years Later." *UPROXX*, 12 May 2012, uproxx.com/hitfix/michael-mann-looks-back-on-the-last-of-the-mohicans-20-years-later/. Accessed 23 Apr. 2020.

Thomson, David. "The Last of the Mohicans." *Have You Seen...?*, 2008, Reprint ed., Alfred A. Knopf, 2010, p. 454.

The Legend of Sleepy Hollow

The Novel
Author: Washington Irving (1783-1859)
First published: 1820

The Film
Year released: 1999
Director: Tim Burton (b. 1958)
Screenplay by: Andrew Kevin Walker
Starring: Johnny Depp, Christina Ricci, Miranda Richardson, Michael Gambon

Context

One of the first fiction authors in the United States to make a living as a writer and to earn fame abroad, Washington Irving has been called the "first American man of letters." He was also an innovator in the short story genre. The story "The Legend of Sleepy Hollow" first appeared in Irving's collection, *The Sketch Book of Geoffrey Crayon, Gent.*, in 1819. Incorporating humor and romanticism, Irving's tales focused on vivid, detailed descriptions of characters and settings more than intricate plotting. Film adaptations, while usually careful to portray protagonist Ichabod Crane and the town of Sleepy Hollow as Irving described them, have typically added numerous embellishments to develop the storyline for feature-length films.

An example of an adaptation that strictly adheres to Irving's plot is *Sketches from Sleepy Hollow* (2014), an eight-minute version of the entire story told with string puppets and intended for children. Other adaptations include the 1999 Canadian full-length television adaptation, *The Legend of Sleepy Hollow*, in which director Pierre Gang bookends Irving's story with the subplot of a traveling journalist, in some ways mirroring Irving's first-person narrator, who had stopped by a local tavern and asked patrons to recount local legends and so heard the tale of the Headless Horseman.

Tim Burton's film adaptation of *The Legend of Sleepy Hollow* is characterized by his quirky, personal directorial style, incorporating both gothic and kitsch, and the use of advanced special effects including vivid depictions of severed heads and the Headless Horseman.

Film Analysis

In *Sleepy Hollow*, Director Tim Burton offers many creative embellishments to Washington Irving's classic story in order to turn Irving's story into a feature film. In his story, Irving established a mood of mystery and suspense, with detailed descriptions of settings and characters. His description of Ichabod Crane, for example, is lengthy, describing everything from the length of his arms, to the size of his feet and even the shape of his head.

Irving's description of Crane is so vivid and clear it has become iconic, and most film adaptations portray Crane as the tall, skinny, scarecrow-like schoolteacher Irving describes. In his adaptation, Burton keeps and builds upon Irving's mood of mystery and suspense while making significant changes to the plot and protagonist, including providing Ichabod Crane (Johnny Depp) with a traumatic backstory in flashbacks, adding an additional plot element involving witchcraft, and providing Crane with a happy, if conventional, ending.

Burton gives a significant re-visioning of Crane. Not only does the actor, Johnny Depp, look nothing like the iconic description of Irving's Crane, but he makes Crane a constable in New York City in 1799 who is sent to Sleepy Hollow by a judge (Christopher Lee) to solve a series of murders. By changing Crane's profession and situation from a schoolteacher hearing a tale told in a village to a big city constable solving a murder case, Burton modernizes the story in ways that entirely obscure Irving's subtle ironies and interest in history, but update the story's trappings for contemporary film audiences.

The townspeople in the film seek to convince Crane that the illusive and legendary phantom, the Headless Horseman (Christopher Walken), was the murderer. They listen to and respect Crane, usually following his lead and acting on his direction in his attempts to solve the murders, and he even gains the trust and assistance of Katrina Van

Tassel (Christina Ricci) as well as Young Masbath (Marc Pickering), a boy who volunteers to help Crane after his father dies as one of the murder victims. Burton's Crane, is mannerist and eccentric, wearing oversized glasses, for example, as magnifying medical equipment to study the corpses, and he is also squeamish. He hides under the covers when he is afraid, cowers in the presence of a spider, and faints after his first encounter with the Headless Horseman.

Burton also incorporates elements of witchcraft, making it an aspect of Crane's past (and future) as well as a contributing factor to the murders in Sleepy Hollow. In Irving's story, Crane has a fascination with scary tales and New England witchcraft, and a copy of Cotton Mather's *History of New England Witchcraft* is one of his few treasured possessions. In Burton's adaptation, interest turns into reality. In an invented backstory told in flashbacks, Crane remembers his loving mother (Lisa Marie) accused of witchcraft by his religious father (Peter Guinness) and tortured to death in an iron maiden. As a child, Crane witnessed his mother's treatment and was deeply traumatized. Additionally, Lady Van Tassel (Miranda Richardson), the second wife of Baltus Van Tassel (Michael Gambon) and stepmother to Katrina, is a practicing witch who has pledged herself to Satan in order to command the Headless Horseman and kill her enemies. With her enemies dead, Lady Van Tassel hopes to inherit their estates and become financially independent.

Crane, relying on logic and rational thought, always suspected a murder conspiracy. His past experience made him deeply skeptical about the existence of the Headless Horseman until he puts the pieces of Lady Van Tassel's puzzle together. Thus, not only is witchcraft an added element of the plot, but Burton uses it to evolve Crane's character. As his understanding and acceptance of the Headless Horseman and witchcraft grow, Crane merges his adherence to rational thought with his mysterious, occult past and the present mystery. As he evolves, so does his relationship with Katrina, who is also a practicing witch, though she conjures good and protection spells rather than evil.

In Burton's adaptation, Brom Van Brunt (Casper Van Dien) dies, and because of Crane's growth, he and Katrina advance their relationship romantically. At the end of the film, Crane, Katrina, and Young Masbath return to New York City at the dawn of the new century, 1800. Crane has been able to put his torturous past behind him and create a new life with Katrina, making the addition of the witchcraft plot an important element of Burton's adaptation and transformative for the Crane character.

Despite the many alterations to Irving's plot and characters, Burton sustains the mystery and suspense of Irving's text through the art direction, cinematography, and special effects. Burton sets the film's mood in the opening scene with an optical illusion. What appear to be drops of blood falling and pooling on a cream-colored surface are eventually revealed to be melted wax, used at the time to seal letters. As he does in many of his films, Burton also mutes the film's color palette, concentrating on blacks, whites, and reds, which provide a sinister edge to the bucolic town of Sleepy Hollow. The special effects remain notable, with the Headless Horseman severing numerous heads and riding at full speed out of the trunk of the Tree of the Dead.

Significance

Tim Burton's *Sleepy Hollow* was released in over three thousand theaters on November 19, 1999 and earned the number two spot at the box office its opening weekend, grossing over $30 million. During its theatrical run, the film ultimately grossed over $200 million in worldwide ticket sales, though some critics attributed the film's initial financial success to its emphasis on gore and violence, which attracted the post-Halloween holiday audience. While *Sleepy Hollow* was nominated for forty-three film awards, including acting awards for Johnny Depp and Christina Ricci, it was most often nominated and won its biggest awards for cinematography, art direction, set design, and costumes. The film won an Oscar for Best Art Direction-Set Direction and BAFTAs (British Academy of Film and Television Arts) for Best Production Design and Best Costume Design.

Sleepy Hollow has many hallmarks of a Tim Burton film: for example, the gothic elements in costume and set design and his reliance on a small group of talented actors—including Johnny Depp, who has had lead roles in eight Burton films. Roger Ebert noted that *Sleepy Hollow* was not a typical horror film and that Burton, "elevates it by sheer style and acting into something entertaining and sometimes rather elegant." Janet Maslin from *The New York Times* found the costumes "sumptuous" and the film infused with "visual cleverness," but ultimately found the film overly gory and "much more conventionally conceived than Mr. Burton's admirers would expect." Some critics noted that the film did not significantly transcend the horror genre. While *Sleepy Hollow* achieved some success at the box office and received generally positive reviews, it did not achieve the wide acclaim of some of Burton's other films, such as *Beetlejuice* (1988), *Batman* (1989), and *Alice in Wonderland* (2010), though it remains one of the most watched adaptations of Washington Irving's classic short story.

—*Marybeth Rua-Larsen*

Further Reading

Greven, David. "Troubling Our Heads about Ichabod: *The Legend of Sleepy Hollow*, Classic American Literature, and the Sexual Politics of Homosocial Brotherhood." *American Quarterly*, vol. 56, no. 1, 2004, pp. 83-110. *JSTOR*, www.jstor.org/stable/40068216. Accessed 29 Apr. 2020.

Ray, Brian. "Tim Burton and the Idea of Fairy Tales." *Fairy Tale Films: Visions of Ambiguity*, edited by Pauline Greenhill and Sidney Eve Matrix, University Press of Colorado, 2010, pp. 198-218. *JSTOR*, www.jstor.org/stable/j.ctt4cgn37.15. Accessed 29 Apr. 2020.

Bibliography

Bernardo, Susan M. "The Bloody Battle of the Sexes in Tim Burton's *Sleepy Hollow*." *Literature/Film Quarterly*, vol. 31, no. 1, 2003, pp. 39-43. *JSTOR*, www.jstor.org/stable/43797095. Accessed 29 Apr. 2020.

Ebert, Roger. "*Sleepy Hollow*." *RogerEbert.com*, 19 Nov. 1999, www.rogerebert.com/reviews/sleepy-hollow-1999. Accessed 29 Apr. 2020.

Kevorkian, Martin. "'You Must Never Move the Body!': Burying Irving's Text in *Sleepy Hollow*." *Literature/Film Quarterly*, vol. 31, no. 1, 2003, pp. 27-32. *JSTOR*, www.jstor.org/stable/43797093. Accessed 29 Apr. 2020.

Maslin, Janet. "Film Review; Headless Horseman with Quite a Head Count." *The New York Times*, 19 Nov. 1999, www.nytimes.com/1999/11/19/movies/film-review-headless-horseman-with-quite-a-head-count.html. Accessed 29 Apr. 2020.

Orr, Stanley. "'A Dark Episode of *Bonanza*' Genre, Adaptation, and Historiography in *Sleepy Hollow*." *Literature/Film Quarterly*, vol. 31, no. 1, 2003, pp. 44-49. *JSTOR*, www.jstor.org/stable/43797096. Accessed 29 Apr. 2020.

Wyrick, Laura. "Horror at Century's End: Where Have All the Slashers Gone?" *Pacific Coast Philology*, vol. 33, no. 2, 1998, pp. 122-26. *JSTOR*, www.jstor.org/stable/1316843. Accessed 29 April 2020.

Lemony Snicket's A Series of Unfortunate Events

The Novels
Author: Daniel Handler (pen name Lemony Snicket) (b. 1970)
First published: The Bad Beginning, 1999; *The Reptile Room*, 1999; *The Wide Window*, 2000

The Film
Year released: 2004
Director: Brad Silberling (b. 1963)
Screenplay by: Robert Gordon
Starring: Jim Carrey, Meryl Streep, Emily Browning, Liam Aiken, Shelby Hoffman, Kara Hoffman

Context

Daniel Handler, under the pseudonym Lemony Snicket, wrote a series of thirteen children's chapter books with the umbrella title A Series of Unfortunate Events between 1999 and 2006. The books proved highly popular and were positively received by critics as well, with much praise for their dark yet comedic, even absurdist, gothic style. Reviewers often likened the series—which recounts the challenges and adventures faced by the orphaned Baudelaire children, Violet, Klaus, and Sunny—to the classic works of Roald Dahl. It also received attention for Handler's use of wordplay, social commentary, and many literary or cultural allusions.

The series' success came amid a broader boom in fantasy books for children and young adults, perhaps represented most famously by J. K. Rowling's Harry Potter series (1997-2007). Many bestselling properties were soon optioned for film adaptation, driving a parallel trend in Hollywood. For some of the most popular franchises, movie versions began to appear even before the respective book series were complete. The eleventh book in A Series of Unfortunate Events, *The Grim Grotto*, was published on September 21, 2004. The film *Lemony Snicket's A Series of Unfortunate Events* was released on December 17, 2004, drawing on the first three books in the series: *The Bad Beginning* (1999). *The Reptile Room* (1999), and *The Wide Window* (2000).

Initially, Handler was put in charge of writing the film script by filmmaker Barry Sonnenfeld, an admirer of the Lemony Snicket novels who had signed on to direct and was known for helming the tonally comparable *The Addams Family* (1991) and *Addams Family Values* (1993). Sonnenfeld ultimately backed out of the project, however, and his replacement as director, Brad Silberling, essentially chose not to use Handler's screenplay. Robert Gordon was brought in to rework the script. Replacing both a director who was an enthusiast of the book series and the book series writer himself resulted in writing and directing that was less faithful to the plot and tone of Handler's novels, to the concern of some fans of the books.

Anticipated as the beginning of a blockbuster film franchise to rival the Harry Potter adaptations (2011-11), *Lemony Snicket's A Series of Unfortunate Events* attracted considerable star power. Comedic chameleon Jim Carrey was attached to the villainous lead role of Count Olaf well before production even began. Esteemed actors such as Meryl Streep and Billy Connolly were eventually cast in prominent secondary roles. Much like with the Harry Potter film series, however, the key parts of the child protagonists went to relative unknown young actors.

Film Analysis

With steampunk-inspired gothic set design and cinematography reminiscent of filmmaker Tim Burton, *Lemony Snicket's A Series of Unfortunate Events* complements the mood of Handler's book series. Other elements of the film, however, such as plot and a decidedly softer approach to violence, veer away from the books and result in a film that is less faithful to its source than most critics and fans expected. While in part this is simply due to the nature of condensing three books into a single movie, it also reflects the style of Silberling and the others involved in the film compared to Handler.

In terms of plot, there are segments of the story line that were abbreviated or moved to another point in the timeline. There is an added scene in which the Baudelaire orphans are put in peril by being locked in a car on railroad tracks with an incoming train. While none of these plot changes affect the audience's overall understanding of Handler's story, they do affect the audience's interpretation of character and theme.

Perhaps the most consequential change is the marriage scene between Count Olaf (Jim Carrey) and Violet (Emily Browning). In this scene, which takes place near the end of the first book, *The Bad Beginning*, the Baudelaire orphans live with their guardian, Count Olaf, as he schemes to get their inheritance. He decides to kidnap the youngest orphan, Sunny (played by Shelby Hoffman and Kara Hoffman in the film), holds her prisoner, and places her in a large birdcage, which he then hangs outside his mansion's top tower window. Count Olaf then blackmails Violet, telling her that if she does not marry him, Sunny would have an "accident" and the cage would fall. Count Olaf also arranges to have Justice Strauss, his neighbor and a judge, unknowingly perform a legal marriage ceremony under the guise of acting out a play. Once the performance is finished, and Count Olaf is legally married to Violet, he believes he will have access to her fortune. In the book, Violet agrees to marry Count Olaf to save Sunny, but then cleverly signs the marriage certificate with her left hand to invalidate it, thus saving Sunny and herself. This scene is the climax of the first book. After the marriage scene, Count Olaf escapes, and the book concludes with the orphans preparing for their next guardian with trepidation.

In the film, however, the marriage scene is placed toward the end of the movie, after the third book, *The Wide Window*, concludes. Not only is the scene moved, but it contains several changes, the most important being that Klaus (Liam Aiken) comes to the rescue by burning the signed marriage certificate with a large, ominous magnifying glass he finds in the tower. Rather than the clever, mechanically minded Violet saving herself as she does in the book, showing her ingenuity and ability to be self-reliant, she must be saved by someone else, in this case her brother. While Violet does have many moments of cleverness in the film, in which she dons her ribbon and ties her hair up to work on a solution to a problem, they are somewhat negated by this last, critical scene, moved to the end of the film as its biggest dramatic moment.

Repositioning this climactic scene to close to the end of the film also leads to a happier conclusion, unlike in the books. In the film, Count Olaf has once again escaped, and Mr. Poe (Timothy Spall), the executor of the Baudelaire parents' estate, drives the sleeping orphans to their new

Jim Carrey. Photo by Ian Smith via Wikimedia Commons.

guardian. The scene that has a relatively uplifting feel emphasized by the narration. In contrast, the books in A Series of Unfortunate Events are known for the many unfortunate events Violet, Klaus, and Sunny suffer, and while the Baudelaire orphans do occasionally have happier moments, each book ends on a note of wariness or uncertainty rather than such hopefulness.

The film downplays the violence and threatening nature of Count Olaf. By reducing the level of danger that the children face, the filmmakers also lessen the stakes and risk giving audiences less reason to be invested in the protagonists' plight. Carrey's more quirky rather than truly villainous portrayal of Count Olaf furthers this difference in tone between film and books. Consequently, reviewers such as Peter Bradshaw, writing for *The Guardian*, criticized the film for its lack of emotional range, noting, "There has to be some sense of menace, some emotional reality to the children's loneliness."

A highlight of the film is its gothic set design. The film has a look both playful and foreboding, and as critic Roger Ebert noted, the art directors and production designer created "wondrous and creepy spaces," such as the kitchen in Count Olaf's mansion. Every kitchen surface is filled with stacks of dirty dishes on every surface and in the cupboards, along with rats and cockroaches scuttling about, and hidden within the filth are the bits of pasta for pasta puttanesca and a large spittoon to cook it in. The film may muddle the plot and downplay the threats and violence, but it is visually successful in creating the absurd world of the source material.

Significance

Lemony Snicket's A Series of Unfortunate Events was made on a budget of $140 million, and was only moderately successful at the box office, grossing over $118 million in the United States and $211 million worldwide. Its performance was likely hampered by mixed reviews. Critics praised the sets and cinematography but little else. They were especially divided on Carrey's performance as Count Olaf; in a review for *The New York Times* Manohla Dargis criticized Carrey's "loud, showboating performance," while CinemaBlend's Jason Wiese found Carrey "devilishly fun." Another common complaint was Roger Ebert's point that Carrey's over-the-top performance negatively affected the emotional impact of the orphans' dire situations. Despite these criticisms, the film won an Academy Award for best makeup and was nominated for several other Oscars, including best original score, best art direction, and best costume design.

Although the film was fairly popular with audiences, there was an underwhelming response from many die-hard fans of the books. The mediocre success of the film effectively ended hopes for an extended film franchise. Another screen adaptation, also called *Lemony Snicket's A Series of Unfortunate Events*, was released as a television series on the streaming platform Netflix from 2017 to 2019. Notably, it provided a second chance for Handler and Sonnenfeld as writer and director, respectively. The Netflix version was ultimately more highly regarded by critics and audiences than the 2004 film, largely due to its greater faithfulness to the books both in terms of level of detail (with two episodes dedicated to each novel but the last) and overall tone.

—*Marybeth Rua-Larsen*

Further Reading

Langbauer, Laurie. "The Ethics and Practice of Lemony Snicket: Adolescence and Generation X." *PMLA*, vol. 122, no. 2, 2007, pp. 502-21, doi:10.1632/pmla.2007.122.2.502. Accessed 1 Mar. 2021.

Purcell, Carey. "7 Things You Didn't Know about 'Lemony Snicket's A Series of Unfortunate Events' Movie." *Mic*, 12 Jan. 2017, www.mic.com/articles/164985/7-things-you-didn-t-know-about-lemony-snicket-s-a-series-of-unfortunate-events-movie. Accessed 18 Mar. 2021.

Bibliography

Bradshaw, Peter. Review of *Lemony Snicket's A Series of Unfortunate Events*, directed by Brad Silberling. *The Guardian*, 17 Dec. 2004, www.theguardian.com/film/News_Story/Critic_Review/Guardian_Film_of_the_week/0,4267,1375023,00.html. Accessed 1 Mar. 2021.

Dargis, Manohla. "Once upon a Gloomy Childhood." Review of *Lemony Snicket's A Series of Unfortunate Events*, directed by Brad Silberling. *The New York Times*, 17 Dec. 2004, www.nytimes.com/2004/12/17/movies/once-upon-a-gloomy-childhood.html. Accessed 1 Mar. 2021.

Ebert, Roger. "Not So 'Lemony' Fresh." Review of *Lemony Snicket's A Series of Unfortunate Events*, directed by Brad Silberling. *Rogerebert.com*, 16 Dec. 2004, www.rogerebert.com/reviews/lemony-snickets-a-series-of-unfortunate-events-2004. Accessed 1 Mar. 2021.

Gartenberg, Chaim. "Netflix's 'A Series of Unfortunate Events' Gets Right What the Movie Got Wrong." *The Verge*, Vox Media, 10 Jan. 2017, www.theverge.com/2017/1/10/14228706/a-series-of-unfortunate-events-netflix-tv-show-review. Accessed 1 Mar. 2021.

Wiese, Jason. "'A Series of Unfortunate Events': Comparing the Show, Movie and Books of Lemony Snicket." *CinemaBlend*, 3 June 2019, www.cinemablend.com/television/2474318/a-series-of-unfortunate-events-comparing-the-show-movie-and-books-of-lemony-snicket. Accessed 1 Mar. 2021.

Life of Pi

The Novel
Author: Yann Martel (b. 1963)
First published: 2001

The Film
Year released: 2012
Director: Ang Lee (b. 1954)
Screenplay by: David Magee
Starring: Suraj Sharma, Irrfan Khan

Context

Both the original novel and the film adaptation of *Life of Pi* are stories of adventure, initiation, maturation, mystery, and survival, as well as of humans in conflict with nature. These are some of the oldest and most enduring themes of literature and cinema, and so it is no surprise that both the book and the movie appealed to readers and viewers on very elemental and visceral levels. Both works, however, are also deeply meditative and philosophical. They deal with some of the largest and most important issues of existence: What are life's purposes and meanings, if any? What does it mean to be human, and how do humans differ, if at all, from other kinds of creatures? What is truth (if truth exists), and how can truth be discerned? Why do evil and suffering exist? How, if at all, can people make sense of either or both? What does it mean to be a good person, if goodness even exists? These are just a few of the questions that both the novel and the film provoke and ponder. Without offering clear, definitive answers to any of them, both works encourage thoughtful responses. Each reader and viewer is ultimately left to answer in his or her own way.

Life of Pi, the first major novel by Canadian writer Yann Martel, was nominated for the 2001 Governor General's Literary Award for fiction and won the prestigious Man Booker Prize in 2002. The film adaptation came after many previous successes by Taiwanese-born director Ang Lee. Lee, one of the most respected filmmakers in the world, is known for making intelligent, probing works that raise important issues about human identity and the achievement of individual freedom but without offering easy or sentimental answers. His Academy Award-winning *Brokeback Mountain* (2005) is one such work. But Lee is also capable of creating films full of excitement, danger, daring, and adventure, such as *Crouching Tiger, Hidden Dragon* (2000) and *The Hulk* (2003). *Life of Pi* falls into both of these categories. Lee has, additionally, shown a real talent for creating films set in non-Western cultures with broad, multicultural, international appeal, such as *Crouching Tiger* and *Lust, Caution* (2007); *Life of Pi* is also successful in this respect. And, finally, in both

Director Ang Lee. Photo by nicolas genin via Wikimedia Commons.

Crouching Tiger and *The Hulk*, Lee demonstrated his gift for creating films full of spectacular special effects, and few films are as impressive in this respect as *Life of Pi*. In fact, *Life of Pi* can be seen as a distillation of many of Lee's very best traits as a filmmaker. In the long arc of Lee's career, *Life of Pi* is one of his most important and most innovative films. It was, for instance, a major advance in the use of computer-generated imagery and 3-D cinematography.

Film Analysis

The film version of *Life of Pi* is inevitably less contemplative than the book. In the novel, most of the words are those of Piscine "Pi" Molitor Patel, a thoughtful middle-aged man (Irrfan Khan) now living in Canada but born in India, where he lived until his mid-teens. Pi both recalls and recounts the major, life-altering adventure of his whole existence: his chance survival of a mid-Pacific Ocean shipwreck that killed almost every other living thing onboard a cargo ship that sank in a ferocious storm. That ship had been carrying the teenaged Pi (Suraj Sharma), his parents and brother, and animals from the family zoo in India to new lives in North America. Pi, in the novel, has literally hundreds of pages in which not only to tell, in first-person narration, what happened during his 227 days in a drifting lifeboat, but also to reflect philosophically on those events. The movie, by contrast, packs his adventure into roughly two hours. Pi's actual voice is heard only intermittently in voice-over in the film but is almost constant in the book. The film, in short, must rely mostly on showing what happened, whereas the novel gives Pi the leisure to tell what occurred, explain his reactions, and interpret the events' potential meanings along the way. In this sense, the book appeals both to the intellect and to the imagination, whereas the appeal of the film is necessarily more imaginative and visual.

The film, however, does follow the plot of the book fairly closely. Both works consist of three main sections: the first deals with the family's life in India; the second, with Pi's frightening existence onboard a lifeboat with a huge Bengal tiger named Richard Parker; and the third, with Pi's time in a Mexican hospital, where he recuperates and tells an entirely different version of the events he has already recounted. Both the book and the movie allow the audience to decide which version they wish to accept as true. The film incorporates many elements of the novel's plot and much of its actual phrasing and dialogue. But the film also differs from the book in various important respects, especially in its emphasis on stunning, spectacular visual imagery and on astounding special effects. The novel had long been considered "unfilmable," and it was partly the sheer challenge of filming it that made the project attractive to, and a source of pride for, Ang Lee.

Many of the most striking differences between the novel and the film involve the middle section dealing with the sudden sinking of the freighter and Pi's subsequent efforts to survive in a small lifeboat with a huge, hungry, carnivorous beast. In the book, the sinking of the boat is initially described very abruptly and unexpectedly, in a single short sentence that opens a new chapter: "The ship sank." In contrast, the film devotes much more extended and spectacular attention to this event. Some of the most harrowing and memorable moments of the film are devoted to showing the ship being thrown around on the turbulent seas and then sinking, slowly, beneath the waters, its lights still glowing as it settles toward the bottom of the ocean. Although this scene and many of the others set at sea were filmed in a huge tank in Taiwan, they are thoroughly convincing, as is nearly every special effect in Lee's movie.

Sometimes, indeed, Lee's film seems more realistic, less sentimental, and therefore more credible than the book on which it is based. In the novel, for instance, Pi at first is eager to have the massive tiger join him as the beast struggles to flee the sinking ship: "Jesus, Mary, Muhammad and Vishnu, how good to see you, Richard Parker! Don't give up, please. Come to the lifeboat," he calls out. He goes on to shout, "What are you doing, Richard Parker? Don't you love life? Keep swimming then!...Kick with your legs. Kick! Kick! Kick!" In the film, on the other hand, Pi immediately realizes that the tiger poses, literally, a big threat. As Pi sees the creature swimming madly toward the lifeboat, he tries to shove the animal away, unsuccessfully, with an oar. Richard Parker nevertheless manages to haul himself into the tiny craft and hide beneath a tarp. (For safety and performance reasons, the realistic-looking tiger was almost completely computer-generated.) In the novel, it is only after Pi has at first been beckoning the beast to join him that he realizes how foolish this behavior is and tries to rectify it, first with the oar and then by jumping overboard. In this respect, Pi in the film seems more sensible and mature than Pi in the book, at least in this situation.

Sometimes, however, the book seems more frankly realistic than the film. In the novel, for example, Pi spends many of his 227 days at sea stark naked, a detail the PG film had to change to avoid a more age-restrictive rating. The book is also often more gruesome in describing gory details, especially the details of injured or half-eaten animals. A zebra, for instance, is another brief survivor onboard the lifeboat, along with a vicious hyena. It is not long before the latter attacks the former, and Pi in the book reports unsparingly the grim results: "The zebra was still alive. I couldn't believe it. It had a two-foot-wide hole in its body, a fistula like a freshly erupted volcano, spewed half-eaten organs glistening in the light or giving off a dull, dry shine." Although Lee's film is sometimes gory, it is rarely as gory as this. Most audiences would have found this sort of close-up too hard to take. Nor does the film depict one of the other grimmer episodes from the novel: Pi's need to clean up Richard Parker's feces and his decision, at one low point, to try eating the animal's waste.

On the whole, the film is more beautiful than the book, especially in its depictions of the sky, the sea, and the myriad creatures the lifeboat encounters. At one point, for instance, Pi looks down into the waters and realizes that a huge whale is steaming up toward the surface. The whale throws itself out of the ocean, soars into the air, and then crashes back into the sea, nearly swamping the boat. In the novel, by contrast, Pi merely looks down into the water and sees the gigantic eye of a whale pass underneath him. The movie is thus a visual feast; the novel is more a feast for the contemplative intellect. Each is memorable in its own distinctive ways.

Significance

The film version of *Life of Pi* was very well received. Most critics praised it highly, and it won numerous honors, including four Academy Awards out of eleven nominations in 2012 and one Golden Globe out of three nominations in 2013. A commercial success, the film earned over $600 million worldwide in its initial release and even more money through subsequent DVD purchases and online rentals.

Life of Pi was almost universally praised as a landmark film in its use of computer-generated special effects as well as for its striking use of 3D cinematography, then an emerging technology. Reviewers also lauded the film for its storytelling, performances by unknown actors, and its refusal to sentimentalize the animals so central to its story,

especially Richard Parker. Some critics, however, found the first and especially the final segments of the three-part film less than compelling and that the movie's last section dragged. Even critics who thought the film unsuccessful in treating philosophical or spiritual themes—perceiving the same flaws in the novel—usually joined the chorus praising its special effects. Some reviewers considered the film's photography to be too unrealistic, however, and thus a distraction or trivialization. But most critics extolled the work for exemplifying the sheer breathtaking magic of moviemaking—the ability of film to make viewers imagine the previously unimagined and believe the unbelievable.

—Robert C. Evans, PhD

Further Reading
Martel, Yann. *Life of Pi*. Harcourt, 2001.

Morace, Robert A. Review of *Life of Pi*, by Yann Martel. *Magill's Literary Annual 2003*, June 2003, pp. 1-3. *Literary Reference Center Plus*, search.ebscohost.com/login.aspx?direct=true&db=lfh&AN=103331MLA.200311070300301960&site=ehost-live. Accessed 6 Mar. 2019.

Palmer, Christopher. *Castaway Tales: From "Robinson Crusoe" to "Life of Pi."* Wesleyan UP, 2016.

Bibliography
Cooper, Rand Richards. "Survivors." *Commonweal*, vol. 140, no. 1, Jan. 2013, pp. 24-5. *Literary Reference Center Plus*, search.ebscohost.com/login.aspx?direct=true&db=lfh&AN=846 52532&site=ehost-live. Accessed 6 Mar. 2019.

Denby, David. "Animal Instincts." Review of *Life of Pi*, directed by Ang Lee, and *Silver Linings Playbook*, directed by David O. Russell. *The New Yorker*, vol. 88, no. 37, Nov. 2012, pp. 86-7. *Literary Reference Center Plus*, search.ebscohost.com/login.aspx?direct=true&db=lfh&AN=83745527&site=ehost-live. Accessed 6 Mar. 2019.

Gilbey, Ryan. "Don't Dream: It's Over." Review of *Life of Pi*, directed by Ang Lee. *New Statesman*, vol. 141, no. 5138, Dec. 2012, p. 84. *Literary Reference Center Plus*, search.ebscohost.com/login.aspx?direct=true&db=lfh&AN=844 62460&site=ehost-live. Accessed 6 Mar. 2019.

Stephens, Gregory. "Feeding Tiger, Finding God: Science, Religion, and 'the Better Story' in *Life of Pi*." *Intertexts*, vol. 14, no. 1, Spring 2010, pp. 41-59. *Literary Reference Center Plus*, search.ebscohost.com/login.aspx?direct=true&db=lfh &AN=54422737&site=ehost-live. Accessed 6 Mar. 2019.

Trachtenberg, Peter. "Inside the Tiger Factory: Behold the Marvel of the Animal's Fabrication." *Virginia Quarterly Review*, vol. 91, no. 3, Summer 2015, pp. 72-90. *Literary Reference Center Plus*, search.ebscohost.com/login.aspx?direct=true&db=lfh&AN=108315992&site=ehost-live. Accessed 6 Mar. 2019.

Little Women (1994)

The Novel
Author: Louisa May Alcott (1832-1888)
First published: 1868

The Film
Year released: 1994
Director: Gillian Armstrong (b. 1950)
Screenplay by: Robin Swicord
Starring: Winona Ryder, Susan Sarandon, Claire Danes, Kirsten Dunst, Trini Alvarado

Context
One of the enduring questions about Louisa May Alcott's *Little Women* is whether or not it should be viewed as a feminist novel. Keeping in mind that the very word "feminist," in the sense of advocating for the rights of women, didn't exist until the end of the nineteenth century, critics have nevertheless noted that Alcott lived an unconventional life for a nineteenth-century woman. She chose not to marry, was an avid abolitionist and a supporter of women's suffrage, and she made a career for herself as a writer. While Alcott chose an untraditional path for herself, the March sisters in *Little Women* follow a traditional path, concentrating on domestic chores, family, and marriage. Some credit for the direction of the novel can be attributed to her publishers, who insisted that Alcott's heroine, Jo March, marry. Alcott herself did not intend for Jo to marry, but she eventually acquiesced. But certainly, many women of acclaim in the twentieth century, such as Simone de Beauvoir, Patti Smith, and Sonia Sanchez, have pointed to Jo March as an early influence for her rebellious and even "feminist" spirit.

Early adaptations, such as the 1933 George Cukor film starring Katharine Hepburn (1907-2003), took a more traditional view of the characters, focusing on the women as self-sacrificing. Marmee (Spring Byington), for example, encourages her daughters to put the needs of others before themselves and give up their Christmas breakfast to the Hummel family, who are in dire need. The scene ends with mother and daughters sharing their bounty with the Hummels. Gillian Armstrong interprets the scene slightly differently: Jo (Winona Ryder) and her sisters learn of the Hummel family's difficulties, and then they give up their breakfast of their own accord. Marmee (Susan Sarandon) is not in the room. Both versions dwell on self-sacrifice, but the Armstrong version focuses on independent thinking. Armstrong also creates a more suffrage-minded Marmee, who encourages her daughters to be true to themselves and follow their dreams. Like Patricia Rozema in her 1999 adaptation of Jane Austen's *Mansfield Park*, Armstrong offers a revisionist *Little Women*, merging biographic elements of Alcott's life, such as her dedication to the suffrage movement, with Alcott's characters to create a feminist interpretation of Alcott's classic, complex novel.

Film Analysis
While director Gillian Armstrong's *Little Women* is a faithful adaptation of Alcott's novel in its adherence to the plot and setting, it also provides a modern and overtly feminist message, especially in terms of its characterizations. Alcott's Jo March, an inspiration to many readers because of her outspokenness, tomboy nature, and career aspirations, becomes even more forthright and unapologetic in Armstrong's film, and some of the most traditional characters in the novel, such as Marmee, are transformed into more assertive, forward-thinking women. Armstrong achieves this transformation through screenwriter Robin Swicord's updated and revised dialogue, with Swicord either deleting some of Alcott's statements of self-sacrifice or revising statements to make them bolder and incorporate elements of Alcott's personal biography, such as her support of women's suffrage. Thus, Armstrong's adaptation has the lush visual appeal of a period drama while re-visioning Alcott's ambivalent perspective and making it decidedly feminist.

On the surface, *Little Women* is a typical period drama. Colleen Atwood's costume design, for which she was

Director Gillian Armstrong. Photo by Eva Rinaldi via Wikimedia Commons.

nominated for several awards, includes elegant and authentic Victorian-era dresses. The set, clearly intended to be Alcott's home, Orchard House, in Concord, Massachusetts, was filmed in British Columbia, Canada, yet accurately portrays the home's brown clapboards and interior details, such as Beth's (Claire Danes) cloth dolls and period-specific Christmas decorations and table settings. Everything about the film, including its warm, sepia-inspired lighting and long, lingering shots of the New England countryside, is authentic to the period and beautifully rendered. The richness of the setting grounds the March sisters fully in the 1860s, during the Civil War, when the novel is set. Armstrong also follows the general plot of *Little Women* in chronological sequence, starting with the March sisters in their later childhood years and following them into adulthood. Alcott's novel, which was originally written in two parts, is lengthy and detailed, and although Amy's (Samantha Mathis) trip to Europe, Jo's adventures in Manhattan, and Meg's (Trini Alvarado) marriage and

pregnancy are abbreviated, all the major events are included in vivid period detail.

It is through characterization and dialogue that Armstrong transforms *Little Women* into a more overt feminist film. Swicord, in her screenplay, drew inspiration from Alcott's biography and made ardent feminists of both Marmee and Jo. While Marmee explains preparing food for the needy at the beginning of the film, much less is made of her volunteer work in this film than in other adaptations or in the novel. In the 1933 adaptation, for example, the film opens with Marmee in town helping the war effort, and she gives the last of the money in her coin purse to a man who has already lost three sons in the war and hopes to visit his remaining son before he succumbs to his injuries. Here, Marmee is emotional to this father's plight and sympathetic to his sacrifice. In Armstrong's version, Marmee is more the compassionate, pragmatic, feminist mother who encourages her daughters to be inquisitive and develop goals while making her views about women's rights known. When her younger daughters are playing outside in the snow with Laurie (Christian Bale), Mr. Brooke, the tutor (Eric Stoltz), notes to a passing Marmee that her daughters are, "unusually active," to which Marmee replies, "It is my opinion that young girls are no different from boys in their need for exertion. Feminine weakness and fainting spells are the direct result of confining young girls to the home bent over their needlework in restrictive corsets." Neither Marmee's statement nor those general feminist ideas are expressed in Alcott's book, and Swicord transfers details from Alcott's personal life as a supporter of the suffrage movement to the film to develop and politicize the character. Marmee is transformed from her self-sacrificing ways in the novel to a forward-thinking mother who expresses her opinion freely and without fear of repercussions. Mr. Brooke is clearly disconcerted by her statement, but Marmee smiles and keeps walking, doing her part to educate both men and women on the equality that should exist between the genders.

In other instances, Swicord invents new dialogue to create more feminist characterizations or modifies existing dialogue, either excising parts that no longer fit the new feminist characterization or combining existing dialogue with new ideas. In the novel, when Jo shares with Marmee her desire to leave Concord and start anew somewhere else, Marmee replies, "You leave to enjoy your liberty till you tire of it, for only then will you find that there is something sweeter." Here, Marmee implies that the "something sweeter" is marriage, and that once Jo gets her "liberty" or freedom out of her system, she will be ready to settle down to a traditional life of marriage and family. In the film, Marmee says only, "embrace your liberty and see what wonderful things come of it." In this response, Marmee does not assume that Jo will tire of her freedom and then revert to a traditional life. She provides encouragement that Jo's move to Manhattan will be the first step in Jo's journey of self-discovery and developing a career and an independent life. Swicord's excising and manipulation of Alcott's writing provide a decidedly feminist perspective on Jo's future.

The character of Jo also benefits from Swicord's re-visioning of Alcott's text, making Jo more assertive and less self-sacrificing, particularly in her relationship with Professor Bhaer (Gabriel Byrne). In the novel, Jo worries about becoming a spinster, stating, "an old maid...a literary spinster, with a pen for a spouse." Jo makes no such pronouncements in the film. She does not worry about marriage, and when she refuses Laurie's marriage proposal, it is not, as is implied in the novel, because Laurie isn't her "perfect match" but because too many compromises would be necessary to make the relationship work, and Laurie would resent her writing. In her relationship with Professor Bhaer, Jo and the professor are shown as equals, and the professor supports Jo's career ambitions, if not her "sensational" stories. She values his opinion, yet she stands up to his criticism, stating her stories will, "buy a new coat for Beth, and I'm sure she'll be grateful to have it." Jo makes no excuses and stands by her work, and when she and Professor Bhaer come together at the end of the film, they come together as equals, and the stage is apparently set for an egalitarian marriage.

Significance

When *Little Women* was released on December 21, 1994, expectations were low. Studio executives did not believe a woman-centered film with a female-led cast would do well at the box office, despite the success of films such as *Beaches* (1988) and *Steel Magnolias* (1989). They were wrong. The film, which was made for $18 million dollars, earned a surprising $50 million dollars worldwide. In addition to doing well at the box office, the film also earned many positive reviews, winning over skeptical critics such as Roger Ebert, who called it "surprisingly sharp and intelligent." Consequently, *Little Women* was recognized with several Oscar nominations, including Best Actress in a Leading Role for Winona Ryder, Best Costume Design, and Best Music, Original Score. The film did not win any major awards, but it has developed a steady and devoted fan base since its release.

Gillian Armstrong was the first woman to direct an adaptation of *Little Women*, and as critic Todd McCarthy notes in his *Variety* review, her version, "surpasses even the best previous rendition, George Cukor's 1933 outing starring Katharine Hepburn." The 1933 version is known for Hepburn's athletic and endearing performance, its faithfulness to Alcott's novel, and its wholesome depiction of family life, which audiences especially appreciated during the Great Depression (1929-39). Despite numerous other film and television adaptations, including two versions from the silent film era, a 1949 adaptation with an all-star cast, including June Allyson (1917-2006) and Elizabeth Taylor (1932-2011), and several television and animated adaptations in the 1970s and 1980s, it was the

1933 version that was most revered until Armstrong's version was released.

—*Marybeth Rua-Larsen*

Further Reading

Blackford, Holly. "Chasing Amy: Mephistopheles, the Laurence Boy, and Louisa May Alcott's Punishment of Female Ambition." *Frontiers: A Journal of Women Studies*, vol. 32, no. 3, 2011, pp. 1-40. *JSTOR*, www.jstor.org/stable/10.5250/fronjwomestud.32.3.0001. Accessed 9 Apr. 2020.

Englund, Sheryl A. "Reading the Author in *Little Women*: A Biography of a Book." *American Transcendental Quarterly*, vol. 12, no. 3, Sept. 1998, pp. 198-219.

Bibliography

Doyle, Katie. "*Little Women* (1994) Retrospective Review." *The Film Magazine*, 5 Sept. 2019, www.thefilmagazine.com/little-women-1994-gillian-armstrong-movie-review/. Accessed 9 Apr. 2020.

Ebert, Roger. "*Little Women*." *RogerEbert.com*, 21 Dec. 1994, www.rogerebert.com/reviews/little-women-1994. Accessed 9 Apr. 2020.

Grasso, Linda. "Louisa May Alcott's 'Magic Inkstand': *Little Women*, Feminism, and the Myth of Regeneration." *Frontiers: A Journal of Women Studies*, vol. 19, no. 1, 1998, pp. 177-92. *JSTOR*, www.jstor.org/stable/3347148. Accessed 9 Apr. 2020.

Hollinger, Karen, and Teresa Winterhalter. "A Feminist Romance: Adapting *Little Women* to the Screen." *Tulsa Studies in Women's Literature*, vol. 18, no. 2, 1999, pp. 173-92. *JSTOR*, www.jstor.org/stable/464445. Accessed 9 Apr. 2020.

McCarthy, Todd. "*Little Women*." *Variety*, 13 Dec. 1994, variety.com/1994/film/reviews/little-women-3-1200439688/. Accessed 9 Apr. 2020.

Spencer, Ashley. "*Little Women*: An Oral History of the 1994 Adaptation." *The New York Times*, 12 Sept. 2019, www.nytimes.com/2019/09/12/movies/little-women.html. Accessed 9 Apr. 2020.

Little Women (2019)

The Novel
Author: Louisa May Alcott (1832-1888)
First published: 1868

The Film
Year released: 2019
Director: Greta Gerwig (b. 1983)
Screenplay by: Greta Gerwig
Starring: Saoirse Ronan, Emma Watson, Florence Pugh, Eliza Scanlen, Timothée Chalamet, Laura Dern, Meryl Streep

Context

Little Women, first published in the 1860s, tells the story of the March sisters—Meg, Jo, Beth, and Amy, each of whom has a distinct personality with her own interests and dreams. Jo, the headstrong second-born sister, is the most fully-rounded character and the one who has captivated and inspired so many readers—especially girls and young women who have seen in her a model of independence. The first part of the book unfolds over the course of a year in Concord, Massachusetts in the early 1860s. The four sisters and their mother, Marmee, are in charge of the house while their father is away serving as a chaplain in the Civil War. The book begins on Christmas Day and ends on the same day one year later, when Mr. March finally comes home from the war. *Little Women* was instantly a hit, bringing Alcott financial security, literary standing, and a deluge of fan mail demanding more stories. She wrote a sequel, which was set three years later and found the March sisters—even the fiercely independent Jo—moving into adulthood and taking husbands. The first book and the sequel were released as a single book in 1868 and have been published in that form ever since.

Greta Gerwig was a well-established actor at work on her directorial debut when she first learned that Sony Pictures was discussing a new version of *Little Women*. The book had last been adapted for the big screen in 1994, and it seemed like the right time for a new production that would appeal to a new generation. Gerwig successfully lobbied the studio to let her make a film that she said would be about "women, art, and money." Gerwig's first film, *Lady Bird*, was subsequently released to overwhelmingly positive reviews, and she began work on her second film. Already familiar with *Little Women* from her own childhood, she did extensive research into Louisa May Alcott's life in the course of writing her screenplay. Gerwig cast Saoirse Ronan, who had starred in *Lady Bird*, in the role of Jo. The supporting cast includes such luminaries as Emma Watson, Florence Pugh, Laura Dern, and Meryl Streep. Released in 2019, Gerwig's version of *Little Women* was extremely well received by critics and audiences alike.

Film Analysis

One of Gerwig's bold decisions in *Little Women* was to intercut the story lines of the two parts of the book. The film begins with Jo, a writer in New York City, bringing a story to a newspaper editor. She has achieved a rare thing for a nineteenth-century woman: economic and artistic independence. The film then cuts to her sisters. The eldest sister, Meg (Watson), has married a teacher and is managing a hardscrabble household in Concord. Having accompanied the family's wealthy Aunt March (Streep) to Europe, Amy (Pugh) is studying art in Paris. Alcott's novel is chronological, with its first part capturing a year in the lives of the March sisters when they are teenagers and children, and a sequel that follows them into adulthood. Fracturing this chronology makes Gerwig's film appeal to modern sensibilities by deepening its tone and complicating its story from the outset. We first encounter Laurie (Chalamet), for example, not as the boy next door, but as a dissolute young man in Paris. Spotting him in a park, Amy is overjoyed to see an old friend, and tells him how sorry she is that Jo rejected him. The viewer is being introduced to characters who already have rich backstories and interconnected lives. As the film cuts between the timelines of the novel's two parts—which Gerwig has separated by seven years rather than three—the viewer is drawn in by a desire to put together the pieces of this narrative puzzle. The film trusts the reader to make connections across the two settings.

Changing the story's chronology also brings out structural parallels between the two halves of the book. Beth (Scanlen), for example, recovers from scarlet fever in the first part, and then succumbs to its complications in the second. Intercutting the two episodes of her illness is a powerful device that builds tremendous pathos during the latter half of the film. Likewise, because Beth's illness has drawn Jo back to Concord, many of the scenes of the girls' childhood are flashbacks as Jo moves back into the family home. The palettes are different for the film's two chronological settings, with the adult scenes washed in grays and browns and the scenes from childhood and adolescence shot in warm, glowing tones. Through scripting and cinematography, Gerwig creates a narratively layered effect that evokes the ways in which childhood memories return to us as adults.

Director Greta Gerwig. Photo by Martin Kraft via Wikimedia Commons.

Literary adaptations are often judged by how faithful they are to their source. In the case of *Little Women*, however, Gerwig has more than one source. Her film effectively triangulates the plot of *Little Women* with the life of its author, Louisa May Alcott. Gerwig did extensive research into Alcott's life, and many lines in the film are adapted from her letters and from her other stories and novels. Alcott was a professional writer who never married; unlike Jo, a stand-in for the author herself, she retained her financial and economic independence. Yet she also needed to bend to market forces, and Alcott's editor made it clear to her that Jo and her sisters must each be married—or dead—by the end of her sequel. Gerwig finds a fascinating way to solve this problem, one that is faithful both to Alcott's novel and to her life.

In her film, Gerwig uses a series of metafictional devices to effectively create two endings for Jo's story. One is the marriage that her editor says the market demands and that Alcott wrote for her: a domestic life with the professor, an end to her literary career, and a future as a teacher and a mother. But by having Jo and her editor break the fourth wall to discuss this ending, it becomes a fiction. A space is created for Jo to instead live an independent, artistic life. Scenes of her marriage are intercut with scenes of her book being printed and bound. When she holds the final product in her hands, its cover proclaims it to be *Little Women* by Jo March. Jo therefore also becomes Louisa May Alcott: an unmarried, financially independent woman and the writer of her own novel. This dual ending is a narrative device that feels both of-the-moment and true to the film's sources, brilliantly dramatizing the inherent conflicts in a story about "women, art, and money." Gerwig's film is ultimately faithful to two sources rather than one: it fuses the story of *Little Women* with its author's own life and with the future she might have imagined for Jo had her Victorian readership allowed for it.

Another of Gerwig's successes in this film is her more nuanced and sympathetic portrayal of Amy, the least sympathetic March sister. Most readers remember Amy as a spoiled and self-centered foil to Jo. She is the jealous upstart who burns Jo's novel, usurps her place on Aunt March's trip to Europe, and ultimately marries the man Jo should have married. Gerwig invests the character with greater depth, seeing in her a young woman who understands the financial realities of the nineteenth century better than her sisters. Amy is the one who understands most clearly how difficult it is to be a woman in the world and who is the most driven to attain security and freedom. Pugh's performance is riveting; her Amy has a clear-eyed intensity and poise that allows her to hold her own against Jo and to emerge as a character who is in many ways the most modern woman of the group. Reimagining Amy and casting Pugh in the role was one of Gerwig's many coups in this film.

The film brilliantly evokes the 1860s, with Concord, New York, and Paris, each coming to life in convincing ways. The costume design and sets are wonderful, and Gerwig has an eye for the subtleties that mark a bygone era. Whether framing a shot through the leaded glass window of an old house, or having the camera linger on the ink stains on Jo's fingers, Gerwig immerses us in an earlier age. The film's great success lies in finding in the past so much that is still relevant to women's lives today.

Significance

Little Women was a box office success that also received rave reviews from critics. Writing for *The New Yorker*, Anthony Lane said, "It may just be the best film yet made by an American woman." Lane sees Gerwig's chronological re-ordering of the novel as a triumph: "The results can be alarming, as weddings adjoin funerals and tantrums melt into firelit peace, but what the mixture yields is a kind of creed: a faith in the fullness of lives that might be deemed unexceptional." In one of several think-pieces about the film published in *The Atlantic*, Alexandra Starr praised Gerwig for stripping away the moralizing that Alcott may have felt pressured to include in her book. Starr argues "When Gerwig deviates from the source material, she's arguably being more faithful to the vision Louisa May Alcott had for her fictional family than she was able to put on the page." Joe Morgenstern, reviewing the film for *The Wall Street Journal*, wrote, "The adaptation is faithful to its historical roots, yet it runs on contemporary energy." Gerwig's bold choices seem to have resonated with most viewers. The aggregating site *Rotten To-*matoes lists the film as scoring equally well with critics and audiences, garnering 95% and 92% positive reviews, respectively.

The film further cemented Gerwig's position as a formidable new director and raised the profiles of the members of its cast. *Little Women* was nominated for six Academy Awards: best picture, actress, supporting actress, costume design, original music score, and adapted screenplay. It only won Best Achievement in Costume Design, and there has been some controversy in the wake of the awards about why it did not fare better and why, in particular, Gerwig was not nominated for Best Director. The controversy over its showing at the Oscars is one more indication that *Little Women*'s focus on "women, art, and money" is as relevant today as it was 150 years ago.

—*Matthew Bolton*

Further Reading

The Selected Letters of Louisa May Alcott, edited by Joel Myerson and Daniel Shealy, Little, Brown and Company, 1987.

Showalter, Elaine. *A Jury of Her Peers: American Women Writers from Anne Bradstreet to Annie Proulx*. Alfred A. Knopf, 2009.

Bibliography

Girish, Devika. "Life's Work." *Film Comment*, Nov.-Dec. 2019, www.filmcomment.com/article/lifes-work/. Accessed 13 Apr. 2020.

Lane, Anthony. "Greta Gerwig's Raw, Startling *Little Women*." *The New Yorker*, 25 Dec. 2019, www.newyorker.com/magazine/2020/01/06/greta-gerwigs-raw-startling-little-women. Accessed 13 Apr. 2020.

Morgenstern, Joe. "*Little Women* Review: Wonder *Women*." *The Wall Street Journal*, 23 Dec. 2019, www.wsj.com/articles/little-women-review-wonder-women-11577143413. Accessed 13 Apr. 2020.

Starr, Alexandra. "What Young Women Need to Know about *Little Women*." *The Atlantic*, 26 Dec. 2019, www.theatlantic.com/ideas/archive/2019/12/what-young-women-need-to-know-about-little-women/604132/. Accessed 13 Apr. 2020.

Lolita

The Novel
Author: Vladimir Nabokov (1899-1977)
First published: 1955

The Film
Year released: 1962
Director: Stanley Kubrick (1928-99)
Screenplay by: Vladimir Nabokov
Starring: James Mason, Sue Lyon, Shelley Winters, Peter Sellers

Context

Both Vladimir Nabokov's 1955 novel *Lolita*, which quickly became a bestseller when it was published in the United States in 1958, and Stanley Kubrick's subsequent 1962 film adaptation were considered highly controversial. In both cases, reviews were positive or negative toward the novel or film depending on whether the critic based their analysis on the elements of humor in the work or on their belief that the book somehow endorsed the actions of its narrator and protagonist, middle-aged Humbert Humbert, in pursuing a sexual relationship with twelve-year-old (or around fifteen in the film) Dolores "Lolita" Haze. Those reviewers who concentrated on the humorous aspects of the works generally praised them, citing clever puns and sight gags, Humbert's over-the-top direct addresses to readers of the novel, or (in the film) Peter Sellers's improvisational and comical turn as Humbert's nemesis, Clare Quilty. Charles Rolo, for example, a book reviewer for the *Atlantic*, wrote of the novel in 1958 that it was "one of the funniest serious novels I have ever read." Rolo, along with other important critics at the time, found Nabokov's word play ingenious and claimed the novel was a "satire of the romantic novel." In a similar vein, forty years later, in an article for *Salon*, the acclaimed author Amy Tan named *Lolita* one of her favorite novels for "its exquisite language" and her belief that "it makes no attempt to serve a higher moral purpose." Readers and critics who admire the novel focus most on Nabokov's skillful satire and engaging wit.

Those critics who rated the novel (or the film) poorly, on the other hand, have tended to focus on the story's sexual aspects, most often claiming it to be pornography or obscene in the way it depicted the predatory nature of pedophiles. Orville Prescott, writing for *The New York Times*, labeled the novel "dull," "repulsive," and "disgusting." He found fault with Nabokov's humor, citing the author's cringe-worthy language and noting that if Nabokov intended farce, he failed. Prescott recognized that Nabokov was writing satire, but he could not ignore the unsavory aspects of the novel. *New York Times* critic Bosley Crowther criticized Kubrick's interpretation of Lolita on screen, claiming that while Kubrick managed the humor well enough, his decision to change Lolita's age—from a pre-teen to a teenager—made her relationship with Humbert seem less aberrant, thereby completely undercutting the wickedly sharp satire. Kubrick, however, had received intense pressure from the Catholic Legion of Decency and enforcers of the Hays Code, a group with the authority to censor a film if their rules were not followed. He therefore felt forced to downplay the erotic elements in the novel to avoid possible censorship and attempted to focus instead on the novel's comedic elements.

Film Analysis

Despite the fact that Nabokov wrote the screenplay, the film adaptation of *Lolita* is significantly different from the novel. This is partly due to the film industry's restrictions on obscenity, enforced through the Hays Code and the Catholic Legion of Decency, and partly due to the fact that Nabokov's original screenplay was four hundred pages long, which would have translated into a seven-hour film. Director Kubrick ultimately had a different vision for the film, and he used only a small percentage of Nabokov's screenplay (with Nabokov still receiving the writing credit). These restrictions and choices resulted in a film that had substantial differences from the novel, including its narrative structure, its narrative voice, the expanded role of Quilty (Peter Sellers), and the maturity of the leading actor, Sue Lyon, in portraying Lolita.

The narrative structure of the film is significantly different from the narrative structure of the novel. In the novel, Nabokov presents the history of the protagonist and narrator, middle-aged Humbert Humbert, including his childhood infatuation with friend Annabel, from which he developed a lifelong attraction to young girls; his early experiences with young prostitutes; and his early marriage to a childlike bride whom he eventually divorces. This extensive backstory is left out of the film, and without the early history of Humbert (James Mason) and the incremental portrayal of his developing perversion, film audiences do not have the benefit of understanding Humbert's neuroses and instead perceive him to be a relatively normal man who has an attraction to "young" women. Additionally, Nabokov's novel is chronological from beginning to end, recounting Humbert's story from his childhood to his incarceration, which ends the novel. In the film, Kubrick uses dramatic compression, or condensing the story and restructuring it. He starts the film where the novel ends, with the tense scene of Humbert hunting down Quilty to kill him after Quilty kidnapped Lolita. The rest of the film is essentially in flashback, ending with the resolution to the confrontation between Quilty and Humbert. In addition to maintaining tension throughout, one result of this change is that beginning with the confrontation between Humbert and Lolita's kidnapper shifts the emphasis from Humbert's growing insanity and perversions to more of a focus on exactly why Humbert commits this murder. Essentially, these changes alter the overall scope and impact of the story.

Another difference that significantly alters the scope and impact of the story is the fact that Humbert rarely addresses the audience in the film and not in the same funny, neurotic way. The film's few voice-overs are much subtler. In the novel, Nabokov has Humbert address the reader directly and often. He begins with, "Lolita, light of my life, fire of my loins. My sin, my soul," and continues a few pages later with, "Or was my excessive desire for that child only the first evidence of an inherent singularity?" Humbert slowly and directly reveals his true nature, his foibles, his desires. After his first sexual encounter with Lolita, he states, "I felt proud of myself. I had stolen the honey of a spasm without impairing the morals of a minor. Absolutely no harm done." He believes himself considerate and rational, which makes it all the more obvious to the

Author Vladimir Nabokov. Photo by Walter Mori, Public domain via Wikimedia Commons.

reader that he is not. Nabokov, in providing these hyperbolic statements, is clearly practicing satire, yet that level of satire is lost in the film. There are few voice-overs and they are emotionally neutral and literary rather than revealing; they move the plot forward, such as when Humbert reads aloud from his diary discussing his lust for Lolita, which the audience has suspected through his actions but which has not yet been stated. These changes result in a film with subtler yet distinct comedy and a potentially more sympathetic protagonist, but one that fails to rise to the level of satire.

Two other decisions related to character also result in significant differences between the novel and the film. In the novel, Lolita is twelve at the onset of the story and someone who is clearly preadolescent. In the film, however, the actor, Lyon, who was around the age of fifteen when the film was produced, looks more like a mature and well-developed teenager. When Humbert first meets Lolita in the film, she is in the garden, clad in a bikini, and her physical appearance seems much more mature than that of a twelve-year-old. The result of an older Lolita is that Humbert's obsession does not seem thoroughly perverse. Another character, Quilty, has a much bigger role in the film than in the novel. Quilty (Peter Sellers) is developed in the film as a local celebrity to whom all women are attracted. Charlotte (Shelley Winters), Lolita's mother, has attended a lecture given by him and adores him. He attends Lolita's play. Along with Vivian Darkbloom (Marianne Stone), who never speaks, he is in one of the hotel lounges watching Humbert and Lolita check in. He is seemingly everywhere in the film, unlike the novel, where he remains a shadowy figure, suggesting he is a doppelganger or Humbert's double. In the film, his ubiquitous presence acts as a foil for Humbert, and since the film bookends their confrontation, it is understandable that he plays a bigger role in the film. The fact that Sellers is a talented improvisational actor adds to the humorous elements, which are more physical and less satiric. While the portrayal of Lolita is considered problematic, Kubrick enlarging Quilty's role and making him Humbert's nemesis is inspired and contributes significantly to the film's success.

Overall, these changes in narrative voice, structure, and characterization result in a movie that differs from the novel in tone and structure. Kubrick would later express in interviews that he regretted that the pressure of meeting censorship standards had also altered the story in the film in that Humbert's feelings of romantic love toward Lolita come across early on, rather than toward the end, as in the novel.

Significance

In part because of the controversy surrounding its content, *Lolita* performed well at the box office. The film was produced on a budget of $2 million and went on to earn more than $9 million after its initial release. Since the United States did not yet have a film rating system, the film had no audience restrictions. In England, however, the film received an X rating, limiting its audience to those age sixteen or older. *Lolita* was also nominated for several film awards, though it only won one. Lyon won a Golden Globe Award for New Star of the Year, Actress, for her portrayal of Lolita. Even though Nabokov's screenplay

was not fully utilized in the film, he was nominated for an Academy Award for Writing (Screenplay-Based on Material from Another Medium), and the Directors Guild of America nominated Kubrick for Outstanding Directorial Achievement in Feature Film. Mason, Winters, and Sellers were also nominated for Golden Globe Awards.

Although Kubrick's film adaptation received mixed reviews upon its release, the film has garnered more appreciation and respect over time. Some early reviewers believed that the threat of censorship from the Hays Code derailed the film and made an accurate depiction of Nabokov's novel impossible, and others criticized the fact that Lolita was played by an older teen rather than a younger one, and the effect of this on the story. Even Kubrick himself was disappointed in the final product. Over time, however, the film has gained admiration. In a review of a collection of Kubrick's work, Brian Tallerico noted that in the case of *Lolita*, he believes the censorship restrictions resulted in a better film, one that is more dream-like rather than a literal translation. Kubrick's *Lolita* is considered a classic, and it is included in the special masterpiece collection of all Kubrick's best films.

—*Marybeth Rua-Larsen*

Further Reading

Connolly, Julian W. "*Lolita*'s Afterlife: Critical and Cultural Responses." *A Reader's Guide to Nabokov's "Lolita,"*, Academic Studies Press, 2009, pp. 141-74.

Trubikhina, Julia. "'Cinemizing' as Translation: Nabokov's Screenplay of *Lolita* and Stanley Kubrick's and Adrian Lyne's Cinematic Versions." *The Translator's Doubts: Vladimir Nabokov and the Ambiguity of Translation*, Academic Studies Press, 2015, pp. 141-205.

Bibliography

Burns, Dan E. "Pistols and Cherry Pies: *Lolita* From Page to Screen." *Literature/Film Quarterly*, vol. 12, no. 4, 1984, pp. 245-50.

Crowther, Bosley. "*Lolita*, Vladimir Nabokov's Adaptation of His Novel." Review of *Lolita*, directed by Stanley Kubrick. *The New York Times*, 14 June 1962, archive.nytimes.com/www.nytimes.com/library/film/061462kubrick-lolita.html. Accessed 29 Nov. 2018.

Harriet Duckett, Victoria. "Letting Lolita Laugh." *Literature/Film Quarterly*, vol. 42, no. 3, 2014, pp. 528-40.

Prescott, Orville. Review of *Lolita*, by Vladimir Nabokov. *The New York Times*, 18 Aug. 1958, archive.nytimes.com/www.nytimes.com/books/97/03/02/lifetimes/nab-r-booksoftimes.html. Accessed 29 Nov. 2018.

Rolo, Charles J. Review of *Lolita*, by Vladimir Nabokov. *The Atlantic*, Sept. 1958, www.theatlantic.com/magazine/archive/1958/09/lolita-by-vladimir-nabokov/304639/. Accessed 29 Nov. 2018.

Tallerico, Brian. "Foreground Material: 'Stanley Kubrick: The Masterpiece Collection.'" Review of *Stanley Kubrick: The Masterpiece Collection*, directed by Stanley Kubrick. *RogerEbert.com*, 8 Dec. 2014, www.rogerebert.com/demanders/foreground-material-stanley-kubrick-the-masterpiece-collection. Accessed 29 Nov. 2018.

Tan, Amy. "Personal Best: *Lolita*." *Salon*, 30 Sept. 1996, www.salon.com/1996/09/30/tan_2/. Accessed 29 Nov. 2018.

Lost Girls

The Novel
Author: Robert Kolker
First published: 2013

The Film
Year released: 2020
Director: Liz Garbus (b. 1970)
Screenplay by: Michael Werwie
Starring: Amy Ryan, Thomasin McKenzie, Gabriel Byrne, Lola Kirke, Oona Laurence, Dean Winters, Reed Birney, Kevin Corrigan

Context

The 2020 drama *Lost Girls* is based on the tragic true story of Mari Gilbert, whose campaign to find her missing daughter led to the discovery of a previously unknown serial killer operating in Long Island's South Shore area between the 1990s and the 2010s. Dubbed Long Island Serial Killer, also known as the Gilgo Beach Killer and the Craigslist Ripper, the suspect is connected to the abduction and murder of four young sex workers. Police believe that the killer, who has never been apprehended, may have murdered as many as ten to sixteen people over a twenty-year span.

Journalist Robert Kolker first wrote an article about the events that led to the discovery of the Long Island Serial Killer for *New York* magazine in May 2011. Two years later, he expanded on the subject in the book *Lost Girls: An Unsolved American Mystery* (2013). The book focuses on Mari Gilbert's search for her missing daughter Shannan, a sex worker and aspiring actor, and uses interviews with Gilbert, police officers, journalists, and many others to piece together the events surrounding the crimes. Shannan Gilbert went missing on May 1, 2010, after visiting a client in the Oak Beach area. Gilbert felt that her daughter's life and safety were being undervalued by the police because she had been working as a sex worker. After months of Gilbert pressuring law enforcement and giving interviews to the press, a new investigation was launched. In December 2010, a police officer working with a police dog in training found the remains of a woman heavily decomposed and wrapped in burlap near Ocean Parkway. Police then uncovered three additional bodies in the same area. This was when law enforcement first told reporters that the deaths might have been the result of a serial killer.

Shannan Gilbert's body was not among those discovered off Ocean Parkway and Gilbert continued to investigate on her own and to pressure law enforcement to continue the case. In March 2011, officers discovered another burial site located near Gilgo and Oak Beach. An additional six bodies were discovered between March and April, most of whom were also female sex workers, though there was an unidentified toddler and an Asian male also found among the bodies buried near Gilgo Beach. At first, it appeared that the remains might have been placed there by different killers, but the police later determined that all the murders were potentially committed by the same person. In December 2011, Shannan Gilbert's body was discovered not far from where she was last seen. Police believed that Shannan's death was unconnected to the other murders, instead stating that she had probably drowned while attempting to navigate a marsh.

The identity of the killer was not discovered, and so Kolker spends much of the book looking at the lives of the five women who were killed and buried near Oak Beach. Using his journalistic eye, Kolker provides a critical examination of America's sex work industry, how young women become prostitutes, and how police treat the abuse and murder of sex workers in America. Kolker's goal in the first half of the book is to refute the myths that prostitutes are degenerate or that prostitution is a "victimless crime." To this end, he not only covers the personal stories of prostitutes abused on the job, but also explores studies and statistics revealing that the leading cause of death for prostitutes is murder by a client. The second half of Kolker's book focuses on Shannan Gilbert, her move into prostitution while pursuing a career in acting, and her mother's efforts to push forward the investigation. Kolker looks at how digital technology, and specifically web services like Craigslist and social media, have transformed the prostitution industry. He also notes how these technological tools helped Gilbert and other mothers and family members whose daughters had gone missing to connect and to advocate for media and police attention to their long-abandoned missing persons cases.

Kolker's *Lost Girls* was a *New York Times* bestselling book and appeared on a number of top-ten book lists for 2013. He published during a time when true crime stories had become increasingly popular. Many major networks were airing true crime series, and podcasts and documentaries about real life crimes were gaining increasing public traction. In 2016, it was announced that a feature film based, in part, on Kolker's book was being produced and directed by Liz Garbus, a director known for her work on documentaries like *The Farm: Angola* (1998) and *What Happened, Miss Simone?* (2015). The film version, entitled *Lost Girls*, was Garbus's first high-profile feature film. The script was written by Michael Werwie, whose screenplay *Extremely Wicked, Shockingly Evil and Vile* (2019), about serial killer Ted Bundy, gained critical acclaim. *Lost Girls* was screened at the Sundance Film Festival in January 2020 before being released by the streaming service Netflix in March.

Film Analysis

Unlike Kolker's book-length investigation of the Long Island Serial Killer case, the film *Lost Girls* only obliquely addresses the social justice issues surrounding prostitution. Instead, it focuses more directly on the material from the second half of the book. The film opens with Mari Gilbert (Amy Ryan) and her daughters Sherre (Thomasin McKenzie) and Sarra (Oona Laurence) struggling with the recent disappearance of Mari's eldest daughter, twenty-four-year-old Shannan (Sarah Wisser). Having heard nothing from police after filing a missing person's case, Gilbert begins investigating on her own. Knowing that her daughter was working as a prostitute, Gilbert tracks down individuals who knew her, including driver Michael Pak (James Hiroyuki Liao), who drove Shannan to a client's house in a gated community the last time she was seen alive. She discovers that her daughter had called 911 on the night of her disappearance, telling the dispatcher, "They are trying to kill me." Police did not arrive at the scene until an hour later, by which time the only sign of Shannan was the young woman's jacket.

Growing increasingly frustrated, Gilbert visits the Suffolk Country Police, accusing them of ignoring her daughter's call because Shannan was a prostitute. She is told by Officer Dean Bostick (Dean Winters) that her daughter's lifestyle meant that her disappearance was not being treated as a homicide. Police later explain that Shannan allegedly did not provide her location, making it difficult for police to investigate. Police only came to Oak Beach after another resident called the police about a young woman banging on his door, screaming for help. Officer Bostick is not based on a real person but was manufactured by the filmmakers to embody the sexism and dismissive attitude towards sex workers representative of some police officers, administrators, and politicians. Bostick's distinctively prejudiced and sexist dialogue is taken from comments that Gilbert reported from different officers on various occasions, but the character streamlines the process of demonstrating how law enforcement ignored and dismissed the case until Gilbert became more closely involved.

In the film, an unnamed officer working with a dog accidentally discovers bodies on the north side of Ocean Parkway, leading to the discovery of the first three victims later assigned to the Long Island Serial Killer. Gilbert learns that none of the discovered young women are her daughter and is told by Commissioner Richard Dormer (Gabriel Byrne) that she should avoid speaking to the press, as the investigation is ongoing. The film then briefly veers to follow the investigation into the crime as police interview Pak and other individuals who may have been witness to Shannan's last night, but new evidence on her whereabouts is not forthcoming. Convinced that she is being dismissed or ignored, Gilbert continues to pressure police.

Using social media, Gilbert also creates a support group for women who have lost daughters, sisters, or friends who had been working as prostitutes before their disappearance. Meetings between the women in this group provide a way for the film to delve into some of the subjects covered in more detail in Kolker's journalistic study of the Long Island Serial Killer. The women discuss, for instance, how Craigslist had been co-opted by the prostitution industry, providing a nigh-untraceable way for prostitutes to market their services. Using burner phones and posting numbers through Craigslist, prostitutes are able to locate clients, but when a prostitute goes missing, there is little way for police to track down the last clients that the prostitute may have visited. In the meetings between Gilbert and the other women, their discussions also focus in on how sex workers are dismissed and devalued, especially by men, who appear to feel that their involvement in prostitution makes them less valuable.

Though many of the women in Gilbert's group have already learned that their loved ones are dead, Gilbert is still tortured, as Shannan's body has not yet been found. With the police still finding nothing, she continues to investigate on her own, tracking down a physician who called her the day after her daughter went missing claiming he had helped Shannan that night. This potential lead provides further room to reflect on police inactivity. In the film, Commissioner Dormer—unlike Bostick's chauvinistic and persistently dismissive character—is portrayed as attempting to engage in a more thorough investigation. Despite his attempts, Gilbert is still not satisfied, frequently pressuring the police through media appearances, and eventually pressing Dormer to search the marsh near Oak Beach, the only place that had not yet been searched.

When the marsh is finally searched Shannan's remains are found at last, but there is little closure. Because her body was located in a different area than the others, police believe that Shannan was not a victim of the same killer, but that she had tried to navigate the marsh and died in the process. Gilbert funds her own autopsy and finds evidence to suggest that Shannan may, in fact, have been strangled, though this evidence was not considered by the police. The identity of the killer is left undiscovered, but the story focuses more on Gilbert and the other women who refused to let the issue go. Speaking in interviews, director Liz Garbus said that the film is above all about "listening to women" and the tendency of men and those in authority to ignore the claims of women or those deemed outside of mainstream or respectable society.

Significance

Some critics found the film version of *Lost Girls* a little dark and cumbersome, but it received a positive response overall. Many found the film notable for its focus on the victims' families, who attempt to come to grips with their losses, rather than on the murders themselves or the crime investigation. Reviewers also found much to appreciate in Amy Ryan's performance. Writing for *Variety*, Owen Gleiberman said that Ryan delivers "ravaged fury" with a resonant performance in which her "anger coats a heart of tragic self-awareness." Even in otherwise negative reviews Ryan's performance was singled out as a highlight.

While Garbus's theatrical version of *Lost Girls* undoubtedly allowed Netflix to capitalize on the growing popularity of the true crime drama, the film's focus on the welfare of the victims and the devaluation of sex workers and women who are seen as "wayward," provided a unique angle for the film and helped to translate some of the deeper social commentary of Kolker's book to the theatrical format.

—Micah Issitt

Further Reading
Kolker, Robert. *Lost Girls: An Unsolved American Mystery*. Harper, 2013.

Kolker, Robert. "Women and Consent: An Interview with Robert Kolker about Lost Girls." Interview by Matthew Turbeville. *Robert Kolker*, Mar. 2018, robertkolker.com/news-and-events/2018/3/16/women-and-consent-an-interview-with-robert-kolker-about-lost-girls. Accessed 26 Mar. 2021.

Mack, Jessica. "'Lost Girls: An Unsolved American Mystery' Is a Tribute to Five Prostitutes." *The Guardian*, 6 Aug. 2013, www.theguardian.com/commentisfree/2013/aug/06/robert-kolker-lost-girls-prostitute-deaths. Accessed 26 Mar. 2021.

Bibliography
Dargis, Manohla. "'Lost Girls' Review: Honoring the Gone Girls, With Sorrow and Rage." Review of *Lost Girls*, directed by Liz Garbus. *The New York Times*, 11 Mar. 2020, www.nytimes.com/2020/03/11/movies/lost-girls-review.html. Accessed 8 Mar. 2021.

Gleiberman, Owen. Review of *Lost Girls*, directed by Liz Garbus. *Variety*, 29 Jan. 2020, variety.com/2020/film/reviews/lost-girls-review-amy-ryan-liz-garbus-1203484766/. Accessed 10 Mar. 2021.

Goldberg, Matt. "'Lost Girls' Review: Netflix Offers a Narrow and Tedious True Crime Retelling." *Collider*, 13 Mar. 2020, collider.com/lost-girls-movie-review-netflix. Accessed 8 Mar. 2021.

Lee, Benjamin. "'Lost Girls' Review—Well-Intentioned But Plodding Netflix True Crime Drama." Review of *Lost Girls*, directed by Liz Garbus. *The Guardian*, 10 Mar. 2020, www.theguardian.com/film/2020/mar/10/lost-girls-review-well-intentioned-but-plodding-netflix-true-drama. Accessed 9 Mar. 2021.

Swartz, Mimi. "Gone Girls." Review of *Lost Girls*, by Robert Kolker. *The New York Times*, 3 July 2013, www.nytimes.com/2013/07/07/books/review/lost-girls-by-robert-kolker.html. Accessed 10 Mar. 2021.

Tallerico, Brian. Review of *Lost Girls*, directed by Liz Garbus. *RogerEbert.com*, 13 Mar. 2020, www.rogerebert.com/reviews/lost-girls-2020. Accessed 9 Mar. 2021.

Love, Simon

The Novel
Author: Becky Albertalli (b. 1982)
First published: 2015

The Film
Year released: 2018
Director: Greg Berlanti (b. 1972)
Screenplay by: Isaac Aptaker, Elizabeth Berger
Starring: Nick Robinson, Josh Duhamel, Jennifer Garner

Context
When gay characters have appeared in mainstream romantic comedies, they have usually appeared in the supporting role that has come to be termed the gay best friend. In films like *Clueless* (1995), *My Best Friend's Wedding* (1997), and *Mean Girls* (2004), a gay man, single, serves to cheer on his straight best friend in her search for true love. *Love, Simon* breaks this mold by focusing on a gay protagonist who comes to find true love himself. The film is therefore a step forward for the genre of the teen romantic comedy.

The film is based on Becky Albertalli's bestselling 2016 young adult novel *Simon vs. The Homo Sapiens Agenda*. Albertalli later published a sequel, *Leah on the Offbeat* (2018), which focuses on Simon's best friend, and has collaborated with Adam Silvera on *What If It's Us?* (2018). Director Greg Berlanti brought vast experience as a producer and director to the film version. Berlanti made his directorial debut with *The Broken Hearts Club* (2001), which centered on a group of gay protagonists, and he later served as an executive producer for several television series aimed at teenagers, including *Dawson's Creek* (1999-2001), *Riverdale* (2016-), and *The Chilling Adventures of Sabrina* (2018-). The screenplay for the film was written by Isaac Aptaker and Elizabeth Berger, showrun- ners for the popular television show *This Is Us* (2016-). *Love, Simon* has been compared to the seminal John Hughes' films from the 1980's, exploring the lives of a group of suburban teenagers who navigate high school and experience the bittersweet nature of growing up. But with its polish and its beguiling cast, it owes at least as much to the teen dramas that Berlanti produced for television. *Love, Simon* is a movie with a lot of heart, with performances that are genuine and moving, and with a storyline that hooks the audience and gets them rooting for Simon's love story.

Film Analysis
Love, Simon draws the viewer into its protagonist's life right from the start, with a conversational voice-over by Simon (Nick Robinson) filling the audience in on the particulars his life. He seems to have it all: a loving family, an affluent but sensible lifestyle, and a group of fun and supportive friends. Simon also has a secret that weighs on him: he is gay, but he is not yet ready to share this truth with his friends and family. The audience is introduced to Simon's parents, Emily (Jennifer Garner) and Jack (Josh Duhamel), and younger sister, Nora (Talitha Eliana Bateman), early in the film. It then follows Simon through a typical day as he carpools to school with his friends Leah (Katherine Langford), Nick (Jorge Lendeborg Jr.), and Abby (Alexandra Shipp), attends classes, and goes to after-school play rehearsal. While Simon suspects that his family and friends would accept him were he to come out, he is not yet ready to disrupt his current life to do so.

Then, an anonymous user in an internet chatroom posts a message that identifies him as a gay student at the same high school that Simon attends. After the user writes about how difficult it is for him to live with his secret, Simon, using a pseudonym of his own, decides to write back. The two begin a deep and heartfelt correspondence. The identity of this other boy, who goes only by the screenname Blue, is the central mystery that runs through the film. In a clever trick of the medium, various characters are seen typing or heard voicing Blue's responses, as Simon considers whether each of these characters might be the boy he is falling in love with. This is only one of several ways in which Berlanti and the film's screenwriters exploit the resources of the medium. A musical dance routine, in which Simon imagines coming out at college, is another effective set-piece, as is a montage of scenes in which Simon imagines what it would be like were his heterosexual friends to have to come out as straight to their parents. The film likewise deftly incorporates text messages, emails, and other artifacts of its characters' digital lives into its visual palette. One of the most touching exchanges in the film, for example, comes in the form of text messages between Simon and his mother, that pop up on the screen the way they might on an audience member's phone. It is a strength of this production that it shows such visual imagination, relating aspects of Simon's story in a way that is only possible through the medium of film.

The film also tones down some of the more explicit or edgy aspects of the novel. As Doreen St. Félix points out in an article for the *New Yorker*, any sexual references or erotic energy in Simon and Blue's email exchanges are edited out in the transition from page to screen. St. Félix writes, "Berlanti's balancing act for the mainstream leaves little room for the physical expression of gay love." Simon's visit to a gay bar in the novel is likewise excised in the screenplay.

The story takes a dramatic turn when Simon leaves his email account open on a school computer, and a fellow student, Martin (Logan Miller), learns his secret. Martin approaches Simon, telling him that unless Simon helps to set Martin up with Abby, he'll tell everyone that Simon is gay. This is actually the scene with which Albertalli's novel opens; she hooks the reader with this predicament and only later does she fill in Simon's backstory and establish the other characters and subplots. The film benefits from its reordering of events, causing the viewer to be already deeply invested in Simon by time Martin begins to blackmail him and disrupt his life.

In a series of scenes, Simon begins to incorporate Martin into his own friend group. Miller turns in one of the film's strongest performances, and his Martin is a complex and eminently watchable character. By turns touching and infuriating, the socially awkward Martin destabilizes the relationships between Simon and his friends. While Abby has no romantic interest in Martin, she does eventually begin to appreciate the empowering and off-kilter energy that he brings to their play rehearsals and to their budding friendship. Simon, meanwhile, actively discourages Nick from pursuing Abby; he makes up a series of stories, from her having a college-age boyfriend to her being in interested in Martin, to dissuade Nick from acting on his crush. Leah has a crush of her own, but Si-

mon encourages her to start dating Nick. Simon's secret therefore begins to weigh on all of his friends and to disrupt the happy equilibrium that the film established in its opening scenes.

Martin eventually makes a disastrous, public confession of his love for Abby at a high school football game. Desperate to shift the public eye toward someone else after he is rejected and bullied online, Martin posts screenshots of Simon's emails with Blue to the school's website. The film's crisis is heartfelt and effective; Simon's hand has been forced and he is outed to the school on someone else's terms rather than choosing to come out on his own. His friends learn that he has been betraying them and subsequently shun him. In perhaps the most devastating turn of events, Blue deactivates his account and effectively disappears.

From this low point, Simon makes a series of decisions regarding what kind of life he will make for himself and what kinds of new relationships he will form with his friends and family. His scenes with his parents are particularly effective and touching. Both Jennifer Garner and Josh Duhamel are compelling in their roles as Simon's mother and father, and Duhamel is particularly effective in a scene where he realizes how his years of jokes and comments must have affected his son. In the inspiring climax to the film, Simon publicly invites Blue, whose identity he still does not know, to meet him at a local amusement park's Ferris wheel. The image of Simon riding the Ferris wheel feels quintessentially cinematic. "I deserve a great love story," Simon says, and by film's end, Blue's identity is revealed and Simon has gotten his love story.

Significance

Love, Simon was a commercial success. Produced for about $17 million, the film made over $40 million domestically and another $25 million internationally by the end of 2018. Critics were generally positive in their appreciation of the film; however, many reviewers criticized aspects of the film as being overly mainstream or homogenized. Nevertheless, critics acknowledged the deftness of its screenplay, the strength of the actors' performances, and the importance its depiction of a gay protagonist.

St. Félix writes, "the film is as sweet as bubble-gum flavored medicine; it arrives as if without cinematic lineage —unburdened by cinema's history of equating gayness with death." Kenny praises the "spectacularly charming cast," and writes of the film's conclusion, "the emotional resonance may be surprising given the movie's relentless gloss, but it's real." Writing for the *Atlantic*, David Sims quibbled with the flatness of Simon, but saw this very ordinariness as "pioneering" in and of itself. Sims writes, "there have been dozens of mediocre studio films about straight teen romances over the decades; it says something about the direction of the film industry to finally see one centered on a young gay man."

Other reviewers saw the mainstream nature of *Love, Simon* as a more wholly positive quality, linking it to great teen films of past generations. Richard Roeper, writing in the *Chicago Sun-Times*, compared *Love, Simon* to such John Hughes films as *Sixteen Candles* (1984) and *The Breakfast Club* (1985). Roeper describes the screenplay as "smart and charismatic" and Berlanti's direction as "nimble." Peter Travers, for *Rolling Stone*, noted that "Greg Berlanti's extraordinary drama is the first mainstream studio release to put a closeted teen front and center." He continued, "*Love, Simon* is a John Hughes movie for audiences who just got woke. And for all its attempts not to offend, it's a genuine groundbreaker."

Many outside of the film industry likewise saw this as an important film. Sarah Kate Ellis, president and chief executive of GLAAD, told George Gene Gustines for *The New York Times* (14 Mar. 2018) that *Love, Simon* is "the *Sixteen Candles* of this generation," and said that the film is "really powerful and will do a whole lot of good." Fans of the film have echoed this praise. Director Greg Berlanti told Gustines in the wake of his film's release, "I've had a lot of people tell me this is the movie they wish they had when they were kids." *Love, Simon* is a critically important step forward in the representation of gay characters on the screen.

—Matthew Bolton

Bibliography

Gustines, George Gene. "A Romantic Comedy about a Teenager? What Took So Long?" *The New York Times*, 1 Mar. 2018, www.nytimes.com/2018/03/14/movies/love-simon-gay-romantic-comedy.html. Accessed 27 Dec. 2018.

Kenny, Glenn. "Review: In 'Love, Simon,' a Glossy Teen Romance, the Hero has a Secret." Review of *Love, Simon*, directed by Greg Berlanti. *The New York Times*, 15 Mar. 2018, www.nytimes.com/2018/03/15/movies/love-simon-review.html. Accessed 27 Dec. 2018.

Roeper, Richard. "'Love, Simon' a Powerful Page Torn from the John Hughes Filmmaking Playbook." Review of *Love, Simon*, directed by Greg Berlanti. *The Chicago Sun Times*, 15 Mar. 2018, chicago.suntimes.com/entertainment/love-simon-a-powerful-page-torn-from-the-john-hughes-filmmaking-playbook. Accessed 27 Dec. 2018.

Sims, David. "Love, Simon is Groundbreakingly Ordinary." Review of *Love, Simon*, directed by Greg Berlanti. *The Atlantic*, 13 Mar. 2018, www.theatlantic.com/entertainment/archive/2018/03/love-simon-review/555422/. Accessed 27 Dec. 2018.

St. Félix, Doreen. "The Chaste Optimism of 'Love, Simon.'" Review of *Love, Simon*, directed by Greg Berlanti. *The New Yorker*, 20 Mar. 2018, www.newyorker.com/culture/culture-desk/the-chaste-optimism-of-love-simon. Accessed 27 Dec. 2018.

Travers, Peter. "'Love, Simon' Review: Gay Teen Romance is 'John Hughes for Woke Audiences.'" Review of *Love, Simon*, directed by Greg Berlanti. *Rolling Stone*, 13 Mar. 2018, www.rollingstone.com/movies/movie-reviews/love-simon-review-gay-teen-romance-is-john-hughes-for-woke-audiences-127832/. Accessed 27 Dec. 2018.

Mansfield Park

The Novel
Author: Jane Austen (1775-1817)
First published: 1814

The Film
Year released: 1999
Director: Patricia Rozema (b. 1958)
Screenplay by: Patricia Rozema
Starring: Frances O'Connor, Jonny Lee Miller, Embeth Davidtz, Alessandro Nivola, Harold Pinter

Context

The 1990s saw a surge of Austen adaptations, including *Sense and Sensibility* (1995), *Persuasion* (1995), *Pride and Prejudice* (1995), and *Emma* (1996). Emma Thompson, lead actress and screenwriter for *Sense and Sensibility*, made numerous changes to the script seeking to stand out from the others and, in particular, hoping to market the film to a broad modern audience and not just to fans of period drama or literary adaptations. Thompson, among things, made the Dashwood sisters, Elinor and Marianne, older, and exaggerating class differences in order to help modern audiences better understand issues like inheritance and the difficulties of women facing the marriage market. While these changes, in total, are significant, and Thompson included scenes entirely invented for the screen, the film nevertheless follows Austen's plot, dialogue, and vision, amplifying at points to help audiences grapple with the historical intricacies.

Rozema believed that Austen's work was more politically astute, in terms of Austen's view of the roles of women and politics in general, than had been previously recognized, and she wanted to convey this belief in *Mansfield Park*. Rozema made the heroine, Fanny Price, stronger both in body and in spirit, emphasized the Bertram family's use of slave labor, and moved sexuality to the forefront. Other directors have tried similar tactics to re-envision Austen's work. Director Amy Heckerling, for example, reworked *Emma* into *Clueless* (1995), a teen comedy starring Alicia Silverstone about a rich high-school student who befriends and provides a makeover to a new girl in her school. Similar to Rozema, director Autumn de Wilde's 2020 film adaptation of *Emma*, starring Anya Taylor-Joy, focused on the comedic aspects of the story, particularly in the manners of the Regency period.

Although all three of these adaptations are considered more revisionist than traditional, Rozema's adaptation distinguishes itself as perhaps the boldest and most overtly political.

Film Analysis

Compared to Austen's other novels, particularly *Pride and Prejudice* (1813) and *Emma* (1815), there are few adaptations of *Mansfield Park*. Many critics find Fanny Price to be a problematic heroine, sickly by nature, stubborn, prim. In her adaptation, Rozema offered a more modern interpretation of the novel and its heroine by merging Austen's Fanny Price with Austen herself and making Fanny Price (Frances O'Connor) a writer. Thus, there are three significant ways Rozema's adaptation of *Mansfield Park* veers from Austen's original text. First, Rozema makes Fanny Price a version of the author and uses Austen's biographical information and juvenile writing as part of the story; second, is her focus on slavery; and third, is her decision to include more explicit sexuality. While these additions did not result in making Mansfield Park a big box office draw, they did produce a modern, enjoyable adaptation.

One of the most significant changes Rozema made in adapting the novel to film was changing Fanny Price's physical attributes. In Austen's novel, Fanny is physically weak and sickly. Activity, even walking, exhausted her, and when young Edmund encouraged her to learn to ride the "old grey pony" her health improved. Subsequently, when the old grey pony was no longer available and there was no other horse to ride, Fanny's health declined until Edmund noticed and remedied the situation by trading in one of his own horses for a horse she could ride. In the film, little is made of Fanny's health or weakness. In fact, there is a boisterous scene in which Edmund (Jonny Lee Miller) and Fanny are teasing each other, tumbling, and running through the house and grounds until they, particularly Fanny, are admonished by Sir Thomas (Harold Pinter). Fanny is physically stronger in the film, and a later scene where Edmund, infatuated with Mary Crawford (Embeth Davidtz), allows Mary to ride Fanny's horse, focuses more on Fanny's quiet jealousy of Edmund's attentions to Mary than issues of her health. In the novel, the jealousy is much more subtle, and Edmund supports Mary's continued riding by explaining, "You [Mary] have been promoting her [Fanny] comfort by preventing her from setting off half an hour sooner: clouds are now coming up, and she will not suffer from the heat as she would have done then." Because worries about Fanny's health are not a significant factor in the film, Fanny is free to focus on romance. Her physical strength also suggests a mental strength and a young woman who is more decisive and less meek than her depiction in the novel.

More important than Fanny's physical health is Rozema's decision to merge Austen's biography into the Fanny Price character. In one of the first scenes in the film, a ten-year-old Fanny (Hannah Taylor Gordon) is in bed reciting one of her own stories to her younger sister, Susan (Talya Gordon). Fanny is reading a short excerpt from Austen's juvenile novella, *Love and Friendship* [sic], and this scene sets the stage for the film's persistent portrayal of Fanny as a writer. In the novel, Fanny is sickly, an avid reader of literature, and a letter-writer to her brother William, but she is not a writer of literature. In the film, Rozema transforms Fanny into a much more spirited character by making her a writer who reads from Austen's early work, which focused on wit and farce, making it harder to see Fanny as the frail, meek character of the novel. Rozema ends the film with Edmund and Fanny discussing the upcoming publication of one of her novels, which Edmund has arranged. Consequently, Rozema's portrayal of Fanny as a robust writer differs significantly from the novel, ultimately making Fanny Price a stronger character and a more modern heroine.

Rozema also chooses to further politicize the film by intensifying the focus on slavery. In the novel, the topic of slavery is only raised once. Sir Thomas uses slave labor to run his plantations in Antigua and maintain the family's wealth. When Fanny mentions the topic of slaves, she is met with silence. Some critics interpret that silence as

Austen's subtle way of criticizing slavery because there is documented evidence that Austen was familiar with arguments against slavery at the time, including the passage of the Slave Trade Act in 1807. Rozema builds on that subtle criticism by adding scenes that were not in the novel to make the criticism much more overt. Slavery is depicted and discussed throughout the film, starting with an early scene in which young Fanny is traveling to Mansfield Park by coach. The coach makes a stop, and Fanny hears chanting. When she asks the coachman about the chanting, he points to the slave ship docked near the coast. Other key scenes center on Tom Bertram's (James Purefoy) illness. While caring for Tom, Fanny finds his sketchbook, which includes graphic drawings depicting torture, the rape of an African female slave by a group of Caucasian men, and Sir Thomas Bertram towering over a female slave. Fanny is shocked, and Sir Thomas takes the sketch pad and burns it in the fire, calling his son "mad." Later, however, Sir Thomas realizes the error of his ways, offering an apology to his gravely ill son, and, in the ending montage that offers updates on all the characters, Fanny announces that Sir Thomas has sold his West Indies assets to invest in tobacco. None of these scenes are in the novel, yet Rozema adds a political awareness and emotional depth that Austen only hints at.

One last significant way in which the novel differs from the film is Rozema's decision to include more sexual innuendo and more sexually explicit scenes. Jane Austen, writing in the early 1800s, makes at best only faint allusions to sex. When Maria Bertram leaves her husband to run off with Henry Crawford, Fanny learns the news through her father as he reads aloud from the newspaper. Austen describes Maria's departure as "having quitted her husband's roof in company with the well-known and captivating Mr. C." This example is Austen at her most explicit. Rozema, on the other hand, portrays Maria's (Victoria Hamilton) affair with Henry Crawford (Alessandro Nivola) vividly and explicitly. Unlike the novel, in which the affair takes place in London, in the film the affair takes place at Mansfield Park and Fanny accidentally happens upon Maria and Henry's intimacy. Both characters are undressed, and the scene includes brief nudity. Other instances of sexuality are frequent but more subtle. On Sir Thomas's return from Antigua, for example, he comments on Fanny's attractiveness in an almost leering fashion and critics have commented on an intimate scene between Fanny and Mary Crawford, when Fanny gets caught in the rain and Mary helps her out of her wet dress in a way that suggests a lesbian attraction. In these scenes, Rozema provides a modern interpretation of Austen.

Significance

Mansfield Park received polarizing reviews. On the positive side, film critic Roger Ebert enthusiastically described it as "an uncommonly intelligent film, smart and amusing too, and anyone who thinks it is not faithful to Austen doesn't know the author but only her plots." Ebert found the film engaging because it was faithful to the spirit of the novel and offered a modern point of view. Critic Derek Elley from *Variety*, on the other hand, found the adaptation too clever. He wrote that the film "too often steps out of its era to adopt a knowing, politically correct, late-20th-century attitude to the society portrayed." While the acting, cinematography, and period costumes were praised, critics were split on Rozema's unique—some have said "eccentric"—re-visioning of the novel.

The split opinion found in the reviews did not help *Mansfield Park* achieve box office success. Released November 18, 1999, the film cost $10 million to make but grossed less than $5 million over its fifty-eight-week run. Compared with 1996's adaptation of *Emma*, starring Gwyneth Paltrow, which grossed $22 million, and 1995's *Sense and Sensibility*, starring Emma Thompson, which grossed over $134 million worldwide during its run, respectively, Rozema's *Mansfield Park* was a box office disappointment. Similarly, while *Emma* and *Sense and Sensibility* won and were nominated for numerous prestigious awards, including Academy Awards and Golden Globes, *Mansfield Park* was excluded from the big awards, although it was nominated for several awards at

smaller film festivals, such as the Chicago International Film Festival and Montreal World Film Festival, which recognized Canadian-born Rozema's efforts. While some critics thought Rozema veered too far away from Austen's vision and intent, Rozema's approach still stands out as fresh and thought-provoking.

—*Marybeth Rua-Larsen*

Further Reading

Bartine, David, and Eileen Maguire. "Contrapuntal Critical Readings of Jane Austen's *Mansfield Park*: Resolving Edward Said's Paradox." *Interdisciplinary Literary Studies*, vol. 11, no. 1, 2009, pp. 32-56.
Despotopoulou, Anna. "Girls on Film: Postmodern Renderings of Jane Austen and Henry James." *The Yearbook of English Studies*, vol. 36, no. 1, 2006, pp. 115-30.

Bibliography

Aragay, Mireia. "Possessing Jane Austen: Fidelity, Authorship, and Patricia Rozema's *Mansfield Park* (1999)." *Literature/Film Quarterly*, vol. 31, no. 3, 2003, pp. 177-185. *JSTOR*, www.jstor.org/stable/43797119. Accessed 15 Mar. 2020.
Ebert, Roger. "*Mansfield Park*." *RogerEbert.com*, 24 Nov. 1999, www.rogerebert.com/reviews/mansfield-park-1999. Accessed 21 Mar. 2020.
Elley, Derek. "*Mansfield Park*." *Variety*, 6 Sept. 1999, variety.com/1999/film/reviews/mansfield-park-2-1200459211/. Accessed 21 Mar. 2020.
Monaghan, David. "Reinventing Fanny Price: Patricia Rozema's Thoroughly Modern *Mansfield Park*." *Mosaic: An Interdisciplinary Critical Journal*, vol. 40, no. 3, 2007, pp. 85-101. *JSTOR*, www.jstor.org/stable/44030266. Accessed 15 Mar. 2020.
Moussa, Hiba, and Patricia Rozema. "*Mansfield Park* and Film: An Interview with Patricia Rozema." *Literature/Film Quarterly*, vol. 32, no. 4, 2004, pp. 255-60. *JSTOR*, www.jstor.org/stable/43797718. Accessed 15 Mar. 2020.

Mary, Queen of Scots

The Novel
Author: John Guy (b. 1949)
First published: 2004

The Film
Year released: 2018
Director: Josie Rourke (b. 1976)
Screenplay by: Beau Willimon
Starring: Saoirse Ronan, Margot Robbie, Jack Lowden, Joe Alwyn, David Tennant, Guy Pearce

Context

There have been many biographies about the remarkable Mary Stuart, queen of Scotland from 1542 to 1567. The sole heir to James V of Scotland, Mary ascended to the throne when she was only six days old. Much of her adult life was spent in rivalry with her first cousin once removed, Queen Elizabeth of England, about who had the right to sit on the English throne. After a Scottish uprising forced her to abdicate in favor of her infant son, Mary fled to England for protection. Elizabeth kept her in custody for eighteen years before having her executed in 1586 for plotting to assassinate the English queen.

Award-winning British historian John Guy, whose work focuses primarily on Tudor England, published *My Heart Is My Own: The Life of Mary Queen of Scots* in 2004. The book would go on to become an international bestseller, appearing in the United States as *Queen of Scots: The True Life of Mary Stuart*. Guy's intention was to clarify many aspects of the received wisdom surrounding Mary and Elizabeth—and many clichés, too, such as that the Scottish queen ruled by her heart while her English cousin ruled by her head, and that Mary was scheming and treacherous while Elizabeth was commanding and decisive. Guy argues that Mary was a pragmatist who made a number of deft political decisions. Furthermore, she was not the murderous adulteress that many have tried to depict her as.

Efforts to adapt Guy's book into a film began in 2007 when Scarlett Johansson agreed to play the titular role. However, after the American actor left the project, it languished until 2012, when actor Saoirse Ronan signed on to play Mary Stuart. Margot Robbie was brought on in 2017 to play opposite Ronan as Elizabeth I in the spring of 2017. Principal photography began several months later

with English director Josie Rourke at the helm. Rourke had been known primarily for her work as an art director in the London theater scene, and *Mary Queen of Scots* would mark her film debut. The task of adapting Guy's biography into a screenplay was given to Beau Willimon. Originally a playwright, Willimon had developed reputation for himself as the politically savvy writer behind the American television show *House of Cards*.

Film Analysis

Mary Queen of Scots is a historical drama, a genre of film that maintained a moderate level of popularity in the early twenty-first century. More often than not, period dramas are produced with the intention of winning awards; they not only require elaborate set design and costumes, they deal with serious human issues. *Mary Queen of Scots* was conceived as a sweeping epic, one that transports audiences to another world. Director Josie Rourke does everything in her power to bring sixteenth-century Scotland and England to life in a way that is appealing and accessible to contemporary viewers. Many historical dramas choose subdued, natural lighting and color palettes. In contrast, the visuals in *Mary Queen of Scots* are bright, polished, and strikingly beautiful. There is a crispness to the film's lighting that comes across as very modern. The characters' costumes, hair, and makeup are glamorous. Unlike many examples of the genre, Rourke's early modern England seems like a faraway fantasy land.

To convey that Mary (Saoirse Ronan) and Elizabeth (Margot Robbie) are one another's equals, Rourke ensures that each woman comes across as powerful in her own way. Mary is shot predominantly in medium and close-up shots, often filling the frame with a cold, stoic beauty. She wears blue and uses friendliness to appeal to others. Meanwhile, Elizabeth is depicted as having a more aggressive energy. She also looms large on screen, but is filmed mostly in medium and wide shots. She is often seen moving quickly around her castle in anger. Given her demeanor, it is not surprising that the color that becomes synonymous with Elizabeth is red. While the women use their intelligence, personalities, strengths, and emotions in different ways, it never seems that one has a clear advantage over the other until the end.

In addition to depicting a political drama, the film attempts to provide nuanced details of sixteenth-century royal life. Mary and her cohort of handmaids are often seen engaging in leisure activities like playing cards or listening to music. At one point, they dress her closest friend, David Rizzio (Ismael Cruz Cordova), in women's clothing as entertainment. These details are not limited to niceties, however. In one scene, for example, viewers see Queen Elizabeth in the aftermath of smallpox. Her once perfect complexion has been disfigured and audiences get a sense of how violent the disease was. In another, Mary has her menstrual blood washed off her legs by her handmaids. Rourke stated in interviews that she had to fight with the studio to include that scene. Here, the director's intention was twofold: Showcasing Mary's bodily functions was a way to demonstrate her humanity—in addition to being a queen, she was also a woman who faced the prospect of procreation. Beyond this, Rourke wanted to destigmatize on-screen menstruation.

Screenwriter Beau Willimon maintains a high level of tension throughout the film by depicting each woman's decision as a deliberate chess move against the other. This battle is present from the film's very first moments, which include a hero shot of Mary getting off of a boat from France and kissing the Scottish ground. She looks like royalty, especially in comparison to the nearby peasants, and radiates steely confidence and determination. It is clear that she intends to become queen, no matter what obstacles she faces. She soon writes her cousin, Queen Elizabeth, requesting a suitor to marry and to be named heir to the English throne. Elizabeth sends her spies and undesirable suitors as a way to deter Mary's plan. Mary chooses to marry an English noble, Lord Darnley (Jack Lowden), which instigates a constitutional crisis. When it turns out that he is gay, as well as lacking in good judgment, she demands that he help her conceive a child anyway. Her resulting pregnancy increases the legitimacy of her claim to the English throne, thus mak-

ing her a bigger threat to Elizabeth. The women's struggle for power continues for years until the film's very last scene, which is of Mary's execution.

While certain elements of the film's plot are true, there are a number of historical inaccuracies. Most historians argue that Mary was not smitten with Lord Darnley and that she would have spoken differently. Ronan plays Mary with a Scottish accent when in fact the young queen had spent most of her early life in France, and she routinely corresponded in French. Perhaps the most controversial change that the film made from the book is creating a scene in which Mary and Elizabeth meet. There is no evidence to suggest that the women ever met in person—their relationship existed solely through written correspondence. However, Willimon and Rourke's decision to have the women in a room together makes for good cinema. The scene takes place in the film's third act. At first, Mary and Elizabeth speak to one another behind sheets. Years have passed since their struggle began, and their meeting is supposed to be a secret. Suddenly, the sheets are pulled down and Elizabeth sees the woman she was threatened by for years is not as formidable as she once feared. In a defiant act of power, Elizabeth takes off her wig and shows her pockmarked face to demonstrate that not only is she not afraid, but she has the upper hand. It is a deeply affecting, resonant scene that brings the conflict between the two characters to its final chapter. Had Willimon stuck to the historical facts, the film may not have been as engaging.

Significance

Mary Queen of Scots premiered on November 15, 2018, at the American Film Institute (AFI) Festival in California and went into wide release in the United States on December 21, 2018. It opened in UK cinemas on January 18, 2019. It did not become especially popular among American audiences, drawing only $16.5 million at the US box office. Combined with the revenue from international screens, the film earned a total of $43 million—a success considering its $25 million budget.

Reception of *Mary Queen of Scots* was mixed, with most of the praise being directed at its cinematography as well as the lead actors' performances. Writing for *The New York Times*, A. O. Scott stated, "That coherence, and the contrast between Robbie's spooky, mannered performance and Ronan's spirited openness, make the movie consistently interesting even if it's not always convincing." Meanwhile, other reviews criticized the film's historical inaccuracy as well as its perceived lack of substance. In her review for the website *Vulture*, Emily Yoshida wrote, "It's these bizarre, ahistorical reads married with the intermittent stabs at a boardroom's idea of millennial values that render Mary a kind of nothing of a film." The film earned a number of award nominations for hair and makeup and costume design, and Margot Robbie scored some nominations for best supporting actress (such as from British Academy of Film and Television Arts [BAFTA] and the Screen Actors Guild), but major wins eluded the film.

Mary Queen of Scots has proved to be a significant film in a number of ways. To ensure that it resonated with modern audiences, Rourke made a number of unorthodox filmmaking choices that resulted in it feeling contemporary despite its historical setting. One such example of this is Rourke's decision to cast actors of color in Caucasian roles. For example, Asian British actress Gemma Chan plays Queen Elizabeth's friend Bess of Hardwick, while black actor Adrian Lester plays Thomas Randolph, her ambassador to Scotland. In interviews, Rourke has said that racial inclusivity was more important to her than historical accuracy. Similarly, the film's feminist undertones come across as atypical for a historical drama. Both Rourke and Willimon's ultimate goal was to provide audiences with an in-depth understanding of the nature of female power and its myriad challenges. *Mary Queen of Scots* demonstrates that despite what is taught in many classrooms, women have played an essential role in shaping the world's political and historical landscape.

—*Emily E. Turner*

Further Reading

Blyth, Antonia. "Mary Queen of Scots: Margot Robbie and Saoirse Ronan on Separation, Smallpox, and the Power behind the Female Throne." *Deadline*, 6 Jan. 2019, deadline.com/2019/01/mary-queen-of-scots-margot-robbie-saoirse-ronan-interview-female-throne-1202529307. Accessed 8 Mar. 2019.

Dunn, Jane. *Elizabeth and Mary: Cousins, Rivals, Queens.* Vintage, 2005.

Bibliography

Higgins, Charlotte. "Josie Rourke: 'I Was Fighting to Put a Period in a Period Movie.'" *The Guardian*, 2 Jan. 2019, www.theguardian.com/film/2019/jan/02/josie-rourke-interview-mary-queen-of-scots-2019-arts-preview. Accessed 8 Mar. 2019.

Loughrey, Clarisse. "*Mary Queen of Scots*: How Historically Accurate is It?" *The Independent*, 15 Jan. 2019, www.independent.co.uk/arts-entertainment/films/news/mary-queen-of-scots-historical-accuracy-meet-queen-elizabeth-margot-robbie-saoirse-ronan-a8666266.html. Accessed 8 Mar. 2019.

Scott, A. O. "*Mary Queen of Scots* Review: Sexy, Spirited, and Almost Convincing." *The New York Times*, 6 Dec. 2018, www.nytimes.com/2018/12/06/movies/mary-queen-of-scots-review.html. Accessed 8. Mar. 2019.

Yoshida, Emily. "*Mary Queen of Scots* Turns Its Queen into a Generic Underdog." *New York Magazine*, 6 Dec. 2018, www.vulture.com/2018/12/mary-queen-of-scots-review.html. Accessed 8 Mar. 2019.

The Men Who Stare at Goats

The Novel
Author: Jon Ronson (b. 1967)
First published: 2004

The Film
Year released: 2009
Director: Grant Heslov (b. 1963)
Screenplay by: Peter Straughan
Starring: George Clooney, Jeff Bridges, Ewan McGregor, Kevin Spacey

Context

A comedy blending elements of reality and fiction, the 2009 film *The Men Who Stare at Goats* was adapted from the 2004 book of the same name by Jon Ronson, a journalist and the author of books such as *Them: Adventures with Extremists* (2001) and *The Psychopath Test: A Journey through the Madness Industry* (2011). Known for exploring lesser-known areas of history and society through research and interviews, Ronson continued in that vein with *The Men Who Stare at Goats*, which describes efforts to study and potentially use phenomena such as psychic powers for military purposes. In addition to the titular individuals, who allegedly sought to kill goats using the power of their minds, the book delves into initiatives such as MK-ULTRA, a secret Central Intelligence Agency (CIA) project focused on controlling and manipulating the mind, as well as the psychological tactics used by the military in the early twenty-first century. In addition to discussing such topics in his book, Ronson starred in the 2004 television documentary *The Crazy Rulers of the World*, which dealt in part with some of the subjects discussed in *The Men Who Stare at Goats*.

The film adaptation of Ronson's work was the second feature film to be directed by Grant Heslov, a director as well as actor and screenwriter who had previously been nominated for the Academy Award for best original screenplay for the 2005 film *Good Night, and Good Luck*, alongside cowriter and star George Clooney. The two went on to become frequent creative collaborators, and Clooney later costarred in *The Men Who Stare at Goats* with Jeff Bridges, Ewan McGregor, and Kevin Spacey. The screenplay for the film was written by Peter Straughan, a playwright and screenwriter who went on to win critical acclaim for his work on the film *Tinker Tailor Soldier Spy* (2011) and the television miniseries *Wolf Hall* (2015). *The Men Who Stare at Goats* premiered at Italy's Venice Film Festival on September 8, 2009.

Film Analysis

In adapting *The Men Who Stare at Goats* for the screen, the filmmakers faced a substantial challenge due to the nature of Ronson's original work. The book *The Men Who Stare at Goats* is neither a fictional narrative nor a single linear narrative focusing on one particular real-world person or event. Rather, the book is a nonfiction work encompassing multiple decades of developments, intersecting yet largely distinct groups of individuals, and a host of different efforts to harness the power of the mind—or exploit its weaknesses—for the purposes of warfare, espionage, and torture. Ronson's work does not fall neatly into a traditional story arc suitable for film, instead moving back and forth between different times and places as Ronson's understanding of the events and programs he discusses grows. To adapt *The Men Who Stare at Goats* for the screen, Straughan was therefore tasked with constructing a compelling narrative arc that incorporated aspects of Ronson's work while translating some of the less cinema-friendly elements of the book into new forms suitable for the screen. Among those elements is Ronson's presence within his narrative, in which he documents in the first person his own attempts to tease out the truth underlying some of his subjects' most unbelievable anecdotes. Straughan transformed the narrative by making a character based somewhat on Ronson—newspaper reporter Bob Wilton (Ewan McGregor)—an active participant in the narrative itself, seeking out the truth and eventually becoming embroiled in it.

Much like Ronson's original book, *The Men Who Stare at Goats* frequently moves between the different eras at hand through the use of flashbacks. The film begins with a flashback taken directly from the first chapter of the book, depicting an army general (Stephen Lang) as he unsuccessfully attempts to overcome the limitations of the physical world and run through a solid wall. The focus then shifts to Bob, who, after being abandoned by his wife, seeks a new calling as a war reporter. He soon meets Lyn Cassady (George Clooney), a former member of the New Earth Army, a military unit dedicated to training its members in psychic skills for a variety of purposes related to espionage and peacekeeping. Through a series of flashbacks beginning in the 1970s, the film chronicles the origins of the New Earth Army, its activities under the leadership of Bill Django (Jeff Bridges), and its eventual downfall at the hands of member Larry Hooper (Kevin Spacey), who sought to find military uses for the psychic powers being explored. In one of the film's largest divergences from its source material, Bob and Lyn go on to travel to Iraq, where they survive various dangers before finding themselves at a research camp run by Larry, who is continuing his work from decades before. Although drawing in part from Ronson's explorations of psychological torture techniques used during the US wars in Iraq and Afghanistan and their connections to government research into psychic abilities and mental manipulation, the portion of the film set in Iraq is largely the invention of the filmmakers, giving the film an adventure plot that is not present in the book. The film's conclusion is drawn in part from Ronson's work, which devotes a chapter to an incident in which an enlightening report on the military's use of music for psychological purposes was largely ignored, with the news media reporting only on the most absurd—and thus seemingly innocuous—part of the story. Although Bob's reporting suffers the same fate at the end of the film, the character himself is convinced that everything he has learned is the truth, and he remains devoted to exploring the realm of psychic powers further.

The film adaptation not only introduces an adventure narrative, establishes strong relationships between characters such as Bob and Lyn, and draws a distinction between those who sought to use psychic abilities to promote peace and those who sought military applications for those abilities, but also takes a different approach to the book in terms of tone. Although comedic at times, such as when recounting the absurdity of certain incidents or conversa-

George Clooney. Photo by Michael Vlasaty via Wikimedia Commons.

tions, Ronson's original work is deeply critical of many of the government and military initiatives it discusses and the toll that such programs have taken on unwitting participants. This is perhaps most obvious in the chapters of the book focusing on Eric Olson, an American man whose father, Frank, died after either falling or jumping out of a hotel window in 1953, when Eric was a child. The circumstances of Frank's death troubled Eric for decades, and in 1975, documents revealed by the Rockefeller Commission in the aftermath of the Watergate scandal suggested that Frank Olson had died by suicide after experiencing a mental breakdown that began when a CIA operator secretly dosed him with the hallucinogenic drug lysergic acid diethylamide (LSD) as part of the CIA's notorious MK-ULTRA project. Eric Olson later came to believe that his father had in fact been murdered by the CIA due to his knowledge of and involvement in deadlier experiments into new interrogation techniques. While Ronson cannot give a definitive answer regarding the circumstances of Frank Olson's death, the book makes it clear that Olson was, in one way or another, a casualty of the CIA's disregard for human well-being. Ronson's critical view of MK-ULTRA and related initiatives remains evident in later chapters, one of which suggests that government and military officials were more concerned with "the trauma of being found out" than with the trauma they had inflicted on individuals such as the Olsons.

Although the story of the Olson family is absent from the film adaptation of *The Men Who Stare at Goats*, the film does explore the negative side of such experiments to a certain extent through the character of Larry. Not only does Larry seek to weaponize the psychic abilities of his fellow soldiers, but he also is shown in a flashback to have caused the death of a New Earth Army recruit who went on a shooting spree and subsequently killed himself after Larry dosed him with LSD. Lyn likewise expresses regrets over an incident in which he killed a goat by staring at it and tells Bob that he believes his actions have cursed the New Earth Army. However, the film version of *The Men Who Stare at Goats* overall has a far more comedic tone than the book, and some events that are played for comedy can be construed as undermining the message of the book. Near the end of the film, for example, the protagonists escape Larry's camp by mixing LSD into the water supply and dosing all the unsuspecting camp personnel. While this contributes to the absurdist tone of much of the film, it seems at odds with the book's negative view of dosing unwitting individuals with LSD. Such incidents, as well as the overall tone of the film, lessen the impact of some of the more disturbing and unethical practices described in the source material, and the serious criticism contained in Ronson's original work is largely absent from the film adaptation.

Significance

Following its debut at the Venice Film Festival, *The Men Who Stare at Goats* was screened at film festivals throughout North America and Europe during late 2009. The film opened in theaters in the United States on November 6 of that year and went on to open around the world through the remainder of 2009 and beginning of 2010. At the box office, *The Men Who Stare at Goats* grossed more than $32 million domestically by January 31, 2010, according to the website Box Office Mojo. The film likewise grossed more than an additional $36 million internationally, performing best among audiences in the United Kingdom, Germany, and Italy. Although the box office performance of *The Men*

Who Stare at Goats was relatively positive, reviews of the film were middling. While many critics identified Ronson's work and the subjects he discusses as offering a fitting premise for a film, they generally found the film to be "a wasted opportunity," as reviewer Peter Bradshaw wrote for *The Guardian*, noting that the film's fictional narrative was lacking in comparison to the original book. Some critics appreciated individual actors' performances and elements of the film's humor, and the film was nominated for the Empire Award for Best Comedy; nevertheless, *The Men Who Stared at Goats* ultimately earned little acclaim from critics and award-granting bodies.

Despite the mixed critical response to *The Men Who Stare at Goats*, Ronson himself approved of the finished film despite having had little involvement in the adaptation process. In interviews following the completion of the film, Ronson noted that the film differed significantly from his book, both in terms of the changes made to render a nonfiction narrative suitable for the screen and in terms of the film's tone, which he described in an interview for the NPR program *All Things Considered* as "unexpectedly gentle, batty, [and] mad." While the change in tone was a particularly large divergence from the original book, Ronson noted that he appreciated the filmmakers' new take on the work and that he viewed the film and book as separate entities. In addition to bringing additional attention to Ronson's work, the process of making *The Men Who Stare at Goats* proved professionally beneficial to the author, who subsequently collaborated with the film's screenwriter, Straughan. The pair cowrote the screenplay for the independent comedy film *Frank*, which premiered in 2014.

—*Joy Crelin*

Further Reading

"Jon Ronson, Staring (at 'Goats') from the Sidelines." *All Things Considered*, NPR, 29 Dec. 2009, www.npr.org/templates/story/story.php?storyId=122006511. Accessed 31 Jan. 2019.

Ronson, Jon. "Catching Up with... *The Men Who Stare at Goats* Author Jon Ronson." Interview with Justin Jacobs. *Paste*, 6 Nov. 2009. www.pastemagazine.com/articles/2009/11/catching-up-with-the-men-who-stare-at-goats-author.html. Accessed 31 Jan. 2019.

Ronson, Jon. *The Men Who Stare at Goats*. Simon, 2009.

Bibliography

Bradhaw, Peter. "The Men Who Stare at Goats." Review of *The Men Who Stare at Goats*, directed by Grant Heslov. *The Guardian*, 5 Nov. 2009, www.theguardian.com/film/2009/

nov/06/the-men-who-stare-at-goats-review. Accessed 31 Jan. 2019.

Dargis, Manohla. "Missing Mind Control in Defense of America." Review of *The Men Who Stare at Goats*, directed by Grant Heslov. *The New York Times*, 5 Nov. 2009, www.nytimes.com/ 2009/11/06/movies/06themen.html. Accessed 31 Jan. 2019.

Ebert, Roger. Review of *The Men Who Stare at Goats*, directed by Grant Heslov. *RogerEbert.com*, 4 Nov. 2009. www.rogerebert.com/reviews/the-men-who-stare-at-goats-2009. Accessed 31 Jan. 2019.

Fischer, Russ. "The Real Documentary That Inspired *The Men Who Stare at Goats*." *Film*, 9 Nov. 2009. www.slashfilm.com/ the-real-documentary-that-inspired-the-men-who-stare-at-goats. Accessed 31 Jan. 2019.

"*The Men Who Stare at Goats*." *Box Office Mojo*, www.boxofficemojo.com/movies/?id=menwhostareatgoats.htm. Accessed 31 Jan. 2019.

Remington, Alex. "*The Men Who Stare at Goats*: Would You Believe the Book Is Better Than the Movie?" Review of *The Men Who Stare at Goats*, directed by Grant Heslov. *Huffington Post*, 18 Mar. 2010. www.huffingtonpost.com/alex-remington/ the-men-who-stare-at-goat_b_383321.html. Accessed 31 Jan. 2019.

Ronson, Jon. "*The Men Who Stare at Goats*: Jon Ronson Interview." Interview by Barry Donovan. *Den of Geek!*, 5 Nov. 2009. www.denofgeek.com/us/movies/15044/the-men-who-stare-at-goats-jon-ronson-interview. Accessed 31 Jan. 2019.

"True Lies: *The Men Who Stare at Goats* Succeeds at Silliness, but Fails at Journalism." Review of *The Men Who Stare at Goats*, directed by Grant Heslov. *Source Weekly*, 4 Nov. 2009. www.bendsource.com/bend/true-lies-the-men-who-stare-at-goats-succeeds-at-silliness-but-fails-at-journalism/Content?oid= 2134567. Accessed 31 Jan. 2019.

Midnight Express

The Novel
Authors: Billy Hayes (b. 1947) with William Hoffer
First published: 1977

The Film
Year released: 1978
Director: Alan Parker (b. 1944)
Screenplay by: Oliver Stone
Starring: Brad Davis, Randy Quaid, John Hurt

Context

Billy Hayes was a young American who was arrested while trying to smuggle hashish out of Turkey. He spent five years in a Turkish prison before escaping and fleeing the country. He published a memoir of his experience in 1977. Hayes had been the victim of the extreme and inhumane sentencing for drug offenders that became the norm in Turkey in the 1970s, a decade during which Turkey was under martial law for several years, with violent factions on both left and right committing extreme acts of terrorism. (The country succumbed to a military coup in 1980, the third in as many decades.) Hayes was approaching the end of a 4 1/2-year sentence for possession when an appeals court changed his crime to smuggling and his sentence was extended to 30 years. The book, penned in conjunction with writer-for-hire William Hoffer, was entitled *Midnight Express*, and it was named after the code word Hayes used in his letters to talk about his escape. A literary sensation of sorts, it was inevitable that the book would soon be turned into a movie.

Not long after *Midnight Express* was published, Columbia Pictures bought the rights to the film. The company turned the reins over to director Alan Parker, a veteran of British television ads with only a single feature film to his credit, and a then barely known young American filmmaker named Oliver Stone, who was charged with writing the screenplay. The filmmakers made some significant changes to the book, altering the chronology, the character of Billy Hayes, and the depiction of his Turkish captors. They also ramped up the violence and offered a more visceral experience overall.

The result was a film that resonated with many people but also proved controversial. Debuting at the Cannes Film Festival in 1978, the movie was among the most talked about at the festival, earning praise for its strong visual style and dramatic narrative but drawing criticism for its portrayal of nearly all the Turkish people as, in the words of critic Andrew Sarris, "fat, greasy, brutal, and perverted." This mixture of enthusiasm and distaste followed the film stateside when it premiered theatrically, with numerous reviewers pointing out the film's flaws alongside its strengths. Nonetheless, the movie proved enormously popular, grossing more than $100 million and earning six Academy Award nominations, including for best picture. It ended up winning Oscars for best writing (adapted screenplay) for Oliver Stone and best music (original score) for Italian composer Giorgio Moroder.

Film Analysis

In crafting a version of his story that would appeal to the widest possible audience, Billy Hayes, along with cowriter William Hoffer, penned a mild, largely inoffensive narrative. *Midnight Express* the book tells the story of an all-American boy who has been caught up in a system beyond his control. He does not accept his fate, but neither does he do anything crazy. He stands up for himself, but he is not a naturally violent person. If, in the end, he does not seem to have much personality, he also does little that could offend a reader.

Similarly, the writers are relatively even-handed in their depictions of Hayes' life in the Turkish prison. While brutal beatings abound—a favorite method is to tie prisoners up by their feet and hit their soles with a stick—there is no suggestion of any kind of sexual assault or any of the more degraded images that readers tend to have of prison life. When dealing with such controversial issues as homosexuality, the writers play it coy as well. The reader learns, for example, that during his time in prison, Billy had an affair with a fellow inmate named Arne, but the writers give out few details, noting, almost in passing, that they "made love."

This loving union is one that the movie refuses. While Billy and the Arne character (here called Erich) kiss, Billy calls things off with a definitive head shake before things can go much further. (Lead actor Brad Davis allegedly pushed for a more ambiguous version of the scene, but while that version was filmed, it ultimately was not used.) In fact, with Erich reduced to a small supporting role from Arne's larger one in the book, there is little tenderness to be found in the film version. Early on in the process of adapting the book, Alan Parker and Oliver Stone decided that the theme of the film would be "man's inhumanity to man" and as such they began to plot out a much darker, more brutal take on the material than Hayes had offered up.

In contrast to the book, which offers a more measured take on the conditions of the prison, the film seems most interested in reveling in the sadistic attitude of the prison guards towards their prisoners. Although Hayes and Hoffer offer up numerous scenes of the beatings perpetrated by the guards, these are much more heavily emphasized in the film and the guards themselves are seen as grotesques, often fat and leering, almost caricatures of Western conceptions of evil-minded Turks. Late in the film, Parker and Stone create a scene that does not exist in the book in which the head guard prepares to rape Billy. He takes off his belt and pulls down his pants, a lascivious look on his face. Billy pushes him away, and as the guard falls back, he is impaled on a hook coming out of the wall, allowing Billy to escape.

Billy's actual escape occurred from a different prison, an island jail from which he swam out to a fisherman's dinghy and rowed away to freedom, but the filmmakers eschew this less dramatic version of events. Instead, they show the worst side of humanity as embodied by an irredeemably bad jailer and further suggest the animalistic side of Billy. Although he was not intending to kill the jailer with his push, the incident nonetheless suggests the capacity to kill that lies dormant in him. If Hayes aimed to make himself a sympathetic character in his book, then Parker and Stone have no such vested interest in perpetuating such a view of his relative goodness. Instead, they are interested in showing the bestial state that Billy is reduced to by his experiences. Even before killing the guard, Billy is shown to be largely unhinged late in his stay in the

prison. In one of the most intense scenes in the film, Billy starts attacking a fellow prisoner who informed on his friend. He knocks him to the ground and then, jumping around like an animal, starts kicking him. Finally, he ends by biting off his tongue, an act that one could scarcely imagine the mild-mannered Billy of the book performing.

Another divergence between the Billy of the book and movie-Billy appears in a different scene earlier in the narrative. In the book, when he is sentenced to life in prison on orders from the high court in Ankara, Billy delivers a calm, rational monologue, in which he waxes eloquent on the relativistic nature of laws, before ending by saying, "All I can do is forgive you." In the movie, Billy begins with the same speech but then works himself up into a frenzy. He yells out in hatred, "For a nation of pigs, it sure is funny you don't eat 'em! Jesus Christ forgave the bastards, but I can't. I hate you, I hate your nation, I hate your people, and I f—— your sons and daughters because they're pigs!"

This scene illustrates the extent of the film's dark vision. The viewer is sympathetic to Billy because what he says seems right in the extreme world of the film. The Turkish justice system is portrayed as beyond the pale, so we can only conclude that Billy is right to be angry. The Turkish people, too, are all portrayed as sinister, grubby people, so the viewer can be forgiven for viewing them as "pigs." As correct as Billy's viewpoint may seem, however, the scene also shows him to be a bit of an unhinged madman. How much of this violent madness is the result of being treated like an animal and how much was latent in his character is a question that the film leaves open, but scenes like this paint a vivid portrait of a world in which everything and everyone partakes of cruelty and hatred.

If the experience of reading *Midnight Express* is one of following a good-hearted young man as he deals admirably with a tough situation that, while the result of his own bad decision, was nonetheless made difficult out of proportion to his actions, then watching the film yields a very different experience. Instead of redemption, Parker and Stone offer up a vision of horror that one imagines Billy will never be able to fully escape from. If Billy gets to return home in the book free of guilt and morally impeccable, the Billy of the movie is far more compromised.

Significance

Midnight Express, the book but especially the movie, brought widespread attention to human rights abuses in

Turkey, and made the words "Turkish prison" something of a cliché. The film contributed to strained relations between the United States and Turkey, and it even affected the Turkish tourism industry. Protests occurred around the world for the release of European foreigners who were being held in Turkish prisons on extreme sentences for drug charges, and Amnesty International issued a report—published in the prominent *New York Review of Books*—decrying the "imprisonment of prisoners of conscience" in Turkey and the practice of "widespread and systematic torture." The group also decried the thousands of assassinations that had occurred in the last five years of the 1970s before the military coup.

Billy Hayes felt that the film had presented a cardboard fictionalization, saying that it was unrealistic in depicting "all Turks as monsters." Hayes later toured with a one-man show called *Riding the Midnight Express with Billy Hayes*, in which he presented a version of the story that was less sanitized than the book version, but nevertheless contained none of the brutality of the movie. In any case, Hayes' book turned out to have been fictionalized as well. Hayes admitted that the book omitted or outright changed events from reality in order to make Hayes himself more palatable as a narrator. For example, the real-life Hayes was not caught on his first attempt at smuggling hashish out of Turkey; he was an established, albeit small-time, smuggler at the time of his arrest. The book also did not reveal that his relaxed attitude toward his circumstances was the result of an epiphany he had while taking LSD. Screenwriter Oliver Stone later said about his screenplay: "I think there was a lack of proportion in the picture regarding the Turks. I was younger. I was more rabid."

The violence and almost mythic brutality in the film can be seen as a reflection of issues that the United States was working through in the 1970s, a time when extraordinary and degraded episodes of violence seemed to be burgeoning at home since the 1960s—not to mention the violence of the Vietnam War. In fact, the year after *Midnight Express*, Francis Ford Coppola's *Apocalypse Now* presented an even more over-the-top—a myth-tinged phantasmagoria—about wholesome American boys acting out with primal violence after exposure to extreme circumstances in a foreign land—this time in Vietnam. *Midnight Express* had a long impact on popular culture. The recent popularity in the United States and Britain of the television program *Banged Up Abroad* (*Locked Up Abroad*) attests to the ongoing influence of the film and its frightening portrayal of foreign prisons.

—*Andrew Schenker*

Further Reading

Stern, Marlow. "The Unbelievable (True) Story of the World's Most Infamous Hash Smuggler." *The Daily Beast*, 14 Nov. 2014, www.thedailybeast.com/the-unbelievable-true-story-of-the-worlds-most-infamous-hash-smuggler. Accessed 7 Jan. 2019.

"The Truth Behind 'Midnight Express.'" *Association for Diplomatic Studies and Training*, adst.org/2013/07/the-truth-behind-midnight-express/. Accessed 7 Jan. 2019.

Bibliography

Ebert, Roger. Review of *Midnight Express*, directed by Alan Parker. *RogerEbert.com*, 6 Oct. 1978, www.rogerebert.com/reviews/midnight-express-1978. Accessed 7 Jan. 2019.

Macnab, Geoffrey. "*Midnight Express*: The Cult Film That Had Disastrous Consequences for the Turkish Tourism Industry." *The Independent*, 17 May 2016, www.independent.co.uk/arts-entertainment/films/midnight-express-the-cult-film-that-had-disastrous-consequences-for-the-turkish-film-industry-a7032161.html. Accessed 7 Jan. 2019.

Midnight Express. *Turner Classic Movies*, www.tcm.com/this-month/article/188689|0/Midnight-Express.html. Accessed 7 Jan. 2019.

Phipps, Keith. Review of *Midnight Express*, directed by Alan Parker. *The AV Club*, 5 Feb. 2008, film.avclub.com/midnight-express-1798203725. Accessed 7 Jan. 2019.

A Midsummer Night's Dream

The Play
Author: William Shakespeare (1564-1616)
First published: 1600

The Film
Year released: 1935
Directors: Max Reinhardt (1873-1943), William Dieterle (1893-1972)
Screenplay by: Charles Kenyon, Mary C. McCall Jr.
Starring: Mickey Rooney, James Cagney, Dick Powell, Olivia de Havilland, Victor Jory

Context

A Midsummer Night's Dream has long been one of Shakespeare's most appealing comedies. By the early 1930s the Austrian-born director Max Reinhardt had been staging the work for decades in European theaters, in ever more elaborate ways. In 1934 one of his exceptionally extravagant productions was performed at the massive Hollywood Bowl, an outdoor atrium attended both by large crowds and by some of the film industry's most important bigwigs. One of these, Jack Warner, was a key executive at Warner Brothers Pictures, a studio most famous for making "tough guy" movies, such as gangster pictures. Warner decided to add some "class" to his studio's reputation by signing Reinhardt to oversee a big-budget adaptation of Shakespeare's play, with the assistance of the veteran movie director William Dieterle.

This movie, released in 1935, was unlike anything that had been tried before with Shakespeare on film. The sets, in particular, were massive and often magical; the lighting (taking full advantage of black, white, and various shades of gray) was striking and memorable; and the huge cast contained some actors whose performances, though sometimes controversial, were frequently effective. Although the film received mixed reviews from critics and had mixed success at the box office, it was one of the first attempts to give Shakespeare the full Hollywood treatment, especially in a "talkie," then the latest innovation in film-making.

Like many later productions of Shakespeare on film, this one raised numerous intriguing questions. The most important of these, as always, was how many of the original words could be retained in a successful film. Accounts of Reinhardt's film almost always assert that half of Shakespeare's phrasing was cut. Purists, of course, dis-

liked this fact, and later purists have criticized other Shakespeare films for the same reason. (Staged versions of the plays also often cut many lines, as many of the plays would run well over two hours if unabridged.) Responses to Reinhardt's film, however, like responses to many later Shakespeare films, often involved not so much what was cut as what was added. Reinhardt and Dieterle had at their disposal a massive budget, advanced technology, hundreds of actors and technicians, and enormous sets and soundstages—the sorts of things entirely unavailable (and probably unimaginable) in Shakespeare's Globe or even in the most modern theaters of Reinhardt's day.

Reinhardt's film, therefore, like many later Shakespeare films, raised the issue of spectacle versus words. At what point might a film version of a Shakespeare play simply overwhelm the play itself? At what point does the film become more the creation of the set designers, costumers, lighting technicians, and cinematographers than the creation of Shakespeare's words in the mouths of talented actors? At what point (if ever) does *A Midsummer Night's Dream* cease to be Shakespeare's play and instead become Reinhardt's spectacle? These are the kinds of questions the film immediately provoked, and they are also the kinds of questions that productions of Shakespeare (whether on film or on stage) often raise. They are especially relevant to the Reinhardt/Dieterle film, which is certainly one of the most lavish Shakespeare films ever attempted. Some critics, in fact, have seen it as a kind of cinematic opera.

Film Analysis

The differences between Shakespeare's script and the Warner Brothers film are immediately obvious. Shakespeare rarely provides elaborate stage directions. Modern readers, therefore, cannot be quite sure how his plays lookedonstage. The text of *A Midsummer Night's Dream*, for instance, opens with a few simple words spoken by the Athenian king Theseus (played in the film by Ian Hunter) to Hippolyta, queen of the Amazons (Verree Teasdale), whom he has defeated in battle and whom he now intends to marry: "Now, fair Hippolyta, our nuptial hour / Draws on apace; four happy days bring in / Another moon." Shakespeare, in short, plunges his auditors right into the midst of things. Reinhardt's film, in contrast, begins with a static "overture" in which Felix Mendelsohn's famous music (inspired by Shakespeare's play) is heard for roughly nine minutes, with little if anything taking place on screen for most of that time. Instead, the screen simply says "Overture" and a sliver of a drawn moon is shown against a drawn gray sky.

With this opening, the film immediately announces itself as a work in which music and visual imagery will be strongly emphasized. The classical music, in particular, instantly implies that this will be a highbrow production. As the Mendelsohn music nears its end, viewers see a printed "Proclamation" giving crucial information about the plot. Then uniformed royal trumpeters are shown; then a massive procession of elaborately costumed figures, including soldiers with gleaming helmets, takes place. Then royal Theseus speaks words to Hippolyta—but not the words he speaks to her at the beginning of Shakespeare's script. His opening words in the film are taken from later in the play. Immediately, then, Reinhardt shows that he is willing to rearrange Shakespeare's text. The director, not the author, is in charge. Reinhardt loved Shakespeare, but he was willing to take liberties to make his own production succeed and to make Shakespeare's plot more instantly comprehensible to modern viewers.

The procession then resumes; joyous singing (like that of an operatic chorus) breaks out; the camera focuses on one key character after another as they all sing along. Their complicated relationships are suggested; and various notes of comedy are implied through bits of silly "funny business." Purists might argue that Reinhardt has already begun to take too many liberties with the play at this point, but admirers of Shakespeare might welcome the effort to get large audiences interested in the play in the first place. In any case, Reinhardt draws on many features of 1930s big-budget Hollywood movie-making—recognizable stars, fancy costumes, interesting sets, vaudeville comedy touches, big musical numbers, tight close-ups,

large crowd shots, and so on. By using these and other methods, he obviously hoped to give his movie greater cinematic appeal. In fact, Reinhardt's film faithfully reflects (and often exceeds) the kind of elaborate productions he had been putting on for years, quite successfully, inside actual theaters. Warner knew exactly what he would be getting when he hired the prestigious Reinhardt.

Reinhardt's film really outdoes itself, however, when it moves from the gleaming city of Athens to the dark surrounding woods. It is here, especially, that the most spectacular visual and musical effects take place. It is here, for long stretches, that the movie comes closest to being a full-blown opera, especially thanks to the presence of scores of richly costumed fairies and dwarves, insistent orchestral music, striking sets, highly choreographed ballet sequences, and magical special effects. Troupes of fairies sometimes seem to dance up into the air, or they and various other characters fly. At one point Bottom the Weaver (James Cagney) seems to transform before the audience's eyes from a human into an ass, as in a 1930s werewolf film.

As was normal for the time, Reinhardt and Dieterle relied on black and white photography. But they worked real magic with this seemingly limited palette, particularly in the ways they often made the screen literally sparkle when certain characters (such as Oberon, the Fairy King, played by Victory Jory) were on screen. When critics and viewers discuss this film, they often comment especially on its visual effects rather than on the skill of its performances. The film was, and is, a feast for the eyes.

But the film is also remembered for the performances of two actors in particular: the high-spirited teenager Mickey Rooney as Puck (who sometimes still looks preadolescent in the film) and the rough-hewn but versatile James Cagney as the incurable ham Bottom. Some critics found fault with both performances: they thought Rooney was too manic and over-the-top (especially with his constant hee-haw laugh), and they thought Cagney was too young, quick-witted, and good-looking to play Bottom, who is usually depicted as a middle-aged dullard. But both Rooney and Cagney had their defenders, and in the twenty-first century critical opinion has warmed considerably toward them, with some hailing them as capturing the spirit of the original play better than the rest of the cast. One of the funniest episodes in the whole film occurs when Rooney echoes and mocks the speech of the play's foolish lovers as those lovers descend, separately, into sleep. These echoes do not appear in Shakespeare's text, but they are the sort of directorial inventions he might well have appreciated.

Significance

Although Reinhardt's film has sometimes been called a box-office disaster, it did make its money back. But the costs of making the film were so great (Reinhardt exceeded his already generous budget) that its profit margin was relatively slim. The movie often failed to draw big crowds in small cities or rural markets, even after many of the ballet sequences and some of the classical musical elements were trimmed to make the movie shorter, tighter, and more focused on the plot and characters than on anything that might strike most movie-goers as extraneous or too "hoity-toity."

Critical opinion about the film was divided right from the start and has remained so over the decades. The film won two Academy Awards, in the technical categories of cinematography and film editing, but the acting was not as well received. Some early critics considered it overblown, tacky, and even tasteless. Some British critics objected to the almost entirely American cast speaking Shakespeare in American accents. Other critics disliked the fact that Hollywood actors—rather than veteran Shakespeareans from the professional stage—had been cast in so many key roles. They especially disparaged the performance of the Hollywood crooner Dick Powell as Lysander (one of the four main romantic leads). Apparently, in fact, even Powell himself immediately suspected that he was not right for the part. Cagney, too, was sometimes considered miscast, but some critics admired his energy and the fact that he was playing against type. Joe E. Brown, as Flute, has been considered either one of the film's great successes or one of its most annoying failures.

More and more critics and scholars, however, seem to appreciate the movie not only for what it tried to achieve but also for what it actually accomplished. In other words, as decades have gone by, the film has been seen more and more as an intriguing, and often engaging, product of its own time. It is not the sort of Shakespeare film that would be made today, but it *is* the sort of Shakespeare film that provides rich insights into the nature of Hollywood movie-making in one of Hollywood's heydays. In the mid-1930s, talkies were relatively new and the Great Depression sent Americans into movie theaters in search of magic, good humor, wonder, and escape. They would have found plenty of all these traits in Reinhardt's film.

—*Robert C. Evans, PhD*

Further Reading

Babington, Bruce. "Shakespeare Meets the Warner Brothers: Reinhardt and Dieterle's *A Midsummer Night's Dream*." *Shakespearean Continuities: Essays in Honor of E. A. J. Honigmann*, edited by John Batchelor, et al, Palgrave Macmillan, 1997, pp. 259-74.

MacQueen, Scott. "Midsummer Dream, Midwinter Nightmare: Max Reinhardt and Shakespeare versus the Warner Bros." *The Moving Image: The Journal of the Association of Moving Image Archivists*, vol. 9, no. 2, 2009, pp. 30-103.

Bibliography

Halio, Jay L. *A Midsummer Night's Dream*. Manchester UP, 2003. Shakespeare in Performance.

Jackson, Russell. "Shakespeare's Comedies on Film." *Shakespeare and the Moving Image: The Plays on Films and Television*, edited by Antony Davies and Stanley Wells, Cambridge UP, 1994, pp. 99-120.

Marx, Peter W. "Max Reinhardt." *The Routledge Companion to Directors' Shakespeare*, edited by John Russel Brown, Routledge, 2008, pp. 374-88.

Rothwell, Kenneth S. *A History of Shakespeare on Screen: A Century of Film and Television*. 1999. 2nd ed. Cambridge UP, 2004.

Van Doren, Mark. "Films: Shakespeare without Words." *The Nation*, 23 Oct. 1935, pp. 491-92.

Mildred Pierce

The Novel
Author: James M. Cain (1892-1977)
First published: 1941

The Film
Year released: 1945
Director: Michael Curtiz (1886-1962)
Screenplay by: Ranald MacDougall
Starring: Joan Crawford, Zachary Scott, Bruce Bennett, Ann Blyth

Context

James M. Cain was a popular 1930's writer who helped innovate the genre of hard-boiled crime fiction. His first three novels—bestsellers *The Postman Always Rings Twice* (1934) and *Double Indemnity* (serialized 1936, published 1943), and *Serenade* (1937)—were all narrated by down-on-their-luck, tough male characters and, collectively, these novels helped define a new American genre and style, one marked by a bleak, cynical outlook; clever, dark humor; and tough main characters in the antihero vein.

For his fourth novel, *Mildred Pierce* (1941), Cain took a different approach. Set between 1931 and 1940, *Mildred Pierce* focuses on a woman, the plucky, obsessive titular heroine, and it tracks her precipitous rise and sudden fall. Cain switched from the first-person narrative voice of his previous three novels to third-person. While the tone is still foreboding, the material is softer. Sexual shenanigans, manipulations, betrayals, financial malfeasance, and generally sleazy behavior abound. But there is little serious crime, and no violence beyond a bit of face-slapping.

The film adaption, released in 1945, was also a departure for its director, Michael Curtiz. After a string of fast-paced, male-oriented hits—including *Captain Blood* (1935), *The Charge of the Light Brigade* (1936), *The Adventures of Robin Hood* (1938), *The Sea Hawk* (1940), *The Sea Wolf* (1941), and *Passage to Marseilles* (1944)—Curtiz turned to *Mildred Pierce*, today recognized as one of his finest. The film is a classic melodrama, a genre characterized by sensational stories, elaborate plots, romance, and strong female audience appeal. It incorporates elements of film noir.

It was the collaborative talents of a succession of screenwriters that elaborated on the murder and crime element in the story. This was done partially to satisfy the Motion Picture Production Code, which specified that transgressors depicted on film must pay for their crimes. Mostly, however, the subplot was intended to add action and suspense to the original soap-opera-like storyline. The change brought the film more into line with the author's expected style, too, as realized in the other film adaptations of Cain's novels—*Double Indemnity* (1944) and *The Postman Always Rings Twice* (1946)—that bookended the release of the movie version of *Mildred Pierce*.

Film Analysis

The structure of the film has little relationship to the print version of *Mildred Pierce*. The novel was written as a character study in which the protagonist devotes herself to pleasing a daughter who can never be satisfied. The book contains a strong subtext of territorial snobbery, concerning the relative social statuses of working-class Glendale, where Mildred lives, and upscale Pasadena, where aristocratic Monty Beragon resides. The high-contrast black-and-white adaptation is a moral tale, illustrating the wages of sin—which are not paid in the novel. Both written and visual forms of the story have merit as products of their particular times and purposes. The novel is steeped in the realities of the beginning of the Depression and the end of Prohibition. The film, however, never refers to either of those historical periods.

The novel thrusts readers into domestic melodrama. Protagonist Mildred Pierce is upset with her unemployed husband Bert, who is having an affair with a neighbor woman. Mildred throws Bert out of the house, then has to figure how to support her family. This leaves her a single mother of two daughters: sweet-natured seven-year-old

Moire (nicknamed Ray), and Mildred's favorite, eleven-year-old Veda, a haughty girl with aristocratic airs. The story proceeds in linear, chronological order for nine years as Mildred toils to succeed in a hostile world. After Ray dies of an infection, Mildred compensates by catering to Veda's increasing demands. Using her cooking skills, physical attributes, and innate business sense, Mildred works her way up from amateur pie-maker to waitress to restaurant owner. She builds a small empire. Then she loses it all trying to buy Veda's love. Her surviving daughter has always despised her mother's common roots and the sweaty, greasy, ordinary way Mildred earns her money. Veda begins an affair with Mildred's new husband Monty, an impoverished blue-blood playboy. Veda and Monty head for New York. Mildred, older and plumper and broke again, reconnects with Bert. With no prospects on the horizon and their future in doubt, they "get stinko."

While highlights of Mildred's history are incorporated into the Curtiz film, information is framed in a different fashion. The film opens with waves lapping upon a beach. As screen credits are superimposed, waves regularly wash them away, suggesting the noirish concept of impermanence. Action begins immediately. The exterior of a beach house is glimpsed. Shots are heard. The camera cuts to the luxurious interior of the house as bullets strike Monte Beragon (Zachary Scott). He falls to the floor. A revolver is tossed beside him. Monty gasps, "Mildred," and dies. Outside, a car drives away in haste.

The next scene shows the back of a broad-shouldered woman in a fur coat walking in deep shadows along a public pier by the oceanfront: it is Mildred Pierce (Joan Crawford). She starts to climb a railing, but is thwarted in her presumed suicide attempt by a policeman. As she walks away, Wally Fay (Jack Carson), lecherous owner of Mildred's former restaurant, now a low-rent bar, beckons her over. They share a drink and talk about old times. He makes a pass. She tells him there is better liquor at the beach house. They go there together. Wally does not realize that Mildred has set him up to take the fall for Monty's murder. Mildred slips away, and Wally finds all doors and windows locked. He uses a chair to break the glass, and escapes—in time to be caught by arriving police. Ultimately, Wally, Mildred, Veda (Ann Blyth), and Bert (Bruce Bennett) are all scooped up to be interviewed by police inspector Peterson (Moroni Olsen).

When it is Mildred's turn to be questioned, the narrative flashes back, with transitions between static scenes assisted by Mildred's voiceover, a film noir standby technique. Flashbacks are periodically interrupted to return to the present, to note the progress of the police investigation.

Events that were minutely examined in Cain's novel—such as Mildred's efforts to sell home-baked pies—are glossed over in a sentence or two of dialogue in the film. Similarly, Mildred's painstaking progress toward financial independence is severely condensed. In one minute, she is working as a waitress, and in the next she is opening her first chicken-and-waffles restaurant. In the book, Mildred slept with Wally occasionally in exchange for cash or favors, but in the film this does not seem to be the case. Some characters are eliminated in the film. For example, Ida Corwin (Eve Arden), Mildred's wise-cracking former waitressing supervisor, is a composite of the book's Ida and Mildred's confidant, next-door neighbor, and eventual partner in the novel, Lucy Gessler. Other characters occupy slightly different roles in the adaptation. In the book, Monty picks up Mildred by chance while she is working as a waitress and is uninvolved in her business affairs. In the film, Monte (the spelling of his name slightly changed) is owner of the first property Mildred wants to turn into a restaurant, and becomes a partner in the enterprise.

Aspects of the on-again-off-again, love-hate relationship between Mildred and Veda are dramatized with original material throughout the film. Veda's hard-to-please nature is emphasized early with an invented scene: a dress Mildred scrimped to buy Veda is delivered. Veda naturally hates it. In the novel Veda is accidentally discovered to have hidden singing abilities and quickly becomes an opera star. In the film, however, she is reduced to belting out popular tunes in Wally's dive to entertain carousing sailors.

The biggest departure, of course, is the addition of the murder plot. It opens the film, and hints of it are threaded through even the flashback sequences. In one scene, Mildred, sorting among overdue bills stuffed into a desk drawer, uncovers a revolver that looks just like the handgun someone tosses alongside Monty's body in the opening scene. The pistol is later seen again when Mildred shoves it into a pocket of her mink coat, an action that makes her appear to be the prime suspect in Monty's murder. At the end of the interrogation, Mildred even confesses to the crime. She is not believed, however, because by then everybody knows who the real killer is.

Significance

Mildred Pierce was an important film for Joan Crawford. The former Lucille LeSeur had begun performing in the early 1920s as a chorus girl. Under contract to Metro-Goldwyn-Mayer (MGM) from 1925, she earned prominent roles in such popular films as *Grand Hotel* (1932), *Rain* (1932), *The Last of Mrs. Cheyney* (1937), and *The Women* (1939). By the time of her last MGM film, *Above Suspicion* (1943), however, her star had faded as she approached her fortieth birthday. Her MGM contract was canceled and she signed with Warner Brothers. Though Crawford wanted to play Mildred Pierce, Michael Curtiz did not want her, preferring Bette Davis or Barbara Stanwyck in the lead. When they proved unavailable, the director insultingly made Crawford screen test for the role —for which she went on to earn her only Academy Award, for best actress. Crawford's comeback added twenty-five years to her career, during which time she memorably performed in such horror-thrillers as *What Ever Happened to Baby Jane?* (1962), *Strait-Jacket* (1964), and *Berserk!* (1967).

The 1945 adaptation was commercially successful, with domestic and foreign revenues quadrupling the $1.4 million production budget. In addition to Crawford's Academy Award, *Mildred Pierce* also received nominations for best supporting actress (Eve Arden and Ann Blyth), best black-and-white cinematography (Ernest Haller), best screenplay (Ranald MacDougall), and best picture. Critics praised the superb photography and singled out the performances of Crawford, Zachary Scott—who had debuted the previous year playing a slimy thief, spy, and murderer in *The Mask of Dimitrios* (1944)—and seventeen-year-old Ann Blyth in her first significant role as evil Veda. Most negative reviews of the time concentrated on the length of the film and the plot's sometimes uneasy mix of melodrama and noir, factors that have not kept *Mildred Pierce* from inclusion on several American Film Institute 100-year lists.

The film has had a long afterlife. In 2011, director Todd Haynes made his own version of *Mildred Pierce* for HBO. As a classic melodrama, it is often studied by film scholars working on that genre, an area that has burgeoned since the 1990s, primarily among feminist scholars of what were once called "women's movies."

—*Jack Ewing*

Further Reading

McKee, Alison. *The Woman's Film of the 1940s: Gender, Narrative, and History*. Routledge, 2018.

Rode, Alan K. *Michael Curtiz: A Life in Film*. UP of Kentucky, 2017.

Spoto, Donald. *Possessed: The Life of Joan Crawford*. William Morrow, 2010.

Bibliography

Als, Hilton. "This Woman's Work: James M. Cain on the Grass Widow." *The New Yorker*, 28 Mar. 2011, www.newyorker.com/magazine/2011/03/28/this-womans-work. Accessed 17 Nov. 2018.

Cain, James M. *Mildred Pierce*. The World Publishing Company, 1945.

Churchwell, Sarah. "Rereading: 'Mildred Pierce' by James M. Cain." *The Guardian*, 24 June 2011, www.theguardian.com/books/2011/jun/24/mildred-pierce-sarah-churchwell-rereading. Accessed 17 Nov. 2018.

Dagan, Carmel. "Remembering Joan Crawford's 'Mildred Pierce' on Its 70th Anniversary." *Variety*, 20 Oct. 2015, variety.com/2015/film/news/joan-crawford-mildred-pierce-70th-anniversary-1201619298/. Accessed 13 Dec. 2018.

Greene, Brian. "Page to Screen: 'Mildred Pierce.'" *Criminal Element*, 21 Feb. 2017, www.criminalelement.com/page-to-screen-mildred-pierce/. Accessed 17 Nov. 2018.

"Mildred Pierce." *American Film Institute*, catalog.afi.com/Catalog/moviedetails/24502. Accessed 13 Dec. 2018.

Ulin, David L. "James M. Cain's 'Mildred Pierce' Is a Realistic Look at a Life, Not Noir." *Los Angeles Times*, 1 Apr. 2011, articles.latimes.com/2011/apr/01/entertainment/la-et-james-cain-20110401. Accessed 17 Nov. 2018.

Millions

The Novel
Author: Frank Cottrell Boyce (b. 1959)
First published: 2004

The Film
Year released: 2004
Director: Danny Boyle (b. 1956)
Screenplay by: Frank Cottrell Boyce
Starring: Alex Etel, Lewis McGibbon, James Nesbitt, Daisy Donovan, Christopher Fulford

Context
The 2004 film *Millions* was directed by Danny Boyle and was based on a script written by Frank Cottrell Boyce. It differs from most adaptations in that the direction was reversed: the screenplay was written first, then the book. Boyce had written the script years before the film went into production, but he did not find a filmmaker who wanted to produce the film until the script fell into Boyle's hands. Boyle, who was best known for films such as the drug-addled dark comedy *Trainspotting* (1996), the action-adventure film *The Beach* (2000), and the zombie horror *28 Days Later* (2002), appeared an odd choice at first to direct a children's Christmas film, but the story and setting had wide appeal for Boyle, whose films across genres were usually centered in working-class British life.

While the two men collaborated on changes to the script, Boyce mentioned over dinner that he had always wanted to write a children's book. Boyle suggested that Boyce adapt his script to a novel in time to release it alongside the film. Boyce jumped at the chance and ultimately the book was published after filming was completed, but prior to the film's release. The book garnered immediate attention in the United Kingdom, where it was awarded the prestigious Carnegie Medal and was one of the books selected for the annual Liverpool Reads campaign in Liverpool, Boyce's hometown.

Originally, Boyle considered filming *Millions* as a musical, but the production team lacked the time and confidence to make the concept work. "If we were approaching *Millions* now, I'd definitely do it as a musical," Boyle said in 2013. "It's the perfect vehicle for singing. There'd be no strangeness about it, you'd just accept it." To play the lead roles of brothers Damian and Anthony, Boyle cast newcomers Alex Etel and Lewis McGibbon, respectively. While McGibbon did have a small prior television role, both actors were new to the big screen, making *Millions* the breakout role for both. To round out the cast, veteran British television and film actors James Nesbitt, Daisy Donovan, and Christopher Fulford, among others, were cast in various supporting roles.

Film Analysis
What is most striking about *Millions*, before one examines the plot, characters, or narrative themes, is the film's setting. The action takes place in Northern England but is transformed from the usual cliché of dreary expanses and crooked teeth, which Boyle is himself sometimes known for. The scenery is green and lush, beneath crisp blue skies. The buildings are bright and cheery. The various characters, who inhabit this world, are good-natured and friendly. The film is a blend of hyperrealism and fantasy, mixing Christian mysticism with themes of loss, charity, and self-actualization.

The story centers on Damian (Etel), a seven-year-old boy with a deep sense of religious faith and compassion. Damian is obsessed with soccer and the lives of the saints, which he studies to the point of obsession. As his mother has recently died, Damian spends much of his time speaking to imaginary friends embodying the very saints he is so obsessed with. Saint Peter (Alun Armstrong), Clare of Assisi (Kathryn Pogson), Saint Francis (Enzo Cilenti), among a score of others, make appearances to Damian, interact with him, and offer guidance and advice. But Boyle does not present the saints that visit Damian as pure and divine. These are eccentric individuals, quirky, maybe crazed. It is while Damian is speaking to one of these saints, Clare of Assisi, discussing her turn as patron saint of television, that a bag of money falls from the sky. The bag of money and the question of what to do with it, becomes the central conflict of the story. Damian, a boy filled with empathy and selflessness, wants to give the money to those in need, while his brother Anthony (McGibbon), older and more world-weary, wants to spend the money on himself, buying things and using it as a way to elevate his social status in school.

In a twist that puts urgency into the boys' actions and choices, Britain is about to switch to the Euro, and so in a matter of days the money they suddenly acquired—made up entirely of British pounds—will be worthless. For Boyle and Boyce, the money is a lens through which to explore the conflict between altruism and cynicism, between charity and selfishness, but the filmmakers are also conscious that even the best intentions are not always clear-cut or easily negotiated. As Damian works to give the money away to those in need, he often struggles with identifying who is in need and getting people to accept his gifts. More often than not, Damian's attempts at selflessness create more problems than they solve.

The heart of the film is the death of Damian's mother and the way each of the survivors cope with the loss. The boys' father, Ronnie (Nesbitt) is barely hanging on, struggling to get through each day in his new role of widower and single father. Anthony is angry at the loss, and his need to buy happiness drives much of his motivation. While for Damian, the loss is more layered, hidden in his good works and his orthodox belief system. He asks the saints he meets if they have seen his mother in Heaven. "She's new," he adds. The action in the film, as well as the moral questions, are upended when the boys learn that the money was not some sort of gift from Heaven, as Damian assumed, but rather the ill-gotten gains from a train robbery. A group of robbers had broken into a train carrying British pounds meant to be destroyed ahead of the switch to the Euro and so they tossed bags of money in various locations along the tracks for collection later. One of these bags just happened to land right next to Damian.

From here the film is less about the conflict between Anthony and Damian, and charity versus selfishness, and becomes one of conflict between the boys and the robber now on their heels, trying to retrieve the money. The film eventually ends with the robber captured by police and Damian choosing to burn the money, deciding that it had

done more harm than good. As the money burns, Damian is visited by his dead mother who assures him he no longer needs to worry about her. It is a poignant scene, which wraps nicely both central threads of the film: the question of what to do with the money, and the grief that sits just beneath the surface. It should be noted also that the film takes place during the Christmas holiday, adding extra emphasis to questions about materialism and greed. At one point, after the robber ransacks the family's home in search of the stolen money, Ronald decides to take the boys on a Christmas shopping spree. Later, it is not just the robber but a group of late-night beggars that ultimately lead Damian to destroy the money rather than just give it to anyone who might need it.

Money cannot buy popularity, or a way out of grief, nor can money alone solve the problems of the world; happiness and prosperity, Boyle and Boyce make clear, come from family, community, and friendship. In the final scenes of the film, Damian, who it is implied is on the road to sainthood himself, dreams of riding a rocket ship to Africa to build water wells. Damian explains through narration that the little money remaining was pooled together to build the wells, which is one of the most effective ways to improve the lives of people in destitute regions.

Significance

Millions premiered on September 14, 2004, at the Toronto International Film Festival and was subsequently picked up for general theatrical release on April 29, 2005. Immediately, the film was hailed by critics who found it to be a funny, sometimes moving, holiday film fit for the entire family. Roger Ebert, in his review of the film, wrote: "Boyce and Boyle have performed a miracle with their movie. This is one of the best films of the year." Audiences agreed. While the film faced some obstacles in theaters, including competition from Steven Spielberg's sci-fi blockbuster *War of the Worlds*, and the fact that it was a holiday film released months prior to Christmas, *Millions* still managed to earn approximately $11 million at the box office, more than covering its original budget.

Both Boyle and Boyce went on to work on more projects, albeit separately, with Boyle finding major critical and commercial success four years later with his Academy Award-winning crime drama *Slumdog Millionaire*. The breakout star of the film, Alex Etel went on to star in more films and television shows, including a leading role in 2007's *The Water Horse: Legend of the Deep. Millions* ended up receiving numerous accolades in the form of award nominations and honors, including a 2005 British Independent Film Award for Best Screenplay, and a 2005 Phoenix Film Critics Association Award for Best Live Action Family Film. Today, it remains an underappreciated but highly cherished holiday and family film, with new audiences discovering it each year around Christmas.

—*KP Dawes, MA*

Further Reading

Chiou, Grace Y. *Feel-Good Giving: The Mythic Construction of Generosity in Millions*, 2015. University of Denver, PhD dissertation, digitalcommons.du.edu/etd/1396. Accessed 25 Mar. 2020.

Dunham, Brent. *Danny Boyle: Interviews*. UP Mississippi, 2011.

Martin, James. *My Life with the Saints*. Loyola Press, 2006.

Bibliography

Dargis, Manohla. "Before Soaring Imagination Is Grounded by Convention." *The New York Times*, 11 Mar. 2005, www.nytimes.com/2005/03/11/movies/before-soaring-imagination-is-grounded-by-convention.html. Accessed 25 Mar. 2020.

Davis, Edward. "Danny Boyle Explains Why *Millions* Should Have Been a Musical, Calls It the Ultimate Genre He Hopes to Tackle." *IndieWire*, 12 Apr. 2013, www.indiewire.com/2013/04/danny-boyle-explains-why-millions-should-have-been-a-musical-calls-it-the-ultimate-genre-he-hopes-to-tackle-99456/. Accessed 25 Mar. 2020.

Ebert, Roger. "Unexpected Riches Abound." *RogerEbert.com*, 17 Mar. 2005, www.rogerebert.com/reviews/millions-2005. Accessed 25 Mar. 2020.

"*Millions*." *IMDb*, www.imdb.com/title/tt0366777/. Accessed 25 Mar. 2020.

Windolf, Jim. "The Danny Boyle Project, Part Three: *Millions*." *Vanity Fair*, 2 Mar. 2009, www.vanityfair.com/news/2009/03/the-danny-boyle-project-part-three-millions. Accessed 25 Mar. 2020.

The Miseducation of Cameron Post

The Novel
Author: Emily M. Danforth (b. 1980)
First published: 2012

The Film
Year released: 2018
Director: Desiree Akhavan (b. 1984)
Screenplay by: Desiree Akhavan, Cecilia Frugiuele
Starring: Chloë Grace Moretz, Sasha Lane, Forrest Goodluck, Emily Skeggs, John Gallagher Jr.

Context

The Miseducation of Cameron Post was author Emily M. Danforth's debut novel. Drawing on her experience of growing up as a lesbian in Montana in the 1990s, it chronicles the adolescence of its title character beginning when she is twelve years old. That was the year her parents die in a car accident and she kisses a girl for the first time. While her parents were not particularly religious, after their death, Cameron is sent to live with an evangelical Christian aunt, who encourages her to attend her church and join its youth group.

The novel follows Cameron through her first several years of high school, which includes her relationship with a temporary transplant from Seattle named Lindsay and her half-hearted attempt to date her male friend Jamie. She then becomes romantically involved with her best friend and longtime crush, Coley, but the two are soon found out. Following this incident, Cameron's aunt sends her to God's Promise, a residential program that practices "conversion therapy," purporting to rid teenagers of same-sex attraction. The book was well received by critics, earning starred reviews in *Booklist*, *Publishers Weekly*, *Kirkus*, and *School Library Journal*. In addition, the editors of *Booklist* selected it as one of the best young adult books of 2012, and it became commonly assigned reading in high schools but was occasionally challenged by parents who objected to its subject matter.

Desiree Akhavan, who adapted the book for the big screen with Cecilia Frugiuele and who also directed the film, had written and directed one previous feature film, *Appropriate Behavior* (2014). The semiautobiographical film tells the story of a bisexual Iranian American woman struggling to come out to her family. In depicting a lesbian woman who is secure in her identity but dealing with the disapproval of more conservative family members, *Appropriate Behavior* covers some of the same thematic ground as *Cameron Post*, albeit in a more comedic way and with less serious consequences.

In 2012, when the novel was published, there were already a number of young adult novels about lesbian or bisexual teenaged girls coming of age and coming out, including Nancy Garden's *Annie on My Mind* (1982), Julie Ann Peters's *Keeping You a Secret* (2003), and Lauren Myracle's *Kissing Kate* (2003). However, conversion therapy was relatively unexplored subject matter for the subgenre. In the film, *Cameron Post*'s most obvious predecessor is *But I'm A Cheerleader* (1999), directed by Jamie Babbit, which also portrays a lesbian teenager's experience in a residential conversion therapy program. However, *Cheerleader* is a dark comedy while *Cameron Post*, despite some humorous scenes, is largely a drama. Several reviews of the film also compared it to *One Flew Over the Cuckoo's Nest* (1975): like the protagonist of that film, Cameron is indefinitely institutionalized in an abusive facility where authority figures attempt to undermine her sense of self, which she eventually rebels against.

Film Analysis

The film version of *Cameron Post*, which has a running time of about ninety minutes, narrows its focus to Cameron's time at God's Promise, a relatively small section of the novel. It opens with Cameron (Chloë Grace Moretz) and Coley (Quinn Shephard) going to their school's homecoming dance with their respective boyfriends, brushing them off to dance with each other, then sneaking off to make out in the back of a car. One of the boyfriends finds them and Cameron is quickly packed off to God's Promise, where she spends the rest of the film.

Unlike most of the teenagers in the program—referred to as "disciples"—Cameron does not believe that there is anything wrong with her. She soon befriends the program's other two skeptics: Jane (Sasha Lane), whose ex-hippie mother recently married a more conservative man, and Adam (Forrest Goodluck), a member of the Lakota nation, whose father converted to Christianity to further his political career. The two often claim to be going on hikes in order to wander the woods surrounding the facility without oversight, and Cameron joins them on these excursions. She also adopts their strategy of telling the program's leaders, Dr. Marsh (Jennifer Ehle) and Reverend Rick (John Gallagher Jr.), what they want to hear in the hope of being allowed to return home sooner. Marsh and Rick do not physically harm the disciples, and Rick, at least, appears friendly and kind, but they are constantly repeating the message that the teenagers are doing something wrong by being themselves. Most of the disciples, including Cameron's roommate Erin (Emily Skeggs), are shown to have internalized this message and to be deeply unhappy as a result.

When another disciple, Mark (Owen Campbell) is hospitalized after an incident of self-harm, the government launches an investigation into God's Promise. Cameron attempts to explain to the investigator that the program is harmful despite appearing innocuous on the surface, saying, "How is programming people to hate themselves not emotional abuse?" However, the investigator does not accept that argument and ultimately nothing comes of the investigation. Realizing that the authorities will not do anything to help them, Cameron, Jane, and Adam decide to run away. In the last scene, they are seen hitchhiking away from the camp toward an uncertain destination.

The novel version of *Cameron Post* is written in the first person, so while Cameron is not a very talkative character, readers are privy to her thoughts. The film does not compensate by increasing Cameron's dialogue or including voice-over narration, instead relying on the actor's facial expressions to convey her thought processes. Some critics felt this worked well, while others found Cameron enigmatic and difficult to connect with. Cameron spends the earlier parts of the film emotionally closed-off, socially isolated, and disconnected from her surroundings, which is communicated by the actor but also supported by the cinematography. For instance, there are many shots of Cameron that are taken from a distance that show her either completely alone or far away from the rest of the disciples.

The film, like the book, is set in the 1990s, which influences the costuming and overall aesthetic, especially in scenes outside of God's Promise, such as Cameron's flashbacks and the disciples' occasional excursions to a nearby town. Within God's Promise, however, the era is harder to pin down. The disciples wear uniforms similar to those that private school students might have worn anytime between 1950 and the early twenty-first century—the girls in cardigans, blouses, skirts, and wool tights and the boys in button-down shirts, sweater vests, and slacks. Dr. Marsh wears 1980s business suits, while Reverend Rick sports a 1970s mustache. The program's ban on secular pop culture removes many of the other cues that might indicate the decade. This serves to highlight the regressive nature of God's Promise but may also encourage audiences not to view the film as a period piece, as the issues it deals with were still relevant at the time of the film's release.

Despite its heavy subject matter, the film retains a sense of optimism, particularly in the scenes that demonstrate Cameron's bonding with Jane and Adam. As with Cameron's isolation in the earlier scenes, the film's visuals are used to reinforce this mood: God's Promise is often shown in a somewhat chilly color palette, but scenes in which the three friends sneak away to the woods to hang out without supervision are shown in a warm, golden light.

Significance

The film debuted in January 2018 at the Sundance Film Festival where it won the Grand Jury Prize, the festival's highest honor. It went on to be shown at nearly thirty film festivals in twenty different countries and was released in theaters in the United States in August of that year. It grossed approximately $1,452,000 on a budget of $900,000.

Reviews of *Cameron Post* were generally positive, with most praising the performances of Moretz, Lane, and Goodluck, as well as Ehle and Gallagher. A number of reviews noted that the scenes of intimacy between Cameron and other girls were tasteful and felt natural, in contrast to the way such scenes are often treated in film. However, some critics felt that the film's pacing was too slow despite its short run time, with Cameron's self-assured nature providing little dramatic tension between her arrival at the camp and the start of her rebellion. Ella Taylor, for example, wrote in a review for *NPR* that "the tone in the middle sections is a bit of a flat plane," while Jesse Hassenger for *The A.V. Club* wrote that the film "stagnates" in the middle, elaborating, "These characters are confined, and the screenplay...doesn't exactly figure out how to generate story momentum from that confinement." Nevertheless, even those who criticized the pacing largely felt that the strong beginning and ending, as well as the excellent performances, made up for the slow middle section.

The film was praised for bringing attention to the issue of conversion therapy by lesbian, gay, bisexual, transgender, and queer (LGBTQ) advocacy organizations.

—Emma Joyce

Further Reading

Clark, Nicole. "*Miseducation of Cameron Post* Explores the Quiet Torture of Gay Conversion Therapy." *Vice*, 3 Aug. 2018, www.vice.com/en_us/article/a3qnq5/miseducation-of-cameron-post-explores-the-quiet-torture-of-gay-conversion-therapy. Accessed 23 Mar. 2020.

Pini, Barbara, et al. "Queering Rurality: Reading *The Miseducation of Cameron Post* Geographically." *Children's Geographies*, vol. 15, no. 3, 13 Nov. 2016, pp. 362-73.

Bibliography

Grobar, Matt. "*The Miseducation of Cameron Post*: After Introspective Hiatus, Chloë Grace Moretz Returns to Her Purpose." *Deadline*, 4 Dec. 2018, deadline.com/2018/12/chloe-grace-moretz-the-miseducation-of-cameron-post-interview-news-1202512949/. Accessed 23 Mar. 2020.

Hassenger, Jesse. "The Affecting *Miseducation of Cameron Post* Sends Chloë Grace Moretz to Gay-Conversion School." *AV Club*, 30 July 2018, film.avclub.com/the-affecting-miseducation-of-cameron-post-sends-chloe-1827970272. Accessed 23 Mar. 2020.

Miller, Hayley. "Video: New Film *The Miseducation of Cameron Post* Focuses on Dangers of 'Conversion Therapy.'" *Human Rights Campaign*, 21 Aug. 2018, www.hrc.org/blog/video-new-film-the-miseducation-of-cameron-post-focuses-on-dangers-of-conve. Accessed 23 Mar. 2020.

Sittenfeld, Curtis. "The Best Novel about a 'De-Gaying Camp' Ever Written." *Slate*, 8 Feb. 2012, slate.com/human-interest/2012/02/the-miseducation-of-cameron-post-by-emily-danforth-a-conversation-between-the-writer-and-novelist-curtis-sittenfeld.html. Accessed 23 Mar. 2020.

Taylor, Ella. "*The Miseducation of Cameron Post*: Lesbian, Interrupted." *NPR*, 2 Aug. 2018, www.npr.org/2018/08/02/634610702/the-miseducation-of-cameron-post-lesbian-interrupted. Accessed 23 Mar. 2020.

Moby Dick

The Novel
Author: Herman Melville (1819-91)
First published: 1851

The Film
Year released: 1956
Director: John Huston (1906-87)
Screenplay by: Ray Bradbury, John Huston
Starring: Gregory Peck, Richard Basehart, Leo Genn, Orson Welles, Friedrich von Ledebur

Context

By the mid-twentieth century, Herman Melville's *Moby-Dick* had come to be regarded as one of the classic novels of American literature. (Melville, oddly, used a hyphen in the title but no hyphen when discussing the whale to whom the title refers.) The massive book had received mixed reviews when it was first published, but, especially after the so-called Melville Revival of the 1920s, *Moby-Dick* came to be considered a powerfully written and profound study of epic ambitions and epic defeat. It had been filmed a number of times before the famous director John Huston undertook the task of filming it again in the 1950s, and it has been filmed several more times in ensuing decades. Although no motion picture can probably ever do justice to the notorious richness of Melville's novel, Huston liked to tackle difficult projects. His film was not the commercial success he hoped and assumed it would be, but it remains, perhaps, the best Hollywood version ever created of Melville's book. Part of the credit for that achievement is due to Ray Bradbury, the film's main screenwriter, although Huston was also given credit for part of the work on the script.

Most people who have watched Huston's film have probably been most intrigued by the sheer adventure of hunting whales in the mid-nineteenth century. This involved the pursuit of massive, dangerous creatures by brave men far out at sea in relatively flimsy boats and ships and with relatively primitive weapons, such as hand-thrown harpoons. (By contrast, modern whaling seems almost a gruesomely industrial enterprise, with few risks for the hunters and almost no chances for the whales.) Films like Huston's arouse an almost archetypal interest in quest narratives featuring daring risk-takers willing to pit themselves against the massive forces of nature, whether these

forces are vast oceans, fearsome storms, huge and dangerous creatures, or, as in *Moby Dick* (the film title also used no hyphen), all of these at once. One archetypal element missing from this narrative, both in the film and in the book, is a heterosexual love interest; but the male bonding, close friendship, and growing maturity in both the book and the film feature provide varied substitutes. Most viewers entering darkened theaters in the 1950s would also have known that *Moby Dick* is a story of initiation (involving a young man called Ishmael, played by Richard Basehart); that it features an especially mysterious and imposing central character (Captain Ahab, played by Gregory Peck); and that it ends in tragedy for practically everyone concerned. Early viewers would also have wanted to see how the moviemaker's special effects could possibly do justice not only to whale hunting in general but to the gigantic, terrifying white whale in particular. All the elements just mentioned, which helped give the film its initial appeal to some viewers, have also helped it retain its interest to the present day. Huston's movie impressed many critics, even if it mostly failed at the box office.

Film Analysis

Perhaps the most immediately striking difference between the novel and the film is the apparent age of Ishmael, the narrator and a main character of both the novel and the movie. Richard Basehart, who was in his early forties when he played the role, will strike some viewers as too old to play Ishmael, whom Melville (who was around thirty when he wrote the novel) depicts as a kind of naive, inexperienced alter ego. Huston wanted a veteran actor, rather than a newcomer, to play this part, but some viewers may wish that he had chosen someone who at least *looked* younger than the middle-aged Basehart. In any case, most critics have felt that the other roles are very well cast. Orson Welles is memorably impressive as an eloquent, commanding Father Mapple; Leo Genn is completely convincing as the sober, morally serious Starbuck; Harry Andrews is full of strength, good humor, and vitality as Stubb; and Friedrich von Ledebur, an Austrian aristocrat, is unforgettable as the heavily tattooed South Sea Islander named Queequeg. In fact, it is hard to think of a role that is badly cast except, perhaps, the role of Ishmael, and even in that case the deficiencies involve simple appearance rather than poor acting.

Some initial reviewers, however, felt that Gregory Peck was badly cast as Captain Ahab. They found Peck too understated, too cerebral, and too similar in appearance to Abraham Lincoln to be convincing as Melville's dark, tormented, mysteriously motivated captain. Even Peck himself doubted that he was right for the part. Huston, however, never regretted his choice of Peck, and it is easy to see why. Huston thought that Peck brought to the role of Ahab a kind of dignity, seriousness, and grandeur that captured, at least in part, the sort of commanding figure Melville had had in mind. Peck could be histrionic when histrionics were called for, but his best scenes, according to his defenders, are those in which he seems most meditative, most thoughtful, most compelled and compelling. His discussion with Stubb, for instance, when he pores over an elaborate sea chart and explains exactly *how* he plans to find Moby Dick in the whole immensity of the Pacific Ocean, is intriguing in several respects. First, admirers considered this scene very well written, especially since much of the phrasing is not Melville's but was concocted by Bradbury, either alone or in consultation with Huston. Melville's own language is notoriously rich, but the screenwriters for the film, in the opinion of many, more than held their own in composing the language for some very important episodes.

The scene involving Ahab and his charts suggests that Bradbury or Huston wanted to explain, to any skeptical modern viewers, precisely *why* Ahab felt so confident that he could know exactly when and where he would find the great white whale. In general, the film can seem even more scrupulous than the book in clarifying (and perhaps simplifying) characters' motives and behavior. Thus, Stubb opposes Ahab's vengeful hunt for Moby Dick partly because the devout Stubb believes that whale hunting should produce as much whale oil as possible in order to benefit

humanity and thereby to please God. In general, the film emphasizes that Ahab is arguably guilty of religious blasphemy, but the movie's defenders felt that it never turned Ahab into a simple villain. They argued that the film, like Melville's novel, presented Ahab as an immensely complex character. Some negative early reviewers, however, apparently wanted an Ahab who would seem merely, and simplistically, crazed with vengeful anger.

In general, Huston sought to achieve a convincing realism, especially in the scenes he set (and often even shot) at sea. He explained that he wanted the film to look gray and dark rather than sharp and colorful. Sometimes, in fact, it is easy to forget that the movie *is* shot in color; it often has a deliberately muted look that helps emphasize the darkness of the novel's characterizations and themes. The scenes shot in the small fishing village from which Ahab's ship departs look completely convincing, as do the scenes shot on the ship itself. (This is less true when the men are shown in small boats.) Huston found and purchased an old wooden ship to use in the filming, and many of the whale-hunting scenes were authentic (with Huston boasting about the large number of whales actually killed). The scenes featuring Moby Dick himself look remarkably realistic for the time: a total of three ninety-foot models supposedly were created and hauled out to sea, and although two of them broke away and were lost, the third survived long enough to allow filming to be completed. Peck was willing and indeed eager to do repeated takes of the final episode, in which he is strapped to the back of Moby Dick as the great whale plunges into and out of the surging water. Although this stunning sequence was shot in a huge tank in a studio, it seems impressively realistic, and in fact realism is at the heart of Huston's film in every way, including in Peck's realistic (rather than overly melodramatic) performance. He is, in more ways than one, a restrained Ahab and is all the more convincing for that reason. Bradbury's dialogue, meanwhile, often has the poetry one expects from Melville. Huston hired Bradbury, in part, because he admired the young man's poetic streak, and there are passages in this film that sound convincingly Melvillean even when they depart from Melville's text.

Although much of the original novel was inevitably cut from the movie (including its philosophical speculations, its frequent humor, and also the character known as Fedallah, whom Bradbury considered a nuisance), the plot of the film stays fairly faithful to the plot of the book. The film emphasizes men's singing much more than the book does, and the scene of lonely women gathered at the dock as the ship pulls out to sea reminds viewers that whalers were members of communities, leaving behind wives, mothers, daughters, and sons. But despite the general realism of the film's style, Huston also manages to create (or recreate) moments of striking symbolism, as when Ahab tempers steel with blood, or when he grasps three harpoons together to make a kind of perverted cross, or when he looks up and sees the ship's masts glowing with the eerie green light of the phenomenon known as St. Elmo's fire. The close-up of Moby Dick's eye is equally eerie and is one of many touches that help make the film seem even more powerful decades after it was first released. The score, especially when Moby Dick is attacking and pummeling the doomed ship, is full of energy and drama, and the almost-final vision of the ship slowly being sucked under the surface as it twists in a whirlpool of its own making is one of those unforgettable moments that make filmmaking so great an artform.

Significance

Much to the disappointment of all involved, *Moby Dick* was not the blockbuster hit its makers had hoped and even assumed it would be. The $4.5 million it had cost to make the film was not recouped upon its initial release. But it *was* praised by some critics (Huston even won the best director award from the New York Film Critics Circle). Huston himself later said that if he had made Moby Dick more the sort of obviously terrifying creature featured decades later in *Jaws*, the film might have been a greater popular success. Perhaps Huston's respect for Melville's novel led him to make a more thoughtful, less obviously exciting, picture than many filmgoers wanted. The scenes in which Ahab speaks with Stubb, which are beautifully written, may not have been the sort of thing audiences were hoping for. In fact, a few of the chase scenes, some of them obviously filmed in a studio rather than at sea, are among the film's least impressive moments. Psychologically and morally, the film seems quite realistic, and most of its special effects remain impressive. But some of the efforts to achieve realistic "action" fall short, especially when the sailors are shown in small boats. Melville's

novel can probably never be turned into a film as great as the book itself, but Huston's film seems more impressive as each decade goes by and new directors try to creator better film versions of *Moby-Dick*.

One aspect of Huston's film that seems especially impressive in retrospect is its emphasis on multiculturalism, particularly in a film from the 1950s. Ahab's crew prominently features an African man, an African American boy, a Native American man, and a Pacific Islander, not to mention people of various European ethnic backgrounds. Huston and Bradbury, like Melville himself, treat all these different kinds of people with respect, showing how each makes his own distinctive contribution to the success of the voyage. The *Pequod*, Ahab's ship, becomes in effect a microcosm of all sorts of people and personalities cooperating to achieve a common goal, even if that goal, eventually, becomes perverted by the vengeful, relentless Ahab.

—*Robert C. Evans, PhD*

Further Reading

McFarland, Douglas, and Wesley King, editors. *John Huston as Adaptor*. SUNY P, 2017.

Peary, Gerald, and Roger Shatzkin. *The Classic American Novel and the Movies*. Frederick Ungar, 1977.

Pratley, Gerald. *The Cinema of John Huston*. A. S. Barnes, 1977.

Bibliography

Bradbury, Ray. *Green Shadows, White Whale: A Novel of Ray Bradbury's Adventures Making Moby Dick with John Huston in Ireland*. Avon Books, 1998.

Metz, Walter C. "The Cold War's 'Undigested Apple-Dumpling': Imaging *Moby-Dick* in 1956 and 2001." *Literature/Film Quarterly*, vol. 32, no. 3, July 2004, pp. 222-28, opensiuc.lib.siu.edu/cgi/viewcontent.cgi?article=1024&context=cp_articles. Accessed 10 Jan. 2019.

Peloquin, David. "John Huston's 1956 Film *Moby Dick*: A 60th-Anniversary Appreciation." *Leviathan*, vol. 19, no. 2, June 2017, pp. 111-14, doi:10.1353/lvn.2017.0030. Accessed 10 Jan. 2019.

Stone, Edward. "Ahab Gets Girl, or Herman Melville Goes to the Movies." *Literature/Film Quarterly*, vol. 3, no. 2, Spring 1975, pp. 172-81. *Academic Search Complete*, search.ebscohost.com/login.aspx?direct=true&db=a9h&AN=7151711. Accessed 10 Jan. 2019.

Monster

The Novel
Authors: Aileen Wuornos (1956-2002), Christopher Berry-Dee
First published: 2004

The Film
Year released: 2003
Director: Patty Jenkins (b. 1971)
Screenplay by: Patty Jenkins
Starring: Charlize Theron, Christina Ricci, Bruce Dern, Lee Tergesen

Context

In 1991 Florida resident Aileen Wuornos was arrested for killing at least seven men beginning in 1989. A drifter who had suffered a violent childhood before turning to prostitution, she took full responsibility for the murders but initially claimed they were done in self-defense. A media frenzy quickly developed around her case, and she was variously portrayed as a cold-blooded psychopath or a sympathetic victim herself. Sentenced to death despite questions over her mental state, Wuornos eventually retracted her claim of self-defense and showed little remorse up to her execution in 2002. She remains one of the most famous female serial killers in US history. Her life has been examined in numerous documentaries and books, including the posthumously published semiautobiographical *Monster: My True Story* (2004), cowritten by Christopher Berry-Dee.

Filmmaker Patty Jenkins had been interested in Wuornos's story for years. Born into a military family, Jenkins's initial foray into the arts was as a painter, but she changed course after taking an experimental film class. She worked as a cameraperson before pursuing a career as a director. After graduating from the American Film Institute (AFI) in 2000, she was told by a contact in the film industry that serial killer films were enjoying a surge of popularity and therefore presented a good opportunity for first-time filmmakers. Jenkins resurrected her idea of a film about Wuornos and chose to write a screenplay herself.

While working on the script for what would become *Monster*, Jenkins began a correspondence with Wuornos, who was incarcerated in Florida at the time. The two developed a trusting relationship, with Wuornos even sharing letters she had written—which Jenkins noted ulti-

mately supported the character portrait she developed. Wuornos reportedly sought fame and attention throughout her life, perhaps accounting for her willingness to discuss her story with figures such as Jenkins and Berry-Dee. However, the filmmaker did not deeply discuss the content of her script with Wuornos. Other sources, including court transcripts and interview footage of Wuornos, helped to fill out the screenplay.

With star Charlize Theron attached in the lead role, *Monster* was shot on location in Florida. It can be compared to other serial-killer-themed films of the era, ranging from the black comedy literary adaptation *American Psycho* (2000) to the nonfiction-based *Zodiac* (2007). Later works such *My Friend Dahmer* (2017) have continued the trend of biopics about serial killers. *Monster* was also part of something of a breakthrough year for women directors, as Sofia Coppola's *Lost in Translation* was also released in 2003 to great critical acclaim.

Film Analysis

The underlying intention of *Monster* is to showcase the humanity of a serial killer. To accomplish this, Jenkins depicts the film's events from the perspective of Aileen "Lee" Wuornos (Charlize Theron), allowing audiences to sympathize with her despite her increasingly immoral behavior. Aileen's point of view is established from the beginning of the film through the technique of voice over narration. In these lines, Aileen describes how her childhood aspirations was to become a movie star but because of a series of hardships it did not work out. When the film begins, she is a prostitute without a place to live, money, or anyone meaningful in her life. She is feeling so hopeless that she is considering suicide. On screen, Aileen immediately comes across as uneducated and generally rough around the edges. However, there is a gentleness buried deep within her as well, a quality that comes out when she meets a young woman named Selby (Christina Ricci).

The romantic relationship between Aileen and Selby is the film's narrative engine, driving the plot from the beginning until the very end. When Selby first sees Aileen at a bar, she tries to flirt with her, but Aileen is overtly hostile and defensive. Later Selby shows her kindness by offering her a place to stay for the night and Aileen develops feelings for her. Jenkins conveys the importance of their feelings for one another with a number of cinematic techniques. Where most of *Monster* is shot in a grittily realistic manner, the scenes focused specifically on their relationship have a more ethereal quality. For example, on their first date Aileen teaches Selby how to roller skate. They hold hands, the lights dim, and romantic pop music swells. Jenkins pushes into medium and closeup shots of the women, creating an atmosphere of deep affection and attraction. In a later scene, in which the two have sex, Jenkins opts for close-ups and soft lighting. This communicates the tenderness and emotional importance of the experience for Aileen, which contrasts with the uncomfortable, transactional sex she engages in with male clients. Ultimately, Jenkins ensures the Selby scenes are to viewers what they are to Aileen—a refuge from the cruelty of the troubled woman's real life.

The film's color palette is intended to provide insight into Aileen's emotional landscape. *Monster* is awash with desaturated browns and greys. This dingy aesthetic consumes every corner of Aileen's world—from the dive bars she frequents to the cheap motels she lives in with Selby. Simply put, everything around her is worn out, broken, and ugly. This is demonstrative of how she feels. As a sex worker who has endured abuse her entire life, Aileen is as emotionally beaten down as her environment. When Selby arrives in her life, offering love and hope, these feelings of despair change, and it is noticeable on screen. There are more scenes shot during the day, for example. In one particular montage sequence, Aileen goes around town looking for a legitimate job. She wears cheerful clothes and walks determinedly. The sun is shining and everything feels optimistic. This feeling ends, however, when a prospective employer laughs in Aileen's face and she is assaulted by a police officer. Without any other choices to make money to support Selby, she returns to prostitution.

In many ways, *Monster* is about the battle for Aileen's soul. There is a struggle between good and evil going on inside her. Jenkins depicts Aileen's descent into evil as a gradual stumble into the darkness. This begins one evening when a client drives her out to the middle of nowhere. She is eager to get the sex over with so that she can return to Selby. The man becomes hostile and knocks her unconscious, and when she comes to, she is being raped. Aileen then shoots her assailant in self-defense and takes his car and wallet. Shortly after, she realizes that she got away with the murder and decides to continue using the gun to kill and rob abusive men because it allows her to provide for Selby. Still, engaging in violence does not initially come easily to Aileen. On one afternoon early on, she almost murders a timid male client but restrains herself because it is clear he is not a bad person. By the end of the film, however, she has lost all of her morality. In a moment of desperation, she murders an innocent man after he offers her a ride. The fact that Jenkins chooses to shoot this last murder at night symbolizes the darkness that has finally taken over Aileen's soul.

While Jenkins does not excuse Aileen's murderous behavior, she does portray her as a victim of circumstances. This is evident in a scene in which Aileen and Selby go to a carnival and ride on a massive red Ferris wheel. Aileen reveals that when she was a child she was simultaneously attracted to and terrified by the ride, which was like a monster. The Ferris wheel is a metaphor for the patriarchy, which shaped Aileen's life from the time she was a young girl. No one ever cared about Aileen or tried to help her because she was mentally ill and a sex worker, meaning her life had less value than others. This constant abuse in turn facilitated her killing spree. In a scene where she confesses abstractly about her crimes to the kindly Vietnam veteran (Bruce Dern) from whom she rents a storage space, Aileen says that she felt she had no choice but to commit those crimes.

Monster the film is quite different from the book *Monster: My True Story*. Jenkins based her script on research as well as personal anecdotes that the real Aileen Wuornos had shared with her in written correspondence, but many names and certain events are changed and otherwise fictionalized. The director also chose to focus the film exclusively on the year of Wuornos's killing spree. On the other hand, *Monster: My True Story* covers the entirety of Aileen's life. The chapters begin with verbatim quotes from her and then biographer Christopher Berry-Dee lays out the details of the significant events of her life. It covers her childhood extensively, providing insight into the abuse that Wuornos suffered at the hands of her family. It also discusses her time at school, her pregnancy at age fourteen, the time she was married to an elderly millionaire, and her experience as a sex worker. Where the film is very much Jenkins's dramatized interpretation of Wuornos and her motivations, the book is more factual and detailed. In this way the two works serve different purposes despite being rooted in the same subject.

Significance

An independent production with a budget of just $8 million, *Monster* premiered in late 2003. After receiving a wide theater release in early 2004, it went on to earn $34.5 million at the domestic box office and a total of $60.4 million worldwide—a resounding commercial success. This performance was driven by predominantly positive reviews, including high praise from many influential critics. For example, Roger Ebert called it the best film of the year and later listed it as the third-best film of the decade. Despite some criticism of the factual inaccuracies of the story, including complaints from relatives of Wuornos's victims, *Monster* has largely maintained its strong reputation.

Much of the praise directed at the film focused on Theron's performance. To play Wuornos, the actor had to gain thirty pounds and wear a significant amount of makeup and prosthetics to make her look more weathered. Many reviewers and even those who had known Wuornos remarked on how close a resemblance was achieved. Beyond her physical transformation, however, Theron was required to play a mentally ill murderer who was simultaneously sympathetic and detestable. Her success in depicting such a complex character earned her a number of awards, including the Academy Award and Golden Globe Award for best actress. The film changed the trajectory of Theron's career, revitalizing her as a serious performer after a number of lighter roles.

Monster also launched Jenkins to fame. She won an Independent Spirit Award and the American Film Institute's Franklin J. Schaffner Alumni Medal for the film, which established her as director of note. She went on to helm several television projects, though for various reasons she struggled to land another feature film before directing the smash-hit superhero blockbuster *Wonder Woman* (2017), which became the highest-grossing film ever directed by a woman.

Monster dealt with issues of mental illness, sexual abuse, and female rage that are rarely seen in popular media. At the time of its release there were also few mainstream films with lesbian protagonists. Similarly, *Monster* is significant in its focus on a complicated female protagonist who is not attractive or likeable in a conventional way. In many ways, the film is groundbreaking in its depiction of a modern cinematic antiheroine.

—Emily E. Turner

Further Reading

Russell, Sue. "More of a Monster Than Hollywood Could Picture." *The Washington Post*, 8 Feb. 2004, www.washingtonpost.com/archive/opinions/2004/02/08/more-of-a-monster-than-hollywood-could-picture/179c7282-5e25-4eb5-8980-c72aa90efdb0/?utm_term=.2506691efe9e. Accessed 1 Apr. 2019.

Wuornos, Aileen. *Dear Dawn: Aileen Wuornos in Her Own Words*. Edited by Lisa Kester and Daphne Gottlieb, Soft Skull, 2012.

Bibliography

Ebert, Roger. Review of *Monster*, directed by Patty Jenkins. *RogerEbert.com*, 1 Jan. 2004, www.rogerebert.com/reviews/monster-2003. Accessed 1 Apr. 2019.

Holden, Stephen. "A Murderous Journey to Self-Destruction." Review of *Monster*, directed by Patty Jenkins. *The New York Times*, 24 Dec. 2004, www.nytimes.com/2003/12/24/movies/film-review-a-murderous-journey-to-self-destruction.html. Accessed 1 Apr. 2019.

Jenkins, Patty. "Behind the Making of a 'Monster.'" Interview by Stephanie Snipes. *CNN*, 19 Jan. 2004, www.cnn.com/2004/SHOWBIZ/Movies/01/19/jenkins.monster/. Accessed 1 Apr. 2019.

———. "An Interview with Patty Jenkins." *IGN*, 24 May 2004, www.ign.com/articles/2004/05/28/an-interview- with-patty-jenkins?page=1. Accessed 1 Apr. 2019.

Theron, Charlize. "The Making of Monster." Interview. *Advocate*, 17 Feb. 2004, www.advocate.com/news/2004/02/17/charlize-theron-making-monster. Accessed 1 Apr. 2019.

Motherless Brooklyn

The Novel
Author: Jonathan Lethem (b. 1964)
First published: 1999

The Film
Year released: 2019
Director: Edward Norton (b. 1969)
Screenplay by: Edward Norton
Starring: Edward Norton, Bruce Willis, Gugu Mbatha-Raw, Bobby Cannavale, Cherry Jones, Alec Baldwin, Willem Dafoe

Context

Motherless Brooklyn is a 2019 film written and directed by Edward Norton based on the book by the same name written by Jonathan Lethem and published in 1999. The novel, a neo-noir, won the 1999 National Book Critics Circle Award and 2000 Gold Dagger award for crime fiction and so there was a lot of interest in Hollywood about a possible adaptation. The film rights were bought by Edward Norton, fresh off his critically acclaimed starring role in the drama *American History X.* In October 1999, it was announced that Norton would produce and likely star in the film, but there was no word on who might direct.

Over the next several years, Norton slowly started planning the film and completed a script. Critically, Norton chose to scrap the novel's contemporary setting in favor of a 1950s setting. Norton reasoned that this made more sense for a noir detective story. For several years, Norton shopped the script around before finally deciding to take on the role of director himself. Norton had repeatedly clashed in the past with writers, directors, and producers over changes to films, and this made him somewhat of a persona non grata in certain circles in Hollywood, complicating his situation.

Production on *Motherless Brooklyn* began years later in February 2018 with numerous high-profile actors signing up for supporting roles, including Willem Dafoe, Bruce Willis, Gugu Mbatha-Raw, and Alec Baldwin, among others. Production was beset with problems from the outset, however, as on March 22, 2018, a fire broke out in the basement of the building where the production was housed. A New York City firefighter died in the blaze, resulting in production delays and a flurry of wrongful death lawsuits against Norton's production company Class 5

Inc., including one by the firefighter's widow. Production did eventually resume in and around New York and all told filming concluded after forty-six days with weeks of production work to follow. Radiohead's Thom Yorke contributed a song to the film and composer Daniel Pemberton wrote the score.

Film Analysis

Motherless Brooklyn is self-consciously film noir, and, unlike the book, set in 1950s New York City. Noir tropes abound, from the heavy use of shadows to the way that shots are framed. The jazz soundtrack adds another "period" element. By moving the setting from 1999 to 1957, the references to 1990s pop culture, so rife in the novel, vanish, and along with them, much of the story's personality. Lionel's (Edward Norton) backstory is minimized in the film, where it stands as a large framing device in the book. In the novel Lionel's outbursts from Tourette syndrome are part of the narration itself. In the film, we only encounter it in dialogue. The basic plot and ending differ, as while Norton's film is a classic if predictable detective noir with a happy ending, the book is a modern, self-aware, tongue-in-cheek homage to classic noir with a bittersweet ending in which Lionel goes back to the detective agency, alone, and most of the people in his life are either dead or have moved on.

The film, *Motherless Brooklyn*, is less an adaptation of the novel with which it shares its name, than it is a reimagining of the novel. The story of the film has a man battling shadowy forces of corruption in order to get to the truth of a highly personal crime: the murder of his mentor and father figure. Along the way he faces foes, suffers reversals of fortune, and endures betrayals. Lionel has a superpower, a photographic memory, which is a strength that is concealed by his Tourette's. But because of his uncontrollable outbursts, he is not considered a real threat, and this gives him room to act.

Laura is the protagonist's main love interest; her mother, a black woman, was raped by Moses (Alec Baldwin), the film's antagonist and a stand-in for the corrupt patriarchy that rules the city. Laura is therefore both the innocent victim of the story and a bridge between Moses and Lionel.

While much of the mystery might be focused on Laura, the story is firmly centered on Lionel. Interestingly, Lionel never defeats Moses but rather negotiates a settlement with him, wherein Moses gets what he wants (the ability to transform and rebuild the city without interference) and Laura is set free. Norton does hint at the possibility that Moses might still be held responsible for his corruption when Lionel sends details of his investigation to a reporter, but Moses's defeat is only implied. It should be noted that Norton goes to great lengths to depict women and people of color with dignity in his film, but this does little to change the fact that ultimately it is a white male hero who must save them.

In *Motherless Brooklyn*, women and people of color are presented as largely ignorant, often struggling against Lionel, not understanding that he is working for their benefit. When he is finally freed from the interference of others, he is able to resolve the main conflicts of the story by solving Frank's murder and saving Laura. In the end, we are left with the impression that Lionel will be made whole by Laura, who through her touch is able to settle his Tourette's outbursts.

Significance

Motherless Brooklyn was released on August 30, 2019, to mixed but generally positive reviews. While critics praised the performances and cinematography, they were not generally excited about the film. Unfortunately, the same could be said for audiences. In its entire theatrical run, *Motherless Brooklyn* earned a total box office of $18.5 million, unable to recoup its $26 million investment. While the film did garner some small award attention, it failed to achieve more than passing interest.

In the end, the film stands as more a testament to its creator than the book it is meant to adapt. Edward Norton has for years been labeled a difficult actor to work with for his insistence on shunning collaboration in favor of changing the work of others to match his specific vision. In *Motherless Brooklyn*, Norton serves as producer, director, writer, and star, and what audiences get in the end is his sole interpretation of Jonathan Lethem's book, what little resemblance it holds in the final result.

—KP Dawes, MA

Further Reading

Hirsch, Foster. *The Dark Side of the Screen*. Tantivy Press, 1981.

Marchese, David. "The Disruptive World of Edward Norton." *The New York Times Magazine*, 7 Oct. 2019, www.nytimes.com/interactive/2019/10/07/magazine/edward-norton-interview.html. Accessed 15 Mar. 2020.

Bibliography

Boone, Brian. "Why Edward Norton Doesn't Get Many Movie Offers." *Looper*, 10 July 2017, www.looper.com/19449/edward-norton-impossible-work/. Accessed 15 Mar. 2020.

Dumaraog, Ana. "Why Mark Ruffalo Replaced Edward Norton as Hulk in the MCU." *Screen Rant*, 12 Feb. 2019, screenrant.com/mark-ruffalo-edward-norton-hulk-replacement-reason/. Accessed 15 Mar. 2020.

Giardina, Carolyn. "Edward Norton on *Motherless Brooklyn*'s 20-Year Journey to Big Screen." *The Hollywood Reporter*, 8 Sept. 2019, www.hollywoodreporter.com/news/edward-norton-motherless-brooklyns-20-year-journey-big-screen-1237734. Accessed 15 Mar. 2020.

"Motherless Brooklyn." *IMDb*, www.imdb.com/title/tt0385887/. Accessed 15 Mar. 2020.

Sims, David. "*Motherless Brooklyn* Is a Passion Project Without Heart." *The Atlantic*, 31 Oct. 2019, www.theatlantic.com/entertainment/archive/2019/10/motherless-brooklyn-review-edward-norton-jonathan-lethem/601069/. Accessed 15 Mar. 2020.

Mudbound

The Novel
Author: Hillary Jordan (b. 1963)
First published: 2008

The Film
Year released: 2017
Director: Dee Rees (b. 1977)
Screenplay by: Dee Rees and Virgil Williams
Starring: Carey Mulligan, Garrett Hedlund, Jason Clarke, Jason Mitchell, Mary J. Blige, Rob Morgan, Jonathan Banks

Context

Hillary Jordan's debut novel, *Mudbound*, was published in March 2008. Positively received by critics, it won several awards, including the Bellwether Prize for fiction as well as the Alex Award from the American Library Association. A work of historical fiction, the novel takes place during the 1940s and explores one of the nation's most deep-rooted themes: racism. Specifically, Jordan examines the tenuous relationships between White and Black communities. The early 2000s saw the success of several works of historical fiction by White female authors that focused on the intersection between White and Black lives. Some of the better-known novels in this wave include the best sellers *The Secret Life of Bees* (2004), by Sue Monk Kidd and *The Help* (2009), by Kathryn Stockett. Yet while *Mudbound* shares some similarities with the other books in this trend, it focuses on specific historical events and has a darker tone. It is also significantly more critical of the role that White Americans play in upholding anti-Black racism.

In 2016, screenwriter-director Dee Rees agreed to spearhead a film adaptation of *Mudbound*. Rees first gained critical acclaim as a director with her semiautobiographical debut *Pariah* (2011), a feature film about a seventeen-year-old Black girl coming to terms with her homosexuality. Her next film was a historical biopic about the blues singer Bessie Smith titled *Bessie* (2015). In interviews, Rees stated that she signed on to write and direct the *Mudbound* film in part because she felt the story shared similarities to the experience of her own grandmother, who was the daughter of sharecroppers like some of the book's characters. Meanwhile, her cowriter on the screenplay, Virgil Williams, was especially drawn to the project because his grandfather fought in World War II in a segregated unit, like the character of Ronsel Jackson.

Ultimately, *Mudbound* (2017) proved to be a part of a 2010s wave of critically acclaimed films by Black directors who used their work to explore the history of racism in America. Other films in this movement include Steve McQueen's *12 Years a Slave* (2013) as well as Ava DuVernay's *Selma* (2014) and Barry Jenkins's *If Beale Street Could Talk* (2018).

Film Analysis

There are several notable differences between the *Mudbound* book and film. Both focus on the lives of the McAllans, struggling White farmers in Mississippi, and the Jacksons, Black sharecroppers who work on the McAllan farm. However, Rees and Williams's script fleshes out the Jackson family further so that audience gets to spend more time with them. This decision ensures that the story feels more balanced in its perspective and provides the Jackson characters with welcome additional depth.

Rees and Williams also put the friendship between Ronsel Jackson (Jason Mitchell) and Jamie McAllan (Garrett Hedlund) at the crux of the story in a way that Jordan does not. It is a choice that amplifies the film's dramatic tension as well as its central theme of how the two communities need one another. As Ronsel and Jamie not only represent their respective families but their races as well, the screenwriters use them to demonstrate just how differently they are treated by society. Both men are decorated heroes when they return from World War II, but Ronsel is treated as a second-class citizen. In a scene where he buys groceries at the store while in his army uniform, the McAllan patriarch Pappy (Jonathan Banks) makes him leave through the back entrance because he is Black. It is a stark contrast to his White counterpart, Jamie, who can go wherever he wants without consequences.

The other changes that Rees and Williams make to Jordan's characters and their arcs provide the narrative with a more hopeful outlook. In the book, for example, the character of Jamie is presented as ignorant toward Black people despite his burgeoning friendship with Ronsel. The film, on the other hand, makes him more understanding and openminded. This change to his character is especially evident in the scene where he reacts to learning that Ronsel has a son with a White German woman. While in the book Jamie is almost horrified, in the film he is congratulatory. It is important to note that Rees and Williams's changes to Jamie do not make him fall into the problematic "White savior" trope often perpetuated in mainstream films, especially by White filmmakers. Instead, they present him as an ally. Another noteworthy change that the screenwriters implement to make the film feel more hopeful than the book is having Ronsel seek out his son in the last act. In addition to providing the film with a happier ending, the imagery of a Black father being reunited with his son is powerful because it is so rarely depicted in media.

To capture the intimacy and unique storytelling style of the *Mudbound* book, Rees uses voice-over. This filmmaking tool successfully emulates Jordan's vignette-like chapters, which shift between each of the six primary characters' first-person narratives. Voice-over also provides the audience with insight into the thoughts of the Jacksons and the McAllans on both their struggles as well as their interactions with each other. For example, when Henry McAllan (Jason Clarke) calls on Florence Jackson (Mary J. Blige) to help Laura McAllan (Carey Mulligan) with their sick children, it is unclear whether or not she obliges out of kindness. Florence's voice-over then reveals that she grew up resenting the fact that her mother was always gone working as the caretaker for White children. Henry's request, however, made her realize that her mother did it out of love for her—not out of love for those White children. Ultimately, Florence articulates what so many Black women of her generation were required to do to take care of their families. If she had refused Henry's request, she would have been putting her own family at risk of his resentment, which could have dire consequences for them.

At its core, *Mudbound* is about the complex, interdependent relationship between Black and White American lives in the mid-twentieth century. The film demonstrates that in the rural South, poor communities of both races were often linked, though Jim Crow laws kept them as far apart as possible. Rees directs the camera to illustrate this reality. White and Black characters are rarely seen in the same frame together, which reflects the existence of societal segregation. When Rees does have characters of different races share the screen, it is either out of a White character's emotional need or a desire to inflict violence. When Laura is grieving a miscarriage, for example, there is a moment when she grabs Florence and weeps. Rees pushes into a close-up of Laura wrapped around Florence's arm, focusing on the contrast of their skin tones as well as the way in which Laura uses Florence as support.

The Black and White characters who are most often shown in the same frame are Ronsel and Jamie, who break the unspoken rules of Jim Crow by riding around in Jamie's truck together. While depicting them together is demonstrative of their friendship, Rees ensures that it always feels somewhat formal and precarious. This is evident in the scene where Ronsel and Jamie drink outside of a barn and reveal their darkest secrets to one another. The camera captures them in a wide shot, but there is a fallen beam across the frame that symbolically suggests that even though they are friends, there is still a significant barrier between them.

Throughout the film Rees further harnesses Rachel Morrison's vivid cinematography to communicate how the characters are at the mercy of forces much larger than them. For the Jacksons, it is the force of racism that is almost inescapable. For the McAllans, it is poverty and nature. To convey their sense of helplessness, Rees often presents the characters in wide shots surrounded by lots of negative space, making them look small. She also emphasizes green and brown tones to emphasize how much power the natural elements have over the characters. Arguably the most significant way that Rees brings the audience into the characters' experiences is by making everything in their world appear as authentic as possible. To accomplish this, she shot many of the scenes in actual sharecropper houses from the late 1800s. Furthermore, the soft color saturation and compositions of many of Morrison's shots emulate photographs taken during the Great Depression in the 1930s and 1940s by photographers such as Dorothea Lange.

Significance

Mudbound premiered at the 2017 Sundance Film Festival and its distribution rights were purchased by the streaming service Netflix. It was released to wider audiences on November 17, 2017, both on Netflix as well as in select theaters. The film's bifurcated debut was demonstrative of the film industry's often difficult relationship with streaming platforms; while the late 2010s saw an increase in prestige cinema being released to audiences directly online rather than through theaters, streaming services were not initially considered legitimate by the Academy of Motion Picture Arts and Sciences. As such, *Mudbound* was required to have a one-week theatrical release to qualify for the Academy Awards.

Once released, the film was met with overwhelmingly positive acclaim. Most critics extolled the actors' performances but focused even more praise on the quality of Rees's filmmaking. Many argued that *Mudbound* was an instant classic thanks to its well-wrought depiction of American history, beautiful cinematography, and epic narrative. In his review for *The Guardian*, critic Peter Bradshaw summed up this view, stating, "There's a rich, arterial force in this film's storytelling: director Dee Rees handles the material with flair and real passion. It's a big, powerful, generational story." Another common point of praise among reviewers was how relevant *Mudbound* felt at the time of its release. For many, racism came to the forefront of American politics in 2017, with a general increase of racist rhetoric and hate crimes after the election of Donald Trump as president in 2016. Specific incidents such as the White supremacist rally that erupted into violence in Charlottesville, Virginia, in August 2017 showed that racial tensions remained very real throughout the country.

Mudbound was nominated for numerous accolades, including best adapted screenplay, best supporting actress, best original song, and best cinematography at the Ninetieth Academy Awards. The film's cinematographer, Rachel Morrison, became the first woman to ever be nominated in that category. Though it did not win any of the Os-cars or Golden Globe Awards it was nominated for, the film did win several other honors, including the Robert Altman Award at the Independent Spirit Awards and the Humanitas Prize. The film also represented Rees's shift from independent cinema to the mainstream film industry. After *Mudbound* she went on to write and direct *The Last Thing He Wanted* (2020), an adaptation of Joan Didion's 1996 novel of the same name, starring Anne Hathaway and Ben Affleck.

—*Emily E. Turner*

Further Reading

Mulligan, Carey, et al. "Mudbound Cast Interview: If This Film Was Directed by a Man, He'd Be Offered the Next Star Wars Film." Interview by Larry Bartleet. *NME*, 16 Nov. 2017, www.nme.com/blogs/tv-blogs/mudbound-interview-carey-mulligan-mary-j-blige-dee-rees-2159656. Accessed 25 Feb. 2021.

Wortham, Jenna. "Dee Rees and the Art of Surviving as a Black Female Director." *The New York Times*, 6 Feb. 2020. www.nytimes.com/2020/02/06/magazine/dee-rees-black-female-director.html. Accessed 25 Feb. 2021.

Bibliography

Blige, Mary J., et al. "Unraveling Racial Hatred in 'Mudbound.'" Interview by Cara Buckley. *The New York Times*, 3 Nov. 2017, www.nytimes.com/2017/11/03/movies/mudbound-mary-j-blige-dee-rees-carey-mulligan-garrett-hedlund.html. Accessed 25 Feb. 2021.

Bradshaw, Peter. "Powerful Tale Set in Jim Crow America Has Real Sinew." Review of *Mudbound*, directed by Dee Rees. *The Guardian*, 16 Nov. 2017, www.theguardian.com/film/2017/nov/16/mudbound-review-powerful-tale-from-jim-crow-america-has-real-sinew. Accessed 25 Feb. 2021.

O'Falt, Chris. "Cinematographer Rachel Morrison on Creating the Lush Realism of 'Mudbound.'" *IndieWire*, 28 Jan. 2017, www.indiewire.com/2017/01/cinematographer-rachel-morrison-mudbound-sundance-2017-1201774117/. Accessed 25 Feb. 2021.

Rees, Dee. "Director Dee Rees Explores Racism in Post-War Mississippi in 'Mudbound.'" Interview by Terry Gross. *NPR*, 2 Feb. 2018, www.npr.org/2018/02/02/582641984/director-dee-rees-explores-racism-in-post-war-mississippi-in-mudbound. Accessed 25 Feb. 2021.

Murder on the Orient Express

The Novel
Author: Agatha Christie (1890-1976)
First published: 1934

The Film
Year released: 2017
Director: Kenneth Branagh (b. 1960)
Screenplay by: Michael Green
Starring: Kenneth Branagh, Michelle Pfeiffer, Penélope Cruz, Willem Dafoe, Judi Dench, Johnny Depp

Context

Murder on the Orient Express is a 2017 film directed by Kenneth Branagh and based on the 1934 novel of the same name written by Agatha Christie. The novel, and the subsequent film, feature the Belgian detective Hercule Poirot as the main protagonist. Poirot was invented by Christie in the 1910s and first appeared in print in her novel *The Mysterious Affair at Styles*, published in 1920. Poirot soon became one of the most beloved characters in English literature and would appear in dozens of novels and short stories throughout the twentieth century. Christie herself grew tired of the pompous Poirot as early as the 1930s, and likewise tired of her fans' unceasing appetite for more Poirot novels. When Christie finally killed off the character in her 1975 novel, *Curtain*, he became the first literary character to receive a front-page obituary in *The New York Times*.

Of all of Christie's Poirot novels, *Murder on the Orient Express* became perhaps the most iconic and therefore the most adapted. Countless radio plays, stage adaptations, and even a video game have been produced in the decades since its initial publication. In 1974, Sidney Lumet directed the first major film adaptation of the novel, featuring an all-star cast that included Hollywood legends Albert Finney, who played the lead, Lauren Bacall, Martin Balsam, Ingrid Bergman, Jacqueline Bisset, Jean-Pierre Cassel, and Sean Connery. The film proved a huge success with critics, fans, and even with Christie, who praised it as one of the few adaptations of her work she liked.

In 2001, a made-for-television adaptation was produced for CBS starring Alfred Molina as Poirot, which greatly altered the story and placed it in a modern setting. In 2010, David Suchet, who had portrayed Poirot for the television series *Agatha Christie's Poirot* since 1989, starred in a film-length episode for the show based on *Murder on the Orient Express*. Another television version of the novel was produced in 2015 for Fuji Television, with the setting changed to 1933 Japan.

Plans for a new big-screen adaptation had been kicked around Hollywood since the Lumet version hit theaters in 1974, but it was not until 2013 that 20th Century Fox announced its intention to develop the project. Veteran television writer, Michael Green, best known for writing for the series *Heroes* and *Everwood* was brought in to complete the script. In late 2015, it was announced that Kenneth Branagh, veteran Irish actor, writer, and director would come onboard to both direct and star in the film. Prior to this, Branagh was perhaps best known for directing and starring in numerous film adaptations of William Shakespeare's plays, including *Henry V* (1989), *Much Ado About Nothing* (1993), *Othello* (1995), *Hamlet* (1996), *Love's Labour's Lost* (2000), and *As You Like It* (2006). By the fall of 2016, much of the cast for the film had been announced, featuring numerous box office heavyweights, including Johnny Depp, Michelle Pfeiffer, and Judi Dench. Principal photography began that November. The film was shot entirely in the United Kingdom.

Film Analysis

The 2017 adaptation of *Murder on the Orient Express* is fairly faithful to the source material. Most of the changes from book to screen involve combining or altering some of the supporting characters, as well as alterations to small details such as locations and relationships. The film is darker in aesthetic though often light in tone, making for a mix of suspense and comedy. Most central to the adaptation is Kenneth Branagh's portrayal of Poirot. Whereas the Poirot of book fame is a bit of a dandy, eccentric in his proclivities, often pompous and seeming almost inept, Branagh chose to focus on Poirot's compulsiveness, giving audiences a recognizable Poirot, though one less buffoonish and more focused on the puzzle of the crime, to an almost obsessive degree. However, what is most remarkable about the film is its rich and striking visual look that adds menace to the overall feel of the film. Branagh, who prior to filming had just completed a role in Christopher Nolan's sweeping 2017 epic, *Dunkirk*, was inspired to use the same 65mm film cameras, a high-resolution film gauge with some of the highest resolution levels available. This way, even small, intimate scenes, of which there are many considering the setting for the film, appear larger and more colorful.

As in the novel, famous Belgian detective Hercule Poirot (Branagh) is en route from Jerusalem to London via the Orient Express, a long-distance passenger train. Poirot, as exemplified by a scene featuring a hardboiled egg, is an obsessive-compulsive who seeks balance and perfection in life. This Poirot views his obsessive need to weed out truth as a curse. The night after meeting con artist Edward Ratchett (Depp), who tries to hire Poirot as a bodyguard, the detective is awakened by strange noises and peers out of his cabin in time to see a figure in a red kimono running down the hallway. The next morning, after an avalanche has stranded the train, it is discovered that Ratchett was murdered in the middle of the night, stabbed a dozen times. From this point on the film follows Poirot as he begins to uncover clues about Ratchett's past, his connections to the other passengers, and what happened on the night of his murder. Eventually, Poirot uncovers that most of the passengers had some connection to Ratchett.

In the climax of the film, in a striking, almost surreal scene, a table is laid out outside on the train tracks where Poirot confronts the suspects. He outlines two possible scenarios. The first, which is not supported by the evidence, suggests that a mysterious assassin came onboard at some point, murdered Ratchett, and got off the train shortly after committing the crime. The second scenario, which is supported by the evidence, points to all twelve suspects having a hand in Ratchett's murder. As the original novel did, the fact that all the suspects are guilty of the crime is a subversion of the standard detective/murder mystery formula. Here the detective must not uncover the murderer among innocent suspects but rather uncover the reason for why these seemingly innocent people might all commit the same crime, together. No longer a "gotcha" moment, the climax instead becomes a meditation on the ethics of the crime.

Ratchett was a deeply immoral man who caused untold pain and suffering. He was a criminal and a murderer. The film then asks us the obvious question: Should the killing of Ratchett be considered murder or justice? Poirot decides to test this conundrum by producing a pistol and asking the suspects to kill him as he would be unable to keep from turning them in. When they fail to do so he decides that the killing of Ratchett was morally justified as those who committed the crime are not murderers. It is a very narrow path the film has to walk. Poirot is a man who believes deeply in balance and order. He has operated within the confines of the law his entire life. The film forces Poirot to confront the rigidity of his beliefs and ponder the true meaning of justice. If he were to turn Ratchett's killers into the authorities he would get justice for an unjust man, while condemning Ratchett's victims to the fate he himself deserved.

In the end, Poirot lies to the authorities to protect the train passengers, blaming Ratchett's death on a mysterious and fictional stranger. This is not an easy choice for Poirot, even though he is morally justified in his decision

Kenneth Branagh. Photo by Giorgia Meschini via Wikimedia Commons.

as it flies counter to his entire belief system. Yet, he does it anyway, because despite the circumstances it is the right thing to do. The moral of the story is that truth is not always analogous to justice. Life is complicated and messy, and while the killing of Ratchett in itself is immoral, the reasons behind it are not. While partly driven by revenge, the twelve train passengers kill Ratchett to also bring justice for his victims, and, as the film teases, as a way to prevent Ratchett from hurting more people in the future.

There is no redemption for Ratchett aboard the Orient Express, nor was it ever a possibility. His death was a matter of fate, the result of a chain of events set into motion by himself years prior to his final night. So, while Poirot may leave the Orient Express conflicted about his choice to let Ratchett's killers go free, ultimately, the decision was never his. Justice had to find a way, and Poirot simply let it play out.

Significance

Murder on the Orient Express was released in November 2017. The film did very well at the box office, taking in $28.7 million in its opening weekend and ultimately earning a cumulative worldwide gross of nearly $353 million, far outpacing its $55 million budget. The film's financial success stood in contrast to its critical reception, with most reviewers praising the style of the film while panning its self-indulgent and convoluted plot. Nonetheless, the film does enjoy a positive score on review aggregator sites such as *Rotten Tomatoes*.

While *Murder on the Orient Express* earned numerous award nominations, mainly in the categories of production and costume design, it failed to win any major honors. Despite this, based on the film's box office and the lavish praise heaped on Branagh by Agatha Christie's estate, a sequel was green lit by 20th Century Fox in 2017, with Branagh returning as both director and star. *Death on the Nile* began production in late 2019 but its release was delayed until 2022 because of the Coronavirus pandemic. In interviews, Branagh has spoken about the possibility of other sequels and even his desire to build a "cinematic universe" around Agatha Christie's famous Belgian detective.

—KP Dawes, MA

Further Reading

Christie, Agatha. *Agatha Christie: An Autobiography*. HarperCollins Publishers, 1977.

Picon, Guillaume. *Orient Express: The Story of a Legend*. ACC Art Books, 2018.

Thompson, Laura. *Agatha Christie: A Mysterious Life*. Pegasus Books, 2018.

Bibliography

"Hercule Poirot." *The Home of Agatha Christie*, www.agathachristie.com/about-christie. Accessed 10 Apr. 2020.

Joint, Laura. "How Agatha Christie Grew to Dislike Hercule Poirot." *BBC*, 27 Oct. 2010, news.bbc.co.uk/local/devon/hi/people_and_places/arts_and_culture/newsid_9131000/9131482.stm. Accessed 10 Apr. 2020.

"*Murder on the Orient Express*." *IMDb*, www.imdb.com/title/tt3402236/. Accessed 10 Apr. 2020.

"*Murder on the Orient Express*." *Rotten Tomatoes*, www.rottentomatoes.com/m/murder_on_the_orient_express_2017. Accessed 10 Apr. 2020.

Pearson, Ryan. "Branagh Teases Return of Old Friends in *Death on the Nile*." *Associated Press*, 26 Dec. 2017, apnews.com/9426db4b7f124a26bcafee2443c99670/Branagh-teases-return-of-old-friends-in-'Death-on-the-Nile'. Accessed 10 Apr. 2020.

My Side of the Mountain

The Novel
Author: Jean Craighead George (1919-2012)
First published: 1959

The Film
Year released: 1969
Director: James B. Clark (1908-2000)
Screenplay by: Joanna Crawford, Jane Klove, Ted Sherdeman
Starring: Teddy Eccles, Theodore Bikel, Tudi Wiggins, Frank Perry, Peggi Loder

Context

This novel was the first in Jean Craighead George's trilogy about life in the mountains, which also includes *On the Far Side of the Mountain* and *Frightful's Mountain*. Based on George's own desire as a child to run away, the novel recounts the efforts of Sam Gribley, a young teen, to live in the wilderness, away from his parents and eight siblings. It was selected as a John Newbery Medal winner and an American Library Association Notable Book award.

George's father was an entomologist; her mother was a storyteller and naturalist. Both influenced their children with trips into nature and pets to tend. George chose a male protagonist because her twin older brothers—who gave her a peregrine falcon when she was thirteen and as adults became noted experts on grizzly bears—were her heroes, and they had just published a book on surviving on both sea and land. George wrote the novel while living near the Catskill Mountains with her three young children, completing the first draft in only two weeks. She later drew the pen-and-ink illustrations.

My Side of the Mountain is one of many novels for young people that relies on the classic tale of a young man who survives in the wilderness, whether by choice or of necessity. *Robinson Crusoe*, Daniel Defoe's 1719 novel, set the fashion for these stories, often linked with coming-of-age stories or quest literature. Such works, which have been popular since the mid-nineteenth century in children's adventure and outdoor stories, are known as "Robinsonades." In this form of literature, there is always a happy ending, with the adventurer reunited with family and civilization, while at the same time more mature and able to survive in the wilderness.

In young adult literature, Gary Paulsen's novel *Hatchet*, published in 1986 and a Newbery Honor book, employs this motif. The hero, Brian Robeson, is thirteen, the sole survivor of a plane crash, who learns to survive in the wilderness for fifty-four days before he is rescued. The book was the first of a trilogy. It was transformed into film in 1990 with *A Cry in the Wild*.

Although George initially felt a boy was more likely to survive in the wilderness, after Outward Bound was established giving girls the opportunity to learn survival skills, she felt it was time to have a female protagonist. She wrote *Julie of the Wolves*, which tells the story of a young Inuit girl who survives by befriending wolves. It was one of the most frequently banned books during the 1990s and 2000s due to violence, sexual content, and offensive language. George traveled to the Arctic and other wilderness places to make sure the book was realistic. That book was also the first in a trilogy.

In 1990, George published the second book of the Gribley family series, *On the Far Side of the Mountain*. This time, her protagonist was Sam's sister, Alice, who remains on the land. This was not a novel written from a first-person point of view; readers learn of Alice's life only through Sam's eyes.

Film Analysis

James B. Clark, who directed the film, was also a noted television director, working on such iconic shows of the 1960s as *Bonanza*, *The Wild Wild West*, and *Batman*. Interestingly, he also directed *Island of the Blue Dolphins*, which was based on Scott O'Dell's novel of the same name and was released in 1964. Based on a true story, it depicts twelve-year-old Karana, who was stranded alone on an island off the California coast for eighteen years.

For the film adaptation of *My Side of the Mountain*, many of the novel's details were changed. Instead of living in New York, Sam (Teddy Eccles) and his family, with only two siblings rather than the novel's eight, live in a high-rise apartment in Toronto. Sam, however, is motivated by the example of Henry David Thoreau, and wants to live alone in the wilderness. There is no mention of land in the Catskills owned by the Gribley family or going to reclaim that land, as the novel says. Instead of taking a train, Sam takes a bus to Knowlton and from there heads into the Laurentian Mountains (which was actually filmed in the Green Mountains) of Québec. In addition, he takes his pet raccoon, Gus, a stand-in for the wild and elusive weasel Sam calls Baron.

Sam's reasons for escaping family and urban living in the film differ from those in the novel. Rather than bidding his family goodbye and telling them his plans, he sneaks away, leaving a note that instructs them not to try to find him. In addition to wanting to emulate Thoreau and proving he is capable of living without other people, Sam wants to become a naturalist. He believes that alone in the wilderness he can continue his research on algae. He even packs a microscope with him to continue his exploration of pond water algae. The viewer also observes his slides of green, moving strands. As the weather becomes colder, however, Sam cannot see the slides, because his breath fogs the lenses.

The character of Bando (Theodore Bikel) is transformed from a college professor on holiday to a collector of folk music and a musician. In the novel, Bando is a nickname created when Sam fears the stranger is a bandit. In the movie, Bando is the man's given name. The relocation to French-speaking Canada gives Bando the opportunity to sing a French tune around the campfire, accompanying himself with a guitar and other simple instruments.

Sam is inspired to burn out a dead tree, which Gus finds, to make a snug dwelling. This is in keeping with the novel, although the Sam of the novel has more sense than to walk away and come back to find an almost dangerous fire in the tree, which he puts out with his coat.

The viewer sees Sam's increasing interest in the falcon he watches flying above. Filled with a desire for his own bird of prey, he hikes back into town, as in the novel, and with the help of a friendly librarian (Tudi Wiggins), finds the information he needs. The most agonizing sequence of the film is watching Sam climb a rock face to reach the falcon's nest and capture a young falcon. As he descends with the bird under his shirt, the mother falcon dive-bombs him, coming extremely close. Just as in the book, Sam tames the bird, which he names Frightful, and teaches her to hunt for him. Perhaps the most poignant scene in the film occurs when a hunter mistakenly kills Frightful, which does not occur in the novel. The motivation for the added scene may be twofold: Frightful's death both heightens Sam's aloneness and jeopardizes his ability to gather food.

In the novel, Sam has guests and visitors, some of whom, like Bando, remain for several days. They include the boy Tom; Matt, a journalist; and Aaron, a songwriter who wandered away from Passover festivities. Sam approaches Aaron first and reflects on doing so. Frightful had "told" him, *You want to be found.* "I began to wonder. I had sought out a human being. This would not have happened a year ago." In the film, by contrast, Sam is solitary, going into town only once after his initial trip to the library. Bando does come, but he is the only human contact the movie allows Sam. In the novel Sam goes into town more frequently and even allows the librarian to cut his hair.

The film also departs from the novel in its ending. The novel reunites Sam with his family when they all come to him in the wilderness. Although he is initially glad to see everyone, he is "stunned and hurt" when he realizes they intend to stay and build a house. His father explained that the newspaper articles that suggested his mother had not "done her duty" with Sam was the real impetus for their move to the land. "Your mother took all those editorials personally.... The nation became her neighbors." When Sam prepares to protest, his mother gets literally the last words in the book: "'That's how it is until you are eighteen, Sam,' she said. And that ended it."

In the film, Sam's solitude ends differently. After a frightening storm during which Sam is snowed in, Bando and the librarian appear with food to celebrate Christmas. Bando gives Sam some newspaper articles relating how his parents are grieving his disappearance; it appears that Sam must finally consider how his disappearance has affected others. He voluntarily returns to his family, saying it was time to go home and that "I learned about myself." Perhaps the movie was influenced by the zeitgeist of the 1960s, which celebrated "doing one's own thing" and "finding oneself." In the final shot of the movie, Sam is looking up at a falcon flying overhead in a blue sky.

Significance

Paramount Pictures filmed the movie on location in Toronto and the Green Mountains of Québec, Canada. The 100-minute Technicolor film was shot in 1967 in Panavision, a relatively new development in widescreen film camera lenses, and was released in 1969. In 1970 the film won the Golden Laurel Sleeper of the Year award. *Parents Magazine* also recognized it with its Gold Medal.

This was not a major motion picture with a high box office return. After all, 1969 saw the release of such blockbusters as *Butch Cassidy and the Sundance Kid*, *Midnight Cowboy*, and *Easy Rider*. In the top twenty highest-grossing films of that year, only one, *A Boy Named Charlie Brown*, was a movie for children or young people.

Reviews of the DVD, which appeared in 2004, reflected the changes in life since the film's release in theaters. Concerns about stranger danger and pedophilia overshadow the innocent friendship of the folksinger/song collector Bando. The unlikelihood of an adolescent leaving home for months without any attempt by his family to locate him or ensure his safety seemed even less likely in the twenty-first century than in 1959, when the book was published, or ten years later, when the movie was made.

Reviewers did note the beauty of the nature scenery as a balance to these plot concerns. One of the film's strengths is its depiction of the beauty of Sam's new world, which capitalized on the use of a relatively recent development, the Panavision lens. Viewers see sweeps of sky; lovely sunsets serve as transition devices and suggest the change of weather and seasons. Surrounding mountains display the changing colors of the leaves and the increasingly bare trees as summer becomes fall. The film's score complements the visuals with simple music, often played on guitar, as if Bando were responsible for it.

—*Judy A. Johnson, MLS, MTS*

Further Reading

Bily, Cynthia A. "Jean Craighead George." *Guide to Literary Masters & Their Works*, Jan. 2007, p. 1. *EBSCOhost*, proxy.ohiolink.edu:9099/login?url=http://search.ebscohost.com/login.aspx?direct=true&db=lkh&AN=103331LM32279790302839&site=ehost-live. Accessed 3 Mar. 2020.

Gerhardt, Lillian N. "Audiovisual Review." *School Library Journal*, vol. 32, no. 6, Feb. 1986, p. 58. *EBSCOhost*, proxy.ohiolink.edu:9099/login?url=http://search.ebscohost.com/login.aspx?direct=true&db=lkh&AN=5573463&site=ehost-live. Accessed 3 Mar. 2020.

Bibliography

Fox, Margalit. "Jean Craighead George, Children's Author, Dies at 92." *The New York Times*, 16 May 2012, www.nytimes.com/2012/05/17/books/jean-craighead-george-childrens-author-dies-at-92.html. Accessed 13 Mar. 2020.

"George, Jean Craighead." *The Essential Guide to Children's Books and Their Creators*, edited by Anita Silvey, Houghton Mifflin, 2002.

Hahn, Daniel. "Robinsonnades." *The Oxford Companion to Children's Literature*. 2nd ed., Oxford UP, 2015.

Hanlon, Tina L. "The Descendants of Robinson Crusoe in North American Children's Literature." *The Presence of the Past in Children's Literature*, edited by Ann Lawson Lucas, Praeger Publishers, 2003, pp. 61-69.

Ygesias, Rafael. "Children's Books; Meanwhile, Back in the Catskills." *The New York Times*, 20 May 1990, www.nytimes.com/1990/05/20/books/children-s-books-meanshile-back-in-the-catskills.html. Accessed 13 Mar. 2020.

The Namesake

The Novel
Author: Jhumpa Lahiri (b. 1967)
First published: 2003

The Film
Year released: 2006
Director: Mira Nair (b. 1957)
Screenplay by: Sooni Taraporevala
Starring: Kal Penn, Tabu, Irrfan Khan, Zuleikha Robinson

Context

The Namesake is the first novel by award-winning author Jhumpa Lahiri. It followed her debut short story collection, *Interpreter of Maladies*, which won a Pulitzer Prize and the Hemingway Foundation/PEN Award. *The Namesake* finds Lahiri building on some of the themes of her earlier collection, while using the novel form to explore her characters' lives in greater depth. The book centers on Gogol, an Indian American boy named for his father's favorite Russian author. Gogol's struggle with his unusual name comes to represent his larger struggle to find his place between the India that is home to his parents and the America in which he has grown up. Lahiri's scope in this novel is ambitious: her novel begins years before Gogol is born, and follows him all the way through childhood, adolescence, and young adulthood. The novel is a window into the immigrant experience and is a compelling portrait of a young man coming of age and coming to terms with his identity and cultural inheritance.

In 2006, Mira Nair released a film version of *The Namesake*, starring Kal Penn as Gogol and featuring a strong ensemble cast that includes Irrfan Khan and Tabu as Gogol's parents. Nair is perhaps best known for *Monsoon Wedding* (2001), one of many films she has made about the Indian and Indian American experience. Prior to *The Namesake*, she had directed a 2004 version of *Vanity Fair* featuring Reese Witherspoon. The *Namesake* was in many ways a return to more familiar territory for Nair and was generally considered to have been a successful undertaking.

Film Analysis

Nair and her screenwriter, Sooni Taraporevala, adeptly worked some of the most cinematic aspects of Lahiri's plot into the film. Nair also evokes the sights and sounds of India, and the viewer who has never been to that part of the world will benefit greatly from her lovely shots of street scenes and interiors. Like the novel, the film opens with Gogol's father, Ashoke Ganguli (Khan), taking a journey by train. He is reading Gogol, his grandfather's favorite author, and shakes off the advice of an older man in his car who encourages him to travel to America while he is still young. Later that night, the train derails—although the actual scene of the disaster is not shown until much later in the film—and Ashoke is in traction for months. When he recovers, he decides that he will, in fact, leave India for America. His parents arrange a marriage for him. Before Ashima (Tabu) meets Ashoke, she finds his shoes outside of the living room in which he and both sets of parents are conversing. She tries them on, a figurative way of trying on marriage.

After getting married in India, Ashoke and Ashima move to America, where Ashoke has a job at a university. Gogol is born while they are living in Queens, New York, during their first year in the country. The tradition in India is to give a child a nickname for his or her first few years; later, he or she will be given a proper "good" name. Not having yet gotten a good name from their grandmother, they put the nickname Gogol on their son's birth certificate—little did they know that it would follow their American son throughout his life. Piece by piece, the Gangulis achieve the American dream, in the form of a split-level ranch in suburbia, financial security, two children, and a host of friends and neighbors. Gogol and his younger sister grow up surrounded by a community of Bengali immigrants who become a surrogate extended family. Nair cast some of author Jhumpa Lahiri's own family members and family friends in these roles. Filming the domestic scenes in an actual house, rather than on a sound stage, lends a sense of realism and authenticity to them. The family's return trips to India are equally detailed and absorbing. These journeys are often full of mixed feelings; one of their first trips home is to bury Ashima's father. Ashima and Ashoke are living lives that straddle two worlds and will always feel some measure of guilt for not being present for their own parents and families back in India.

While the book spends more time on Gogol's childhood and college years, Nair's film compresses the storyline and focuses on a few key periods of the protagonist's life. It jumps from Gogol as a young boy to a sulky, long-haired, pot-smoking teenaged Gogol, played by Kal Penn. At the time, Penn was best known for comedic roles in films like *Harold & Kumar Go to White Castle*. He shows depth and range as Gogol, displaying an understated charm that helps to define the role, and he does a fine job of transitioning from a brooding adolescent to a young man in his twenties. Nair and her screenwriter deftly refocused the narrative on Gogol's relationship with his father. As a teenager, Gogol seems vaguely embarrassed and bored by his infinitely gentle, patient father. When Ashoke gives him a copy of stories by his favorite Russian author, Gogol, as a graduation present, he can barely rouse himself to thank his father, much less to read the book. In fact, he is moving ever further from his father's love of the author. He changes his own name from Gogol to Nikhil, which friends will later shorten to Nick. Upon Gogol's graduation from high school, the family takes a trip to India. Here again, Nair is able show the continuities and contrasts in the Ganguli family's lives. These return trips to India ultimately make a big impression on Gogol. On a trip to the Taj Mahal, for example, he decides that he will study architecture in college.

The film jumps over Gogol's college years, excising several episodes and characters from the book, to focus next on Gogol as a young architect. He has become an urbane Manhattanite, dating a young woman named Maxine. He makes little time for his family and has scrupulously avoided telling them about his American girlfriend. A brief trip back home with Maxine is brilliantly realized; Gogol's dismay when she kisses his parents on the cheek is palpable. It is on this trip that Ashoke finally tells Gogol the origin and importance of his name. Nair shrewdly waits until this point in the film to show the aftermath of the train wreck; it is a scene of destruction and

carnage that makes Ashoke's survival—and hence Gogol's very existence—seem miraculous. Ashoke subsequently takes a semester-long appointment at a university in Cleveland, which leaves Ashima living on her own for the first time. He calls her from the emergency room, complaining of a stomachache. Nair's eye for color again pays off. The washed-out, fluorescent lighting of the hospital contrasts dramatically with the warm glow of the Ganguli's suburban home. It turns out to be a farewell, as he dies of a massive heart attack in the hospital.

Nair has structured her film around parallel events—funerals, celebrations, weddings, trips to India—and Ashoke's funeral echoes that of Ashima's father when Gogol was a boy. Maxine tries to support Gogol, but he pushes her away. He has decided, belatedly, to embrace his Bengali heritage and to be a dutiful son, and he perhaps sees severing his relationship with Maxine as the first step in this process. In reality, he enters a period of regression, moping around the family home with his mother, who even goes so far as to encourage him to resume seeing Maxine. Instead, Gogol agrees to meet the daughter of a family friend, a young woman name Moushumi who is studying French in New York. We have seen her before as a pretentious twelve-year-old who proclaims to "detest" American television. As a worldly adult played by Zuleikha Robinson, she captivates Gogol, and the two of them are soon dating. Gogol and Moushumi's marriage seems to bring the story full circle. Like his parents before him, Gogol marries in a traditional ceremony someone who his mother picked out for him, and both sides of the family, as well as the extended family of Bengali expats, are thrilled about the match.

Yet nothing is that simple for Gogol. He finds his wife's smug, hip friends grating, and feels betrayed when she tells them that Nikhil is not his real name. Moushumi, for her part, seems trapped in her marriage to Gogol. The real blow comes a year into their marriage, on a train ride to spend one last Christmas at the family house before Ashima sells it and moves to India. In a conversation with Gogol, Moushumi mentions someone named Pierre. It is a textbook Freudian slip: she has essentially just ended her marriage, and it takes Gogol all of two lines of dialogue to ask, "Are you having an affair?" Moushumi is not a wholly unsympathetic character; her fear that she is turning into her own dutifully married mother is a genuine one that speaks to a search for identity that, on one level or another, mirrors Gogol's own.

His marriage over, Gogol visits the family home, alone once again. His younger sister, meanwhile, has married a young man named Ben, who is not Bengali and yet makes her happy and whom Ashima seems to wholly accept. Somehow, Gogol has not yet found a way to integrate the different facets of his identity, to balance respect for his parents with an attunement to his own volitions, and to live life on his own terms. Gogol finds the book his father once gave him, and on the train ride back to New York City, begins to read it.

Significance

The Namesake was released in 2006 and turned a considerable profit; the film was produced for just under $10 million and grossed a little over $20 million worldwide. *The Namesake* was well received by critics and by casual viewers. Writing in *The New York Times*, Stephen Holden said that it "conveys a palpable sense of people as living, breathing creatures who are far more complex than their words might indicate." Holden singled out Kal Penn for his "crackling star performance." The film certainly revealed a depth to Penn's acting abilities and showed that he could take on a dramatic role rather than the comedic ones he was best known for. In *The Wall Street Journal*, Joe Morgenstern called it "strikingly original, superbly acted and profoundly satisfying."

The film was made during the time in which Mira Nair alternated between bigger, studio productions like *Vanity Fair* (2004) and *Amelia* (2009), and smaller ones like *The Namesake*. *The Namesake* shows that a thoughtful, character-driven drama about immigration and identity can find an audience and be a success.

—*Matthew Bolton*

Further Reading

Gogol, Nikolai V. *The Overcoat and Other Tales of Good and Evil*. W. W. Norton & Company, 1965.

Shukla, Sandhya. *India Abroad: Diasporic Cultures of Postwar America and England*. Princeton UP, 2003.

Bibliography

Ebert, Roger. "Gogol? How Did I Get a Name Like Gogol?" *RogerEbert.com*, 6 Dec. 2007, www.rogerebert.com/reviews/the-namesake. Accessed 19 May 2020.

Holden, Stephen. "Film Review: Modernity and Tradition at a Cultural Crossroads." *The New York Times*, 9 Mar. 2007, www.nytimes.com/2007/03/09/movies/09name.html. Accessed 13 April 2020.

Morgenstern, Joe. "*Namesake* Is a Richly Spiced Immigrant Saga." *The Wall Street Journal*, 9 Mar. 2007, www.wsj.com/articles/SB117339757711731537. Accessed 13 Apr. 2020.

Nair, Mira, and Jhumpa Lahiri. *The Namesake: A Portrait of the Film Based on the Novel by Jhumpa Lahiri*. Newmarket Press, 2006.

Nappily Ever After

The Novel
Author: Trisha R. Thomas (b. 1964)
First published: 2000

The Film
Year released: 2018
Director: Haifaa al-Mansour (b. 1974)
Screenplay by: Adam Brooks and Cee Marcellus
Starring: Sanaa Lathan, Ernie Hudson, Lynn Whitfield, Ricky Whittle, Lyriq Bent

Context
The 2018 Netflix romantic comedy *Nappily Ever After*, directed by Haifaa al-Mansour, is an adaptation of the 2000 novel of the same name, by Trisha R. Thomas. The book is the first in Thomas's bestselling Nappily series. Thomas had worked in a variety of careers, including marketing and teaching in a middle school, before trying her hand at writing novels. It took her several years to find a publisher willing to take a chance on her work, but the warm reception the book received was enough to propel Thomas through a bestselling series.

The series follows the adventures of Venus Johnston, an African American woman who spent much of her life pursuing a certain beauty ideal, especially involving her hair. When she decides to embrace the texture of her natural hair, it sets off a series of events that cause Johnston to reexamine many different aspects of her life, career, and relationships. Thomas's debut book was well reviewed and put the author on a number of "best new author" lists around the country. It was short-listed for the National Association for the Advancement of Colored People (NAACP) Image Award for Outstanding Fiction, and the Black Writers Alliance nominated Thomas for the 2001 Gold Pen Award for Best New Author. Over the next sixteen years Thomas penned and published eight more books following Venus Johnston. Though few of the later Nappily books received the same level of critical acclaim as Thomas's debut, many of her follow-up books also proved popular.

A year after Thomas's debut was published, in 2001, actor Halle Berry optioned the rights to create a theatrical version of the book, with the intention to star in the lead role as Venus Johnston. The film was in development for Universal Pictures, and Patricia Cardoso, known for her film *Real Women Have Curves*, was chosen to direct the feature. Tina Gordon Chism, known for writing *Drumline* (2002) and *ATL* (2006), reportedly drafted the initial adaptation. However, due to the film's high budget and its expected niche audience, Universal ultimately abandoned the project, and Berry moved on to other films. Around 2005 veteran producer Tracey Bing was first approached about it, but Warner, where she was working, also passed on it. In 2010 Bing recalled the idea and developed it for eOne before pitching it successfully to the streaming service Netflix. In the summer of 2017, it was announced that Saudi Arabian feminist director Haifaa al-Mansour would direct the film, while Sanaa Lathan, the award-winning star of such films as *Love & Basketball* (2000), *Brown Sugar* (2002), and *Alien vs. Predator* (2004), signed on both as a producer and lead actor, with the character's name changed from Venus Johnston to Violet Jones.

The final screenplay was credited to Adam Brooks, known for his work on the romantic comedy *Bridget Jones: The Edge of Reason* (2004), and debut screenwriter Cee Marcellus. Bing recalled in interviews that six writers were involved with the adaptation between 2001 and its release in 2018. Notably, additional revisions were provided by Lisa Loomer, of *Girl, Interrupted* (1999) fame, and Gina Prince-Bythewood, who had scripted *Love & Basketball* and *Beyond the Lights* (2014) and adapted *The Secret Life of Bees* (2008).

Film Analysis
In the film version of *Nappily Ever After*, Violet Jones (Lathan) has a difficult relationship with her mother, Pauletta (Lynn Whitfield), who believes that straightened hair is more attractive than "natural" hair on a Black

woman. Audiences witness Pauletta forcing her young daughter into a weekly routine of ironing and straightening her hair, sometimes being burned by the iron in the process. One day in the summer of 1993, a young White boy at a public pool challenges eleven-year-old Violet to see who can hold their breath longer underwater. Violet jumps into the pool, despite her mother's warning, and when she comes out, the White children tease her for her frizzy hair.

The film then fast-forwards to an adult Violet, on the eve of her birthday, believing that her British physician boyfriend, Clint (Ricky Whittle), is about to propose. She is visited by her mother, who helps her prepare her hair for the big day, and the audience learns that Violet has embraced her mother's standards of beauty, to the point that she is terrified of rain and getting her hair wet. Through dialogue, it is suggested that this standard is ultimately unhealthy for Black women, as it forces them to conceal their natural physical qualities and to conform to standards based on White women and their hair. (The beauty ideal is arguably unhealthy for White women as well, but this is not the primary subject of the film.) The audience learns that Violet's father, Richard (Ernie Hudson), has left her mother.

During the preparations for her birthday night, Violet is accidentally sprayed with water by neighbor children playing with a hose. Her wet hair begins to curl and frizz, and she visits a friend's hair salon, where the owner, Will Wright (Lyriq Bent), is attempting to convince another customer to embrace her natural curls. Violet meets Will's daughter, Zoe (Daria Jones), a precocious child whose dialogue is largely adult in nature. Violet's comments on Zoe's natural hair hurts the preteen's self-image.

With her own hair fixed, Violet attends her birthday party. When the expected proposal turns out to be simply the gift of a small dog, Violet ends her relationship with Clint and sinks into a depression. Seeking to try something new, she experiments with blond hair and a shorter cut and clubbing but still feels depressed and frustrated. In a decisive moment, Violet shaves her head; onscreen, this occurs after a drunken outing goes awry, whereas in print, she makes a sober, deliberate choice. With her newly shorn head, Violet encounters very different reactions from the people in her life. Her father embraces her and tells her she still looks beautiful and that this rebellion was something that had been building in her for some time. Violet then visits hairdresser Will and strikes up a friendship

with him and his daughter, apologizing for the comments she made about Zoe's appearance. In her discussions with Will, he explains more about his philosophy on hair and helping women embrace a beauty image that aligns with their bodies, rather than artificially imposed ideals.

Trouble begins again when Violet's mother reenters the picture. She disparages Will and his career choice, causing Will to leave Violet. Then, at the advertising agency where she works, the beer campaign she has created featuring women sports fans fails to win over executives. She quits her job, realizing that she does not want to conform to the company's male-dominated beauty ideals. Shortly after, she reconciles with Clint, who proposes marriage. Pauletta is pleased, but Violet feels unfulfilled. She realizes that she is with Clint for the wrong reasons when Clint asks her to straighten her hair when meeting his parents. At the engagement party, Violet blows up her relationship, jumping in a pool. Her friends join her, and her father pulls Pauletta in with him as well, wrecking her perfectly straightened hair and telling her she has never looked more beautiful. They reconcile. In the concluding segment, Violet pitches Will's plant-based hair products for African American customers to a major beauty company, and it is implied that the two will reunite romantically as well.

Many details of the book *Nappily Ever After* were changed for the film version, from names to the order of plot points, and in some cases, this led to predictability in the construction of the plot. Violet's relationship with Will and his daughter, Zoe, for instance, leverages an often-used trope in which an initially hostile meeting blossoms into attraction on one hand and a predictable mentor-mentee relationship with the daughter, who, audiences are told explicitly, needs a "mother." There is also little in the way of context given for Violet's controlling and image-obsessed mother. In the novel, her mother's nuanced relationship to her own standards of beauty was a focal point, but in the film version, the origin of Pauletta's feelings about hair, beauty, and the value of physical perfection is left unexplored.

Significance

Writing for *Vulture*, Angelica Jade Bastién called the film *Nappily Ever After* a "well-intentioned misfire" that embraces a "reductive understanding of black womanhood" and fails to capture enough chemistry to develop into a compelling story. Bastién argued further that Violet's character is never truly explored and that audiences are left with little to understand her, save her mother's oppressive presence in her life. Other critics agreed that the primary characters in the film seem underdeveloped. Several argued the story relies too heavily on romance-genre plot tropes and conventions, while reviewers for the *Hollywood Reporter* and *Black Girl Nerds* noted it is ultimately more a coming-of-age tale. Other reviewers were more accepting of the film, though few felt it offered a deep reflection on the tangled world of Black beauty standards or the cultural phenomena that have shaped them.

Though critics found many flaws in Netflix's adaptation of the beloved first book of the Nappily series, many critics and journalists applauded the addition of a new story focusing on Black experience and, more specifically, Black female experience. Much of the press surrounding the film focused less on the performances of Lathan and her costars and more on the sociological subjects raised by the film and the book. In this way the film, like the book before it, provided a platform for a conversation about the evolution of Black beauty standards and the way that these standards have been shaped by White culture. Critics pointed out that as the film trailed the book by almost twenty years, much had changed with regard to standards of beauty and hairstyles in the nation's African American community, and varying representations of Black hair, including celebrations of artistry, had appeared in television shows by then. Despite that, the film and book both encouraged conversation about this important aspect of the ongoing echoes of acculturation and prejudice.

—*Micah Issitt*

Further Reading

Sandoval, Lapacazo. "'Nappily Ever After' Producer, Tracey Bing, Is an African American Woman Who Understands the Politics of Hollywood and Hair!" *Los Angeles Sentinel*, Oct 12. 2018, lasentinel.net/nappily-ever-after-producer-tracey-bing-is-an-african-american-woman-who-understands-the-politics-of-hollywood-and-hair.html. Accessed 11 Mar. 2021.

Thomas, Trisha R. *Nappily Ever After*. Crown, 2000.

Bibliography

Bahr, Robyn. "'Nappily Ever After:' Film Review." Review of *Nappily Ever After*, directed by Haifaa al-Mansour. *The Hollywood Reporter*, 30 Sept. 2018, www.hollywoodreporter.com/review/nappily-ever-review-1148103. Accessed 13 Mar. 2021.

Bastién, Angelica Jade. "*Nappily Ever After* Is a Well-Intentioned Misfire." Review of *Nappily Ever After*, directed by Haifaa al-Mansour. *Vulture*, 22 Sept. 2018, www.vulture.com/2018/09/nappily-ever-after-movie-review.html. Accessed 13 Mar. 2021.

French, Asha. "What Was Lost in Nappily Ever After's Journey from Book to Film—Women's Media Center." *Women's Media Center*, 28 Sept. 2018, www.womensmediacenter.com/news-features/what-was-lost-in-nappily-ever-afters-journey-from-book-to-film. Accessed 29 Mar. 2021.?

Kang, Inkoo. "*Nappily Ever After* Is Smarter about Womanhood Than It Is about Black Hair." Review of *Nappily Ever After*, directed by Haifaa al-Mansour. *Slate*, 26 Sept. 2018, slate.com/culture/2018/09/nappily-ever-after-review-netflix-movie-black-hair.html. Accessed 12 Mar. 2021.

Kroll, Justin. "Sanaa Lathan to Star in Netflix Adaptation of 'Nappily Ever After.'" *Variety*, 15 Aug. 2017, variety.com/2017/film/news/sanaa-lathan-nappily-ever-after-netflix-1202528753. Accessed 11 Mar. 2021.

O'Malley, Sheila. Review of *Nappily Ever After*, directed by Haifaa al-Mansour. *Roger Ebert*, 21 Sept. 2018, www.rogerebert.com/reviews/nappily-ever-after-2018. Accessed 13 Mar. 2021.

Native Son

The Novel
Author: Richard Wright (1908-1960)
First published: 1940

The Film
Year released: 2019
Director: Rashid Johnson (b. 1977)
Screenplay by: Suzan-Lori Parks
Starring: Ashton Sanders, Margaret Qualley, Nick Robinson, KiKi Layne, Bill Camp, Sanaa Lathan

Context

Rashid Johnson's 2019 film adaptation of *Native Son* was the third time the book had been turned into a motion picture, not to mention being variously adapted for the stage. The book, although first published in 1940, is commonly considered not only a literary classic but also a narrative continuously relevant to race relations in the United States. For that reason, Johnson's adaptation was deliberately set in contemporary times; it clearly reflects, for instance, the impact of the presidency of Barack Obama, the first African American to hold the nation's highest office.

Oddly, race relations were often particularly tense during Obama's eight years as president, especially during his second term, which saw the rise of the Black Lives Matter (BLM) movement. That movement condemns police brutality against Black people, especially young Black men. The concerns of the BLM movement are especially relevant to the closing scene of Johnson's *Native Son*. In that scene, the main character is gunned down and killed by police, although he *may* have committed the kind of suicide sometimes called "death by cop." In any case, Johnson intentionally wanted to "update" Wright's novel in various ways to show that the book was far from irrelevant to the contemporary era.

Another way the film reflects contemporary times involves the ways the main character, Bigger ("Big") Thomas (Ashton Sanders), is presented and the ways he presents *himself*. Big dyes his hair bright green; wears a distinctive painted jacket that associates him with the punk rock scene; and prefers that sort of rock music (as well as Beethoven) over the kind of hip-hop music that would have made him a more stereotypical African American youth of the twenty-first century. He is slender rather than well-built, and although he carries a gun, he is also inter-

ested in literature. In fact, in the film's opening scene, he places his gun squarely on top of a copy of *Invisible Man*, Ralph Ellison's famous novel about race relations in the United States. In appearance, behavior, interests, and language, Big defies many of the stereotypes often associated with many young Black men of his time and place, especially those living in urban areas and particularly those living in Chicago, with its vicious gangs and sky-high murder rate.

Big represents, in many ways, the growing emphasis on sheer individualism that characterizes the values of many people living today. He wants to be his own person, live by his own values, and not have to conform to others' expectations, whether those others are Black, White, rich, poor, or something else. In fact, he is mocked by some of his Black friends for wanting to chart his own distinctive path and for rejecting what Big himself at one point calls "lowest common denominator stereotypical negro s—." The film, in short, tries to avoid making Big a young Black male who conforms to—and thus confirms—many common expectations about young Black men. Some critics, in fact, have suggested that in trying to reject stereotypes, the filmmakers were responding to James Baldwin's famous criticism that *Native Son* the novel had reinforced many racist assumptions about African Americans. Johnson's "Big" is, in some ways, himself a stereotype, but not necessarily in some of the commonly expected ways.

Film Analysis

The 2019 film version of *Native Son* resembles the 1940 novel in numerous ways. The "Bigger" Thomas of the book becomes the "Big" Thomas of the film. Both are young Black men who live in the ghetto of Chicago; both have young Black girlfriends named Bessie; both eventually find work, as drivers, for a wealthy white liberal family known as the Daltons; both are befriended but also patronized by the Daltons' daughter, Mary, and her white boyfriend Jan (both of whom are "woke" political radicals); and in both the novel and the film, Big accidentally kills Mary and is then himself killed as the result of this unintentional murder. In a resemblance that was widely mocked by film critics, Big in the 2019 film disposes of Mary's body by cramming it into a coal-fired furnace, which destroys most of the corpse but leaves enough evidence among the ashes to help establish Big's guilt. This plot twist was perfectly plausible in the 1940s, but the idea that any large house in Chicago in 2019 still uses a coal-fired furnace struck many commentators as preposterous and severely damaging to the film's credibility. In fact, many critics thought that this incident, as well as the rest of the film in general, made its final act far less effective than the film's first two thirds had been.

Indeed, another significant change between the novel and the film involves the film's ending. In the novel, Bigger is arrested, jailed, and put on trial. He is defended by a prominent left-wing white attorney for whom he develops real respect. In fact, the lawyer in some ways becomes the hero of the final part of the novel. In the 2019 film (unlike the 1986 teleplay), Big is gunned down by police before there is any opportunity for a trial. His death, although criticized by some reviewers as too melodramatic, struck others as memorably tragic and particularly relevant to the lives of young Black men in contemporary America. In any case, the absence of the imprisonment and trial, which take up a large proportion of the novel, is perhaps the most significant change made by Johnson in adapting the book to the screen.

Also significantly different is the way the film presents the final moments of Big's relationship with Bessie (Kiki Layne). In the novel, Bigger rapes and then kills Bessie. In the film, he is angry with her, attempts to strangle her, but then gets control of his emotions and not only lets her live but expresses real remorse for trying to kill her. He seems as shocked by his behavior as she is. Therefore, in the film Big is inadvertently responsible for the death of one young white woman—Mary (Margaret Qualley). He is not also guilty of the deliberate murder of his young Black girlfriend, and he certainly does not rape her. (Early in the film, they have sex that is quite clearly consensual.) The filmmakers seem to have wanted to make Big, in general, a

less stereotypically violent character than Bigger can seem in the novel, and they also seem to have wanted to make Big less misogynistic. In the latter respect, especially, they made their film more acceptable to audiences of the late 2010s.

Some critics thought that the relatively passive Big who appears early in the film was unlikely to kill anyone under any circumstances. Others, however, thought that the killing Big *does* commit in the film is plausible and, in fact, almost inevitable given his racial and socioeconomic circumstances. On the other hand, still other critics thought that even the one killing he does commit seems far less believable as an event in 2019 than as an event committed by Bigger in the late 1930s. According to this argument, the Big of 2019 would have felt under less pressure to kill Mary than the Bigger who appears in the novel. Presumably, the idea of a Black man being found in Mary's bedroom would have been easier for everyone, including or perhaps especially her liberal parents, to accept in 2019 than in 1940.

Various aspects of the 2019 film provoked reviewers' either favorable or unfavorable comments. For example, several reviewers noted that the film sometimes effectively resembles a horror movie, especially in scenes set in the Dalton mansion, where Big often feels nervous and out of place. Some commentators objected to the film's occasional use of narrative voice-overs, although others found the voice-overs (which often involve quotations from famous texts, such as W. E. B. Du Bois's *The Souls of Black Folk*) perfectly appropriate. One of the most interesting and distinctive elements of the film involves several scenes in which Big stands motionless while other people are shown in very rapid, almost blurred movement around him. Some critics admired these brief segments, suggesting that they implied how Big was figuratively out of touch with the life around him. Others, however, considered these segments too self-consciously artsy and distracting. Johnson, the director, is himself an artist, and many critics noted how often and how obviously artworks by contemporary Black painters and sculptors are featured in the film. The Daltons clearly collect contemporary "Black" art—a fact that some critics found variously meaningful, suggesting either their tony admiration for Black culture, their tendency to fetishize and appropriate that culture, or both.

The scene in which Big unintentionally kills Mary by smothering her with a pillow was sometimes called especially effective. It is so striking, in fact, that some members of the audience at the initial screening let out audible gasps of horror, and some even left the theater. In the two previous film versions of *Native Son*, as in the book, Bigger smothers Mary while Mary's blind mother is actually in the room as the smothering takes place. Johnson makes the accidental killing far more plausible: Big hears Mary's mother *approaching* the room. That fact alone terrifies him enough that he tries to keep the drunken Mary quiet by covering her face with the pillow. When Mary's mother leaves and Big's fear subsides, he discovers that he accidentally pressed too hard with the pillow and that Mary is dead. This scene will make many viewers recall similar scenes from filmed versions of Shakespeare's *Othello*, especially the scene from the 1995 film starring Laurence Fishburne and Kenneth Branagh. Surely Johnson must have intended the *Othello* allusion. In that respect, this moment in the film exemplifies all the various ways in which the 2019 film is full of allusions to other works, whether they are works of visual art, written works, and even various works of music.

Significance

Reactions to the 2019 film of *Native Son* were decidedly mixed. HBO, the television streaming service, purchased exclusive rights to the film just before it was premiered at the prestigious Sundance Film Festival. Thus, the film, rather than heading for conventional theaters, was first aired on television. It never stood the test of seeing how many people would buy tickets to see it on a big screen, and therefore it never received the kind of widespread reviews it would have attracted if it had been released into theaters. The reviews of the film that *were* published tended to be negative, often severely so.

The film's final section, set in motion by Mary's death, was especially condemned, even by critics who otherwise admired what Johnson had attempted. But some reviewers did enthusiastically praise the film not only for what it had attempted to do but for what it had often achieved. Critics widely admired the performance of Ashton Sanders as

Big; even commentators who disliked the film in general had good things to say about Sanders' performance. Kiki Layne, as Bessie, also received widespread praise. In fact, most of the film's actors were commended. When it was faulted, most of the blame was laid at the feet of the director, with many critics noting that this was Rashid Johnson's first attempt at directing a film. Some critics admired the innovative screenplay by Suzan-Lori Parks, although others found the script too self-consciously literary, especially in its use of voice-overs. The use of contemporary Black artwork was widely discussed and broadly admired, with some critics noting that Johnson had even incorporated some of his own art into various shots. Overall, the film was considered a work of real potential, with some critics claiming that that potential had largely been achieved but most suggesting that the film had not fully lived up to its promise.

—*Robert C. Evans, PhD*

Further Reading

Del Barco, Mandalit. "*Native Son* Is Reborn, in 'Still Kind of the Same America.'" *Morning Edition* (*NPR*), Apr. 2019. *EBSCOhost*, search.ebscohost.com/login.aspx?direct= true&db=n5h&AN=6XN201904031008&site=ehost-live. Accessed 26 Apr. 2020.
Lewis, Miles Marshall. "Song of Suzan-Lori." *Essence*, vol. 50, no. 1, May 2019, p. 24. *EBSCOhost*, search.ebscohost.com/ login.aspx?direct=true&db=f6h&AN=136064379&site= ehost-live. Accessed 26 Apr. 2020.
Uyehara, Mari. "Art Dad, Art Son." *GQ: Gentlemen's Quarterly*, vol. 89, no. 4, May 2019, p. 24. *EBSCOhost*, search.ebscohost.com/login.aspx?direct=true&db=f6h&AN =135945262&site=ehost-live. Accessed 26 Apr. 2020.

Bibliography

Gleiberman, Owen. "Sundance Film Review: *Native Son*." *Variety*, 25 Jan. 2019, variety.com/2019/film/reviews/native-son- review-sundance-film-festival-1203117692/. Accessed 26 Apr. 2020.
Phillips, Michael. "*Native Son* Review: Modern-Day Chicago's Gonna Need a Bigger Thomas." *Chicago Tribune*, 4 Apr. 2019, www.chicagotribune.com/entertainment/tv/sc-tv-native-son-hbo-review-0404-story.html. Accessed 26 Apr. 2020.

Nineteen Eighty-Four / 1984

The Novel
Author: George Orwell (Eric Arthur Blair, 1903-50)
First published: 1949

The Film
Year released: 1984
Director: Michael Radford (b. 1946)
Screenplay by: Michael Radford
Starring: John Hurt, Richard Burton, Suzanna Hamilton, Cyril Cusack

Context

Events of the twentieth century—two world wars, the apparent success of totalitarian states, atomic bombs, and more—created an atmosphere of uncertainty and fear that inspired an outpouring of literary speculations—and warnings—about what the future might bring. Writers such as Karel Capek (*Rossum's Universal Robots*, 1921), Franz Kafka (*The Trial*, 1925), Aldous Huxley (*Brave New World*, 1932), Sinclair Lewis (*It Can't Happen Here*, 1935), and others contributed to a multitude of possible scenarios. One of the most popular and enduring dystopian works was created by George Orwell with *Nineteen Eighty-Four*, first published in 1949.

Most of Orwell's body of work—novels, memoirs, essays, articles, reviews, criticism, letters, wartime propaganda broadcasts—was steeped in political thought. From 1936, when he was seriously wounded fighting for the Republican army in the Spanish Civil War, until his early death from tuberculosis, he vehemently opposed totalitarianism and staunchly supported democratic socialism. The last full-length work published in his lifetime was *Nineteen Eighty-Four*, which presented such principles in fictional form. Orwell created a dismal world in which ordinary worker Winston Smith quietly rebels to save his own humanity. He commits forbidden acts to show his disdain for a cruel regime under the leadership of a semidivine presence known as Big Brother. The elite Inner Party uses surveillance, intimidation, torture, brainwashing, scapegoating, and murder to stamp out anyone perceived as a threat, and Outer Party member Smith knows he will eventually be caught and punished.

The story of an individual fighting alone against impossible odds allowed Orwell to explore numerous issues, including the effects of totalitarianism on individuals and groups, the nature of truth, and the depths of love and hate. A chief element is the use of language to manipulate people, events, and the very perception of reality. The novel was a critical success and proved hugely popular—with strong sales well into the twenty-first century—as well as culturally influential. It was first adapted for radio in 1949, for television in 1953, and for film in 1956.

The second film version of Orwell's classic is distinguished for being released in the very year of the title. *1984* (originally rendered as *Nineteen Eighty-Four*, and like the book known in both formats) was just the second feature film Michael Radford wrote and directed. It followed his debut with the World War II drama *Another Time, Another Place* (1983). Radford subsequently became a noted filmmaker, writing and directing more than a dozen films. Included among his filmography are such well-received works as *White Mischief* (1987), *Il Postino: The Postman* (1994), *The Merchant of Venice* (2004), and *The Music of Silence* (2017).

Film Analysis

Radford's *1984* sacrifices Orwell's surreal opening line: "It was a bright cold day in April, and the clocks were striking thirteen." Radford starts his film by superimposing, in stark white-on-black type, a key objective of those at the top of society's pyramid, who lust for power and ruthlessly defend their hold on it. "Who controls the past controls the future," the words read, "Who controls the present controls the past."

The theory and practice of that message is illustrated throughout the film, which is structured differently from Orwell's original. Rather than start at the beginning of the book, the director creates a dramatic opening extrapolated from passages midway through the first chapter of the novel. The Two Minutes Hate (which actually lasts about five minutes on-screen before the credits roll) is a brilliantly conceived piece of propaganda that also serves as a means of exposition. By moving the sequence forward in the narration, Radford efficiently provides solid cornerstones on which the story is built. The hate session shows how power manipulates: a large audience, dressed identically in blue coveralls, sits attentively facing a huge screen. There the Ingsoc (Newspeak for English Socialism) banner flies. The plot is launched with a presentation that moves the crowd to feel patriotic ("This is our land. Oceania. These are our people."). The mood is bent toward jingoism with hyperbole recapping the current situation: "fighting...against the dark murdering armies of Eurasia." The audience is motivated to act when the subject switches again to the "evil tumor spreading in our midst." As the visual changes to a still shot of a mild-looking bearded man, the viewers stand and angrily shout his name: "Goldstein!" Individual members of the audience gesticulate, curse, and make a crossed-wrist sign of solidarity. The camera travels across the faces, lingering to visually introduce three principal characters: Winston Smith (John Hurt), Julia (Suzanna Hamilton), and O'Brien (Richard Burton).

Except for similar temporal rearrangements, extended flashbacks, lush dream sequences, and small, insignificant changes in details, Radford's *Nineteen Eighty-Four* follows Orwell's original quite closely in virtually all of the important plot particulars. (Winston's secret diary in the film, for example, is hidden behind a loose brick in a wall instead of in a desk drawer as written. Evocative symbols, like a piece of coral embedded in crystal, a relic of a redacted past, remain.) Many whole sections of dialogue have been lifted from novel to movie. Crucially, much of the political thought has been transferred from one medium to the other. Thematically important discussions between Smith and O'Brien about power are intact. O'Brien still transmits the startling image Orwell had envisioned: "If you want a picture of the future, imagine a boot stamping on a human face—forever!"

The look and feel of the film are especially well-matched to the tone of the novel. The color is appropriately faded; the setting of London (the capital of the Oceania province known as Airstrip One) is a dirty, grungy place for most inhabitants. Streets are filled with rubble and trash. Rats scurry about. Party slogans are part of the scenery:

War Is Peace, Freedom Is Slavery, Ignorance Is Strength. Posters of Big Brother hang everywhere, and the Leader's hypnotic gaze seems to follow pedestrians. Telescreens continually output information and input data on individuals. Ordinary citizens, like Smith, who work at the Ministry of Truth, "rectifying" history to his superior's specifications, have to scrounge for everyday items like razor blades and cigarettes. Government-provided cafeteria meals are sludgy, but the gin is free.

The film includes a few snatches of Newspeak—the iconic, restrictive language Orwell invented for Oceania —such as "thoughtcrime," "doubleplusgood," "blackwhite," "doublethink." However, there is no attempt to incorporate the "Principles of Newspeak" appendix from the end of the novel. That section of the book has been interpreted by some critics as a hopeful ending, because it is written in past tense as though Newspeak is no longer in use and contains critical remarks about "rubbishy entertainment" and "spurious news," suggesting the government under Big Brother has fallen. No such optimism is apparent in the film.

The technological ambiance of Radford's film is steampunk-like. (Earlier adaptations of Orwell's work had more futuristic-looking gadgets and more stylish costumes.) Smith's cubicle at work features, in addition to the omnipresent telescreen, a rotary dial-type device to call up particular articles to be changed. The articles are delivered by a crude pneumatic tube, verbally edited through something resembling a dictaphone, and are then destroyed by fire after being inserted into a slot nicknamed "a memory hole." The Thought Police rely upon uniformed thugs with rubber truncheons to control suspects. Even the torture device O'Brien uses to persuade Smith to rethink is primitive, like an updated medieval rack upon which a victim is painfully stretched into confessing.

The casting of *Nineteen Eighty-Four* is inspired. John Hurt's angular, world-weary visage and gaunt physique lend an Everyman aspect to his portrayal. His Winston Smith has been beaten down by life but has an inner strength that has allowed him to resist surrender to the powers that be. O'Brien, played by a subdued Richard Burton (in his last film role before his death), makes good use of the actor's powerful voice. Julia, reportedly based on Sonia Brownell (1918-80), a woman with whom Orwell had a fling and married a few months before he died, is appropriately depicted as young and sensuous, but not especially interested in political nuances.

Because Radford's film was released in the late twentieth century, by which time social standards had changed since the novel's publication, there are a number of brief scenes of full-frontal female nudity, and one sequence featuring full dorsal male nudity. This seems perfectly natural given the situation: clandestine lovers enjoying each other physically in a time and place fraught with danger, where a frisson of risk adds to the pleasure. With their clothes off, the lovers embody the malnourished nature of a repressive society: she is not voluptuous, but thin; he is not muscular, but wiry.

Significance

Radford's *1984* was well-received critically and broke just about even commercially, returning box office revenues of $8.4 million on an investment of $5.5 million. It garnered the *Evening Standard*'s award as Best British Film of the Year and earned high honors at the Istanbul International Film Festival. It did generate some controversy for the studio's decision to include music by the pop group Eurythmics rather than the complete score composed by Dominic Muldowney. Subsequent soundtrack albums and home video releases would variously feature the Eurythmics songs or the original score.

Radford's film remains considered a relatively strong adaptation of Orwell's iconic novel, though it never reached the cultural influence of the original. In general, *Nineteen Eighty-Four* continues to be widely studied and taught as one of the great classics of Western literature. Indeed, the work saw a new wave of popularity in the early twenty-first century, as many commentators identified similarities to contemporary social and political trends. Fears of rising authoritarianism and nationalism—especially amid concerns over disinformation and propaganda—brought fresh attention to Orwell's dystopian vision. Growing economic inequality and Big Brother-like threats to privacy created by ever-advancing technology have also been cited as evidence that the world of *Nineteen Eighty-Four* is hardly far-fetched. Whether in Orwell's timeless writing or an adaptation such as Radford's appropriately bleak film, the tragic tale of Winston Smith stands as an important warning to humanity about its darkest potential.

—Jack Ewing

Further Reading

Hitchens, Christopher. *Why Orwell Matters*. Basic Books, 2003.

Lynskey, Dorian. *The Ministry of Truth: The Biography of George Orwell's 1984*. Doubleday, 2019.

Ricks, Thomas E. *Churchill and Orwell: The Fight for Freedom*. Penguin Publishing Group, 2018.

Bibliography

Lief, Ruth Ann. *Homage to Oceania: The Prophetic Vision of George Orwell*. Ohio State UP, 1969.

Orwell, George. *All Art Is Propaganda: Critical Essays*. Compiled by George Packer, Houghton Mifflin Harcourt, 2008.

———. *1984*. Plume/Harcourt Brace, 2009.

———. *Orwell on Truth*. Houghton Mifflin Harcourt, 2018.

Packer, George. "Doublethink Is Stronger Than Orwell Imagined." *The Atlantic*, July 2019, www.theatlantic.com/magazine/archive/2019/07/1984-george-orwell/590638/. Accessed 6 Feb. 2020.

Schlueter, Nathan. "The True Lessons of *1984*." *National Review*, 9 Feb. 2017, www.nationalreview.com/2017/02/george-orwell-1984-trump-not/. Accessed 6 Feb. 2020.

Spurling, Hilary. *The Girl from the Fiction Department: A Portrait of Sonia Orwell*. Counterpoint/Perseus Books Group, 2003.

Nothing Lasts Forever / Die Hard

The Novel
Author: Roderick Thorp (1936-99)
First published: 1979

The Film
Year released: 1988
Director: John McTiernan (b. 1951)
Screenplay by: Jeb Stuart, Steven E. de Souza
Starring: Bruce Willis, Bonnie Bedelia, Alan Rickman, Alexander Godunov, Reginald VelJohnson

Context

Author Roderick Thorp published the critically acclaimed novel, *Nothing Lasts Forever* in 1979. The book reprised the hard-boiled character Joe Leland, introduced in the 1966 bestseller *The Detective*. Leland is a World War II fighter ace and former police officer, turned private eye. *The Detective* was adapted for film under the same title in 1968 starring Frank Sinatra as Joe Leland.

In the second novel, Leland has become a security consultant and terrorism expert who travels widely as a featured guest at corporate seminars and conferences. Enthusiastically received, the novel was quickly optioned with the idea that Sinatra would reprise the lead role in the film. However, Sinatra, then in his mid-60s, turned down the offer. The rejection began an almost decade-long effort to transform the novel into a film. Adaptations, under various titles and with different slants, were rewritten multiple times in an attempt to attract a suitable actor to play Joe Leland. The list of potential candidates reads like a who's who of Hollywood action figures. Actors who turned down the role included James Caan, Harrison Ford, Richard Gere, Mel Gibson, Al Pacino, Burt Reynolds, Arnold Schwarzenegger, and Sylvester Stallone.

Finally, in 1987, the perfect actor was found to play the protagonist. He was Bruce Willis, the wisecracking costar to Cybill Shepherd on the television series *Moonlighting* (1985-89). It was a popular comedy-mystery television series based upon the exploits of a fictional detective agency. During the show's nearly three-month production hiatus to accommodate Shepherd's pregnancy (she gave birth to twins), Willis was able to tackle the rigorous film role. For his work, Willis was paid $5 million, an enormous amount at the time for someone who was practically unknown on the big screen. The *Nothing Lasts Forever* adaptation, written by Jeb Stuart and Steven E. de Souza, was retitled *Die Hard* (1988). The adaptation forever severed the formal connection between the novel's Joe Leland character and his much younger film counterpart, renamed John McClane.

Film Analysis

The major plot points of *Nothing Lasts Forever*—on Christmas Eve a lone man fights a small army of well-armed terrorists holding hostages in a thirty-five-story building in Los Angeles, California—were transferred intact from page to screen. A number of specific incidents (the hero cuts his bare feet on broken glass, uses flimsy straps to lower himself into an elevator shaft, and employs a fire hose to rappel down the building) were reproduced from descriptions in the novel. Almost everything else was changed for the adaptation to *Die Hard*.

One major difference between novel and film was the tone of the finished product. *Nothing Lasts Forever* is dark and noirish. From the start, aging protagonist Joe Leland broods about yesteryear and is a bitter bundle of regrets. He is a recovering alcoholic. His wife divorced him, remarried, and died. His relationship with his only child, a daughter living alone with two children on the West Coast, is fragile. Leland, who has spent most of his life in life-or-death occupations, is portrayed as a cynic who expects the worst, usually finds it, then excoriates himself afterward. This is one of several of Leland's typically jaundiced impressions of Los Angeles: "...you came away with the conclusion that, if the billboards were removed, the power lines buried, and the business signs restricted to a modest size, the city would look like a shaved cat."

Die Hard, by contrast, is considerably more upbeat and positive, despite all the explosions and bullets, despite all the blood and killing that ensue. The lighthearted, adventurous mood is indicated from the beginning of the film, when Leland stand-in John McClane (Bruce Willis) carries a giant teddy bear, a Christmas gift for one of his young children. McClane is not laden with the baggage of the past. He is capable of sloughing off setbacks and moving on with an aggressive, forward-looking attitude. He actually has a good time finding new ways to thwart and eliminate bad guys. McClane's snide comments about the West Coast whenever he witnesses something outrageous are confined to a wry smile, a head shake, and a muttered, "California." There are numerous tension-lightening moments throughout the film, like jokes about Twinkies, comments about Western legend Roy Rogers, and colorfully profane expressions. Midway through the film there is a clever parody of a live television talk show centered around the ongoing hostage crisis, with "Dr. Hasseldorf, author of *Hostage Terrorist, Terrorist Hostage*" (George Christy), talking about "the Helsinki Syndrome." Quips fly, and even the terrorists engage in banter about seasonal miracles and earning twenty percent on their ill-gotten gains: $640 million in negotiable bearer bonds. Unlike the novel, where Christmas is merely a date marked off in chapter headings by hours and minutes, in the film it is an occasion. There are visual reminders throughout—trees, wreaths, Santa hats, decorated tape. The music reinforces the spirit of the holidays, with hip-hop carols, pop standards like Vaughn Monroe's "Let It Snow!" (accompanied by sheets of paper drifting down from the burning Nakatomi Building like giant flakes), and soaring passages of the "Ode to Joy," from Ludwig van Beethoven's *Symphony No. 9*, competing with sirens from emergency vehicles.

Die Hard also modernizes the trappings of the story in *Nothing Lasts Forever*. The film is a product of the late 1980s, whereas the novel belongs firmly in the 1970s. Typewriters in the older work become desktop computers. An old-fashioned safe in the original turns into a vault with sophisticated electronic safeguards. There are armored police vehicles and handheld guided missiles. In the novel, Leland attaches himself to a friendly stewardess and often speaks with her by citizens band (CB) radio for moral support during the hostage crisis. McClane of the film adaptation is married but separated from his wife by circumstances: she has a prestigious, high-paying job with

Bruce Willis. Photo by Gage Skidmore, CC BY-SA 3.0, via Wikimedia Commons.

a Japanese American firm. Her executive position necessitated relocation west; he could not move with the family because he is still committed to his profession—protecting and serving on the East Coast. The terrorists are similarly modern. The villains of the novel (which included several young women who Leland dispatched as if they were men) were genuine radicals willing to die for their cause. The film villains, however, are only pretending—they are really just high-class thieves.

Perhaps the biggest difference between the novel and the adaptation is the development of secondary characters. *Nothing Lasts Forever* is told in close third person from Leland's point of view, so the supporting cast is largely two-dimensional. Friends or foes of the protagonist are often remembered in flashbacks, heard as voices, glimpsed during a firefight, or seen as lifeless bodies. In *Die Hard*, many of these shadows have real substance. Although the main perspective is McClane's, an omniscient viewpoint gives others a chance to strut their stuff. Holly Gennaro McClane (Bonnie Bedelia), for example, serves as a focal point to provide whispered asides about McClane's antics. Top architectural executive, elegant Takagi (James Shigeta), replaces his sleazy novel counterpart, an illegal arms dealer. Lead terrorist Hans Gruber (Alan Rickman, in his first film role) is greatly expanded, becoming a glib, clever, worthy foe. His second-in-command, Karl Vreski (Alexander Godunov), brings balletic grace and a menacing presence to a formerly offstage role. Many of the walk-on roles in the novel are likewise built into more important parts in the film. An elderly black chauffeur who vanishes early after one scene in the novel becomes hip young Argyle (De'voreaux White), who plays a key part in a late plot twist not contained in the novel. Sergeant Al Powell (Reginald VelJohnson), McClane's radio link, takes on added qualities and importance, and is even given a backstory. Several new characters have also been added to further complicate the plot. A pair of Federal Bureau of Investigation (FBI) agents named Johnson ("no relation"), one white (Robert Davi), one black (Grand L. Bush), provide an opportunity to satirize governmental overconfidence. Obnoxious newsman Richard Thornburg (William Atherton) symbolizes the intrusiveness of the media.

Significance

Die Hard launched both Bruce Willis's career as a bankable big-screen action star and a feature film franchise. The film received mixed reviews upon release—though critical reception has improved over the years. *Die Hard* was nominated for four technical Academy Awards (Best Sound, Best Film Editing, Best Sound Effects Editing, and Best Visual Effects), but earned no Oscars. The adaptation did well commercially, more than quintupling its $28 million budget with over $140 million in box office receipts.

Although he had appeared in only two significant film roles before *Die Hard* (*Blind Date*, 1987 and *Sunset*, 1988), Willis was soon in demand as a lead actor in action films, and he has appeared in a string of features of varying quality since then.

Willis starred as John McClane in four further permutations of the *Die Hard* adaptation. *Die Hard 2* (1990), *Die Hard with a Vengeance* (1995), *Live Free or Die Hard* (2007), and *A Good Day to Die Hard* (2013) all revolve around stories that feature spectacular stunts and explosive pyrotechnics. The second installment carried over the strong Christmas theme and several actors from the first film (Bonnie Bedelia, William Atherton, and Reginald VelJohnson), but later sequels eliminated the seasonal tie-in and phased out recurring secondary characters.

—*Jack Ewing*

Further Reading

Lichtenfeld, Eric. *Action Speaks Louder: Violence, Spectacle, and the American Action Movie*. Wesleyan UP, 2007.

Mottram, James, and David S. Cohen. *Die Hard: The Ultimate Visual History*. Insight Editions, 2018.

Bibliography

Abrams, Brian. "*Die Hard*: How Bruce Willis Changed the Movies." *Daily Beast*, 13 Apr. 2017, www.thedailybeast.com/die-hard-how-bruce-willis-changed-the-movies. Accessed 2 Apr. 2020.

Bailey, Jason. "How *Die Hard* Changed the Action Game." *Vulture*, 10 July 2018, www.vulture.com/2018/07/how-die-hard-changed-the-action-game.html. Accessed 2 Apr. 2020.

Collins, K. Austin. "*Die Hard* Is as Brilliantly Engineered as a Machine Gun, Even 30 Years Later." *Vanity Fair*, 13 July 2018, www.vanityfair.com/hollywood/2018/07/die-hard-30th-anniversary-bruce-willis-john-mcclane. Accessed 2 Apr. 2020.

Connelly, Sherryl. "Before Bruce Willis' *Die Hard* There Was the Book *Nothing Lasts Forever*." *New York Daily News*, 18 Feb. 2013, www.nydailynews.com/entertainment/music-arts/book-behind-die-hard-packs-punch-article-1.1265319. Accessed 2 Apr. 2020.

Smith, Kevin Burton. "Joe Leland (also John McClane)." *The Thrilling Detective Web Site*, www.thrillingdetective.com/eyes/leland.html. Accessed 2 Apr. 2020.

Thorp, Roderick. *Nothing Lasts Forever*. W. W. Norton & Company, 1979.

The Old Man and the Sea

The Novel
Author: Ernest Hemingway (1899-1961)
First published: 1952

The Film
Year released: 1958
Directors: John Sturges (1910-92), Fred Zinnemann (1907-97)
Screenplay by: Peter Viertel
Starring: Spencer Tracy, Felipe Pazos Jr., Harry Bellaver

Context

American author Ernest Hemingway was a celebrity during his lifetime, famous not only for his fiction but for his adventurous life. After serving as an ambulance driver in World War I, he came to prominence as a key member of "the Lost Generation" of writers, living in Paris where he befriended Gertrude Stein, Ezra Pound, and others. He was a war correspondent, filing stories from the Spanish Civil War and World War II. He left Havana just ahead of the Cuban revolution, after which Fidel Castro's government confiscated the author's restored farm, Finca Vigía. A famous womanizer, he married four times and fathered several children, some of whom became famous in their own right. He drank to excess. He survived two plane crashes. In the end, he committed suicide like his father before him and his granddaughter, the actress and supermodel Margaux Hemingway, after him.

As a writer, Hemingway developed a distinctive, modern prose style—terse, direct, pared down, and declarative—that influenced many writers. When he was awarded the Nobel Prize in 1954, the prize committee cited "the influence that he has exerted on contemporary style." His narratives tended to be straightforward and direct as well, and he favored a reduction to elemental conflicts: the protagonist versus antagonist, or versus the self, or versus nature.

The last full-length work that Hemingway published during his lifetime was a novella, *The Old Man and the Sea* (1952). Inspired by a true account, the author produced a timeless story about the battle of a solitary individual (said by some critics to represent the author himself) against the implacable forces of nature and his struggles to maintain his dignity against the creeping weaknesses of age. Considered by many—including Hemingway—to be his best work, *The Old Man and the Sea* was an immediate critical and commercial success—a bestseller. It won the 1953 Pulitzer Prize, and was named as a key factor in the author's selection as Nobel Laureate the following year.

Film Analysis

Because of its widespread popularity, it was inevitable that *The Old Man and the Sea*, like several previous Hemingway novels, would be adapted for the screen. Unlike some of the author's other works, however, the story (essentially a fish tale about the big one that got away), except for a few brief action sequences, is contemplative, internalized, uncinematic. The bulk of the text consists of the old man of the title sitting patiently alone in a little skiff far out to sea. He clings desperately to a line connected to a sizable, but unseen hooked fish. While he waits to learn whether he or his prey will win the battle, whether he will be lucky or unlucky, nothing much happens. He observes, thinks, dreams, hopes, remembers—and holds on for dear life.

Despite such moviemaking uncertainties, Warner Brothers okayed the project. Fred Zinnemann—known for such films as *High Noon* (1952), *From Here to Eternity* (1953), and *Oklahoma!* (1955)—was initially assigned to direct. When Zinnemann bowed out partway through production (and lost his film credit in the process), John Sturges replaced him. The new director's recent successes included directing Spencer Tracy in *Bad Day at Black Rock* (1955).

Among those who contributed to the final product was composer Dimitri Tiomkin, who won an Oscar for the score of *High Noon*. The cinematographer was James

Wong Howe, Academy Award winner for *The Rose Tattoo* (1955). Screenwriter Peter Viertel, who scripted Hemingway's *The Sun Also Rises*, was tapped to bring *The Old Man and the Sea* to life on-screen. The author himself was involved in production, primarily trying to shoot original footage of hooking an enormous marlin. (Ultimately, as noted at film's end, the production company used shots from an earlier world record catch off the coast of Peru.)

The film adhered closely, even reverently, to the source material from start to finish. The plot motivation is laid out in the first paragraph of the first chapter. An old fisherman, Santiago, has not caught a fish for eighty-four straight days. For the first forty days, he went out with a young boy, Manolin, who adores and cares for the old man. Because of his fishing drought, Santiago is considered *salao*, unlucky, in the Cuban village where they live, so Manolin's parents order him to switch to a different, luckier boat. Santiago rows out on the eighty-fifth day, feeling hopeful—what else can a poor man do but keep trying?

While little was added to Hemingway's original plot or dialogue, the film eliminates extraneous material to streamline an already spare story. Chit-chat between the boy and the old man is pared to essentials; most of their conversation about American big-league baseball is omitted. Certain explanatory passages are cut down. Footage for some of the natural events that were mentioned (such as descriptions of turtles encountering Portuguese Man-of-War) was skipped. An obvious change from Hemingway's text was the deletion of the description of Santiago as "thin and gaunt." This change was necessitated by the casting of Spencer Tracy as Santiago. A reliable leading man, Tracy had taken home acting Oscars in successive years for *Captains Courageous* (1937) and *Boys Town* (1938). But he was neither thin nor gaunt. Nor was he Hispanic. (Apparently, he wore a prosthetic to suggest poor dental care, which slightly altered his well-known features in close-up shots.) Although he had an accent for the seafaring saga *Captains Courageous*, Tracy did not attempt to alter his voice to portray Santiago. It would have been difficult trying to match the subtle phrasing and linguistic lilt of a character (whose exotic history is revealed throughout via flashbacks) native to the Canary Islands who has long resided in Cuba.

Tracy's unaltered voice provides almost continuous narration, as though reading aloud Hemingway's lightly edited manuscript. Unfortunately, the author's poetic prose did not always translate well from page to screen. His experimental narrative technique, written sometimes in third-person omniscient ("...the old man could feel the line..."), sometimes in first person ("I could give the fish more line..."), makes the continuity feel sloppy. This is complicated by the fact that the old man also talks to himself, and to various passing creatures on-screen. While devotion to the original source is commendable, *The Old Man and the Sea* film contains scenes where narration becomes a distraction. In many places Tracy's voice-over describes exactly what the camera shows: "The old man stood the mast up outside the shack... inside the shack there was a bed, tables and chairs...," or "the sun was going down." The inclusion of so much superfluous narration makes the usually terse Hemingway seem positively wordy.

Director Sturges, aided by cinematographer Howe, took good advantage of the few opportunities provided in the text to include several dramatic sequences in an otherwise leisurely, low-key film. The colorful flashback to an epic arm-wrestling contest from Santiago's youth could have been lifted from an Indiana Jones movie. Scenes showing an enormous marlin leaping from the water are genuinely exciting, and in general are well-matched to cuts showing Tracy in his little boat—which were actually shot in a studio tank. Tracy is most convincing as Santiago when fighting off gangs of sharks. Well-photographed and edited scenes mix stock shots of dorsal fins cutting through waves with underwater footage, as the predators swarm in to attack the old man's great fish from below. Viewers are shown the frolicking African lions of which Santiago often dreams, though they are romping on grass, rather than on a sandy beach as originally written.

Significance

The Old Man and the Sea, shot in WarnerColor, is an attractive film, thanks to the efforts of cinematographer Howe (who was nominated for a 1959 Academy Award). There are sweeping shots of seascapes, sunsets, birds, flying fish, and other animals. These images reinforce one of the author's major themes: the elemental, eternal force of nature. Other themes—such as verbal (Hail Marys and Our Fathers) or visual (the cross-like mast and spars) religious motifs—were included intact. A particularly memorable sequence shows fishermen, looking like fireflies with their dim lanterns, moving through the predawn toward the sea. The film also sounds good, due to the score by Tiomkin (who won an Oscar for his work); his music for the fishermen's procession is reminiscent of a mass. Tracy was nominated as best actor for the sixth out of nine times he was so honored during his career but lost out to David Niven in *Separate Tables*.

The strengths of the film, however, were not enough to counterbalance the relatively static pace, compared to most other films adapted from Hemingway's major novels and short stories—such as the excellent noir film *The Killers* (1946) or *The Snows of Kilimanjaro* (1952). Critics were lukewarm, and from the box office revenues, it was clear that audiences agreed that the 1958 film did not do justice to the novel.

The potential difficulties of adapting Hemingway's sea tale have not stopped other artists from trying. The story, a clash between indomitable forces, is compelling, like much of Hemingway's work. The author's works have been adapted for dozens of film and television productions. Since 1958, two other adaptations have been developed of *The Old Man and the Sea*. In 1990, Anthony Quinn starred in a made-for-television feature that garnered three Emmy nominations, and a twenty-minute animated Russian-Canadian-Japanese production directed in 1999 by Aleksandr Petrov won the Academy Award in its category.

—*Jack Ewing*

Further Reading

Godfrey, Laura Gruber. *Hemingway's Geographies: Intimacy, Materiality, and Memory*. Palgrave Macmillan, 2016.

Hendrickson, Paul. *Hemingway's Boat: Everything He Loved in Life, and Lost, 1934-1961*. Vintage Books, 2012.

Mazzeno, Laurence W. *The Critics and Hemingway, 1924-2014: Shaping an American Literary Icon*. Camden House, 2015.

Bibliography

Barson, Michael. "John Sturges, American Director." *Encyclopaedia Britannica*, 1 Jan. 2020, www.britannica.com/topic/The-Old-Man-and-the-Sea-film-by-Sturges. Accessed 10 Feb. 2020.

Billock, Jennifer. "Follow Ernest Hemingway's Footsteps Through Havana." *Smithsonian Magazine*, 10 Oct. 2019, www.smithsonianmag.com/travel/follow-ernest-hemingways-footsteps-through-havana-180967659/. Accessed 10 Feb. 2020.

Crowther, Bosley. "Hemingway; *Old Man and the Sea* Stars Spencer Tracy." *The New York Times*, 8 Oct. 1958, www.nytimes.com/1958/10/08/archives/hemingway-old-man-and-the-sea-stars-spencer-tracy.html. Accessed 10 Feb. 2020.

De Koster, Katie, editor. *Readings on Ernest Hemingway*. Greenhaven Press, 1997.

Hemingway, Ernest. *The Old Man and the Sea*. 1952. Scribner Classics, 1995.

Stamant, James. *Competing Stories: Modernist Authors, Newspapers, and the Movies*. Lexington Books, 2020.

Stamberg, Susan. "The Enduring Depths of *Old Man and the Sea*." *NPR*, 4 Mar. 2006, www.npr.org/templates/story/story.php?storyId=5245376. Accessed 10 Feb. 2020.

Oliver Twist

The Novel
Author: Charles Dickens (1812-70)
First published: 1837-39

The Film
Year released: 1948
Director: David Lean (1908-91)
Screenplay by: David Lean, Stanley Haynes
Starring: John Howard Davies, Alec Guinness, Robert Newton, Kay Walsh, Anthony Newley

Context

The primary inspiration for Dickens's *Oliver Twist* (serialized between 1837-39) was the passage of England's Poor Law Amendment Act in 1834, still commonly called the New Poor Law. Intended to reduce costs and curb perceived abuse of the system of public assistance for paupers that had been established 300 years earlier, the new law promoted "workhouses" as the solution to the problem. There, the nation's poorest were forced to live and work much like indentured servants. Conditions were prison-like, with stone walls and barred fences. The notoriously poor conditions were a deliberate strategy, intended to keep the poor from applying for assistance in the first place. Making matters worse, inmates often received the barest sustenance because unscrupulous workhouse managers tended to extract maximum profits from the allowances the government provided to feed, clothe, and shelter indigent individuals.

Against that bleak backdrop, as a form of impassioned social commentary, Charles Dickens spun a tale of an orphan boy raised in the system. Born to a destitute unmarried mother who died in the workhouse, the young protagonist, Oliver Twist, endures and ultimately thrives. The author noted in the preface to the novel's third edition in 1841, "I wished to show, in little Oliver, the principle of Good surviving through every adverse circumstance, and triumphing at last."

"Despised by all, and pitied by none," Oliver is tested by a series of challenges over the course of several years. His struggles begin in earnest on his eighth birthday. After a brief interview with a board of gentlemen that treat him more like an object than a person, Oliver is assigned to perform hard but useless menial labor. Months later, nearly starving, he asks for a second helping of gruel. Speaking up earns him daily floggings and he is sold into service as an apprentice. Oliver is insulted and abused while serving as a mute mourner at children's funerals, and fights back, striking his tormenter. Facing probable demotion to service at sea, where he would likely die, he runs away to London, seventy miles away.

Outside the city, Oliver encounters Jack Dawkins, also known as the Artful Dodger, a brash thief who recruits young people for criminal enterprise. Through Dodger, Oliver meets Fagin, a dealer in stolen goods. The clever, unctuous Fagin heads a slum-based ring of youthful pickpockets—like Dodger and his pal, Charley Bates—adult burglars, teenage prostitutes, and other assorted miscreants. Among the motley crew are several who will be instrumental in Oliver's rollercoaster ride from the depths of despair to the heights of joy. Important figures are a couple: Bill Sikes, a violent burglar, and his prostitute girlfriend, Nancy. Another is a tall, dark, mysterious man named Monks who for some reason holds a grudge against poor young Oliver Twist.

Film Analysis

In adapting *Oliver Twist* for the big screen, David Lean used the strategy he had employed in directing another well-realized Dickens adaptation, *Great Expectations* (1946). He gathered the same key behind-the-scenes people—coproducers Ronald Neame and Anthony Havelock-Allen; and Guy Green, Jack Harris, and John Bryan were cinematographer, editor, and designer. Casting, as usual, was impeccable. Nine-year-old John Howard Davies, in the first of only a few film roles, perfectly represented Oliver's innocence. Alec Guinness—despite a distracting nasal prosthetic modeled after George Cruikshank drawings accompanying the novel that emphasized stereotypical "Jewish features"—made a convincing Fagin. (Guinness, who debuted in film in *Great Expectations*, would also figure prominently in later David Lean features: *The Bridge on the River Kwai*, 1957; *Lawrence of Arabia*, 1962; and *Doctor Zhivago*, 1965.) Bill Sikes (Robert Newton) was snarly and brutal enough to land a similar role as a pirate in *Treasure Island* (1950). Kay Walsh, Lean's wife at the time, who had appeared in her husband's *In Which We Serve* (1942) and *This Happy Breed* (1944), played a Nancy more mature, but no less passionate or fatalistic than the teenager imagined by Dickens. Fine character actors smoothly filled other important roles, such as Mr. Brownlow (Henry Stephenson), Mr. Bumble (Francis L. Sullivan), and the Artful Dodger (Anthony Newley).

Most importantly, the complex novel was streamlined without losing the tone, essence, or message. Several subplots (in fact, the bulk of Book Two, the middle third of *Oliver Twist*) were shorn away. One extended storyline—when Sikes forces Oliver to participate in a burglary and Oliver is shot and later recovers at the scene of the crime—is missing. While there, Oliver becomes deeply involved with the Maylie family. The character of 17-year-old Rose Maylie, the virtuous female counterpart of Oliver, was based on Dickens's beloved sister-in-law, Mary Hogarth, who died tragically young in 1837.

Several characters who figure larger in print, are reduced to walk-on roles on-screen. These include Dodger's jolly chum Charley Bates (John Potter) and the landlord (Peter Bull) of the dank pub where criminals plan their capers. The important role of Monks (Ralph Truman) is greatly diminished. Noah Claypole (Michael Dear) in the film only appears as an employee at the Sowerberry establishment. In the novel, he later travels with devoted companion Charlotte (Diana Dors) to London and joins Fagin's gang. It is Noah, not Dodger (caught stealing and about to be transported to a convict colony), who follows Nancy to her fateful meeting on London Bridge. It is Noah who overhears and repeats to Fagin and Sikes the conversation that results in Nancy's violent death.

Numerous incidents were condensed for the sake of fluidity. Some dramatic scenes were transposed from one medium to the other virtually intact, especially those featuring the pompous Bumble. Several sequences, not in the original, were created to add emotional impact. The ultimate fates of various characters, summarized in the novel's final chapters, are left unseen. Such changes, which showcased the visual storytelling skills Lean continued to refine throughout his illustrious career, always work to keep the film aligned with the second part of the original novel's title, "The Parish Boy's Progress."

The director's touch is evident from the start in the adapted *Oliver Twist*. The film opens with a tense, memorable sequence. A distant figure struggles across a stark landscape during a thunderous, lightning-lit downpour. Silhouettes of gnarled branches threaten. Thorny stems claw at the wind. The figure nears: it is a young woman. Blinding bolts of lightning reveal details: she is drenched, exhausted, pregnant. She staggers toward a distant light and rings a bell at the gate. Taken inside the building, a workhouse, she gives birth, fondly kisses her baby, and collapses. The first words of dialogue are not spoken until almost the seventh minute, when a doctor pronounces her dead. Lean's script makes the woman, Oliver's mother (Josephine Stuart), important. She has been shown as brave, determined, and sympathetic (Dickens does not reveal her heritage and qualities until late in the novel). Because she does not survive, the viewer's sympathy is subconsciously transferred to her child. Such faith will not be misplaced. Oliver is the personification of purity and goodness. Many characters—undertaker Sowerberry (Gibb McLaughlin), criminals Dodger, Fagin, Nancy, benefactor Brownlow—remark on his guileless appearance. He also sounds and acts as he looks. Through every trial, he clings to a code of behavior that distinguishes right from wrong.

One of the more interesting differences between novel and film is the treatment of Bill Sikes's dog, Bull's-eye. In the novel, although he is routinely cursed, beaten, or kicked for no reason, the dog, like Oliver Twist, remains true to his nature. Bull's-eye accompanies his cruel master everywhere and runs away only after Sikes, in fear of being connected with his four-legged companion, prepares to drown the dog following Nancy's murder. The animal, however, shows up at the Fagin gang's hideout. Sikes, running from a bloodthirsty, torch-bearing mob led by the law, and fleeing from the haunting apparition of Nancy conjured by his conscience, appears seeking shelter. It is Bull's-eye that inadvertently causes Sikes's demise. The murderer flees across the rooftops (without Oliver, as in the film), intending to lower himself by a rope affixed to a chimney. He looks back to see eyes glowing in the dark—the ghost of Nancy, in his fevered mind. Startled, he slips and accidentally hangs himself. In reality, the luminescent eyes belong to the dog, who followed Sikes onto the roof. Faithful to the end, Bull's-eye tries to jump onto the shoulders of the swinging body below, but misses, and like his master is killed; both man and beast essentially commit suicide. In the film, the dog (uncredited) is an active agent of doom and outlives his master. After Sikes attempts to drown him, Bull's-eye takes canine revenge. He runs off, finds the assembled citizens and lawmen, and leads them to Sikes's hideout, barking all the way.

Significance

Lean's version was popular with the British public on its release and is today considered the best of many adaptations. Lean's *Oliver Twist* is still listed among the best British films, along with several of the director's other efforts including *Brief Encounter* (1945), *Lawrence of Arabia*, *Great Expectations*, and *The Bridge on the River Kwai*. The British Academy of Film and Television Arts (BAFTA) nominated *Oliver Twist* for best film, but it lost the award to Carol Reed's *The Fallen Idol*.

Despite the acclaim it achieved in the United Kingdom, it was not as well received in the United States, largely a result of reaction to Guinness's portrayal of Fagin. Though accurate to Dickens's depiction of the wily character in the novel, the film role was deemed offensive by several Jewish groups that were given a private screening prior to its release in America. Several Jewish organizations, including the Anti-Defamation League, condemned the film. Its opening in Berlin, Germany, the following year was picketed by Jewish Holocaust survivors. In order to avoid an outright ban, the American release, which was originally scheduled for September 1948, was delayed for nearly three years. During the interim, the film was edited and about ten minutes were removed—mostly close-ups of Guinness as Fagin. The shorter film, given the Production Code Administration seal of approval, was released in May 1951. Like the British version, it was also widely acclaimed, but failed to receive a single Academy Award nomination. Some twenty years later, the missing footage was restored.

—Jack Ewing

Further Reading

Ackroyd, Peter. *Dickens' London: An Imaginative Vision*. Headline Publishing Group, 1987.

Hitesh, Joshi. *Charles Dickens as a Social Reformer: A Study of Some of His Novels*. Lambert Academic Publishing, 2019.

Bibliography

Ackroyd, Peter. *Dickens*. HarperCollins, 1991.

Dickens, Charles. *Oliver Twist*. Penguin Classics, 2002.

Diniejko, Andrzej. "Charles Dickens as Social Commentator and Critic." *The Victorian Web*, www.victorianweb.org/authors/dickens/diniejko.html. Accessed 13 Mar. 2020.

Drazin, Charles. "Dickens's Jew—from Evil to Delightful." *The Jewish Chronicle*, 3 May 2013, www.thejc.com/comment/comment/dickens-s-jew-from-evil-to-delightful-1.44612. Accessed 13 Mar. 2020.

Garnett, Robert. *Charles Dickens in Love*. Pegasus Books, 2012.

Hazlitt, Henry. "The Poor Laws of England." *Mises Institute*, 7 Dec. 2018, mises.org/library/poor-laws-england. Accessed 13 Mar. 2020.

Richardson, Ruth. *Dickens & the Workhouse: Oliver Twist & the London Poor*. Oxford UP, 2012.

One Flew Over the Cuckoo's Nest

The Novel
Author: Ken Kesey (1935-2001)
First published: 1962

The Film
Year released: 1975
Director: Miloš Forman (1932-2018)
Screenplay by: Lawrence Hauben, Bo Goldman
Starring: Jack Nicholson, Louise Fletcher, Will Sampson, Danny DeVito

Context

Writer Ken Kesey published his first and best-known novel, *One Flew Over the Cuckoo's Nest*, in 1962. Kesey, who died in 2001, is mostly remembered as a Merry Prankster—the name he gave his intrepid band of friends and followers—and one of the most prominent figures of 1960s counterculture. *Cuckoo's Nest* was published before Kesey's most famous exploits, chronicled by Tom Wolfe in *The Electric Kool-Aid Acid Test* (1968), but it is also a powerful literary emblem of his prankster philosophy. An allegory about conformity and the oppression of shame, *Cuckoo's Nest* captures Kesey's unease with stifling social conventions. As a writing student, he volunteered in a study funded by the government exploring the effects of psychoactive drugs including lysergic acid diethylamide (LSD). He also worked as a night aide in the psychiatric ward of the same hospital. His experiences led him to question the nature of insanity. What was the difference between the nurses and the patients, he wondered. What was the difference between someone who was merely eccentric, like Kesey, and someone who was insane? His line of thinking, Michael Schulman wrote for *Vanity Fair*, followed that of philosopher Michel Foucault, who argued "that insanity was a construct designed to sequester undesirables from society." In the 1960s, one could still be committed for any number of divergences from the norms of society that today seem normal. Women and homosexual men, in particular, could face institutionalization for not embracing traditional roles or behaving in ways considered proper according to societal expectations.

Kesey's concept for *Cuckoo's Nest* mimics his experience taking hallucinogenic drugs. Like the inmates in *Cuckoo's Nest*, most of whom remain at the hospital by choice, Kesey was introduced to a scope of the world beyond his own imagining. He achieved this view with LSD while the inmates in the novel are able to do so through their introduction to a swaggering, rebellious character named Randle Patrick McMurphy. Actor Kirk Douglas bought the rights to the story shortly after publication and starred as McMurphy in a Broadway adaptation that ran for a short time between 1963 and 1964. Due to miscommunication, among other things, it took more than a decade for the film project to start to come together. By that time, Michael Douglas, Kirk's son, had taken over as producer and hired director Miloš Forman, a leading artist of the Czech New Wave of cinema in his home country of Czechoslovakia. Forman, who would go on to enjoy an illustrious Hollywood career, had only made a handful of films at that point, including only one unsuccessful theatrical release in America, but the type of work that he did on projects such as *The Fireman's Ball* (1967) seemed like a good fit to Douglas. Forman was attracted to the project for reasons rooted in his own familial experience. Both of his parents had died in Nazi concentration camps, and he had come of age under and ultimately fled oppressive authoritarianism that he had criticized through some of his New Wave projects. The film finally hit theaters in 1975.

Film Analysis

Actor Jack Nicholson, who was cast as McMurphy in the film adaptation (Kirk Douglas had aged out of the role), has largely become the "face" of *Cuckoo's Nest* in the popular imagination; in the book, however, a character named Chief Bromden is the narrator and protagonist. Chief Bromden is a half-white, half-American Indian man. He is nearly seven feet tall, and the entire ward believes that he can neither

Jack Nicholson. Photo by AP Wire via Wikimedia Commons.

speak nor hear. In the book, the reader understands Chief Bromden's ruse as they can see and hear the world through his eyes. With his point of view comes an added layer of awareness. Prone to hallucinations, he imagines Nurse Ratched, the strict head nurse, with snake-like mechanical arms. He also sees something called the Combine. In his mind, Nurse Ratched is an "adjuster," who tends to a web of nearly invisible wires connecting all of the patients in the ward to the Combine, an efficient social correction machine. The Combine is integral to the world of the book as it is a metaphor for the crushing machinery of conformity and oppression. Chief Bromden's narrative is colored by the Combine and other distinctly hallucinogenic visions, but the film strictly adheres to realism and therefore has a different tone. Chief Bromden (played by Will Sampson) becomes a more secondary character while McMurphy moves to the fore. These decisions rankled Kesey, who later sued the film's producers.

In the book, McMurphy is almost mythological in his vigor. He is a physical representation of individuality, a tall tale. When he bets the men of the ward that he can lift the control panel in the tub room, they believe him, if only for a transcendent moment, because McMurphy is an alien figure—he could be capable of anything. This scene also occurs in the film, but the audience sees it from McMurphy's perspective, as a quixotic attempt to change the shape of the world in which he finds himself; he is rattling the proverbial bars of his cage. In the film, McMurphy could not be mistaken for a metaphor—he is a flesh-and-blood human being. He has arrived at the ward after pleading insanity to escape the prison work farm. Played by Nicholson, he is devilishly charming in a taunting and lecherous kind of way. Surrounded by a talented cast of character actors—including Christopher Lloyd, Vincent Schiavelli, and Danny DeVito—his charisma is the engine that drives the film. *Cuckoo's Nest* typifies the era of actor-driven films—such as *Dog Day Afternoon* (1975), starring Al Pacino—in which it was made. Adding to the authenticity desired in translating the setting of the novel to the screen, Nicholson and other actors spent time at the Oregon hospital where the film was shot prior to beginning production, observing therapy and routines, and some of the patients were allowed to be part of the crew.

McMurphy's foil, Nurse Ratched, is played by Louise Fletcher, then a relatively little-known television actor. Fletcher worked with Forman to shape the role into a slightly different form than traditionally interpreted from the page. Like McMurphy, the Nurse Ratched of the book is a larger-than-life character, the overt personification of shame and orderly oppression. As she explained to Schulman, Fletcher, who had grown up as the daughter of white, deaf missionaries in the Jim Crow South, saw in Nurse Ratched the perverted sense of power inherent in the systemic racism upheld by everyday white people—Nurse Ratched, Fletcher and Forman felt, must think that her actions are just. Fletcher's Nurse Ratched is softspoken, but there is still something sinister in her civility. Though her manner is different, the character effectively remains part of the unsettling tableau Kesey creates in his story. However, while Kesey imagines oppression, in part, as a woman with power and, further, imagines a woman with power as emasculating to men, this aspect did not carry through in Fletcher's portrayal. In the world of the story, the balance of power is a perversion of the real world.

Despite having trouble finding a studio interested in financing or distributing the film, the filmmakers did not accept one studio's distribution offer due to the condition that was proposed. In order to distribute the film, the largely tragic ending, which the producers had kept true to the novel, would need to be reconfigured to conclude on a happier note. The novel's powerful finish rests on the system proving at least partly victorious in its literal lobotomization of McMurphy, even as Chief Bromden manages to escape. Therefore, the filmmakers, unwilling to alter this ending to keep McMurphy alive instead for the potential sake of Hollywood audiences, maintained the original concluding scene and went with a different distributor.

Significance

Larger themes—the concept of freedom as well as the subversion of authority and conformity—resonated with audiences, particularly given the political context of recent years in the United States, and *Cuckoo's Nest* became one of the highest-grossing films of the time. Critics were reservedly intrigued; Vincent Canby of *The New York Times* was drawn to the humanity of the characters, if not the larger metaphors in the story. He took particular issue with the film's tragic and symbolic ending, writing, "America is much too big and various to be satisfactorily reduced to the dimensions of one mental ward in a movie like this." However, he praised the film's actors, writing that Nicholson "slips into the role of Randle with such easy grace that it's difficult to remember him in any other film." *Chicago Sun-Times* film critic Roger Ebert took Canby's criticisms further, writing, "There are long stretches of a very good film to be found in the midst of Forman's ultimate failure." He took issue with the scene where McMurphy steals a bus and takes his friends on a fishing trip. (The fishing trip happens in the book, too, but under slightly different circumstances.) Describing it as a "serious misstep," Ebert wrote that the scene's "idealized fantasy" broke the film's careful realism. He noted the importance of the ward, with its rules and codes of behavior, to the construction of the film as a whole. "The ward is the arena in which they'll win or lose, and it's not playing fair—to them, as characters—to give them a fishing trip," he wrote.

Regardless, *Cuckoo's Nest*, considered a time-tested classic, was nominated for nine Academy Awards. It is one of only three films in American cinematic history to sweep all five major categories including Best Picture, Best Directing, Best Writing (Adapted Screenplay), Best

Actor in a Leading Role (for Nicholson), and Best Actress in a Leading Role (for Fletcher). In addition to McMurphy, the film elevated Nurse Ratched as a recognizable figure in popular culture, with writers interested in exploring her origin story. The film also had a profound impact on how Americans viewed electroshock therapy and psychiatry in general. Overall, the picture's success proved especially powerful due to the fact that its producers had struggled to secure funding and distribution due to industry reservations about the subject matter.

—Molly Hagan

Further Reading

Arbeiter, M. "15 Things You Might Not Know about *One Flew Over the Cuckoo's Nest*." *Mental Floss*, 19 Nov. 2017, mentalfloss.com/article/63639/15-things-you-might-not-know-about-one-flew-over-cuckoos-nest. Accessed 18 Dec. 2018.

Wolcott, James. "Still *Cuckoo* after All These Years." *Vanity Fair*, Dec. 2011, www.vanityfair.com/news/2011/12/wolcott-201112. Accessed 18 Dec. 2018.

Bibliography

Canby, Vincent. "Jack Nicholson, the Free Spirit of *One Flew Over the Cuckoo's Nest*." Review of *One Flew Over the Cuckoo's Nest*, directed by Miloš Forman. *The New York Times*, 28 Nov. 1975, archive.nytimes.com/www.nytimes.com/packages/html/movies/bestpictures/cuckoo-re.html?scp=6&sq=sampson&st=cse. Accessed 18 Dec. 2018.

Douglas, Michael, and Louise Fletcher. "Michael Douglas: How We Made *One Flew Over the Cuckoo's Nest*." Interview by Phil Hoad. *The Guardian*, 11 Apr. 2017, www.theguardian.com/film/2017/apr/11/michael-douglas-and-louise-fletcher-how-we-made-one-flew-over-the-cuckoos-nest-interview. Accessed 18 Dec. 2018.

Ebert, Roger. Review of *One Flew Over the Cuckoo's Nest*, directed by Miloš Forman. *RogerEbert.com*, 1 Jan. 1975, www.rogerebert.com/reviews/one-flew-over-the-cuckoos-nest-1975. Accessed 18 Dec. 2018.

Lehmann-Haupt, Christopher. "Ken Kesey, Author of *Cuckoo's Nest*, Who Defined the Psychedelic Era, Dies at 66." *The New York Times*, 11 Nov. 2001, www.nytimes.com/2001/11/11/nyregion/ken-kesey-author-of-cuckoo-s-nest-who-defined-the-psychedelic-era-dies-at-66.html. Accessed 18 Dec. 2018.

Schulman, Michael. "Louise Fletcher, Nurse Ratched, and the Making of *One Flew Over the Cuckoo's Nest*'s Unforgettable Villain." *Vanity Fair*, Aug. 2018, www.vanityfair.com/hollywood/2018/07/louise-fletcher-nurse-ratched-interview. Accessed 18 Dec. 2018.

Swaine, Jon. "How *One Flew Over the Cuckoo's Nest* Changed Psychiatry." *The Telegraph*, 1 Feb. 2011, www.telegraph.co.uk/news/worldnews/northamerica/usa/8296954/How-One-Flew-Over-the-Cuckoos-Nest-changed-psychiatry.html. Accessed 18 Dec. 2018.

Peter Pan

The Play
Author: James Matthew (J. M.) Barrie (1860-1937)
First published: 1904

The Film
Year released: 2003
Director: P. J. Hogan (b. 1962)
Screenplay by: P. J. Hogan, Michael Goldenberg
Starring: Jeremy Sumpter, Rachel Hurd-Wood, Jason Isaacs, Lynn Redgrave, Richard Briers

Context

Scottish writer J. M. Barrie's character Peter Pan—a mischievous, ageless boy who can fly and has adventures in the fantastical world of Neverland—has become a cultural icon and even a kind of psychological archetype, symbolizing the desire for youthful freedom from responsibilities. Barrie first introduced Peter in the adult novel *The Little White Bird* (1902), and popularized the character through the play *Peter Pan, or The Boy Who Would Not Grow Up* (1904) and its novel version, *Peter and Wendy* (1911). Over the years the tale had a deep influence on both children's and adult literature, reflecting its central theme of growing up.

The popularity of the Peter Pan story is evident in the numerous adaptations that have appeared over the decades. Barrie himself revised his work multiple times and developed versions in many formats aimed at audiences of all ages. The first film version was a silent picture released by Paramount in 1924, which stayed highly faithful to the stage version. Later adaptations often took considerable liberties with the source material, however. Notably, the Walt Disney-produced animated version in 1953—which became a classic in its own right—toned down the romantic tension between Peter and fellow lead character Wendy Darling, and made other family-friendly changes. Other film adaptations of Barrie's story include Steven Spielberg's *Hook* (1991), Disney's animated sequel *Peter Pan 2: Return to Neverland* (2002), Damion Dietz's *Neverland* (2003), and Joe Wright's 2015 *Pan*. Often these (and other works in television and other media) introduce various twists to the core story, along with other changes such as addressing racist characterizations from the original.

The 2003 live-action film *Peter Pan* in many ways represented a return to a more direct adaptation of Barrie's work.

Screenwriters P. J. Hogan and Michael Goldenberg based their script on the original play and novel. Hogan also directed, following his work helming films such as *Muriel's Wedding* (1994) and *My Best Friend's Wedding* (1997).

Film Analysis

Hogan's *Peter Pan* closely follows Barrie's play and novel. It even opens with the text "All children grow up, except one," which is altered only slightly from the first line of the book. In both cases, this sets up the overarching themes of the work: the joy of childhood and the bittersweet nature of growing up.

The general plot will be familiar to many viewers. Wendy Darling (Rachel Hurd-Wood), a twelve-year-old girl in Edwardian London, tells her younger brothers John (Harry Newell) and Michael (Freddie Popplewell) stories of the fantastical Peter Pan. Peter himself (Jeremy Sumpter) is listening at the window, entranced by Wendy's stories, and later his shadow is captured by the Darlings' dog, Nana. Returning to retrieve his shadow, Peter befriends Wendy and convinces her and her brothers to go with him to Neverland to join his group of Lost Boys. Using fairy dust from Peter's fairy companion, Tinker Bell (Ludivine Sagnier), they fly to Neverland and soon find themselves facing off against Peter's nemesis, the one-handed pirate Captain Hook (Jason Isaacs). They have various adventures, including some caused by Tinker Bell's jealousy of Wendy. Eventually the pirates are defeated and the children return home, though Peter goes back to Neverland. Wendy, as an adult, notes that she passes the story of Peter on to the next generation.

Despite its overall faithfulness to the source material, the film does introduce some changes. For example, the character of Aunt Millicent (Lynn Redgrave) does not appear in the book. In Hogan's adaptation Aunt Millicent serves to bring up the subject of Wendy's transition from girlhood to womanhood, noting for example that she should no longer be sharing a room with her brothers. Another addition in the first act of the film shows Wendy at school, where she gets into trouble for drawing a picture of Peter hovering over her in bed. The teacher sends a note to her father (also played by Isaacs, continuing a stage tradition of casting the same actor as Mr. Darling and Captain Hook), resulting in a humorous chase as Wendy sends Nana after the message boy. Other minor alterations include Peter's ability to affect the weather and the princess Tiger Lily's (Carsen Gray) attraction to John rather than Peter.

A notable aspect of the 2003 adaptation is its inclusion of sensual themes that are present in Barrie's work but were removed in many other versions, including the Disney-animated feature. Wendy's burgeoning physical attraction to Peter is made clear, and their relationship drives the narrative. The camera emphasizes the romantic theme early on, as the heart-shaped cut-out in the footboard of Wendy's bed becomes a frame for each child's face and they exchange innocent "kisses" (a thimble from Wendy and an acorn from Peter). Their interactions continue to walk a fine line between innocent and flirtatious and the chemistry between Hurd-Wood and Sumpter is played up at every chance. There are multiple scenes where the two are face to face, looking poised to kiss. In one instance, Peter takes Wendy to see a fairy wedding (another scene not present in the novel) and the two dance romantically in mid-air.

Ultimately, however, Wendy and Peter's relationship runs into the problem of Peter's endless childhood. The filmmakers embrace Barrie's theme that while never growing up may seem appealing, the scary aspects of adulthood are balanced out by the ability to experience romantic love. Both Wendy and Peter struggle with this in different ways. Wendy is initially drawn to Neverland in rebellion against the grownup world, but eventually cannot deny her developing adult feelings. Peter, meanwhile, is intrigued by real-life family relationships, but continues to resist emotional maturity. Wendy asks Peter about his feelings, especially love, but he runs away, telling her to go home. Captain Hook also recognizes Peter's immaturity and attempts to use it against him, telling Wendy, "Oh, no, he cannot love. It is part of the riddle of his being." When Wendy again confronts Peter about emotional attachment and he responds poorly, she compares him negatively to Hook, but

J. M. Barrie, creator of Peter Pan. 1902. Photo by George Charles Beresford via Wikimedia Commons. [Public domain.]

his response is "You can't catch me and make me a man. I want always to be a boy and have fun."

The film also explores sensuality beyond the dynamic between Peter and Wendy. The addition of a relationship between the shy John and Tiger Lily further emphasizes the theme of romance. Meanwhile, Tink's jealousy can be interpreted as stemming from her sexual attraction to Peter, as also hinted in the novel, though this is never stated outright. Another layer of subtle—and potentially uncomfortable—sexual tension is seen in Hook's interactions with Wendy, as he caresses her cheek and gently plays with her hair. The competition between Peter and Hook is therefore even more psychologically complex, as the themes of childhood versus adulthood and innocence versus sexuality intertwine. Finally, nonromantic familial love is also highlighted. As Wendy realizes that she and her brothers are forgetting the real love for their family, she decides it is time to go home.

While more serious than many adaptations of the Peter Pan story, Hogan's film does not focus wholly on complex themes. There is a lighthearted note throughout with comedic scenes that follow the novel or provide new humor. The pirates are the focus of many of the jokes, including visual gags such as a balding parrot who stomps around deck on a wooden peg leg and one crewmember who becomes oddly attached to Michael's teddy bear. As in other versions, Hook's first mate, Smee (Richard Briers), is a particular source of comic relief.

Swashbuckling adventure is another hallmark of *Peter Pan*. Indeed, the film carries over a level of violence found in the book that is sometimes toned down in other adaptations. For instance, a jealous Tinker Bell attempts to have Wendy killed by the Lost Boys upon her arrival in Neverland. Hook also remains the violent criminal he is in the novel, killing several pirates throughout for no apparent reason and threatening to kill the children each time he captures them. His attempt to poison Peter, which results in Tinker Bell's death (and resurrection) is also faithfully depicted. The special effects, which were cutting-edge for the time, contribute to the excitement of the action scenes as well as the overall fantastical atmosphere of Neverland.

The film does make some attempts to revise outdated aspects of Barrie's original, mainly in the form of sexist stereotypes. Wendy is depicted as less passive, with her own sense of adventure. In the novel, she prominently serves as a mother figure to Peter's group of misfit children, and even Hook and the other pirates covet a mother. This is mentioned briefly in the film, but its significance is downplayed. While Peter does tell the boys that he brought them a mother, Wendy becomes more of a story-teller and adventurer, even claiming the identity of Red-Handed Jill, a storytelling pirate. Tiger Lily is also presented as a more progressive figure than in many other versions. Yet despite these efforts, the film's treatment of gender roles remains largely traditional. Wendy is still mainly viewed as a romantic interest, mother figure, or a storyteller rather than an active hero. She gets into messes where she must be saved by a male, whether it is Peter or even Hook. Tiger Lily and even Tinker Bell are also saved largely by males. While faithful to the original story, these elements may be seen as problematic by some viewers.

Significance

The 2003 film version of *Peter Pan* was an expensive production, with an estimated budget of at least $100 million, but it grossed just $48.4 million in the United States and about $122 million in total, making it a box-office bomb. The disappointing return was considered in part due to competition with films such as *The Lord of the Rings: The Return of the King* (2003) and *Cheaper by the Dozen* (2003).

Despite its commercial failure, the film received generally positive critical attention. Many reviewers praised its faithful take on Barrie's classic, especially in the complex characterizations and underlying tensions that are often purged from other adaptations. For example, noted critic Roger Ebert wrote, "I walked in anticipating a sweet kiddie fantasy and was surprised to find a film that takes its story very seriously indeed, thank you, and even allows a glimpse of underlying sadness." In a review for *Newsweek*, David Ansen also found that the film remains "faithful to Barrie's Edwardian spirit without making him feel musty," though he pointed out that some viewers might be uneasy with "a subtly eroticized *Peter Pan*." In contrast, Andrew Osmond presented a negative take in *Sight and Sound*, arguing that the movie is "let down by indifferent performances and some frustratingly half-hearted plot tinkering."

—*Theresa L. Stowell, PhD*

Further Reading

Hollindale, Peter. "A Hundred Years of Peter Pan." *Children's Literature in Education*, vol. 36, no. 3, Sept. 2005, pp. 197-215.

Valentova, Eva. "The Betwixt and Between: Peter Pan as a Trickster Figure." *The Journal of Popular Culture*, vol. 51, no. 3, June 2018, pp. 735-53.

Bibliography

Ansen, David. "Peter Pans Out." Review of *Peter Pan*, directed by P. J. Hogan. *Newsweek*, 18 Dec. 2003, www.newsweek.com/peter-pans-out-131635. Accessed 14 July 2020.

Ebert, Roger. Review of *Peter Pan*, directed by P. J. Hogan. *RogerEbert.com*, 24 Dec. 2003, www.rogerebert.com/reviews/peter-pan-2003. Accessed 14 July 2020.

Hermansson, Casie. *A Study of Film Adaptations of James Barrie's Story Peter Pan*. The Edwin Mellen Press, 2016.

Osmond, Andrew. Review of *Peter Pan*, directed by P. J. Hogan. *Sight & Sound*, vol. 14, no. 3, Mar. 2004, pp. 56-57. *Biography Reference Bank*, search.ebscohost.com/login.aspx?direct=true&db=brb&AN=505062498&site=eds-live. Accessed 14 July 2020.

"Peter Pan (2003)." *IMDb*, 2020, www.imdb.com/title/tt0316396/. Accessed 14 July 2020.

The Pianist

The Novel
Author: Wladyslaw Szpilman (1911-2000)
First published: 1946

The Film
Year released: 2002
Director: Roman Polanski (b. 1933)
Screenplay by: Ronald Harwood
Starring: Adrien Brody, Thomas Kretschmann, Frank Finlay

Context

In 1946, Polish Jewish pianist Wladyslaw Szpilman published a memoir called *Death of a City* describing his harrowing survival in Warsaw, Poland, during World War II. For the *Washington Post*, historian Anne Applebaum wrote that Szpilman, who died in 2000, did not mythologize his experiences during the war: "There are no hero or enemy nations in his memoir," she wrote. "Szpilman encountered brave Jewish resistance fighters and corrupt Jewish ghetto policemen, courageous Poles who risked their lives to hide him and thieving Poles who cheated him out of his meager rations. In the final days of the war, Szpilman also received help from a German officer." This kind of realism, refusing the expected good guy/bad guy typology and over-determined characters, did not sit well with postwar Polish censors—Poland became a Soviet satellite state after the war—and the book was suppressed for years. Szpilman's son, Andrzej, helped republish the book in the late 1990s as *The Pianist: The Extraordinary True Story of One Man's Survival in Warsaw, 1939-1945*. It became an international best seller. A reviewer for *Publishers Weekly* compared Szpilman's restraint—some have suggested that the authorial tone was influenced by shell shock—to the Italian writer and Holocaust survivor Primo Levi. Szpilman, born in 1911, was already a famous musician when Germany invaded Poland in 1939. He was imprisoned with his family and nearly 400,000 other Jewish adults and children in the Warsaw ghetto. (Only a fraction of that number survived the war.) His parents and siblings were all murdered in the Holocaust, but in his book, Szpilman recounts the bizarre tale of his survival thanks to his fame, talent, and luck.

The film's director, Roman Polanski, is today best known for the horror film *Rosemary's Baby* (1968) and the classic noir *Chinatown* (1974). In 1977, he pled guilty to raping a thirteen-year-old girl but fled the United States for France before he was sentenced. Polanski has never returned to the United States, where there remains a warrant for his arrest, though he was arrested in Switzerland in 2009 and served a brief sentence of house arrest for his crime. American audiences have an uneasy relationship to the director, who continues to work and win accolades around the world.

Polanski was born in Poland and, like Szpilman, survived the Holocaust. He and his family were forced into the Krakow ghetto, where the young Polanski witnessed countless horrors. His mother was murdered at Auschwitz, and his father, who ultimately survived, was imprisoned at a labor camp. He spent the war in hiding; he was only twelve when it ended. Polanski's films explore dark themes inspired by these traumatic experiences: fear, isolation, and cruelty. Polanski turned down Steven Spielberg's offer to direct the Holocaust epic *Schindler's List* (1993), set in Krakow, because the story cut too close to his personal experience. But years later, Polanski found himself drawn to Szpilman's memoir, he told *The New York Times*, because it was "very dry, without sentimentalism or embellishments." He hired British playwright Ronald Harwood, known for adapting *Cry, the Beloved Country* (1995) and, later, *The Diving Bell and the Butterfly* (2007), to write the script. When Harwood first read the book, he too was struck by its "objective" tone, he told Peter M. Nichols for *The New York Times*. "Although it's autobiography, it's as if the man is writing about someone else," he said. "We were determined to keep that approach."

Film Analysis

The film opens with a prophetic moment in Szpilman's life. Employed as the Polish Radio house pianist,

Szpilman (played by Adrien Brody) is giving a Fryderyk Chopin recital on September 23, 1939, when the station is bombed by Germany. It was the station's last broadcast before the war. Part of Szpilman's program that day was Chopin's Nocturne in C-Sharp Minor. He would play the same song, both in life and onscreen, for German officer Wilm Hosenfeld (Thomas Kretschmann) in a bid to save his life. It was also the song Szpilman played as the first postwar broadcast from Polish Radio in 1945. Like the book, the film goes on to capture Szpilman's experiences moving to the Warsaw ghetto and playing piano in a café to support his family. Polanski includes one moment, directly from the book, in which Szpilman is asked to stop playing so that a patron might test the authenticity of gold coins by bouncing them off a marble table. In the book Szpilman writes that he hated walking to and from work because the streets were littered with corpses, wrapped in paper, waiting to be buried. These images are included in the film as well.

Other moments of extreme violence occur without fanfare. In 1942, Szpilman's family is expelled from the ghetto and sent to their deaths at Treblinka. Szpilman is spared after a Jewish police officer recognizes him and pulls him out of the line to board the train. Szpilman spends the rest of the war in hiding. He witnesses the ghetto uprising and the Warsaw uprising and, after an interminable period of hiding in abandoned buildings, survives thanks to the mercy of Hosenfeld. (Excerpts of Hosenfeld's diary are included in the 1999 version of Szpilman's book.)

Polanski and Harwood took a few liberties with Szpilman's story, most notably adding a character named Dorota (Emilia Fox), a Polish woman and, at the beginning of the film, a potential love interest. Dorota represents the blindness and intermittent sympathy of the Polish gentiles. She is shocked to discover, early in the film, the myriad restrictions placed on Jews, and later, helps Szpilman hide from the Nazis.

The film captures the confusion and disorienting ambiguity of Szpilman's experience. When bombs start to fall on Warsaw as the German invasion begins, Szpilman writes of the energy in the streets: "There was no panic. The mood swung between curiosity—what would happen next? —and surprise: Was this the way it all began?" Particularly chilling about this observation is Szpilman's ignorance of what exactly "all" would entail. Polanski captures this queasy uncertainty by alternating scenes of violence and destruction with scenes of everyday life. When the audience first meets Szpilman's family, they are rushing around their apartment, frantically packing their bags to flee the city. After a radio broadcast—Great Britain declares war on Germany—they unpack and enjoy a luxurious, celebratory dinner. Without the benefit of hindsight, their reaction seems reasonable—surely it is crazier to leave one's home than to stay in it? ("If I'm to die, I'd prefer to die in my own home," Szpilman says flippantly.) Similarly, Polanski includes an early scene in which the family argues about where to hide extra money and valuables—under the flowerpot or in the violin? They are unable to imagine a world in which everything they own, everything their neighbors own, everything they have ever loved or even merely seen, will be destroyed. But then again, Polanski implicitly asks, who could? These scenes are painfully contrasted later in the film, when Szpilman's father (Frank Finlay) meticulously divides a single candy caramel so that they may all have something to eat.

A recurrent theme for Polanski is isolation, and *The Pianist* explores it thoroughly. A significant portion of the film finds Szpilman alone, dependent on his own wits to survive. Polanski also emphasizes the horror of Szpilman's dependency on strangers. An underground resistance helps house him, but Szpilman is often left alone in empty apartments for weeks at a time without food. One helper, a former radio technician who is miffed that Szpilman does not recognize him, takes Szpilman's watch with the promise of selling it to buy food and never returns. During the Warsaw uprising, Szpilman is trapped in the same apartment, locked in from the outside, as the building is blasted by German tanks. He miraculously escapes the shelling only to find himself in a deserted and crumbling city. Polanski's incredible wide shot at this moment, revealing destruction as far as the viewer can see in every direction, suggests that Szpilman is more alone than he ever realized.

Significance

The Pianist was released in 2002 to enthusiastic reviews, though it counted a few prominent detractors. A. O. Scott, critic for *The New York Times*, expressed admiration for the film for the same reasons the *New Yorker*'s David Denby expressed distaste. Both noted Polanski's decision to depict Szpilman's incredible survival, not as sentimental or particularly miraculous, but as so lucky as to be almost absurd. Polanski, as Scott put it, "presents

Szpilman's story with bleak, acid humor and with a ruthless objectivity that encompasses both cynicism and compassion. When death is at once so systematically and so capriciously dispensed, survival becomes a kind of joke." Denby, by contrast, found this remove "unsettling." He was troubled by Szpilman's impassivity and his complacent return to Polish Radio. "Is he ashamed, guilty, defiant, disgusted? Grateful for his luck? We don't have a clue," Denby wrote. Still, he praised Polanski's filmmaking, writing, "This is a big movie made utterly without strain, large-scaled when it needs to be, intimate when intimacy is called for."

The Pianist won the coveted Palme d'Or at the Cannes Film Festival, as well as three Academy Awards, including best actor for Brody, best adapted screenplay, and best director for Polanski. Being a fugitive, Polanski was not present to accept the award, though it and the film itself went a long way toward redeeming his image in the United States. Reports of other sexual assaults among film directors and actors motivated the US Academy of Motion Picture Arts and Sciences to expel Polanski from their ranks in 2018.

—*Molly Hagan*

Further Reading

Nichols, Peter M. "Home Video; Reality Elides with Drama." Review of *The Pianist*, directed by Roman Polanski. *The New York Times*, 30 May 2003, www.nytimes.com/2003/05/30/movies/home-video-reality-elides-with-drama.html. Accessed 17 Jan. 2019.

Scott, A. O. "Film Review; Surviving the Warsaw Ghetto Against Steep Odds." Review of *The Pianist*, directed by Roman Polanski. *The New York Times*, 27 Dec. 2002, www.nytimes.com/2002/12/27/movies/film-review-surviving-the-warsaw-ghetto-against-steep-odds.html. Accessed 17 Jan. 2019.

Bibliography

Applebaum, Anne. "War without Myth." Review of *The Pianist*, directed by Roman Polanski. *The Washington Post*, 15 Jan. 2003, www.washingtonpost.com/archive/opinions/2003/01/15/war-without-myth/ce4e82ff-bb57-4f16-a44a-d169cbf27699. Accessed 16 Jan. 2019.

Denby, David. "Nocturnes." Review of *The Pianist*, directed by Roman Polanski, and *25th Hour*, directed by Spike Lee. *The New Yorker*, 13 Jan. 2003, www.newyorker.com/magazine/2003/01/13/nocturnes. Accessed 17 Jan. 2019.

Review of *The Pianist: The Extraordinary True Story of One Man's Survival in Warsaw, 1939-1945*, by Wladyslaw Szpilman. *Publishers Weekly*, 30 Aug. 1999, www.publishersweekly.com/978-0-312-24415-6. Accessed 17 Jan. 2019.

Pride & Prejudice

The Novel
Author: Jane Austen (1775-1817)
First published: 1813

The Film
Year released: 2005
Director: Joe Wright (b. 1972)
Screenplay by: Deborah Moggach
Starring: Keira Knightley, Matthew Macfadyen, Brenda Blethyn, Donald Sutherland, Judi Dench

Context

Jane Austen's six novels have all been adapted for the screen numerous times. Although class relations are central to Austen's novels, as is a kind of irony that leaves the works open to suggestions that they strongly critique the relations they observe, adaptations have chosen variously to highlight or to deemphasize class over the years. More overtly "political" adaptations—foregrounding feminist issues, or race, or sometimes class—have grown in popularity since the 1990s. In the 1996 television adaptation of *Emma* starring Kate Beckinsale, class differences are quietly but vividly addressed. In the Box Hill picnic scene, for example, director Diarmuid Lawrence includes a wide-angle shot of servants laboriously carrying all the picnic food, blankets, and accessories up the hill for the landed gentry to enjoy, showing the hard, unacknowledged, behind-the-scenes toil required for what seems a simple picnic. Other adaptations, including director Joe Wright's 2005 version, focus on exaggerating class differences so audiences will better see and understand them and their effects, particularly on women. In 1995's *Sense and Sensibility*, sisters Elinor (Emma Thompson) and Marianne (Kate Winslet) Dashwood, who were part of the landed gentry when their father was alive, fall on hard financial times after his death when his estate is entailed to their older half-brother. In the film, before they leave the family estate for their new home at Barton Cottage, Elinor gathers the servants and tells them she must leave most of them behind because they can no longer afford their salaries with the sisters' reduced circumstances. Additionally, Barton Cottage is much smaller and more congested than the family estate, which, though an exaggeration of what they would have experienced in the Regency period, make clear their fall in economic status. In *Pride & Prejudice*,

Wright makes similar choices, particularly in his depiction of the Bennets' home, replete with barnyard animals roaming about the yard, marking their social rank as decidedly below the Darcys of Pemberley. While some adaptations of Austen's novels ignore issues of class and gender, many more address—as they believe Austen intended—those issues in subtle and not-so-subtle ways.

Film Analysis

Joe Wright's adaptation of *Pride and Prejudice* is a mostly faithful adaptation of Jane Austen's novel in terms of plot and character. Wright distinguishes his version by casting younger, more age-appropriate actors in the lead roles, setting the film earlier than the Regency period, focusing on romance, and showing more family warmth, particularly between Mr. and Mrs. Bennet (Donald Sutherland and Brenda Blethyn). The resulting film is a relaxed, charming, and well-regarded adaptation of Austen's classic.

Unlike earlier adaptations, which cast twenty-year-old Elizabeth Bennet with significantly older actresses such as Jennifer Ehle (late twenties) and Greer Garson (mid-thirties), Wright cast twenty-year-old Keira Knightley in the lead role. Knightley was not an unknown, having had hits with key roles in *Bend it Like Beckham* (2002) and *Pirates of the Caribbean* (2003), and Wright wanted both someone young and exuberant as well as someone who would be a box office draw to create a new generation of Austen fans. With her youth and acting skills, Knightley brought a freshness and playfulness to the role that critics admired, particularly Roger Ebert, who credited Knightley with taking the story from "well-mannered 'Masterpiece Theatre'" to a romance where "strong-willed young people enter life with their minds at war with their hearts."

Wright also heightened the romance and relaxed atmosphere by setting the film in an earlier time, before the Regency period. During the Regency period, people were expected to follow specific social conventions of manners, rules of courtship, and fashion, resulting in highly formal personal interactions and social obligations. Because most film adaptations aspire to depict these conventions accurately, some films unintentionally alienated audiences with an overdeveloped sense of formality. Wright wanted a more relaxed, informal atmosphere, and by setting the film in the late 1700s, before the French Revolution when social conventions and dress were less rigid, he achieved a more casual, romantic setting that appealed to audiences. This more relaxed environment is evidenced in a number of ways but especially through Wright's use of animals and choice of costumes. The Bennet home is less an estate and more a country farm, with a family dog that wanders through the house, ducks and pigs ramble throughout the grounds, and wet laundry hangs in the yard to dry. When the Bennet sisters go to Meryton for ribbon, there are horses at the water trough in the center of town and chickens walking through the street. None of the characters interact with the animals. They are all included in background shots as part of everyday life, not a life of servants, teas, and balls, but one filled with daily domestic tasks. The costumes are also, with the exception of the ball scenes, significantly less formal with fewer bonnets and accessories. By relaxing the formality of the costumes and allowing animals to roam freely throughout the film, Wright achieves a breezy, bucolic sense of romance.

In an effort to heighten the romance further, Wright makes additional choices to support his vision, including relying less on Austen's witty dialogue and focusing more on the characters' hands, rather than their eyes, as a romantic symbol. In the novel, when Elizabeth Bennet arrives to check on the health of her sister, Jane, Miss Bingley comments on the dirty hem of Elizabeth's dress and asks Mr. Darcy (Matthew Macfadyen) if he was thinking about her dress as well. Mr. Darcy replies, "Your conjecture is totally wrong, I assure you. My mind was more agreeably engaged. I have been meditating on the very great pleasure which a pair of fine eyes in the face of a pretty women can bestow." Throughout the novel, Mr. Darcy continues to reference Elizabeth's eyes and they become symbolic of how his love for Elizabeth quietly grows. In the film, Wright focuses on the character's hands, with Mr. Darcy using his hand to help Elizabeth

into a carriage after her visit to Jane. Elizabeth reacts with surprise to his gesture, and Mr. Darcy walks away, stretching out the fingers of his hand as if they had been tingling. At the end of the film, when Elizabeth and Mr. Darcy meet, at sunrise, in the open field and he asks her, once again, to marry him, she responds by kissing his hand. In both of these examples, Wright relies on the character's hands as a more tangible and easily recognized romantic symbol.

Lastly, Wright heightens the novel's romance in the way he depicts the marriage of Mr. and Mrs. Bennet. In her novel, Austen implies Mr. Bennet did not make the best match in marrying Mrs. Bennet, who is described as a woman of "mean understanding, little information, and uncertain temper." She is perceived as silly and shallow, overly conscious of upward social mobility for her daughters, and she has an attack of nerves when she does not get her way. Mr. Bennet realizes he married hastily, yet he has resigned himself to the situation and endures by teasing his wife or ignoring her. In the film, their relationship is much more affectionate and even intimate. Both near the beginning and toward the end of the film, they have quiet scenes together in their bedroom. The scenes are shot through their bedroom window and are lit by candlelight, further emphasizing their intimacy. In the first scene, they are in bed together, with Mrs. Bennet discussing Mr. Bingley and all the possible marriage opportunities for their daughters while Mr. Bennet listens attentively. In the second, they are again in bed together, this time discussing Jane's upcoming marriage to Mr. Bingley with whispered joy and laughter. Earlier, Mrs. Bennet even rewarded Mr. Bennet with an affectionate kiss after he made arrangements for the family to meet Mr. Bingley. Thus, Wright shows a decidedly different version of the Bennet marriage, but like other aspects of the film, he focused on portraying the romantic side of Austen, filled with warmth and charm.

Significance

Pride & Prejudice was an award-winning film, earning box office success and many favorable reviews. The adaptation was nominated for fifty-nine awards in the United States and England, ranging from well-known, prestigious awards to much smaller state, city, and film festival awards. Actress Keira Knightley was nominated for an Oscar and Golden Globe as Best Actress, and Joe Wright was nominated for, and won, a BAFTA (British Academy of Film and Television Arts) award for Best Director. The film also received numerous nominations for Original Musical Score, Costume Design, and Feature Film. Although the film did not win any Oscars or Golden Globes, it did win a total of thirteen awards in the smaller categories. In terms of overall awards, Joe Wright's adaptation of *Pride and Prejudice* compares favorably with other Austen adaptations, surpassing the highly regarded *Sense and Sensibility* (1995) in the number of nominations, if not wins.

The film was equally successful at the box office, reaching the number one spot in the United Kingdom the week it was released in September 2005. The film also performed well in the United States during its saturation booking through the holiday season in 2005, earning close to $40 million in ticket sales. By the time the film left cinemas in February 2006, it had earned over $121 million at the box office worldwide, largely attributed to Joe Wright finding a new audience for Jane Austen by casting Knightley in the lead role, which brought a "millennial girlhood to the megaplex."

In general, critics praised *Pride & Prejudice* for its fresh, youthful approach to Austen's most famous novel and for Wright's casting of Knightley in the lead role. Some critics, however, lamented Wright's decision to exaggerate class differences between the Bennets and the Darcys, which were not nearly so pronounced in the formal and austere Regency period Austen captured so vividly in her novels. Other critics believed Wright's emphasis on romance overshadowed Austen's subtlety and wit regarding relations between the sexes. Overall, however, most critics appreciated the warmth and accessibility of Wright's adaptation, with its more relaxed, romantic approach to Austen's beloved novel.

—*Marybeth Rua-Larsen*

Further Reading

Fricke, Christel. "The Challenges of *Pride and Prejudice*: Adam Smith and Jane Austen on Moral Education." *Revue Internationale de Philosophie*, vol. 68, no. 269 (3), 2014, pp. 343-72. *JSTOR*, www.jstor.org/stable/24776806. Accessed 15 Mar. 2020.

Suzuki, Mika. "Sharing One's Story and 'a Faithful Narrative of Every Event.'" *Critical Survey*, vol. 26, no. 1, 2014, pp. 59-75. *JSTOR*, www.jstor.org/stable/24712589. Accessed 15 Mar. 2020.

Bibliography

Ebert, Roger. "Miss Knightley Meets Mr. Darcy." *RogerEbert.com*, 10 Nov. 2005, www.rogerebert.com/reviews/pride-and-prejudice-2005. Accessed 29 March 2020.

Elley, Derek. "*Pride & Prejudice*." *Variety*, 11 Sept. 2005, variety.com/2005/film/awards/pride-prejudice-2-1200523317/. Accessed 29 Mar. 2020.

Grandi, Roberta. "The Passion Translated: Literary and Cinematic Rhetoric in *Pride and Prejudice* (2005)." *Literature/Film Quarterly*, vol. 36, no. 1, 2008, pp. 45-51. *JSTOR*, www.jstor.org/stable/43797397. Accessed 15 Mar. 2020.

Hume, Robert D. "Money in Jane Austen." *The Review of English Studies*, vol. 64, no. 264, 2013, pp. 289-310. *JSTOR*, www.jstor.org/stable/42003625. Accessed 15 Mar. 2020.

Neckles, Christina. "Spatial Anxiety: Adapting the Social Space of *Pride and Prejudice*." *Literature/Film Quarterly*, vol. 40, no. 1, 2012, pp. 30-45. *JSTOR*, www.jstor.org/stable/43798812. Accessed 15 Mar. 2020.

Raitt, George. "'Lost in Austen': Screen Adaptation in a Post-Feminist World." *Literature/Film Quarterly*, vol. 40, no. 2, 2012, pp. 127-41. *JSTOR*, www.jstor.org/stable/43798823. Accessed 15 Mar. 2020.

Sadoff, Dianne F. "Marketing Jane Austen at the Megaplex." *NOVEL: A Forum on Fiction*, vol. 43, no. 1, 2010, pp. 83-92. *JSTOR*, www.jstor.org/stable/27764374. Accessed 15 Mar. 2020.

The Prime of Miss Jean Brodie

The Novel
Author: Muriel Spark (1918-2006)
First published: 1961

The Film
Year released: 1969
Director: Ronald Neame (1911-2010)
Screenplay by: Jay Presson Allen
Starring: Maggie Smith, Robert Stephens, Pamela Franklin

Context

Muriel Spark was the author of twenty-two novels, but it was her slim 1961 offering *The Prime of Miss Jean Brodie* that proved to be her breakthrough and became, by far, her most read book. Originally published as a short story in the *New Yorker*, *Jean Brodie* was loosely based on the author's own experiences attending James Gillespie's School for Girls in Edinburgh, Scotland, with the title character based on Spark's teacher Christina Kay, who encouraged Spark to become a writer. "What filled our minds with wonder and made Christina Kay so memorable," she later wrote, "was the personal drama and poetry within which everything in her classroom happened."

In taking the facts of her own life and turning them into fiction, Spark transformed her circumstances into far more dramatic form, turning the inspirational figure of Kay into the volatile and ambiguous Jean Brodie. For example, while Spark noted in an article that she wrote for *The New Yorker* that Kay hung a poster of Italian dictator Benito Mussolini on the wall of her classroom, the author took this much further in the book by having Brodie, unlike Kay, actively embrace fascism. Similarly, it seems unlikely that Kay manipulated her students in quite the questionable ways that Brodie does. Such are the ways fiction operates, though; the author draws on her life and makes it more dramatic, and hopefully readers take notice.

Take notice they did, in this case, as *Jean Brodie* proved to be something of a sensation. In 1966, the American playwright, screenwriter, producer, and director Jay Presson Allen adapted the book into a play, which met with great success. Starring Vanessa Redgrave in the title role, the theatrical version debuted in London in 1966 and moved to Broadway two years later. With Zoe Caldwell replacing Redgrave, the Broadway version was a certifi-able hit, and Caldwell went on to win a Tony for her performance. This led Allen to adapt her play into a screenplay, which was produced by 20th Century Fox and directed by venerable English filmmaker Ronald Neame. The film, with Maggie Smith portraying Jean Brodie, likewise met with much acclaim, taking home the Academy Award for best picture. The film also won two BAFTA Awards, with Smith winning best actress and Celia Johnson winning best supporting actress.

Film Analysis

The movie version of *The Prime of Miss Jean Brodie*, like the play it was based on, offers a far more straightforward experience than the original novel. A linear, streamlined retelling of the events of Spark's book, it dispenses with some of the high modernist techniques employed by the Scottish novelist and turns the story into a more conventional tale of thwarted love.

In telling the story of an unconventional teacher and her pet students against the backdrop of 1930s Edinburgh and the rise of European fascism, Spark weaves a complicated narrative that asks the reader to get to know and keep track of a wide range of characters in a short period of time. To do this, she assigns specific qualities to the characters and then repeats these qualities over and over again. For example, the reader is repeatedly told that one of the students, Rose Stanley, will later become "famous for sex." In employing these characteristics as identifying tags, Spark often gives away what will later happen to her characters. She frequently employs flash forwards and informs the reader from early on which characters will meet a tragic fate. For example, the dim-witted Mary McGregor, is, the reader learns early on, fated to die in a hotel fire. Spark's insistence on heavy repetition and somewhat perverse spoiling of the plot not only allows the reader to better differentiate the characters, it gives to the whole proceedings a certain fatalism, which, given the book's setting in the years leading up to World War II and what the reader knows about world history, seems entirely appropriate.

In contrast, the movie (as with the play before it) proceeds in strictly linear fashion, no detail given away before its time. The film also simplifies the action and characters, reducing the number of girls in "the Brodie set" from six to four and amalgamating several characters from the book into composites. As in the book, the movie tells the story of Jean Brodie (Maggie Smith), an unconventional teacher at the highly conservative Marcia Blaine School in Edinburgh. Rejecting the rote learning instruction style of her fellow teachers, she ignores lesson plans altogether, sharing instead her experiences and her reflections on art, hoping to inspire her charges with her romantic worldview.

The headmistress (Celia Johnson) naturally hates Miss Brodie and wants her gone from the school, but her students do love her. She takes a special interest in a group of girls, known as the "Brodie set," from the time they are very young. When the book begins in the early 1930s, the girls are ten, and readers follow them over the course of the next several years. Although the timeline of the movie is less specific, it seems to follow roughly the same path. The six girls in the book are reduced to four, with Jenny Gray (the "pretty one" in both texts; played by Diane Grayson in the film) also taking on the qualities and role of Rose Stanley in the movie (in which Rose is absent). In both book and film, the principal character among the "Brodie set" is Sandy Stranger (Pamela Franklin), a smart young girl whom Miss Brodie takes a special interest in, crediting her with great powers of "insight."

If the book, though, proceeds nimbly through Spark's time jumping and repetition, the movie occasionally feels like a filmed piece of theater, which in some respects it is. Director Ronald Neame does his best to liven up the proceedings, particularly in his color scheme. Against the mostly drab background of the school, Miss Brodie herself always wears bright colors, making her a symbolically rich source of life amidst the conformity of her surroundings. At the end of the movie, when Miss Brodie is finally brought down, it is symbolically significant that she wears a gray suit.

Another asset that Neame brings to the table are the talents of his cast. Maggie Smith won an Oscar for playing Miss Brodie, and she is a lively presence throughout, half inspiring, half pathetic, both qualities of which Smith captures fully. With her exaggerated, over-the-top way of speaking, heavy on trilling r's, Smith shows Miss Brodie to be an affected individual, a petty bourgeois who longs for more in life without gaining much understanding. But it is also easy to see how she could prove an exciting presence to a group of impressionable young girls. Smith is ably matched by Pamela Franklin, who, in portraying Sandy, communicates both the awkwardness of youth and the fierceness that comes from a dawning adult-level understanding.

Both book and movie turn on Jean Brodie's love for a married art teacher, Teddy Lloyd (Robert Stephens), which is reciprocated by Teddy but is unable to be properly fulfilled. Frustrated at the situation, Miss Brodie both takes up with another, less desired teacher, the bachelor music instructor Gordon Lowther (Gordon Jackson), and attempts to have one of her students sleep with Teddy as a proxy. (In the book, this is Rose Stanley; in the movie, Jenny Gray.) Instead, Sandy ends up becoming Teddy's lover, and as a result of this attempted manipulation on Miss Brodie's part and the teacher's subsequent misguided encouragement of a student—Joyce Emily Hammond in the book, Mary McGregor (Jane Carr) in the movie—to go fight in Spanish dictator Francisco Franco's army, Sandy ends up betraying Miss Brodie to the headmistress.

The filmmakers seem to take much more satisfaction in Miss Brodie's defeat than Spark does. Spark herself called the character of Sandy a "little b——," but in the movie, not only does Sandy seem fully justified in her actions, she is given a triumphant speech to seal the deal. She denounces Miss Brodie to her face, in a way that, while it may be not off the mark, seems more cruelly concocted than in the book. As critic Lisa Rosman points out, the cruelty is sealed when the camera moves in close on Maggie Smith's mouth and eyes as she receives this denouncement. Miss Brodie may be pathetic, but the viewer is also invited to feel triumph in her defeat, even if the final shot of the film shows a tearful Sandy, perhaps somewhat remorseful for her actions. This tendency is less prevalent in the richer, more ambiguous novel, which ends on a note of tribute, with Sandy, much older, now a nun who wrote a successful book on psychology, acknowledging the influence of her former mentor, leaving the reader with an entirely different sensation than the viewer of the movie version that came out eight years later.

Significance

The *Prime of Miss Jean Brodie*, and particularly the character of Jean Brodie, have held a fascination for those interested in the arts since the publication of Muriel Spark's short novel in 1961. Miss Brodie herself is a perpetually compelling figure, a prototype for the inspirational teachers that would come to populate the film world of the 1980s and 1990s. Unrestrained, unorthodox, imperious, she is a more challenging character than the likes of John Keating in *Dead Poets' Society* (1989) or LouAnne Johnson in *Dangerous Minds* (1995). Miss Brodie is arguably both actually dangerous and a light in the lives of her immature and impressionable students.

This carefully crafted, carefully observed ambiguity, as if to say "because life is like that," is what gives Jean Brodie and the various works based around her their charge. Virtually any actor who took on the meaty role of the unconventional teacher met with great acclaim, be it Zoe Caldwell's Tony-winning performance in the 1968 Broadway production or Maggie Smith's Oscar-winning turn in the 1969 movie. The material and the character continued to fascinate beyond the 1960s, with a seven-episode television serial appearing in 1978 on Britain's ITV with Geraldine McEwan starring as Miss Brodie. The program crafted new situations for its characters, beyond those outlined in the book, showing the material to be endlessly adaptable years after its original publication.

—*Andrew Schenker*

Further Reading

Smith, Ali. "'Vital, Witty, Formidably Blithe': Ali Smith on Muriel Spark at 100." *The Guardian*, 29 Jan. 2018, www.theguardian.com/books/2018/jan/29/ali-smith-on-muriel-spark-at-100. Accessed 10 Dec. 2018.

Taylor, Alan, and Cal Flynn. "The Best Books by Muriel Spark." *Five Books*, fivebooks.com/best-books/muriel-spark-best-novels/. Accessed 10 Dec. 2018.

Bibliography

Canby, Vincent. Review of *The Prime of Miss Jean Brodie*, directed by Ronald Neame. *The New York Times*, 3 Mar. 1969, movies2.nytimes.com/books/01/03/11/specials/spark-brodiefilm.html. Accessed 10 Dec. 2018.

Rosman, Lisa. "Why 'The Prime of Miss Jean Brodie' Still Matters." *Signature Reads*, 17 June 2016, www.signature-reads.com/2016/06/why-the-prime-of-miss-jean-brodie-still-matters/. Accessed 10 Dec. 2018.

Spark, Muriel. "The Teacher Who Inspired 'The Prime of Miss Jean Brodie.'" *The New Yorker*, 25 Mar. 1991, www.newyorker.com/magazine/1991/03/25/the-school-on-the-links. Accessed 10 Dec. 2018.

Ready Player One

The Novel
Author: Ernest Cline (b. 1972)
First published: 2011

The Film
Year released: 2018
Director: Steven Spielberg (b. 1946)
Screenplay by: Zak Penn, Ernest Cline
Starring: Tye Sheridan, Olivia Cooke, Ben Mendelsohn, Lena Waithe, Simon Pegg, Mark Rylance

Context

When Ernest Cline's first novel, *Ready Player One*, was published in 2011, it became an instant bestseller and was named to numerous best books of the year lists. It also earned the 2012 Prometheus Award and a 2012 Alex Award from the Young Adult Library Services Association of the American Library Association (ALA). Critics and science-fiction fans alike were thrilled by Cline's take on a dystopian future (a subgenre of science fiction) in which humanity spends most of its waking hours living in an artificial reality known as the Ontologically Anthropocentric Sensory Immersive Simulation (OASIS). The OASIS had been created by eccentric video game developer James Halliday, who filled this virtual reality with endless popular culture references from his childhood in the 1970s and 1980s. The success of *Ready Player One* enabled Cline to write a second science-fiction novel, *Armada*, which was published in 2015. Like its predecessor, it became a bestseller, but it did not enjoy favorable critical reviews.

Cline spent almost a decade writing the book, never expecting that it would be developed into a film due to the vast number of references to registered trademarks of toys, video games, films, and television shows. After the rights to the book were purchased, however, the film rights to *Ready Player One* were sold in less than forty-eight hours. Director Steven Spielberg soon announced his intentions to direct the film. Spielberg's works were much beloved by Cline throughout his childhood, so much so that he made significant references to them in *Ready Player One*. Among Spielberg's most notable films from the time are *Jaws* (1975), the Indiana Jones series, *E.T.: The Extra-Terrestrial* (1982), *Jurassic Park* (1993), and *Schindler's List* (1993).

Cline wrote the initial draft of the screenplay, which was then further developed by screenwriter Zak Penn. The screenplay differed significantly from the novel, in part to make the film more visually stimulating but also to eliminate references to Spielberg's own movies as well as products the film did not obtain the rights to use.

Director Steven Spielberg. Photo by Gage Skidmore via Wikimedia Commons.

Film Analysis

The movie version of *Ready Player One* differs significantly from the novel in that the timeline is tightened; characters' motivations, descriptions, and backstories are changed; and many of the popular culture references have been altered, either because of rights issues or personal preferences on the part of Spielberg as director. Yet the main thrust of the story remains the same: a quest to solve a puzzle inside a virtual reality.

It is 2045. Most of humanity spends its time plugged into the virtual reality known as the OASIS, because the real world has been ravaged ecologically and economically. Among the denizens of the OASIS is Wade Watts (Tye Sheridan), known inside the OASIS by his avatar moniker Parzival. Watts is an orphan, living in the stacks —trailer homes piles atop of one another—in Columbus, Ohio, with his aunt. He spends much of his time trying to win a contest announced a few years earlier via prerecorded message on the day of game creator James Halliday's death.

Halliday (Mark Rylance) and his partner Ogden Morrow (Simon Pegg) cocreated the OASIS through their company, Gregarious Games. In his message, Halliday announces that the first person to find a golden Easter egg hiding in the game would win ownership of the OASIS itself—a business worth a vast fortune. To find the egg, players need to complete secret quests to earn three keys to open three gates, each containing a riddle to find the next key. Legions of people compete in the contest, including Nolan Sorrento (Ben Mendelsohn), the boss of a competitive company named Innovative Online Industries (IOI), who has a vast army of employees and indentured servants, known as Sixers, playing on his behalf. Players looking for the egg are known as egg hunters, or gunters for short.

Watts spends much of his time in the game studying Halliday's life and popular culture interests in the Archives, a virtual journal of Halliday's life, with the aid of its Curator (later revealed to be Morrow). In the novel, Halliday's journal is a written manuscript called Anorak's Almanac that contains the clue to finding the Copper Key. In the film, the challenge that must be completed to get the first key is widely known, but seems impossible to beat. After Watts obsessively replays scenes from Halliday's life in the Archives—including the moment in which Halliday forces Morrow to leave the company, ending their friendship—he discovers a hint about how to beat the challenge. Watts becomes the first person to find the Copper Key. In Cline's novel, Watts wins the first key by going on a Dungeons and Dragons quest—the 1974 fantasy role-playing game—and then beating Halliday's avatar, known as Anorak, at the video game *Joust*. He then finds the First Gate and the clue leading to the next key by acting out Matthew Broderick's role in the film *WarGames* (1983). In the film, he succeeds by winning a race through an ever-shifting Manhattan cityscape, complete with a King Kong crushing cars. The gate with the clue appears directly after he receives the Copper Key, with no added challenge.

After finding the first key, he shares his hint with his friend Aech (Lena Waithe) and fellow gunter Art3mis (Olivia Cooke), who seems to be his single greatest competitor. In the film version, the competition between these three gunters and another pair, Daito (Win Morisaki) and Sho (Philip Zhao), is downplayed in favor of collaboration. Because of their scores in the game, the group becomes known as the High Five. They work together to find and complete the quest for the Jade Key. In the film, Watts and the others win the Jade Key by completing a challenge inside a virtual reality inspired by *The Shining*, a 1980 horror film directed by Spielberg's friend Stanley Kubrick. In the novel, Watts wins the key alone by playing an immersive version of the adventure game *Zork*.

With Watts's success as Parzival bringing him fame and fortune inside the OASIS, he comes to the attention of Sorrento, who hires another player, named I-R0k (T. J. Miller), to learn Parzival's true identity. When he does, Sorrento has Watts's home in the stacks bombed, killing his aunt, her boyfriend, and a score of other people. Watts, not being home at the time, is rescued by someone working with Art3mis, whose real name is Samantha Cook.

After Samantha helps Watts, IOI operatives track them down. Watts escapes, but Samantha is captured and forced into indentured servitude as a Sixer. In the book, Watts intentionally gets himself arrested by IOI to sabotage their system from the inside. In the film, however, much of this sabotage plotline is given to Samantha. Later, with the help of the rest of the High Five—whom he also meets in real life—Watts helps to break Samantha out of IOI custody.

The movie quest for the Crystal Key also departs from the book version. In the novel, the gunters must use a

Voight-Kampff machine from the film *Blade Runner* (1982) and other clues to find the key. Because the film company could not get the rights to *Blade Runner*, the gunters instead find an Easter egg inside of Halliday's favorite Atari 2600 game, *Adventure*, on a frozen planet called Planet Doom.

After the location of the final quest is revealed, Sorrento places an impenetrable force field around the planet. Watts, as Parzival, rallies all of the gunters he can to do battle with Sorrento and his legion of Sixers, while Art3mis works within IOI to deactivate the force field. Now desperate, Sorrento explodes a bomb called the Catalyst to wipe out all of the avatars attacking the force field. Miraculously, Parzival survives; he had won a quarter in a bet with the Curator earlier in the film that grants him an extra life. With the extra life, Parzival is able to find the Easter egg inside *Adventure* and win the Crystal Key. Once he does, Anorak meets him through the final gate and presents him with the contract to take over Gregarious Games. Parzival refuses to sign, remembering that Halliday had forced Morrow to sign his portion of the company away the same way. Anorak admits to Parzival that it was a final test for the winner and transforms into Halliday, where he appears alongside Watts in Halliday's childhood room. Halliday hands Watts the golden egg, and with it, the ownership of the OASIS.

A similar happy ending occurs in the real world: Sorrento and his minions are arrested for bombing the stacks and Morrow visits Watts, revealing himself to be the Curator and offering his help. Watts accepts it, provided that he can share control of the OASIS with the rest of the High Five. In a voiceover, Watts tells of how he makes IOI give up forcing people into indentured servitude to pay off their debts; how he shuts down the OASIS twice a week, so people can spend more time in the real world; and how he and Samantha move in together to enjoy more of the real world.

Significance

Ready Player One, released on March 29, 2018, was the number one movie in the United States during its opening weekend. Made on a budget of about $175 million, it earned more than $137 million in the United States alone, and another $445 million in foreign markets, bringing its worldwide take to more than $582 million.

In addition to being a commercial success, the film received generally favorable reviews. Writing for *Rolling Stone* (27 Mar. 2018), critic Peter Travers declared: "The gamer kid in Steven Spielberg lets his VR freak flag fly in *Ready Player One*, a mindbending joyride that jacks you into a fantasia bursting with CGI wonders, dazzling cyberscapes mixed with live action, hidden Easter eggs and infinite pop-culture shoutouts to the 1980s." While admiring Spielberg's skill, Travers admitted that the CGI sequences were more engaging than the live-action scenes, stating, "Spielberg's visual inventiveness is unflagging. He stumbles only when trying to warm up the tech gadgetry with a personal touch.... Sheridan and Cooke bring genuine romantic longing to their few scenes together. But the live-action segments of the movie are more buzz kill than bracing." Some critics, however, did not believe it was Spielberg's best work. In the *New Yorker* (9 Apr. 2018), Anthony Lane wrote: "it was the meagre emotional charge that shocked me most. Toward the end, as in many Spielberg movies, there are tears, but, for once, they feel unearned."

—*Christopher Mari*

Further Reading

Cline, Ernest. "'Imagining the Future Is Dangerous.'" Interview by Jacob Brogan. *Slate*, 14 July 2015, slate.com/technology/2015/07/an-interview-with-ernest-cline-author-of-ready-player-one-and-armada.html. Accessed 14 Dec. 2018.

Shepherd, Jack. "Ernest Cline Interview on *Ready Player One*, Working with Steven Spielberg, and the Future of Virtual Reality." *Independent*, 28 Mar. 2018, www.independent.co.uk/arts-entertainment/films/features/ready-player-one-ernest-cline-interview-steven-spielberg-virtual-reality-vr-a8277996.html. Accessed 14 Dec. 2018.

Bibliography

Jackson, Josh. "22 Differences Between the *Ready Player One* Book and Movie." *Paste*, 29 Mar. 2018, www.pastemagazine.com/articles/2018/03/difference-between-ready-player-one-book-and-movie.html. Accessed 14 Dec. 2018.

Lane, Anthony. Review of *Ready Player One*, directed by Steven Spielberg, and *Lean on Pete*, directed by Andrew Haigh. *The New Yorker*, 9 Apr. 2018, www.newyorker.com/magazine/2018/04/09/ready-player-one-and-lean-on-pete. Accessed 14 Dec. 2018.

Murphy, Mekado. "How They Made the Movie References Pop in 'Ready Player One.'" *The New York Times*, 27 Apr. 2018, www.nytimes.com/2018/04/27/movies/ready-player-one-visual-effects.html. Accessed 14 Dec. 2018.

Rottenberg, Josh. "How the Team behind 'Ready Player One' Wrangled a Bonanza of Pop Culture References into a Single Film." *Los Angeles Times*, 1 Apr. 2018, www.latimes.com/entertainment/movies/la-et-mn-ready-player-one-references-20180401-story.html. Accessed 14 Dec. 2018.

Travers, Peter. "'Ready Player One' Review: Spielberg's Overwhelming Blockbuster Hearts the '80s." Review of *Ready Player One*, directed by Steven Spielberg. *Rolling Stone*, 27 Mar. 2018, www.rollingstone.com/movies/movie-reviews/ready-player-one-review-spielbergs-overwhelming-blockbuster-hearts-the-80s-204608/. Accessed 14 Dec. 2018.

The Red Pony

The Novel
Author: John Steinbeck (1902-1968)
First published: 1937

The Film
Year released: 1949
Director: Lewis Milestone (1895-1980)
Screenplay by: John Steinbeck
Starring: Myrna Loy, Robert Mitchum, Louis Calhern, Shepperd Strudwick, Peter Miles

Context

The film version of *The Red Pony*, like the book of the same title, explores various archetypal themes—that is, issues that practically anyone, of any place, period, race, or gender, can relate to. Such themes, in this case, include the transition from childhood to adolescence; the complex relationships between children and their parents; the complicated relationships of children with other children; the complications of relationships between husbands and wives; the tensions that sometimes exist within families and between different generations; the disillusionment that often accompanies the process of growing up; and the growing realization as one grows up, of the inevitability of death. Other universal issues especially relevant to both versions of *The Red Pony* involve humanity's complex relationship with nature; the desire and need to feel both respected and loved; the need to feel fulfilled in one's social and familial roles; and the need to cope with rivalries that sometimes arise, even within tightly knit communities, including families.

For all these reasons, both the film and the book seem designed to interest not only adolescents but also adults. Both explore various rites of passage. More broadly, they suggest the ways the United States itself has changed over the years—from a country whose western territories were settled (often at the expense of Native Americans) by immigrants from the east; to a country whose western territories were then mainly rural and agricultural, with an emphasis on ranches and the raising of crops and livestock; to a country whose western territories were, by the time the film was produced, increasingly urban, with an emphasis on trade and other modern forms of money-making, including film production. Both the book and the film look back, nostalgically, to earlier, more "innocent" times in the lives of individuals and in the life of the country as a whole.

Both the book and the film deal not only with a young boy growing up but also with the changes occurring in the nation itself, and especially in the west, evolving in ways that could be viewed as a loss of innocence—a kind of "paradise lost," never to be recovered. Even more broadly, both can be seen as concerned with the westward expansion of the United States, an expansion that finally came to an end when immigrants from the east reached the Pacific Ocean and could not (almost) go any further. In many ways, the book and film deal with issues of change that often involve not only growth but also the pain of leaving childish things behind.

Film Analysis

For various reasons, Steinbeck's *The Red Pony* is a complicated work. The book is not a novel but instead four loosely connected short stories: "The Gift," which recounts how Jody is given a red pony that dies after being exposed to cold rain; "The Great Mountains," which is about an old Mexican man who grew up near the ranch and returns there, all alone, not long before his death; "The Promise," which tells how Billy Buck promises Jody a newborn colt as a substitute for the dead pony; and "The Leader of the People," which describes how Jody's grandfather annoys Jody's father by repeating, again and again, the same old stories about his distant past as the leader of a wagon train. The Gift introduces many of the most important characters, including a young boy named Jody Tiflin —changed to Tom in the film (Peter Miles); his mother (Myrna Loy); his father (Shepperd Strudwick); and the family's omnicompetent ranch hand, Billy Buck (Robert

Mitchum). "The Leader of the People" emphasizes another of the film's important characters—Jody's maternal grandfather (Louis Calhern).

Steinbeck, who wrote the film's screenplay, included all but one of the short stories—"The Great Mountains" was omitted. He also has the grandfather appear much earlier in the film than he does in the book. He is present on the ranch to see the red pony grow and die and to see the newborn colt replace the pony. As the title of the film suggests, the tale about the red pony is the dominant story in the film.

In the film, Steinbeck also adds various episodes and characters that are only implied in the book. These include Tom's elaborate fantasies about being a medieval knight and a circus star; his repeated interactions with young friends, who are often hostile and include a girl who is a conventional tomboy; his tense interactions with a stereotypical old maid schoolteacher (played by Margaret Hamilton, famous for her earlier role as the Wicked Witch of the West in *The Wizard of Oz*); and his father's decision to visit a nearby city for an extended period when he feels dissatisfied with life on the ranch. This episode implies real tension in the relationship between Tom's parents. In the film, Tom seems more obviously responsible for the death of the red pony than he does in the book: he teaches the pony, as a trick, how to open the barn door, and he twice falls asleep when the pony does exactly that during bad rainstorms. Yet Tom, in the film, does not acknowledge much, if any, responsibility for these events; instead he prefers to blame Billy Buck for failing to accurately predict the weather and for being absent during the pony's first escape into a violent storm. Meanwhile, the actor Peter Miles seems smaller—and perhaps more childish—than many readers of the book may have imagined the character Steinbeck depicted in the stories.

The film graphically depicts an incident only described in the story: little Tom, furious when he sees buzzards picking apart the corpse of the pony, grabs one of the giant birds by the neck, awkwardly wrestles with it, and eventually manages to beat it to death. This incident, in the book, is already quite memorable, but in the film, it is so shocking and so violent (Tom's skin is ripped and torn, and he bleeds profusely) that some early reviewers thought it should never have been depicted on-screen. They found it too horrific to watch. However, if in this scene Steinbeck chose to present unflinchingly the horrors of violence, bloodshed, and death, by the end of the film he went to an altogether different extreme.

In the book, the boy gets his colt only after Billy Buck is forced to slit open the colt's mother and remove the badly positioned baby from her insides. On the other hand, in the film the mare gives birth with no serious complications. The film closes by showing all the main characters gathered in the barn, laughing uproariously together as they admire the beautiful newborn colt. In the book, the need to kill the mother so that the colt can be born safely helps teach Jody yet another lesson about the hard facts of life. In the film, Tom gets his new horse fairly easily, and everyone is very pleased. Perhaps Steinbeck felt that three shocking deaths—first the pony, then the buzzard, then the mare—would literally have been overkill. In any case, he eliminated the third incident and gave the film a happy ending that seems almost too happy to be believed, especially as it is somewhat overacted. Some critics faulted the film for its sentimental conclusion; others, however, faulted it for being too dark earlier on.

One of the most effective aspects of the film was, and remains, its use of a richly developed score by Aaron Copland, perhaps the greatest American composer of the twentieth century. Reviewers frequently singled out the score as especially memorable and effective, and in fact, Copland later developed the score into a full-blown orchestral suite that remains immensely appealing. Less effective—again, for being perhaps too sentimental—is the scene in which Tom imagines himself as a squire on horseback serving Billy Buck as a medieval knight and the scene in which Tom imagines himself as the red-coated, top-hat-wearing, whip-flicking ringleader of a circus.

However, the scene with grim, prune-faced Margaret Hamilton playing yet another scary old schoolteacher is a delight to anyone who remembers her unforgettable performance as the witch in *The Wizard of Oz*. She nicely (if only briefly) counterbalances the performance of Louis Calhern as a sentimental old grandfather with flowing white hair and a long white beard. The grandfather and Billy Buck are the two adult males whom Tom comes close to idolizing, while his relationship with his stiff, humorless father and silent mother are anything but sentimental in the film—at least until the very end.

Significance

Although early reactions were mostly positive, some reviewers did censure different aspects of the film. Positive reviews praised the refreshing theme, the restrained tone, the quiet pace, the heartwarming plot and down-to-earth characters, and the appeal the film would likely have not only for children but also for adults. The film was extolled for its simplicity, sensitivity, laconic dialogue, poignant plot, and strong visual flavor. Many reviewers especially commended the realistic ranch setting, the striking Technicolor photography, and Copland's inventive music. On the other hand, the reviewers who disliked the film found it too slow, too predictable, too sentimental, too rambling, too devoid of suspense, and a bit too corny in depicting Tom's grandfather. Bosley Crowther, in *The New York Times*, was especially negative in assessing the film, but a far more positive (and much more typical) review came from Lew Sheaffer in the *Brooklyn Eagle*.

Reviewers strongly disagreed about the wisdom of including the bloody scene in which Tom battles a ferocious buzzard. Some found this episode far too horrible to watch, while others thought it was valuably realistic and unforgettable and helped contribute to the film's larger, unromantic view of nature. Meanwhile, assessments of the acting were also mixed. Some reviewers admired every performance, especially that of young Peter Miles. But while some critics praised the restraint of the actors playing Tom's parents and Buck, others thought they were restrained to the point of being wooden and even depressing. Some critics considered Louis Calhern just right as the lovable, loquacious grandfather, but others considered his performance overdone and even hammy.

—Robert C. Evans, PhD

Further Reading

Bernardo, Anthony. "*The Red Pony*." *Masterplots II: American Fiction Series, Revised Edition*, Jan. 2000, pp. 1-3. *EBSCOhost*, search.ebscohost.com/login.aspx?direct=true&db=lkh&AN=103331AMF14000011000400?&site=ehost-live. Accessed 12 May 2020.

McConnell, Jean. "*The Red Pony*." *Masterplots II: Juvenile & Young Adult Fiction Series*, Mar. 1991, pp. 1-2. *EBSCOhost*, search.ebscohost.com/login.aspx?direct=true&db=lkh&AN=103331JYF13469270000381?&site=ehost-live. Accessed 12 May 2020.

Shuman, R. Baird. "*The Red Pony*." *Magill's Survey of American Literature, Revised Edition*, Sept. 2006, p. 1. *EBSCOhost*, search.ebscohost.com/login.aspx?direct=true&db=lkh&AN=103331MSA25929830001591&site=ehost-live. Accessed 12 May 2020.

Bibliography

Crowther, Bosley. "The Screen in Review; *Red Pony*, Based on Steinbeck Novel, New Bill at Mayfair—Mitchum, Loy in Cast." *The New York Times*, 9 Mar. 1949, www.nytimes.com/1949/03/09/archives/the-screen-in-review-red-pony-based-on-steinbeck-novel-new-bill-at.html. Accessed 12 May 2020.

Loeb, Theresa. "*Red Pony* Is Excellent Film Fare." *Oakland Tribune*, 7 Feb. 1949, p. 14. newspapers.com/clip/51204679/oakland-tribune/. Accessed 12 May 2020.

Sheaffer, Lew. "Steinbeck's *The Red Pony* Turned into an Appealing Film." *Brooklyn Eagle*, 9 Mar. 1949, newspapers.com/clip/51202549/the-brooklyn-daily-eagle/. Accessed 12 May 2020.

Red Sparrow

The Novel

Author: Jason Matthews (b. 1951)
First published: 2013

The Film

Year released: 2018
Director: Francis Lawrence (b. 1971)
Screenplay by: Justin Haythe
Starring: Jennifer Lawrence, Joel Edgerton, Matthias Schoenaerts, Charlotte Rampling, Jeremy Irons

Context

In 2013, former Central Intelligence Agency (CIA) officer Jason Matthews published his first spy novel, *Red Sparrow*, which was informed by many of his experiences during his thirty-three-year tenure at America's preeminent spy agency. During his time serving at postings in the Mediterranean, Asia, and the Caribbean, Matthews developed a healthy understanding of the ways in which Soviet—and later Russian—operatives handled themselves. In his retirement, he decided to pen a novel based on his work. Like all other former officers who go on to author books, Matthews had to run the manuscript past the publication review board at the CIA, in order to ensure that he did not inadvertently reveal CIA sources and methods. Apart from changing a few sentences, the novel he submitted remained remarkably intact, giving readers interesting insights into the modern world of espionage.

Because of his extensive experience, Matthews imbued *Red Sparrow* with a level of authenticity rarely seen but always celebrated in spy novels. In reviews he was favorably compared to authors like Graham Greene, Ian Fleming, and John le Carré, all of whom worked for the British intelligence services. Art Taylor, in the *Washington Post* (15 Oct. 2013), called *Red Sparrow* a "sublime and sophisticated debut." Writing for *The New York Times* (31 May 2013), Charles Cummings declared that "Matthews offers the reader a primer in twenty-first-century spying."

The film rights were quickly snatched up by Hollywood, where Twentieth Century Fox tapped Francis Lawrence, who had directed three of the four films in the popular *Hunger Games* series, to direct. Initially an in-demand music video director, Lawrence transitioned to big-budget filmmaking with *Constantine* (2005), based on the DC Comics character, and then directed the postapocalyptic horror film *I Am Legend* (2007) and the romantic drama *Water for Elephants* (2011), before moving on to the *Hunger Games* adaptations. Screenwriter Justin Haythe was given the task of adapting the book for the screen. The director saw the film as a starring vehicle for the acclaimed actress Jennifer Lawrence (no relation), with whom he had worked in the *Hunger Games* films, and who won the 2012 Academy Award for Best Actress for her performance in *Silver Linings Playbook*.

Film Analysis

In order to adapt the novel to the screen, a number of aspects were eliminated or altered. The novel alternates points of view between the various main characters; in the film, viewers generally follow the viewpoint of Dominika Egorova (Jennifer Lawrence), a former ballerina who is forced to work in Russian intelligence in order to get care for her ailing mother. Also in the book, Dominika has a form of synesthesia, a condition in which one kind of sensory stimulus is experienced as another, for example hearing color or smelling sound. In Dominika's case, she sees music, words, and people's moods as colors, which aids her both as a ballerina and later when she must seduce men as a spy. Another (minor) difference is that Russian president Vladimir Putin appears briefly in the book but not in the movie.

Opening in contemporary Russia, the film quickly introduces the two main protagonists, Dominika and a young American CIA officer. Dominika, while performing in a ballet, is grievously injured, ending her career. Her uncle, Vanya Egorov (Matthias Schoenaerts), the deputy director of the Russian intelligence agency SVR, then suggests she come to work for him. She is reluctant to enter his deceptive world, but agrees in order to get government care for her sickly mother. During her first assignment, a Russian gangster tries to sexually assault her but is killed by an SVR assassin named Matorin (Sebastian Hülk). Her uncle then gives Dominika a choice: work for the SVR full time or be executed because she witnessed the gangster's assassination.

At the same time, an American agent named Nate Nash (Joel Edgerton) is contending with the fact that his high-ranking asset in the Russian government, code-named Marble, was nearly captured by the Russian police during their meeting. Nash is chastised by his superiors and then assigned to Budapest, hoping that Marble will again be able to make contact.

Meanwhile, Dominika is sent to State School 4, run by a matron (Charlotte Rampling) who educates her and the other male and female "Sparrows" in the arts of spying and seduction. Despite her disgust at being there and nearly being sexually assaulted by another Sparrow,

Jennifer Lawrence. Photo by NASA/Joel Kowsky, Public domain, via Wikimedia Commons.

Dominika proves to be an excellent recruit, impressing both the matron and her superior, General Korchnoi (Jeremy Irons). She is then assigned to Budapest to make contact with Nash, whom the Russians know is a CIA agent, and get him to reveal Marble's identity.

While in Budapest, Dominika rooms with another Sparrow and makes contact with Nash. In short order he realizes she is a spy like him; she in turn tells him that her mission is to seduce him and get Marble's identity. She reveals this to demonstrate she is willing to work as a double agent, in order to get back at her uncle and the Russian system that turned her into a Sparrow. Nash takes her to his superiors so they can ask her questions while connected to a lie detector. They believe she is telling the truth, but remain wary of her.

Dominika then discovers that her Sparrow roommate is attempting to buy US secrets from Stephanie Boucher (Mary-Louise Parker), the chief of staff to a senator. Dominika gets her uncle to believe that she is working with her roommate to get the secrets; when the roommate is killed, Dominika replaces her at the meeting where the money and information exchange is to take place. She tells Nash of the meeting. He then has it arranged so that she will give the Russian government floppy disks that the CIA will supply instead of the real ones, thereby allowing the United States to keep its secrets. But the meeting goes wrong. After successfully exchanging the disks, Dominika leaves to give the disks to her uncle, but Boucher is killed when she is spooked by CIA agents and accidently walks out into traffic.

Back in Moscow, Dominika is tortured for days to see if she is a double agent. Nash is frantic with worry about what has happened to her. Ultimately, the Russian government is persuaded that she is not a traitor. When she returns to Budapest, she asks Nash to help her and her mother defect. Nash agrees to help. They have sex and spend the night together.

In the morning, Dominika wakes up to find the assassin Matorin torturing Nash in gruesome ways. In order to convince Matorin that she is loyal, she initially takes part in the torture, but then kills Matorin, after a horrific fight in which she and Nash battle for their lives. When Dominika regains consciousness in a hospital, General Korchnoi is waiting for her. He then admits that he is Nash's asset, Marble. When she asks him why he is revealing being a double agent, he explains that he believes he will be executed soon, once her uncle figures out who he is. He advises her to give her uncle his name and then take his place as Nash's highly placed operative in Russian intelligence.

Initially, it appears she will do just that. At a spy swap, a hooded figure is unmasked—but it is not General Korchnoi, but rather her uncle. In flashbacks it is revealed that Dominika has framed her uncle as the spy, by placing a glass with Nash's DNA in her uncle's apartment during one of their meetings. As the spy swap commences, an unseen Russian sniper shoots and kills her uncle.

In the film's coda, Dominika receives a commendation and a promotion for her work as a Sparrow. She is later seen caring for her mother in their apartment. Then her phone rings. When she answers, "Grieg's Piano Concerto in A Minor" is playing. Previously, Nash and Dominika had used this piano concerto as a signal. The viewer is left believing that Dominika has become the new Marble for the CIA.

Significance

The novel *Red Sparrow* met with considerable acclaim and won the 2014 Edgar Award for Best First Novel. It also generated two sequels: *Palace of Treason* (2015) and *The Kremlin's Candidate* (2018).

The novel, which impressed critics as a richly textured first effort and a standout in its genre, was better received than the film, which garnered decidedly mixed reviews. Many critics judged the film harshly for its thick overlay of sex and violence and its convoluted plot, which the undeniably talented cast had a hard time carrying. The roles of Lawrence and Edgerton were seen as poorly written, and the couple as lacking on-screen chemistry. Rex Reed, writing in the New York *Observer* (8 Mar. 2018), declared: "Unbearable violence so graphic you endure most of it with your hands covering your eyes, over-written script and hysterical direction so over-the-top it's incomprehensible, and Jennifer Lawrence wallowing in full-frontal nude scenes—the trashy, convoluted *Red Sparrow* has plenty of everything it doesn't need and very little of what it does." In the *Toronto Sun* (1 Mar. 2018), Liz Braun wrote: "As *Red Sparrow* unfolds, you see Dominika get brutalized in various ways...and it's immensely off-putting; there's a voyeuristic element to the violence in *Red Sparrow* that's really creepy." But while many reviewers were put off by the violence, especially centered on a woman protagonist, Manohla Dargis of *The New York Times* was more philosophical: "It's both appealing and crucial that *Red Sparrow* doesn't soft sell Dominika.

There's an attractive, recognizable toughness to her as well as a febrile intensity born from need and circumstances, including the existential reality of being a woman in a man's world."

The film was profitable but not a box-office smash, grossing a worldwide total of $151.5 million, against a production budget of $69 million. Industry analysts speculated whether those numbers would justify adapting the other two novels in Matthews' trilogy.

—*Christopher Mari*

Further Reading

Kilkenny, Katie. "How *Red Sparrow* Author Made the Film More 'Authentically CIA.'" *Hollywood Reporter*, 1 Mar. 2018, www.hollywoodreporter.com/heat-vision/red-sparrow-author-jason-matthews-made-film-authentically-cia-1089625. Accessed 26 Feb. 2019.

McGrath, Charles. "Shadowing Jason Matthews, an Ex-Spy Whose Cover Identity Is Author." *The New York Times*, 27 May 2015, www.nytimes.com/2015/05/28/books/shadowing-jason-matthews-the-ex-spy-whose-cover-identity-is-author.html. Accessed 26 Feb. 2019.

Bibliography

Braun, Liz. "Jennifer Lawrence Can't Save Dull Thriller." Review of *Red Sparrow*, directed by Francis Lawrence. *Toronto Sun*, 1 Mar. 2018, torontosun.com/entertainment/movies/red-sparrow-review-jennifer-lawrence-cant-save-dull-thriller. Accessed 26 Feb. 2019.

Cummings, Charles. "Spy vs. Spy." Review of *Red Sparrow*, by Jason Matthews. *The New York Times*, 31 May 2013, www.nytimes.com/2013/06/02/books/review/red-sparrow-by-jason-matthews.html. Accessed 26 Feb. 2019.

Dargis, Manohla. "'Red Sparrow' Has Spies, Lies and Dirty Dancing." Review of *Red Sparrow*, directed by Francis Lawrence. *The New York Times*, 1 Mar. 2018, www.nytimes.com/2018/03/01/movies/review-red-sparrow-has-spies-lies-and-dirty-dancing.html. Accessed 26 Feb. 2019.

Matadeen, Renaldo. "Red Sparrow's Twist Ending, Explained." *CBR.com*, 3 Mar. 2018, www.cbr.com/red-sparrow-movie-ending-explained/. Accessed 26 Feb. 2019.

Reed, Rex. "'Red Sparrow' Really Makes You Question Jennifer Lawrence's Career Choices." Review of *Red Sparrow*, directed by Francis Lawrence. *Observer*, 8 Mar. 2018, observer.com/2018/03/review-jennifer-lawrence-and-joel-edgerton-fizzle-in-red-sparrow/. Accessed 26 Feb. 2019.

Taylor, Art. "'Red Sparrow,' a Fantastic New Spy Thriller by Former CIA Operative Jason Matthews." Review of *Red Sparrow*, by Jason Matthews. *The Washington Post*, 15 Oct. 2013, www.washingtonpost.com/entertainment/books/red-sparrow-a-fantastic-new-spy-thriller-by-former-cia-operative-jason-matthews/2013/10/15/3f7f9672-cc50-11e2-8845-d970ccb04497_story.html. Accessed 26 Feb. 2019.

The Remains of the Day

The Novel
Author: Kazuo Ishiguro (b. 1954)
First published: 1989

The Film
Year released: 1993
Director: James Ivory
Screenplay by: Ruth Prawer Jhabvala
Starring: Anthony Hopkins, Emma Thompson, Christopher Reeve

Context

The Remains of the Day, a novel by Nobel Prize-winning British novelist Kazuo Ishiguro, was published in 1989. The story begins in 1956, and is told from the perspective of an aging English butler named Stevens. In an article about the book for *The Guardian*, writer Peter Beech described Stevens not as an unreliable narrator, which some readers have called him, but as an "unwitting" narrator: one who remains "trapped in self-preserving fictions." The novel's central achievement is sometimes said to be the skill and sensitivity with which Ishiguro conveys the quiet anguish behind Stevens's unruffled narrative voice. Most of the book is written in the form of a journal, but even at his most private, Stevens remains unable to shake an ethical code that relies on extreme propriety and trust in authority. In flashbacks, the reader watches Stevens lose out on a chance at romantic love and pledge his life, in the form of eager and unquestioning subservience, to a British Nazi sympathizer. (Most of the events of the novel take place in the years before World War II.)

Ishiguro was awarded the Nobel Prize in 2017. He has authored seven novels, among them *A Pale View of Hills* (1982) and *The Unconsoled* (1995). He wrote a well-known and award-winning science fiction novel called *Never Let Me Go* in 2005. Though Ishiguro has explored various genres, he tends to return to the same themes. *The New York Times* aptly described them as the "fallibility of memory, mortality and the porous nature of time." *The Remains of the Day*, Ishiguro's third novel, was published to critical acclaim. It won the Man Booker Prize in 1989. Lawrence Graver, who reviewed it for *The New York Times*, called it "a dream of a book," and "a beguiling comedy of manners that evolves almost magically into a profound and heart-rending study of personality, class and culture." The book is regularly included on lists of contemporary classics. It was fitting, then, that the film adaptation fell into the hands of director James Ivory, producer Ismail Merchant, and screenwriter Ruth Prawer Jhabvala. The Nobel Prize-winning British playwright Harold Pinter, known for works both existential and absurd, optioned the film rights after reading Ishiguro's book in galleys. He wrote an early draft of the script and brought on legendary director Mike Nichols. Unable to secure adequate funding, Nichols stepped down as director, remained as a producer, and offered the directing job to Ivory. Ivory, Merchant, and Jhabvala had previously collaborated on two Academy Award-winning films, *A Room with a View* (1985) and *Howards End* (1992), both adaptations of E. M. Forster novels set among the wealthy in Edwardian England. A similar sensibility—tradition and a studied performance of class distinction—shapes *The Remains of the Day*.

Film Analysis

Jhabvala, the film's Academy Award-winning screenwriter, remains largely faithful to Ishiguro's text. There are however, a few key differences between the stories. The film combines two American characters, making Mr. Lewis (played by Christopher Reeve) both the congressman who expresses reservations about Nazi appeasement in the 1930s and also the man who buys Darlington Hall (Mr. Farraday in the book), thus becoming Stevens's new employer, in the 1950s. The book also offers a more complex portrait of Stevens's father (Peter Vaughan). The film makes little use of an important theme in the book—Stevens's inability to "banter" with Mr. Lewis—which drastically alters the story's ending. In the book, Stevens breaks down in front of a stranger; in the film, he has a more enigmatic conversation with Miss Kenton (Emma Thompson), Darlington Hall's former housekeeper and the object of his affection.

The novel, the story is narrated in the first person—conveyed in Stevens's precise and restrained voice—making his inner conflict that much more agonizing for the reader. In the film, the responsibility for presenting this dramatic irony (the way Stevens sees the world and the way the audience does) is left entirely to Academy Award-winning actor Anthony Hopkins. Hopkins was nominated for an Oscar for his masterful performance. Much of what Stevens says directly in the book is communicated in the film through Hopkins's gestures and facial expressions. His unknowable inner thoughts are manifested in the way he pushes in Lord Darlington's chair, uncharacteristically drops a bottle of wine, or turns his head away from his dying father. Without such a subtle and thorough performance, the film would not work. In this respect, the film bears a similarity to the Academy Award-winning 2017 film *Call Me by Your Name*, also adapted for the screen by Ivory. The original 2007 novel by André Aciman is told from the perspective of an adult man looking back on his teenage romance. The film is more immediate; in it, seventeen-year-old Elio (Timothée Chalamet) experiences first love in real time. Ivory had initially included voice-over narration in his script, acknowledging that the voice of adult Elio was at the heart of the novel. Ultimately, though, the narration was dropped in favor of a more visual language. The same choice was made, successfully, in *The Remains of the Day*.

Stevens represents an old England that disappeared, or at least, lost considerable influence, after the war. At the beginning of the film, Lord Darlington, the last aristocratic owner of Darlington Hall, has died in disgrace and the contents of his vast estate are up for auction. Mr. Lewis, a former American congressman, buys Darlington Hall and in the film, appears to go to some trouble to reassemble it, buying up old paintings and effects. Stevens throws himself into the task of building the estate to its former glory, mildly complaining of the "staffing" problems that prevent him from doing so more efficiently. Director Ivory gives the audience hints that these "staffing" problems are less benign than they might seem. As Stevens bustles from room to room—snake-like passageways and secret servant doors hidden in bookshelves suggest the immensity of the hall's former operation—he sees loafing young butlers and Miss Kenton walking at a brisk clip. When Stevens passes through the space they are in, however, their figures disappear. In the film's first flashback, Ivory deftly reveals both the estate's and Stevens's former glory. In that scene, Lord Darlington is hosting a foxhunt. Dogs, horses, and riders crowd the frame, presenting a marked difference from the emptiness of the film's present day. In the middle of the bustle is Stevens, patiently holding up a silver cup to a man on horseback who does not notice him. The scene conveys Stevens's perverse ideal of "dignity in keeping with one's position." Subservience and loyalty: these are the qualities Stevens has been trained to value, but also the values he will come to question over the course of the film.

The Remains of Day is, in part, about regret. Most obviously, Stevens regrets not expressing his feelings for Miss Kenton, but the well runs a bit deeper than that; thus, the unquantifiable regrets of an old man become a metaphor for the folly of the English aristocracy. The bulk of the film explores the twilight of Darlington Hall in the 1930s. Aristocrats like Lord Darlington wield tremendous power; regretful over the terms of World War I, Darlington aims to use his power to engineer an appeasement deal between England and Germany. At the celebratory dinner that follows this informal summit, the American representative Mr. Lewis gives an uncomfortable but prescient toast. He criticizes the aristocrats as "amateurs." They are not "professional," he argues, meaning that they are not career politicians knowledgeable about negotiation, foreign policy, or war. English tradition and the rules that govern rich men are meaningless in the real world, he says. This sentiment echoes through the rest of the film, as Darlington becomes more sympathetic to Hitler's cause. In one scene, he instructs Stevens to fire two servant girls who are German Jewish refugees. Stevens complies, deferring to an ethical code built upon the innate righteousness of his employer. Miss Kenton is furious—Why is Stevens unable to stand up for what is right when the stakes are so high? The question, manifested in various ways throughout the story, is one Stevens will be left to grapple with as he nears the end of his life, or in the parlance of the novel and film, the "remains" of his day.

Significance

The Remains of the Day premiered in 1993 to critical acclaim. Chicago *Sun-Times* critic Roger Ebert, who awarded the film three and a half out of four stars, wrote that he had thought the book "unfilmable, until I saw this film." He described Ivory, Merchant, and Jhabvala as being "at the height of their powers." Comparing it to Martin Scorsese's subtly heartbreaking adaptation of *The Age of Innocence* (1993), he wrote: "The whole movie is quiet, introspective, thoughtful: A warning to those who put their emotional lives on hold, because they feel their duties are more important." Vincent Canby, for *The New York Times*, described *The Remains of the Day* as "an exquisite work" and "a spellbinding new tragi-comedy of high and most entertaining order." He went further, offering that nothing Ivory, Merchant, and Jhabvala had done before (including two Academy Award-winning films) "has the psychological and political scope and the spare authority of this enchantingly realized film." Years later, this has become a popular opinion; *The Remains of the Day* is widely considered the trio's best film. In addition to the film's artistic merits, Canby also praised it for its "riveting, almost documentary-like sequences showing how such great houses once functioned, how dozens of guests were accommodated, how elaborate meals were prepared, how the servants preserved order among themselves through their own hierarchies." This attention to detail was thanks to Ivory, who hired a former personal attendant to Queen Elizabeth as a consultant.

The Remains of the Day was nominated for eight Academy Awards, including best picture, best director, best actor for Hopkins, best actress for Thompson, and best screenplay adaptation. Hopkins won a British Academy of Film and Television Arts (BAFTA) Award for best actor.

—*Molly Hagan*

Further Reading

Canby, Vincent. "Review/Film: *Remains of the Day*; *Blind Dignity: A Butler's Story*." *The New York Times*, 5 Nov. 1993, www.nytimes.com/1993/11/05/movies/review-film-remains-of-the-day-blind-dignity-a-butler-s-story.html. Accessed 7 Jan. 2019.

Rushdie, Salman. "Salman Rushdie: Rereading *The Remains of the Day* by Kazuo Ishiguro." *The Guardian*, 17 Aug. 2012, www.theguardian.com/books/2012/aug/17/rereading-remains-day-salman-rushdie. Accessed 3 Jan. 2019.

Bibliography

Alter, Alexander, and Dan Bilefsky. "Kazuo Ishiguro Is Awarded the Nobel Prize in Literature." *The New York Times*, 5 Oct. 2017, www.nytimes.com/2017/10/05/books/nobel-prize-literature.html. Accessed 4 Jan. 2019.

Beech, Peter. "*The Remains of the Day* by Kazuo Ishiguro—A Subtle Masterpiece of Quiet Desperation." *The Guardian*, 7 Jan. 2016, www.theguardian.com/books/booksblog/2016/jan/07/the-remains-of-the-day-by-kazuo-ishiguro-book-to-share. Accessed 3 Jan. 2019.

Ebert, Roger. Review of *The Remains of the Day*, directed by James Ivory. *RogerEbert.com*, 5 Nov. 1993, www.rogerebert.com/reviews/the-remains-of-the-day-1993. Accessed 7 Jan. 2019.

Graver, Lawrence. "What the Butler Saw." Review of *The Remains of the Day*, by Kazuo Ishiguro. *The New York Times*, 8 Oct. 1989, www.nytimes.com/1989/10/08/books/what-the-butler-saw.html. Accessed 3 Jan. 2019.

Miller, Frank. "50 Years of Merchant-Ivory: *The Remains of the Day*." *TCM*, 2019, www.tcm.com/this-month/article/430514%7C29865/The-Remains-of-the-Day.html. Accessed 7 Jan. 2019.

Requiem for a Dream

The Novel
Author: Hubert Selby Jr. (1928-2004)
First published: 1978

The Film
Year released: 2000
Director: Darren Aronofsky (b. 1969)
Screenplay by: Darren Aronofsky and Hubert Selby Jr.
Starring: Ellen Burstyn, Jared Leto, Jennifer Connelly, Marlon Wayans

Context

The 1970s was a grim decade for New York City, with white flight, an economic recession, and the drug trade hollowing out many once vibrant neighborhoods. It was against this backdrop of urban decay that Hubert Selby Jr. published his harrowing 1978 novel *Requiem for a Dream*. A native of Brooklyn who dropped out of high school and who struggled with drug addiction himself, Selby wrote in an unorthodox style of people at the bottom of his borough's social and economic ladder. He had faced obscenity charges—and his publisher had been arrested—for his 1961 short story "Tralala," which depicts a prostitute being gang raped. That story became part of his debut novel, *Last Exit to Brooklyn* (1964), which itself faced an obscenity trial in Great Britain. *Requiem for a Dream*, like its predecessor, would explore the darkest realms of human degradation, following four characters who descend into their own versions of hell on earth through the trials of addiction.

Another Brooklynite, Darren Aronofsky, discovered Selby's books in college and was deeply inspired, even drawing on them for a short project while in film school. He went on to become regarded as something of a filmmaking wunderkind; his critically acclaimed first feature, *Pi* (1998) was made on a budget of only around $60,000 but earned $3.2 million. That success gave him many options when looking for a subject for his second feature film, but he turned again to Selby's works. With the encouragement of Pi producer and cowriter Eric Watson, he eventually chose to adapt *Requiem*.

Aronofsky collaborated with Selby himself to write the screenplay, which hews closely to the plot of the novel and includes much of Selby's dialogue. In fact, Selby had previously written a version of his novel for the screen, but he only rediscovered it after already expressing approval of Aronofsky's project; the two compared their drafts and found they were highly similar. Though better financed than he had been for *Pi*, Aronofsky had what was still by Hollywood standards a very low budget for *Requiem*, about $4.5 million. He would later enjoy a much higher-profile status as a director, finding critical and commercial success with bigger-budget films such as *The Wrestler* (2008), nominated for two Academy Awards, and *Black Swan* (2010), nominated for five.

Film Analysis

Like Selby's book, Aronofsky's film begins with protagonist Harry Goldfarb (Jared Leto) hocking his mother's television set to get money for heroin. This has become something of a routine for the two, with his mother, Sara (Ellen Burstyn), following him to the pawn shop to pay to get her set back. It also gets to the heart of their respective addictions: while Harry is hooked on heroin, his mother is no less in thrall to a predatory weight-loss infomercial and to the promise of love and fulfillment that it holds out for her. A supertitle reading "Summer" announces the setting of this first part of the film. It finds its characters at their most innocent and hopeful stage, while the subsequent Fall and Winter sections will follow them down the spiral of addiction.

Harry spends most of his time in the company of his friend Tyrone (Marlon Wayans) and his girlfriend Marion (Jennifer Connelly). All three are heroin addicts, but at this point in the film they are still functional and are able to precariously manage their addictions. Tyrone and Harry are operating a small-time drug dealing operation that is making them money and keeping them supplied with her-

REQUIEM FOR A DREAM

Director Darren Aronofsky. Photo by Andriy Makukha via Wikimedia Commons.

oin. Marion, with Harry's help, is pursuing her dream of opening a dress shop that would showcase her fashion designs. All of this unfolds in the Brighton Beach and Coney Island area of Brooklyn, New York, and Aronofsky's on-location filming captures the faded glory of these seaside neighborhoods.

Selby's text is a demanding one. Its absence of quotation marks, lack of paragraphs, and its multi-page sentences put demands on the reader to interpret and reorder what he or she encounters on the page. The film is equally demanding, and Aronofsky's use of techniques such as split-screens and extreme close-ups challenges the viewer to track these four characters' overlapping lives. As Peter Travers wrote in his review for *Rolling Stone*, "Aronofsky, cinematographer Matthew Libatique and editor Jay Rabinowitz assault the senses with jump cuts, split

screens and jarring, distorted images to show lives spiraling out of control." Indeed, the highly stylized editing and other filmmaking techniques not only effectively portray the experiences of the characters, but also directly engage viewers in the chaotic sensations. Perhaps most notable is the rapid-fire montage used to represent the characters taking heroin and the high that accompanies.

While Harry, Marion, and Tyrone's growing heroin addiction is visceral, it is in many ways typical of narratives about drug abuse. Yet when speaking about the film, Aronofsky repeatedly suggested it is not at its core about drugs or drug users, but rather addiction itself, love, and the negative effects of trying to escape reality. Selby, too, argues in the preface to the novel that his real subject is the destruction that comes from giving up one's own personal vision for the pursuit of wealth or accomplishment. The materialistic American Dream is depicted as a poor substitute for the love and fulfillment that people truly desire. This is where Sara Goldfarb's story proves vital as a counterpoint to the heroin story line. Already arguably addicted to television, she starts using prescription diet pills—amphetamines—after getting a phone call about the possibility of appearing on her favorite TV show, hoping to lose enough weight to fit into the red dress she once wore to her son's graduation. Her addictions are clearly different from those of Harry and his friends, but no less damaging. Meanwhile, Aronofsky's infomercial-within-the-movie, with its ingratiating host and earworm buzzwords and catchphrases, is a powerful satire of commercialism.

As summer gives way to fall and then winter, all four of the film's protagonists slide ever further into addiction and degradation. In a scene that is reported secondhand in the book, but that the film portrays explicitly, Tyrone witnesses the execution of his heroin supplier by a rival gang. He is arrested as he escapes the scene, forcing Harry to use most of their earnings to bail him out. With the city's supply of the drug suddenly drying up, Harry, Tyrone, and Marion begin to suffer withdrawal and to consider ever more desperate measures to get their next high.

Sara, too, slips into a nightmarish state. In her first few weeks of taking pills, she was filled with energy and with a manic optimism; now, she has become paranoid and delusional. Like the novel, the film collapses the line between objective reality and Sara's hallucinations. Her refrigerator begins to menace her, and eventually lurches away from the wall and attacks her. The host of her favorite TV show begins talking to and about her, and a more glamor-

330 NOVELS INTO FILM: ADAPTATIONS & INTERPRETATIONS

ous, composed Sara—wearing the red dress—begins to appear on the show. Towards the climax of Sara's storyline, stagehands enter her apartment to remove the walls and furniture, revealing that she is on a television soundstage. The success of all of these surreal scenes is grounded in the strong performance of Burstyn, which earned high praise from Aronofsky and others involved in the production. She reportedly spent four hours each day having makeup and prosthetics applied to perfect her various looks throughout the film, and also wore two different weight-adding suits and many different wigs.

The final scenes of the film find each of the four characters in desperate circumstances that closely follow the book. Sara puts on her red dress and goes to the Manhattan office of a television studio to plead to be on her show. Clearly delusional, she is taken away and committed to a psychiatric ward to undergo electric shock therapy. Harry and Tyrone set off on a disastrous road trip to Florida to try to score heroin directly from the source. However, Harry's heavily injected arm becomes seriously infected, forcing them to stop at a hospital, where they are arrested for drug use. Tyrone ends up facing racist taunts in a Southern prison while going through withdrawal, while Harry has his arm amputated in the hospital. Marion, suffering withdrawal and without any source of heroin, sells herself into sexual slavery in exchange for drugs. Aronofsky cuts between these four stories in rapid-fire fashion, creating a montage-like climax that unites the four protagonists in the misery of their fates even as they are otherwise isolated from each other.

While the strong acting, bold direction, and stylized editing are key to the successful film adaptation of *Requiem*, the film's sound design is also important. Composer Clint Mansell, who had worked with Aronofsky on *Pi* and went on to collaborate with him on later films as well, was crucial in developing the affecting score. While the director originally envisioned a soundtrack filled with hip-hop music, Mansell eventually suggested some instrumental ideas that fit with the idea of the film itself as a requiem. The final soundtrack, performed by the Kronos Quartet, mirrors the building intensity throughout the film.

Significance

Requiem for a Dream was screened at the Cannes Film Festival in early 2000, where it immediately began attracting controversy for its graphic drug use and sexual imagery. That summer the Motion Picture Association of America (MPAA) labeled the film NC-17, primarily because of a sequence toward the end of the film in which Marion and another woman put on a degrading sex show for a crowd of men. Aronofsky and Artisan Entertainment, the studio that had produced the film, contested the decision, but were unable to get the rating overruled. They ultimately decided to release both an unrated version of the film and an edited version that carried an R rating. For the edited version, Aronofsky substituted less graphic alternate footage for the closing scenes.

Upon its general release in the fall of 2000, reviews were highly polarized and it performed modestly at the box office, earning about $3.6 million domestically and $7 million worldwide. Some critics saw it as a masterpiece. Travers, for example, wrote that "no one interested in the power and magic of movies should miss it." He and other reviewers commended all four of the main actors, noting Leto's dramatic weight loss for the role and suggesting that both Connelly and Wayans surpassed any of their previous work. But Burstyn received the most accolades, and was nominated for an Academy Award for best actress. However, some critics saw Aronofsky's filmmaking as showy or self-indulgent. Writing for the *Washington Post*, Stephen Hunter implored, for example, "Can't you just make the movie and forget about the style?" Yet even many of the film's detractors agreed that it marked Aronofsky as a virtuoso filmmaker.

Indeed, *Requiem* launched Aronofsky's career into bigger-budget productions. In the years following its release, the film garnered something of a cult status and is cited frequently as an important film that was underappreciated in its own time. A 2016 BBC poll of international critics even selected it as one of the greatest films of the twenty-first century. The soundtrack also proved to have great staying power of its own, and has been used in a variety of other media.

—*Matthew Bolton*

Further Reading

Giles, James Richard. *Understanding Hubert Selby, Jr.*. U of South Carolina P, 1998.

Laine, Tarja. *Bodies in Pain: Emotion and the Cinema of Darren Aronofsky*. Bergahn Books, 2015.

Skorin-Kapov, Jadranka. *Darren Aronofsky's Films and the Fragility of Hope*. Bloomsbury Academic, 2016.

Bibliography

Aronofsky, Darren, and Hubert Selby. *Requiem for a Dream: Screenplay*. Faber, 2000.

Goodridge, Mike. "MPAA Slams NC-17 Rating on Artisan's Requiem." *Screen Daily*, 22 Aug. 2000, HYPERLINK www.screendaily.com/mpaa-slams-nc-17-rating-on-artisans-requiem/403357.article. Accessed 5 Dec. 2018.

Hunter, Stephen. "'Requiem:' An Overdose of Tricks." Review of *Requiem for a Dream*, directed by Darren Aronofsky. *The Washington Post*, 3 Nov. 2000, www.washingtonpost.com/wp-srv/entertainment/movies/reviews/requiemforadreamhunter.htm. Accessed 20 November 2018.

Mitchel, Elvis. "Film Review; Addicted to Drugs and Drug Rituals." Review of *Requiem for a Dream*, directed by Darren Aronofsky. *The New York Times*, 6 Oct. 2000, www.nytimes.com/2000/10/06/movies/film-review-addicted-to-drugs-and-drug-rituals.html. Accessed 20 November 2018.

Selby, Hubert, Jr. *Requiem for a Dream*. 1978. Penguin, 2012.

Snider, Eric D. "12 Addictive Facts about Requiem for a Dream." *Mental Floss*, 16 Sept. 2015, mentalfloss.com/article/68660/12-addictive-facts-about-requiem-dream. Accessed 5 Dec. 2018.

Travers, Peter. Review of *Requiem for a Dream*, directed by Darren Aronofsky. *Rolling Stone*, 11 December 2000, www.rollingstone.com/movies/movie-reviews/requiem-for-a-dream-118844/. Accessed 5 Dec. 2018.

The Revised Fundamentals of Caregiving / The Fundamentals of Caring

The Novel
Author: Jonathan Evison (b. 1968)
First published: 2012

The Film
Year released: 2016
Director: Rob Burnett (b. 1962)
Screenplay by: Rob Burnett
Starring: Paul Rudd, Craig Roberts, Selena Gomez, Jennifer Ehle

Context
The Revised Fundamentals of Caregiving (2012) was author Jonathan Evison's third novel, after *All about Lulu* (2008) and the bestselling *West of Here* (2011), which established his reputation for handling heavy topics in a sensitive and humorous manner. *Fundamentals* follows Ben, who is dealing with a tragic loss, a separation from his wife, and difficulty finding a job. Desperate for something to do, he takes the titular course, a twenty-eight-hour training that certifies him to serve as a full-time caregiver to a person with a disability. Assigned to a hostile nineteen-year-old named Trevor, or Trev, Ben finds the job harder than he expected, but when he agrees to embark on a cross-country road trip to reunite Trev with his long-absent father, it proves to be a healing experience for them both.

Like his protagonist, Evison was recently divorced; struggling in his career, having tried for years to get a book published without success; and had suffered a tragedy, the death of his older sister in a car accident at the age of sixteen. He is also a certified caregiver, working three years as a full-time caregiver for a boy who, like Trev, had Duchenne muscular dystrophy (DMD). During that time, the two did take a road trip together. The further details of the plot, however, are not autobiographical.

Director Rob Burnett is best known as the longtime executive producer of the *Late Show with David Letterman*. He had directed only one film prior to *The Fundamentals of Caring* (2016), the independent *We Made This Movie* (2012), which was released to little fanfare. *We Made This Movie* follows five twelfth graders who, seeing limited prospects for their future in their poor, rural town, try to gain stardom by making a comedy film. The film shares with *Fundamentals* a blend of comedy and drama and a focus on teens in difficult situations.

Fundamentals was widely compared by critics to *Me Before You* (2016), which also focuses on the relationship between a person with disabilities and his caregiver; however, the relationship in *Me Before You* is romantic, and the film is less comedic. *Fundamentals* also provoked comparisons to the French buddy drama *The Intouchables* (2011), which also features a caretaker and charge who form something of a mentoring or pseudo-parental relationship. In that film, however, the younger man is the caretaker, which results in somewhat of a different dynamic between the two men.

Film Analysis
The Fundamentals of Caring roughly follows the plot of the book, but it does make some changes. In the film, Trevor, sometimes called Trev (Craig Roberts), sticks to a strict schedule that keeps him mainly in his living room; however, he has an interest in odd roadside attractions, such as the biggest cow and the deepest pit in the United States. While he maps these out, Trevor expects never to see them for himself. It is this that prompts Ben (Paul Rudd) to take Trev on a road trip. Only once underway does Trev decide that he wants to visit his father, whose attempts to get in touch Trev has been studiously ignoring up to this point. The film also places greater emphasis on Trev's romance with Dot (Selena Gomez), a hitchhiking runaway whom Trev and Ben pick up during the trip.

In the book, Trev's character is heavily defined by his anger and crassness. The reader may have sympathy for his situation, and he does come to show more emotional vulnerability later on, but he is a difficult character to like. The film may have intended to make the character more immediately endearing by introducing his quirky hobby of researching roadside attractions and giving an immediate hint, through his initial refusal to take the trip, that his hostility is a layer of bravado covering up sadness and fear. The emphasis on the romance similarly softens his character, especially as he is notably shy around Dot.

In both the book and the film, Ben goes from refusing to sign divorce papers at the beginning to agreeing to sign them at the end, symbolizing his move from denial to acceptance of the tragedy in his past. Trev, while not a static character in the novel, does not have such a straightforward, clear-cut journey. The film gives him an arc that somewhat mirrors Ben's, as he initially refuses to move past his hurt and anger at his father leaving when he was young, but at last comes to terms with the situation and is therefore willing to accept his father's tentative efforts to mend the relationship. The decision to have him avoid contact with his father for most of the film before finally agreeing to see him during the trip provides a clear arc of character growth for Trev. In combination with the film's move away from Ben's perspective (he is the novel's first-person narrator), this makes Trev seem like more of a coprotagonist in the film than in the book.

The film also makes changes to Ben, albeit somewhat less extensively. Ben in the novel had two children, one of whom died in a freak accident and the other of whom lives with Ben's estranged wife; the film cuts the surviving child and spends less time on the ex-wife in general. This seems to serve as a way to streamline the plot for the restrictions of the medium; the book is long and slow-paced in a way that a film cannot be. (The road trip portion of the book is, in fact, only about half of its length.)

In both the film and the book, Ben is a former stay-at-home father, but in the film he is also a novelist who "retired" after his son's death but is shown at the end to have written a novel based on his experiences with Trev. This makes him slightly more of a stand-in for Evison than Evison's own version of the character; the change may have been meant as a tribute to the author, but its impact on the film is limited to providing an additional way, beyond the signing of the divorce papers, of demonstrating that Ben has moved past his trauma by the film's end.

Perhaps the most significant change is that in the novel, Ben and Trev bond largely through long conversations in which they objectify women in very explicit terms. In the film, this is replaced with a sort of friendly rivalry in which the two engage in an escalating series of pranks against one another. Dirty jokes or comments about women do appear several times in the film—including a conversation about an attractive weather forecaster and an off-color joke about singer Katy Perry—but are far less prominent. While the novel was well regarded, some reviewers did find the conversations between Ben and Trev to be off-putting, so the film may have wanted to reduce the prominence of this somewhat controversial aspect. The prank war aspect then serves to retain the novel's sense that Ben and Trev's relationship is built on a foundation of edgy, inappropriate humor.

The filmmaking techniques used are largely unobtrusive, encouraging viewers to remain focused on the dialogue and acting. However, there are a few scenes in which the camerawork and editing aim to be something other than simply transparent. For example, a scene in which Ben (retaliating for an earlier prank by Trev) plays a joke on Trev that goes too far is shot in long takes that drag out the moment and underscore the awkwardness. The early scenes showing Ben's integration into Trev's unglamorous daily routines make use of montage, which makes the pre-road trip portion of the film shorter than the corresponding section of the book. In addition, the film slices together the broadly shot current events with closely shot flashbacks in order to slowly reveal what happened to Ben's son. This tactic proves to underscore Ben's current actions with events of the past, while leaving the audience guessing at the full scope of events until the very end of the film.

The decision to spend less time on Ben and Trev's daily life and more time on the road trip may be due to the fact that the road trip is more visually interesting. It provides an opportunity for many landscape shots that showcase natural beauty, which emphasizes what Trev has previously been missing by refusing to leave the house.

Significance

Fundamentals premiered at the Sundance Film Festival and was subsequently released for streaming on Netflix. The book received mostly positive reviews, but responses to the film were more mixed. Many critics praised Rudd's acting in the lead role, and Roberts's performance was also well regarded, although several reviewers pointed out the film's place in a trend of actors without disabilities portraying characters with disabilities. Regardless, reviewers largely felt that the two actors played off one another well.

There was also praise for the opening scenes of the film, which focus on the unpleasant minutiae of caregiving and establish that Trev is a sarcastic, foul-mouthed, prank-loving teenage boy rather than a saintly, tragic figure. Once the road trip begins, however, these elements are downplayed, and many felt that this portion of the film became saccharine and formulaic. Katie Rife, for the *AV Club*, for example, commented positively on the early parts of the film for "irreverently depicting the humiliating-yet-hilarious minutiae of Ben and Trevor's daily routines," but noted that "the story starts to take a turn for the precious" when the road trip begins. Brian Tallerico, for RogerEbert.com, agreed that the film "really loses focus" at that point.

Critics also noted that the aesthetic was unoriginal: from the camerawork (described by Geoff Berkshire for *Variety* as "adequate") to the soundtrack of soft indie rock (which, Rife noted, "even has ukulele," a well-established cliché of indie dramedies).

The film's greatest significance may be as an indicator of Netflix's then-nascent ambitions of establishing itself as a player in the film industry and not merely a licensor of others' content. *Fundamentals* was the company's seventh original film. The first five were lightweight comedies that were not released anywhere outside of Netflix; the sixth was the acclaimed war drama *Beasts of No Nation* (2015), which premiered at the Venice Film Festival and went on to be screened at independent film festivals around the world. *Fundamentals*, with its Sundance premiere, signaled Netflix's continued interest in producing serious independent films.

—*Emma Joyce*

Further Reading

Evison, Jonathan. "Filling Holes." *Jonathan Evison: The Revised Fundamentals of Caregiving*, s3.amazonaws.com/algonquin. site.features/revisedfundamentals/author-essay.html. Accessed 9 Apr. 2021.

Gilmore, Jennifer. "Assisted Living." Review of *The Revised Fundamentals of Caregiving*, by Jonathan Evison. *The New York Times*, 7 Sept. 2012, www.nytimes.com/2012/09/09/books/review/the-revised-fundamentals-of-caregiving-by-jonathan-evison.html. Accessed 12 Apr. 2021.

Bibliography

Berkshire, Geoff. "Sundance Film Review: *The Fundamentals of Caring*." Review of *The Fundamentals of Caring*, directed by Rob Burnett. *Variety*, 23 Jan. 2016, variety.com/2016/film/reviews/the-fundamentals-of-caring-film-review-sundance-1201686813. Accessed 9 Apr. 2021.

Rife, Katie. "*The Fundamentals of Caring* Is a Quirky Trip to a Familiar Destination." Review of *The Fundamentals of Caring*, directed by Rob Burnett. *AV Club*, 23 June 2016, film.avclub.com/the-fundamentals-of-caring-is-a-quirky-trip-to-a-famili-1798188208. Accessed 9 Apr. 2021.

Tallerico, Brian. "*The Fundamentals of Caring*: Two Stars." Review of *The Fundamentals of Caring*, directed by Rob Burnett. *RogerEbert.com*, 24 June 2016, www.rogerebert.com/reviews/the-fundamentals-of-caring-2016. Accessed 9 Apr. 2021.

The Road

The Novel

Author: Cormac McCarthy (b. 1933)

First published: 2006

The Film

Year released: 2009

Director: John Hillcoat (b. 1961)

Screenplay by: Joe Penhall

Starring: Viggo Mortensen, Charlize Theron, Kodi Smit-McPhee

Context

Cormac McCarthy is widely regarded as one of the greatest novelists of the late twentieth and early twenty-first centuries. His dense, complex writing style has been compared to Shakespeare, Herman Melville, and the Bible, and he is known for focusing on parables of good and evil, marked by intense violence. After several early efforts, including *Suttree* (1979), McCarthy achieved a career breakthrough with the highly praised *Blood Meridian* (1985), about a frontier gang in the mid-1800s. He continued to explore Western settings in what became known as the Border Trilogy, consisting of the National Book Award-winning *All the Pretty Horses* (1992), *The Crossing* (1994), and *Cities of the Plain* (1998). These were followed by *No Country for Old Men* (2005), another violent Western but in a contemporary setting.

McCarthy published his tenth novel, *The Road*, in 2006. Like his earlier works it was critically acclaimed, and among other awards it won the Pulitzer Prize. It also continued his exploration of both the bleak and hopeful sides of humanity, while at the same time introducing new dimensions to his writing. The story concerns an unnamed protagonist and his young son making their way across a postapocalyptic North America. Though much of the broader context is ambiguous—What disaster preceded this apocalypse? What will happen once the characters reach their destination, the coast?—many reviewers considered it one of McCarthy's more accessible books. This was in part due to its powerful depiction of the bond between father and son. While McCarthy earned a reputation as a recluse by rarely granting interviews, he noted at the time of the book's release that the idea for *The Road* came to him while traveling with his own young son and imagining what the landscape might be like in the future.

Much of the pleasure of reading McCarthy lies in his compelling, artful prose. For example, from *The Road*:

He walked out in the gray light and stood and he saw for a brief moment the absolute truth of the world. The cold relentless circling of the intestate earth. Darkness implacable. The blind dogs of the sun in their running. The crushing black vacuum of the universe. And somewhere two hunted animals trembling like ground-foxes in their cover. Borrowed time and borrowed world and borrowed eyes with which to sorrow it.

Elsewhere, the demands on the reader are enhanced by a trademark minimalism regarding punctuation. Because of its literariness, critics for years maintained that his work was poorly suited for film adaptation. However, the popularity of his books made attempts at adaptation all but inevitable. The first example was the film version of *All the Pretty Horses* (2000), which earned largely negative reviews and flopped at the box office. Far more successful was *No Country for Old Men* (2007), directed by Joel and Ethan Cohen, which won four Academy Awards. A 2013 adaptation of McCarthy's 1973 novel *Child of God* was mostly panned.

After earning attention with his Australian-set Western *The Proposition* (2005), director John Hillcoat took on the task of bringing *The Road* to the screen. British playwright Joe Penhall, who adapted Ian McEwan's novel *Enduring Love* for film in 2004, was hired to write the screenplay. In part because of Hillcoat's Australian background, the filmmakers sought to deliberately avoid similarities to the well-known Australian Mad Max films starring Mel Gibson, which portray a highly stylized postapocalyptic world. Instead, they aimed for realism, in everything from the sets and costumes to the dialogue and performances.

Hillcoat communicated extensively with McCarthy while working on the project, though the author did not directly contribute to the script and gave his approval of the film developing as its own work.

Film Analysis

Penhall's script is remarkably faithful to the novel, following the same plot arc of a Man (Viggo Mortensen) and Boy (Kodi Smit-McPhee) traveling southward across a devastated landscape vaguely recognizable as the eastern United States. The main alteration is an expanded story line involving the Woman—the Man's wife and the Boy's mother—played in flashbacks by Charlize Theron. The film opens with colorful shots of a house surrounded by trees and flowers. The viewer is offered a glimpse of the Man and Woman in blissful domesticity. But then the Man wakes up in the middle of the night. Outside the window there are flashes of light and sounds of people yelling. He begins filling buckets of water. Hillcoat intercuts these scenes—the run-up to the disaster and the early fallout from it—with the main plot of the film involving the travels of the Man and his son.

As in the book, the pair are working their way toward the coast with a grocery cart holding their few possessions. The most important of these is an old revolver with only two remaining bullets—one for the Man and one for the Boy. Why should the two need to shoot themselves? The answer soon presents itself in the form of a marauding gang. With the collapse of society and ecological devastation, scarcity of food has become dire, and many survivors have turned to cannibalism. It is revealed that fear of falling victim to such a gang led the Woman to give up hope and ultimately commit suicide. In the present, the Man is forced to shoot a gang member in a confrontation, using one of their precious bullets.

In the book, the story is told in short, brutal episodes. The film strings these episodes together alongside the expanded backstory to illustrate the duo's journey toward the sea. The filmmakers dutifully re-create most of the violence of McCarthy's book, though they omit a particularly gruesome scene in which the Man and the Boy come across a newborn infant roasting on a spit. They do include, however, the scene in which the Man and Boy stumble across a locked cellar door in an old Victorian house while searching for supplies. In the cellar they discover a roomful of people being held captive, some missing limbs because their captors are eating them one ap-

Author Cormac McCarthy. Photo by David Styles, Public domain via Wikimedia Commons.

pendage at a time. The Man and Boy narrowly escape. Such depraved imagery is McCarthy's hallmark. His visions of violence do not merely disgust but disturb; he provokes his readers to imagine human nature as inherently evil. The film version of *The Road* does not delve quite as far into this darkness, but it remains capable of shocking.

Yet *The Road* is a rarity among McCarthy's works in that it also offers a hopeful glimpse of true goodness, and this too is carried over in the film. Unlike the Man, the Boy bristles at every act of violence, even when it is committed against one of the so-called bad guys. He is a Christlike figure, forcing his father to help people, such as the Old Man (Robert Duvall) they encounter, when the Man would prefer not to. The Boy also makes his father promise that they will never eat anyone, no matter how hungry they get. He anxiously reminds himself of the enigmatic phrase he father once told him: that they will survive because they are "carrying the fire."

This undefined fire is metaphorical in a world where even flames appear leached of color. McCarthy's story describes an environment almost wholly gray with ash and soot, and cinematographer Javier Aguirresarobe, known for his work on *The Others* (2001) and *Vicky Cristina Barcelona* (2008), played a major part in bringing this bleak scenery to life. Aguirresarobe and Hillcoat realized that they needed to begin by blocking out the light of the sun, a formidable task. This guiding principle makes every scene appear suffused in gray shadow. Any brighter light (other than in the flashbacks) is created by fire—from matches, candles, bonfires, or in one scene near the end of the film, flames from a flare gun. Of course, changing weather across more than fifty shooting locations made this sunless illusion difficult to maintain. Sometimes, the film was treated in processing to remove any errant color.

Although *The Road*, unlike many of McCarthy's best-known novels, does not take place in the Old West or even the western United States, both the book and movie versions nevertheless make use of certain themes and characteristics of classic and revisionist Westerns. Chief among these is the emphasis on the landscape, both natural and human-made. The cinematography and sets highlight the barrenness of the world the characters must face, from freezing woods to abandoned hulks of cars and ships. The eerily empty buildings echo the ghost towns of the West, and the Man and Boy engage in a classic struggle against nature as they try to stay warm and fed. Meanwhile, the cannibal gangs resemble the bandits of countless Westerns, taken to an extreme of total lawlessness. Indeed, the postapocalyptic world is like a heightened Wild West in the way social norms hold little value, illustrated by images such as heads on spikes and the actions of various characters. Just as many other Westerns and science fiction works before it, *The Road* uses its physical and social setting in symbolic and metaphorical ways to explore desperation and human nature.

Significance

Upon its premiere in 2009, *The Road* was not a box office success. It earned just $8.1 million domestically against a $25 million production budget, though it performed better internationally to bring its total gross to $27.6 million. Industry analysts suggested that a late decision to postpone its release until near Thanksgiving in the hopes of earning

Oscar considerations backfired, as most holiday moviegoers were not interested in the bleak, R-rated film. It also failed to garner any Academy Award nominations, though Aguirresarobe was nominated for a British Academy of Film and Television Arts (BAFTA) Award for best cinematography.

Despite these disappointments, McCarthy himself was reportedly happy with the adaptation, and the film was met with mostly positive reviews. Though some critics felt it did not live up to the original novel, many others suggested it did an admirable job of visualizing very difficult source material. Leading reviewers tended to praise the film, especially the lead performances and the story's social commentary, while acknowledging that a few flaws kept it from being a masterpiece. For example, writing for *The New York Times*, A. O. Scott commended "just how fully the filmmakers have realized this bleak, blighted landscape of a modern society reduced to savagery," and noted the influence of zombie movies. Yet he felt the film, while quite dark, did not find the same extremes of horror and utter despair that make the final notes of hope so powerful in the book. "'The Road' is engrossing and at times impressive, a pretty good movie that is disappointing to the extent that it could have been great," Scott concluded. In a review for *The Guardian*, Peter Bradshaw offered a similar take, describing the film as a "respectful" adaptation. "This is undoubtedly a serious, powerful, well-acted movie," he wrote, "but I can't fully share the critical enthusiasm it has widely gained elsewhere because of what seemed to me its fractional reluctance to confront the nightmare fully."

—*Molly Hagan*

Further Reading

Hage, Erik. *Cormac McCarthy: A Literary Companion*. McFarland, 2010.

Ibarrola-Armendariz, Aitor. "Cormac McCarthy's *The Road*: Rewriting the Myth of the American West." *European Journal of American Studies*, vol. 6 no. 3, 2011, doi:10.4000/ejas.9310. Accessed 5 Feb. 2019.

Peebles, Stacey. *Cormac McCarthy and Performance: Page, Stage, Screen*. U of Texas P, 2017.

Bibliography

Adams, Tim. "Cormac McCarthy: America's Great Poetic Visionary." *The Guardian*, 19 Dec. 2009, www.theguardian.com/theobserver/2009/dec/20/observer-profile-cormac-mccarthy. Accessed 5 Feb. 2019.

Bradshaw, Peter. Review of *The Road*, directed by John Hillcoat. *The Guardian*, 7 Jan. 2010, www.theguardian.com/film/2010/jan/07/the-road-review. Accessed 5 Feb. 2019.

Hart, Hugh. "*The Road* Takes Desolate Journey from Page to Screen." *Wired*, 24 Nov. 2009, www.wired.com/2009/11/the-road-page-to-screen/. Accessed 4 Feb. 2019.

Hillcoat, John. "John Hillcoat, *The Road*." Interview by Damon Smith. *Filmmaker Magazine*, 24 Nov. 2009, filmmakermagazine.com/1396-john-hillcoat-the-road/. Accessed 5 Feb. 2019.

McGrath, Charles. "At World's End, Honing a Father-Son Dynamic." *The New York Times*, 27 May 2008, www.nytimes.com/2008/05/27/arts/27iht-27road.13242016.html. Accessed 5 Feb. 2019.

Scott, A. O. "Father and Son Bond in Gloomy Aftermath of Disaster." Review of *The Road*, directed by John Hillcoat. *The New York Times*, 24 Nov. 2009, www.nytimes.com/2009/11/25/movies/25road.html. Accessed 5 Feb. 2019.

Smith, Joelle. "A Q&A with *The Road* Cinematographer Javier Aguirresarobe." *New York Film Academy*, 19 June 2017, www.nyfa.edu/film-school-blog/a-qa-with-the-road-cinematographer-javier-aguirresarobe/. Accessed 5 Feb. 2019.

The Secret Garden

The Novel
Author: Frances Hodgson Burnett (1849-1924)
First published: 1911

The Film
Year released: 1993
Director: Agnieszka Holland (b. 1948)
Screenplay by: Caroline Thompson
Starring: Kate Maberly, Maggie Smith, Heydon Prowse

Context

English author Frances Hodgson Burnett published her novel *The Secret Garden* in 1911. A classic of children's literature, the book tells the story of a young girl named Mary Lennox. An English child born and raised in colonial India, ten-year-old Mary is the only survivor of a deadly cholera outbreak. She moves to England an orphan. Mary's adventures at her reclusive uncle's estate, Misselthwaite Manor, and her discovery of a locked and overgrown garden constitute the heart of Burnett's coming-of-age tale. *The Secret Garden* sold well when it was first published but was largely forgotten for several decades before enjoying a renaissance beginning in the 1960s. Dinitia Smith wrote for *The New York Times* that the novel gives children, especially young female readers, "the hope that somewhere there is a secret place away from adult scrutiny, where they can find order in the chaos of their loneliness." In her time, author Burnett's fame, Smith wrote, could be likened to that of J. K. Rowling, the author of the Harry Potter series, in the early twenty-first century. Burnett is also the author of the well-known book *Little Lord Fauntleroy* (1886) as well as the enduring classic *A Little Princess* (1905). Biographers have suggested that *The Secret Garden* sprang from tragedy; Burnett's sixteen-year-old son, Lionel, died from tuberculosis in 1890. A decade later, she ended her violently abusive second marriage and, in the process, lost her beloved English manor, where she had tended to a garden and tamed a robin. Readers of *The Secret Garden* will recognize both details from the book.

The Secret Garden has enjoyed numerous adaptations for the stage and screen. Before the 1993 version, there was a film adaptation in 1949, a 1975 BBC special, and an Emmy Award-winning television movie in 1987. A new version of the story began filming in 2018. The 1993 adaptation was directed by Polish filmmaker Agnieszka Holland. Holland, who was attracted to the project because she had loved the book as a child, was then best known for writing and directing the German Holocaust drama *Europa, Europa* in 1990. She was nominated for an Academy Award for Writing (Screenplay Based on Material Previously Produced or Published), though Germany, controversially, did not submit the film for consideration for Best Foreign Language Film. Holland later directed a number of films and episodes of television shows in different languages to critical acclaim. There are no common themes that define her diverse body of work outside, as Holland has stated, a lack of sentimentality. This sensibility was particularly important to *The Secret Garden*, a familiar and beloved story that, poorly told, could easily become saccharine.

Film Analysis

Screenwriter Caroline Thompson—known for a handful of young-adult classics such as *Edward Scissorhands* (1990), *The Addams Family* (1991), and *The Nightmare Before Christmas* (1993)—changed a few large aspects of Burnett's story, in addition to a number of small ones. The film begins in India, where the unhappy ten-year-old Mary Lennox (Kate Maberly) tries desperately to win her aloof mother's affection. One night, a dangerous earthquake strikes, and both of her parents die. In the book, they die of cholera, and Mary, the only survivor, is left alone and forgotten in her crypt-like house for several days. Holland and Thompson capture this sense of terrible isolation in a scene in which Mary breaks one of her mother's prized objects, a small ivory elephant, and dives under the bed to avoid getting caught. She watches her parents come into the room, only to leave again and die in the crumbling palace. Thompson also changes the story so that Mary's mother and the late Lady Craven, the owner of the secret garden, are twin sisters. Mary later discovers a matching ivory elephant that belonged to her aunt; the connection between the two dead women suggests that when Mary learns about her aunt, it brings her closer to her mother. These changes allude to a bond between Mary and her mother that is absent in the book. Otherwise, the change has little effect on the story.

Both the book and the film explore, literally and metaphorically, concepts of illness and health. In the book, Burnett suggests that physical illness in India springs from a larger moral illness inherent in the culture. Thompson expunges Burnett's racism in her decision to have Mary's parents die in an earthquake. After her parents' death, Mary arrives at Misselthwaite Manor in the winter. The grounds are dead and bare, and the imposing manor itself is cold and austere. Most of the hundred rooms are closed off, in quarantine after the death of Lady Craven ten years before. The grief felt by Lord Craven (John Lynch) is contagious; it spreads through the house like a disease. This metaphor is made literal in the form of ten-year-old Colin (Heydon Prowse), Lord Craven's sickly son. It is unclear exactly what disease Colin is supposed to be suffering from, but he is too weak to walk or even see sunlight. Household servants must wear a face mask in his presence. It is unlikely that he has ever left his bedroom. In the film, Colin's diligent caretaker is the housekeeper, Mrs. Medlock (Maggie Smith). Determined to keep him alive, she insists on all manner of so-called modern treatments for her charge. In one scene, she gives his legs a jolt with an electric device operated by a hand crank. Mary's ailments, also borne of grief and loneliness, manifest themselves in different ways. She is selfish, spoiled, and cruel. She does not know how to treat people who are not hired to serve her.

The advent of spring marks an awakening for the film's characters. As plants and animals emerge from hibernation, so too do the characters choose to embrace a spring-like vitality. Mary pours her energy into nursing the secret garden back to life and in the process, makes her first real friend, her maid's little brother, Dickon (Andrew Knott). Dickon has an uncanny knack with animals; rabbits, horses, deer, and birds will follow him anywhere. His peculiar talent is mirrored in Mary's newfound abilities as

a gardener. Working together, the garden flourishes beyond their wildest dreams. This sense of wonder—or "Magic," as the children call it in the novel—is beautifully captured in the film, under the guidance of director Holland and Academy Award-winning production designer Stuart Craig. The garden in the film is characterized by wildness, Craig told Matt Wolf for *The New York Times*, stating that "the house is a prison, so you want to escape into the wilderness." The set still fits with Holland's unsentimental vision, though: "This is a story about something very real," Holland told Wolf. "Yorkshire is Yorkshire; the garden is a garden. You want something symbolic without becoming too theatrical." Veteran cinematographer Roger Deakins, who won an Academy Award in 2017, further captures the transformative effects of the garden through time-lapse photography of flowers budding.

Author Frances Burnett. Photo by Herbert Rose Barraud via Wikimedia Commons.

After befriending her lonely and tyrannical cousin, Mary becomes determined to cure him. She and Dickon scheme to bring Colin to the garden and let the Magic do its work. Mary never believed that Colin was truly ill, or, as Mrs. Medlock believes, dying. As the two spend more time together, Colin becomes braver, sitting in the sunlight, sneaking to meet Mary in other parts of the house, and ultimately deciding to venture into the garden himself. He orders Mrs. Medlock to allow him to go outdoors. Holland captures the climactic scene with humor, arranging Mary, Dickon, and Colin in his wheelchair at the top of the grand staircase, and the entire household staff, wearing absurdly unnecessary face masks, blocking their path at the bottom. The children win out, of course, and soon Colin's health improves and harmony is restored to the manor. There are problems with Burnett's rendering of illness and health—people can be ill and disabled; ability has no bearing on one's moral character—but the effects of the garden do not merely cure Colin, they awaken him to the beauty that can be found in life, nature, and loving relationships with other people.

Significance

The film, released in 1993, was popular with audiences and most critics. In 2005, the British Film Institute listed it among fifty films that children should see before they turn fourteen. Critics who were unimpressed by the film, such as Owen Gleiberman for *Entertainment Weekly*, tended to describe it as inferior to its source. Gleiberman wrote that the film lacked the book's "aura of spectral enchantment, the sense that the overgrown garden literally has a life of its own." The late film critic, Roger Ebert, however, was effusive in his praise of the film, awarding it four out of four stars. "Some 'children's films' are only for children," he wrote. "Some can be watched by the whole family. Others are so good they seem hardly intended for children at all, and *The Secret Garden* falls in that category. It is a work of beauty, poetry and deep mystery, and watching it is like entering for a time into a closed world where one's destiny may be discovered." Janet Maslin, writing for *The New York Times*, described the film as "elegantly expressive" but also "discreet." Both critics identified Holland's skill as a visual storyteller, and her canny avoidance of "the preciousness that is this story's greatest liability," as

Maslin put it. In Mary's curious wanderings, the audience understands the depth of her loneliness; in her furious weeding and planting, how determinedly she has chosen to cling to hope.

—*Molly Hagan*

Further Reading

Bowman, Sabienna. "A New *Secret Garden* Movie Is Happening & It'll Take '90s Kids Right Back to Their Childhoods." *Bustle*, 12 May 2018, www.bustle.com/p/a-new-secret-garden-movie-is-happening-itll-take-90s-kids-right-back-to-their-childhoods-9068509. Accessed 26 Nov. 2018.

Clark, Anna. "*The Secret Garden*'s Hidden Depths." Review of *The Secret Garden*, by Frances Hodgson Burnett. *The Guardian*, 5 Aug. 2011, www.theguardian.com/books/2011/aug/05/secret-garden-frances-hodgson-burnett. Accessed 26 Nov. 2018.

Bibliography

Ebert, Roger. Review of *The Secret Garden*, directed by Agnieszka Holland. *Roger Ebert*, 13 Aug. 1993, www.rogerebert.com/reviews/the-secret-garden-1993. Accessed 21 Nov. 2018.

Gleiberman, Owen. Review of *The Secret Garden*, directed by Agnieszka Holland. *Entertainment Weekly*, 13 Aug. 1993, ew.com/article/1993/08/13/secret-garden-2/. Accessed 26 Nov. 2018.

Gritten, David. "On Location: Tending Her Dark 'Garden:' Agnieszka Holland, Who Explored the Horrors of the Holocaust in 'Europa, Europa,' Is Finding Murky Depths in a Children's Classic." *Los Angeles Times*, 1 Nov. 1992, articles.latimes.com/1992-11-01/entertainment/ca-1589_1_europa-europa. Accessed 26 Nov. 2018.

Maslin, Janet. "Review/Film; Blossom Time for a Lonely Girl." Review of *The Secret Garden*, directed by Agnieszka Holland. *The New York Times*, 13 Aug. 1993, www.nytimes.com/1993/08/13/movies/review-film-blossom-time-for-a-lonely-girl.html. Accessed 21 Nov. 2018.

Smith, Dinitia. "Books of the Times; In a Topsy-Turvy Life, Finding Her Secret Garden." Review of *Frances Hodgson Burnett: The Unexpected Life of the Author of The Secret Garden*, by Gretchen Holbrook Gerzina. *The New York Times*, 28 July 2004, www.nytimes.com/2004/07/28/books/books-of-the-times-in-a-topsy-turvy-life-finding-her-secret-garden.html. Accessed 21 Nov. 2018.

Wolf, Matt. "Film; *The Secret Garden* and How It Grew." Review of *The Secret Garden*, directed by Agnieszka Holland. *The New York Times*, 8 Aug. 1993, www.nytimes.com/1993/08/08/movies/film-the-secret-garden-and-how-it-grew.html. Accessed 21 Nov. 2018.

The Secret Life of Walter Mitty

The Novel
Author: James Thurber (1894-1961)
First published: 1939

The Film
Year released: 2013
Director: Ben Stiller (b. 1965)
Screenplay by: Steve Conrad
Starring: Ben Stiller, Kristen Wiig, Jon Daly, Kathryn Hahn, Terence Bernie Hines, Shirley MacLaine

Context

The 2013 film *The Secret Life of Walter Mitty* was based on the short story of the same name written by the American author and cartoonist James Thurber. It was published in *The New Yorker* in March 1939. Thurber had been a contributor to the magazine since 1927, when he began serving as its managing editor and staff writer. His first illustration appeared in the magazine in 1930. After leaving *The New Yorker* in 1933, he continued to contribute to it regularly for much of the remainder of his life.

Thurber's writings and illustrations often portrayed the frustrations of life in the modern world through humor. Walter Mitty is a quintessential Thurber character: a mild-mannered man pestered by a nagging wife, who escapes into elaborate, heroic daydreams. Although Thurber published numerous short stories, which were later collected in such volumes as *Fables for Our Time* (1940), *My World—and Welcome to It* (1942), *The Thurber Carnival* (1945), and *Credos and Curios* (1962), "The Secret Life of Walter Mitty" is ranked among his most popular.

The story has been adapted twice for the silver screen, each time taking liberties with its source material. The first version, released in 1947, starred Danny Kaye as the title character. In it, Mitty is no longer a henpecked husband but is an editor of the popular pulp fiction magazines of the era. In the 2013 film version directed by and starring Ben Stiller, Mitty is a socially awkward but incredibly responsible office worker who is in charge of *Life* magazine's photo negatives department. Just before the magazine is about to end its print run and turn into a digital platform, he must attempt to find a missing negative that will be the photo cover of the final issue.

Stiller, who is a prolific comedic actor, has also directed a number of films, including *Reality Bites* (1994),

Zoolander (2001), *Tropic Thunder* (2008), and *Zoolander 2* (2016). He brought a new version of *Walter Mitty* to the screen after it had been in development for many years. According to reports, noted comedians such as Jim Carrey, Mike Myers, and Sacha Baron Cohen have wanted to be featured in a new version.

Film Analysis

The 2013 film *The Secret Life of Walter Mitty*, directed by and starring Ben Stiller, is markedly different from its source material. Its tagline, "Stop Dreaming, Start Living," reveals that much. In the original story, Mitty cannot get out of his own head to live a better life. In the film version, Mitty must get out of his own head in order to start living. When he does, he discovers that he has incredible courage and drive.

In the Thurber story, Mitty's first fantasy—being a commander of a hydroplane—is interrupted when his wife interrupts him to say she thinks he's driving too fast. After he pulls up to the building where she's getting her hair done, she orders him to buy overshoes. Before he pulls away, he puts on gloves—at his wife's insistence—which then sends him into a fantasy about removing his gloves as a famous surgeon. Mitty goes from one daydream to another. When he leaves the surgeon fantasy behind, he becomes a murder suspect, then a war hero, and finally, he faces a firing squad with a smile.

As previously noted, the 2013 film jettisons the specifics of Thurber's tale of Mitty and instead re-imagines it. The film's Mitty cares for his aging mother Edna (Shirley MacLaine) and his sister Odessa (Kathryn Hahn), while managing the negatives of *Life* magazine's photo department. The viewer discovers Mitty had planned to travel the world when he was younger, but then his father died, leaving him to provide for his family. Because of this, Mitty has an active fantasy life in which he imagines himself as a superhero capable of zipping into fires or as a dashing mountain climber. What he is unable to do is ask out his coworker Cheryl Melhoff (Kristin Wiig), either in person or via an online dating site.

The story begins in earnest when he arrives at work to discover that *Life* is being closed and will survive only as an online version. It also means that he and many of his fellow workers will likely be fired. However, they must still print the final issue, with a cover photo by legendary photojournalist Sean O'Connell (Sean Penn), who still shoots on film. Although Mitty and O'Connell have never met, they have considerable respect for each other; O'Connell even gives Mitty a wallet with *Life*'s motto inscribed inside.

Ben Stiller. Photo by Eva Rinaldi via Wikimedia Commons.

After opening O'Connell's last set of negatives, Mitty discovers that the one O'Connell wants to use—number 25—is missing. What's more, O'Connell himself is missing. Because O'Connell never uses a cell phone while out on assignment, Mitty must come up with a way to find him. At Cheryl's suggestion, Mitty uses the clues left on his last role of negatives to track O'Connell down. The photos are of a ship, a person's thumb with a strange ring on it, and a curved piece of wood. The photo of the ship leads Mitty to Greenland, where the ship is docked. There at a bar he discovers that O'Connell has been there. He also meets a drunken pilot, who tells Mitty that he is flying out to that particular ship to deliver the mail. Initially, Mitty is reluctant to get on the helicopter, but then he's inspired to do so when he imagines Cheryl singing David Bowie's "Space Oddity."

Mitty reaches the ship and learns that O'Connell is no longer onboard. When the crew offers him Clementine cake—his mother's favorite—he learns of O'Connell's next destination through an itinerary scratched out on the cake's wrapping paper. Mitty then travels to Iceland, where he attempts to find O'Connell photographing a volcano. In order to get there, he trades with a local boy for his skateboard and he uses his skateboarding skills from his youth to get there in record time. Unfortunately, just as he's about to close in, the volcano erupts. Shortly thereafter, *Life*'s new bosses demand that he produce the negative and call him back to New York.

Upon his return, he's fired and goes to visit Cheryl, who was fired earlier, and her young son, who he knows enjoys skateboarding. When he arrives at her front door, however, he finds her ex-husband there. Believing the former spouses have reconciled, he leaves the skateboard he got in Iceland. He returns to his apartment, where his mother is staying. He tosses the wallet O'Connell gave him in the garbage, then sits in the living room, where he recognizes that the curved piece of wood he saw in one of O'Connell's photographs is actually the curve of his mother's piano. He asks his mother about it; she confirms that she met O'Connell and that she had told him about it earlier but that he was off in a daydream. His mother helps him learn that O'Connell is in the Himalayas attempting to photograph a snow leopard.

Mitty begins an arduous trek up the Himalayas and finds O'Connell who he then asks about the missing negative. O'Connell explains to him that he tucked the negative inside the wallet he had given Mitty. Mitty returns home and tells his mother what happened. She hands over the wallet that she had retrieved from the garbage. Mitty then returns to *Life* with the negative, criticizes the new management for the heartless way they treated the longtime employees, and departs. He is soon reunited with Cheryl, who is not making up with her ex, and was there simply to help her repair her broken refrigerator. They then pass a newsstand where they see the cover of the final issue of *Life*: a picture of Mitty himself outside the *Life* magazine offices holding up a contact sheet. They then take one another's hands and walk down the avenue.

Significance

The critical response to *The Secret Life of Walter Mitty* was somewhat mixed but generally favorable. In a review for *Time*, Richard Corliss called it "a lovely romantic comedy—the portrait of a man, nearly swallowed by the gulf between the world he lives in and the world he dreams of, who manages to bridge the two and to find Ms. Right in the workplace he cherishes." Chris Nashawaty, in *Entertainment Weekly*, was more critical, noting, "Stiller seems to lack the confidence as a dramatic actor to fully commit to the emotional potential of his story. Too often he aims at our funny bones when he should be targeting our heartstrings."

The film was a commercial success. With a $90 million budget, it earned box-office receipts of about $188 million. It premiered at the New York Film Festival in October 2013 and received a wide release on Christmas Day. It was also named one of the top 10 films of the year by the National Board of Review. Whether this film version of *The Secret Life of Walter Mitty* proves to have the enduring popularity of Thurber's short story remains to be seen.

—*Christopher Mari*

Further Reading
Editors of the Encyclopedia Britannica. "James Thurber: American Writer and Cartoonist." *Britannica.com*, 4 Dec. 2019, www.britannica.com/biography/James-Thurber. Accessed 15 Apr. 2020.
Setoodeh, Ramin, and Dave McNary. "Ben Stiller on Hollywood's Long Journey with *The Secret Life of Walter Mitty*." *Variety*, 3 Dec. 2013, variety.com/2013/film/news/ben-stiller-on-hollywoods-long-journey-with-the-secret-life-of-walter-mitty-1200911759/. Accessed 16 Apr. 2020.

Bibliography
Corliss, Richard. "*The Secret Life of Walter Mitty*: Ben Stiller's Dream of Life." *Time*, 23 Dec. 2013, entertainment.time.com/2013/12/23/the-secret-life-of-walter-mitty-ben-stillers-dream-of-life/. Accessed 15 Apr. 2020.
Nashawaty, Chris. "*The Secret Life of Walter Mitty* Movie." *Entertainment Weekly*, 7 Jan. 2014, ew.com/article/2014/01/07/secret-life-walter-mitty-movie/. Accessed 15 Apr. 2020.
Scott, A. O. "He Can Balance a Checkbook, but Not His Imagination." *The New York Times*, 24 Dec. 2013, www.nytimes.com/2013/12/25/movies/the-secret-life-of-walter-mitty-stars-ben-stiller.html. Accessed 15 Apr. 2020.
"*The Secret Life of Walter Mitty*." *IMDb.com*, www.imdb.com/title/tt0359950/?ref_=ttfc_fc_tt. Accessed 16 Apr. 2020.
Thurber, James. "*The Secret Life of Walter Mitty*." *The New Yorker*, 18 Mar. 1939, www.newyorker.com/magazine/1939/03/18/the-secret-life-of-walter-james-thurber. Accessed 15 Apr. 2020.

Shiloh

The Novel
Author: Phyllis Reynolds Naylor (b. 1933)
First published: 1991

The Film
Year released: 1996
Director: Dale Rosenbloom (b. 1964)
Screenplay by: Dale Rosenbloom
Starring: Michael Moriarty, Blake Heron, Scott Wilson, Ann Dowd, Bonnie Bartlett, Rod Steiger

Context
Shiloh is a 1996 film written and directed by Dale "Chip" Rosenbloom and based on the 1991 Newbery Medal-winning children's book of the same name written by Phyllis Reynolds Naylor. A prolific children's book author who had by 1991 written no less than sixty-four books, Naylor became inspired to write *Shiloh* after encountering an abused dog while on a walk with her husband along a river near Shiloh, West Virginia. Emotionally devastated by the encounter, Naylor resolved to take action by making animal cruelty, and the ethics of animal abuse, central to the plot of her next book. The resulting novel was an instant critical and commercial success, and Naylor was the recipient of numerous honors. It became an instant favorite with libraries and a fixture in many elementary English classrooms.

The book eventually came to the attention of Dale Rosenbloom, a graduate of the University of Southern California Film School, who had begun his independent filmmaking career in 1990 with the release of the teen drama *Across the Tracks* starring a young, up-and-coming Brad Pitt. Rosenbloom followed up his debut with made-for-television movies *Nails* and *Ride with the Wind* and was looking for new stories to develop for the screen when he discovered Naylor's novel. *Shiloh* looked well-positioned to take advantage of the family drama craze sweeping Hollywood in the mid-1990s. Films such as *Beethoven* (1992), *Homeward Bound* (1993), and *Wild America* (1997), featuring child actors and animals, and developed on relatively small budgets, were proving highly profitable for studios.

Rosenbloom secured the rights to the novel from Naylor and wrote the script. Rosenbloom would also go on to produce and direct the film himself. Blake Heron, a

child actor best known for his starring role in 1995's *Tom and Huck*, was cast in the lead of Marty, with Frannie, a trained Beagle, brought in to play the title role. Veteran character actors Michael Moriarty of *Law & Order* fame, Scott Wilson, best known for his roles on *In the Heat of the Night* and *The Great Gatsby*, and Ann Dowd, of *Green Card* and *Lorenzo's Oil*, were brought in to round out the cast. Joel Goldsmith, up to that time best known for his work on *The Untouchables* television series, was tapped to write and compose the musical score. Filming took place primarily in Topanga, California.

Film Analysis
While the primary message remains intact, the film version of *Shiloh* departs from the book in its form, structure, and plot. First and foremost, the book is written from the perspective of Marty (Heron). It is written in the first person, complete with the sorts of grammatical errors and hayseed tone one would expect from a boy growing up in the rural South.

The film, necessarily dispensing with a first-person perspective, is shot traditionally as a fast-paced action drama. Furthermore, while much of the plot of the book's story plays out through conversation, the film is much more action-packed, with Rosenbloom having added several action sequences, including a fight between Judd (Wilson), the owner of the puppy and Marty's father Ray (Moriarty). The action in the film, just as in the book, begins when a puppy escapes from his abusive owner and is found by Marty. The boy takes the puppy home and remodels an abandoned shack for the dog. Despite clear evidence of abuse and the fact that Marty has started bonding with Shiloh (Frannie), Marty's strict father demands that Marty return the dog to its rightful owner. The relationship between father and son is juxtaposed with the relationship between boy and dog, and the latter is used as a catalyst by which to define the former. Marty decides to hide Shiloh in the abandoned shack in defiance of his father, but his secret is soon discovered by his mother Louise (Dowd). Here again the relationship between father and son is made more complicated, with the mother figure coming into the fray between them. Louise's help is immediately undermined when Shiloh is attacked by another dog. Again, the power and authority of the father at the expense of that of the mother is confirmed. To find resolution, father and son must reach accord, or at least the father must give his blessing. After a trip to the doctor, Ray, who is still insistent on returning the puppy to Judd, also begins to bond with Shiloh.

Eventually, Marty approaches Judd with a deal: he will work on Judd's property, doing odd jobs and chores, until he has earned the right to keep Shiloh outright. Judd agrees. The way events transpire in this crucial scene depart greatly from those in the book. In the book, Marty approaches Judd about making a deal over Shiloh, but as he's approaching Judd's house, he witnesses the hunter shoot a deer. This is consequential as Marty is then able to use the killing of the deer—which was illegal as Judd shot the deer during off season—as leverage to get Judd to agree to the deal over the dog. By removing the blackmail from the film, Rosenbloom creates a Marty who is much less morally complex. Although the blackmail doesn't really go very far in the book, the threat is completely eliminated with the removal of the deer scene.

In the book, Marty and Judd have clear motivations and are willing to use various means to get what they want. The film simplifies some of the moral complexity of the novel. It also expands the story somewhat. While in the book the conflict is strictly about Marty and Judd, the film reframes it to include Rick, who Marty chastises for not standing up to Judd. We eventually learn that Judd was abused by his father, which in turn made him abusive toward his animals. When Marty tells Judd that dogs are like kids, and if you mistreat them, they are bound to run away, to which Judd responds that he never ran away when his father beat him. After Marty works hard on his property, Judd tells Marty that their deal is off as there were no witnesses to their agreement. Judd and Marty fight, but Marty continues to work on Judd's property, determined to force Judd into holding up his end of their agreement.

The final resolution comes when Judd shows up at Marty's house in an attempt to take his dog back by force. An argument between Judd and Ray ensues, which then devolves into a physical altercation. Judd manages to grab Shiloh all the same and tries to escape in his truck, but at the last minute, reconsiders his position. Glancing at Marty in his rearview mirror, Judd decides to open his car door allowing Shiloh to run back into Marty's arms. The film closes with the Sheena Easton song "Are There Angels" over images of Marty and Shiloh walking together, happily side by side.

The book contains no fight between Judd and Ray. The focus of the book is entirely on the relationship between Judd and Marty, and Judd's slow redemption. At the end of the novel, it is Judd's budding friendship with Marty that convinces him to give up Shiloh, and we would hope, become a better man in the end. By reframing the conflict to ultimately involve Ray, the film centers the story on Marty's relationship with his father. In this telling, more of the character development rests with Ray, who we see turn from a strict, distant father into one who will stand up for his son. In this sense, Shiloh is a stand-in for Marty. While Ray does not physically abuse Marty, his emotional distance makes him seem like an uncaring father, abusive through neglect. And so, the act of Ray fighting for his son and Judd releasing Shiloh have much of the same emotional resonance.

Significance

Shiloh premiered at the Heartland Film Festival on November 8, 1996 and was released for wide distribution on April 25, 1997. Generally, the film was well-received by critics, who applauded the film for its examination of animal cruelty and complex moral questions. It went on to have an opening weekend box office of $115,710 and grossed a cumulative $1 million worldwide.

Based on the success of the film, Rosenbloom decided to adapt two more books from the Shiloh series, Shiloh 2: Shiloh Season, which was released in 1999, and Saving Shiloh, released in 2006. While Rosenbloom did write and produce both films, directing was passed to Sandy Tung. Blake Heron did not make an appearance in the sequels; however, Scott Wilson and Ann Dowd reprised their roles in both. Tragically, Heron, who would have some limited acting successes in the years that followed Shiloh's release, died of a drug overdose in 2017.

While Shiloh failed to receive much award attention, the film did pick up a few notable honors. These included a Crystal Heart Award from the Heartland International Film Festival, a 1998 Genesis Award presented by the Humane Society, and a Children's Jury Award from the Chicago International Film Festival. While *Shiloh* did not break any records at the box office, nor did it reinvent filmmaking, *it does* remain a much-liked classic coming-of-age story about a boy and his dog, and the imperative to treat all living things humanely.

—*KP Dawes, MA*

Further Reading

Beech, Linda Ward. *Scholastic Book Guides: Shiloh by Phyllis Reynolds Naylor*. Scholastic, 2003.

Mills, Claudia. "The Structure of the Moral Dilemma in *Shiloh*." *Children's Literature*, 1999, Johns Hopkins UP, vol. 27, pp. 185-97.

Morris, Timothy. *You're Only Young Twice: Children's Literature and Film*. University of Illinois Press, 2000.

Bibliography

Ebert, Roger. "*Shiloh*." *RogerEbert.com*, 25 Apr. 1997, www.rogerebert.com/reviews/shiloh-1997. Accessed 14 Apr. 2020.

Gates, Anita. "A Mistreated Dog and a Boy with a Mission." *The New York Times*, 25 Apr. 1997, www.nytimes.com/1997/04/25/movies/a-mistreated-dog-and-a-boy-with-a-mission.html. Accessed 14 Apr. 2020.

McNary, Dave. "*Shiloh* Star Blake Heron Dies at 35." *Variety*, 8 Sept. 2017, variety.com/2017/film/news/blake-heron-dead-dies-shiloh-1202552485/. Accessed 14 Apr. 2020.

"Shiloh." *IMDb*, www.imdb.com/title/tt0120118/. Accessed 14 Apr. 2020.

"Shiloh." *Rotten Tomatoes*, www.rottentomatoes.com/m/shiloh. Accessed 14 Apr. 2020.

Silver Linings Playbook

The Novel
Author: Matthew Quick (b. 1973)
First published: 2008

The Film
Year released: 2012
Director: David O. Russell (b. 1958)
Screenplay by: David O. Russell
Starring: Bradley Cooper, Jennifer Lawrence, Robert De Niro, Jacki Weaver, Brea Bee, Chris Tucker

Context

In 2006, Matthew Quick was a tenured New Jersey high school English teacher who also coached basketball and soccer. Suffering from anxiety and depression, Quick quit his job to begin writing his first novel. The result was *Silver Linings Playbook* (2008). The novel is told from the point of view of narrator Pat Peoples, a former high school history teacher who is being released from the "bad place," a neural health facility in Baltimore. He does not know how long he has been confined. He does not remember what he did to be placed there, nor how he got a scar on his face. All he knows is that he wants to end "apart time," separation from his wife Nikki. To accomplish that goal, he will do anything necessary to improve himself enough for Nikki to take him back, so that the movie of their life will have a happy ending, a "silver lining." His loving, supportive mother, Jeanie, drives him home to Collingswood, New Jersey, where he becomes an inmate of a different sort of asylum. Pat's father, Pat Senior, district manager of a grocery chain, is a violent, taciturn man obsessed with the fortunes of the Philadelphia Eagles football team. Upon his return home, Pat suspects his family and friends—also rabid Eagles fans, who drag him to weekly home games—are hiding information about his immediate past. He experiences frightening hallucinations, and has to adapt to a new psychiatrist, Dr. Patel, an Indian American.

Pat embarks upon his self-improvement campaign. To become buff, he exercises compulsively and jogs wearing a trash bag for maximum perspiration. He reads books his wife teaches in her English classes. Along the way, he meets Tiffany, a troubled new widow. Tiffany makes a bargain with Pat. If he will train to perform with her in a dance contest, she will circumvent restraining orders to serve as a liaison between Pat and his estranged wife.

However, the budding relationship between Pat and Tiffany has unexpected consequences.

In 2007, before publication, *Silver Linings Playbook* was optioned by Sydney Pollack and Anthony Minghella for production by The Weinstein Company. David O. Russell was named director—this would be his first adaptation. Russell's credits include the critically acclaimed film *The Fighter* (2010). Unfortunately, beginning in 2008, bad luck caused several delays, beginning with the deaths of both Pollack and Minghella. Vince Vaughn and Zooey Deschanel, for whom the adaptation was initially written, had other commitments. Another pair of potential leads, Mark Wahlberg and Anne Hathaway, also bowed out. Finally, after numerous rewrites, Bradley Cooper and Jennifer Lawrence agreed to do the film. A thirty-three-day shoot was planned for Philadelphia and its environs in the fall of 2011.

Film Analysis

While the film adaptation of *Silver Linings Playbook* (2012) remains essentially the story of how two damaged people with the capacity to heal one another got together romantically, much was changed in the process of bringing the novel to the big screen. A number of key scenes in the novel—such as a dinner date built around a single-serving box of Raisin Bran and a cup of tea—were reproduced exactly. Some dialogue was transferred verbatim. Certain plot points were also eliminated, and new subplots were added. The chronology of events was shifted to a significant degree so secrets could be revealed sooner. The subtle humor of the novel (such as a clumsy explanation of why the hero's wedding photos are missing) was replaced by broad humor and visual gags sometimes tending to slapstick. Though the fanaticism of the community for the local professional football team (a constant thread throughout the novel) is retained, it is toned down and redirected into a new subplot. There are no groups spelling out "E-A-G-L-E-S!" with gestures akin to the Village People's rendition of "YMCA." Pale imitations (face painting, jerseys, team merchandise) represent the simmering intensity of home games against particularly hated rival National Football League (NFL) teams.

The novel is told in the first person by an unreliable narrator suffering from bipolar disorder; he even sees and hears things that the reader knows aren't there. Because the narration focuses to a great extent on the protagonist's inner experiences in an profoundly intimate way, modifications were necessary to tell the story in the language of cinema. Russell's adaptation, using mostly Steadi-cam in enclosed spaces, creates its own experience of intimacy, a sort of "fly on the wall" experience (the director of photography was Masanobu Takayanagi). The final script spotlights the film's greatest strength—an excellent cast. A storytelling device important in the novel—a series of letters exchanged between Pat (Bradley Cooper) and his estranged wife Nikki (Brea Bee) via new friend Tiffany (Jennifer Lawrence)—also have presented cinematic production problems. These communications are condensed to one typed letter, which contains a vital clue to a plot twist.

Significant differences exist between novel and film in the treatment of major characters. For example, Pat (for no obvious reason his surname switched in ethnicity from Irish American, Peoples, to Italian American, Solitano), is confused, fragile, almost childlike in Quick's novel. He does not learn until late in the story that he actually spent four years in the asylum, and the real reason he was put there. In the adaptation, Pat is considerably more confident and assertive. He has spent only eight months in the mental hospital and knows exactly why he was confined. At home, there is no basement equipment that his devoted mother bought him for his daily ten-hour workout, only his sweaty trash bag-encased ten-mile runs. One jogging sequence presents an unresolved issue with continuity. In the film, Pat is shown being discharged from Baltimore State Mental Hospital (because Baltimore is where he and his wife lived and taught, and where he committed the offense that caused him to be legally institutionalized). Yet on his runs around his New Jersey hometown, he stops by the high school to terrorize the principal, Nancy (Patsy

Bradley Cooper. Photo by Georges Biard via Wikimedia Commons.

Meck), and visits the house he and his wife owned before their breakup.

Tiffany, too, is both younger and more outspoken than initially written. Her backstory is largely intact (wife of sex addict cop husband, wracked by guilt when he was killed, who lost her job when she slept with everybody in the office). The adaptation hints Tiffany may still be sleeping around because three different new characters hit on her in ways that suggest they know about her promiscuous reputation.

There are a number of secondary characters original to the adaptation. One is a bookie, Randy (Paul Herman), who figures prominently in a fresh plot diversion. Another is a cop, Officer Keogh (Dash Mihok) who shows up at several disturbances at different places. It's as if he is the only policeman in town and is always on duty. He interacts with Tiffany as the widow of a brother law enforcer. Nikki, an unobtainable object of desire, is only seen from a distance late in the novel, is physically present at several venues, and offers the possibility of reunion with Pat, an unrealistic outcome. Some existing roles were expanded, like Pat's best friend Ronnie (John Ortiz), and Pat's fellow former asylum inmate Danny (Chris Tucker). One missing character is Emily, simply called "the baby" on-screen. Emily is the young daughter of Ronnie and wife Veronica (Julia Stiles), Tiffany's niece, with whom Pat interacts in the novel in a tender and fatherly fashion.

The most startling transformations in the film are Pat's parents. The former football-hating Jeanie Peoples, now Dolores Solitano (Jacki Weaver), once a vital contributor to her son's well-being, has been reduced to a caricature: the maternal stereotype, who mainly smiles or cries on cue. More radical is the portrayal of Patrizio Solitano (Robert De Niro). Certainly, casting someone of De Niro's stature as a silent, brooding figure would not take full advantage of his considerable talents. However, the quality of his character is completely changed. He is charming, talkative, caring, and his violent tendencies have vanished—he even sings a duet of "Young at Heart" with his wife, something entirely out of character for Pat Peoples Sr. Moreover, Patrizio is now an illegal book-maker, even more compulsive and superstitious than originally conceived, and willing to risk everything on a sucker's bet.

Significance

Silver Linings Playbook gained wide approval among cinema fans and reviewers, becoming a critical and commercial success. In addition to Academy Award nominations for Best Picture and Best Director, it was the first film since *Reds* (1981) to be nominated for all four lead (Cooper and Lawrence) and supporting (De Niro and Weaver) acting roles. Jennifer Lawrence, after being nominated for her work in *Winter's Bone* (2010), took home her first acting Oscar and also collected top honors from the Screen Actors Guild (SAG) and the Golden Globes. Both the film and director Russell garnered recognition at several other awards venues. *Silver Linings Playbook* also did well at the box office, returning gross revenues of over $235 million, a more than tenfold return on a budget of $21 million.

An unexpected advantage of the acclaim was that the popular film helped raise public awareness of mental health challenges. This was a significant factor in David O. Russell's enthusiasm for the project from the start. He has a bipolar son, who as a teenager was cast as a neighbor, Ricky (Matthew Russell) in the film. Russell and members of the cast appeared before federal legislators to promote mental health care reform and discuss related issues.

Author Matthew Quick went on to write a string of bestsellers. Since his debut, he has published several young adult novels, beginning with *Sorta Like a Rock Star* (2010). He has also written adult novels, including *The Good Luck of Right Now* (2014), which has been optioned for adaptation and is in development at DreamWorks.

—*Jack Ewing*

Further Reading

Fast, Julie A., and John D. Preston. *Loving Someone with Bipolar Disorder: Understanding and Helping Your Partner*. 2nd ed., New Harbinger Publications, 2012.

Seger, Linda. *The Art of Adaptation: Turning Fact and Fiction into Film*. Henry Holt & Company, 1992.

Bibliography

Brownfield, Paul. "Oscars: The 'Very Specific World' of *Silver Linings Playbook*." *Deadline*, 23 Dec. 2012, deadline.com/2012/12/oscars-silver-linings-playbook-389548/. Accessed 15 Apr. 2020.

Hughes, Mark. "Director David O. Russell Talks *Silver Linings Playbook* and What It Means to Him." *Forbes*, 18 Feb. 2013, www.forbes.com/sites/markhughes/2013/02/18/director-david-o-russell-talks-silver-linings-playbook-what-it-means-to-him/#505683af33df. Accessed 15 Apr. 2020.

Orr, Christopher. "*Silver Linings Playbook*: A Clear-Headed Comedy about Mental Illness." *The Atlantic*, 16 Nov. 2012, www.theatlantic.com/entertainment/archive/2012/11/silver-linings-playbook-a-clear-headed-comedy-about-mental-illness/265327/. Accessed 15 Apr. 2020.

Poling, Margaret. "*Silver Linings Playbook*." *The Encyclopedia of Greater Philadelphia*, 2018, philadelphiaencyclopedia.org/archive/silver-linings-playbook/. Accessed 15 Apr. 2020.

Quick, Matthew. *Silver Linings Playbook*. Sarah Crichton Books/Farrar, Straus and Giroux, 2012.

Siegel, Tatiana. "Making of *Silver Linings Playbook*." *The Hollywood Reporter*, 4 Dec. 2012, www.hollywoodreporter.com/news/making-silver-linings-playbook-397396. Accessed 15 Apr. 2020.

Strecker, Erin. "Q&A with *Silver Linings Playbook* Author Matthew Quick." *Entertainment Weekly*, 6 Feb. 2013, ew.com/article/2013/02/06/silver-linings-playbook-matthew-quick-jennifer-lawrence/. Accessed 15 Apr. 2020.

Slumdog Millionaire / Q & A

The Novel
Author: Vikas Swarup (b. 1963)
First published: 2005

The Film
Year released: 2008
Director: Danny Boyle (b. 1956), Loveleen Tandan
Screenplay by: Simon Beaufoy
Starring: Dev Patel, Freida Pinto, Madhur Mittal, Anil Kapoor, Irrfan Khan

Context

Slumdog Millionaire is a 2008 film directed by Danny Boyle and Loveleen Tandan and was based on the 2005 book *Q & A* written by Vikas Swarup, a career diplomat who began writing as a hobby. He was inspired by the works of fellow Indian authors V. S. Naipaul and Suzanna Arundhati Roy to write a book exploring societal issues, but he wanted to combine these themes with a more action-filled, thriller-like plot. *Q & A*, Swarup's first novel, was a surprise success, receiving widespread critical acclaim and winning the Boeke Prize, a South African award modeled on the Man Booker Prize. It was also shortlisted for the Commonwealth Writers' Prize. Swarup went on to write *Six Suspects* (2008) and *The Accidental Apprentice* (2013), both of which feature the same combination of social commentary and exciting plots.

Boyle, a British director with a somewhat eclectic career, first came to prominence in the mid-1990s with the black comedy crime films *Shallow Grave* (1994) and *Trainspotting* (1996). *Shallow Grave* won the British Academy Film Award (BAFTA) for Best British Film and earned Boyle the 1996 British Newcomer of the Year award from the London Critics Circle, while *Trainspotting* provoked slightly less immediate enthusiasm, it proved more enduring. In 1999, the British Film Institute named *Trainspotting* the tenth-best film of the twentieth century. Boyle's next success was *28 Days Later* (2002), a horror film about zombies. He then went on to direct *Sunshine* (2007), a science-fiction thriller that flopped at the box office. In many ways, *Slumdog Millionaire*'s tone, style, and subject matter were a departure for Boyle, but its frenetic pace is a characteristic it shares with many of the director's earlier works .

Tandan, an Indian filmmaker, had served as second assistant director on the international hit romantic comedy *Monsoon Wedding* (2001). *Slumdog Millionaire*'s success failed to launch her career, however, and she had no subsequent credits.

Slumdog Millionaire is in many ways a traditional rags-to-riches story, widely compared by reviewers to Charles Dickens's *Oliver Twist* (1838) for its portrayal of urban poverty and children in desperate situations being drawn into the criminal underworld. It also stands as part of a trend in the first decade of the twenty-first century of

Director Danny Boyle. Photo by gdcgraphics via Wikimedia Commons.

films about India made primarily for Western audiences, including *Monsoon Wedding* as well as such films as *Bride and Prejudice* (2004) and *The Darjeeling Limited* (2007). While many of these films, including *Slumdog Millionaire*, were well received by critics, the trend also drew criticism for what some saw as a tendency to portray India in a shallow and exoticized fashion and to treat serious issues in Indian society as opportunities for melodrama.

Film Analysis

Q & A and *Slumdog Millionaire* share a basic premise: a young man from the slums of Mumbai becomes a contestant on the Indian version of the game show *Who Wants to Be a Millionaire?* and is arrested on suspicion of cheating due to his success. To prove his innocence, he recounts the events that led to him learning the answer to each of the questions he was asked, in the process revealing his life story to readers or viewers. Swarup stated in an interview that he considered the novel's structure—the narrative unfolding in flashbacks prompted by questions from a game show—to be the most important aspect of the book to preserve in an adaptation, and *Slumdog Millionaire* indeed preserves it. Otherwise, however, the film's narrative diverges significantly from that of the book. The film version is generally lighter and more uplifting; more of the characters are fundamentally decent people, and while they undergo hardships, these tend to be less severe than those in the original novel.

In the novel, for example, the protagonist, Ram, becomes a contestant on the game show as part of a revenge plot against the host, Prem Kumar (Anil Kapoor in the film). Kumar assaulted a woman Ram used to work for, who then killed herself. Ram decides against killing Kumar during the break before the final question, but the host ultimately dies anyway; it is implied that the producers arranged his death because he failed to prevent Ram from winning. Meanwhile, the film's protagonist, Jamal (Dev Patel), becomes a contestant in an attempt to be reunited with his lost love Latika (Freida Pinto), who watches the show regularly. Kumar tries to rig the outcome by feeding Jamal a wrong answer but does not seem to have committed any worse crimes than this.

The film's more positive tone is enhanced by a vibrant color palette and brightly sunlit scenes. This visual style draws heavily on Bollywood films, the product of India's mainstream, big-budget film industry; *Slumdog Million-*

aire even features a song-and-dance number at the end as a nod to these films, which are often musicals. Boyle cited the Bollywood crime films *Deewaar* (1975), *Satya* (1998), *Company* (2002), and *Black Friday* (2004) as particular inspirations.

Color also serves, at times, to create a sense of visual continuity for the central characters of Latika, Jamal, and Jamal's brother Salim, who are each played by three different actors at various ages. Latika, for example, wears a yellow dress as a child and a yellow scarf as an adult at the end of the film. Her association with the color, in addition to giving the character a distinct visual identity, marks her as a bright spot in Jamal's life.

A constantly moving camera and fast-paced editing maintain a sense of breathlessness and tension. The score, composed by A. R. Rahman, uses driving beats and hip-hop influences to supplement the film's feeling of relentless motion. Boyle had previously used these techniques to portray the jittery energy of heroin addiction in *Trainspotting* and the constant threat of pursuing monsters in *28 Days Later*; in *Slumdog Millionaire*, they create a sense of the pressure that Jamal is under. Whether on the set of the game show, being interrogated by police, or simply trying to survive his childhood, Jamal is constantly required to think and act fast; he is always just one step ahead of disaster.

Despite the heightened nature of the plot and the more fantastical elements such as the musical finale, the film also makes an effort to maintain a core of authenticity; this realism is key to audiences' acceptance of the less probable aspects of the film. Much of *Slumdog Millionaire* was filmed on location in Mumbai. Camera people moved around the city on foot, taking the same shortcuts that locals took, and recorded on handheld digital cameras. This technique provides the viewer with a sense of what it is like to walk through Mumbai's streets.

The film was initially intended to be entirely in English, but Tandan felt that it would be more realistic for the characters to be speaking Hindi at times, especially in the flashbacks to Jamal's childhood. Tandan translated roughly one-third of the script into Hindi; Boyle later said that "as soon as she did it, the scenes just transformed." In addition, though Boyle planned to cast professional child actors for the younger versions of Jamal, Salim, and Latika, he found their performances too polished, and instead cast local children from the slum in which filming took place.

Significance

Shot on a budget of just $15 million, *Slumdog Millionaire* grossed over $378 million worldwide, becoming one of Fox Searchlight's highest-grossing films ever. Critical reception was largely positive, with many reviewers praising the film's cinematography, pacing, and soundtrack. Critics were impressed with the performance of Patel, a relative newcomer, in the lead role. For example, writing for *Entertainment Weekly*, Owen Gleiberman said that Patel "holds the camera while appearing to do nothing —the mark of a star." Some also offered compliments to Bollywood veterans Kapoor and Irrfan Khan, who played the menacing police inspector in charge of Jamal's interrogation.

The film also earned praise for striking a balance between optimism and serious treatment of its heavy subject matter. Peter Travers, reviewing the film for *Rolling Stone*, pointed to the film's elements of magical realism as the reason it was able to "[let] in hope without compromising integrity." "Even in the Bollywood musical number that ends the film," Travers wrote, "joy and pain are still joined in the dance."

A few reviewers were less impressed, finding the film too heavy-handed in its attempts to stir up emotion; Manohla Dargis's review for *The New York Times*, for example, praised many elements of the film, but concluded that "its joyfulness feels more like a filmmaker's calculation than an honest cry from the heart about the human spirit." Some Indian critics also argued that the film did little to distinguish itself from the Bollywood films it drew on for inspiration and only seemed innovative to Western audiences unfamiliar with those older films. Acclaimed director Priyadarshan, for example, called it a "mediocre version of those commercial films about estranged brothers and childhood sweethearts" that were popular in India in the 1970s. Many Indian audiences also felt that the film portrayed the country in a bad light by focusing on poverty and crime. However, many reviewers for prominent Indian publications praised the film.

Slumdog Millionaire was nominated for ten Academy Awards and won eight of them: best film, best director, best adapted screenplay, best original score, best original song (for the closing musical number "Jai Ho"), and technical awards for cinematography, film editing, and sound mixing. The best Achievement in Directing award provoked some minor controversy for being given only to Boyle and not Tandan, although she said that she did not think her contributions merited equal credit to Boyle's, stating, "I am greatly honored by the credit I have been accorded. It would be a grave injustice if the credit I have should have the effect of diminishing Danny Boyle's magnificent achievement." The film also won seven BAFTA Awards, along with numerous other accolades.

The film's success also made Dharavi, the slum in which much of the film is set, a destination of interest to tourists, prompting the establishment of guided tours and a museum showcasing the work of local artists.

—Emma Joyce

Further Reading

Mendes, Ana Cristina. "Showcasing India Unshining: Film Tourism in Danny Boyle's *Slumdog Millionaire*." *Third Text*, vol. 24, no. 4, 2010, pp. 471-79.

Tzanelli, Rodanthi. *Mobility, Modernity, and the Slum: The Real and Virtual Journeys of* Slumdog Millionaire. Routledge, 2015.

Bibliography

Dargis, Manohla. "Orphan's Lifeline Out of Hell Could Be a Game Show in Mumbai." *The New York Times*, 11 Nov. 2008, www.nytimes.com/2008/11/12/movies/12slum.html. Accessed 27 Apr. 2020.

Gleiberman, Owen. "*Slumdog Millionaire*." *Entertainment Weekly*, 12 Jan. 2009, ew.com/article/2009/01/12/slumdog-millionaire/. Accessed 27 Apr. 2020.

Handley, Emily. "Interview: Vikas Swarup—The Author of *Q&A*, the Novel behind the Oscar-Winning Film *Slumdog Millionaire*." *TCS*, 24 Jan. 2013, www.tcs.cam.ac.uk/interview-vikas-swarup-the-author-of-qa-the-novel-behind-the-oscar-winning-film-slumdog-millionaire/. Accessed 27 Apr. 2020.

Hill, Logan. "Slumdog's Underdog." *New York Magazine*, 6 Nov. 2008, nymag.com/movies/features/52003/. Accessed 27 Apr. 2020.

Iqbal, Nosheen. "Dev Patel: 'I Didn't Know What I Was Getting Myself Into.'" *The Guardian*, 21 Feb. 2015, www.theguardian.com/film/2015/feb/21/dev-patel-didn-t-know-what-getting-into-slumdog-marigold-hotel. Accessed 27 Apr. 2020.

Travers, Peter. "*Slumdog Millionaire*." *Rolling Stone*, 13 Nov. 2008, www.rollingstone.com/movies/movie-reviews/slumdog-millionaire-120433/. Accessed 27 Apr. 2020.

The Snows of Kilimanjaro

The Novel
Author: Ernest Hemingway (1899-1961)
First published: 1936

The Film
Year released: 1952
Director: Henry King (1886-1982)
Screenplay by: Casey Robinson
Starring: Gregory Peck, Susan Hayward, Ava Gardner, Hildegard Knef, Leo G. Carroll

Context

The film version of *The Snows of Kilimanjaro* was released in 1952. It focuses on an American named Harry Street (Gregory Peck) who has risen to international prominence and achieved enviable success. Although the film shows him, through flashbacks, as a younger man struggling to win fame and to earn a living as a writer, viewers know at the outset that Street has succeeded on both counts. Ironically, however, his success in both respects fails to satisfy him. Being wealthy, he says, is not especially satisfying (although being poor would definitely be worse), and, more importantly, he feels that he has not yet met his own high aspirations as a writer. There is much more writing—and much *better* writing—that he would like to do.

At the beginning of the story, Street senses that he will never have the chance to accomplish anything more as an author than he has already achieved. He expects to die, very shortly, from an infection that is destroying his leg and weakening his entire body. That infection, ironically, began with a mere scratch that he failed to properly sanitize. Having survived actual combat in earlier years, including being shot in the leg, while volunteering in Spain during the Spanish Civil War, he now seems likely to die from a mere scratch.

The story can be seen as emblematic of the dissatisfactions that were lurking under the surface of America's postwar economic—and military—position. Street, despite his worldly success, seems unhappy and unfulfilled. He faces his likely death with bitterness rather than stoic acceptance. He lashes out at his wife instead of taking comfort from her devotion. Street, obviously the center of his own attention and concerns, never asks his wife very convincingly for any forgiveness. Street seems to live in a world in which Street is the most important figure. When he faces death, he finds himself to be consoled by nothing, and especially not by any hope of a happy afterlife. He symbolizes, in some ways, the kind of existential philosophy that had become increasingly influential in the first half of the twentieth century—the idea that each person creates his or her own values and lives in his or her own universe, beyond which nothing else exists. Many people watching the film today will be struck by Street's essential egotism—an egotism relieved, in part, only by memories of one romantic relationship. Ironically, those memories may strike many viewers as cloyingly sentimental. Street, in some ways, seems a typical American of his era, in ways both appealing and unappealing.

Film Analysis

The film version of *The Snows of Kilimanjaro* differs considerably from the short story, although the two works do begin in roughly the same way. In both works, Harry Street is lying on a cot in Africa with Mount Kilimanjaro, that continent's highest mountain, visible in the distance. In both works, Harry is near death, having injured his leg. He and his wealthy wife Helen (Susan Hayward)their relationship obviously tense—are hoping that a plane may yet arrive to take Harry away for medical treatment. In both the story and the film, Harry is a renowned, successful writer who has come to Africa to hunt big game. He is a stereotypical tough guy and has been involved, over the years, with numerous women. For him, hunting is a metaphor for life: everything, including writing, is a hunt—a pursuit of big, impressive targets. In the story, he often describes women as "bitches," whereas in the film his relationships with women—especially with Cynthia (Ava

Gardner), whom he met long ago in Paris—are more stereotypically romantic. The filmmakers drastically played down the story's cynicism about women. In the story, Harry seems far more egocentric than he does in the film. Gregory Peck presents a far more likeable Harry than the one who dominates the story.

As Harry, in both works, lies on the cot anticipating his death, he begins to reminisce about the events of his life. It is in these memories that the film differs most obviously from the story. In the story, most of Harry's memories revolve around his service as a soldier in World War I. (In this way, as in many others, Harry resembles Hemingway, who drove an ambulance in that war and was injured during his service.) Harry, in the story, recalls his comrades in arms, his sometimes-ugly experiences as a witness of brutal combat deaths, his experiences as a talented skier, his skills as a street fighter battling another man for a woman. Harry picked up and then quickly abandoned, his pride in his sexual prowess, his experiences as a fisherman, his love of his early life in the poor section of Paris, his sympathies for the poor, and even his complicated relationship with a mentally handicapped American boy who had shot an antagonistic older man—a boy whom Harry had had to turn in to the police. Almost none of these memories from the story appear in the film.

Instead, the film emphasizes Harry's recollections about his relationships with various women. These include an unnamed girl from his youth; a beautiful, thoughtful, devoted young woman named Cynthia, whom he met in Paris but who eventually left him and whom he never forgot; a beautiful but frosty and self-centered German aristocrat (Hildegard Knef), whom he quickly ditched; and then, finally, Helen, whom he married partly because she reminded him of the long-lost Cynthia. In the film, Harry also reminisces about satisfying times spent with Cynthia in Paris and Spain; her unexpected pregnancy; her hopes for a settled life when Harry wants a life of adventure; her loss of the baby; and eventually her heartbreaking death, years later, while driving an ambulance in the Spanish Civil War. In a remarkable coincidence, Harry and Cynthia happen to meet up, as volunteers, on the very same battlefield during that war; unfortunately, Cynthia dies despite Harry's best efforts to save her. The film, then, was written in a way that would make female viewers much more interested than they might have been in a faithful rendition of the story, which revolves around Harry and other men. The story is basically about Harry; the film is basically about Harry's romantic relationships in exotic locales.

In the film, Harry is a far more appealing character than he is in the story. He genuinely loves Cynthia; seems capable of loving Helen; does not treat Helen nearly as contemptuously as he does in the story; and is clearly more sinned against than sinning in his relationship with the arrogant German countess. He is beloved by his lovable Uncle Bill (Leo G. Carroll)—a character invented for the film and one who, oddly, speaks with a British accent but who is often there to support Harry when Harry seems glum. However, in the most remarkable departure of all from the story, at the end of the film Harry apparently survives, much to the delight of Helen and everyone else, including a jubilant Harry himself. At the end of the film, he flies off in the long-awaited airplane, which arrives just in the nick of time, and there is every reason to assume that he will escape death and perhaps have a genuinely happy future with Helen.

In contrast, in the story, it seems clear that the airplane flight is merely Harry's latest and last fantasy. He dies, leaving Helen essentially alone and thoroughly terrified and devastated. The film, then, is in every way far less grim and depressing than the story. Hemingway expressed contempt for the film, especially because it ultimately rejected the dark vision with which his story concluded. In the story, almost no one, least of all Harry, enjoys a happy ending. In the film, even the only truly devastating event—Cynthia's death on the battlefield—is heavily sentimentalized, as she and Harry enjoy an improbable reunion right before she dies. She dies knowing that he still loves her and always has, and Harry seems genuinely devoted to at least one other person besides himself.

No wonder the film was so popular: it had adventure and tough stuff for men, and it had romance and true love for women. In this sense, it was a typical Hollywood film of its era. Most of the rough edges of the story had been rubbed smooth; most of the story's disturbing notes had been drastically toned down. Viewers of both genders could enjoy the vivid settings that showed, by turns, exciting scenes of wildlife in Africa, the beauties of Paris, and the excitement of Spanish bullfighting and flamenco dancing. The film allowed viewers a chance to glimpse intriguing locales, vicariously participate in big-game hunting, and walk out of the theater feeling that good luck, true love, and attractive people (especially wealthy Americans) could triumph in the end.

Significance

Critical reaction to the film version of *The Snows of Kilimanjaro* was generally positive but sometimes mixed. Bosley Crowther, in *The New York Times*, spoke for many other reviewers when he praised the wildlife scenes in Africa, the effectiveness of the film's music, the "vivid performance" by Gregory Peck, and the visual qualities of what he called a "generally absorbing" and "taut, eye-filling film." He did find the film "spasmodically" episodic, noted its emphasis on Street's love affairs, found the location shots both literally and figuratively "colorful," and called the film as a whole stimulating, nostalgic, and well-acted by Peck, Gardner, and Hayward. The film was praised for exploring the workings of Street's mind rather than overemphasizing mere action and adventure, and Peck was admired by some critics (but not all) as the perfect actor for this romantic, ruminative role. The photography was often praised as beautiful; the score by Bernard Herrmann was frequently commended; the script was admired for its intelligence; the expansion of the original story and the segues between episodes were frequently praised as inventive; and the scenes in Africa involving the hunt for big game were almost universally extolled.

On the other hand, some reviewers did find various causes for complaint. Even Crowther called some roles "soggy and ambiguous," while other reviewers found Peck, as Harry, aloof, unsympathetic, and not the right choice for this often-gloomy part. Other critics called some sections distracting in their unconvincing use of location shots badly projected as background images on a Hollywood stage. The pace was sometimes criticized as too jumpy, too rambling, and/or too rushed; the script was sometimes called too talky; and the episodes involving Paris and the Spanish Civil War were occasionally found unconvincing for a variety of reasons. On the whole, however, the film was well received by critics and was popular at the box office. It was nominated for two Academy Awards (for cinematography and art direction) but won neither. Otherwise, it was neglected by the Academy of Motion Picture Arts and Sciences.

—*Robert C. Evans, PhD*

Further Reading

Hartman, James. "The Defamiliarization of Death in Hemingway's *The Snows of Kilimanjaro*." *Hemingway Review*, vol. 35, no. 2, Spring 2016, pp. 120-23. *EBSCOhost*, search.ebscohost.com/login.aspx?direct=true&db=lkh&AN=114259306&site=ehost-live. Accessed 12 May 2020.

Johnston, Kenneth G. "*The Snows of Kilimanjaro*: An African Purge." *Studies in Short Fiction*, vol. 21, no. 3, Summer 1984, p. 223. *EBSCOhost*, search.ebscohost.com/login.aspx?direct=true&db=lkh&AN=9271288&site=ehost-live. Accessed 12 May 2020.

Little, Anne C. "*The Snows of Kilimanjaro*." *Short Fiction: A Critical Companion*, Jan. 1997, pp. 104-11. *EBSCOhost*, search.ebscohost.com/login.aspx?direct=true&db=lkh&AN=24576500&site=ehost-live. Accessed 12 May 2020.

Shul'ts, Sergei. "Hemingway and Tolstoy: *The Snows of Kilimanjaro* and *Death of Ivan Il'ich*." *Tolstoy Studies Journal*, vol. 25, Jan. 2013, pp. 82-89. *EBSCOhost*, search.ebscohost.com/login.aspx?direct=true&db=lkh&AN=113960078&site=ehost-live. Accessed 12 May 2020.

Shuman, R. Baird. "*The Snows of Kilimanjaro*." *Masterplots II: Short Story Series, Revised Edition*, Jan. 2004, pp. 1-2. *EBSCOhost*, search.ebscohost.com/login.aspx?direct=true&db=lkh&AN=103331MSS21889240001476&site=ehost-live. Accessed 12 May 2020.

Bibliography

Bourke, George. "*Kilimanjaro* Film Briefly: Don't Miss It." *The Miami Herald*, 23 Oct. 1952, newspapers.com/clip/46879898/the-miami-herald/. Accessed 12 May 2020.

Crowther, Bosley. "*Snows of Kilimanjaro*, Based on Hemingway's Story, Is New Feature at Rivoli." *The New York Times*, 19 Sep. 1952, timesmachine.nytimes.com/timesmachine/1952/09/19/84356914.html. Accessed 12 May 2020.

"The New Pictures." *Time Magazine*, vol. 60, no. 12, Sept. 1952, p. 102. *EBSCOhost*, search.ebscohost.com/login.aspx?direct=true&db=f6h&AN=54169318&site=ehost-live. Accessed 12 May 2020.

"*The Snows of Kilimanjaro*." *Variety*, 31 Dec. 1951, variety.com/1951/film/reviews/the-snows-of-kilimanjaro-2-1200417125/. Accessed 12 May 2020.

Travers, James. "*The Snows of Kilimanjaro*." *FrenchFilms.org*, 2012, www.frenchfilms.org/review/the-snows-of-kilimanjaro-1952.html. Accessed 12 May 2020.

Sophie's Choice

The Novel
Author: William Styron (1925-2006)
First published: 1979

The Film
Year released: 1982
Director: Alan J. Pakula (1928-98)
Screenplay by: Alan J. Pakula
Starring: Meryl Streep, Kevin Kline, Peter MacNicol

Context
Novelist William Styron published *Sophie's Choice*, about a Polish Catholic survivor of the Holocaust, in 1979. Styron's previous novel, *The Confessions of Nat Turner*, won the 1968 Pulitzer Prize for Fiction but elicited controversy for his choice to write a fictionalized story from the perspective of Turner, a real-life enslaved man who led a rebellion against Virginia slave owners in 1831. The book, vigorously praised and vigorously derided, raised important questions about empathy, art, and race. Did Styron, a white man, have the right to tell Turner's story? Prominent African American authors like James Baldwin and Ralph Ellison defended Styron. Similar issues were raised in the reaction to *Sophie's Choice*, which focuses on a non-Jewish person who suffered in the Holocaust. For the most part, however, the book was critically well-received. It won the US National Book Award for Fiction in 1980, and it spent six weeks on *The New York Times* Best-Seller List.

Novelist John Gardner, who reviewed the book for *The New York Times*, described it as a "courageous, in some ways masterly book." Like Styron's other novels, he wrote, it explores "the nature of evil in the individual and in all of humanity." He described it as Southern Gothic in its tone and structure, though suggested that the trappings of this genre undercut the story Styron seeks to tell. In 2004, scholar Sylvie Mathé offered a critique of the book that dovetails with Gardner's criticism. She argued that Styron sensationalized Sophie's choice by couching it within the larger context of a love triangle and otherwise sexualizing her trauma. She also cites a frequent, though controversial, criticism of the book, that Styron's choices mitigate, rather than illustrate, the horrors of the Holocaust itself.

Alan Pakula, who directed the Academy Award-winning film *All the President's Men* in 1976, bought the rights to *Sophie's Choice* when the novel was still in galleys. He wrote the screenplay—his first—with minimal suggestions from Styron. (At least one executive producer suggested that he change the story and give it a happy ending; he declined.) *Sophie's Choice* had already become a bestseller by the time shooting began in Brooklyn. For the scenes set at Auschwitz (shot in Zagreb, Yugoslavia), Pakula hired a consultant who was a survivor of that death camp. When asked if he was worried that most audience members might be familiar with the story's ultimate revelation, Pakula was undaunted, though he expressed some doubts about claiming the story. "There are times when I've worried whether I have the right to do this—I don't want to theatricalize this, there are dangers," he told Janet Maslin for *The New York Times*. "In the end, I did it because I thought, 'My God, it's going to take several years of my life to make this film. What a wonderful way to spend several years.'"

Film Analysis
As the book, the film *Sophie's Choice* is narrated by and told from the perspective of a young Southern man named Stingo (Peter MacNicol). Widely understood to be a surrogate for a twenty-two-year-old Styron, Stingo has just moved from his home in Virginia to Brooklyn in the hope of completing his first novel. It is the summer of 1947. He takes a room in a sprawling Brooklyn rooming house, painted army surplus pink. The book begins a bit earlier and chronicles Stingo's short-lived adventure as a manuscript reader for the McGraw-Hill publishing company. Stingo quickly becomes acquainted with his upstairs

neighbors, a Jewish scientist named Nathan Landau (Kevin Kline in his film debut) and his girlfriend, a Polish refugee named Sophie Zawistowska (Meryl Streep). They leave him a copy of Walt Whitman's *Leaves of Grass*—the film, like the book, is rife with references to classic literature—and invite him to dinner. But before that official meeting happens, Stingo witnesses a violent fight between them. Nathan mocks Stingo and storms out of the house. Sophie brings Stingo dinner on a tray, and he notices the numbered tattoo on her wrist, indicating that she is a Holocaust survivor. The next day, Nathan apologizes to Stingo, marking the beginning of a fierce and turbulent friendship among the three. Pakula condenses Styron's tome but remains quite faithful to it. One major omission is tonal and harder to capture on screen. The book includes a number of explicit sexual descriptions, both of actual acts undertaken by the characters and of dreams. Pakula suggests the vibrant sex life between Sophie and Nathan, but otherwise, the characters are drained of the sleaziness Styron imbued them with in the novel.

In the book, Stingo's coming-of-age as a writer and a sexual being is the frame through which the reader learns about Sophie and her mysterious past. The film, however, places less emphasis on Stingo and, by extension, his lurid imaginings. In the book, an older Stingo recalls the summer; intermittent voice-over in the film only suggests that this is the case. The events of the summer happen in real time, and large swaths of the film are devoted to Sophie alone. Stingo's intellectual and sexual awakening takes a necessary backseat to her story. Stanley Kauffman, famed critic of the *New Republic*, described Streep's performance as the film's "sole achievement." She creates, he wrote, "a psychological verity for Sophie that she reveals through patterns of motion." Indeed, Streep's subtly evasive body language is the audience's first clue that she is not telling the truth about her past. Despite Kauffman's distaste for the film, he suggested that Streep's studied portrayal gives Sophie more depth than Styron does in the book. (Streep, who won her second Academy Award for the role, learned Polish and some German for the film and, as Maslin attested, kept Sophie's halting Polish accent throughout the entire shoot, both on camera and off.) Whether or not it was Pakula's original intention, the film's elements seem to coalesce around her. In several scenes, Kauffman writes, "the camera fixes on her in medium close-up and, virtually without any change of shot, she tells a long story." (It

is worth noting that the lingering camera offers no hint of salaciousness, as opposed to the book, in which Stingo admiringly compares her various body parts to food.) This particular shot, Kauffman wrote, is reminiscent of one employed by Swedish filmmaker Ingmar Bergman with his muse, actor Liv Ullmann.

The most memorable scene in which Pakula and cinematographer Néstor Almendros employ this shot occurs three-quarters of the way through the film, when Sophie, seated in shadow, framed in the moonlit window of her Brooklyn apartment, begins to tell Stingo about her experiences at Auschwitz. Critic Keith Phipps, who reviewed the film years later for the now-defunct film website the *Dissolve*, wrote that the scene "ranks among the best moments in the careers of all those involved." Almendros, who had just won an Academy Award for his work on Terrence Malick's *Days of Heaven* (1978), casts the film's Brooklyn present in glowing, nostalgic light. In many scenes, Streep, like a Renaissance painting, appears to be illuminated from within. Elsewhere the sun and moon stream through the countless windows of Sophie and Nathan's apartment. In Stingo's loving remembrance, each day of the summer appears as a sparkling, perfect day. By contrast, Almendros opts for a colorless, almost sepia-toned light in Sophie's flashbacks. Everything at Auschwitz is grey-brown, until a guard opens a forbidden door for Sophie to enter the property of Rudolf Höss, the Nazi commandant of the camp who is based on the real-life figure of the same name. On the other side of the door is a private garden in full bloom.

Significance

Sophie's Choice received mostly positive reviews when it premiered in 1982, though Kauffman and, famously, the *New Yorker*'s Pauline Kael hated it. Streep's performance received near-universal praise, though it inspired Kael to accuse her, to paraphrase, of acting only from the neck up. Maslin, in her review for *The New York Times*, praised Streep's ability to gather the disparate threads of Sophie's character. "Streep accomplishes the near-impossible, presenting Sophie in believably human terms without losing the scale of Mr. Styron's invention," she wrote. She described the film overall as "far from flawless" but "unified and deeply affecting." Much of her critique sprang from problems inherent in Styron's novel. Though the film sheds the "windiness" of that work, she wrote, it retains many of the book's contrivances, including the revelation of Nathan's secret and the narrative's unquestioning reverence for Stingo's talent as a writer. Similarly, Kauffman's displeasure with the film was mostly rooted in his displeasure with the book and Styron's overwrought style. Roger Ebert gave the film a rave review, awarding it four out of four stars. He described it as "a fine, absorbing, wonderfully acted, heartbreaking movie." Unlike other critics at the time, he did not see the film as belonging more to Sophie than to Stingo or Nathan. "It is about three people who are faced with a series of choices, some frivolous, some tragic," he wrote.

Streep won the Academy Award for Best Actress in a Leading Role, and *Sophie's Choice* was also nominated for the categories of best adapted screenplay, best cinematography, best costume design, and original musical score. The film was included among the American Film Institute's 100 Greatest American Films of All Time in 2007. An opera based on the novel by British composer Nicholas Maw premiered at the Royal Opera House in London in 2002. It was also performed in Washington, Berlin, and Vienna. In the same year, Styron received the Auschwitz Jewish Center Foundation's Witness to Justice Award.

—Molly Hagan

Further Reading

Gardner, John. "A Novel of Evil." Review of *Sophie's Choice*, by William Styron. *The New York Times*, 27 May 1979, www.nytimes.com/1979/05/27/archives/a-novel-of-evil-styron.html. Accessed 6 Feb. 2019.

Maslin, Janet. "Bringing *Sophie's Choice* to the Screen." *The New York Times*, 9 May 1982, www.nytimes.com/1982/05/09/movies/bringing-sophie-s-choice-to-the-screen.html. Accessed 6 Feb. 2019.

Bibliography

Ebert, Roger. "Reviews: *Sophie's Choice*." *RogerEbert.com*, Ebert Digital, 1 Jan. 1982, www.rogerebert.com/reviews/sophies-choice-1982. Accessed 8 Feb. 2019.

Kauffman, Stanley. "TNR Film Classics: *Sophie's Choice* (January 10, 1983)." *New Republic*, 10 Jan. 1983, newrepublic.com/article/103307/tnr-film-classics-sophies-choice-january-10-1983. Accessed 8 Feb. 2019.

Lehmann-Haupt, Christopher. "William Styron, Novelist, Dies at 81." *The New York Times*, 2 Nov. 2006, www.nytimes.com/2006/11/02/books/02styron.html. Accessed 6 Feb. 2019.

Mathé, Sylvie. "The 'Grey Zone' in William Styron's *Sophie's Choice*." *Études Anglaises*, vol. 57, no. 4, 2004, pp. 453-66. *Cairn.info*, www.cairn.info/revue-etudes-anglaises-2004-4-page-453.htm. Accessed 6 Feb. 2019.

Phipps, Keith. "Review: *Sophie's Choice*." *The Dissolve*, 28 Apr. 2014, thedissolve.com/reviews/751-sophies-choice. Accessed 8 Feb. 2019.

Still Alice

The Novel
Author: Lisa Genova (b. 1970)
First published: 2007

The Film
Year released: 2014
　　Directors: Richard Glatzer (1952-2015) and Wash Westmoreland (b. 1966)
Screenplay by: Richard Glatzer, Wash Westmoreland
Starring: Julianne Moore, Alec Baldwin, Kristen Stewart, Kate Bosworth, Hunter Parrish

Context

The novel *Still Alice* (2007) had an unusual path to success. Author Lisa Genova, who held a doctorate in neuroscience but had not previously written fiction, was inspired to write a novel about the inner life of a woman with Alzheimer's disease by both professional and personal experience—her grandmother had struggled with the condition for many years. Genova submitted it to numerous agents and publishers, all of whom turned it down because they felt its subject matter would be of interest only to a niche audience. Undeterred, Genova self-published the book in 2007.

Still Alice received a favorable review in the *Boston Globe* in 2008, bringing it to the attention of a wider audience than is typical for a self-published book. Subsequently, Genova signed with a literary agent, and the book was republished by a Simon and Schuster imprint in 2009. Genova went on to publish a number of novels revolving around characters with other neurological disorders, including *Left Neglected* (2011), *Love Anthony* (2012), and *Inside the O'Briens* (2015).

Directors Richard Glatzer and Wash Westmoreland, a married couple, had previously codirected three moderately successful independent films, *The Fluffer* (2001), *Quinceañera* (2006), and *The Last of Robin Hood* (2013). Their body of work is eclectic in tone, theme, and subject matter. *Quinceañera*, about a teenage girl who moves in with her gay cousin after becoming pregnant and being thrown out of her home by her conservative father, bears the most resemblance to *Still Alice*. The films share a heartfelt, earnest tone and an interest in depicting family relationships being turned on their heads following an upheaval in the protagonist's life. The protagonists are dis-

tanced from family members they were previously closest to, while developing a renewed relationship with a previously estranged relative.

At the time that Glatzer and Westmoreland began work on *Still Alice* in 2011, Glatzer had been experiencing symptoms related to the neurodegenerative disease amyotrophic lateral sclerosis (ALS), and this was part of the directors' motivation for adapting *Still Alice* to film. While ALS and Alzheimer's are different in many ways, with the former affecting physical capabilities more than memory and intellect, both are irreversible, incurable diseases that are constantly confronting the patient with new challenges as they progress. *Still Alice*, which premiered at the Toronto International Film Festival in 2014 before receiving a wider theatrical release in 2015, was Glatzer's last film before his death from complications of ALS in 2015.

The subject of Alzheimer's disease was relatively uncommon for mainstream films at the time but had previously been explored in such well-received independent films as *Traveling Companion* (1996), *Iris* (2001), and *Away from Her* (2006). All of these, however, focus on the experience of spouses or children of Alzheimer's patients as they come to terms with what is happening to their loved one and attempt to maintain some kind of closeness. Perhaps in part to justify the focus on the distress of their relatives, characters with Alzheimer's are often portrayed as insulated from the pain of the condition by the condition itself—they are not aware enough of what is happening to them to be upset by it. In reality, however, this level of detachment from reality is often preceded by years of gradual decline with substantial periods of lucidity, and it is this period of time that *Still Alice* is concerned with. While the film cannot inhabit the perspective of its protagonist as thoroughly as the book does, it still sets itself apart from its predecessors by keeping the focus firmly on the protagonist's feelings about her own condition.

Film Analysis

The film follows Alice (Julianne Moore), a linguistics professor who, as she says, has "always been so defined by [her] intellect." Her sense of self is challenged when she is diagnosed with early-onset Alzheimer's disease when she is just fifty years old. The disease also throws a wrench into her relationships with her husband, John (Alec Baldwin), and her adult children Anna (Kate Bosworth) and Tom (Hunter Parrish). They seem hesitant to make any personal sacrifices for Alice's sake. For example, Alice asks John, who is a physician involved in research, to take a year off work so that they can spend time together while she is still able to appreciate it, but he is not willing to risk the possible damage to his career.

Alice's youngest daughter, Lydia (Kristen Stewart), was previously the family disappointment, having eschewed college in favor of moving to Los Angeles to pursue an acting career, but she proves to be the only one who can offer her mother unconditional love and support. John, Anna, and Tom, the film suggests, struggle with the disruption to their carefully ordered lives; they have planned everything out for themselves, and Alice's condition was not part of the plan. Lydia is, of course, also upset by her mother's illness. However, unlike the rest of her family, she does not have a specific idea of the course for the rest of her life, so she is more able to accept what has happened and adapt to it.

The film largely stays close to the plot and details of the book but does make some small changes. Perhaps the most notable is that Alice now uses a smartphone—a device less common in 2007 but ubiquitous in 2014—to compensate for her failing memory. She also uses it to track the progress of the disease, writing on it a series of questions about herself that she must answer every morning. This touches on the growing role of technology in everyday life in the 2010s and the double-edged nature of its ability to mitigate issues like Alice's. Used intentionally for this purpose, technology is a valuable tool, but reliance on it before her diagnosis may have masked her symptoms. However, this is not a major focus of the film. The smartphone, and particularly the questions Alice writes

for herself, are mainly present to support the film's overarching goal: to portray the disorientation and distress that Alice feels as her condition worsens.

The filming techniques and background music used in the film are also carefully chosen to evoke these feelings. Many scenes are shot with a shallow depth of field, leaving Alice in focus while everything around her is blurry. This provides a visual illustration of Alice's sense that her surroundings are constantly unfamiliar, even in her own home. Overlapping shots and shots that spin around Alice are also sometimes used to highlight her confusion.

Composer Ilan Eshkeri uses a string trio for much of the score to notable effect. The limitation of having only three instruments leads to incomplete harmonies, in which a note seems to be missing from a chord, creating an unsettling atmosphere. Describing this, Peter Debruge, in his review of the film for *Variety*, wrote that the score "doesn't tell you how to feel, but rather how [Alice] feels: lost, emotional and anxious most of the time." Other musical pieces in the film center around the piano, which, in accordance with Eshkeri's view of the instrument's place in the home, highlight Alice's family-oriented nature.

These choices support Moore's understated performance in the lead role, which relies heavily on facial expressions to communicate the character's mental and emotional state. In preparation for the role, Moore spoke with women with early-onset Alzheimer's. Moore stated in interviews that while the public perception of the disease focuses on the tragedy of the memory loss itself, many of the women to whom she spoke considered the most significant problem to be the constant anxiety and stress that they felt due to lacking the context to understand what was going on around them. Moore's performance clearly draws on this knowledge, emphasizing the anxiety that Alice experiences in her less lucid periods.

Significance

Still Alice grossed over $44 million worldwide on a budget of about $5 million, making it a considerable commercial success. Critical response was mostly positive, though some reviewers found elements of the story contrived. Liam Lacey, for the *Globe and Mail*, wrote that "the script appears to be following the checked boxes on a medical chart" in its formulaic depiction of family drama. Another common criticism was that the secondary characters were poorly fleshed out; A. O. Scott, for *The New York Times*, wrote that "the film, concentrating on the accurate portrayal of Alice's condition, leaves the other characters undeveloped." Several reviews compared the film to a television special due to its low budget and focus on eliciting a dramatic emotional response from viewers.

However, the praise for Moore's performance was almost unanimous. "Moore's gift is her transparent emotional presence," Lacey wrote. *"Even when Alice is trying to cover up, she's wonderfully readable."* Kenneth Turan, for the *Los Angeles Times*, wrote that Moore's performance allows the audience "to see through the changing contours of her face what it is like when your mind empties out." Moore won a number of awards for the film, including the Academy Award for best actress. Many reviewers also commended Stewart's performance as Lydia. Turan, for example, wrote that the film "wouldn't be nearly as emotionally effective as it is" without Stewart.

Reviewers also praised the film's focus on Alice rather than her family, and the fact that the film did not depict her as handling the situation perfectly—she is shown to get angry and lash out at times, and at other times to use her condition in a calculated play for sympathy in order to get her way. In addition to the critical acclaim, the film was recognized by some people with Alzheimer's as a particularly true-to-life depiction of the subject matter, and some advocacy groups praised the film for raising awareness about the condition.

—Emma Joyce

Further Reading

Bailey, Catherine. "Films Like Still Alice Are Crucial to Keeping Debate about Dementia Alive." *The Conversation*, 12 Mar. 2015, theconversation.com/films-like-still-alice-are-crucial-to-keeping-debate-about-dementia-alive-38675. Accessed 19 Mar. 2021.

Westmoreland, Wash. "Richard Glatzer and Wash Westmoreland on the Catharsis of 'Still Alice.'" Interview by Steven Zeitchik.

Los Angeles Times, 12 Mar. 2015, www.latimes.com/entertainment/movies/moviesnow/la-et-mn-richard-glatzer-dies-wash-westmoreland-still-alice-20150312-story.html. Accessed 19 Mar. 2020.

Bibliography

Buckley, Cara. "Yearning to Make the Connection." *The New York Times*, 26 Nov. 2014, www.nytimes.com/2014/11/30/movies/the-makers-of-still-alice-have-their-own-story-of-illness.html. Accessed 19 Mar. 2021.

Debruge, Peter. "Toronto Film Review: *Still Alice.*" Review of *Still Alice*, directed by Richard Glatzer and Wash Westmoreland. *Variety*, 9 Sept. 2014, variety.com/2014/film/reviews/toronto-film-review-julianne-moore-in-still-alice-1201301421. Accessed 19 Mar. 2021.

Eshkeri, Ilan. "The Beautiful Music of *Still Alice*: A Q & A with Composer Ilan Eshkeri." Interview by Xaque Gruber. *HuffPost*, 12 Jan. 2015, www.huffpost.com/entry/the-beautiful-music-of-st_b_6449660. Accessed 19 Mar. 2021.

Lacey, Liam. "Julianne Moore Masters Alzheimer's Disappearing Act in *Still Alice.*" Review of *Still Alice*, directed by Richard Glatzer and Wash Westmoreland. *The Globe and Mail*, 23 Jan. 2015, www.theglobeandmail.com/arts/film/film-reviews/julianne-moore-masters-alzheimers-disappearing-act-in-still-alice/article22581318. Accessed 19 Mar. 2021.

Scott, A. O. "Losing Her Bearings in Familiar Places." Review of *Still Alice*, directed by Richard Glatzer and Wash Westmoreland. *The New York Times*, 4 Dec. 2014, www.nytimes.com/2014/12/05/movies/in-still-alice-a-professor-slides-into-alzheimers.html. Accessed 19 Mar. 2021.

Seymour, Tom. "*Still Alice* Is 'Shockingly Accurate'—People Living with Dementia Give Their Verdict." *The Guardian*, 10 Feb. 2015, www.theguardian.com/film/2015/feb/10/still-alice-alzheimers-accurate-dementia-sufferers-verdict. Accessed 19 Mar. 2021.

Turan, Kenneth. "Review: 'Still Alice' Powerfully Presents a Mind Falling to Alzheimer's." Review of *Still Alice*, directed by Richard Glatzer and Wash Westmoreland. *Los Angeles Times*, 4 Dec. 2014, www.latimes.com/entertainment/movies/la-et-mn-still-alice-movie-review-20141205-column.html. Accessed 19 Mar. 2021.

A Streetcar Named Desire

The Play
Author: Tennessee Williams (1911-1983)
First published: 1947

The Film
Year released: 1951
Director: Elia Kazan (1909-2003)
Screenplay by: Tennessee Williams (1911-1983)
Starring: Marlon Brando, Vivien Leigh, Kim Hunter, Karl Malden

Context

A Streetcar Named Desire, which centers on the complex interactions of a young man named Stanley Kowalski (Marlon Brando), his young wife Stella (Kim Hunter), and Stella's older sister, Blanche DuBois (played by Jessica Tandy in the original Broadway production and by Vivien Leigh in the film), made an important impact on American culture, both as a play in 1947 and then as a film in 1951. Both were examples of gritty realism and honest explorations of the sometimes-dark, violent underbelly of post-war American society. They were also seen as sexually frank at a time when such candor was much less common than it is today. Stanley Kowalski was played both on stage and on-screen by Marlon Brando, who became one of the most popular and influential actors of his generation, partly because of his smoldering performance in this role. The young, well-built Brando played Kowalski as an often shirtless, sweaty, and dangerous male sex symbol, equally attractive to straight women and gay men.

Playwright Tennessee Williams was in fact, gay, and both the film and especially the play touch on gay themes and issues at a time when such matters were far less openly discussed. But this emphasis on male sexuality was balanced by an equally strong emphasis on sexual desire in women. Although this desire is most obvious in Stella, whose erotic yearning for Stanley is frequently stressed, it is also shown in Blanche, both in her tense, ambivalent reactions to Stanley and in her relations with other young men, not only in her present life but also in her past. Some critics have suggested that edits to the film were deliberately designed to de-emphasize the sexual yearnings of the play's women, especially Stella. Yet despite such edits, both the play and the film struck Williams's contemporaries as definitely intended for "mature audiences."

Streetcar, both as a play and as a film, explores a wide variety of social issues relevant both to its own day and to more recent times. Stanley Kowalski's Polish ancestry is stressed in ways that imply that the United States was already a multicultural society and was becoming more multicultural with every passing year. Hispanic as well as African American characters and cultures play interesting—and often symbolic—roles, and other ethnic groups (such as Italian Americans) are also significant. The play is deliberately set in New Orleans, one of the most multicultural cities in America at that time, and the sounds of jazz and blues music can be heard throughout the drama. Stanley symbolizes the nation's multicultural present and future; Blanche symbolizes its more traditional past (although even Blanche has French ancestors); while Stella is in many senses a transitional figure. She shares a past with Blanche but a present and, presumably, a future with Stanley. She is, in every sense, a mediating figure—someone who tries to prevent and quell, often unsuccessfully, any conflicts between her sister and her husband.

Film Analysis

The film adaptation of *Streetcar* is remarkably faithful to the play, including its dialogue and structure. The characters in the film are all strikingly similar to the characters in the play, and the filmmakers seem to have done almost everything possible to bring Williams's original work to the big screen. At the same time, the film is obviously a film rather than merely a recording of a stage performance. The film's sets are realistic, and New Orleans is as much a character as any of the people. Every so often—as in the improbable depiction of a Mexican woman selling mourning flowers late at night—the film sticks a bit *too* closely to the play's script and the symbolism becomes a bit *too*obvious and mechanical. For the most part, however, the film tones down the play's sometimes blatant symbolism and some of its more blatant staginess, such as the various menacing special effects (both aural and visual) Williams describes. The film rarely seems unconvincing and is a fine homage to the play. Most viewers are unlikely to feel that any damage has been done to the drama in its transition to the screen. In fact, some critics have called the adaptation one of the best play-to-film transformations ever made. Indeed, some have claimed that the film is superior to the drama. The fact that Williams wrote both the play and the screenplay definitely helped in this respect.

One major change between the play and the film involves Blanche's description of her relationship with the handsome young man (whom she usually calls a "boy") she married when she was very young. He later kills himself and she feels haunted both by his tenderness and by his death. The reasons for his suicide, however, are far less clear in the film than in the play. In the film, Blanche describes his death by saying that at the edge of a lake he had

...stuck a revolver into his mouth...
...and fired. It was because...
...on the dance floor...
...unable to stop myself, I'd said:
"You're weak. I've lost respect for you. I despise you."

Why had Blanche lost respect for him? Why did a mere accusation of weakness lead him to kill himself? In the film, the "boy's" response to her accusation makes little obvious sense. She had earlier mentioned hearing him crying at night, but crying at night, even if regarded as a sign of weakness, hardly seems enough to provoke a suicide. In the play, however, everything is much clearer as Blanche explains, "Then I found out. In the worst of all possible ways. By coming suddenly into a room that I thought was empty—which wasn't empty but had two people in it... the boy I had married and an older man who had been his friend for years." The boy, in other words, was a closeted homosexual. He had married Blanche on impulse, and out of genuine love on some level, but he had been unable to completely suppress his real sexual desires. Although both he and Blanche subsequently "pretended that nothing had been discovered," Blanche later, on a dance floor (perhaps under the influence of alcohol, but in any case, "unable to stop" herself), had "suddenly said—'I know! I know! You

disgust me.'" The film could not deal as openly with "the boy's" homosexuality as the play did. Clearly the play is, on one level, a plea for kindness, not only toward people like Blanche, who famously says that she has always depended "on the kindness of strangers," but also toward people like Blanche's young husband—which is to say, toward people like Williams himself.

A Streetcar Named Desire is a multicultural drama not only in the way it implies the need for tolerance toward ethnic and racial minorities but also in the way it implies the need for tolerance for gays, who were at the time perhaps the most despised group in the United States. Blacks, Italians, and others could all seek open affirmation among themselves, but gays during most of Williams's lifetime had almost no such solace. Even the kind-hearted Stella later says about Blanche's first husband, "that beautiful and talented young man was a degenerate." Stella, who treats practically everyone else in the play with genuine compassion and respect, nonetheless sees the beautiful, talented "boy" as merely a "degenerate." Sadly, he would have been unable to depend even on the kindness of a fundamentally good and decent person like Stella.

Press publicity photo of Marlon Brando and Vivien Leigh in A Streetcar Named Desire, *1951. Public domain via Wikimedia Commons.*

Some critics have seen Blanche as a version of Williams, who could never afford to be quite as open about his sexuality as would have been possible if he had been born a few decades later. Blanche has to hide her sexuality, which nevertheless finds covert expressions in ways that ultimately disrupt her life and destroy her reputation in her own hometown. She has been involved with various young men, including young soldiers and even a seventeen-year-old student. Meanwhile, the contempt Stanley feels for Blanche has been read, by some, as the kind of contempt a stereotypical self-defined and hyper-masculine straight man might feel for a male he perceived as too effeminate and "refined." However one interprets this homosexual subtext in the play and film, the subtext is definitely there and would probably have been much more overt if both productions had been products of the 1990s or early 2000s.

Significance

The film version of *Streetcar* was generally well received by early critics and has, over the years, come to be considered a classic film of the 1950s. In particular, Brando's portrayal of Stanley is seen as trailblazing—a legendary performance that seems more and more impressive with time. Brando once claimed that Stanley was the only character that he had ever portrayed whom he fully despised. After re-reading the play today, or re-watching the film, it is easy to see why. The rise of the women's liberation movement in the 1960s and '70s and its enormous impact on present-day culture has made Stanley seem not only obviously crude but genuinely cruel. On some levels his honesty and contempt for pretensions (especially class snobbery) still seem appealing, but his verbal abuse and violence, not to mention the strong likelihood that he actually rapes Blanche near the end of the play, make him seem in some ways thoroughly repulsive. Overall, however, the film (like the original play) presents its major characters as complicated human beings. It is difficult to judge any of them in completely negative or positive ways.

It seems safe to say that the film version of *A Streetcar Named Desire* helped accelerate some key changes that were already occurring in American culture at the time. If Stanley as played by Brando seems a crude, plain-spoken, self-assertive "bad boy" with little respect for conventional middle-class values, he seems in those respects an embodiment of many impulses that became increasingly common in American culture in the second half of the twentieth century. Stanley was an early forerunner of later "bad boy" figures in pop culture, not only on film but also in popular music. If Stanley in the 1950s seemed an uncouth nonconformist, someone with little tolerance of bourgeois niceties, by the end of the twentieth century he no longer seemed very unusual. By that point society had become much less restrained and well-mannered than it had once aspired to be. Sexually explicit language, conduct, and popular culture have become much more common today than in 1951; Stanley seems positively tame by today's standards. Indeed, recent critics have frequently noted that a film that shocked many people when it was first released now seems mild by comparison. Blanche may have felt superior to Stanley in 1947 and 1951, but Stanley has clearly won the day.

The film was nominated for twelve Academy Awards and won four—for Best Actress (Leigh), Best Supporting Actor (Karl Malden as Mitch), Best Supporting Actress (Hunter), and Best Art Direction-Set Direction (Black-and-White). It has often been listed in various rankings of the hundred best films ever made, and certain moments from it—especially Brando bellowing in anguish for "Stella!" after he physically assaults her, or Blanche saying that she has always depended on the kindness of strangers—have become iconic in film history.

—*Robert C. Evans, PhD*

Further Reading

Dorwick, Keith. "Critical Readings: Stanley Kowalski's Not So Secret Sorrow: Queering, De-Queering and Re-Queering *A Streetcar Named Desire* as Drama, Script, Film and Opera." *Interdisciplinary Humanities*, vol. 20, no. 2, 2003, p. 80.

McCann, John S. *The Critical Reputation of Tennessee Williams: A Reference Guide*. G. K. Hall & Co., 1983.

Tischler, Nancy M. "Critical Readings: 'Tiger—Tiger!' Blanche's Rape on Screen." *Magical Muse: Millennial Essays on Tennessee Williams*, edited by Ralph F. Voss, University of Alabama Press, 2002, p. 50-69.

Bibliography

The Tennessee Williams Encyclopedia, edited by Philip Kolin, Greenwood, 2004.

Williams, Tennessee. *A Streetcar Named Desire*. New Directions, 2004.

Williams, Tennessee. *A Streetcar Named Desire. Scripts*, 1951, www.scripts.com/script/a_streetcar_named_desire_2037. Accessed 30 Mar. 2020.

Swiss Family Robinson

The Novel
Author: Johann David Wyss (1743-1818)
First published: Der schweizerische Robinson, 1812 (*The Swiss Family Robinson*, 1814)

The Film
Year released: 1960
Director: Ken Annakin (1914-2009)
Screenplay by: Lowell S. Hawley
Starring: John Mills, Dorothy McGuire, James MacArthur, Janet Munro, Sessue Hayakawa

Context

English author Daniel Defoe's novel *Robinson Crusoe* (1719) is the prototypical shipwreck adventure narrative, based on the true-life ordeal of Scottish sailor Alexander Selkirk, who had endured a solitary castaway's existence on a desert island between 1704 and 1709. Defoe's book proved so popular and influential that scholars have coined the term "robinsonade" to refer to any story of survival in isolation. One of the most famous robinsonades was written by Swiss pastor Johann David Wyss in 1812. His German-language novel pays direct homage to Defoe's work in its title, *Der schweizerische Robinson*, which could be translated as "Swiss people living like Robinson"—Robinson is not a typical surname in Switzerland. Wyss also included various other references to *Robinson Crusoe* in his novel, which he wrote to entertain and instruct his four sons when they were young. Yet rather than featuring a single castaway hero, Wyss built an adventure around an entire family that is shipwrecked, with his own family serving as models for the book's characters. In the story, an unnamed Swiss family is bound for New Guinea to establish a colony but are caught in a typhoon. Their ship is wrecked off an uncharted tropical island, with the family the only survivors. Fortunately, they are able to salvage much from the wreck, including numerous domesticated animals, and settle into the work of establishing a self-sufficient community they call New Switzerland. Their island, uninhabited by other humans, is a paradise of exotic flora and fauna to be explored and exploited. Narrated by the family patriarch, the novel incorporates Enlightenment philosophy and Christian ethical and moral principles as the four sons learn lessons and grow into adulthood.

Wyss's manuscript was edited by his son Johann Rudolf Wyss. Like its predecessor *Robinson Crusoe*, it immediately caught the public's fancy and became hugely popular. The novel was first translated into English in 1814 and as *The Swiss Family Robinson* in 1818, and over the years it became an international classic. However, the text was often abridged or otherwise altered as it was translated into various languages. Other authors freely adapted or extended the plot, and sequels were created to continue the story in fresh directions. Many alterations became accepted parts of the narrative and were incorporated into later versions, making Wyss's original text fairly obscure.

The story remained highly popular, however, as generation after generation of readers dream of getting away from it all and starting over. *The Swiss Family Robinson* would inspire many adaptations across various media, from stage productions to comic books to computer games, and of course television series and films. These have had varying degrees of faithfulness to the source material. Some of the more popular loosely inspired versions have updated the castaway concept to outer-space science fiction, including the television series *Lost in Space* (1965-68) and its various remakes. Other films have retained the nineteenth-century shipwreck concept. The first notable feature-length film was RKO's 1940 production, directed by Edward Ludwig and starring Thomas Mitchell, Edna Best, Freddie Bartholomew, and Tim Holt, with narration by Orson Welles. Film industry titan Walt Disney and producer Bill Anderson reportedly saw this version and were inspired to make their own take on the story. The 1940 adaptation was ultimately withdrawn from circulation before the release of the Disney film *Swiss Family Robinson* in 1960.

Film Analysis

Disney's adaptation streamlines Wyss's story, but keeps highlights of the original: Swiss family, shipwreck, use of local resources, conquest and domination of the island. The script, by longtime Disney writer Lowell S. Hawley, leaves out slow, repetitive, visually boring parts of *The Swiss Family Robinson*. Gone are most allusions suggestive of a religious mission, such as quotations from scripture, biblical-style parables, resting from labor on Sundays. Only once does the family kneel together in prayer in the film: to commemorate their safe arrival on dry land. Likewise absent are the book's many encyclopedic information dumps concerning new plant or animal discoveries. Also missing are the lengthy, detailed descriptions of how the family collectively imagines, plans, and executes various projects designed to improve efficiency or comfort. Instead, montages show rather than tell family deeds, such as building seaworthy craft, rescuing stranded animals with improvised flotations devices, and constructing an elaborate treehouse with amenities like skylights and running water.

In the Disney film, the family numbers five members, with three boys instead of four. Lead roles are played by reliable actors associated with the studio. For example, John Mills, who took the role of Father, was a respected British actor and real-life father of actor Hayley Mills, who would star in numerous Disney films. Dorothy McGuire, who played Mother, was known for similar maternal roles, including in Disney's *Old Yeller (*1957). The part of eldest son Fritz went to James MacArthur, who had appeared in the earlier Disney releases *The Light in the Forest* (1958), *Third Man on the Mountain* (1959), and *Kidnapped* (1960). Tommy Kirk was a former star of the *Mickey Mouse Club* series *The Hardy Boys* and was cast as the lead in *Old Yeller* and *The Shaggy Dog* (1959) before playing scholarly middle son Ernst. Kevin Corcoran took the role of youngest son Francis—Franz in the original—after parts in many Disney productions, including *Old Yeller* and *The Shaggy Dog.*

Behind the camera stood director Ken Annakin, an adventure-comedy veteran who had helmed the Disney features *The Story of Robin Hood and His Merrie Men* (1952), *The Sword and the Rose* (1953), and *Third Man on the Mountain.* Annakin reportedly insisted on breaking from the 1940 RKO adaptation's exclusive use of studio sets and instead shooting primarily at a real tropical location, for which Disney settled on the island of Tobago, near Trinidad off the northern coast of South America. (Some process sequences were completed at Pinewood Studios in London, England.) The production would be Disney's first full-color, live-action widescreen film to use Panavision lens technology.

The Disney version of Wyss's classic adds considerable drama, tension, and pace by expanding two subplots barely mentioned in the source material. The first is the inclusion of pirates. The original manuscript hinted of their presence but they were only a vague threat and never made a physical appearance. *Swiss Family Robinson* changes this by making a pirate band an important antagonist. Early in the film, a ship is seen in the distance as the family ashore collects flotsam and jetsam from the shipwreck. As it nears, the colorfully dressed pirate captain (Sessue Hayakawa) can be seen through a telescope, surrounded by a cutthroat crew (Andy Ho, Milton Reid, and Larry Taylor). They are initially driven off when the outnumbered, outgunned family hoists a quarantine flag, tricking the pirates into avoiding the threat of disease. The pirates will return in force, however, twice more. Once they land elsewhere on the island to divide booty from a captured ship, and are encountered by Fritz and Ernst. Later they return again to attack the colonists in an epic battle. The preparation and execution of that confrontation consumes a significant portion at the back end of the film's 126-minute running time.

The other major change the film adaptation makes is the expansion of a second female character, who serves as a love interest for the older two boys. Late in the Wyss novel a young English castaway named Jenny Montrose is introduced through a clumsy device. Fritz, exploring the island in his handmade boat, clubs a passing albatross and finds a message tied to the bird's leg, which leads him to Jenny, a fellow shipwreck survivor, whom he brings back to the family. The Disney film instead features a young woman named Roberta (Janet Munro, another Disney veteran), who is brought into the story much sooner by incorporating her into the pirate subplot. Disguised as a cabin boy, she is a captive of the pirates along with her grandfather, Captain Moreland (Cecil Parker), when Fritz and Ernst come across them while exploring the island. The brothers free her and all three flee from the pursuing buccaneers. In the course of their escape, her true sex is revealed, causing conflict between the formerly oblivious brothers as they afterward vie for her affection.

Another notable difference between novel and film is how the Swiss family interacts with the unbelievably diverse menagerie of animals found on the island. In the novel, the Robinson men slaughter great numbers of creatures for their meat and pelts or feathers. They preserve the heads of some for the "museum" they create in a cave fortress where they take refuge during monsoon season. They even use plant-derived poison to kill troops of marauding apes that trashed one of their many residences. Their prolific killing demonstrates their survival skills, but also implies a mastery over nature with clear spiritual undertones that reflects a nineteenth-century mindset with little concern for the environment. The Disney adaptation downplays the animal massacre, as even dangerous creatures such as sharks, snakes, and tigers are driven away rather than shown to be killed. Instead, the film builds up the family's collection of wildlife specimens to serve as pets, often for comic effect. The boys, led by animal-lover Francis, trap and tame a monkey, an ostrich, a zebra, an elephant, and other animals, some of which figure in a humorous race.

The result of all the changes is a film that is much lighter and less serious in tone than the novel. The Disney production, focusing more on adventure than on morality, was meant to be entertaining for audiences of all ages.

Significance

Released in late 1960, *Swiss Family Robinson* became a major hit. Though it had gone over budget at a cost of about $5 million, it turned a profit soon after premiering and became the fourth-highest-grossing film of the year. It was re-released several times over the years, ultimately collecting over $40.3 million in box-office receipts. Adjusting for inflation, the film took in more than a half-billion dollars by 2020 standards, making it one of the top-earning American films of all time. Critical reception was also highly favorable, as seen in a glowing review from Howard Thompson for *The New York Times*, who declared the production a "grand adventure yarn" that was "stunningly photographed."

With its family-friendly approach to a classic adventure tale, Disney's *Swiss Family Robinson* remained popular decades after its release. The family's treehouse became a popular attraction at the Disneyland and Disney World theme parks. Director Ken Annakin was honored as a Disney Legend in 2002. However, the film's reputation faded somewhat as tastes changed in the late twentieth and early twenty-first centuries. The rosy image of colonialism and the racist depictions of people of color were also heavily critiqued by later critics. Nonetheless, the film typically retains high approval ratings from review aggregators such as Rotten Tomatoes and Metacritic as well as family-oriented outlets such as Common Sense Media, with mild reproval for stereotypes or certain scenes depicting animal abuse.

The 1960 Disney film also proved a strong influence on many later adaptations of *The Swiss Family Robinson*. Audiences are largely more familiar with the swashbuckling adventure of the film than the moralistic message of the original novel. In 2020 Disney itself announced a remake, planned as a television series for the Disney+ streaming service.

—*Jack Ewing*

Further Reading

Annakin, Ken. *So You Wanna Be a Director?* Tomahawk, 2001.

Sanna, Antonio, editor. *Pirates in History and Popular Culture.* McFarland, 2018.

Thomas, Nicholas. *Islanders: The Pacific in the Age of Empire.* Yale UP, 2012.

Bibliography

Butler, Margaret. "Annakin, Ken (1914-2009)." *BFI ScreenOnline*, www.screenonline.org.uk/people/id/479412/index.html. Accessed 9 Mar. 2021.

Murray, Noel. Review of *Swiss Family Robinson*, directed by Ken Annakin. *AVClub*, 17 June 2002, film.avclub.com/swiss-family-robinson-dvd-1798197612. Accessed 9 Mar. 2021.

Spiegel, Josh. "Revisiting 'Swiss Family Robinson,' Disney's Problematic Box Office Smash from 1960." *SlashFilm*, 30 Oct. 2020, www.slashfilm.com/revisiting-swiss-family-robinson/. Accessed 9 Mar. 2021.

"Swiss Family Robinson." *Turner Classic Movies*, www.tcm.com/tcmdb/title/25093/swiss-family-robinson#overview. Accessed 9 Mar. 2021.

"Swiss Family Robinson (1960)." *AllMovie*, 2021, www.allmovie.com/movie/swiss-family-robinson-v48188. Accessed 9 Mar. 2021.

Thompson, Howard. "New Version of 'Swiss Family Robinson.'" Review of *Swiss Family Robinson*, directed by Ken Annakin. *The New York Times*, 24 Dec. 1960, www.nytimes.com/1960/12/24/archives/new-version-of-swiss-family-robinson.html. Accessed 9 Mar. 2021.

White, Peter. "'Swiss Family Robinson' TV Remake in the Works at Disney+." *Deadline*, 10 Dec. 2020, deadline.com/2020/12/swiss-family-robinson-tv-remake-in-the-works-at-disney-1234654443/. Accessed 9 Mar. 2021.

A Tale of Two Cities

The Novel
Author: Charles Dickens (1812-70)
First published: 1859

The Film
Year released: 1935
Director: Jack Conway (1887-1952)
Screenplay by: W. P. Lipscomb (1887-1958), S. N. Behrman (1893-1973)
Starring: Ronald Colman, Elizabeth Allan, Basil Rathbone, Blanche Yurka, Donald Woods

Context

Although serialized novels existed earlier, it was not until the early nineteenth century that they became common. The person chiefly responsible for their rise in popularity was Charles Dickens. His first novel, *The Pickwick Papers* (1835-37) was published in monthly installments, accompanied by illustrations of dynamic scenes. The novel appeared in a periodical that also featured paid advertisements, which helped defray publishing costs. Serialization—a precursor of comic books, graphic novels, and series television—was a smashing success. Dickens's only true historical novel, *A Tale of Two Cities*, was likewise serialized in 1859. While dark in tone, the novel has remained popular. The plot, silhouetted against factual conditions leading up to the French Revolution, is melodramatic, sometimes violent, and often moving.

Such qualities, combining romance and action, made *A Tale of Two Cities* a perfect vehicle for producer David O. Selznick. He had returned to Metro-Goldwyn-Mayer (MGM) in 1933 after a stint at Radio-Keith-Orpheum (RKO) Pictures. During his two-plus years at MGM, before he formed his own production company in 1936, Selznick produced at least ten films. His historical feature *Viva Villa!* (1934) was directed by Jack Conway, who was selected to lead the first adaptation with synchronized sound. Selznick had already overseen production of a highly successful film based on Dickens's work, *David Copperfield* (1935), earlier that year. Although the stories told were quite different, the two adaptations would have a similarly crisp look and style thanks to Oliver T. Marsh, who was chosen to serve as cinematographer on both films. The connection between *Copperfield* and *Two Cities* was further enhanced by the presence of character actors Edna May Oliver and Basil Rathbone, who appeared in key roles in both Dickens adaptations.

Silent film star Ronald Colman, a heroic figure in such films as *Beau Geste* (1926), *Bulldog Drummond* (1929), and *Raffles* (1930) was cast as the doomed Sydney Carton. Colman had long coveted the role and for the sake of historical accuracy sacrificed his trademark trim mustache.

Selznick, in his final film for MGM, wanted Colman to portray the roles of both Carton and Darnay, an approach sometimes used in other film productions. Although he had played two parts previously in *The Masquerader* (1933) and would do so again in *Prisoner of Zenda* (1937), Colman had reservations about the dual roles in Selznick's film. Instead, Donald Woods was chosen to play Charles Darnay, and the remarkable resemblance between the two characters, as envisioned by Dickens, would be downplayed in the adaptation.

Film Analysis

Although shorter than many Dickens novels, *A Tale of Two Cities* nonetheless required judicious editing to keep the film at a reasonable length for theatrical release. Screenwriter W. P. Lipscomb, who had worked on the historical features *Cardinal Richelieu* (1935) and *Les Misérables* (1935), teamed up with playwright/screenwriter S. N. Behrman, who scripted such historical/costume/romantic adventures as *Queen Christina* (1933) and Selznick's *Anna Karenina* (1935). Together, they performed delicate surgery on the novel. Condensing and rearranging, they produced an adaptation that retained major plot points, kept the atmosphere intact, and cut material that slowed narrative flow. The finished film was 128 minutes.

Both the novel and the adaptation start and finish at the same point but occasionally diverge with slight structural shifts. An abbreviation of the author's memorable opening is superimposed on the screen, ending with an edited lead-in, "In short, it was a period very like the present." The film uses superimposed words to act as silent movie title cards, "The Dover Road. A certain evening late in the Eighteenth Century" (the novel specified the year 1775). The Dover mail coach is struggling to climb a muddy hill, when a rider gallops out of the dark. It is an employee from fictional Tellson's Bank, who imparts important news to a passenger, banker Jarvis Lorry (Claude Gillingwater): He is to wait at an inn for a woman. Lorry in turn, passes along a cryptic message for the bank, which launches the plot, "Recalled to life."

The message underscores a major theme of the story—rebirth. The messenger himself, Jerry Cruncher (Billy Bevan), is referred to several times as a "resurrection man"—he gives bodies new life by illegally disinterring fresh cadavers to sell to scientists for dissection. The theme is reiterated and reinforced throughout by symbolic images such as churches and crucifixes. Key character Dr. Manette (Henry B. Walthall), thought dead, is actually alive. After being held in the bowels of the Bastille fortress for eighteen years, Manette has been released and is awaiting the reunion with his beautiful young daughter Lucie (Elizabeth Allan) in Paris. France itself will be reborn through violent revolution, when the peasants overthrow the aristocracy. In the upheaval, overindulgent lawyer Sydney Carton (Ronald Colman), transformed by love, will seize upon an opportunity to be spiritually redeemed by keeping a promise he made years earlier.

When the story transitions from England to France, several related threads are cinematically brought forward. Soft-spoken, blonde Lucie, a paragon of kindness and virtue, contrasts visually with swarthy, vengeful Madame Thérèse Defarge (Blanche Yurka, in her first feature film role) in a classic analogy of light-versus-dark. Tattered French peasants, blameless for their poverty, are shown lapping spilled wine from the gutters in a scene lifted from the novel. They are contrasted with the recklessly extravagant lifestyles of the evil aristocracy. Representative of the haughty nobles is Marquis St.

Author Charles Dickens, c. 1860. Public domain via Wikimedia Commons.

Evrémonde (Basil Rathbone). When his fancy coach runs down a child in the street, the marquis expresses more concern for the state of his horses than the condition of his victim. The depths of Evrémonde's depravity are shown in his willingness to frame his principled young nephew, Charles Darnay (Donald Woods), for treason simply because he rejected his inheritance.

A close-up of a newspaper clipping neatly summarizes Darnay's forthcoming trial. In the novel, the event unfolds much later. Altering the chronology allows the film's popular leading man to appear on screen much sooner. It also foreshadows the subterfuge to be employed at the conclusion, based on the supposed resemblance between Carton and Darnay. From his entrance, Colman's Sydney Carton dominates the film—although he relinquishes the spotlight long enough for Rathbone and Yurka to take their villainous turns.

A series of sequences leading to the revolution are especially well-conceived. Evrémonde, in his nightclothes, remarks snidely that the rent he receives from the peasants is barely enough to pay his perfume bill. He complains that one tenant was impertinent enough to die of hunger before paying rent. The marquis is stabbed to death in his bed that very night. Oblivious fellow aristocrats ignore the warning signs of revolt. The wealthy continue to attend balls in elegant dress and elaborate wigs, confident they are safe. They believe German and Swiss mercenaries hired by the king—seen marching in ranks through the streets—will help protect them. A culminating incident announced by superimposed type, "The Footsteps of July 14, 1789," causes the people to rise up in rage. To the stirring strains of "La Marseillaise" (an anachronism, because the anthem was not written until 1792), a crowd of starving peasants surges forward to get at chunks of meat being fed to a rich man's pack of dogs. The desperate people knock down a barred fence only to be thwarted by soldiers on horseback wielding sabers.

The filmed attack on the fortress prison of the Bastille is a highlight. Second unit directors/sequence arrangers Val Lewton and Jacques Tourneur used a combination of closeups of individual characters—like Madame Defarge exhorting the crowd—and long shots showing hundreds of extras waving swords, clubs, and other improvised weapons to capture the excitement, chaos, and mayhem of pitched battle. The turmoil following the surrender of the fortress prison is nicely staged. Brief scenes of destruction are enhanced by superimposed type. A jubilant mob serves as backdrop to "Liberty! Equality! Fraternity!" Bonfires and flaming châteaus silhouette brief written messages foreshadowing what is to come, "Death to the Aristos! Death to all their friends! Death to their servants! Death to the innocent as well as the guilty!" The last line sets up the closing scenes of the innocent and guilty alike being led to the guillotine. When it is Carton's turn to mount the steps, the camera does not follow the blade's descent, but rises as he utters his immortal closing sentences, "It is a far, far better thing..." As the sky fills the screen, a biblical quote recalls the main theme of the story. "I am the Resurrection and the Life: he that believeth in me, though he were dead, yet shall he live."

Significance

Because of the author's innate skills for developing unique, realistic, colorful characters and then setting them in motion in suspenseful situations, virtually the entire Charles Dickens canon has been adapted across a full range of media, from radio to television, from musical to opera, and from comic books to graphic novels. *A Tale of Two Cities* had been previously adapted for silent films in 1911, 1917, and 1922. Another black-and-white adaptation featuring Dirk Bogarde as Sydney Carton was released in 1958. In 1980, a full-color, made-for-television version starred Chris Sarandon in both the Carton and Darnay roles. The 1935 Selznick-produced version is generally considered the best adaptation to date. This was largely due to a well-written script, a corps of excellent actors, the efforts of Jack Conway (plus several uncredited replacements who took over when the director fell ill), and the cinematography of Marsh—a collaboration that created a gorgeous black-and-white production. Released in the middle of the Great Depression, the film delivered a powerful, uplifting message of hope, courage, honor, and compassion that still resonates today.

Critically acclaimed, *A Tale of Two Cities* earned about twice its $1.2 million budget at the box office. It was nominated for best picture and best film editing (by Conrad A. Nervig) but lost to other productions. *A Tale of Two Cities* was named among the Ten Best Pictures of 1936 (because it was not released until December 27, 1935). Despite his excellent work, Ronald Colman was not recognized in a year that featured a plethora of outstanding films. He would later star in such features as *Under Two Flags* (1936), *Lost Horizon* (1937), and *Random Harvest* (1942) before earning an Academy Award for best actor for *A Double Life* (1947).

—*Jack Ewing*

Further Reading

Bryfonski, Dedria. *Class Conflict in Charles Dickens's A Tale of Two Cities*. Greenhaven Press, 2013.

Lester, Valerie Browne. *Phiz: The Man Who Drew Dickens*. Random House, 2011.

Bibliography

"*A Tale of Two Cities* (1935)." *American Film Institute Catalog*, catalog.afi.com/Catalog/moviedetails/3914. Accessed 15 Feb. 2020.

Ackroyd, Peter. *Dickens*. HarperCollins, 1990.

Dickens, Charles. *A Tale of Two Cities*. Oxford UP, 1994.

Garnett, Robert. *Charles Dickens in Love*. Pegasus Books, 2012.

McClurg, Jocelyn. "Serial Novels Were the Craze in the 19th Century." *Hartford Courant*, 11 Sept. 1994, www.courant.com/news/connecticut/hc-xpm-1994-09-11-9409110110-story.html. Accessed 15 Feb. 2020.

Merritt, Stephanie. "Deferred Gratification Is Dead? Tell That to Fans of Serialised Novels." *The Guardian*, 13 Mar. 2018, www.theguardian.com/commentisfree/2018/mar/13/serialised-novels-podcasts-serial-readers. Accessed 15 Feb. 2020.

Stein, Daniel, and Lisanna Wiele, editors. *Nineteenth-Century Serial Narrative in Transnational Perspective, 1830s-1860s: Popular Culture—Serial Culture (Palgrave Studies in Nineteenth-Century Writing and Culture)*. Palgrave Macmillan, 2019.

The Talented Mr. Ripley

The Novel

Author: Patricia Highsmith (1921-95)
First published: 1955

The Film

Year released: 1999
Director: Anthony Minghella (1954-2008)
Screenplay by: Anthony Minghella
Starring: Matt Damon, Gwyneth Paltrow, Jude Law, Cate Blanchett, Philip Seymour Hoffman

Context

Author Patricia Highsmith made her debut in the literary world with her novel *Strangers on a Train* (1950). The book quickly established her as one of the most preeminent psychological thriller writers of her generation, and its classic status was further established after it was adapted into a film by famed director Alfred Hitchcock in 1951. Highsmith had a penchant for telling stories about people succumbing to their worst instincts, some transgressive tendency, leading to crime or violence. *The Talented Mr. Ripley* (1955) is perhaps most her most famous. She followed up the novel, a story about a serial killer and con man named Tom Ripley, with four sequels. Together, the five books in the Ripley series are known as the Ripliad.

The Talented Mr. Ripley shares its worldly, cynical, "noir"-ish qualities with other popular noir novels of the era, including Jim Thompson's *The Killer Inside Me* (1952), Charles Willeford's *Pick-Up* (1955), and Chester Himes's *The Real Cool Killers* (1959). However, *The Talented Mr. Ripley* is distinctive among these works, at least some literary critics have argued, in part due to Highsmith's personal background. As a woman who struggled with her attraction to women—she lived and wrote at a time when the larger societal attitude toward homosexuality was overtly hostile—some have suggested that she weaved her own experience as a social outsider into the character of Ripley, a man who longs to be someone else.

The Talented Mr. Ripley, or at the least its concept, has been adapted for the screen several times, including a full-length feature French film directed by René Clément titled *Plein soleil* (*Purple Noon*; 1960). The most well-known adaptation, however, is the 1999 film by director Anthony

Minghella. A British filmmaker, Minghella was best known for directing *The English Patient*, (1996) which won nine Academy Awards, including for best picture. *The Talented Mr. Ripley* (1999) represented a tonal shift in Minghella's work, as it is not a sweeping romantic epic like *The English Patient* but, rather, a twisted thriller.

Film Analysis

As director and the writer of the screenplay, Minghella made several significant changes to *The Talented Mr. Ripley* when translating the story to the screen. Like the book, the film is a portrait of Tom Ripley (Matt Damon) as a serial killer obsessed with upward mobility. However, the way that Minghella presents this character differs greatly from its source material. When Highsmith first introduces Ripley to her readers, he is already a seasoned con man who dupes rich people into giving him money by impersonating an Internal Revenue Service (IRS) employee. As the novel continues, his desire for a privileged life results in him unremorsefully plotting to kill Dickie Greenleaf so that he can steal his identity. Contrarily, Minghella's Ripley initially comes across as a somewhat sympathetic character. A piano accompanist who longs to be part of the upper echelon of society, he kills Dickie (Jude Law) in a moment of passion and is seemingly regretful afterwards. When he murders again, it is out of desperation to not get caught.

Additionally, the film sees Ripley form a close, seemingly lover-like relationship with Peter Smith-Kingsley (Jack Davenport), a more minor character in the novel. This would not have been characteristic of Highsmith's Ripley. Ultimately, Minghella presents Ripley as human as possible throughout the film, likely because he wanted audiences to find the character more relatable.

The 1999 film version of *The Talented Mr. Ripley* is similar to the book in that its central message is how dangerous society's obsession with wealth and status can be. Most of the characters whom Ripley encounters throughout his journey were born into significant means. Although many try to shirk the snobby stigma that accompanies their wealth by living ostensibly bohemian lives in Europe, they are still elitists. The character of Dickie, for example, pretends to be a jazz musician who wants nothing to do with his shipping-magnate father's empire. Minghella demonstrates the ironic falseness of Dickie's identity by surrounding him with luxuries like a sailboat, a well-furnished house, and tailored clothes. The way Minghella's camera lingers on and celebrates the beauty of the Italian landscape and architecture demonstrates that even Dickie's location is an enviable indulgence. It is through Ripley's interactions with Dickie and his friends that Minghella makes commentary about the elusiveness of status. Although the American Dream narrative is meritocratic in its suggestion that anyone can achieve the "ultimate" goal of excessive wealth, the old money characters of Dickie, Freddie Miles (Philip Seymour Hoffman), and Meredith Logue (Cate Blanchett) are insular and unwelcoming to anyone born into a different class—so much so that Ripley must kill to become one of them.

Minghella employs strategic imagery to signify Ripley's evolution into a new identity. When audiences first see Ripley, he is shot as an outsider observing the privileged from a distance. In these early scenes, Minghella alternates between close-ups of Ripley's face to wide shots of the people he is spying on. He begins to infiltrate their ranks, however, when he meets the exceptionally wealthy Herbert Greenleaf (James Rebhorn), who offers to pay him to go to Italy to bring his son Dickie back to New York. Minghella depicts Ripley's acceptance of this generous offer as a transformative moment from being a "nobody" into a "somebody" by having him climb the stairs up from his dingy basement apartment to the street, where a limousine waits for him. Once in Italy, Ripley's knack for impersonation and forgery allows him to quickly adopt the air and mannerisms of the well-bred Dickie and Marge (Gwyneth Paltrow). He becomes obsessed with Dickie and wants to become both him and his lover. When he kills Dickie in the heat of an argument on a

boat, Minghella showcases an overhead shot of him nestling with the body. Bathed in Dickie's blood for hours, the scene is symbolic of a baptism or rebirth. When Ripley emerges, he begins his new life as Dickie by getting himself a beautiful apartment filled with the finest things—a far cry from the basement hovel that he first emerged from.

The Talented Mr. Ripley is in many ways an homage to horror director Hitchcock's oeuvre. This is evident in everything from the opening credits, in a mid-century style, and the film's musical cues to its casting. While Highsmith's book presents the character of Marge as somewhat unappealing in both her looks and personality, Minghella rewrites her as the quintessential Hitchcockian "icy blonde." Played by Paltrow, who has a similar appearance to Hitchcock actors like Grace Kelly and Tippi Hedren, Marge embodies this cinematic archetype by be-

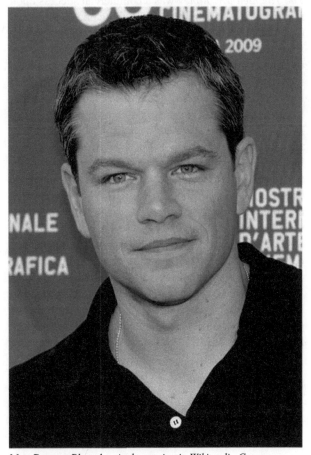
Matt Damon. Photo by nicolas genin via Wikimedia Commons.

ing stylish, sophisticated, and poised. A more significant way that Minghella captures the Hitchcock aesthetic, however, is the way in which he uses the camera to create feelings of dread and suspense. These techniques are especially evident in the film's last sequence (which deviates from the book's ending), when Ripley is worried about being found out by Peter and confronts him in the cabin of a steamship. The lighting in this scene, reminiscent of noir films, gives it a grim, ominous feeling. To convey Ripley's feelings of panic, Minghella switches back and forth between over-the-shoulder shots from Ripley's perspective to close-ups. This technique was utilized by Hitchcock in films like *Psycho* (1960) to generate a foreboding sense of uneasiness in audiences. It successfully creates the same ambiance in *The Talented Mr. Ripley*.

Significance

The Talented Mr. Ripley was a commercial success upon release. Shot on a budget of $40 million on location in Italy, it went on to earn a respectable $129 million worldwide at the box office. It was well received by the majority of critics, who extolled Minghella for his writing and direction. Most reviews commended the film for capturing the complicated themes of identity and longing as effectively as Highsmith's novel. Others pointed to the way Minghella blended suspense with astute social commentary. Roger Ebert wrote about this in his 1999 review, stating that the film is "insidious in the way it leads us to identify with Tom Ripley." The film was also considered a breakout role for Damon, as it successfully demonstrated his ability to play complex antagonists or antiheroes.

In the years since its release, *The Talented Mr. Ripley* has become a minor classic. Furthermore, it has become a cultural touchstone when it comes to discussing the issue of identity deception in America. This is thanks largely to Minghella, whose depiction of Ripley is often referred to by academics and essayists as a kind of patron saint of grifters with whom to compare real-life con artists like Bernie Madoff or Elizabeth Holmes. The film's enduring reputation ultimately led to the idea for a reboot, this time for the small screen. In 2019, Showtime announced plans for a television series based on the Ripliad. The first season of *Ripley* was scheduled to air in 2020, but the Coronavirus pandemic delayed production.

—*Emily E. Turner*

Further Reading

Clapp, Susannah. "The Simple Art of Murder." *The New Yorker*, 13 Dec. 1999, www.newyorker.com/magazine/1999/12/20/the-simple-art-of-murder. Accessed 28 Feb. 2021.

Mlotek, Haley. "The Most Stylish Scammer: 20 Years of *The Talented Mr. Ripley*." *The Ringer*, 23 Dec. 2019, www.theringer.com/movies/2019/12/23/21034364/talented-mr-ripley-anniversary-20-years. Accessed 25 Feb. 2021.

Willmore, Alison. "Let's Torture Ourselves with the Beautiful, Murderous Italy of *The Talented Mr. Ripley*." *Vulture*, Vox Media, 29 Apr. 2020, www.vulture.com/2020/04/why-the-talented-mr-ripley-is-a-perfect-quarantine-watch.html. Accessed 25 Feb. 2021.

Bibliography

Davis, Sandi. "The Talented Mr. Minghella 'Ripley' Director Reflects on Film That Studies Envy." *Oklahoman*, 2 Jan. 2000, oklahoman.com/article/2681312/the-talented-mr-minghella-ripley-director-reflects-on-film-that-studies-envy. Accessed 25 Feb. 2021.

Ebert, Roger. Review of *The Talented Mr. Ripley*, directed by Anthony Minghella. *RogerEbert.com*, 24 Dec. 1999, www.rogerebert.com/reviews/the-talented-mr-ripley-1999. Accessed 25 Feb. 2021.

Minghella, Anthony. "Looking Back on Misters Minghella and Ripley." Interview by Alex Simon. *HuffPost*, 6 Dec. 2017, www.huffpost.com/entry/looking-back-on-misters-m_b_7102760. Accessed 25 Feb. 2021.

Montgomery, Hugh. "The Talented Mr. Ripley Is a Sociopath for Our Instagram Age." *BBC*, 11 Dec. 2019, www.bbc.com/culture/article/20191211-the-talented-mr-ripley-is-a-sociopath-for-our-instagram-age. Accessed 25 Feb. 2021.

O'Grady, Megan. "How *The Talented Mr. Ripley* Foretold Our Era of Grifting." *The New York Times*, 16 Nov. 2020, www.nytimes.com/2020/11/12/t-magazine/mr-ripley.html. Accessed 25 Feb. 2021.

The Taming of the Shrew / 10 Things I Hate About You

The Play
Author: William Shakespeare (1564-1616)
First published: 1594

The Film
Year released: 1999
Director: Gil Junger (b. 1954)
Screenplay by: Karen McCullah, Kirsten Smith
Starring: Julia Stiles, Heath Ledger, Joseph Gordon-Levitt, Larisa Oleynik, Andrew Keegan

Context

Written between the years 1590 and 1592, *The Taming of the Shrew* has historically been one of William Shakespeare's most popular comedies. The play follows the story of Petruchio, a man who transforms Katherine Minola, a feisty, willful, unmarried woman, into an obedient wife. The popularity of *The Taming of the Shrew* led to collaborator John Fletcher writing *The Tamer Tamed*, in which a widowed Petruchio is worn down into submission by his next wife, Maria. Beginning in the late twentieth century, questions about whether or not the play endorses the misogyny it represents became prominent, and to what extent the farcical, comedic, and ironic elements in the play undercut an easy "yes" answer that question. While certain feminist critics have maintained a fairly straightforward "yes," others have strongly argued the case for the opposite—that the play is, in fact, protofeminist.

The adaptation of *The Taming of the Shrew* into the film *10 Things I Hate About You* (1999), a romantic comedy geared toward teenagers, was partially inspired by the enormous critical and commercial success of the film *Clueless* (1995). Written by Amy Heckerling, *Clueless* is an updated adaptation of Jane Austen's *Emma* (1815). In interviews, *10 Things I Hate About You* screenwriters Karen McCullah and Kirsten Smith have stated that their goal was to write a gender reversed-version of *The Taming of the Shrew* in which it was the men whose behavior needed to be changed and conversely the women were never "tamed."

The screenplay was purchased by Walt Disney Studios, which hired Gil Junger to oversee the film's production. *10 Things I Hate About You* was Junger's debut as a feature director, and he joined the project because of his admiration of the script. The film's cast would eventually include veteran teenage actors including Joseph Gordon-Levitt and Larisa Oleynik. The film would also launch the careers of its then unknown leads, Julia Stiles and Heath Ledger.

Film Analysis

10 Things I Hate About You is a film inspired by *The Taming of the Shrew* rather than an adaptation of it. Set in twentieth-century Seattle, Washington, and with a script that doesn't employ any of Shakespeare's dialogue, the film is a teen romantic comedy written from a contemporary and straightforwardly "feminist" perspective.

The premise of the play is the domestication of the titular shrew, Katherine Minola. Outspoken and unwilling to submit to a man, Katherine is considered an unmarriageable woman. Her father becomes so desperate to marry her off that he declares that his conventionally desirable daughter, Bianca, is not allowed to wed until her sister does. In turn, three of Bianca's suitors, Gremio, Hortensio, and Lucentio, decide to pay a stranger named Petruchio to marry Katherine. Delighted by the prospect of marrying into the wealthy Minola family, Petruchio agrees and embarks on a quest to transform the strong-willed Katherine into a meek, obedient spouse.

The story of the film revolves around the love lives of sisters Kat (Stiles) and Bianca (Oleynik). Like the play, *10 Things I Hate About You* presents these two young women as the embodiments of different styles of femininity. Popular among her peers, Bianca is sweet, feminine, and conciliatory; Kat is defiant, outspoken, and refuses to act conventionally simply to fit in. Just as Katherine was considered unmarriable, Kat is perceived as undateable—her male classmates are afraid of her. Furthermore, she is not interested in finding a boyfriend. When new student

Cameron (Gordon-Levitt) falls for Bianca and discovers that her father will not allow her to date unless her sister does, he finds a potential match for Kat in Patrick, the school outsider (Ledger). Cameron, whose character is based on Lucentio in the play, tricks another one of Bianca's suitors, Joey (Andrew Keegan), to pay Patrick to take Kat out on a date. Although Patrick initially only agrees to date Kat in exchange for compensation, after winning her over, he eventually falls for her.

Despite the broad similarities of its premise, characters, and plot elements, *10 Things I Hate About You* is quite different. *The Taming of the Shrew* delights in irony and farcical elements, and when Katherine delivers a monologue at the play's end showing herself a compliant woman, it isn't clear that this itself isn't simply farce. *10 Things I Hate About You*, thought a comedy, plays things straight and offers a moral obvious and salutary for young viewers: Kat is rewarded for being a strong, independent woman who challenges gender norms. She wins Patrick's love and is granted permission from her father to attend the East Coast college of her dreams simply for being true to herself.

Tonally, *10 Things I Hate About You* is somewhat akin to *The Taming of the Shrew*. The film is a comedy with bold, outlandish characters who engage in elaborate schemes to achieve their goals. For example, Cameron pretends to be a French tutor in order to spend more time with Bianca. Meanwhile, Patrick's character is similar to Petruchio because he is a mischievous rebel who is willing to break the rules to get what he wants. In *The Taming of the Shrew*, this involves ridiculous techniques to trick Katherine into becoming subservient. In *10 Things I Hate About You*, Patrick sings Frankie Valli's "Can't Take My Eyes Off You" while being accompanied by the school marching band, despite knowing that it is going to get him sent to detention. Furthermore, much of the comedy of the film pays tribute to *The Taming of the Shrew's* over-the-top farce through an almost cartoonish, surreal quality. At one point, for example, Bianca accidentally shoots an arrow into her gym teacher's leg without even noticing what she has done. In another scene, a stampede of students takes over a stuffy gathering and turns it into a wild party. In the film's final shot, Kat's favorite band is inexplicably playing on top of the school's roof.

Significance

10 Things I Hate About You was a moderate commercial and critical success. Filmed on a $16 million budget, it ultimately earned $53 million at the box office. Its profitability is especially impressive considering that the film opened the same weekend as *The Matrix* (1999), one of the most popular and highest-grossing science fiction films of the time. Most critics' reviews praised the actors' performances as well as the film's avoidance of many stereotypical high school tropes. Scott Tobias described the movie's appeal in a review for *The A.V. Club*: "Quirky, inventive, and brimming over with clever visual gags and colorful supporting characters, *10 Things* uses Shakespeare as a jumping-off point to playfully send up a society that doesn't know what to do with a strong woman."

10 Things I Hate About You would go on to gain a cult-like following from fans who kept it part of the cultural conversation many years after its initial release. This continued popularity eventually led to a television adaptation in 2009. The true legacy of *10 Things I Hate About You*, however, is the successful careers of its cast and crew. The film demonstrated Stiles's depth and range as a performer, and introduced Australian actor Ledger to American audiences. Both actors became household names as a result of their roles in *10 Things I Hate About You* and would go on to land major parts in critically acclaimed, Oscar-nominated films. *10 Things I Hate About You* also proved to be a vehicle for its screenwriters' careers. It was the debut script of Karen McCullah and Kirsten Smith, who would go on to write more popular romantic comedies with strong female leads, including *Legally Blonde* (2001) and *Ella Enchanted* (2004).

—Emily E. Turner

Further Reading
Kaplan, Ilana. "*10 Things I Hate About You*: When Heath Ledger Was Just Breaking Through." *The New York Times*, 27 Mar. 2019, www.nytimes.com/2019/03/27/arts/10-things-i-hate-about-you-heath-ledger.html. Accessed 20 Feb. 2020.
Wilkinson, Alissa, et al. "*10 Things I Hate About You* Is as Fresh as Ever, Even 20 Years Later." *Vox Media*, 29 Mar. 2019, www.vox.com/culture/2019/3/29/18287403/10-things-i-hate-about-you-20-anniversary-heath-ledger-julia-stiles-shakespeare. Accessed 20 Feb. 2020.

Bibliography
Blickley, Leigh. "The Full Story Behind Heath Ledger's Famous Bleacher Scene in *10 Things I Hate About You*." *The Huffington Post*, 29 Mar. 2019, www.huffpost.com/entry/10-things-i-hate-about-you-bleachers-scene_n_5c990c60e4b057f7330e3190. Accessed 20 Feb. 2020.

McCullah, Karen, and Kirsten Smith. "The *10 Things I Hate About You* Writers Reflect on the Film's Feminist Legacy." Interview by Kaitlin Reilly. *Refinery 29*, 20 Jun. 2019. www.refinery29.com/en-us/2019/06/235767/10-things-i-hate-about-you-rom-com-fest-writer-interview. Accessed 20 Feb. 2020.

Tobias, Scott. Review of *10 Things I Hate About You*, directed by Gil Junger. *The A.V. Club*, 31 Mar. 1999, film.avclub.com/10-things-i-hate-about-you-1798192034. Accessed 20 Feb. 2020.

Tex

The Novel
Author: S. E. Hinton (b. 1948)
First published: 1979

The Film
Year released: 1982
Director: Tim Hunter (b. 1947)
Screenplay by: Charles S. Haas, Tim Hunter
Starring: Matt Dillon, Jim Metzler, Meg Tilly, Bill McKinney, Ben Johnson

Context

Tex (1979) was the fourth novel written by American author S. E. Hinton, who first came onto the literary scene twelve years earlier with her debut novel *The Outsiders* (1967). Published when Hinton was still in high school, *The Outsiders* grew popular among adolescent readers and eventually became a staple of middle- and high-school English class curricula. With *Tex*, Hinton continued her exploration of themes introduced in her first novel and then continued with the two that followed—*That Was Then, This Is Now* (1971) and *Rumble Fish* (1975). All four books follow a young male protagonist who is struggling to find his place among his family and in the world. *Tex* also examines the nature of male friendship and the disconnect that exists between teenagers and adults. Unlike most of Hinton's other books, which are set predominantly in urban settings like Tulsa, *Tex* takes place in a rural suburb. *Tex* was the first of Hinton's books to be adapted into a film, followed by *The Outsiders* and *Rumble Fish*, both of which were directed by Francis Ford Coppola and released in 1983.

The director that ultimately brought *Tex* to the cinema was American filmmaker Tim Hunter. A graduate of the American Film Institute (AFI), Hunter started his career by writing the screenplay for the coming-of-age drama *Over the Edge* in 1979. The film was American actor Matt Dillon's debut and told the story of a group of unruly teenagers causing chaos in a planned suburban community. While doing research for *Over the Edge*, Hunter discovered Hinton's work and felt that she was one of the only writers who could accurately capture the American teenage experience. He reached out to her publishers to see if she had anything else in the pipeline and was sent a copy of her upcoming novel *Tex*. After their review of the

novel, Hunter and his writing partner Charles S. Haas quickly optioned the film rights for the book. Hunter was able to parlay his writing credit from *Over the Edge* as well as his relationship with Matt Dillon into an opportunity to write and direct the film *Tex* for Walt Disney Productions. This was significant considering that he had never directed anything before.

In some ways, *Tex* was a traditional story for the time in that it followed a boy in a rural setting who loves horses. It also exemplified a trend toward edgier topics and themes for young audiences then becoming popular. Although produced by Disney, *Tex* depicted teenagers discussing sex, violence, and drug use in a frank, realistic fashion.

Film Analysis

The plot of film stays largely true to its source material. In part, this is because Charles Haas's screenplay lifts nearly all of the scenes and much of the dialogue directly from the novel. Like the original iteration, the film follows fifteen-year-old Tex (Dillon) through several formative weeks of his life. He lives in Bixby, Oklahoma, a rural suburb of Tulsa, with his older brother Mason (Metzler) in a dilapidated house with a few acres of land and two horses. A troublemaker, Tex does not do well in school and is often getting called to the principal's office. He is happiest when he is riding his horse Rowdy, spending time with his best friend Johnny Collins (Emilio Estevez), or admiring Johnny's sister Jaime (Tilly). The Collins family is wealthy and is ruled by a strict patriarch named Cole (Johnson) who despises Tex and Mason.

Although he is only seventeen years old, Mason acts like a father figure to Tex. This is largely because their actual father (McKinney) is away for months at a time working on the rodeo circuit and rarely sends money home. Unable to pay the bills or buy food, Mason has no choice but to sell the horses one day while Tex is away at school. This proves to be the pivotal incident of the film—the event that launches Tex's storyline into new and uncharted territory.

The film sensitively explores issues of masculinity and male friendship. Tex's identity is defined in many ways by the relationships he has with other male characters. For example, his troublemaker tendencies seem to be the result of both his father's absence and Cole Collins repeatedly telling him that he is a bad influence on his children. Tex's self-worth is upheld by his brother, who clearly cares about him despite their constant arguing, and his best friend Johnny's adoration. Throughout the film, Tex is trying to figure out who he is and what his place is in the world. He looks to older boys for inspiration on how to be a man but has a difficult time finding anyone who is like him. Mason is a basketball star who wants to leave Bixby as soon as possible. Then, there is their friend Lem (Phillip Brock) who got his girlfriend pregnant and started dealing drugs to support his new family. Tex does not want to run away like Mason, but also does not want to turn out like Lem. Tex's decision of who to become provides the film with its central conflict.

A noticeable difference between Hunter's film and Hinton's novel is the role that the character of Jaime plays in Tex's life. In the novel, his feelings for Jaime are overwhelming. The two spend a lot of time together as she often hangs out with Johnny. At one point, in Hinton's version, they go on a date together and Tex kisses her and tells her that he loves her. She replies that while she loves him too, she is not ready to have sex. This sequence is omitted from the film and, similarly, their love for one another is never discussed outright. Instead, Hunter presents the two characters' relationship as a kind of fun flirtation. Jaime becomes a symbol of Tex's growing interest in girls as well as the classism that he feels suffocated by. This is because Jaime is smart and lives in a nice house and feels out of reach. Tex is not an aspirational character who seeks upward mobility like Mason, but is instead searching for inner peace.

Hunter's film explores the insidious nature of anger and how harmful it can be. Tex feels angry because of the many difficult circumstances in his life: he is poor, his mother is dead, and his father does not care very much about him. However, most of this anger is directed toward his brother for selling his horse. For Tex, anger is some-

thing that must be expressed physically. When he learns that he cannot get his horse back, he and Mason get into a physical fight.

In a later scene, he learns that he is not his father's biological son, and Tex becomes so overwhelmed with fury that he goes with Lem to a drug dealer's house. There, confrontation builds, and the drug dealer pulls a gun on them. Instead of walking away, Tex starts to fight the man and wrestles the gun away from him. He is shot in the process and almost dies. Hinton's book explores the idea that anger is dangerously toxic even further; in an earlier scene, Tex and Mason are held at gunpoint by a deranged hitchhiker. The entire time he is driving, Tex keeps wondering who the hitchhiker reminds him of. After the police come to the rescue, he realizes that the hitchhiker reminds him of himself. It is then that he begins to understand how his anger has the potential to fester like a poison.

Tex was shot on location in Oklahoma with cinematographer Ric Waite. Under Hunter's direction, the film is defined by many long, loose takes. In other words, Hunter allows the scenes to continue for long stretches of time rather than cutting and transitioning to different angles. This stylistic choice becomes evident in the film's first few sequences. Specifically, it is used when viewers are first introduced to Tex riding his horse Rowdy and later when he is interacting with his brother in their kitchen. Perhaps the most iconic scene that exemplifies Hunter's style is after Tex is shot and gets out of Lem's car to call for help. Hunter allows this scene to continue in one long take rather than cutting away to a close-up or medium setup. The result is a scene that feels more rooted in reality, which in turn allows audiences to experience in real time the fear and suspense that Tex is feeling.

Significance

Tex was released on July 30, 1982, to mostly positive reviews. A common point of praise was the film's realistic, sensitive depiction of teenagers. Roger Ebert wrote, "There is a shock of recognition almost from the beginning of *Tex*, because we're listening to the sound of American voices in an authentically American world, the world of teenaged boys trying to figure things out and make the right decisions. The voices sound right but may be a little unfamiliar, because adolescents on television are often made to talk in pseudo-hip sitcom nonspeak." Like Ebert, most other critics argued that it was a believable portrait of small-town youth and the struggles they face.

Although not a flop, the film was also not a huge commercial success, earning only $7.4 million at the box office. It did not receive any major awards with the exception of earning Jim Metzler a nomination for best supporting actor at the Golden Globes. The film's biggest legacy, however, was in how it elevated many of its cast and crew's careers. As a result of *Tex*, Matt Dillon became a teenage heartthrob and then a major Hollywood actor. He also starred in other adaptations of Hinton's novels, including *The Outsiders* (1983) and *Rumble Fish* (1983).

The film also provided a launching pad for director Tim Hunter. After *Tex*, he directed another film about a teenager and their horse called *Sylvester* (1985) before making the controversial but critically acclaimed teenage cult classic, *The River's Edge* (1986). Much of Hunter's early work focused on the adolescent experience. As his career developed, he became a highly respected television director known for his work on shows like *Twin Peaks*, *Beverly Hills 90210*, *Mad Men*, *Breaking Bad*, and *Deadwood*.

—*Emily E. Turner*

Further Reading

Biedenharn, Isabella. "S. E. Hinton on *The Outsiders'* Success: It Gave Me Writers Block for Four Years." *Entertainment Weekly*, 24 Apr. 2017, ew.com/books/2017/04/24/the-outsiders-anniversary-s-e-hinton/. Accessed 24 Apr. 2020.

Ebert, Roger. "Interview with Matt Dillon." *RogerEbert.com*, 24 Apr. 1983, www.rogerebert.com/interviews/interview-with-matt-dillon. Accessed 24 Apr. 2020.

Bibliography

Ebert, Roger. "*Tex*." *RogerEbert.com*, 1 Jan. 1982, www.rogerebert.com/reviews/tex-1982. Accessed 24 Apr. 2020.

Halskov, Andreas. "It All Begins with the Story: An Interview with Tim Hunter." *16:9*, 24 Nov. 2018, www.16-9.dk/2018/11/interview-with-tim-hunter/. Accessed 24 Apr. 2020.

Ihnat, Gwen. "*Outsiders* Author S. E. Hinton Is Still Gold after 50 Years." *AV Club*, 16 May 2017, film.avclub.com/outsiders-author-s-e-hinton-is-still-gold-after-50-yea-1798262219. Accessed 23 Apr. 2020.

Rickman, Gregg. "An Interview with Tim Hunter." *Film Quarterly*, vol. 47, no.1 (Autumn, 1993), pp. 8-14. www.jstor.org/stable/1213105?read-now=1&seq=3#page_scan_tab_contents. Accessed 23 Apr. 2020.

The 39 Steps

The Novel
Author: John Buchan (1875-1940)
First published: 1915

The Film
Year released: 1935
Director: Alfred Hitchcock (1899-1980)
Screenplay by: Charles Bennett, Ian Hay
Starring: Robert Donat, Madeleine Carroll, Lucie Mannheim, Godfrey Tearle, Peggy Ashcroft

Context

When Scottish author John Buchan published his first "shocker," *The Thirty-Nine Steps* (1915) featuring protagonist Richard Hannay, World War I was still raging in Europe. The novel centers on a plot by German spies set a few months before the outbreak of the war. Its complicated plot involves the assassination of an important Greek politician on British soil, the impersonation of an Admiralty officer, and a scheme to spirit British military plans out of the country so the United Kingdom can more easily be defeated once the fighting begins. But while elements of Buchan's novel were highly topical, the basic concept and the characterization of the hero proved timeless and influential. Indeed, the book is often credited with establishing the innocent-hero-on-the-run subgenre of suspense and even the entire category of the modern thriller.

The character of the falsely accused but resourceful everyman hero was based partially on Buchan's own history. Like his creation Hannay, Buchan was an avid outdoorsman and spent many years in southern Africa working for colonial administrations. Buchan also borrowed aspects of Hannay's personality from renowned soldier William Edmund Ironside (1880-1959), who served more than forty years in the British Army, rising to the rank of field marshal. Ironside was famous for his exploits, including operating in disguise, during the Boer War. The military connections of *The Thirty-Nine Steps* helped make it highly popular among the soldiers serving in World War I.

By the time filmmaker Alfred Hitchcock began to adapt Buchan's novel, almost twenty years had passed. This meant the film version was formed in a very different social and political climate than the one that had shaped the book. Though there were again major rumblings of war in the mid-1930s following the rise of Adolf Hitler in Germany, the British government's policy at the time was appeasement. This consisted of the periodic granting of concessions to Germany in an attempt to prevent or forestall combat until British land, sea, and air forces could be strengthened enough to compete against the presumed enemy-to-be's military might. When it was publicized that Hitchcock had begun filming Buchan's novel, the British government grew alarmed that a faithful adaptation of a work in which Germans were presented as villains might contribute to prematurely unleashing the aggression building on the continent. The British Foreign Office therefore directly urged against the kind of negative portrayal of Germany that Buchan's book contained. Whether for this reason or through pure artistic license, Hitchcock's 1935 film—stylized as *The 39 Steps*—does away with much of the source material's political context, focusing instead on more universal action and intrigue.

Film Analysis

While Hitchcock retained some of the structure, setting, and cast of Buchan's novel, many plot points were developed quite differently for the film. Though Buchan's Richard Hannay is likeable and lighthearted, *The Thirty-Nine Steps* has a fairly serious tone overall. This is in keeping with the reality of the widespread death and destruction of war in 1915, which the author hinted could be the consequence of a successful espionage scheme. The Hitchcock film, however, with less at stake—not war, but the loss of unknown but "vital" information to an unspecified spy organization—blends comedy and suspense from beginning to end. The tragicomic atmosphere expands the appeal of a manly adventure to a broader audience. Hitchcock also arguably improves upon the source material. The complicated plot is streamlined and simplified, and the most jarring coincidences and improbabilities are eliminated. Considerable action is packed into a running time of eighty-six minutes.

One of the most crucial changes made in the adaptation is Hitchcock's insertion of women into prominent roles; in Buchan's novel, women are relegated to the background, where they are occasionally seen but seldom heard. This change begins from the start of *The 39 Steps*. Whereas in the novel, it is an American man named Scudder who tells the hero about the espionage plot, in the film it is a woman named Annabella Smith (Lucie Mannheim) who informs Richard Hannay (Robert Donat). (While Hitchcock avoids any overt mention of Germany, the presence of the German-born Mannheim provides a subtle reference). The expanded role of women in the film also highlights themes of sexuality and gender dynamics that are largely absent in the novel.

The way Smith and Hannay meet is made an integral part of the story. Hannay is first seen entering a local music hall, where a featured performer is "Mr. Memory" (Wylie Watson), whose specialty becomes an object of humor. Hannay is identified as a Canadian when he queries, "How far is Winnipeg from Montreal?" The proceedings are interrupted by gunshots. As patrons run screaming, Hannay and Smith are thrust together. She asks, in an exotically accented voice, if she can come home with him. At Hannay's flat, she tells him she is a freelance spy, working for England because they pay well. She is trying to prevent military information from being taken out of the country, and asks for a map of Scotland, where she is supposed to find the head of the enemy spy network, a man missing the top of his little finger.

Hannay is skeptical of her story, but begins to believe her when he sees suspicious men lurking outside the apartment, who make annoying calls from a phone booth that go unanswered. Hannay is awakened in the night as Smith lurches into his room and falls dead, a knife embedded in her back. A map of Scotland, with a place circled, is clutched in her hand. Hannay, likely to be accused by the police of her murder, and a probable target of the spies, decides to flee to Scotland to search for the head spy as a means to extricate himself from a doubly dangerous situation.

Hitchcock quickly launches the chase that consumes the rest of the film. Hannay escapes his watched flat by impersonating a milkman. Hitchcock bridges to the next scene with a clever device: A woman discovers the body of Smith in Hannay's flat, and as she opens her mouth to scream, the scene dissolves to a shot of the Flying Scotsman locomotive as the train's whistle shrieks. The technique would become something of a trademark for the filmmaker. Hannay's trip north—a passive sequence in the novel, when the hero attempts to decipher Scudder's coded notebook—provides Hitchcock with opportunities to add humor, provide information, build suspense, and introduce romance. Hannay shares a carriage compartment with two businessmen—one is a ladies' underwear salesman who proudly displays his products. Hannay reads about the murder in a newspaper on the train: a close-up shows his picture in outdoor gear, and a caption confirms he is Canadian, a wealthy rancher.

When the train stops and uniformed and plainclothes police board to search for him, Hannay has to duck and dodge to avoid discovery. He darts into a compartment where a blonde woman, Pamela (Madeleine Carroll) is reading and greets her familiarly, embracing and kissing her as policemen parade by in the corridor. He then hastily tells the shocked woman of his problem and his innocence, and pleads for her not to give him away. When the police return, however, Pamela gives him up. Hannay manages to daringly escape from the train as it crosses a bridge, a memorable piece of action that was not part of the book.

Several sequences only suggested in the novel are fully developed by Hitchcock for the film. Hannay, tramping cross-country, stays with jealous older farmer (John Laurie). The farmer's pretty young wife (Peggy Ashcroft) becomes aware of and sympathetic to the fugitive's plight, and gives him her pious husband's best overcoat. This gesture becomes significant later when Hannay, running from a line of policemen searching the moors, encounters the head spy at the spot Annabella Smith circled on the map. The ringleader is country gentleman Professor Jordan (Godfrey Tearle), who proves his identity by showing his mutilated finger. Jordan promptly shoots Hannay. Immediately afterward, it is revealed that Hannay's life was saved by a hymnal in the breast pocket of the borrowed overcoat.

Later, Hannay, wearing a handcuff on one wrist after escaping from the law, is mistaken for a scheduled speaker and pressed into giving a rousing political oration. Pamela is also on the program at the same hall, and is manipulated by spies impersonating police detectives into accompanying Hannay. The two are ultimately handcuffed to one another and so are forced to participate together in further adventures—including a long, semierotic sequence at an inn, where they pose as a runaway couple—while eluding both police and villains disguised as police. Ultimately, Pamela comes to believe in Hannay's innocence. She aids him in figuring out how the stolen information is to be transmitted, and works to help him prevent it from falling into enemy hands as the plot circles back to where it began: a music hall. Like the novel, the film concludes with the revelation of what the "39 Steps" actually means—though the answer is quite different from Buchan's version—and the foiling of the espionage plot.

Significance

Buchan's *The Thirty-Nine Steps* was an instant bestseller and remained constantly in print into the twenty-first century. It was greatly influential in the development of modern thrillers and spy fiction, but perhaps the most obvious sign of the work's lasting impact is the frequency with which it has been adapted. In addition to the famous 1935 film, versions include a 1959 film, a 1978 film, a 2008 television film, a comic play that premiered in 1995, and multiple radio programs.

Hitchcock's *The 39 Steps* became one of the most popular British films of the year upon its release. Some British film critics, who were familiar with Hitchcock's work and held him to a high standard, took issue with things like the combination of humor and suspense—which was to become a Hitchcock trademark for the remainder of his long career—and certain fortuitous coincidences in the film (most of them stemming from the source material, which is propelled by a series of improbabilities). But most reviewers lauded the film, and it was one of Hitchcock's first works to earn major success in North America. *The 39 Steps* was released in Canada in conjunction with Buchan assuming the role of Canada's governor-general (he served from 1935 until his death in 1940), and by early 1936 was the highest-earning British film ever in Canada. In the United States, reviews were overwhelmingly positive, with the pacing, performances and cinematic storytelling receiving particular attention. The enthusiastic reception contributed to Hitchcock earning a seven-year contract in Hollywood in 1939. He stayed in the United States beyond the contract, expanded his repertoire into television, and became a US citizen in 1955.

Hitchcock's adaptation has held up well over the years. Twenty-first century reviewers generally consider *The 39 Steps* one of the best films of Hitchcock's British period and one of the best British films of all time. It is seen as an early masterpiece from one of the twentieth century's most visionary and influential directors, and a cinematic originator of the ever-popular man-on-the-run film trope.

Hitchcock used themes featured in *The 39 Steps*—espionage, a false accusation, a chase, a blonde woman in jeopardy, suspicion and distrust of law enforcement, set pieces involving notable landmarks—many times in later films. Examples include *Foreign Correspondent* (1940), *Saboteur* (1942), *Strangers on a Train* (1951), *To Catch a Thief* (1955), *The Man Who Knew Too Much* (1956), *The Wrong Man* (1956), and *Frenzy* (1972). Perhaps most notable was the masterpiece *North by Northwest* (1959), regarded by many critics as essentially an American version of *The 39 Steps*.

—Jack Ewing

Further Reading

Buchan, Ursula. *Beyond the Thirty-Nine Steps: A Life of John Buchan*. Bloomsbury Publishing, 2019.

Duncan, Paul, editor. *Alfred Hitchcock: The Complete Films*. Taschen, 2018.

Bibliography

Buchan, Ursula. "The Many Lives of John Buchan." *The Spectator*, 10 Oct. 2015, www.spectator.co.uk/2015/10/the-many-lives-of-john-buchan/. Accessed 7 Nov. 2018.

Caterson, Simon. "A Century of *The Thirty-Nine Steps*." *Quadrant Online*, 23 Jan. 2016, quadrant.org.au/magazine/2015/12/century-thirty-nine-steps/. Accessed 7 Nov. 2018.

Dirks, Tim. Review of *The 39 Steps*, by Alfred Hitchcock. *AMC Filmsite*, www.filmsite.org/thirt.html. Accessed 15 Nov. 2018.

Glancy, Mark. *The 39 Steps: A British Film Guide*. I. B. Taurus, 2003.

House, Christian. "How *The Thirty-Nine Steps* Invented the Modern Thriller." *The Telegraph*, 11 Oct. 2015, www.telegraph.co.uk/books/what-to-read/thirty-nine-steps-modern-thriller-john-buchan/. Accessed 7 Nov. 2018.

Rimington, Stella. "John Buchan and *The Thirty-Nine Steps*." *The Telegraph*. 11 Jan. 2011, www.telegraph.co.uk/culture/books/bookreviews/8243300/John-Buchan-and-The-Thirty-Nine-Steps.html. Accessed 7 Nov. 2018.

Tinker Tailor Soldier Spy

The Novel
Author: John le Carré (1931-2020)
First published: 1974

The Film
Year released: 2011
Director: Tomas Alfredson (b. 1965)
Screenplay by: Bridget O'Connor, Peter Straughan
Starring: Gary Oldman, Colin Firth, Mark Strong, Tom Hardy, Benedict Cumberbatch

Context

Long a topic of interest, the subject of espionage flourished in literature and film in the decades following World War II as Cold War-era tensions between the Soviet Union and its allies and Western nations, such as the United States and United Kingdom, brought the practices of surveillance, intelligence gathering, and infiltration to the forefront of popular culture. As the era progressed, writers with personal experience in espionage became particularly popular, among them British novelists Ian Fleming, a former naval intelligence officer and the creator of the secret agent James Bond, and John le Carré, born David John Moore Cornwell, a former intelligence officer with the United Kingdom's domestic and foreign intelligence services. Whereas Fleming's works, and especially the multitude of films based on them, popularized the image of the spy as a flashy womanizer armed with a host of outlandish gadgets, le Carré's novels and their film and television counterparts became known for depicting a more realistic view of the world of espionage, focusing on observation and analysis more than physical conflict, and earned widespread acclaim for their complex narratives and compelling characters.

Among le Carré's most influential works was the 1974 novel *Tinker, Tailor, Soldier, Spy*, one of several novels focused on the character of former spy George Smiley. The character originated in le Carré's 1961 debut novel, *Call for the Dead*, and went on to appear in *The Honourable Schoolboy* (1977) and *Smiley's People* (1979), both of which were sequels to *Tinker, Tailor, Soldier, Spy*. Le Carré's novels proved popular sources of inspiration for film and television projects, and *Tinker, Tailor, Soldier, Spy* was adapted into a seven-part television miniseries that debuted on British television in 1979. The miniseries earned critical acclaim, and actor Alec Guinness received the British Academy of Film and Television Arts (BAFTA) TV Award for best actor for his portrayal of Smiley.

The 2011 adaptation of the novel, titled *Tinker Tailor Soldier Spy*, was directed by Tomas Alfredson, a Swedish director who was then best particularly known for directing the 2008 vampire film *Let the Right One In* (*Låt den rätte komma in*), an adaptation of a novel by John Ajvide Lindqvist. *Tinker Tailor Soldier Spy* marked Alfredson's English-language directorial debut. The screenplay for the film was written by Peter Straughan and Bridget O'Connor, a married couple and writing duo who had previously collaborated on the films *Sixty Six* (2006) and *Mrs. Ratcliffe's Revolution* (2007). O'Connor died during the period between writing the screenplay and the film's release, and *Tinker Tailor Soldier Spy* was ultimately dedicated to her. Starring Gary Oldman, Colin Firth, Mark Strong, Tom Hardy, and Benedict Cumberbatch and also featuring Ciarán Hinds, David Dencik, Toby Jones, John Hurt, and Kathy Burke, among others, the film premiered at the Venice Film Festival in Italy on September 5, 2011.

Film Analysis

Much like the original novel, *Tinker Tailor Soldier Spy* begins by introducing not its central character, George Smiley, but a different character whose experiences will prove key to the plot of the narrative to come. The novel begins seemingly far from the realm of international espionage, as a schoolboy named Bill Roach observes the arrival of a mysterious new temporary teacher at his school. The teacher is revealed to be Jim Prideaux, a former agent with the British foreign intelligence service—known as the Circus—who was betrayed and shot during a mission a year before, the failure of which cost Smiley and Circus leader Control their jobs. It is only after this first chapter that Smiley is introduced, and the reader is thus already poised to better understand the events that have led him to his current state.

While some films adapted from similarly structured novels might reconfigure the events of the narrative to ensure that the central character is introduced immediately, the film adaptation of *Tinker Tailor Soldier Spy* retains the delayed introduction of Smiley, who is not seen on-screen until nearly seven minutes into the film and does not speak until more than ten minutes later; the film instead begins with Prideaux (Mark Strong). However, the opening of the film differs significantly from that of the novel in terms of events. Rather than beginning with Prideaux's arrival at the school, the film depicts the events leading up to and during Prideaux's failed mission, including his meeting with Control (John Hurt), who tasks him with determining the identity of a Soviet mole within the Circus, and the subsequent incident in Budapest, in which Prideaux is shot and presumed dead. In the novel, these events happened in the past and are discussed in conversation rather than presented directly; in the film, however, they are seen as they occur, providing the film with an engaging opening that hints at the twisting espionage narrative to come.

The film's opening scenes signal a creative choice made in translating the events of the novel to the screen that continues throughout the remainder of the film. Due to the nature of the original novel, much of the plot, backstory, and relationships between the characters are explained through conversations between characters or through the focal characters' own memories as Smiley and his allies work to piece together the truth about the mole, a narrative strategy that is appropriate for a novel but less so for a film. While Smiley's intelligence gathering represents a significant part of *Tinker Tailor Soldier Spy*, the filmmakers render the work more visually engaging by presenting much of the information originally gleaned from such conversations as scenes in their own right. While the opening sequence depicting Prideaux's mission in Hungary is perhaps the most substantial of those, that strategy continues throughout the film, adding further visual interest to Smiley's ensuing search for the identity of the mole and at times enabling the filmmakers to present additional information key to the narrative. Following the

John le Carré. Photo by Krimidoedel via Wikimedia Commons.

attack on Prideaux, for example, the film moves on to a sequence in which Control and Smiley, after meeting with their colleagues in the wake of the Budapest incident, depart their office after being forced to retire. In addition to visualizing an event that is discussed at length but not depicted in a scene within the novel, the sequence provides a brief introduction to many of the film's other significant characters, including potential mole suspects Bill Haydon (Colin Firth), Percy Alleline (Toby Jones), Roy Bland (Ciarán Hinds), and Toby Esterhase (David Dencik), and Smiley allies Peter Guillam (Benedict Cumberbatch) and Connie Sachs (Kathy Burke), all of whom go on to play substantial roles in later events.

Discussing the screenwriters' strategy when adapting the novel, Straughan later described the process as "a kind of mosaic work" in which the original narrative was "broken into pieces" that were then shifted "around endlessly until it felt right," with the goal of creating "a new version of the narrative that would bear a close family resemblance to the source material, but have its own cinematic personality." The bulk of the film reflects that strategy, closely following the core of the novel's original plot while shuffling events and details as needed for thematic and cinematic effect. The scene in which Prideaux arrives at the school, for example, is moved from the very beginning of the novel to nearly forty minutes into the film, thus allowing the viewer to realize that Prideaux is still alive just after Smiley himself does. The filmmakers likewise continue to make use of enlightening flashbacks as Smiley continues to gather information about the rumored mole. His conversations with both Connie Sachs and spy Ricki Tarr (Tom Hardy) are intercut with scenes depicting the events they are telling Smiley about: Sachs reveals that she was fired after alerting Alleline that a Soviet official in London, Polyakov (Konstantin Khabensky), was likely a spy and may have been working with a mole, while Tarr tells Smiley about his encounter with a woman who claimed to know the mole's true identity. Smiley's conversations with Prideaux and with former colleague Jerry Westerby (Stephen Graham) likewise offer further opportunities to segue into flashbacks that provide Smiley and the audience with a greater understanding of how the events following Prideaux's failed mission played out.

As evidence accumulates, Smiley comes to realize that the mole has been passing key British and American information to the Soviets through Polyakov and devises a plan to lure the mole to Polyakov's location. The mole is revealed to be Haydon, whom Prideaux later kills for his betrayal. At the film's conclusion, the filmmakers again diverge from the original text in terms of details, although not entirely in spirit. Prior to the end of the novel, the work states that Alleline has been placed on leave indefinitely and that Smiley has been tasked with returning to the Circus to "help sweep up what was left." However, the novel does not depict Smiley returning to the Circus and instead focuses on his complicated relationship with his estranged wife before returning to Prideaux, who slowly recovers from his traumatic experiences and continues his unlikely friendship with Bill Roach. While the film does suggest that Smiley's wife has returned to him, the conclusion primarily places Smiley back at the Circus, where he takes his place in the chair once filled by Control. Despite the lingering specter of Haydon's betrayal, *Tinker Tailor Sol-dier Spy*—much like the original novel—thus ends on an optimistic note.

Significance

Following its premiere at the Venice Film Festival, *Tinker Tailor Soldier Spy* opened in the United Kingdom and Ireland later in September 2011 and went on to screen at various film festivals and in cinemas in several countries over subsequent months. The film debuted in a limited number of US theaters in December 2011 and opened in theaters throughout the country in January 2012. *Tinker Tailor Soldier Spy* grossed more than $24 million during its US and Canadian cinema run, according to the website Box Office Mojo. The film grossed an additional $56 million abroad, nearly $23 million of it from the United Kingdom, the home country of le Carré as well as the majority of the film's cast.

Tinker Tailor Soldier Spy was received well by critics, who largely appreciated the film's ability to distill the narrative of the original novel into a more concise one suitable for the screen as well as its overall tone and atmosphere. While some critics noted that elements of the 1979 miniseries, such as Guinness's performance as Smiley, were difficult for any subsequent adaptation to measure up to, those reviewers nevertheless widely praised Oldman's work in the film as well as the filmmakers' success in creating a work that is both related to yet distinct from its predecessors. Le Carré himself likewise commented in interviews that he approved of the film and highlighted Oldman's performance as particularly intriguing. In addition to winning the approval of author and critics alike, *Tinker Tailor Soldier Spy* received widespread recognition from award-granting organizations. The film was nominated for several European Film Awards and, at the BAFTA Awards, won the Alexander Korda Award for Best British Film and the BAFTA Film Award for Best Adapted Screenplay. The film also earned recognition in the United States, including nominations for the Academy Awards for adapted screenplay, best actor in a leading role, and best original score.

—*Joy Crelin*

Further Reading

Le Carré, John. *Tinker, Tailor, Soldier, Spy*. Penguin, 2011.
Levin, Robert. "The Director of *Tinker, Tailor, Soldier, Spy*: 'It's a Demanding Film.'" *The Atlantic*, 9 Dec. 2011, www.theatlantic.com/entertainment/archive/2011/12/the-

director-of-tinker-tailor-soldier-spy-its-a-demanding-film/ 249724/. Accessed 31 Jan. 2019.

Straughan, Peter. "*Tinker Tailor Soldier Spy*: What John Le Carré Really Thought of the Movie Adaptation." *Huffington Post*, 15 Dec. 2011, www.huffingtonpost.com/peter-straughan/ tinker-tailor-solider-spy-adaptation_b_1149007.html. Accessed 31 Jan. 2019.

Bibliography

Bradshaw, Peter. "*Tinker, Tailor, Soldier, Spy*—Review." Review of *Tinker Tailor Soldier Spy*, directed by Tomas Alfredson. *The Guardian*, 15 Sept. 2011, www.theguardian.com/film/2011/ sep/15/tinker-tailor-soldier-spy-film-review. Accessed 31 Jan. 2019.

Brooks, Xan. "'We Agreed *Tinker Tailor Soldier Spy* Was Probably Totally Impossible to Film.'" *The Guardian*, 4 Sept. 2011, www.theguardian.com/film/2011/sep/04/tinker-tailor-soldier-spy-film. Accessed 31 Jan. 2019.

Crompton, Sarah. "Thirty Years On, *Tinker Tailor* Still Rings True." *The Telegraph*, 19 Sept. 2011, www.telegraph.co.uk/ culture/film/8772807/Thirty-years-on-Tinker-Tailor-still-rings-true.html. Accessed 31 Jan. 2019.

Dargis, Manohla. "The Spy Who Emerged from the Fog." Review of *Tinker Tailor Soldier Spy*, directed by Tomas Alfredson. *The New York Times*, 8 Dec. 2011, www.nytimes.com/2011/12/ 09/movies/tinker-tailor-soldier-spy-with-gary-oldman-review. html. Accessed 31 Jan. 2019.

Le Carré, John, and Gary Oldman. "*Tinker, Tailor, Soldier, Spy*: Interview with John le Carré and Gary Oldman." Interview by Will Lawrence. *The Telegraph*, 29 July 2011, www.telegraph.co.uk/culture/film/starsandstories/8668955/ Tinker-Tailor-Soldier-Spy-interview-with-John-le-Carre-and-Gary-Oldman.html. Accessed 31 Jan. 2019.

Parker, James. "The Anti-James Bond." *The Atlantic*, Dec. 2011, www.theatlantic.com/magazine/archive/2011/12/the-antijames-bond/308708/. Accessed 31 Jan. 2019.

"Tinker, Tailor, Soldier, Spy." *Box Office Mojo*, www.boxofficemojo.com/movies/?id=tinkertailorsoldier spy.htm. Accessed 31 Jan. 2019.

To All the Boys I've Loved Before

The Novel
Author: Jenny Han (b. 1980)
First published: 2014

The Film
Year released: 2018
Director: Susan Johnson (b. 1970)
Screenplay by: Sofia Alvarez
Starring: Lana Condor, Noah Centineo, John Corbett, Anna Cathcart

Context

Jenny Han is an American writer of young adult and children's fiction. She published her first novel *Shug* (2006) while working on her Master of Fine Arts degree at The New School in New York City. She found success with her next book, *The Summer I Turned Pretty* (2009), and its two sequels. A coming-of-age story about a girl named Isabella, the novel explores themes of independence and love. The Summer trilogy became a *New York Times* bestseller and established the author's reputation among readers.

Han's depiction of romance and adolescent self-discovery continued in *To All the Boys I've Loved Before* (2014), which depicts the love life of a sixteen-year-old girl named Lara Jean Song Covey. Han, who grew up in a Korean household, felt that there was not enough Asian American representation in young adult literature and so made her protagonist half-Korean. *To All the Boys I've Loved Before* spent forty weeks on *The New York Times* Young Adult Best Seller list and went on to be published in thirty different languages. It was followed by two sequels, *P.S. I Still Love You* (2015) and *Always and Forever, Lara Jean* (2017).

The rights to *All the Boys I've Loved Before* were optioned by actor Will Smith's Overbook Productions in 2014. In interviews, Han noted that she declined other production companies that were interested in adapting the book because they wanted to "white-wash" the character of Lara Jean. Ultimately, Lana Condor, a Vietnamese American actor, was cast in the lead role. Filmmaker Susan Johnson was brought on to direct. Johnson began her career as a film and music video producer. Her previous works include the young adult film *Carrie Pilby* (2016) a comedy drama about a depressed nineteen-year-old prodigy.

To All the Boys I've Loved Before represented a new trend in the young adult film genre. Following the release of *Harry Potter and the Sorcerer's Stone* in 2001, many films directed at people under the age of eighteen were about teens fighting against oppressive fictional regimes. The genre was bolstered by film series like the Twilight Saga (2008-12) and the Hunger Games series (2012-15). By contrast, *To All the Boys I've Loved Before* lacks supernatural or dystopian themes and shares more in common with 1980s John Hughes films like *Sixteen Candles* (1984) and *Pretty in Pink* (1986).

Film Analysis

Screenwriter Sofia Alvarez did not take many liberties with Han's book, staying as close to the original story as possible. Both iterations of the story follow sixteen-year-old Lara Jean Song Covey (Lana Condor), a romantic who spends much of her time daydreaming and reading about love. Whenever she develops strong feelings for a boy, she writes them a love letter. She does not send the letter, however, keeping them for herself in an old hat box. Lara Jean does not have the courage to actually pursue love—she is content living in her fantasies. When her little sister, Kitty (Anna Cathcart), secretly sends out the letters, Lara Jean is forced to confront the boys she once had feelings for, including her former crush Peter Kavinsky (Noah Centineo) and her sister's ex-boyfriend, Josh Sanderson (Israel Broussard).

The book places more importance on the love triangle between Lara Jean, Peter, and Josh, while the film focuses predominantly on Lara Jean's relationship with Peter. Alvarez employs the character of Josh primarily as a catalyst; most of the film's narrative is powered by Lara Jean's decision to start a fake relationship with Peter in order to convince Josh that she does not love him. When Lara Jean and Josh move past the letter and rekindle their childhood friendship, he learns the truth about her relationship with Peter. Josh then effectively becomes a sounding board for Lara Jean and a tool for the audience to learn Lara Jean's inner most thoughts.

The other differences between the book and the film are minimal. Alvarez makes Kitty older and omits several scenes between Lara Jean and Peter, such as when they attend a Halloween party together and an antique shopping date. Additionally, the screenplay adds a scene between Lara Jean and her father, Dr. Dan Covey (John Corbett), where they discuss how her late mother would dance in public without caring what other people thought. The conversation is intended to empower Lara Jean and speaks to the film's central theme of the importance facing fears. From the beginning, it is clear that Lara Jean's biggest fear is getting close to other people. Johnson demonstrates this during the opening shot of the film: Lara Jean is dressed in a Victorian dress in a field waiting to be kissed by a boy. The scene is a fantasy, depicting what the character wishes she could do but is too afraid to. The film's inciting incident—Kitty mailing the love letters—forces Lara Jean to interact with Peter and subsequently allow herself to be vulnerable. By taking risks and facing her fears, she grows. The last scene of the film demonstrates this growth, with Lara Jean meeting Peter on a lacrosse field. She confesses her feelings for him and the two kiss, mirroring her original fantasy.

To All the Boys I've Loved Before has a quiet, dreamy tone. It is intended to provide audiences with the experiences of being a sweet but insecure sixteen-year-old-girl looking for love. Johnson succeeds in crafting this experience by employing a number of different filmmaking techniques. The use of voice over, for example, is an effective way to provide readers with a direct channel into Lara Jean's mind. Her inner monologue has a confessional, vulnerable quality that captures the adolescent experience and subsequently is highly relatable. By having Lara Jean directly reveal her inner most desires and fears, Johnson creates a deep sense of empathy for the character.

At times, Johnson utilizes point-of-view shots that have the actors look directly into the camera. Johnson typically employs it during heartfelt moments, when characters are their most vulnerable. The shots create intimacy and ensures that Lara Jean and her crushes feel accessible rather than unobtainable. Johnson furthers the film's unique aesthetic through its saturated blue and pink color palette. This choice gives Lara Jean's world a rich, dreamlike quality that is both feminine and romantic. The colors are atypical for a young adult film, which often are bright and sterile looking. Here, the muted shades of blue and pink foster the film's emotional depth and in turn speak to Lara Jean's experience navigating complex romantic feelings.

Throughout *All the Boys I've Loved Before*, there is evidence of a myriad filmic influences. The film's quirky, well-composed look is reminiscent of the works of Michel Gondry and Wes Anderson in some ways. Furthermore, the respectful manner in which Johnson depicts the adolescent protagonist's conflict, thoughts, and emotional journey is clearly influenced by the work of John Hughes. Known for his 1980s teenage romantic comedies, Hughes treated his characters' feelings and perspectives with great respect. Johnson does the same with Lara Jean. There is never a moment where the character's plight is depicted as silly or unimportant. The film also nods to its John Hughes influence by referencing his classic film *Sixteen Candles*.

Significance

To All the Boys I've Loved Before was released on August 17, 2018, on the streaming platform Netflix. It became an instant critical success, garnering predominantly positive reviews. Linda Holmes wrote for *National Public Radio* (17 Aug. 2018) that, "The film is precisely what it should be: pleasing and clever, comforting and fun and romantic." These qualities made it exceptionally popular among viewers. This popularity was publicly noted by Netflix when the company, which does not generally provide ratings information on its streamed content, announced that the film was one of its most watched and rewatched ever. Netflix ordered its sequel, *P.S. I Still Love You*, in December 2018.

To some critics, *To All the Boys I've Loved Before* represented a new wave of romantic comedies. This was significant considering that the genre had been somewhat dormant in the 2010s. From films like Frank Capra's *It Happened One Night* (1934) to *Pretty Woman* (1990), romantic comedies were an enormous part of the American cinematic culture for years. The genre, however, diminished in popularity beginning in the early 2000s due to changes in society and moviegoing culture. *To All the Boys I've Loved Before* was considered a part of Netflix's so-called Summer of Love, a release of six original romantic comedies, which also included the films *Set It Up* (2018) and *The Kissing Booth* (2018).

Upon its release, critics were quick to praise the film for its Asian American representation, remarking that it demonstrated an exciting shift in the cultural zeitgeist. Gina Mei wrote for *Vanity Fair* that *To All the Boys I've Loved Before* is significant because it, "features a young Asian-American protagonist without centering the story on her race. Lara Jean and her two sisters are half Korean and half white, yet even though their ethnic-racial identity is a large part of their lives, it isn't the only thing that defines them." Notably, *To All the Boys I've Loved Before* followed the release of the romantic comedy *Crazy Rich Asians* (2018), which earned $238 million at the box office, by two days.

—*Emily E. Turner*

Further Reading

Han, Jenny. "Jenny Han Says Some Hollywood Execs Tried to Whitewash *To All the Boys I've Loved Before*, Too." Interview by Karen Han. *Teen Vogue*, 16 Aug. 2018, www.teenvogue.com/story/jenny-han-interview-to-all-the-boys-ive-loved-before-movie. Accessed 15 Jan. 2019.

Ngyuen, Hanh. "*To All the Boys I've Loved Before* Cast and Crew Discuss That Surprise Ending and a Possible Sequel." *IndieWire*, 20 Aug. 2018, www.indiewire.com/2018/08/to-all-the-boys-ive-loved-before-sequel-ps-i-still-love-you-book-differences-1201996123/. Accessed 15 Jan. 2019.

Bibliography

Holmes, Linda. "Here's to the Romantic Comedy Pleasures of *To All the Boys I've Loved Before*." *National Public Radio*, 17 Aug. 2018, www.npr.org/2018/08/17/639213124/heres-to-the-romantic-comedy-pleasures-of-to-all-the-boys-i-ve-loved-before. Accessed 15 Jan 2019.

Johnson, Susan. "*To All the Boys I've Loved Before* Director on Social Media's Role in New Rom-Com." Interview by Jillian Forstadt. *The Hollywood Reporter*, 16 Aug. 2018, www.hollywoodreporter.com/news/all-boys-ive-loved-before-director-susan-johnson-interview-1134228. Accessed 15 Jan. 2019.

Mei, Gina. "*To All the Boys I've Loved Before* is an Extraordinary Rom-Com About Ordinary Teens." *Vanity Fair*, 16 Aug. 2018, www.vanityfair.com/hollywood/2018/08/to-all-the-boys-ive-loved-before-netflix-romantic-comedy-jenny-han-interview. Accessed 15 Jan. 2019.

Wright, Tolly. "*To All the Boys I Loved Before*: The Biggest Changes from Book to Movie." *Vulture*, 24 Aug. 2018, www.vulture.com/2018/08/all-the-boys-ive-loved-before-book-to-movie-changes.html. Accessed 15 Jan. 2019.

True Grit

The Novel
Author: Charles Portis (b. 1933)
First published: 1968

The Film
Year released: 2010
Director: Joel Coen (b. 1954), Ethan Coen (b. 1957)
Screenplay by: Joel Coen, Ethan Coen
Starring: Jeff Bridges, Hailee Steinfeld, Matt Damon, Josh Brolin, Barry Pepper

Context

The Arkansas-based novelist and author Charles Portis has earned cult status for his deadpan humor, oddball characters, and lyrical evocation of time and place. Of his novels, *True Grit*, released in 1968, is undoubtedly the most famous and the one that has secured for him a minor place in the American literary pantheon. Set in Arkansas during the 1870s, the western comic novel tells the story of a brassy fourteen-year-old girl named Mattie Ross, who hires a ruthless one-eyed US marshal, Rooster Cogburn, to track down her father's killer. Recounted decades later in Mattie's idiosyncratic first-person voice, the novel received widespread critical acclaim and became a best seller upon its release. Many critics hailed the novel as a masterpiece and compared it to Mark Twain's *The Adventures of Huckleberry Finn* (1884) for its Wild West grittiness and picaresque charm. It was quickly adapted into an eponymous 1969 feature film starring John Wayne, whose memorable, blustery turn as Cogburn landed him his only Academy Award for best actor.

The popularity of the Wayne film, directed by Western auteur Henry Hathaway, quickly overshadowed its source material and Portis's novel faded into obscurity. However, it was the novel, not its film adaptation, that first drew the Oscar-winning directing team of Joel and Ethan Coen—known as the Coen brothers—to the idea of remaking *True Grit* for the screen. Both Coens discovered the Portis novel as adults and began hashing out ideas for the remake while shooting their much-lauded neo-Western crime thriller *No Country for Old Men* (2007), which is based on the same-titled 2005 novel by Cormac McCarthy. Drawn particularly to Portis's florid language, the Coens developed a script that restored Mattie as the focal point of the story, unlike the original adaptation, which was dominated by Wayne's Cogburn. They approached their film without consulting the first movie at all and without consciously having the classical Western genre in mind.

In casting the pivotal role of Mattie, the Coen brothers looked at prospective young actors around the country. They ultimately settled on thirteen-year-old Hailee Steinfeld, who, despite having only a few minor film and television roles to her credit at the time, beat out fifteen thousand girls for the part. Meeting the Coens' intentions, Steinfeld was nearly identical in age to the fictional Mattie—and visibly younger than the 1969 film's Kim Darby, who was twenty-one years old when cast in the role. Steinfeld was cast just weeks before shooting for the film commenced in Texas and New Mexico in early 2010.

Taking the iconic role of Cogburn was veteran star Jeff Bridges. He was then coming off his Oscar-winning turn as a fading country music star in Scott Cooper's *Crazy Heart* (2009). The Coen brothers rounded out their cast with stars including Matt Damon, Josh Brolin, and Barry Pepper. After meeting a tight production schedule, *True Grit* debuted on December 14, 2010.

Film Analysis

From the outset of *True Grit*, the Coen brothers illustrate their intent of remaining faithful to Portis's novel. The film opens with an epigraph taken from the Old Testament—"The wicked flee when none pursueth"—before slowly fading in on a dimly lit, snow globe-like vignette of Frank Ross, the murdered father of Mattie Ross (Hailee Steinfeld). Mattie concurrently begins to recount her tale in a brief voice-over prologue, in which she utters the novel's famous opening lines. This opening sequence helps establish the film's dark and vengeful tone and highlights its principal protagonist in Mattie. It is also quite unlike the original film adaptation, which begins with a voiceover-free sequence that depicts the events that lead up to Frank Ross's death. By using narration, the Coen brothers limit superfluous scenes in favor of striking visual images.

As recounted in the novel, Mattie travels from her home in Yell County, near Dardanelle, Arkansas, to Fort Smith, a town located on the state's western edge, to recover her father's body. Mattie arrives there by train with her family's African American farmhand, Yarnell. After the two watch a public hanging, they claim Mattie's father's body from the town undertaker. After sending Yarnell home with her father's coffin, Mattie visits the town sheriff to gather information on the whereabouts of Tom Chaney (Josh Brolin), the dim-witted miscreant responsible for killing her father. She is told that Chaney has ventured west into Indian territory with a band of outlaws led by Lucky Ned Pepper (Barry Pepper), and as a result, has fallen under the jurisdiction of the US marshals. Through the sheriff Mattie learns of US deputy marshal Reuben "Rooster" Cogburn (Jeff Bridges), a "pitiless man, double-tough" who "loves to pull a cork." Intrigued, Mattie seeks out and soon hires the cantankerous Cogburn to help her track down Chaney. The two are eventually joined by a flashy Texas Ranger named LaBeouf (Matt Damon), who is after Chaney for murdering a Texas state senator.

Like the original film adaptation, the 2010 version fleshes out these early scenes with dialogue taken directly from Portis's novel. However, the Coens go further, extending this faithfulness for much of the film. Portis's distinct contraction-free language often appears verbatim, illustrating the directors' reverence for their source material. Still, they condense and at times adjust the novel's sequence of events to present a more straightforward story. When Cogburn is first introduced, for instance, he is delivering testimony inside a courthouse. In the novel, this scene, in which Mattie spots the US marshal for the first time, runs for fifteen pages, but the Coens effectively tighten the dialogue by cutting out extraneous details not pertinent to the screen narrative. The scene is initially framed from Mattie's perspective, as she is shown trying to get a clear view of Cogburn, helping to reemphasize to viewers that they are seeing the story through her eyes. Meanwhile, LaBeouf's entry into the picture differs slightly from the novel, as he is first shown smoking on the porch of Mattie's boardinghouse before turning up again later at the foot of Mattie's bed, upon which he presents his case to her.

It is with the character of LaBeouf, in fact, that the Coens take the most dramatic license. As in the novel, Cogburn and LaBeouf initially come to terms together and embark on their manhunt for Chaney without Mattie, who they try to leave behind in Fort Smith. Mattie, however, catches up to Cogburn and LaBeouf, and soon creates a rift between them. In the novel, LaBeouf's dandy ways make him a good foil to the unrefined, hard-drinking Cogburn, and the constant conflict and one-upmanship that the two engage in helps drive the plot of the story forward. Though essentially a tagalong character with his own motivations, LaBeouf serves a vital role in Mattie's mission to find and apprehend Chaney. That role is emphasized by the Coens, but in a different manner. Unlike the novel and earlier film, the Coens have LaBeouf leave Mattie and Cogburn on two separate occasions due to conflict with Cogburn. He nonetheless finds his way back to them both times, first during a shooting encounter with the Pepper gang and later when Mattie is about to be knifed by Chaney. LaBeouf's two absences allow the Coens to add more narrative heft to scenes featuring only Mattie and Cogburn, while also creating greater emotional audience resonance for the LaBeouf character as he reappears during opportune times.

For the most part, the Coen brothers adhere closely to the rest of the novel's plot, but they add their own signature comic and absurdist flourishes. Prior to seeing Cogburn in the courthouse for the first time, for example, Mattie humorously confronts him outside of an outhouse while he is doing his "business." Later, when LaBeouf leaves Mattie and Cogburn the first time, the Coens show Mattie and Cogburn riding through a grove of leafless cottonwood trees before coming upon an unknown dead body suspended high up on one of them. During this sequence the two encounter a trail doctor adorned in a bearskin coat who directs them to a dugout shelter. Such bizarre scenes and characters do not appear in the novel, but they allow the Coens to put their own unique stamp on the source material. Many other aspects of the film—including Roger Deakins's cinematography, which is characterized by stark, bleached-out color schemes, and Mary Zophres's costume design, which emphasizes a toned-down, lived-in approach—reflect the Coens' desire for utmost authenticity. In this way they effectively capture

Portis's gritty vision of the late-nineteenth-century Wild West.

That vision is further realized in the film's third act, in which the Coens essentially follow Portis's novel beat for beat. During her initial encounter with Chaney, Mattie shoots the fugitive, but ultimately fails to kill him. He takes her to Ned Pepper, who is hiding out up a nearby hill with his band of outlaws. The commotion catches the attention of Cogburn, who agrees to leave the scene after Pepper threatens to kill Mattie. On Pepper's orders, Mattie is left alone with Chaney, who, despite being told otherwise, attempts to kill her. LaBeouf, however, suddenly reappears and thwarts Chaney by hitting him over the head. Meanwhile, Cogburn engages in a final standoff with Pepper and his gang; Pepper is ultimately sniped to death by LaBeouf.

After regaining consciousness, Chaney knocks out LaBeouf, but Mattie then shoots him dead with the latter's rifle. However, the recoil sends her into a rattlesnake pit. Cogburn retrieves her, but not before she suffers a life-threatening rattlesnake bite. Consequently, LaBeouf, whose injuries are not fatal, is left behind, as Cogburn embarks on a frantic days-long horseback journey with Mattie to reach a doctor. Restoring the framing device of the novel, which was omitted in the original screen adaptation, the film ends with a voiceover coda set a quarter century later. Mattie, whose left forearm is amputated as a result of the snakebite, chronicles the aftermath of the ordeal, shedding light on Cogburn's recent death and LaBeouf's unknown whereabouts.

Significance

With *True Grit*, their fifteenth feature film, the Coen brothers turned to the Western genre, strictly defined, for the first time. However, themes and tropes of Western films, and a vision of America and Americana informed by these, are recognizable in much of their previous body of work, including Oh Brother, Where Art Thou?, Raising Arizona, No Country for Old Men, and even The Big Lebowski with the character of "The Stranger" (played by Sam Elliott). Often referred to as the quintessential American film genre, Westerns were Hollywood's most popular form of screen entertainment from the early twentieth century to the 1960s before falling out of favor with the public for much of the next thirty years. In the late 1960s, a group of intelligent films emerged sometimes called "Revisionist Westerns" or Anti-Westerns that reflected sensitively on the meaning of the genre in American culture. The Coens' True Grit can be properly understood only against this film-historical backdrop. In fact, their *True Grit* came at a time when Westerns were again enjoying somewhat of a resurgence in Hollywood. Twenty-first-century interest in the genre can be considered part of a nostalgic yearning for core American values driven by events such as the September 11, 2001, terrorist attacks. It can also be seen alongside other, contemporaneous developments, such as the rise of the new folk music and "weird America" themes, reflecting historical worries about American identity and decline.

Critics generally agreed that the Coens succeeded in their maiden venture into the genre, with many hailing their remake as being greatly superior to the original and oft-maligned 1969 film adaptation in regard to tone, emphasis, and overall artistic value. Reviewers also pointed out that the film, which was rated a more audience-friendly PG-13 (a rarity for the Coen brothers), felt much more straightforward and hopeful than other Coen films, which frequently subvert genre expectations and are marked by varying degrees of irony, cynicism, and violence. Positive reviews helped *True Grit* pulled in an estimated $38.6 million at the box office during its opening weekend, the highest ever for a movie directed by the Coen brothers. It ultimately earned $252 million in worldwide box-office receipts, making it the most commercially successful Coen film to date. The film also landed, among numerous other accolades, ten Academy Award nominations, including for best picture, best director, and best adapted screenplay, and acting nods for Bridges and Steinfeld. It proved to be a breakout role for Steinfeld, who drew universal praise for her steely, intuitive performance.

Though *True Grit* failed to win a single Oscar, the film has been regarded as an important addition to the Coen brothers' highly lauded, eclectic oeuvre. Most importantly, the film has been responsible for introducing Portis's original classic novel to a new generation of readers, and for reawakening interest in the famously elusive author's other works. In an article for *Newsweek* released in conjunction with the Coen brothers' film adaptation, Malcolm Jones called *True Grit* "one of the great American novels, with two of the greatest characters in our literature and a story worthy of their greatness."

—*Chris Cullen*

Further Reading

Jones, Malcolm. "Did You Know That *True Grit* Is a Book Too?" *Newsweek*, 9 Dec. 2010, www.newsweek.com/2010/12/09/did-you-know-that-true-grit-is-a-book-too.html. Accessed 21 Mar. 2019.

Portis, Charles. *True Grit*, 1968. Overlook Press, 2010.

Shone, Tom. "The Coen Brothers: The Cartographers of Cinema." *The Guardian*, 27 Jan. 2011, www.theguardian.com/film/2011/jan/27/coen-brothers-interview-true-grit. Accessed 21 Mar. 2019.

Bibliography

Dargis, Manohla. "Wearing Braids, Seeking Revenge." Review of *True Grit*, directed by Joel Coen and Ethan Coen. *The New York Times*, 21 Dec. 2010, www.nytimes.com/2010/12/22/movies/22true.html. Accessed 21 Mar. 2019.

Lawrence, Will. "Joel and Ethan Coen on *True Grit*: We Completely Ignored the Original." *The Telegraph*, 28 Jan. 2011, www.telegraph.co.uk/culture/film/filmmakersonfilm/8287138/Joel-and-Ethan-Coen-on-True-Grit-We-completely-ignored-the-original.html. Accessed 21 Mar. 2019.

McCarthy, Todd. Review of *True Grit*, directed by Joel Coen and Ethan Coen. *Hollywood Reporter*, 1 Dec. 2010, www.hollywoodreporter.com/review/true-grit-film-review-55300. Accessed 21 Mar. 2019.

Miller, Stuart. "'The American Epic': Hollywood's Enduring Love for the Western." *The Guardian*, 21 Oct. 2016, www.theguardian.com/film/2016/oct/21/western-films-hollywood-enduring-genre. Accessed 21 Mar. 2019.

Patterson, John. "With *True Grit*, the Coen Brothers Have Given the Western Back Its Teeth." Review of *True Grit*, directed by Joel Coen and Ethan Coen. *The Guardian*, 7 Jan. 2011, www.theguardian.com/film/2011/jan/08/coen-brothers-true-grit. Accessed 21 Mar. 2019.

Thomson, David. "David Thomson on Films: *True Grit*." Review of *True Grit*, directed by Joel Coen and Ethan Coen. *New Republic*, 24 Dec. 2010, newrepublic.com/article/80284/coen-brothers-true-grit-review. Accessed 21 Mar. 2019.

Turan, Kenneth. Review of *True Grit*, directed by Joel Coen and Ethan Coen. *Los Angeles Times*, 22 Dec. 2010, www.latimes.com/archives/la-xpm-2010-dec-22-la-et-true-grit-420101222-story.html. Accessed 21 Mar. 2019.

25th Hour

The Novel
Author: David Benioff (b. 1970)
First published: 2000

The Film
Year released: 2002
Director: Spike Lee (b. 1957)
Screenplay by: David Benioff
Starring: Edward Norton, Philip Seymour Hoffman, Barry Pepper, Rosario Dawson, Anna Paquin

Context

Spike Lee's 2002 feature film, *25th Hour*, is based on the 2000 novel by the same name written by David Benioff, author, screenwriter, and producer. Benioff wrote the novel as the thesis for his master of fine arts in creative writing at the University of California, Irvine. He wrote the novel when, upon returning home to New York City from a job in Wyoming, he found himself suffering from appendicitis; as a result, he was kept from many experiences he wanted to enjoy. The feeling of frustration was the impetus for the novel's plot.

Before the book's release, actor Tobey Maguire, who had read an advance copy, approached Benioff about adapting the novel for the big screen. Maguire purchased the rights to the book and asked Benioff to write the screenplay. After Benioff had completed the script, Maguire, who had been interested in playing the book's protagonist, stepped back from the project because he was about to begin production on *Spider-Man*. The script for the film eventually found its way into the hands of Spike Lee, a lifelong New Yorker best known for urban dramas such as *Do the Right Thing* and *Summer of Sam*. Lee was interested in the script for two main reasons: first, New York City was featured so prominently that it was almost a character within the narrative; and second, Lee was intrigued by a profanity-laced monologue delivered by the main protagonist.

The film was picked up by Disney, with Lee as director and Maguire as producer. Edward Norton, star of the acclaimed David Fincher film, *Fight Club*, was given the lead role, with Philip Seymour Hoffman, Barry Pepper, Rosario Dawson, and Anna Paquin rounding out the cast. Jazz composer Terence Blanchard, who had previously worked with Lee on *Jungle Fever* and *Malcolm X*, would compose the score. With a budget of $5 million, principal filming began in the summer of 2001. The film was in postproduction when terrorists attacked the United States on September 11. The immediate reaction of most filmmakers who had shot films in New York City just prior to the attacks was to remove the World Trade Center through postproduction edits. Maguire's *Spider-Man*, which had also been filmed in New York City that summer, did just that. Lee, however, decided to incorporate the attacks into his film, which required him to reshoot large portions of it. As Norton said in an interview with the BBC, "We were making a film about loss and about the consequences of choices and taking things for granted. To not allow that new emotional reality into the background just seemed like an insane kind of denial."

Film Analysis

Both the book and the film share the same basic plot. Montgomery "Monty" Brogan (Norton) is a convicted drug dealer who has twenty-four hours to report to prison to begin serving a seven-year sentence. Monty plans to spend his last day of freedom with his girlfriend Naturelle Riviera (Dawson) and his two closest friends, Frank Slattery (Pepper), a Wall Street trader and Jacob Elinsky (Hoffman), a high school teacher.

The film begins with a flashback showing Monty and Russian mobster Kostya Novotny (Tony Siragusa) trying to decide whether to shoot a stray dog they find lying in the street. The animal has been mauled and Monty wants to put it out of its misery but decides instead to take the dog to a clinic. Back in the present (2002), Monty begins his last day of freedom by visiting his father James, a recovering alcoholic and former firefighter turned bar owner, who will drive him to prison the next day. Monty helped his father save the bar with his drug money—a fact that has led James back to drinking. While in the bathroom, Monty stares into the mirror and delivers an angry, profanity-laced monologue tearing into the various groups that make up New York City. He then turns his focus inward, berating himself for being greedy and mostly for getting caught. A flashback shows us how Monty got arrested and that the Drug Enforcement Administration (DEA) agents who burst into his apartment knew exactly where to find the drugs. The implication is clear—Monty was betrayed. Kostya tells Monty that it was probably Naturelle who betrayed him, and Monty begins to grow suspicious of her, asking Frank to find out if she was responsible. In another flashback, we see how Monty and Naturelle met, and how happy they were together.

As night descends, Monty, Frank, and Jacob head to a club for Monty's going away party. Outside, the three meet Mary (Paquin), one of Jacob's high school students over whom he has been obsessing, and invite her in. Inside the club, Monty and Frank discuss prison and soon Frank and Naturelle begin to argue. Frank accuses her of taking Monty's money despite knowing where it comes from, and Naturelle accuses Frank of being a hypocrite. After Frank insults Naturelle with a racial slur, she slaps him and storms out of the club. Meanwhile, Jacob kisses Mary, an awkward moment that shocks them both, leaving him terrified that he just endangered his career. Because the party is derailed, Monty and Kostya go to see the Russian mob boss, Uncle Nikolai (Levan Uchaneishvili), for whom they both work. Nikolai tells Monty how to survive in prison, but also reveals to him that it was Kostya who betrayed him. Nikolai gives Monty the option of killing Kostya in exchange for protecting his father's business, but Monty refuses and leaves Kostya to his fate at the hands of Nikolai. Monty makes amends with Naturelle and as daylight approaches meets up with Jacob and Frank, whom he asks to beat him up so that he looks too ugly to be raped in prison. Initially, Frank refuses but Monty gets under his skin and Frank beats him savagely, breaking his nose.

The film ends with Monty in his father's car on his way to prison. James offers to keep driving west, past the prison, so that Monty might be able to start a new life with Naturelle. In a series of images, we see the life Monty could have on the lam, including children and a nice home. But it is all just fantasy, and in an ending far less ambiguous than in the book, Monty goes to prison, leaving his life behind.

Outside of flashbacks and its overall structure, the film adaptation is fairly true to the novel with one major exception—the omnipresent specter of the 9/11 attacks. Rather than minimize or ignore the horror that were the terrorist attacks of September 11, Lee goes out of his way to emphasize the scar left on New York City and the people who live there. The opening credits focus on the twin pillars of light that were set up in place of the twin towers, and the characters in the film discuss the attacks on more than one occasion. In one scene in particular, as Frank, Jacob, and Monty discuss Monty's fate, they look down on Ground Zero, the national wound open before them, flooded in light. In this way, Monty's story is tied to 9/11. His grief is our grief. His anger is our anger. This anger, epitomized by Monty's monologue, ranting and raving against stereotypical New Yorkers before eventually turning his ire on himself, captures the mixed feelings of many Americans after the attacks. Monty is both sad and angry with himself for his fate. It was his choice to be a drug dealer and get mixed up with the Russian mob, which led to his arrest.

In the final scenes, Monty fantasizes about a life outside of prison with his father narrating a montage featuring an American flag and a multiracial family all dressed in white. "We drive west, keep driving until we find a nice little town," James says in this fantasy. "These towns out in the desert—you know how they got there? People wanted to get away from something else." His father recounts the promise of America—that no matter how bad things get; one can always pick up and start over by going west to the new frontier. But as the fantasy fades, Monty is resigned to his new reality, as we are faced with a trauma that we cannot escape. In so doing, the film breaks down the old optimistic American mythos of self-determination in favor of self-reflection and an acceptance of the things we as individuals and as a people cannot change.

Significance

25th Hour premiered exactly fifteen months after the September 11 attacks. It was immediately hailed by critics and audiences alike and became arguably the most important film produced in response to the attacks. Writing for the *San Francisco Chronical*, film critic Mick LaSalle wrote, "*25th Hour* is as much an urban historical document as Rossellini's *Open City*, filmed in the immediate aftermath of the Nazi occupation of Rome." Several other critics, including Roger Ebert, added the film to their lists of greatest films ever made. It was nominated for dozens of awards and won honors from the Central Ohio Film Critics Association, the Italian Online Movie Awards, the Las Vegas Film Critics Society Awards, and the Sant Jordi Awards. Although not a blockbuster, the film was very profitable, with a box office totaling $23.9 million. In the years since its release, *25th Hour* continues to be rediscovered by audiences and has been praised as one of the best films made in the first decade of the twenty-first century. Edward Norton followed this role with successes throughout the 2000s, while Spike Lee followed this feature with several more films focused on life in New York City, including 2006's *Inside Man*. Benioff published another novel and a book of short stories following *25th Hour*, but found his greatest success in television, when he became co-showrunner on HBO's *Game of Thrones* in 2011.

—*KP Dawes, MA*

Further Reading

Alsultany, Evelyn. *Arabs and Muslims in the Media: Race and Representation after 9/11*. New York UP, 2012.

Bragard, Varonique, editor. *Portraying 9/11: Essays on Representations in Comics, Literature, Film and Theatre*. McFarland & Company, 2011.

Stubblefield, Thomas. *9/11 and the Visual Culture of Disaster*. Indiana State University, 2015.

Bibliography

Ebert, Roger. "*25th Hour*." *RogerEbert.com*, 16 Dec. 2009. www.rogerebert.com/reviews/25th-hour-2002. Accessed 27 Feb. 2020.

Keeble, Arin. "Why Spike Lee's *25th Hour* Is the Most Enduring Film about 9/11." *The Conversation*, 8 Sept. 2017. theconversation.com/why-spike-lees-25th-hour-is-the-most-enduring-film-about-9-11-82020. Accessed 27 Feb. 2020.

LaSalle, Mick. "9/11: FIVE YEARS LATER / Spike Lee's *25th Hour*." *SF Gate*. 10 Sept. 2006. www.sfgate.com/entertainment/article/9-11-FIVE-YEARS-LATER-Spike-Lee-s-25th-Hour-2469808.php. Accessed 27 Feb. 2020.

Papamichael, Stella. "Edward Norton." *BBC*, 25 Feb. 2003. www.bbc.co.uk/films/2003/02/25/edward_norton_25th_hour_interview.shtml. Accessed 27 Feb. 2020.

Tobias, Scott. "The Ruins and Reckoning of *25th Hour*." *The Dissolve*, 24 Feb. 2015. thedissolve.com/features/movie-of-the-week/935-the-ruins-and-reckoning-of-25th-hour/. Accessed 27 Feb. 2020.

Up in the Air

The Novel

Author: Walter Kirn (b. 1962)
First published: 2001

The Film

Year released: 2009
Director: Jason Reitman (b. 1977)
Screenplay by: Jason Reitman, Sheldon Turner
Starring: George Clooney, Vera Farmiga, Anna Kendrick, Danny McBride, Jason Bateman

Context

Up in the Air is a 2009 film directed by Jason Reitman based on the 2001 novel of the same name written by Walter Kirn. The novel was written while Kirn was spending a winter in Montana, the majority of which he spent snowed-in on a ranch. The novel tells the story of protagonist Ryan Bingham, who is a "Career Transition Counselor" working in "human resources," meaning that his job is to travel the country and fire people in corporations. He has come to despise his work, but he loves the inhuman, sleek, professionalized environment and culture that he ironically calls "Airworld," an environment of airports, stewardesses, executive hotel rooms, and suitcases. Bingham yearns to reach one million frequent-flier miles. The book was praised for its wit, intelligence, and sensitive depiction of rootlessness and its psychic costs.

Soon after the novel's publication, it was adapted for the screen by Sheldon Turner, the screenwriter who wrote *The Longest Yard* (2005) and was quickly sold to Steven Spielberg's production company DreamWorks. Independently, Jason Reitman happened upon the novel and convinced his father, legendary filmmaker Ivan Reitman to purchase the film rights. Incorporating elements from Turner's adaptation, Jason Reitman wrote his own version of the script, and soon after a conflict developed over proper script credit. In the end, the Writers Guild of America ruled that Reitman must share credit with Turner. Another crisis hit in 2008, just before filming was set to start, after the mortgage housing crisis rocked financial centers across the globe sending stocks plummeting and forcing millions of Americans into unemployment. As it was no longer appropriate to approach the subject of layoffs and job loss with humor

and sarcasm, Reitman made major changes to the script, even deciding to include in the film the voices of real people who had experienced layoffs and downsizing. For the lead, Reitman cast George Clooney, who at that point was at the height of Hollywood celebrity, with Vera Farmiga, Anna Kendrick, and Jason Bateman, among others, rounding out the cast. Principal photography began in early 2009, with scenes filmed across the interior of the country, focused mainly on St. Louis, Detroit, and Omaha. All told, filming took fifty days, including eight days spent on aerial photography.

Film Analysis

Ryan Bingham (Clooney), charming and handsome, is successful in his career, but he has nothing meaningful to show for it. His apartment, which he rarely sees, is barren and lacks even the most basic touches of personality. He is estranged from his family, including his sisters Kara (Amy Morton) and Julie (Melanie Lynskey). With little to focus on besides his job, Ryan becomes obsessed with frequent-flyer miles.

The only tangible results of Ryan's efforts are the misery and stress he causes in others. Some of the people he fires cry, others get angry, some turn to retaliation or self-harm. The only hope—aside from frequent-flier miles—for meaning that Ryan encounters is in the form of Alex (Farmiga), a no-nonsense businesswoman who flies nearly as much as he does. For several months, Ryan and Alex meet each other in airport terminals and at hotel bars. They become lovers, though sharing little intimacy. The two agree to share no personal details and to keep their two worlds apart. But Ryan wants more and attempts to force a closer relationship with Alex, a move that ultimately causes everything to unravel. She is married with children, and Ryan is only a diversion for Alex.

Ryan's journey in the film is mirrored by Natalie (Kendrick), a twenty-three-year-old ambitious up-and-comer. She is like Ryan was at the beginning of his journey, and much of the film is spent with Ryan imparting his wisdom on his protege. But Natalie sees more than Ryan thinks to show her and through the film becomes increasingly aware of the reality of Ryan's world. Beyond the embellishments of success lies emptiness. Yes, Ryan has an impressive job and gets to travel the country, but isn't his sister, about to marry her "loser" boyfriend Jim (McBride), the one who is ultimately happier?

Interestingly, a recurring theme throughout the film is the 1922 children's book, *The Velveteen Rabbit*. The story, which chronicles the desire of a stuffed rabbit to become real by virtue of the love of its owner, is analogous to Ryan's journey. While extolling the virtues of an uncomplicated life, hammered home by Ryan's moonlighting as a motivational speaker, Ryan in reality wants love and friendship. He no longer wants to live out of a backpack or a suitcase. While the velveteen rabbit is ultimately transformed into flesh and blood, Ryan's arc is less fulfilling.

After Natalie rejects Ryan's lifestyle and his job, following the suicide of a woman she and Ryan had laid off, Ryan finally accomplishes his goal of earning ten million frequent-flyer miles. After his accomplishment is announced onboard a plane, a legendary airline pilot (played by Sam Elliott) comes to congratulate Ryan. He asks the pilot for advice, hoping the personification of his life's one pursuit might finally lead him to meaning. But the pilot has little to offer Ryan beyond platitudes and kind words of congratulation. Here is the goal Ryan has been working toward all this time, and it too is empty, bringing neither relief, nor joy, nor catharsis.

Toward the end, the film features a montage of real people discussing the impact on them of having been laid off or fired, and the strength they drew from friends and family in their darkest moments. Then we see Ryan, back on the road, as he stares blankly at a vast destination board at an airport. As he looks up, with sadness in his eyes, he lets go of the handle of his carry-on and his gaze falls to the floor. The scene cuts to a rolling shot of clouds, eventually growing silent and then dark. Ryan has accepted the lack of meaning in his life; what happens to him next remains a mystery, but the symbolism suggests that Ryan dies in un-

happiness, while in his closing narration he says that he accepts his lot in life.

After seeing the film adaptation, Kirn said in an interview with *NPR* that he was "entirely pleased" with the film. He also described his own understanding of the difference between novels and films, and the process of adaptation: "Novels tend to come from the inside of a character and movies tend to look at them from the outside in relation to others in their world. And so, I fully understood that for this book to make it onto film it had to be sort of opened up, unfolded." He continued, "...you're able to do things in novels: introduce subplots, other characters, thematic layers and so on, in a way that you simply can't in a movie. A movie really has to choose its battles. And most adaptations end up having to really edit out a lot of the book and bring forward those elements that they think play dramatically."

In the same interview, Kirn highlighted a key difference between the novel and the film, the film's introduction of the character Natalie. Kirn remarked, "...if they'd filmed the novel completely faithfully, it would've been a lot of voice-over and a lot of the shots of planes crossing the sun." In the novel, the reader overhears what Ryan is thinking about his world and his experience, while in the film, the character Natalie allows Ryan to speak out loud to another character, explaining or debating his thoughts. As Kirn said in the *NPR* interview, again praising the adaptation, "...it sounds as though it was a device, but it ended up in the movie being one of the richest and, I think, most amusing and potent elements of the script."

Significance

Up in the Air was previewed at the Telluride Film Festival on September 6, 2009 and later premiered at the Toronto International Film Festival on September 12. It was released for wide distribution that December. The film proved a hit with audiences and critics alike, earning $1.1 million in its opening weekend and eventually hitting $166 million in its total worldwide box office, well outpacing its $25 million estimated budget. Thanks to its success, the film received numerous accolades and award nominations. Among the most impressive honors, *Up in the Air* received six Academy Award nominations, including nominations for both Farmiga and Kendrick for Best Supporting Actress. Unfortunately, it did not win in any category. The film was also nominated for six British Academy Film Awards, of which it won one award for

Best Screenplay-Adapted. And finally, the film was also nominated for six Golden Globe Awards, with Reitman and Turner again taking the award for Best Screenplay-Motion Picture.

Since its original premier, *Up in the Air* has been featured on numerous best films lists, including those compiled by Roger Ebert, the American Film Institute, and *The New York Times*. The film marked a bit of a peak for both Reitman and Clooney. While Reitman continues to work as a producer, writer, and director, none of his films since have achieved the same level of critical and commercial success. Much of the same could be said for Clooney, who while appearing in numerous films since 2009, has seen his celebrity decline in recent years. As for the film itself, it continues to endure as a critical success, remaining an important example of films attempting to make sense of a capitalistic American society in which the search for meaning is in stark contrast to the meaninglessness of corporate anonymity.

—KP Dawes, MA

Further Reading

Coelho, Paulo. *The Alchemist, 25th Anniversary: A Fable about Following Your Dream*. 1988. HarperCollins Publishers, 2014.

Frankl, Viktor E. *Man's Search for Meaning*. 1959. Beacon Press, 2006.

McCarthy, Cormac. *No Country for Old Men*. Alfred A. Knopf, 2005.

Bibliography

Clyman, Jeremy. "*Up in the Air*: The Anti-Mid Life Crisis." *Psychology Today*, 6. Jan. 2010, www.psychologytoday.com/us/blog/reel-therapy/201001/in-the-air-the-anti-mid-life-crisis. Accessed 12 May 2020.

Lane. "Nowhere Man." *The New Yorker*, 30 Nov. 2009, www.newyorker.com/magazine/2009/12/07/nowhere-man-2. Accessed 12 May 2020.

Nemiroff, Perri. "Interview: *Up in the Air*'s Jason Reitman, Vera Farmiga, Anna Kendrick and Walter Kirn." *Cinema Blend*, 5 Nov. 2009, www.cinemablend.com/new/Interview-Up-In-The-Air-s-Jason-Reitman-Vera-Farmiga-Anna-Kendrick-and-Walter-Kirn-15568.html. Accessed 12 May 2020.

"*Up in the Air*." *IMDb*, www.imdb.com/title/tt1193138/. Accessed 12 May 2020.

"*Up in the Air*." *Rotten Tomatoes*, www.rottentomatoes.com/m/up_in_the_air_2009. Accessed 12 May 2020.

Who Goes There? / The Thing

The Novella
Author: John W. Campbell Jr., writing as Don A. Stuart (1910-71)
First published: 1938

The Film
Year released: 1982
Director: John Carpenter (b. 1948)
Screenplay by: Bill Lancaster
Starring: Kurt Russell, Wilford Brimley, T. K. Carter, David Clennon, Keith David, Richard Dysart

Context

John Carpenter's *The Thing* (1982) is one of the most critically celebrated sci-fi/horror films in history. Its story began as a science fiction novella titled *Who Goes There?*, which was first published in a 1938 issue of *Astounding Science Fiction*. It was written by science fiction editor John W. Campbell Jr., under the pen name of Don A. Stuart, and is frequently considered one of the most memorable sci-fi stories ever written. It has been anthologized numerous times, including in *The Science Fiction Hall of Fame, Volume Two* (1973), for which members of the Science Fiction Writers of America ranked their favorite stories of all time.

Prior to Carpenter's film effort, Campbell's novella was adapted for the screen in 1951 as *The Thing from Another World*, directed by Christian Nyby. Instead of employing a shape-shifting alien, Nyby created a vegetable monster that seemed to have more in common with the monster in Mary Shelley's *Frankenstein* (1818), which is sometimes considered the first science fiction novel.

Prior to *The Thing*, John Carpenter had been known for directing phenomenal horror films and thrillers, including *Halloween* (1978), *The Fog* (1980), and *Escape from New York* (1981), before he took a shot at adapting *Who Goes There?* Unfortunately, *The Thing* was critically panned when it debuted, effectively wrecking Carpenter's career for a time. While some found much to praise about the special effects, many critics were repulsed by their goriness and believed the paranoid viewpoint of the film and its supposedly flat characters made it nothing but a shock fest. Ultimately, both Carpenter and his film have come to be seen as creative and visionary. Today, *The Thing* is regarded as one of the greatest horror-tinged sci-fi films ever made. Carpenter has since made a number of cult classics, including *Christine* (1983), which is based on the Stephen King novel of the same name; as well as *Big Trouble in Little China* (1986), *Prince of Darkness* (1987), *They Live* (1988), and *In the Mouth of Madness* (1994). He expanded his interests into making music after experiencing a decline as a commercial director in the mid-1990s, but in 2018 he rejoined the Halloween franchise when he was the composer and executive producer for the same-titled sequel *Halloween*.

Film Analysis

Because Carpenter wanted to honor the paranoid claustrophobia of Campbell's novella, the plot of *The Thing* stays true to its source material. Many of the characters remain mostly the same, including their names, but Carpenter decreased the number of individuals at the Antarctic research station from thirty-seven members with sixteen named characters, to twelve named characters in the film. Those twelve characters are MacReady (Kurt Russell); Dr. Blair (Wilford Brimley); Nauls (T. K. Carter); Palmer (David Clennon); Childs (Keith David); Dr. Copper (Richard Dysart); Norris (Charles Hallahan); Bennings (Peter Maloney); Clark (Richard Masur); Garry (Donald Moffat); Fuchs (Joel Polis); and Windows (Thomas Waites).

Some important differences in the shift from page to screen include the elimination of the Thing's telepathic ability; the removal of the flashback at the story's start, which explained how the members of the expedition came across the creature; and the change from making MacReady a larger-than-life character as he was in the novella, into more of an "everyman" attempting to stay alive along with the rest of the team. Carpenter also begins the film by introducing the Thing into the American expedition's camp in the form of a sled dog, who is being chased and shot at by two men in a Norwegian helicopter. The Norwegians are not in the original story. Additionally, the Norwegians are the ones who discover the crashed alien ship, not the Americans, as had been the case in the novella.

The film opens with the Norwegian helicopter pilot and passenger attempting to kill a sled dog racing through the brutal Antarctic landscape with a rifle and grenades. As they approach the American research station, one of them inadvertently kills himself and blows up the helicopter. The other then rushes toward the Americans, brandishing a rifle and attempting to kill the dog. Garry, the American station commander, then kills the pilot, fearing for the lives of his men. Clark brings the dog to the kennel, where it is soon revealed to be an alien that can change its shape. Garry sends his pilot, MacReady, and Dr. Copper to the Norwegian station to find out what had happened. While there, the two men discover a burned-out husk where the Norwegian station had been, along with members of the station crew frozen in the snow. They also find what appears to be the body of a misshapen human being, which they bring back to their station.

Back at the station, Childs and the other men discover that some of the dogs are being eaten and transformed into hideous creatures by the imposter sled dog. Childs then burns all of the alien creatures with a flamethrower. Dr. Blair, the biologist, conducts an autopsy on the dog and discovers that the creature can perfectly mimic a real organism. Similarly, when MacReady and Copper bring the misshapen human body back to the station, Blair discovers that the corpse contains perfectly healthy human organs.

Data recovered from the Norwegian research site helps them understand that they are dealing with something of extraterrestrial origins. They find an enormous alien spacecraft, buried in the ice for possibly 100,000 years, that the Norwegians have partly excavated. All of these revelations cause Blair to break down mentally. Believing that the Thing is capable of infecting them all and escaping to plague the rest of the planet, he destroys all of their vehicles, smashes the radios, and kills off all of the unaffected sled dogs. The other men then lock him in a shed to prevent him from doing more harm. They also take precautions about being alone, fearing that any of them might be infected and changed at any moment. Copper suggests doing a blood test of each man against uncontaminated blood they have in stores, but they discover it is all destroyed as well. They then relieve Garry of his command, fearing he might have done it, and put MacReady in charge.

Things continue to spiral out of control and into full-blown terror when the malformed body returns to life and begins to absorb Bennings. MacReady then burns the creature. Later, MacReady, along with Nauls and Windows, comes across Fuchs' burned body and suspect that he killed himself to keep from being absorbed by the Thing. MacReady and Nauls go to MacReady's quarters to investigate as Windows heads back to the main base. Finding ripped-up clothes there, Nauls rushes away in a snowstorm, convinced he has been transformed and replaced. The expedition then refuses to let MacReady in, believing he has been taken, but he breaks in, holding them at bay with dynamite.

As they argue, Norris looks like he is having a heart attack. Copper sets him on the table and attempts to stabilize him with a defibrillator. But then Norris's chest caves in, transforms into a mouth, and kills Copper, biting his arms off in the process. MacReady is able to burn the Thing on the table, but its head falls off and sprouts spider legs in an attempt to escape. Clark is then killed by MacReady when he tries to knife him in the back.

In a quiet moment, the remaining men speculate that each separate part of the Thing is a living individual, and that infected blood, separated from the original body, might recoil from a hot wire. The men agree to test each of their blood in this fashion. MacReady and all of the others pass inspection, but Palmer's blood scurries away from the live wire. Palmer transforms, then attacks Windows. MacReady then incinerates them both.

The remaining men agree they must test Blair, who has been locked away all this time. At his shack, they discover Blair has also been transformed and has been attempting to construct some kind of spaceship from the undamaged parts of their vehicles. When they return to base, the generator has been destroyed and Childs is nowhere to be seen. MacReady, Nauls, and Garry then make a grim decision: in order to ensure the Thing is destroyed, they have to use explosives to blow up their base. As they get ready to do this, the transformed Blair appears and morphs into a huge, hideous creature. The Blair creature then kills Garry and Nauls and vanishes. MacReady uses a stick of dynamite to blow the charges they had set. He somehow survives and stumbles around outside, watching their station burn to the ground. He drinks deeply from a bottle of liquor as Childs appears, claiming he was lost in the snow while chasing the Blair creature. He is also drinking from a bottle. The two men face off, grimily wondering if the other is the Thing, as the film ends.

Significance

When *The Thing* was released in 1982, it was skewered by critics and generally ignored by the moviegoing public. The reviews across major publications were uniformly brutal. In his review, Roger Ebert wrote, "*The Thing* is...just a geek show, a gross-out movie in which teenagers can dare one another to watch the screen.... Because this material has been done before, and better, especially in the original *The Thing* and in *Alien*, there's no need to see this version unless you are interested in what the Thing might look like while starting from anonymous greasy organs extruding giant crab legs and transmuting itself into a dog." Similarly, Dave Kehr wrote that "although the group members are played by familiar, well-defined character actors, the terse banality of the dialogue makes them all sound and seem alike—it's hard to tell who's being attacked, and hard to care. Carpenter's direction is slow, dark, and stately; he seems to be aiming for an enveloping, novelistic kind of effect, but all he gets is heaviness."

Carpenter took the criticism very hard. In an article for *SyFy Wire*, Christopher Mahon quoted Carpenter as saying: "I take every failure hard. The one I took the hardest was *The Thing*. My career would have been different if that had been a big hit.... The movie was hated. Even by science-fiction fans. They thought that I had betrayed some kind of trust, and the piling on was insane." It was not until the film was released on home video and shown on television that it began to acquire a cult following. At that point, audiences began to appreciate the film for being cleverly crafted and psychologically complex. Before long, it was being viewed as one of the finest horror/science-fiction films ever made. It has since spawned numer-

ous offshoots, including a video game and a board game. By 2008, it was ranked on *Empire* magazine's 500 Best Films of All Time. A prequel of the same name, describing what happened to the Norwegian team, was released in 2011. On *Reelviews.net*, James Berardinelli perhaps best described why the film proved to be so successful: "A paranoia-choked atmosphere is the primary reason why *The Thing* works as well as it does. The setup is standard stuff, establishing that the characters are isolated and can expect no help from the outside. The realization there could be an alien among them, and any one of them might not be human, is what launches *The Thing* into a spiral of escalating tension."

—*Christopher Mari*

Further Reading

DeNardo, John. "Review: *Who Goes There?* by John W. Campbell." *SF Signal*, 1 Sept. 2009, www.sfsignal.com/archives/2009/09/review_who_goes_there_by_john_w_campbell/. Accessed 14 May 2020.

Campbell, John W. "*Who Goes There?*" *Goldenageofscifi.info*, www.goldenageofscifi.info/ebook/Who_Goes_There.pdf. Accessed 14 May 2020.

Bibliography

Berardinelli, James. "*Thing, The* (United States, 1982)." *Reelviews.com*, www.reelviews.net/reelviews/thing-the. Accessed 14 May 2020.

Ebert, Roger. "*The Thing*." *RogerEbert.com*, 1 Jan. 1982, www.rogerebert.com/reviews/the-thing-1982. Accessed 14 May 2020.

Kehr, Dave. "*The Thing*." *Chicago Reader*, 2 Aug. 1985, www.chicagoreader.com/chicago/the-thing/Film'oid=2587533. Accessed 14 May 2020.

Mahon, Christopher. "How John Carpenter's *The Thing* Went from D-List Trash to Horror Classic." *SyFy Wire*, 16 Jan. 2018, www.syfy.com/syfywire/how-john-carpenters-the-thing-went-from-d-list-trash-to-horror-classic. Accessed 14 May 2020.

"*The Thing*." *IMDb*, www.imdb.com/title/tt0084787/. Accessed 14 May 2020.

The Willoughbys

The Novel
Author: Lois Lowry (b. 1937)
First published: 2008

The Film
Year released: 2020
Director: Kris Pearn (b. 1958)
Screenplay by: Kris Pearn, Mark Stanleigh
Starring: Will Forte, Maya Rudolph, Alessia Cara, Terry Crews, Martin Short, Jane Krakowski, Seán Cullen, Ricky Gervais

Context

Directed by Kris Pearn for the streaming service Netflix, *The Willoughbys* is a 2020 film based on Lois Lowry's 2008 novel of the same name. Both the book and movie take a tongue-in-cheek approach to the orphan trope so common in children's literature, as well as other themes typical of "old fashioned" books, such as neglectful parents, nannies, and eccentric millionaires. Lowry created the story to poke good-natured fun at the classics of her own youth, such as *Heidi* (1880-81) and *The Bobbsey Twins* (1904), as well as more modern tales by Roald Dahl and Lemony Snicket. Additionally, her pen-and-ink illustrations call to mind the work of Edward Gorey.

Lowry is known for her prolific and varied contributions to children's literature ranging from lighthearted coming of age stories, like *Gooney Bird Greene* (2002), to poignant realistic fiction, including *A Summer to Die* (1977) and *The Silent Boy* (2003), and everything in between. She won the Newbury Medal in 1990 and 1994, for *Number the Stars* (1989) and *The Giver* (1993), respectively. Overall, *The Willoughbys* novel received positive reviews with some criticism of the overly exaggerated silliness of the novel compared to the author's more serious works. Lemony Snicket, author of *A Series of Unfortunate Events* (1999-2006), wrote a rather glowing review of it for *Publishers Weekly*—while directly panning other critics—stating, "There are those who will find that this novel pales in comparison to Ms. Lowry's more straight-faced efforts, such as *The Giver*. Such people are invited to take tea with the Bobbsey Twins. Ms. Lowry and I will be across town downing something stronger mixed by Anastasia Krupnik." (Anastasia Krupnik is the titular character in Lowry's *Anastasia Krupnik* (1979) series,

which met with criticism due to the introduction of adult themes, including alcohol, as Snicket's comment implies.)

In 2015, Bron Studios acquired the animated film rights to the novel. The computer-animated comedy was cowritten by Kris Pearn and Mark Stanleigh and directed by Pearn with the vocal talents of comedians Ricky Gervais, Will Forte, Maya Rudolph, and others. It was released in April 2020.

Film Analysis

The plot of *The Willoughbys* film, while similar to the book, takes a fair amount of creative license with the source material. While many of the characters are the same in the movie, their portrayal compared with their book counterparts tend to have overexaggerated features. Certain plot elements are also changed or eliminated. Screenwriters Pearn and Stanleigh make Lowry's story their own with a witty script filled with wordplay, physical humor, and unexpected plot twists.

In keeping with the theme of a children's book that pokes fun at other children's books, Pearn does the same with the movie, incorporating clear references to other children's films such as *Mary Poppins* (1964) and *Willy Wonka & the Chocolate Factory* (1971). The animation style is similar to films like *Hotel Transylvania* (2012) and brings the "old-fashioned" theme to life. In a review for *Variety*, Peter Debruge wrote, "The spindly family shares a tendency to move with almost manic speed, the way hand-drawn cartoon humans might." He further explained, "In traditional animation, artists use what are called key frames for efficiency—strong poses that characters strike and hold—and Pearn and his team bend the digital tools to imitate that aesthetic, giving *The Willoughbys* its 'old-fashioned' look."

The film opens with the Willoughbys' cat (Ricky Gervais), who acts as the narrator of the film, saying, "If you like stories about families that stick together and love each other through thick and thin, and it all ends up happily ever after, this isn't the film for you, OK?" The choice of the cat as narrator is a clever one as, coupled with Gervais' droll linguistic style, it immediately sets a comic tone to what could prove to be a rather dark story. As the cat explains, while the family has an impressive ancestry, the current Willoughby parents, Mother and Father (Martin Short and Jane Krakowski), have no interest in their own four children. These are Tim (Will Forte), Jane (Alessia Cara), and the twins named Barnaby (Sean Cullen)—the latter being of so little consequence that their parents could not even be bothered to give them individual names.

Tim is the oldest of the quartet and takes on something of a pseudoparental role for his younger siblings, although often his direction is misguided. He is particularly attached to the Willoughby ancestral legacy, as it is his only real knowledge of family due to his parents' dismissive attitude toward him and his siblings. Despite his attempts to ingratiate himself with—or at least not attract negative attention from—his parents, Tim often finds himself locked in the coal bin, a nod to Harry Potter's cupboard under the stairs. Jane is a more sensitive soul—described as "whiny" in the book—who wants nothing more than to sing, but is forever being silenced by her family who look at her talents with disdain. The "creepy" twins (as the cat refers to them) are budding inventors and do almost everything in unison. One of their defining traits is their shared sweater; like with their shared name, Mother could not be bothered to knit them each an individual sweater. This becomes a running gag throughout the film with one twin shivering while he awaits his turn with the shabby pullover. While Mother is described as an avid knitter in the book, the film takes this a step further. She collects yarn grown from Father's mustache, and even the children's hair has the appearance of being made of yarn.

The Willoughby parents are even more over the top than in books in their parental negligence, nearly starving their children and relegating them to the darkest corners of their gloomy old-fashioned house. Despite the dreariness of it all, the sheer ridiculousness of the family makes the film humorous in its eccentricity. The two parents are so lovestruck and full of themselves that they barely acknowledge their children's existence unless they do something overtly "annoying," such as taking food from the table. They do not even notice when one morning a box is left on their doorstep containing a baby girl.

The discovery of the baby by the Willoughby children leads to the introduction of Commander Melanoff (Terry Crews), an eccentric candymaker who resembles Willie Wonka and a runs a magical rainbow-spewing factory. This is a major departure from the character's book portrayal as a lonely hermit in a dilapidated vermin-infested home who is mourning the apparent loss of his wife and son in a Swiss train accident. In the book, the Commander's family is later discovered to be alive and there is an entire subplot about his son and their eventual reunion. This is completely left out of the film version in favor of a more focused approach on the adventures of the Willoughby siblings.

After initially wanting to keep the baby, Jane is convinced by Tim to leave the baby on the Commander's doorstep as one would do in an old-fashioned book. She pens a letter to the Commander giving the baby the name of Ruth due to them being the "ruthless Willoughbys." The moniker later takes on a new meaning when the Commander adopts the child, who becomes known as Baby Ruth. Ruth's plight gives the Willoughby children the idea to escape their parents neglect by becoming orphans themselves. Planting a travel brochure from the aptly named "Reprehensible Travel Agency" in view of their generally oblivious parents does the trick, and the couple sets out on a journey full of treacherous adventures sure to bring on their swift demise. Tim, Jane, and the Barnabys, however, encounter an unexpected wrinkle when they discover that their normally irresponsible and uncaring parents have hired a nanny (Maya Rudolph) to look after them.

Not only is the nanny the complete opposite of the children's parents, seemingly acting in the children's best interests because she actually cares, but she is also a former orphan herself and clearly is empathetic to the plight of the children and the neglect they have faced. It does not take long for the younger children to warm up to her, but Tim, used to being disappointed by the adults in his life, remains suspicious of her motives. This leads to a subplot, unique to the film version, involving the nefarious Orphan Services, a Men in Black type agency who not only made Nanny's life miserable as a child but who are determined to do the same to the Willoughbys. What follows is a zany adventure in which the siblings attempt to rescue their parents from a mountaineering debacle in order to escape the clutches of the evil orphan brigade. Once again, the yarn comes into play as the children use the trail of their mother's knitting to lead them to their nearly frozen parents, visually tying the family together. While for a moment it almost seems as if the parents have had a change of heart, it is not to be the case, but, the Willoughbys do find a happily ever after of sorts with a family of their own choosing.

The ability to choose is at its heart the theme of this story. The song "I Choose" was specifically written for the film and sung by Alessia Cara as Jane, "Through the lows and the highs I will stay by your side/There's no need for goodbyes now I'm seeing the light/When the sky turns to grey and there's nothing to say/At the end of the day, I choose you." Despite the difficult hands they were dealt in life, the Commander, Nanny, the Willoughby siblings, and Ruth overcome impossible obstacles to find each other and finally come to realize the true meaning of family.

Significance

The Willoughbys received reviews ranging from lukewarm to positive. Monica Castillo, writing for *RogerEbert.com*, opined that "For all its candy-colored silliness, *The Willoughbys* is a surprisingly sweet story about chosen families." Other reviewers criticized the flashy absurdness of the film as merely sugar-coating more macabre themes. For example, in a review for the *Los Angeles Times*, Michael Ordoña stated, "The film's bright colors and blaring happy music may not be enough for viewers to overcome the rather unfunny themes of neglect ('Back up the abuse caboose') routinely excused in more engaging fare." Overall, review aggregators such as Metacritic and Rotten Tomatoes showed that the film received generally positive but somewhat mixed reviews from both professional critics and audiences. In general, it is likely that *The Willoughbys* as a film will not stand out as an instant classic, but rather a fun, darkly humorous, and oddly touching movie based loosely on a lesser-known work by a beloved author.

—Aimee Chevrette Bear

Further Reading

Lowry, Lois. *The Willoughbys*. Houghton Mifflin Company, 2008.
———. "Lowry Spins Mischievous Tale of *The Willoughbys*." Interview by Liane Hanson. *National Public Radio*, 6 July 2008, www.npr.org/transcripts/92267961. Accessed 27 Feb. 2021.

Bibliography

Castillo, Monica. "Review of *The Willoughbys*, directed by Kris Pearn." *RogerEbert.com*, 22 Apr. 2020, www.rogerebert.com/reviews/alice-in-wonderland-2010. Accessed 27 Feb. 2020.
Debruge, Peter. "*The Willoughbys* on Netflix: Film Review." Review of *The Willoughbys*, directed by Kris Pearn. *Variety*, 20 Apr. 2020, variety.com/2020/film/reviews/the-willoughbys-review-netflix-1234584685. Accessed 27 Feb. 2021.
Lee, Benjamin. "*The Willoughbys* Review—Imaginative Animated Netflix Adventure." *The Guardian*, 20 Apr. 2020, www.theguardian.com/film/2020/apr/20/the-willoughbys-review-netflix-animated-movie. Accessed 5 Mar. 2021.
Ordoña, Michael. "Review: *The Willoughbys* is Loud, Colorful and Frantic, but At Least It's a Distraction." Review of *The Willoughbys*, directed by Kris Pearn. *The Los Angeles Times*, 20 Apr. 2020, www.latimes.com/entertainment-arts/movies/story/2020-04-20/willoughbys-review-animated-netflix. Accessed 27 Feb. 2021.
Snicket, Lemony. Review of *The Willoughbys*, by Lois Lowry. *Publishers Weekly*, 4 Feb. 2008, www.publishersweekly.com/978-0-618-97974-5. Accessed 27 Feb. 2021.

The Wolf of Wall Street

The Novel
Author: Jordan Belfort (b. 1962)
First published: 2007

The Film
Year released: 2013
Director: Martin Scorsese (b. 1942)
Screenplay by: Terence Winter
Starring: Leonardo DiCaprio, Jonah Hill, Margot Robbie

Context

The Wolf of Wall Street was a 2007 memoir by Jordan Belfort, a former stockbroker who defrauded investors by artificially inflating the prices of low-value stocks known as "penny stocks," which he promoted heavily through the brokerage Stratton Oakmont during the 1980s and 1990s. Although Belfort amassed extensive wealth and led a lavish lifestyle, his fraudulent activities attracted the attention of law enforcement, and he later served twenty-two months in prison and paid required restitutions to the victims of the crimes. Following his release from prison, Belfort published *The Wolf of Wall Street*, which documents his entrance into the world of stock trading and subsequent illegal activities, as well as the 2009 *Catching the Wolf of Wall Street*, which focuses on his arrest and prosecution.

The Wolf of Wall Street became a bestseller and quickly attracted attention from the film industry. After several years of stalled development, it was officially announced in April 2012 that Martin Scorsese had joined the project as director, as had actor Leonardo DiCaprio, who was set to portray Belfort. Scorsese, a veteran filmmaker, had directed now-classic films dealing with organized crime earlier in his career, including *Goodfellas* (1990) and *Casino* (1995), and which were often based on real events and extensive historical research. *The Wolf of Wall Street* both builds upon and diverges from Scorsese's earlier work, trading the world of organized crime for the more socially acceptable, yet no less criminal, realm of financial crime.

The film was the fifth collaboration between Scorsese and DiCaprio, who had previously worked with the director on critically acclaimed films such as *The Aviator* (2004) and *The Departed* (2006). The screenplay for the film was written by Terence Winter, an Emmy Award-winning writer and producer best known for his work on acclaimed television shows such as *The Sopranos* and *Boardwalk Empire*. Starring DiCaprio as well as Jonah Hill and Margot Robbie, *The Wolf of Wall Street* premiered in the United States on December 17, 2013.

Film Analysis

As a film directed by Scorsese, focused on criminal activity and the lives of those who partake in it, and based on real-world events, *The Wolf of Wall Street* invites comparisons to earlier Scorsese films such as *Goodfellas* and *Casino*, which established Scorsese as a leading director of such films. However, a key difference in the origin and process of adapting the film immediately sets *The Wolf of Wall Street* apart from those earlier works. For both *Goodfellas* and *Casino*, the screenplays were cowritten by Scorsese and the journalist and screenwriter Nicholas Pileggi and based upon nonfiction books by Pileggi, which in turn drew from extensive research and interviews with the primary personages involved, their associates, and, at times, members of law enforcement. While the first-person voices of some major figures made it into the films thanks to those interviews and other documentary evidence, their perspectives were filtered through several layers of additional storytelling and tempered somewhat by the conflicting perspectives also presented. *The Wolf of Wall Street*, on the other hand, is adapted not from a theoretically objective work, such as Pileggi's *Wiseguy* (1985) or *Casino* (1995), but from the wholly subjective memoir of protagonist Jordan Belfort himself. The film is not simply an adaptation of the events surrounding Stratton Oakmont's rise and fall; rather, the narrative presented on screen is one constructed by Belfort.

Although the influences of the screenwriter, director, and actors shape the film adaptation of *The Wolf of Wall Street*, as do practical and legal considerations—for example, the names of several of the figures involved were changed for the film, and some characters were created as composites of multiple individuals with whom Belfort interacted—Belfort's voice is the dominant force throughout the narrative. This was a strategic choice on the part of the filmmakers, who identified the preservation of Belfort's narrative voice and unique perspective as essential to the film. In a 2013 interview with Eric Spitznagel for *Esquire*, Winter described *The Wolf of Wall Street* as "a movie about a con man, told from his perspective," and went on to explain, "Jordan is talking directly to you. You are being sold the Jordan Belfort story by Jordan Belfort, and he is a very unreliable narrator. That's very much by

Leonardo DiCaprio. Photo by Christopher William Adach via Wikimedia Commons.

design." Indeed, both the subjective nature of the narrative and the unreliability of the narrator himself are evident from as early as the opening sequence in the film, which begins in *medias res* during the height of Stratton Oakmont's success. Following a commercial that seeks to cast the brokerage as a reliable firm of unimpeachable integrity, the scene shifts to show Stratton Oakmont as it was: a raucous firm that encouraged a host of illegal and unethical acts. The juxtaposition between how the firm presents itself and how it operates is the first evidence of the many layers of deception taking place, and the subsequent sequences aptly illustrate Belfort's role in developing and maintaining those deceptions.

After the film reveals the reality of Stratton Oakmont, the footage on-screen freezes, and Belfort (DiCaprio) begins to speak directly to the viewer, introducing himself and his background. Rather than simply introduce Belfort as he wishes to be perceived, however, the ensuing montage hints that both Belfort the character and the narrative itself may not be entirely trustworthy. As the montage shows a shot of Belfort driving down the highway in a red Ferrari, he interrupts his narration to assert that his Ferrari was "white, like Don Johnson's in *Miami Vice*," rather than red, and the car's color shifts from red to white on-screen. That transformation aptly demonstrates to the viewer that the events taking place on screen may not be entirely accurate. At the same time, the sequence raises an additional question: was Belfort's Ferrari ever truly white, or did he simply wish that it had been? While Belfort's memoir asserts that he did, in fact, own the same variety of white Ferrari used in the television show *Miami Vice*, the film's treatment of that assertion makes for a degree of ambiguity.

The unreliable nature of Belfort as a narrator and of *The Wolf of Wall Street* as a work becomes increasingly apparent as the film progresses, particularly as the film demonstrates the ways in which Belfort's extensive drug use influenced his behavior and perception of the world around him. In one scene, Belfort drives home while high on Quaaludes, and he tells the viewer that he drove slowly in an attempt to drive safely. The film depicts him doing so successfully; however, police later arrive to arrest him and show him his car, which displays clear signs of having been in multiple accidents. In addition to lying to the viewer through Belfort's voice-over narration, the film again misleads the viewer by presenting an inaccurate visual depiction of the events that took place. Although the film goes on to reveal what truly happened during Belfort's ride home, the initial deception emphasizes the narrator's unreliability and raises doubts about the narrative as a whole: if drugs could cloud Belfort's perceptions so much that he mistook a drive full of collisions for a collision-free one, what other falsehoods might be present in the film and, indeed, in Belfort's entire personal narrative?

Ultimately, the version of Belfort and his life story presented in *The Wolf of Wall Street* are as much a sales pitch as those he gives his clients throughout the film, which the film's final scene emphasizes. By the end of the film, Belfort has served nearly two years in prison and subsequently established himself as a motivational speaker; the film ends with a scene set at one of his speaking engagements. There, an announcer, in fact played by the real Belfort, introduces the fictionalized Belfort, likening him to "rock stars, professional athletes, gangsters" before going on to describe him as "the world's greatest sales trainer." While the film visually depicts Belfort entering a new career that—though still profitable—is far less glamorous than his previous lifestyle, the real Belfort is shown having the final opportunity to sell the audience on the vision of himself as a figure of legend—a vision shown to be as much the result of Belfort's manipulations as anything sold to his clients.

Significance

Following its premiere, *The Wolf of Wall Street* opened in theaters in the United States, Canada, and France on December 25, 2013. The film went on to open in numerous additional countries between December 2013 and February 2014, ultimately screening in more than fifty countries worldwide. Popular among audiences, the film achieved a domestic gross total of nearly $117 million and grossed an additional $275 million internationally, performing particularly well in the United Kingdom, Germany, and France. The highest-grossing Scorsese film to date worldwide, *The Wolf of Wall Street* also had the third-highest domestic gross earning among the director's films.

The critical response to *The Wolf of Wall Street* was generally positive, with critics praising its entertainment value, DiCaprio's performance, and the film's ability to maintain an engaging pace despite its three-hour run time. Critics disagreed, however, over whether the film ultimately condemned or glamorized Belfort's crimes and the debauchery in which he and his colleagues indulged. Critics correctly identified the film as offering a critique, intel-

lectually, of unrestrained capitalism and consumption, but many also felt that the critique was contradicted by the way the film's pleasure, its fast pace and levity and vigor, are based on the vicarious enjoyment of, and a reduplication of, Belfort's own pleasures. Further, these critics felt that the film's ending—showing him still in charge, as it were—ultimately only glamorized Belfort. Not insignificantly, the film became the center of controversy among individuals who had been personally victimized by Belfort, some of whom publicly criticized Scorsese, DiCaprio, and others involved with the project for romanticizing Belfort and ignoring his victims. Despite such controversy, *The Wolf of Wall Street* was nominated for five Academy Awards, including the awards for Best Writing (Adapted Screenplay), Best Picture, and Best Directing. DiCaprio and Hill were also recognized for their performances as lead actor and supporting actor, respectively, and DiCaprio ultimately won the Best Actor award at the 2014 Golden Globes.

—*Joy Crelin*

Further Reading

Belfort, Jordan. *The Wolf of Wall Street*. Bantam, 2007.

Winter, Terence. "Screenwriter Terence Winter Talks *The Wolf of Wall Street*, His First Draft of the Script, Adapting the Memoir, His Plans for *Boardwalk Empire*, and More." Interview by Steve Weintraub. *Collider*, 24 Dec. 2013, collider.com/terence-winter-wolf-of-wall-street-interview. Accessed 31 Jan. 2019.

Bibliography

Bradshaw, Peter. Review of *The Wolf of Wall Street*, directed by Martin Scorsese. *The Guardian*, 16 Jan. 2014, www.theguardian.com/film/2014/jan/16/wolf-of-wall-street-review. Accessed 31 Jan. 2019.

Brody, Richard. "The Wild, Brilliant 'Wolf of Wall Street.'" Review of *The Wolf of Wall Street*, directed by Martin Scorsese. *The New Yorker*, 24 Dec. 2013, www.newyorker.com/culture/richard-brody/the-wild-brilliant-wolf-of-wall-street. Accessed 31 Jan. 2019.

Child, Ben. "Real-Life Wolf of Wall Street Says His Life of Debauchery 'Even Worse' Than in Film." *The Guardian*, 28 Feb. 2014, www.theguardian.com/film/2014/feb/28/wolf-of-wall-street-jordan-belfort-sex-drugs. Accessed 31 Jan. 2019.

Haglund, David. "How Accurate Is *The Wolf of Wall Street*?" *Slate*, 31 Dec. 2013, slate.com/culture/2013/12/wolf-of-wall-street-true-story-jordan-belfort-and-other-real-people-in-dicaprio-scorsese-movie.html. Accessed 31 Jan. 2019.

Scott, A. O. "When Greed Was Good (and Fun)." Review of *The Wolf of Wall Street*, directed by Martin Scorsese. *The New York*

Times, 24 Dec. 2013, www.nytimes.com/2013/12/25/movies/dicaprio-stars-in-scorseses-the-wolf-of-wall-street.html. Accessed 31 Jan. 2019.

Winter, Terence. "Q&A: Terence Winter on *The Wolf of Wall Street*'s Infamous Candle Scene." Interview by Eric Spitznagel. *Esquire*, 23 Dec. 2013, www.esquire.com/entertainment/ interviews/a26525/terence-winter-interview. Accessed 31 Jan. 2019.

"The Wolf of Wall Street." *Box Office Mojo*, www.boxofficemojo.com/movies/?page=main&id=wolfof wallstreet.htm. Accessed 31 Jan. 2019.

Wonderstruck

The Novel

Author: Brian Selznick (b. 1966)
First published: 2011

The Film

Year released: 2017
Director: Todd Haynes (b. 1961)
Screenplay by: Brian Selznick
Starring: Oakes Fegley, Julianne Moore, Millicent Simmonds, Jaden Michael, Michelle Williams

Context

Author and illustrator Brian Selznick began his career in 1991 with the book *The Houdini Box*. His Caldecott Medal-winning *The Invention of Hugo Cabret* (2007) remains one of his best-known works, combining narration with illustrations to tell the story. *Wonderstruck* (2011) was published four years later and uses a similar technique. The book intertwines two distinct stories, moving back and forth between the years 1977 and 1927.

Wonderstruck tells the story of two children separated by fifty years but tied together by a shared experience and surprising family connections. The text portion of the novel takes place in 1977; Ben is living with his aunt, uncle, and cousins after his mother's death. He is deaf in one ear, which often leads to mockery by Robby, the cousin with whom he has been forced to share a room. One night he sees lights on in the neighboring house where he had lived with his mother. He sneaks out with the hope that his mother may have returned, but instead he finds his cousin, Janet, who is also grieving. After he talks her into allowing him to stay by himself, he discovers a few of his mother's treasures, including a book about a New York museum, which contains a bookmark that leads to a quest to find his father. The illustrated portions of the novel take place in 1927. Rose lives in Hoboken, New Jersey, with a strict father who cannot understand his deaf daughter or her desire to be with the woman who left him for another man. The novel traces the events of the next few weeks for Ben and an undetermined amount of time for Rose until the two are united and discover that the adult Rose is the grandmother Ben did not know he had.

Film Analysis

Wonderstruck was directed by Todd Haynes, but the screenplay was written by Selznick himself. As a result, the storyline between the two versions is very close, with just a few minor differences that do not detract from the story itself.

One of the main thematic elements of both the novel and the film intertwines the semiorphaned experience with running away. Ben (Oakes Fegley) was orphaned when his mother died, leaving him with his aunt and uncle but no knowledge of his father or his father's family. Rose (Millicent Simmonds), although she lives with her father, has been abandoned by the mother she worships from afar. Both leave home in an effort to reunite with the missing parent. For Selznick this theme is linked to the fact that as we mature, we search for a place to belong in the larger world. This element is seen in the way the film closely mimics the novel's representation of Ben's experiences with his aunt and uncle as well as his relationship with his mother (Michelle Williams). The main difference between the two is in Ben's curiosity about his father. The novel tells readers that Ben asked his mother about his father but did not receive straight answers. As a result, he fantasizes about his father, and Selznick ties his fantasies into the song "Space Oddity" by David Bowie while the child pictures Major Tom as an incarnation of his father. His curiosity is gentle, not interfering with a strong maternal relationship. In contrast, the film shows Ben more aggressively asking his mother about his father's identity, and although Bowie's song is playing quietly in the background, it is nowhere near as significant in the film. Instead, Haynes uses Eumir Deodato's "Also sprach Zarathustra," a version of the composition by Richard Strauss made famous in Stanley Kubrick's *2001: A Space Odyssey* as a repeated background to highlight Ben's journey. The parental relationship for

Rose is also similar in both the novel and in the film, but the film leaves out some detail about her relationship with her mother, softening the representation of Lillian Mayhew (Julianne Moore) from the novel's self-centered actress who abandoned her family for stardom and another man to an actress who was separated from her family but not as completely selfish. In contrast, the film emphasizes her father's strict attitude, showing him admonishing her at several points. The separation between the children and the missing or absent parents becomes the stimulus behind each child's journey away from home.

This journey is problematic in the novel and in the film because both of the children are deaf. Ben was born with deafness in one ear, but an electrical accident leaves him completely deaf while Rose is characterized as having been deaf since birth. Because Ben's full disability is not realized until late in the first section of either the novel or the film, we do not see how others react to it. However, the film does enhance the reactions between Rose's parents and the girl as a result of her hearing impairment with both her father and mother seemingly unable to handle what they viewed as a defect. Fortunately for both children, there is someone who cares for them anyway. For Rose, her older brother Walter (Cory Michael Smith) steps in to care for the girl and to make sure she receives an appropriate education and moves on to have a full life. In contrast to the memories of Rose's full life, only one year of Ben's life is closely shared. This limits our understanding of his family relationships before his flight to New York to find his father. However, we are introduced to his friend Jamie (Jaden Michael) while he is in the city. The film successfully uses diegetic sound to take viewers into the silent worlds where the children live, often illustrating their experiences through moments of no sound or through snatches of muffled noise. This cinematic effect emphasizes the mood of the story, especially the moments when the children are frightened or feeling alone. The fact that Rose's portion of the story is completely without words further emphasizes the world that Rose must navigate through.

Another successful connection between the novel and the film is the transition between the intertwined stories seen particularly in the filmmaking. In the novel, Ben's story is told through text, but Rose's story is told mostly through black-and-white pencil illustrations. Haynes maintains this back and forth with color filming of the scenes revolving around Ben and black-and-white filming of scenes revolving around Rose's childhood. Haynes's camerawork, including a variety of tracking shots, long shots, and close-ups, mimics the early days of silent film to reflect Rose's experiences in 1927 as well as film styles from the late 1960s and early 1970s to reflect Ben's experiences in 1977. The film also successfully uses lighting to present the mood of the moment. For instance, the film opens with the scene where Ben is having a nightmare. Blue tones, jerky camerawork, and blurred lines add to the sense of discord the child feels as his dream self is chased by wolves through a wooded landscape. This tone is repeated later in the film when Ben sees the museum diorama created by his father, further suggesting a dream-like state. Darkness is also used to create mood as the film ends with Ben, the now adult Rose, and Jamie standing on the roof of the Queens Museum, silently watching a city blackout. In this instance, the darkness and lack of sound are reassuring, promising a happier future for grandmother and grandson.

Two additional elements of the story handled carefully in the film are worth mentioning. First, the children both seek friendship. Ben finds a friend in Jamie, a child whose father works at the American Museum of Natural History. The story's mood is lightened as the two scamper through the museum after closing hours, discovering a variety of fascinating exhibits and historical artifacts. Rose finds friendship in a slightly different way, as she is found in the same museum by her older brother. Once Rose joins Walter, he changes her life, adding humor, education, and friendship, something that is expanded in the film more than in the novel. Second, the museum itself is central to both main characters. Ben's lifelong fascination with collections links him to the museum book *Wonderstruck*, a tome sent to his mother by his father, which contains a bookmark with a message that sets him on his journey to the city. Rose's connection to the museum is first found in her brother's employment there, but then leads to her own adult occupation both at the same institution as well as at the Queens Museum where she was still employed when she and Ben find each other.

Significance

The film was produced by Amazon Studios and is distributed in the United States through Roadside Attractions. The box office sales during opening weekend of October 20-22, 2017, equaled $65,822; however, the total gross has added up to $1.060 million, and the international gross income is almost $3.3 million.

Both versions of Selznick's work were recognized for awards. The 2011 novel received the American Library Association's Notable Children's Book Award and was on *The New York Times* Best Seller list. It was also a *USA Today* bestseller, a Publisher's Weekly Best Book of 2011, a Booklist Editor's Choice of 2011, a *Kirkus Reviews* Best Children's Book of 2011, and a School Library Journal Best Book of 2011. The film was nominated for three 2018 Saturn Awards by the Academy of Science Fiction, Fantasy & Horror Films and for the 2018 Critics Choice Award by the Broadcast Film Critics Association. Todd Haynes was nominated for the Palme d'Or award at the 2017 Cannes Film Festival. In addition, Selznick received several nominations for his screenplay, and both Millicent Simmonds (who played Rose) and Oakes Fegley (who played Ben) received several notable recognitions.

Despite this acclaim, *Wonderstruck* received mixed reviews. Writing for RogerEbert.com, Christy Lemire lauded Haynes for "using his formidable abilities to explore the universal need for human connection" but felt the film was disappointing overall. *The New York Times* review by Manohla Dargis, on the other hand, was much more positive, noting Haynes's skill in combining the children's stories "with craft and wit." She argued that the film "becomes a Haynesian exploration of identity, desire and imagination," despite being slow getting to its point.

—*Theresa L. Stowell, PhD*

Further Reading

Eastland, Katherine. "Deaf Meets *Wonderstruck*." *Humanities*, vol. 33, no. 1, Jan. 2012, pp. 38-42. *EBSCOhost*, search.ebscohost.com/login.aspx?direct=true&db=f6h&AN=71408441&site=ehost-live. Accessed 27 Mar. 2020.

Metz, Walter. "The Sounds of Silence: Todd Haynes' Film Adaptation of Brian Selznick's *Wonderstruck*." *Film Criticism*, vol. 42, no. 4, Nov. 2018, pp. 1-6. *EBSCOhost*, search.ebscohost.com/login.aspx?direct=true&db=lkh&AN=134308408&site=ehost-live. Accessed 27 Mar. 2020.

Reichl, Susanne. "Turning Brian Selznick's Pages: A Multimodal Celebration of the Visual and the Textual." *Fractures and Disruptions in Children's Literature*, edited by Ana Margarida Ramos, et al., Cambridge Scholars Publishing, 2017, pp. 262-75. Accessed 27 Mar. 2020.

Bibliography

Dargis, Manohla. "Review: *Wonderstruck*, Todd Haynes's Imitations of Life." *The New York Times*, 19 Oct. 2017, www.nytimes.com/2017/10/19/movies/wonderstruck-review-todd-haynes.html. Accessed 27 Mar. 2020.

Hudson, Hannah Trierweiler. "Talking with Brian Selznick." *Instructor*, vol. 121, no. 2, Fall 2011, pp. 55-57. *EBSCOhost*, search.ebscohost.com/login.aspx?direct=true&db=f6h&AN=66659848&site=ehost-live. Accessed 27 Mar. 2020.

Lemire, Christy. "*Wonderstruck*." *RogerEbert.com*, 20 Oct. 2017, www.rogerebert.com/reviews/wonderstruck-2017. Accessed 27 Mar. 2020.

Metz, Walter. "The Sounds of Silence: Todd Haynes' Film Adaptation of Brian Selznick's *Wonderstruck*." *Film Criticism*, vol. 42, no. 4, Nov. 2018, pp. 1-6. *EBSCOhost*, search.ebscohost.com/login.aspx?direct=true&db=lkh&AN=134308408&site=ehost-live. Accessed 27 Mar. 2020.

"*Wonderstruck*." *IMDb*, www.imdb.com/title/tt5208216/?ref_=ttawd_awd_tt. Accessed 27 Mar. 2020.

World War Z

The Novel
Author: Max Brooks (b. 1972)
First published: 2006

The Film
Year released: 2013
Director: Marc Forster (b. 1969)
Screenplay by: Matthew Michael Carnahan, Drew Goddard, Damon Lindelof
Starring: Brad Pitt, Mireille Enos, Daniella Kertesz, Fana Mokoena, David Morse

Context

Max Brooks's bestselling novel, *World War Z: An Oral History of the Zombie War* (2006), acknowledges three people who particularly inspired him. First, is Louis "Studs" Terkel (1912-2008), whose Pulitzer Prize-winning *The Good War: An Oral History of World War II* (1985) provided the format. Brooks's work presents an unidentified reporter who, years after the end of the Zombie War, travels around the world to interview survivors for their unique perspectives on the battle for survival. Second, is General Sir John Hackett (1910-97), a much-decorated World War II British military officer. Hackett wrote two novels—*The Third World War: August 1985* (1979) and *The Third World War: The Untold Story* (1982)—which posited a deadly new global conflict. Third, is George A. Romero (1940-2017), whose series of seven films, beginning with *Night of the Living Dead* (1968), launched the concept of a zombie apocalypse. Zombies were enthusiastically embraced, and their existence has been celebrated by writers, artists, and filmmakers ever since.

Brooks's contribution to the horror subgenre was to inject semiplausible, semiserious styles of discourse drawing on expert language not only from contemporary science but from the fields of government, politics, and the military. The concept for the book was appropriate to an era of "war games" and disaster event modeling. The popularity of the novel made *World War Z* a natural for film. Brad Pitt's production company, Plan B Entertainment, won a bidding war for the option rights. Because the novel had no central character around which to stage the action, screenwriter J. Michael Straczynski was hired to write an adaptation, the first of numerous drafts turned out by several writers. Straczynski created lead character, Gerry Lane. A retired United Nations (UN) investigator, Lane—in exchange for sanctuary for his family—globe-hopped in an attempt to find the origin of the virus so an antizombie vaccine could be developed. In 2008, Marc Forster was hired as director. In 2010, Pitt accepted the lead role, and also became a first-time producer. Shooting for the film began the following year.

Film Analysis

The adaptation of *World War Z* (2013) was troubled throughout a tortuous, drawn-out production process. Multiple issues inflated costs on what was already a big-budget film. Delays were the result of a comedy of errors, including the illegal importation of real working weapons, rather than harmless props, into a foreign country. Tempers flared between members of cast and crew over the conflicting directions the film was taking. Paramount studio executives and allied investors fretted there was an expensive, potentially reputation-destroying bomb in the making.

Even as cameras began rolling in Malta (a stand-in for Israel), where memorable sequences would be shot—like a flood of zombies scrambling up and over a high wall—the story was still in development. The zombies themselves underwent metamorphosis. Brooks's traditional shambling undead moaned, oozed black pus from open wounds, and became more tattered as they aged. Disintegrating scraps of rotten flesh, they were driven by unearthly hunger. The film zombies, however, looked comparatively fresh. Upon being bitten by the infected, they changed from human to ravenous cannibals within twelve twitching seconds. They moved at normal speed. Their hearing was acute. Blood vessels stood out dark against their skin. They typically attacked in overwhelming numbers.

While a hero had been born and a rough plot sketched in, there were some shaky spots in the adaptation. Other than borrowing the title and including vast quantities of zombies, the film eliminated much of what made Brooks's novel compelling to readers. Large portions of the script had to be created from whole cloth, resulting in a patchwork effect, as though the film could not decide what it wanted to be. Sometimes it was a straightforward horror story and sometimes it was a medical mystery based upon dubious science. A race-against-the-clock adventure/ thriller had undertones of bureaucratic satire and family drama. The rewrite process continued into post-production and beyond. The first director's cut—which ended with Gerry Lane (Brad Pitt) transformed into a blood- thirsty warrior leading troops into battle in Russia against an army of zombies—was less than satisfying to all concerned. A total rewrite of the last third of the adaptation and extensive reshoots not only added millions to the price of production, but also shoved back the release date by months.

The scope of the novel—which was truly global, traveling to interview survivors living in remote spots from Antarctica to Siberia and from American outposts to Pacific atolls—was greatly reduced. The finished film uses just a handful of major settings. Each, as in the novel, is indicated by name and place. Only three of these (a United Nations [UN] command ship on the ocean, the Demilitarized Zone in South Korea, and Jerusalem, Israel) are contained in the novel. Four are North American (Philadelphia, New York, Newark, Nova Scotia). The East Coast cities are the sites of several exciting set pieces featuring zombie attacks that are representative of what is transpiring everywhere on Earth. One new site, a World Health Organization (WHO) laboratory in Wales, serves as a final battleground where humankind makes a stand.

To make up for the lack of first-hand observations from elsewhere about the progress of the zombie plague, the adaptation inserts information where possible. A snatch of a news broadcast is overheard: "...the virus changes in a way that allows transmission to humans." Quick cuts show people in different environments wearing face masks to avoid contamination. Footage of various creatures—armies of ants, snarling wolves—symbolize nature's fierce rule: kill or be killed. A counter in a war room spins too fast for the eye to follow, tallying "projected losses" of humans to zombies in the billions. Gerry's friend, UN Deputy Secre-

tary-General Thierry Umutoni (Fana Mokoena), summarizes conditions in the now fallen national capital: the president is dead, the vice president is missing.

The novel's multiple viewpoint technique was also changed. Brooks included dozens of individual voices, some humorous, some brash, many unreliable because they were traumatized in the zombie war. Each contributor poignantly recalled personal experiences which, like jigsaw pieces, helped reveal the size and shape of the overall puzzle. In the film, however, almost everything is filtered through Gerry Lane's perspective. While this sacrifices local color, it actually improves clarity of purpose and story focus. The single point of view greatly simplifies a complex story line. It boosts the importance of the lead character and increases viewers' sympathies toward him, an ordinary individual caught in a dilemma. Anyone can understand Gerry's reluctance to risk his life, balanced against his desire to find a way to stop the zombies. The health and safety of wife Karin (Mireille Enos) and young daughters Rachel (Abigail Hargrove) and Connie (Sterling Jerins) are at stake. Gerry's qualifications for setting out on his quest are enumerated by the American naval commander (David Andrews). He was on the ground during the Liberian civil war, investigated Chechen war crimes, participated in Sri Lanka in 2007—so he is made for the present catastrophe. If Gerry does not agree to use his skills in pursuing a zombie cure—first with virologist Dr. Fassbach (Elyes Gabel) then on his own after the doctor imparts a valuable clue before accidentally shooting himself to death—his family will lose their sanctuary aboard the command ship. The interim authorities cannot protect "nonessential personnel."

A significant difference between novel and film is the time element involved. Brooks set his work in a postwar era, after humans regained the upper hand. A greatly diminished world population has reorganized into such entities as the West Indies Federation, the Holy Russian Empire, and the Federated States of Micronesia. Resetting *World War Z* in the present was a wise cinematic decision. It kept flashbacks to a minimum and gave the story immediacy. The horror unfolds in real time and viewers can live it vicariously, through noble Gerry Lane. The danger feels real. Even at the end of the film, the future is uncertain.

Significance
Overcoming myriad problems, *World War Z* opened seven months later than initially intended, in June 2013.

While critical reception was mixed, reviewers in major media outlets (like *The Washington Post* and Rex Reed in *The Observer*) gave glowing recommendations. Commercially, the film earned more than $540 million worldwide, making it the highest-grossing Brad Pitt feature to date. Net profits are unknown. The initial production budget was estimated to be in the range of $125-$150 million. This figure rose sharply (by at least $50 million in some reports and by more than $100 million in others), primarily due to reshoots. The elevated costs mostly involved photographing brand-new material to replace the final 45 minutes of the original screened film. One extended sequence showed the effects of zombies on a plane. Another sequence illustrated humans versus zombies in a laboratory. Judicious editing of the first part of the production was also necessary to remove references that might offend the lucrative but highly restrictive Chinese film import market.

—Jack Ewing

Further Reading

Brooks, Max. *The Zombie Survival Guide: Complete Protection from the Living Dead*. Random House, 2003.

Geiser, Kelsey. "Stanford Scholar Explains Why Zombie Fascination Is Very Much Alive." *Stanford News*, 20 Feb. 2013, news.stanford.edu/news/2013/february/why-zombie-fascination -022013.html. Accessed 7 Apr. 2020.

Bibliography

Brodesser-Akner, Taffy. "Max Brooks Is Not Kidding about the Zombie Apocalypse." *The New York Times Magazine*, 21 June 2013, www.nytimes.com/2013/06/23/magazine/max-brooks-is-not-kidding-about-the-zombie-apocalypse.html. Accessed 7 Apr. 2020.

Brooks, Max. *World War Z: An Oral History of the Zombie War*. Random House, 2006.

Holson, Laura M. "Brad's War." *Vanity Fair*, 9 May 2013, www.vanityfair.com/hollywood/2013/06/brad-pitt-world-war-z-drama. Accessed 7 Apr. 2020.

Masters, Kim. "Brad Pitt's Zombie Nightmare: Inside the Troubled *World War Z* Production." *The Hollywood Reporter*, 12 June 2012, www.hollywoodreporter.com/news/brad-pitt-world-war-z-production-nightmare-336422. Accessed 7 Apr. 2020.

Mendelson, Scott. "Brad Pitt, *World War Z 2* and Why Not Every Blockbuster Deserves a Sequel." *Forbes*, 7 Feb. 2017, www.forbes.com/sites/scottmendelson/2017/02/07/brad-pitts-world-war-z-2-pulled-from-schedule-hopefully-for-good/# 280071134057. Accessed 7 Apr. 2020.

Reed, Rex. "*World War Z*: Apocalyptic Zombie Flick Towers above Every Other Alleged Summer Blockbuster." *Observer*, 18 June 2013, observer.com/2013/06/doomsday-apocalyptic-zombie-flick-towers-above-every-other-alleged-summer-blockbuster/. Accessed 7 Apr. 2020.

Stanton, Dan. "Virus Fights Virus for Control of Brad Pitt's Brain, but Is This Science?" *Biopharma Reporter*, 10 Jan. 2014, www.biopharma-reporter.com/Article/2014/01/10/World-War-Z-scientifically-duff-experts-say. Accessed 7 Apr. 2020.

Troy, Tevi. "What *World War Z* Can Teach Us." *Politico*, 27 June 2013, www.politico.com/story/2013/06/what-world-war-z-can-teach-us-about-pandemics-093497. Accessed 7 Apr. 2020.

A Wrinkle in Time

The Novel

Author: Madeleine L'Engle (1918-2007)
First published: 1962

The Film

Year released: 2018
Director: Ava DuVernay (b. 1972)
Screenplay by: Jennifer Lee, Jeff Stockwell
Starring: Storm Reid, Oprah Winfrey, Reese Witherspoon, Mindy Kaling, Chris Pine

Context

A favorite among generations of young readers since its publication in 1962, Madeleine L'Engle's classic novel *A Wrinkle in Time* has long stood out relative to most science fiction of the mid-twentieth century. First of all, L'Engle featured a teenaged girl as the book's protagonist, a refreshing innovation for the genre. In addition to having an awkward, but ultimately triumphant girl, Margaret "Meg" Murry, as the protagonist, the book included an array of female characters: Meg's mother, Mrs. Murry, faithfully holds the Murry family together on Earth while her husband remains imprisoned on the evil planet Camazotz, waiting to be rescued. And the three mysterious supernatural guardians—Mrs. Whatsit, Mrs. Who, and Mrs. Which—shepherd Meg, her schoolmate Calvin O'Keefe, and her precocious, brilliant younger brother, Charles Wallace, through space-time to rescue Mr. Murry.

A second reason the book stood out is because it presented an intriguing, and then-novel mix of science fiction and fantasy with spiritual themes. The children and their guides travel through the universe by tessering, a method of time travel that shortens, or wrinkles, space and time—a phenomenon that Meg's parents had studied in their work as scientists. L'Engle uses time travel and the tropes of science fiction to explore the oldest and most primal material in human stories: the battle between good and evil, darkness and light. It is up to Meg to overcome her adolescent angst, deepened by the trauma of having lost her father, to rescue him and save the vulnerable Charles Wallace from IT, the evil force that rules Camazotz and casts a shadow (called the "Black Thing") over the universe.

The author's quirky treatment of these themes, along with the book's targeting of a young female audience, earned it many loyal readers over the years, and so it generated great anticipation when the film version was announced. Although the film received mixed reviews and arguably failed to translate the book's complexity and appeal to the screen, director Ava DuVernay mobilized star power, gifted actors, and exciting cinematography to create an engaging, socially current experience of L'Engle's classic.

Film Analysis

The casting of *A Wrinkle in Time* is one of its strengths, but at the same time, the extent to which the characters work in this visual adaptation varies quite a bit. Newcomer Storm Reid, as the character of Meg Murry, brilliantly conveys the sullen resistance of the adolescent protagonist—a stubbornness that Meg must learn to harness in her battle against the evil intelligence of IT. Balancing the casting of an unknown actor as the story's protagonist, DuVernay packed several of the other main roles with a star-studded group: Oprah Winfrey, Mindy Kaling, and Reese Witherspoon play Mrs. Which, Mrs. Who, and Mrs. Whatsit, respectively, and Rowan Blanchard, of *Girl Meets World* fame (2014-17), departs from her perfect-girl television role to play a bully who torments Meg at school.

These choices meet varying degrees of success. The most obvious triumph is the way the film's cast expands the book's diversity by including numerous women of color as main characters, including Reid, Kaling, Winfrey, and Gugu Mbatha-Raw, who plays Meg's mother, named Kate Murry in the film. This diversity, extending to Meg's interracial family, offers welcome progress through the film's accurate reflection of different races as a simple fact of life. The effect of this is powerful, as audiences see a girl of color as the lead character traveling through space and defeating forces of evil.

Two of the guardian angel figures give strong performances that embellish the characters in the book. Witherspoon brings great personality to the character of Mrs. Whatsit, the youngest of the guides, through humorous lines and an engaging youth that counterweights the negative energy of Meg. Likewise, Kaling's tranquil rendering of Mrs. Who nicely interprets the book's wise character, whose words consist almost entirely of quotations from famous sages throughout history, much as her counterpart in the book does. The most significant of these for Meg is Mrs. Who's quoting of the ancient Persian poet Rumi: "The wound is the place where the light enters you." This bit of wisdom helps Meg in the film to understand the words of Mrs. Whatsit, who, in announcing her gift to Meg, says, "I give you your faults." Through these two guides, Meg comes to understand that she must transform her suffering into strength; she must use her deep sense of alienation and stubbornness to match the power of IT.

Winfrey's character in the film, however, is somewhat disappointing, a deficiency derived more from the script and direction than from Winfrey's performance. In the book, Mrs. Which is the oldest and most mysterious guide, and L'Engle renders her ancient formality by making her somewhat inaccessible—for example, by drawing out her speech through labored syllables. Winfrey certainly could have conveyed this odd majesty, but the film reduces Mrs. Which to a sort of clichéd grand, earth-mother type who directs the other two guides but fails to earn the audience's sympathy.

The script reflects other deficiencies that involve character but ultimately result in a drastic simplification of the book's themes. The film effectively portrays Meg's struggle with self-esteem, but it reduces the battle with IT almost entirely to this individual level. For example, Meg and her fellow travelers visit the Happy Medium (played by Zach Galifianakis), a sort of prophet, who shows them IT's dark forces in the world, in the form of Calvin's abusive father and the school bully, Veronica, who is shown castigating herself for her weight. The medium also trains Meg to open up, take risks, and trust others, in preparation for her battle against IT. These scenes are not problematic per se, but L'Engle's rendering of IT went much deeper by including spiritual, cultural, and even political elements. The film avoids this depth entirely, most prominently by representing IT as a vaguely spider-like monster rather

than the disembodied brain that haunts the original story. This change fundamentally alters the story's thematic possibilities. In the book, IT threatens to take over the universe, casting its shadow on Earth and other plants, but has already conquered the planet Camazotz. The power of IT on Camazotz manifests in the robotic, identical behavior of the planet's inhabitants. The film effectively captures one of the book's most frightening scenes, when Meg and her companions find a neighborhood of people acting in perfect, chilling unison: children bounce balls in exactly the same rhythm until their mothers step outside and call them in for dinner, in exactly the same voice.

Yet, by altering the source of this behavior, the film destroys not only the book's thematic logic but also some of its key significance. In the book, the citizens' robotic behavior literally matches the rhythm of IT as a cold, pulsing brain, and this correspondence, it turns out, enables the story's primary symbolism and rich themes. Readers come to realize that the brain is not simply an evil force that causes people to be mean; it comes to represent pure, corrupted human intelligence, devoid of love, spirituality, or any consciousness of freedom or free will. Literally disembodied, the brain is divorced from the spirit and from love, a contrast that L'Engle communicates in part by inserting references to spiritual figures, including Jesus, and quotes from the New Testament in the Christian Bible. While the book also cites many other religious and cultural thinkers, it has long been recognized as containing strong Christian allusions. The brain's symbolism enables this contrast, which drives much of Meg's intellectual and spiritual journey: her discovery of love, understood through ancient wisdom, as the ultimate weapon against IT.

L'Engle's use of the brain also allows her to advance a powerful cultural and political commentary. In the context of the Cold War era and the "military-industrial complex," in full force during the 1960s when the book was first published, L'Engle's representation of IT's absolute control over the people of Camazotz clearly invokes the threatening, totalitarian aspects of highly regulated, modern technological society. Fear of its most extreme forms, in the Soviet Union or in East Germany, weighed heavily on the minds of Americans during this period. In this sense, the book went far beyond the personal realm to signify a cultural and political struggle that deeply resonated with Americans. Finally, the brain emphasizes, in a way that the film's monster does not, the human source of the evil wrought by IT.

Stripped of the larger meanings behind L'Engle's construction of good and evil, the film resorts to watered-down versions of these concepts—hence, the overemphasis on personal goodness in the form of self-esteem, kindness, and courage. Still, despite the script's many weaknesses, the film's visual direction, cinematography, and actors' performances give much to the viewing experience. The costumes of the three guides are dazzling, colorful, and shimmering, while some of the computer-animated effects are stunning, such as the gossiping flowers dancing and flying on the planet Uriel and Mrs. Whatsit's transformation into a winged creature who carries the children through the sky.

Significance

The film was released in March 2018. It faced competition for audience attention from the blockbuster *Black Panther*, an all-black comic-book adaptation that dominated sales for many weeks during this period. Despite that, *A Wrinkle in Time* was received reasonably well overall by critics and viewers. While some, such as Michael Dirda, highlighted the book's flaws even before the movie was released, critics such as Richard Brody and Katy Waldman praised the book while recognizing the script's conceptual weaknesses, such as shallow characterizations, but appreciating other aspects of the film, such as its cinematography, diverse casting, and musical choices. *New York Times* critic A. O. Scott was more enthusiastic, calling the film "demonstratively generous, encouraging and large-spirited." Scott also noted the historical significance of the production itself, not only its inclusive casting but its status as "the first $100 million movie directed by an African-American woman."

—Ashleigh Imus, PhD

Further Reading

Egan, Kate. *The World of* A Wrinkle in Time: *The Making of the Movie*. Farrar, Straus and Giroux, 2018.

Larson, Hope. *A Wrinkle in Time: The Graphic Novel*. Farrar, Straus and Giroux, 2012.

Bibliography

Brody, Richard. "Ava DuVernay's *A Wrinkle in Time*, Reviewed." Review of *A Wrinkle in Time*, directed by Ava DuVernay. *The New Yorker*, 7 Mar. 2018, www.newyorker.com/culture/richard-brody/ava-duvernays-a-wrinkle-in-time-reviewed. Accessed 28 Dec. 2018.

Dirda, Michael. "*A Wrinkle in Time*: Let's Hope the Movie Is Better Than the Book." Review of *A Wrinkle in Time*, by Madeleine L'Engle. *The Washington Post*, 27 Feb. 2018, www.washingtonpost.com/entertainment/books/a-wrinkle-in-time-lets-hope-the-movie-is-better-than-the-book/2018/02/27/48e1a260-1b19-11e8-b2d9-08e748f892c0_story.html. Accessed 28 Dec. 2018.

Kelley, Sonaiya. "*A Wrinkle in Time* Fails to Best *Black Panther*." *Los Angeles Times*, 11 Mar. 2018, www.latimes.com/entertainment/movies/la-et-mn-box-office-wrinkle-in-time-black-panther-20180311-story.html. Accessed 28 Dec. 2018.

L'Engle, Madeleine. *A Wrinkle in Time*. Farrar, Straus and Giroux, 2012.

Scott, A. O. "Review: *A Wrinkle in Time* Gives a Child of the Universe Powerful Friends." Review of *A Wrinkle in Time*, directed by Ava DuVernay. *The New York Times*, 7 Mar. 2018, www.nytimes.com/2018/03/07/movies/a-wrinkle-in-time-review-ava-duvernay-oprah-winfrey.html. Accessed 28 Dec. 2018.

Waldman, Katy. "Rereading *A Wrinkle in Time* after a Childhood Enthralled by Madeleine L'Engle." Review of *A Wrinkle in Time*, by Madeleine L'Engle. *The New Yorker*, 8 Mar. 2018, www.newyorker.com/books/page-turner/rereading-a-wrinkle-in-time-after-a-childhood-enthralled-by-madeleine-lengle. Accessed 28 Dec. 2018.

Wuthering Heights

The Novel
Author: Emily Brontë (1818-48)
First published: 1847

The Film
Year released: 1939
Director: William Wyler (1902-81)
Screenplay by: Charles MacArthur, Ben Hecht
Starring: Merle Oberon, Laurence Olivier, David Niven, Flora Robson, Geraldine Fitzgerald, Hugh Williams

Context

Emily Brontë's only novel, *Wuthering Heights*, was first published in 1847, under the pseudonym Ellis Bell. (Like her sisters, Anne and Charlotte, who respectively published *Agnes Grey* and *Jane Eyre* that same year, Emily wrote under a male pseudonym.) Few contemporary critics knew what to make of *Wuthering Heights* upon its initial publication. While some found its moorland setting and gothic fiction elements entertaining, more were bothered by its disorganized and wandering plot, disturbing characters, and bizarre ending. When Emily Brontë—about whom personal information is scarce—died at age thirty in 1848, Charlotte edited the novel so that a second posthumous edition, published in 1850, made the Yorkshire accents more intelligible. The book would eventually earn widespread acclaim, and since the 1930s, at least, it is often considered one of the great works of English literature. This reversal of its fortunes was established in a reappraisal by English critic Lord David Cecil in *Early Victorian Novelists: Essays in Revaluation* (1935). But even before Cecil's book, perceptive twentieth-century readers like Virginia Woolf had come to similar conclusions. Woolf, who had made a pilgrimage in 1904 to Haworth, England, home of the Brontës, wrote in the 1920s of Charlotte Brontë: "She looked out upon a world cleft into gigantic disorder and felt within her the power to unite it in a book. That gigantic ambition is to be felt throughout the novel—a struggle, half thwarted but of superb conviction..."

Wuthering Heights was first adapted for film in a 1920 British production. American producer Walter Wanger then planned an adaptation before abandoning the project. Famed Hollywood mogul Samuel Goldwyn eventually acquired the screen rights to the novel, including a script written by Charles MacArthur and Ben Hecht, in the mid-1930s despite his reported dislike for the gloominess of the story. By the 1930s Goldwyn was an independent producer known for his difficult personality, but he managed many successes by focusing on high-quality, often literary-inspired projects. He appointed director William Wyler, whom he had under contract, to head *Wuthering Heights*, with Merle Oberon starring as Cathy and Laurence Olivier as Heathcliff, the doomed lovers.

Wyler had begun his career directing silent films, moving on to successes such as *The Good Fairy* (1935), *These Three* (1936) and *Jezebel* (1938). He would eventually become one of the most acclaimed directors in Hollywood, winning Academy Awards for best director for *Mrs. Miniver* (1942), *The Best Years of Our Lives* (1946), and *Ben Hur* (1959) and being nominated eight other times. He was known for his exacting standards, but also for helping novices in their breakout roles—for example, Audrey Hepburn in *Roman Holiday* (1953) and Barbra Streisand in *Funny Girl* (1968). *Wuthering Heights*, however, was a notoriously difficult production. Wyler demanded dozens of shoots for many scenes, exasperating the actors. Olivier in particular was often contemptuous and also clashed with Oberon. Wyler and Goldwyn were often in direct conflict, with the producer even threatening to replace the director over a disagreement on the film's ending.

Film Analysis

Wuthering Heights details the lifelong torturous love affair between Catherine "Cathy" Earnshaw and Heathcliff, an orphaned boy found on the streets of Liverpool and taken in by her father at a young age. Throughout their lives, Cathy is divided between wanting to be wild and free, like Heathcliff, or like the more refined Edgar Linton. When Cathy eventually agrees to marry Edgar, Heathcliff vows revenge against all who have wronged him, and when he becomes a man of means as an adult, he enacts his revenge on everyone, including the next generation of Earnshaws and Lintons. After Cathy's early death, Heathcliff treats his own son, Cathy's daughter, and the son of Cathy's brother in ways that make him appear to both the characters in the novel and to many readers as something close to a monster. He takes all the cruelty that was unjustly inflicted upon him and turns it back on the world in equal measure.

Wyler's adaptation of *Wuthering Heights* differs from the novel in many aspects, but primarily in its omission of this second generation's story, instead focusing on the story of Heathcliff (Laurence Olivier) and Cathy (Merle Oberon). Wyler also softens the temperaments of both main characters, maintaining to a degree their selfish and vengeful streaks, but making them far more palatable for the screen. Also notable is that the story's time period shifts from the late eighteenth and early nineteenth centuries in the novel to the mid-nineteenth century in the film. This change was reportedly because Wyler preferred the clothing styles of the later period.

The film opens with a traveler named Lockwood (Miles Mander) lost on the moors in a snowstorm. He finds a house, Wuthering Heights, and enters, only to be shocked by the cold reception he receives from the master of the house, Heathcliff, his wife, Isabella (Geraldine Fitzgerald), and the servants. The only one who treats him with any kindness is the housekeeper, Ellen Dean (Flora Robson). That night Lockwood awakes from a fitful sleep and thinks he sees the ghost of a woman outside. After Heathcliff comes to the room and is told what happened, he rips open the shutters and calls out "Cathy!" then rushes off into the still raging snowstorm. Ellen then tells Lockwood the bulk of the story in a long flashback. In this way the film follows the general structure of the novel, although in the book Lockwood hears the tale over a long period while recovering from an illness.

Ellen's narrative describes how Heathcliff (played as a child by Rex Downing) was brought home by Cathy's father, Mr. Earnshaw (Cecil Kellaway), and is treated as a member of the family by everyone except Cathy's brother,

Hindley (played by Douglas Scott as a child and Hugh Williams as an adult), who sees him as nothing more than a "gypsy beggar." After Hindley hits Heathcliff with a rock, Heathcliff swears revenge on him. Meanwhile, Heathcliff and Cathy become close friends, especially after playing on the rocks of Peniston Crag, which they pretend is a castle where they live as king and queen. The crag becomes their special place, where they continue to meet secretly into young adulthood.

After the death of Mr. Earnshaw, Hindley becomes the master of Wuthering Heights and forces Heathcliff into the role of stable boy. Although mistreated by Hindley, who grows up to be a gambler and a drinker, Heathcliff stays at Wuthering Heights to be near Cathy. She urges him to run away, make a fortune, and come back for her. One day an injured Cathy is taken in by the wealthy neighbors, the Lintons, but they scorn Heathcliff, who vows revenge. Cathy again tells him to run away and come back for her with better prospects. He leaves as Cathy recuperates at the Linton home.

Detail of Emily Brontë, from painting by her brother, Patrick Branwell Brontë. Photo by National Portrait Gallery via Wikimedia Commons.

After several weeks living at the Lintons', Cathy returns to Wuthering Heights entranced by wealth and beauty. She discovers that Heathcliff did not run away for long but returned because he missed her so badly. When Heathcliff sees Cathy with Edgar Linton (David Niven), who is now in love with her, he is appalled by her haughtiness with him. However, Cathy also lashes out at Edgar when he criticizes Heathcliff in front of her. She meets Heathcliff on Peniston Crag, where they again declare their love for each other and she talks of his running away to make a fortune. A classic love triangle is established, in which Cathy is drawn to both Heathcliff and Edgar, who represent different sides of her own personality and desires. These opposing natures are highlighted by the cinematography and sets, which contrast the wild moors (in fact shot in California) and the comfortable domestic life of the Lintons.

Cathy later invites Edgar to Wuthering Heights, leading to a violent argument between her and Heathcliff. After Edgar asks Cathy to marry him, she discusses the proposal with Ellen, who knows Heathcliff is eavesdropping. Heathcliff hears Cathy say that it would degrade her to marry him and leaves without hearing her conclude that, regardless, they are soulmates. Heathcliff runs away, and after Cathy searches for him fruitlessly, she is found near death by Edgar. With Heathcliff gone, Cathy agrees to marry Edgar, though not without some inner turmoil. At this point the camera briefly returns to present-day Ellen, setting up a time jump in the main narrative.

The flashback resumes with Cathy and Edgar seemingly happily married. As in the book, Heathcliff then returns, now a wealthy and refined gentleman. Though many details from the source material are rearranged or omitted, two key elements of Heathcliff's revenge plan are retained. He reveals that he has bought Hindley's gambling debts and is now master of Wuthering Heights, allowing him to turn the tables by taunting Hindley. Heathcliff also marries Edgar's sister, Isabella, and then neglects her, purely to torment both Edgar and Cathy.

When Cathy becomes gravely ill, Heathcliff rushes to her bedside, where they argue about the tortures inflicted upon each other but eventually admit their mutual love. Heathcliff carries Cathy to the window to see Peniston Crag once more, and she dies in his arms. When Edgar and Dr. Kenneth (Donald Crisp) enter the room, Heathcliff curses Cathy that she might not rest until he dies, too. The powerful scene showcases many of the film's strengths, including the acting skills of Oberon and Olivier, Wyler's nuanced direction, and the crisp black-and-white cinematography of Gregg Toland. It also highlights the major changes made in adaptation; while in the novel Cathy's death comes about halfway through and sets the stage for Heathcliff's ongoing revenge against a new generation, the film makes it the major climax and the final scene of the flashback.

The present-day narrative concludes with Ellen and Lockwood joined by Dr. Kenneth, who says that he found Heathcliff's body out in the snowstorm after believing he saw Heathcliff walking with a woman. Ellen suggests that Heathcliff was with Cathy's spirit, and the film ends with their ghosts walking in the snow toward Peniston Crag. The shot of the ghosts, filmed with doubles after Olivier and Oberon had gone on to other projects, was added over the objections of Wyler, at the behest of producer Goldwyn, who wanted a more upbeat ending.

Significance

The 1939 film version of *Wuthering Heights* is a highly regarded adaptation of a classic, and still popular, novel. Although the book has been adapted for film and television numerous times, no other version has garnered the esteem that the 1939 film has achieved in the decades since its initial release.

Wyler's film was widely acclaimed as one of the best pictures of 1939—a year considered to be one of the greatest in the history of Hollywood, producing such classics as *Gone with the Wind*, *The Wizard of Oz*, *Stagecoach*, and *Mr. Smith Goes to Washington*. Despite such stiff competition, *Wuthering Heights* was nominated for eight Academy Awards, including best picture, best director, best leading actor (Olivier), best supporting actress (Fitzgerald), and best screenplay. It ultimately won just a single Oscar, with Gregg Toland winning for best black-and-white cinematography. The movie also won the 1939 New York Film Critics Circle Award for best film. Contemporary critics generally considered the adaptation to match or even surpass the novel in artistic quality. Fred S. Nugent, writing for *The New York Times*, declared, "Goldwyn and his troupe have fashioned a strong and somber film, poetically written as the novel not always was, sinister and wild as it was meant to be." Similarly, a reviewer for *Variety* wrote that "Goldwyn's film version retains all of the grim drama of the book," and praised the central performances, but also suggested that "it's rather dull material for general audiences."

Although neither Wyler nor Goldwyn won major awards for *Wuthering Heights*, it remains regarded as one of the best films of their illustrious careers. Goldwyn even reportedly considered it his favorite production. The film is also credited with establishing Olivier, already a renowned stage actor, as a true film star. In 1998, *Wuthering Heights* was included on the American Film Institute's list of the hundred best films of all time, and in 2007 the Library of Congress selected it for preservation in the US National Film Registry.

—*Christopher Mari*

Further Reading

Hazette, Valerie V. Wuthering Heights *on Film and Television: A Journey across Time and Cultures*. Intellect, 2015.

Miller, Gabriel. *William Wyler: The Life and Films of Hollywood's Most Celebrated Director*. UP of Kentucky, 2013.

"William Wyler." *Turner Classic Movies*, 2019, www.tcm.com/tcmdb/person/210004%7C156648/William-Wyler. Accessed 6 Mar. 2019.

Bibliography

Dirks, Tim. "Wuthering Heights (1939)." *AMC Filmsite*, 2019, www.filmsite.org/wuth.html. Accessed 6 Mar. 2019.

McCrum, Robert. "The 100 Best Novels: No 13—Wuthering Heights by Emily Brontë (1847)." Review of *Wuthering Heights*, by Emily Brontë. *The Guardian*, 16 Dec. 2013, www.theguardian.com/books/2013/dec/16/emily-bronte-wuthering-heights-100-best. Accessed 6 Mar. 2019.

Nixon, Rob, and Margaret Landazuri. "Wuthering Heights (1939)." *Turner Classic Movies*, 2019, www.tcm.com/tcmdb/title/96324/Wuthering-Heights/articles.html. Accessed 6 Mar. 2019.

Nugent, Frank S. "THE SCREEN; Goldwyn Presents Film of 'Wuthering Heights' at Rivoli—'The Hardys Ride High' at the Capitol." Review of *Wuthering Heights*, directed by William Wyler, and *The Hardys Ride High*, directed by George B. Seitz. *The New York Times*, 14 Apr. 1939, www.nytimes.com/1939/04/14/archives/the-screen-goldwyn-presets-film-of-wuthering-heights-at-rivolithe.html. Accessed 6 Mar. 2019.

"Wuthering Heights (1939)." *American Film Institute*, catalog.afi.com/Catalog/moviedetails/8187. Accessed 6 Mar. 2019.

Review of *Wuthering Heights*, directed by William Wyler. *Variety*, 28 Mar. 1939, variety.com/1939/film/reviews/wuthering-heights-2-1200412239. Accessed 6 Mar. 2019.

Index of Print Works by Title

Index of Print Works by Author

Index of Print Works by Date of First Publication

Index of Films by Screenwriter

Index of Films by Director

Index of Films by Release Date